KT-485-592

Good Housekeeping

COMPLETE BOOK OF THE HOME

Good Housekeeping

COMPLETE BOOK OF THE HOME

The Ultimate Home Reference Guide

General Editor: Suzanne Wilkinson
Contributors: Caroline Bloor, Linda Gray,
Stewart Patterson, Patricia Schofield

LONDON NEW YORK SYDNEY TORONTO

First published 1994
1 3 5 7 9 10 8 6 4 2

This edition published in 1994 by BCA by arrangement with Ebury Press

CN 3459

Editor: Margot Richardson
Illustrations: David Eaton
Design: Martin Lovelock

Printed and bound in Zaragoza (Spain) by Edelvives

CONTENTS

INTRODUCTION

Wouldn't it be wonderful if, in every aspect of our lives, someone else would do all the work around the home, leaving us with precious extra time to spend as we please? This is exactly what this book does. Within it, you will find a distilled version of the Good Housekeeping Institute's practical expertise, built up over many years.

These days time is of the essence, and the less time you spend running your home, the more time you have for other activities. You need to take on numerous roles – without any formal training – from financial manager when buying a home and consumer expert when equipping it, to being the sole cleaning and maintenance worker to keep it in top condition.

Most of us are more choosy than ever about spending and want to make sure we're getting good value, whether it's buying bedding, a whole new bathroom, kitchen equipment or garden lighting. Here also is easy reference to the quick solutions for almost every household problem, whether getting grease out of a silk shirt or unblocking a sink.

In addition, the book contains practical, creative ideas for making curtains and soft furnishings, and instructions for unusual painting techniques.

To cope with the increasing need to protect your home and possessions – from burglary, fire or water – there is information on home security and what to do in an emergency: from coping with major flooding to a chip-pan fire.

And as it's essential to understand your rights in relation to your home and the law, there's a whole chapter arming you with answers to some of the more frequently asked legal questions. Do I need planning permission to extend my home? What should I do when the noise from my neighbour's stereo is keeping the entire family awake at night?

We've also included over 250 useful contacts for further information, which you'd be unlikely to come across in one volume elsewhere.

The Good Housekeeping Institute forms the backbone of the highly successful Good Housekeeping magazine. This book marks the Institute's 70th year. Our seal proudly proclaims the words 'Tried, Tested and Trusted'.

In 1924, when the Institute was launched, housewives were struggling with the transition into a servant-less society. Now, women need independent advice they can trust in an increasing number of fields, especially as almost as many women as men now work outside the home. However, despite this outside interest, most women haven't been able to totally relinquish their domestic workload.

The Good Housekeeping Institute has an exceptionally talented and experienced team of experts ready to talk about any area covered in the book. Do give us a call on 0839 141414* for one-to-one advice.

Finally, this book is full of hints and tips. Perhaps the most important of all is to delegate the advice in these pages to your partner, children or paid help!

Suzanne Wilkinson
General Editor

*Costs 49p per minute; open 9.30 to 5, Monday to Friday.

INTRODUCTION

BUYING A HOME

MOVING HOUSE

There's nothing quite like the excitement of stepping over the threshold into your new home. But with months of house-hunting, arranging a mortgage, negotiating a price and carrying out the move, few would deny how stressful the whole process can be.

Buying a house is probably the most complicated and costly purchase you will ever have to make. Whether the move is to accommodate a family, a change in financial position or a new job, it takes weeks of planning, costs hundreds of pounds and results in a very large commitment for 20 to 25 years. Yet, with careful planning and a basic understanding of the processes involved, you can make the whole operation run relatively smoothly. The following pages show you how best to approach the entire undertaking.

ARRANGING A MORTGAGE

One of the first steps for most people when buying a new house is to approach a building society, bank or other lending institution to find out how much, in principle, you can borrow. You'll find it useful to get a mortgage certificate from your lender. This will tell anyone considering selling to you that (subject to a valuation and status – see pages 33 and 19 respectively), you are guaranteed a mortgage up to a certain sum. It will reassure people that you are a serious buyer.

A mortgage adviser will be able to give you an idea of how much you could borrow, based on your income/s (see page 18). Add your own

HOW MUCH CAN YOU AFFORD?

Before you decide the price range for possible properties, consider what you spend on all your other regular commitments. Use our check-list to help organise your monthly budget:

Monthly income

Take-home pay (after tax)	£ .
Partner's take-home pay (after tax)	£ .
Other regular income, eg investment	£ .
TOTAL £	**.**

Monthly outgoings

Present mortgage/rent	£ .
Second mortgage repayments (if applicable)	£ .
Home repairs/maintenance	£ .
Hire purchase/ other loan repayments	£ .
Credit-card repayments	£ .
Council tax	£ .
Endowment/life assurance premiums	£ .
Food/drink	£ .
Clothing	£ .
Services (eg electricity, gas, telephone)	£ .
Petrol/car maintenance	£ .
Car insurance/road tax	£ .
Savings	£ .
Social life	£ .
Travel expenses	£ .
Holidays	£ .
TV licence/rental	£ .
TOTAL £	**.**

savings to this and you'll have a rough guide to the price range of properties open to you. It's also useful to take into account the other costs involved in house purchase: fees for valuation, survey, legal expenses, Stamp Duty, Land Registry, and removal expenses (see page 15).

WHERE TO BUY

You probably have a reasonable idea already of the area in which you want to live, and the sort of house you're looking for, but it's worth bearing in mind the differences between town and country, and flats and houses, that may not at first be obvious.

TOWN OR COUNTRY

If you are moving into the countryside, you will need to take the following factors into account:

- Usually less crime in country areas, so insurance rates are lower for home contents and car security.
- Reduced accessibility in the winter if the weather turns bad or there are problems with public transport.
- Better leisure facilities.
- Greater variety of housing.
- Health and welfare facilities are spread more thinly due to a sparser population.
- Greater distance from the nearest school/hospital/shops.

Likewise, if you are moving to a town or city, consider:

- More frequent and more accessible public transport.
- Larger, more convenient shops.
- Higher house prices.
- Larger insurance premiums. For example, for the contents of a three-bedroomed house, insurance cover has been quoted as five times more expensive in London than in a Dorset village. Similarly, car insurance in London was nearly 50 per cent more expensive than in the country.

HOUSE OR FLAT

If you were previously in rented accommodation and are now buying your own flat, consider:

- Maintenance costs and buildings insurance. If the freehold of the building is owned by a separate freeholder, these will probably be handled by a managing agent who will charge a management fee, as well as passing on the costs of insuring and running the communal areas of the building. If the freehold is controlled by the flat-owners' own management company, you will have to deal collectively with these items.
- Organisation of cleaning communal areas, gardening, etc.
- Terms of the lease, eg restrictions on pets, parties, noise after 11pm, etc.

If you are moving from a house to a flat, you need to consider:

- You may need less furniture.
- Close neighbours within the building may need more consideration.
- Maintenance costs and buildings insurance, see above.
- Terms of the lease, see above.

If you are moving from a flat to a house, consider:

- The additional expense of furnishing.
- Higher heating costs.
- Having a garden for the first time, which may entail extra expense of tools and plants.
- More housework.
- Higher maintenance and repair costs.
- Sole responsibility for insuring the building.

NEW OR OLD

NEWLY BUILT HOUSES

Over the last few years, brand-new homes have become increasingly popular with house-buyers. They save on repair and maintenance (at least for the first few years) and are becoming increasingly energy efficient: new homes use up to 50 per cent less energy than homes built in the 1980s. Most house builders offer you a choice of colour schemes, fixtures and fittings, so you shouldn't have the costs of redecorating to suit your own taste.

Disadvantages include some teething problems, such as plaster cracks, for the first couple of years. And if you decide to move again within one or two years, it is unlikely that you would be able to sell at the same price as you paid for the house.

Mortgate lenders require a structural warranty. Check that your builder is offering, and is entitled to offer, a warranty before exchanging contracts on a new home. The National House-Building Council runs Buildmark structural warranty, which covers new houses for ten years. The Zurich Municipal company provides insurance cover for newly built homes, called a Newbuild Home Building Guarantee, which is also for a basic period of ten years, although in some cases it can be extended by a further five years.

OLD HOUSES

Buying an old, run-down property for a song and renovating it isn't a job which appeals to everyone. It can, however, be extremely rewarding if you have the time, patience and dedication to follow the job through. Just getting the right planning permission and any improvement grants on offer could take up to a year before building work can start.

Planning permission

To find out what, if any, planning permission you need for the work you would like to do, such as extensions or structural alterations, ask the planning department and the environmental health department of the local authority for advice. Conservation officers working for district or county councils can also sometimes help with general advice.

Renovation grants

It's always worth checking whether you are entitled to any financial help with modernising and renovation. Local authorities administer and give improvement or renovation grants such as House Renovation Grants (formerly the improvement grant) or Common Parts Grants (covering the cost of repairs or improvements to common parts of buildings containing one or more flats). Grants are now means-tested. *House Renovation Grants* is a useful booklet giving further information. Copies are available from the Department of Environment, (see Useful Addresses).

Living in a listed building or in a conservation area can be a boon or a blight. The Department of National Heritage compiles lists of buildings of special architectural or historic interest. This means that you cannot alter or extend the property in any way which would affect its character, without getting permission from the local planning authority. If you are moving into a conservation area (such as the city of Bath), be aware that there are restrictions on alterations to houses.

You can check whether a house is in a conservation area, or is a listed building, by going to the local authority offices to inspect the list. Do this before buying a house if you have any big ideas about changing things, such as installing double glazing or a conservatory at the back. On the positive side, your listed building may be eligible for a local authority grant if it is in need of structural repair, or to retain certain aspects of architectural interest.

SELF-BUILD HOUSES

Every year, an increasing number of people design or build their own house. It is a way to get a home designed exactly to your specifications, such as a traditional structure but with all the modern fixtures and fittings.

Self-build doesn't necessarily mean you do all the work yourself. You don't have to be a master builder to create the home of your dreams. There are a variety of options enabling you to do as little or as much of the work yourself as you choose. Whichever option you choose, be prepared to spend *at least* nine months on the project.

OPTIONS FOR SELF-BUILD

- Employ an architect to do the design, specifications, and oversee the work. His fee will be around 10 per cent of the overall cost.
- Go straight to a builder, who can advise on the project and do the work. Make sure he is registered with the National House Building Council or Zurich Home Building Guarantee. These mean the house is built to specific standards and provide a means of redress should there be any problems in the future.
- Get a self-build 'package'. More than 70 companies specialise in mid to top-quality house packages. They will help you estimate your budget, assist in co-ordinating the project and recommend builders and subcontractors.
- Organise everything yourself, and use a design consultant for as much or little as required. (If the designer is not subject to The Royal Institute of British Architects or Architects' Registration Council, check that he/she has professional indemnity insurance.)

Choosing your own subcontractors and doing some work yourself can save 20 to 25 per cent of the cost, but is only an option if you don't need the NHBC Buildmark Warranty or Zurich Home Building Guarantee for a mortgage. Bear in mind that if you plan to sell within ten years, your buyers may have difficulty getting a mortgage.

FINANCIAL CONSIDERATIONS

First, you must have the land on which to put your house. You'll need to shop around for a lending institution that will give you a mortgage to buy land. For further help see *Blay's Mortgage Guide* in your local library. For land, try public exhibitions or estate agents. Plots with buildings due for demolition are also suitable. Talk to the local building inspectorate before purchase because some ground requires expensive foundations.

It is possible to get a mortgage for a self-build project, provided you meet the lender's conditions, such as using a builder who is NHBC registered.

When dealing with builders, *always* get several quotes, so that you can get the best deal for your available money. If a builder is given the entire contract, he can zero-rate the VAT, and therefore need not charge you VAT at all. Check this before work starts. Once work has begun, don't hand over large amounts of money without checking progress. Keep back most of the builder's payment until an architect or surveyor has checked the work.

With all self-build projects, you must be covered by public and employers' liability, and contract works insurance.

Finally, you will also need a solicitor to check planning permission, searches, availability of electricity, gas and water, and to apply for a building-regulations certificate.

THE COST OF MOVING HOUSE

The expense of moving house, or setting up home for the first time, can seem enormous. Taking into account a deposit, legal fees and other charges, it costs much more than it initially appears just to get the keys of your new home.

For example, to buy a £50,000 home, you would need to pay out approximately £4,000, as well as repaying the mortgage itself.

WHAT CAN YOU AFFORD?

To give yourself a rough guide on the maximum that you can realistically afford to spend on a new house, add together all the following amounts:

1 The likely net proceeds from the sale of your present home, after repaying your present mortgage. (Find out what other similar properties in your area are selling for or use an estate agent's valuation as a guide to what your home is worth.)

2 The maximum mortgage you can comfortably afford (see pages 18–19).

3 Any other available capital or savings that could swell the amount available.

Then deduct:

1 The cost of selling through an estate agent, who will charge from 1 to 3 per cent of the sale price, plus VAT (see page 36).

2 The cost of solicitor's or licensed conveyancer's fees for selling your old home.

3 The cost of buying a new property: valuation fee, survey fee, legal expenses, stamp duty, Land Registry fee, removal expenses and VAT.

4 The cost of essential repairs, redecoration and improvements to the new house.

FINDING A DEPOSIT

You may be asked for a deposit of 5 to 10 per cent of the purchase price to put down on the house when you exchange contracts.

If you don't have enough for the deposit in ready money, you may be able to get a bridging loan from your bank, but they can be extremely expensive. It would have to be repaid on completion of the sale of your present house.

Alternatively, it may be possible to use a deposit guarantee scheme, arranged through a solicitor or licensed conveyancer (who specialises in house purchase transactions). Instead of paying a deposit, you pay an insurance premium related to the purchase price of the house, which covers a deposit of 10 per cent up to a set maximum. The insurance policy guarantees that the 10 per cent deposit will be paid if you default under the contract. However, first check that the seller is willing to accept the guarantee instead of a deposit, as deposit guarantees are far less common at present than they used to be.

If you are selling a property, it may be possible to use your sale deposit towards your purchase deposit.

FEES TO PAY

The various fees that are involved in house buying are considerable, and must be taken into account when planning your purchase. They are as follows:

LEGAL FEES

Solicitors and, in England and Wales, licensed conveyancers, can charge what they choose.

The cost is based on the complexity of the transaction (ie, the skill, number of hours, and the number and importance of documents) plus other local factors, such as the place and circumstances of the conveyancing, and whether the land is registered or unregistered.

If you don't already have a solicitor or conveyancer in mind, get estimates from several before choosing one. The Law Society should have a list of solicitors' practices in your area and, likewise, the Council for Licensed Conveyancers lists its members (who specialise solely in house purchase and sale transactions). Many solicitors and conveyancers charge a fixed fee plus disbursements (stamp duty, local authority searches, Land Registry fee) for all the work involved. As a rough guide, allow up to 1 per cent of the price (plus VAT).

SELLING YOUR PRESENT HOME

You will probably need an estate agent to sell your current property. Most charge a fee of between 1 and 3 per cent of the selling price (plus VAT). (See Selling Your Home, page 36.)

Alternatively, if you decide to sell privately, you must allow for your own advertising costs (see page 36–7).

There may be a mortgage redemption charge if you already have a mortgage on your existing property. This is a penalty for repaying it within a short period (eg, less than four years), and may be up to three months' interest and/or administration or legal fees.

STAMP DUTY

This is a statutory 1 per cent tax on property purchases. It only applies to purchases of over £60,000, but it is charged on the whole amount once this threshold is passed. For example, on a house costing £60,000, the Stamp Duty is nil. But a house at £60,001 would cost £601 in stamp duty.

The following table shows what is payable on amounts over £60,000:

Purchase price (£)	**Duty (£)**
60,001 - 60,100	601
60,101 - 60,200	602
60,201 - 60,300	603
60,301 - 60,400	604
60,401 - 60,500	605
60,501 - 60,600	606
60,601 - 60,700	607
60,701 - 60,800	608
60,801 - 60,900	609
60,901 - 61,000	610
61,001 - 61,100	611
61,101 - 61,200	612
61,201 - 61,300	613
61,301 - 61,400	614
61,401 - 61,500	615
61,501 and above	£1 on each £100 or part of £100

LAND REGISTRY FEE

This has to be paid on all purchases on a scale related to the purchase price.

Value (£)	**Fee (£)**
30,001–35,000	60
40,001–45,000	80
50,001–60,000	120
60,001–70,000	140
70,001–80,000	160
80,001–90,000	190
90,001–100,000	230
100,001–150,000	260
150,001–200,000	300

LOCAL AUTHORITY SEARCHES

These fees are payable to the local authority for information about, for example, planning in the area. In England and Wales this is about £40 to £100. In Scotland this fee is nominal.

OTHER SEARCH FEES

This includes a whole range of possible searches, from company searches to mining searches, but not all are applicable to every transaction. Check with your solicitor what will be needed and ask him to give you an idea of the cost.

LENDER'S LEGAL FEES

Usually your solicitor will act for the lender as well as for you. His/her fee for the purchase will include all the work on the mortgage. You should check the costs of this with your solicitor. A few lenders require their own solicitors to act for them. You may have to pay their fees (in addition to your own solicitor's fees for acting on your side of the mortgage) and for this your solicitor may make a separate, additional charge.

VALUATION FEE

This pays for the lender's surveyor's valuation, and is based on the price of the house. It varies according to the lender's arrangements with the valuers. Add on approximately £120 (plus VAT) as an estimate.

TOP-UP LOAN

This may be needed if you are unable to raise enough money from your lender to cover the whole cost of the purchase (see Top-up Loan, page 20).

MORTGAGE INDEMNITY POLICY

After the deposit, this is likely to be the biggest cost. It is a one-off charge which the lender uses to buy an insurance policy if your loan is over 70 per cent of the property's value. It compensates the lender if they have to repossess your home and are unable to sell it for enough to clear the loan and any arrears. This may be added to your mortgage, or paid separately, depending on your lender. The cost can vary from lender to lender, so if you need a 90 or 95 per cent mortgage, you should also take into account the cost of mortgage indemnity when comparing the different mortgage quotations.

MORTGAGE-ARRANGEMENT FEE

This is payable on almost all fixed-rate mortgages. Costs vary depending on the type of mortgage. Budget for around £250.

BRIDGING LOAN

If such a loan is required, interest on it will be charged at 3 to 4 per cent above the current bank base rate.

SURVEY FEE

It is wise to allow for more than one survey during house-hunting, as you may find a property which fills all your criteria, but is structurally unsound. If this happens, you will have to keep looking, and eventually pay for another survey on a different building.

Most building societies offer you the choice of a full structural survey, a Home Buyer's Survey and Valuation, or just a valuation. It is important to have at least a Home Buyer's report, which should highlight any major defects in the property. A valuation is just that: it will highlight only significant defects such as would affect the value of the property.

For a full survey, allow from £250 to £1,000 (plus VAT). The cost relates to the size, value of the property, and amount of time spent by the surveyor. Get a quotation before instructing the surveyor. There could be a reduction if it is combined with a valuation.

If buying an old property, budget for possible extra charges in case tests by specialist firms (such as for wood rot) are needed.

INSURANCE

For a freehold property, the first premium for building insurance is payable in advance. Ring your insurance broker for a quotation. You may also wish to consider contents insurance.

REMOVAL EXPENSES

Will you be using a professional removal firm or hiring a van? Either way, get at least three quotations, and arrange insurance cover for your possessions while in transit. If hiring a van, budget for packing materials, petrol for several journeys, plus food and refreshment for your helpers.

If your possessions are going into storage for a period of time, budget for this too. (For costs, see Storage Costs, page 40).

SERVICES

Check if you need to arrange the following:

- Gas: disconnection charges at your old home and reconnection at the new one.
- Electricity: disconnections and reconnection charges, inspections, tests, or installing additional circuits.
- Telephone: you may have to pay for the installation of a phone at your new home or for taking over the existing line if disconnected. (There is no connection charge if a line remains unbroken between one owner and another.)
- Redirection of letters.
- Plumber: disconnection and reconnection of a washing machine or dishwasher.

REPAIRS AND REDECORATION

As well as the expense of the move itself, also consider the cost of any immediate repairs, improvements or redecoration.

If you are buying a brand new house you will have an initial outlay on many items that would be considered fixtures in a second-hand property, such as kitchen units and curtain rails, but you probably won't have the cost of decoration and carpets.

CHECK-LIST OF MOVING EXPENSES

Expense	£	Expense	£
Advertisements (if DIY selling)	£ .	Removal insurance cover	£ .
Bridging loan	£ .	Repairs and redecoration	£ .
Building insurance premium	£ .	Services disconnection	£ .
Carpet laying	£ .	Services reconnection	£ .
Contents insurance premium	£ .	Solicitor's/conveyancer's fee	£ .
Estate agent's fee	£ .	Specialist structural tests	£ .
Land Registry fee	£ .	Stamp Duty	£ .
Lender's legal fee	£ .	Storage	£ .
Local authority searches	£ .	Structural survey	£ .
Mail redirection	£ .	Top-up loan charges	£ .
Mortgage arrangement fee	£ .	Valuation fee	£ .
Mortgage indemnity policy	£ .	Van hire	£ .
Mortgage redemption penalty (if relevant)	£ .	Other	£ .
Removal company	£ .	**TOTAL**	**£ .**

GETTING A MORTGAGE

One of the first steps for most people, when buying a new house, is to approach a building society, bank or other lending institution to find out how much can be borrowed. Visit several lenders to discuss a loan and their terms because they each have different lending criteria.

When you have decided which lender to use, ask them to give you a mortgage certificate. This will show that you are guaranteed a mortgage up to a certain amount (subject to valuation and status – see page 19) and will be useful when house-hunting to show you are a serious buyer.

WHAT IS A MORTGAGE?

A mortgage is any loan which is secured on property, whether it's the home you wish to buy or, in the case of a re-mortgage, the property you are living in.

The usual term of the loan is 20 or 25 years, but it can be longer. Lenders may insist that a mortgage is paid off by the time you reach retirement age – but many now offer shorter-term loans for retired people (see Home-Income Plans, page 23). If the loan is not repaid, the lender has the right to repossess and sell the property.

HOW MUCH CAN YOU BORROW?

A mortgage adviser will be able to give an approximate loan figure. This may differ slightly between lenders, but the calculations are based on your income. If you are in employment, your gross income, before tax, forms the basis of calculations. If you are self employed, your net income (that is, gross income minus the expenses of running your business) is used for calculations.

MORTGAGE BORROWING A ROUGH GUIDE

1 Kate is single, and earns £10,000 per year. Her lender is prepared to let her borrow three times her salary. So she can borrow 3 x £10,000 = £30,000.

2 Mr and Mrs Brown want to take out a joint mortgage. He earns £15,000 per year and she earns £10,000 per year. Assuming that the lender is prepared to let them borrow three times the major income plus once the other income, the amount they can borrow is 3 x £15,000 + £10,000 = £55,000.

In general, if you are single, you might be allowed to borrow between 2½ and 3 times your basic annual income. If you are a couple who are both earning, you would usually be able to borrow up to 2½ to 3 times the higher income plus 1 to 1½ times the lower income. Take note that mortgage lenders don't usually take into account any overtime or bonuses. Some lenders will be more flexible if you are able to put down a big deposit.

TIP Check your finances carefully. Just because the lender is prepared to give you a mortgage of a certain size, don't automatically assume that you can afford it. Lenders work on averages, but you need to take into account any heavy or long-term financial commitments, such as the cost of equipping your new home, your family and travel costs. (See The Cost of Moving House, pages 14–17.)

Before making a firm commitment to lend you any money, the lender will want to make sure you can keep up the repayments and that the house you want to buy is worth enough to cover the loan if you default on your repayments. When you make your formal mortgage application the lender will make certain 'status enquiries', such as seeking confirmation of your salary from your employer and getting details of your existing mortgage account. He/she will also consult a credit reference agency and have a valuation carried out on the property.

THE DEPOSIT

The lender will probably expect you to put down a deposit of 5 per cent or more; although some may give a 100 per cent mortgage, where you borrow the full value of your home.

TIP A 95 per cent loan doesn't automatically equal 95 per cent of the purchase price. The lender will be letting you have 95 per cent of the value that *the lender believes* your house is worth – which may not be the same sum.

For example, if you agree to buy a home for £50,000 on a 95 per cent loan, you should be able to borrow £47,500 with a deposit of £2,500 covering the rest. If the house is only valued at £47,000 then a 95 per cent loan will only give you £44,650, and you will have to find the rest yourself, ie, £5,350.

If the valuation is considerably lower than the buyer's asking price, it may be worth trying to negotiate a price reduction with the buyer.

MORTGAGE INDEMNITY POLICY

Generally, lenders are prepared to lend more than 75 per cent of a property's value if you pay for them to take out a mortgage indemnity policy. This guarantees to pay the lender the outstanding balance of the loan if the home has to be repossessed and sold for less than the amount of the mortgage. Be warned, it can be expensive to take out such a policy: an extra £10,000 may cost as much as £700 (usually payable in a lump sum up front, but in some cases it may be added to the mortgage loan).

INTEREST RATES

The size of the monthly mortgage payment will depend on the sum you borrow, the length of the mortgage and the current rate of interest. You'll find the initial rate of interest and monthly repayments set out clearly in your mortgage offer.

After that, any changes in the interest rate will be reflected in your mortgage payments, unless you have a fixed-interest agreement (also called a fixed-rate mortgage) where the interest rate, and therefore your payments, stay the same for a fixed period. Some lenders adjust the amount you pay on an annual basis so that changes which occur during the year take effect when calculating the following year's repayments. With any mortgage, you will be notified of any change in the level of your repayments.

MAKING A FORMAL APPLICATION

Once you have found a suitable property, you will have to apply formally for the mortgage and pay for the lender to value the property. If the lender decides not to give you a loan as a result of the valuation, you will not get the valuation fee back.

When the valuation has been done and the status enquiries are complete, the lenders will let you know whether they are prepared to lend, how much and on what terms (for example, not letting it out or altering the property without the permission of the lender).

TURNED DOWN?

If your mortgage application is turned down, it may be worth trying a different lender with different lending criteria. You could also enlist the help of a mortgage broker, who is not linked to any one lending institution and may have a better idea which companies are more likely to give you a loan.

If the lender has received a bad report about your financial background from a credit-reference agency, you should ask the lender for the address of the agency concerned. The large agencies keep computer records on every address in the UK.

You can write to them (with your full name, address, and postcode for the last six years) and ask them for a copy of your file. You will usually be charged a nominal fee of approximately £1. If the facts are incorrect you can ask the agency to change them. If the company refuses to change your details or allow you to include a correction, complain to The Office of Fair Trading (see Useful Addresses).

If the lender is experiencing a shortage of funds, they may be prepared to commit themselves to granting your mortgage in the near future.

TOP-UP LOAN

You may be able to get a top-up loan from an insurance company or bank if the sum that the lender is prepared to grant you falls short of what you need to borrow. The first lender will normally have to give permission.

You may have to pay a higher interest rate on the top-up loan than on the main mortgage, and may have to take out an additional insurance policy to cover it.

TYPES OF MORTGAGE

With all mortgages, you have to pay back the money borrowed (the capital) and something towards the cost of borrowing the money (the interest). There are two main methods:

Repayment mortgage Every month you pay back some of the capital, plus interest on the outstanding loan.

Interest-only mortgage Each month you pay just the interest to your lender, and make a separate payment into a savings plan that is eventually used to pay off the mortgage.

TIP Be wary about taking out an interest-only mortgage without having a suitable savings plan alongside it. This may seem like a nice, cheap option, but you may come unstuck eventually. The longer you wait to set one up the more you'll have to pay.

REPAYMENT MORTGAGE

You pay a monthly instalment to the lender that is made up of the interest on the loan and some of the capital. The longer the term of the loan, the less capital you pay in the early years. Initially, most of the monthly payment will be paying off the interest, but as the years pass more will go towards capital repayments.

Pros

- The cost of the mortgage is not related to your age or health.
- If times are hard, you can often extend the term to reduce monthly payments.
- Your loan is guaranteed to be paid off at the end of the term.
- You reduce the amount you have borrowed with regular payment.

Cons

- Once your outstanding mortgage falls below £30,000, tax relief is reduced.
- It can work out more expensive than an interest-only mortgage with savings plan scheme, if the mortgage rates are lower or you move frequently.
- If you are buying a home with a partner, have a family or other financial dependants to think about, you ought to take out life assurance to run alongside the loan so that the mortgage would be repaid if you or your partner should die. This is called mortgage protection insurance.

INTEREST-ONLY MORTGAGES

You pay the interest only to the lender and simultaneously you pay a monthly premium into an insurance company's savings plan, which eventually pays off the capital sum of the mortgage. The savings plans fall into three main groups: endowment policies, pension plans or personal equity plans.

LOW-COST ENDOWMENT

This is the most popular type of savings plan. The insurance company makes assumptions about the future rates of return on investment. If those assumptions are accurate, the mortgage will be repaid in full, and there may even be some money left over. If the returns are not as high, then there may be a shortfall which you would have to repay. Alternatively, you could take out a full endowment policy which guarantees to repay the loan at the end of the term. This is much more expensive.

Pros

- The savings plan may repay your loan early.
- Life assurance is included automatically.
- You can move home and take the existing endowment policy with you, rather than taking out a completely new mortgage, as with a repayment mortgage.

For example, you buy a house for £50,000 with an endowment policy for £50,000 over 25 years. In ten years' time you sell up and buy a new house for £70,000, taking your existing policy with you and topping it up with another policy for £20,000. After 15 years of the new mortgage the first policy will mature and pay off £50,000 of the mortgage. You will be left with the balance, £20,000 to pay off over the next ten years.

Cons

- The minimum term of the mortgage is usually ten years.
- A new mortgage lender may not accept an existing endowment policy.
- If you cash in the policy in the early years it won't be worth much.
- The amount of the original loan remains the same throughout the mortgage term, so the interest payments remain the same.
- With a low-cost endowment, there's no guarantee that the loan will be repaid at the end of the term.

PENSION MORTGAGES

You pay interest on the whole amount borrowed throughout the term of the loan. In addition, you pay regular premiums to a pension plan. When you start drawing your pension, part of it can be taken as a lump sum and used to pay off the mortgage, while the remainder provides a regular pension.

Pension mortgages are most suitable for people who have, or are eligible for, a personal pension plan: that is, people who are self employed and those not in occupational pension schemes.

Pros

- Tax relief on contributions is extensive, especially for high earners.
- The fund grows tax free.
- Low-cost life cover can usually be included within the pension plan; these contributions also gain full tax relief.

Cons

- As you are using part of your pension fund to repay your mortgage loan, the sum available for your pension will be smaller.
- The loan is not designed to be repaid until retirement, and it remains the same throughout the mortgage term.
- Personal pension plans cannot be written in joint names.
- You can only get the lump sum at the same time as you take the pension.

PEP MORTGAGES

You pay to the lender interest only on the loan, and also make contributions to a Personal Equity Plan that builds up tax free over the years. This should provide a lump sum which you use to pay off the loan.

Pros

- The main advantage is that it's a tax-efficient way of building up a fund to pay off the mortgage.
- Suits high-rate taxpayers.

Cons

- PEPs invest in company shares, often via unit trusts, so there is no guarantee that there will be enough to repay the mortgage at the end of the term (as the value of shares and units trusts can go down or up).
- Maximum contribution permitted is £6,000 per year.
- No built-in life cover.

TAX RELIEF

When you borrow to buy your own home, you currently get tax relief of 20 per cent on the interest payable on the first £30,000 of your mortgage. (The tax-relief rate was formerly 25 per cent.) From 1995–96, tax relief will only be available at a rate of 15 per cent.

Tax relief is usually given 'at source', which means that it is taken off the interest, before you pay it, with no need to claim it back from your tax office. It is usually known as MIRAS (Mortgage Interest Relief At Source).

MORTGAGES ON NEW HOMES

If you are buying a house in the process of construction, you will not receive all the money you are borrowing at once. The payments will be made at various stages, and most building societies or other lenders will not release the final loan until all the work is complete.

You will also find that lenders normally only lend on a new house built under the supervision of an architect or surveyor employed solely by the buyer, or by an NHBC or Zurich Municipal-registered builder.

If you are commissioning a house to be built, most building societies or other lenders will not release any money until the ground floor of the house is complete (or, if a bungalow, once you get to the roof stage). They will then send a valuer to inspect the work. The next instalment will be made when the second floor of the property has been completed and inspected. A final payment will be made when the property is complete and has been inspected. You will be charged about £50 for each inspection.

HOME-INCOME PLANS

Home-income plans, often called mortgage annuity schemes, are arrangments made with financial institutions through which older home owners (over retirement age) can raise an annual income for life from the capital value of their home, while still remaining the owner. The interest payable on the loan has to be deducted from the annuity and because of this many people are disappointed to find that the extra income is not as much as they hoped it would be (although the loan interest does attract tax relief). The loan is repaid when the home owner dies or sells the property.

Get independent financial and legal advice before making any commitment to such a plan, and look for companies who are part of the Safe Home Income Plan (SHIP) campaign. *Using Your Home as Capital* by Cecil Hinton and David Bookbinder (£4.50) available from bookshops or Age Concern has a useful fact sheet on the subject (see Useful Addresses).

TIP A home-income plan may not be worthwhile if you are receiving a means-tested social security benefit, as the income from the plan could jeopardise the benefit.

INSURANCE AND REGULATION

Anyone can adopt the title of mortgage broker or insurance consultant, whereas to be called an insurance broker you have to be registered with the Insurance Brokers Registraton Council.

There are a number of organisations regulating companies in the area of insurance and investment, many of which overlap in their role, which can be confusing for the uninitiated. As a rough guide, independent financial advisers and their appointed representatives should be regulated by FIMBRA (Financial Intermediaries, Managers and Brokers Regulatory Association). Insurance companies, life companies and financial advisers tied to one insurer should be regulated by LAUTRO (Life Assurance and Unit Trust Regulatory Organisation). The newly formed Personal Investment Authority will effectively take over the roles of LAUTRO and FIMBRA in regulating the private savings market as a whole (from October 1994).To find out who authorises a particular company you can contact the Securities and Investments Board (SIB), which has a central register and monitoring service.

GETTING GOOD MORTGAGE ADVICE

There are well over 200 institutions in the mortgage market so take some time to shop around. Make sure you know what sort of loan you are being offered; check the costs involved; find out whether life assurance is included or not. Study the literature from different building societies, banks, insurance companies and other financial institutions. Try to find an adviser who has a computerised mortgage database, to find the best deal for you quickly.

Under the Financial Services Act, companies that sell endowments, pension plans or personal equity plans have to be authorised to carry out their business, and have to abide by a set of rules. One important feature of these rules is that the company has to make it clear whether it is giving completely independent advice to its customers, or whether it is tied to selling one company's products. (If so, look for a sign in the window stating this.)

MORTGAGE BROKERS

Mortgage brokers make arrangements for you to borrow from someone else. If mortgages are not in short supply, or you want to buy a fairly ordinary house with an average sort of mortgage, there is little point in paying a broker. Go straight to a lender. But if you are hoping to buy an unusual house, or one which most lenders aren't too keen on (for example, a flat combined with shop) or if you want a very large loan, or mortgages are in short supply, a broker could be useful.

A good broker should give you a choice of mortgages to suit your circumstances. Get written quotations setting out all the payments involved and study the figures carefully.

If a broker offers you a repayment mortgage you will usually have to pay an arrangment fee of 1–2 per cent of the loan. If you are offered an endowment mortgage or pension mortgage you should not have to pay a fee as the broker will get commission from the insurance company that provides the endowment or pension policy. Be warned: some brokers may charge if you lapse the policy before a certain time has elapsed, eg, four years.

COMPARING QUOTES

When calculating how much you can afford to pay each month, remember that mortgage interest rates fluctuate. A change in interest rates can make a substantial difference to your monthly outgoings. As a rough guide, over the last ten years building society rates have averaged around 12.5 per cent.

It isn't easy to compare like with like between mortgage quotations. They all have to show the Annual Percentage Rate (APR) in their printed information. This tells you the true cost of your mortgage but spreads all the upfront charges involved in buying a house (such as arrangement fees, valuation and legal fees) across the term of the loan (usually 25 years). In reality, few mortgages last as long as this so the up-front fees have to be spread over a much shorter term than the APR calculation implies. So the best way to compare costs is to ask for a written quotation which clearly shows how much you will have to pay each month and details all the initial charges.

Also, you can compare current interest rates and conditions for mortgages in specialist mortgage magazines.

MORTGAGE INTEREST RATES

In addition to the different types of mortgage available, interest can be calculated and charged in various different ways.

VARIABLE

Most people have a mortgage with a variable rate of interest which reflects the general ups and downs of the interest rates in the economy. This means that when bank interest rates go up and down, so do your mortgage repayments. Your lender will always notify you of a change in advance.

FIXED-RATE

Alternatively, it may help you to budget more effectively if you opt for a fixed-rate mortgage. This gives you a guaranteed rate of interest for an agreed period of time, usually between three and five years. However, with a fixed-rate loan you are, in effect, gambling on future interest rates. At best, it guarantees that payments won't rise, but at worst, it may leave you paying over the odds if the interest rates fall. This type of mortgage can be expensive, too, if you want to switch to a different type of loan or repay the mortgage early.

CAPPED

Similar to a fixed-rate loan but you have a ceiling above which the interest on your loan will not rise for a set period.

DEFERRED RATE

These mortgages allow you to pay less interest each month than is actually being charged on your loan. The difference between what you pay and what you are charged is then added to the outstanding capital for a set period.

DISCOUNTED

Discounted rates are often used to entice first-time buyers to place their business with a particular lender. With this, a percentage discount is offered off the current mortgage rate for a specified period, eg, a 2 per cent discount on the standard rate for a year. A discount can substantially reduce outgoings for a short period, but the increase at the end of the discount period can take you by surprise.

TIP Look out for early redemption penalties. Some lenders make a special charge if you want to pay your mortgage off early. It can be as much as three months' extra interest.

PROBLEMS WITH MORTGAGE PAYMENTS

If you find that you cannot keep up your mortgage payments, do not assume that you will automatically lose your home. Ask your mortgage adviser for advice. With a repayment mortgage, the lender may agree to extending the term of a mortgage possibly by up to 35 or 40 years; or to you paying only the interest for a short period. There is less flexibility with an endowment mortgage, but you may be able to extend the term of the loan, and so reduce the amount you have to pay each month.

If you are out of work, or too ill to work and eligible for income support, the DSS may pay the interest on your mortgage for you. Ask for details at your local social security office.

Some lenders offer insurance policies that pay the mortgage payments if you are unable to earn because of illness or unemployment. These policies aren't cheap, so the wider the circumstances in which you are eligible to claim, the better.

Read the contract carefully. Many policies will only pay out for a fixed period (eg, one year) and the money paid under the policy will also be taken into account if you are claiming means-tested state benefit.

HOUSE-HUNTING

Looking for the home of your dreams can involve weeks of hunting which may at times be exhausting and demoralising, trailing round estate agents and viewing disappointing and unsuitable properties. So, take a deep breath … and be prepared to use all available methods: visiting estate agents, looking at advertisements in property magazines and newspapers, driving round the area, and even word of mouth.

ESTATE AGENTS

Look for local estate agents' names in the local paper or local directory. Most in England and Wales are members of professional associations such as the National Association of Estate Agents, The Incorporated Society of Valuers and Auctioneers, and the Royal Institution of Chartered Surveyers.

GETTING THE BEST FROM AN ESTATE AGENT

- At first, be prepared to spend time calling in or ringing up regularly in order to establish a good relationship with the agent. Ask to be put on the mailing list.
- If it's a seller's market, property may be bought up so quickly that the agent barely has time to print the particulars or put up a 'For Sale' board outside the house, so go straight to the agent's office and leave your name and your requirements.

MOVING FAR?

If you are planning to move into a completely new area, too far away for any regular on-the-spot house-hunting, it's worth getting your name on the mailing lists of the estate agents in the locality. Call on an agent in your home town and ask if he has any contact with fellow agents in the other area. He/she may have the *Estates Gazette,* which publishes a monthly regional directory of agents.

Also contact the National Association of Estate Agents' national Homelink Service, which provides a national network of estate agents. If you want to buy or sell a property in a different area it helps you to do it from a distance. You deal with your local estate agent, who will liaise with the estate agent in the area on your behalf. There is no charge for this service. (See Useful Addresses.)

There are a number of agencies which offer a national relocation service. These can take on much of the groundwork for you, from viewing properties and negotiating the price. They may even help you choose the children's schools. Expect to pay from around 1 per cent of the house purchase price. (Some charge a registration fee from about £200, which may be deductable from the final payment.) These agencies advertise in the national press and may be members of the Association of Relocation Agents.

SOLICITORS IN SCOTLAND

In Scotland, more properties are sold by solicitors than by estate agents.

Solicitors' property centres are run on a co-operative basis, and are usually situated in shopping areas to provide details of all properties being sold by local solicitors. The property centres are often part of chains owned by UK insurance companies or building societies.

For further information see Buying in Scotland, pages 34–5.

ADVERTISEMENTS

Find out which day the local newspaper devotes to property advertising. The paper will usually carry notices with details of property developments, and lists of recently granted planning permission may appear with the names of builders and developers. The local authority planning officer and building control officer know about future developments. There are also some monthly magazines which contain information on new estates being built and have regular articles on different areas of the country.

TIP If looking for a newly built house, ask local builders or national companies whether they have any future plans for putting up houses in the area. Ask local estate agents not only for details of houses being built or just completed, but also about any plans for the building of future estates.

AUCTION

The requirements for buying or selling at auction are somewhat different from ordinary sales. You must be aware of these before committing yourself in a sale room.

SELLING

If the estate agent finds it difficult to value your house because it is so unusual, or there is nothing similar to compare it to locally, he/she may suggest that the best way of getting the best price is at auction. The actual cost of selling is more expensive by auction, but you may get this back through a better sale price.

The estate agent will prepare detailed particulars, or a brochure, and extensive advertising. Prospective buyers will want to have surveys and valuations carried out before the auction, and you will need to be accommodating about these. The agent will help you to decide what the reserve price should be.

BUYING

Usually, the seller gains more benefit by going to auction than the buyer. Repossessed homes, or properties being sold by the executors after the death of the owner, often come to auction.

If you find that a property in which you are interested is going to auction, check immediately whether it must definitely go to auction, or if offers might be accepted beforehand.

Buying at auction is quite different to the normal method of sale, 'by private treaty' as it is known. By the day of the auction you must have carried out all the usual preparation work up to exchange of contracts on the property (see page 34).

You should have viewed the property, had a valuation survey carried out, raised a mortgage and had your solicitor carry out all the usual conveyancing. You will also probably be competing with other interested parties for the property. It's important to fix yourself a maximum price and stick to it at all costs. If your bid is accepted, you will be expected to exchange contracts there and then with the auctioneer, and pay at least 10 per cent of the purchase price. You will have vacant possession usually within 28 days after the auction.

THE RIGHT PROPERTY

Once you have found a property you want to see, make an appointment to view it as soon as possible, preferably with your partner, a friend, or a relative to give you a second opinion. Before you go to see it, make up a short check-list of things that are important to you, such as number of bathrooms, whether it has a garage, etc. Take a pen and paper and measuring tape with you, and the agent's particulars, so you can check the dimensions of the rooms.

Try to imagine your own decorations/furnishings/family/dogs in the house. Take your time when looking round – it's a big decision that you will live with for a long time.

SELECTING A PROPERTY

Here's a check-list for the kind of details you'll need to help you make an informed decision about a property:

Location

- How heavy is the traffic?
- Is it near a school, shops, police station, hospital, sports ground?
- Are traffic lights, road junctions, bends, hills, etc, close by?
- Do you share gateways, drives, hedges with neighbours?
- How secluded is the house? Are there footpaths or rights of way across your land?
- Do cars regularly park outside on weekdays?
- Do trains/planes pass within unpleasant hearing distance?

Accommodation

Does it have the right number of bedrooms, bathrooms, a large enough kitchen, separate toilets, etc?

Structure

Obviously, if you like the property and decide to put in an offer, a professional survey will have to be carried out. But try to get as good an impression as you can of the structural condition of the building when you visit it. If there is a great deal to be done, the cost of repairs may not justify the cost of the house. You could save yourself a survey fee. It's worth conducting your own 'mini MOT':

- Ask which way the property faces. A north-facing living room or kitchen is likely to be cold and gloomy if it gets no sun at any time of the day.
- If the house is less than ten years old, ask whether it has a National House-Building Council Buildmark or Zurich Home Building Guarantee and, if so, how long is left on it.
- Look for flaking outside brickwork, cracks, crumbling pointing, etc.
- Six inches/15cm above ground level, look for the damp-proof course.
- Look out for damp patches on ceilings and walls which may indicate a leaking roof, broken rainwater pipe or gutter, or perished pointing to the brickwork. Areas of lighter wallpaper or tide marks above the skirting boards may indicate rising damp.
- Timber defects: Are the floors springy? Be wary if the carpets or vinyl are firmly fixed down so inspection is difficult. There could be timber defects; get your surveyor to check this out carefully.

ROTTEN PROBLEMS

Dry rot

Look for cube-shaped cracking in the structural timbers, and in advanced stages, matted greyish-white strings, rusty red spores, pancake-like fungus and a mushroomy smell.

Wet rot

Check the basements and along bases of exterior doors, sills and window frames. Look for brittle wood with dark brown or black strands of fungus.

HOUSE-HUNTING AND THE WEATHER

Most houses look at their best when it's warm and sunny, so bear this in mind if house-hunting in the summer. If you like the look of a property on a cold, wet, winter's day, there's a good chance you won't be making a rash choice. Also, in cold weather the heating will probably be on, so you can judge for yourself how efficient it is.

- Open and close doors and windows to see if they stick.
- Dry and wet rot: If the house is old, ask about any timber treatments or damp courses which may have been inserted, how long ago and what guarantees go with them. The present owner may even insure against such defects. Wood preservation wasn't standard until the early 1970s.
- Subsidence has become a common problem, particularly in the South-east. Look for cracks in the main supporting walls, running diagonally through brick joints; walls that are obviously out of plumb; the tops of internal door linings that are not level and doors that stick in their frames.
- General decor: in what state are the doors, window frames, plasterwork, skirting boards and staircases?

Fixtures and fittings

Does the vendor intend to leave the carpets, curtains and light fittings, etc? Make sure all extra items that you see on your tour are included in the contract.

Light fittings, curtain rails, bathroom fitments, fitted bookcases, plants in the garden, etc, are often disputed. Look for a solicitor using The Law Society's TransAction Scheme. It is designed to make clear exactly what is included in the purchase price. The seller is provided with a comprehensive list of items and must indicate on it what is and what is not included.

Services

- Heating: ask the owners about the past year's fuel consumption and heating costs. Ask if the loft is properly insulated; and if the cavity walls have been insulated by foam or other fillings, and by whom.
- Water supply: is it on direct mains water? Check that both hot and cold water taps run clean. Discoloration could indicate a rusting storage tank and pipework. Ask how hard or soft the water is. If it's very hard, you may need to consider water-softening measures in your central heating and water systems to stop the pipes from furring up. If the water is naturally soft, it shouldn't be a problem as long as the water pipework isn't lead. Most lead

WHAT TO CHECK IN A FLAT

- Tap the walls to establish how thick they are. Try to make your visit on a weekday evening when neighbours are most likely to be in, to assess noise levels, car-parking space, etc.
- If it is a basement flat, how much natural light can you expect on a dull day? Is there on-street parking, and if so, will the windows be obstructed?
- Take a good look at the general condition of the property. You may be liable for major repairs if it hasn't been properly maintained in the past.
- Check the facilities for storage/dustbins/drying clothes/car-parking.

BUYER'S AND SELLER'S MARKETS

There are times when it is easier to sell than to buy (a seller's market) and times when the reverse is true (a buyer's market).

A seller's market occurs when more people want to buy than there are properties, and when loan finance is comparatively easy to obtain. At these times you will probably be able to sell your property within a few weeks at a good price.

A buyer's market is when there are more properties than prospective purchasers, and loan finance may be difficult to obtain or interest rates high. It may take a long time before you find a purchaser prepared to pay the price you want.

plumbing has been replaced now. If it hasn't, you may be able to get a grant from the local authority to help with costs.

- Council Tax: how much?
- Electricity: how old is the wiring? Anything older than 25 years will definitely need replacing. Newer wiring systems will have a consumer unit (a box of minature circuit breakers which don't blow) instead of an old-fashioned box of fuses.
- Drainage: is the house connected to mains drainage or is there a septic tank or cesspool?

Parking

- Is there a garage, and is it big enough?
- Is there parking for more than one car?

Vacant possession

When could you move in?

TAKING A SECOND LOOK

If you are still interested in the property, it is essential to go back again to see it at a different time of the day, on a different day of the week and in different weather conditions if possible. It is easy to gloss over the faults in your enthusiasm and a second look will ensure you've covered all the points on the check-list.

THE MECHANICS OF BUYING

Once you have chosen your property, there is a series of steps which must be followed:

1 CONSIDER MAKING AN OFFER

Once you have seen the house you like, you will be considering putting in an offer. Now, you need to ask yourself about the likely changes it would make to your standard of living and outgoings:

- What is the house going to cost in monthly mortgage payments?
- How will the mortgage affect your life insurance premiums (if payable on endowment or a mortgage-protection policy)?
- House contents insurance: is the premium higher for this area than where you are currently living? Ring your insurers for a quotation on the new property.
- Fuel consumption and travel costs: how much will it cost to get to work/the children to school. Will you need a second car?
- Will you have to spend out on redecoration or is the decor 'liveable with'?

BUYING A FLAT

- Is it leasehold or freehold? If leasehold, ask the current owner or estate agent who handles the general administration and maintenance of the building.

In Scotland, leasehold as such doesn't exist. Responsibility for repairs, the proportion of costs to be borne by each owner and the rights of owners to instruct repairs are dealt with in the title deeds of the property.

- Find out what ground rent is payable.
- Get an idea of the annual maintenance charges for repairs or redecoration. Is there any major expenditure to come?

If the flat comes with a share of the freehold, there will still be these common bills to pay, but they will be the joint responsibility of all the flat owners. Ask to see the lease and find out how the bills are divided between the flats.

- In the case of converted and freehold flats, check with your mortgage lender before proceeding too far towards buying to see whether they will accept it.
- Are there any restrictions in the lease such as hanging out washing, making a noise after 11pm, keeping pets, or having parties?

2 FIND A SOLICITOR

If you are ready to put in an offer and haven't already found a solicitor, choose one now. In England and Wales, you will also have the choice of going to a licensed conveyancer who specialises in house purchase transactions. Tell them about the offer.

Conveyancing is covered in more detail in Chapter 7, Legal Matters, but in essence your solicitor or conveyancer will:

- Advise you on the draft contract.
- Explain the details of the mortgage deed.
- Check that there are no developments planned (such as a road widening scheme) that might adversely affect the value of the property under consideration.
- Go through the title documents to ensure that proper title to the property is obtained.
- Check restrictions on the way the property is used, compliance with building regulations and planning legislation
- Check legal aspects of facilities such as sewers serving the property.
- Arrange the exchange of contracts.
- Arrange for completion, when the balance of the mortgage is paid to the seller and the buyer moves into the property.

PROBLEMS WITH SOLICITORS

If you experience any disputes with your solicitor, you can use the Law Society's Arbitration Scheme. For problems with a licensed conveyancer turn to the Council for Licensed Conveyancers.

See Useful Addresses.

3 MAKE AN OFFER

Make sure you have a clear understanding of exactly what the property includes and that the particulars are all correct. Put your offer in quickly, either direct to the seller if being sold privately, or to the seller's estate agent. Don't forget to take into account how much you can afford, the state of the property market (ie, whether you have any bargaining power) and how much you are prepared to raise your offer. Let the estate agent or vendor know if you:

- Are a cash buyer.
- Already have a buyer for your own property.
- Have a mortgage certificate guaranteeing the offer of a loan.

Any of these will make your offer much more attractive to the seller.

Be prepared: you may be asked to pay a deposit (£100–250) as a token of your interest. This deposit isn't binding in law so if you are unwilling to pay it it shouldn't jeopardise your chances of buying. If you do pay it, make sure you get a receipt saying 'subject to contract and survey'. If the sale then falls through before contracts are exchanged, that money has to be returned.

Once you have put in your offer you will be asked for the details of your solicitor or conveyancer. The average period, from putting in your offer to the date when the keys are handed over, is about 12 to 16 weeks, but this can vary considerably.

4 SELL YOUR CURRENT HOUSE

Put your own house on the market if you haven't already done so. (See Selling Your Home, pages 36–8.)

5 CONFIRM YOUR OFFER

Confirm your offer in writing 'subject to contract and to survey' either direct to the seller or to his/her estate agent. Liaise with your solicitor or conveyancer over this.

You may have to wait some time for the offer to be considered by the seller, or you may have to put in a new offer. If you are lucky, your offer may be accepted straight away. If so, the house is 'under offer', and you can ask the seller not to take offers from any other potential buyers – but he is under no obligation to do so. While the sellers may not look like the kind of people to accept a higher offer after accepting yours, it may well be the estate agent who is keen to get as much for the property as possible. 'Lock-out' agreements are now used by some solicitors, where both sides agree in writing not to withdraw from the offer. The seller agrees not to deal with anyone else for a fixed period, and the buyer agrees to take active steps to proceed with the purchase.

The time between making an offer and exchanging contracts is always an anxious one, as in England and Wales, simply making an offer and having it accepted isn't legally binding on either side.

6 MAKE A FORMAL MORTGAGE APPLICATION

Return the mortgage application form to the lender with the fee for valuation.

The lender will require considerable information about the house (most of which can be obtained from the particulars provided by the estate agent or seller) and also about you, the borrower.

7 THE VALUATION

In order to check the value of a property, the lender will commission a qualified valuer to inspect it. You will be expected to pay for this even if you don't subsequently buy the property. There is no set scale of fees for valuation, but an average fee would be in the region of about £120. Ask the lender for an exact figure.

The valuation assesses whether the condition and value of the house is adequate security for the loan. If the building society feels the house is worth less than the purchase price, the proportion that will be lent may be calculated on the valuation price, not the purchase price.

For a lender's valuation, the valuer takes into account factors such as the age, and type of property; its fixtures and features, construction, general state of repair and amenities. It will provide some idea of the condition of the 'visible' parts of the property. The lender is not legally bound to disclose the contents of the report. but may recommend that certain work is done, such as repointing a chimney or putting in a damp proof course, before the loan is given. He/she may even recommend that an amount of the loan is withheld until the work has been carried out.

8 GET A SURVEY

The lender's valuation is no substitute for a full structural survey on the property. Only about 20 per cent of buyers arrange even a House Buyer's report, and the result is that around 4 per cent of house purchases involve a property with a defect such as subsidence and dry rot.

You can organise the survey yourself, or in most cases get the building society's surveyor to do your survey at the same time as the valuation. This may reduce the overall fees for both survey and valuation slightly.

Tell the surveyor as much as you know about the house and its history, and any plans you have for changing the structure, such as knocking down walls, opening up fireplaces or building an extension. Of course, it will be easier for your surveyor to be thorough if the house is empty (and therefore floorboards, etc, accessible). If it's still occupied try to get an idea how much prodding and upheaval the owners are prepared to put up with, as they may already have had to put up with other prospective buyers' surveys.

Alternatively, you will need to find a qualified surveyor to carry out the work for you. Contact the Royal Institution of Chartered Surveyors, or the Architects and Surveyors Institute for names of any of their members in your area. Otherwise, get a recommendation from a friend.

Full Structural/Building survey

If the property is old, or clearly in need of repair, or you are contemplating alterations such as extensions, you should definitely commission a full structural/building survey. There is no scale of fees for structural surveys. Costs depend on the property's size and age, but may well be about £500 on a property under £100,000. It's expensive, but it can be invaluable to ensure that there are no major structural faults that may prove expensive to repair. It will also tell you in detail about minor defects which, in the long run, you can't ignore.

An inspection lasts several hours and provides a detailed examination and report of all visible parts of the building, including testing walls for dampness and timber for damage. It is important to discuss with your surveyor exactly what is to be covered in the survey before he proceeds.

Home Buyer's Survey and Valuation

The Royal Institution of Chartered Surveyors (RICS) and the Incorporated Society of Valuers and Auctioneers now offer the Home Buyer's Survey and Valuation (HBSV), which is less detailed than a full structural survey but is more than a valuation. Buyers are advised to commission this type of independent survey at the very least. It will tell you about:

- The general condition of the property.
- Any factors likely to affect materially the value of the property.
- The true, current value of the property in the open market.
- The estimated reinstatement cost for insurance purposes. This is the cost of rebuilding the house if it burns down.

The HBSV is suitable and sufficient for most purchases of second-hand property. If a problem is spotted, you can then arrange a more detailed examination with the agreement of the existing owner.

For more advice on the different surveys available, ring the RICS Information Centre and ask for their leaflet called *Buying a new home: Mortgage valuation report or survey?*

The surveyor may recommend that you have specialist tests carried out if the property is of a particular age. He may also recommend specialist treatment such as damp proofing is carried out. Get at least three estimates and then bear this in mind: you may want to offer less to take into account the work needed.

9 EXCHANGE CONTRACTS FOR SALE AND PURCHASE

Now you are legally committed to buying. You will have to pay a deposit of 5 to 10 per cent, and arrange a completion date. Ensure that any life policy runs from the date you exchange contracts. Also arrange buildings and contents cover from this date.

10 COMPLETION

This is when you pay the balance of the purchase price, and in return you get the keys and title deeds (usually done via the solicitors). Your mortgage lender is then sent the deeds.

BUYING IN SCOTLAND

The house buying and selling process is rather different in Scotland than England or Wales. There are two major advantages of the system in Scotland:

1 It avoids the difficulties of delays resulting from 'chains'. (These can arise under the English and Welsh system if one sale is delayed, thereby affecting a whole series of transactions.)

2 Formal offers are legally binding, so you cannot be gazumped (where someone offers more for the property) or gazundered (where someone can act more quickly on the transaction than you can).

If you are thinking of buying a property in Scotland, you should seek advice from your legal adviser before you take any steps at all.

THE SCOTTISH SYSTEM

This is the basic process:

1 Even before you have found a house, you should establish your eligibility for a mortgage on the intended type of property.

2 When you have found a house you like, tell your solicitor. He will then notify the seller's solicitor or estate agent of your interest.

3 The survey is usually carried out before you make a formal offer for a property.

4 If the survey report is favourable, make a written offer (with a time limit for acceptance) to buy the property through your solicitor. This is a formal document specifying all the conditions on which you are willing to buy the property right down to when you want to move in and what extras you want to buy (such as carpets, curtains or cooker). If your offer is accepted, it is a binding contract under Scottish Law and you will not have an opportunity for second thoughts. You may be penalised if you do break the contract.

5 If there is more than one interested party, there will be a closing date by which all interested parties must have made their offer. The highest offer is normally the one accepted, but the seller may take other factors into consideration such as the moving date. (The offer will be subject, among other things, to local authority and property searches. If they disclose anything adverse, you can withdraw your offer or re-negotiate the price.)

6 Usually, the seller's solicitor will tell your solicitor if the offer has been accepted with any modifications to the terms of your offer, such

as the date of entry. These written modifications along with the offer are called 'the Missives'. This bargaining process should only take a few days. From the date of signing the Missives to the date on which you get the keys is a matter of negotiation.

7 Your solicitor will then start the conveyancing procedure and you must formalise your mortgage arrangements.

8 On the date of settlement, the money for the full price will be handed over in return for the title deeds and the keys.

The Law Society of Scotland has a series of leaflets on buying and selling a house in Scotland. Send an SAE with a 45p stamp – see Useful Addresses.

GENERAL HOUSE-BUYING TIPS

- Keep all the paperwork to do with your house transactions together in a file. Keep a copy of every letter you send and take a note of every conversation relating to the buying or selling transaction. Note the date, time, who you spoke to and what was said.
- Keep a record of financial details and all the money you spend.
- If possible, type letters and documents and use a fax machine to speed up the process. Send any important communications by registered post.
- Stay in regular contact with your solicitor.

SELLING YOUR HOME

If you already own a home, you'll know that the first step to finding your new home is to get a good idea of your current property's value and then put it on the market.

It's also a good idea, at this stage, to make a list of the items you are prepared to leave (such as carpets, curtains, a washing machine), then to include the cost of buying new items in the calculations for your new property.

USING AN ESTATE AGENT

The estate agent's role is to value your property in line with others of a similar nature in your area, advise on how to prepare the house for sale, handle enquiries and receive offers on your behalf. He/she should guide you through all aspects of your sale and have a good relationship with other professionals such as banks and building society managers, mortgage advisers, solicitors and accountants. The estate agent's fee is usually about 1 to 3 per cent of the selling price, plus VAT.

Ideally, go to an estate agent who has been recommended to you or in whom you already have confidence. Since the implementation of the Estate Agents Act 1979, the industry has had to clean up its act. It is, however, still permissible for anybody to set up as an estate agent without training. So ask if the estate agent of your choice is a member of a professional body. There is also an ombudsman to deal with complaints. The Properties Misdescription Act also curbs the natural tendency towards flowery descriptions, such as 'bijou' when they mean cramped.

If you don't have a particular firm in mind, look for estate agents who are members of The National Association of Estate Agents (or RICS, or the Incorporated Society of Valuers and Auctioneers). The NAEA insists on a certain level of training for its members, has a code of practice and a grievance procedure for dissatisfied customers.

Ask at least three estate agents to value your house (this is usually free of charge) and get an idea of how long they think it will take to sell. Choose one that will co-ordinate your sale carefully, not just the one that offers the highest valuation or the lowest fees.

SOLE OR JOINT SELLING RIGHTS?

You can instruct more than one estate agent to sell your property. If you ask just one, he/she may reduce his fee, say to 1 per cent. Don't give them sole selling rights, as you will have to pay them commission even if you sell privately without their help. Joint sole agency is more usual. Two agents take the property on their books and split the commission, say 1.5 per cent each, whoever arranges the sale.

DIY SELLING

If you are prepared to organise advertising and viewing of your home yourself, you could save an estate agent's fee. On a property worth £120,000, this could be as much as £3,600. Around 5 per cent of homes in the UK are sold successfully in this way. As long as you don't hand over sole selling rights, you could even try to sell privately as well as having an estate agent working on your behalf.

However, selling privately involves effort, and depends on a number of factors:

- You. Are you resilient enough to put up with derogatory comments about your home, or insultingly low offers?
- The time you have available to organise

appointments and show viewers round.

- The area in which you live, ie, sought after or run down.
- Market conditions, ie, buyer's or seller's market.
- The type of property you are selling. It is probably easier to sell DIY at the lower end of the market.

STEPS TO SELL PRIVATELY

Setting the price

If you have already had your house on the market through an estate agent you will know how much it is worth. You may have a rough idea from similar properties in the area. If not, for about £120, you could ask a professional valuer to give you a valuation and highlight any obvious defects. Shop around for a surveyor and choose one who is a member of either the Royal Institution of Chartered Surveyors, the Architects and Surveyors Institute or the Incorporated Society of Valuers and Auctioneers.

Advertising

This is the most expensive part of selling privately, but is crucial in order to get a result. People moving into a new area will often buy the local or regional paper to give them a feel for what properties are available. Check out the advertising rates and set yourself a budget. It may also be worth investigating the cost of advertising in the national press.

There are also a number of property magazines which often print pages of classified house sale advertisements at a nominal fee.

If you are putting up your own signs, check with the local authority about the number of signs and the size they are allowed to be. This is now regulated by the local authority Town and Country Planning Act. Erect the sign on your own land in a prominent position so it is easily visible to passing traffic.

Once you have found a buyer it is best to let your solicitor deal with the formalities of transferring the ownership of land and property (ie, conveyancing).

SELLING IN SCOTLAND

If you are selling a house in Scotland you may be familiar with the Scottish system already, where more properties are sold by solicitors than estate agents (see Buying in Scotland, pages 34–5).

First, you should contact your solicitor before putting your house on the market, to give him/her time to get your title deeds in good order, and get local authority searches under way.

You can advertise your house for sale either using a solicitor, which is the usual way; using an estate agent; or by doing it yourself.

The first thing to decide is when you are going to sell, how much you want for the property, and what items you are prepared to leave behind. In Scotland it is normal to advertise at 'offers over' a certain figure, in anticipation of receiving a higher bid.

It is usual for any interested parties, whom you may have shown round your house, to tell their solicitor that they are interested. They will then notify your solicitor. You should then not sell to anyone without giving everyone who has notified an interest to you, your solicitor, or your estate agent, an opportunity of making an offer.

Noting interest is usually followed by a visit from the surveyors of interested parties. If the reports are favourable they will probably be followed by an offer which will be made in writing by the buyer's solicitors. The offer – usually the highest is accepted – will form the basis of the sale contract and will usually contain a large number of conditions.

Sometimes a number of letters are required to adjust the details for your and the purchaser's contractual obligations. Only once all the conditions are agreed is there a binding contract. The offer and letters are known as 'the Missives'.

When more than one person wants to make an offer for your property it will be appropriate for your solicitor to fix a closing date for offers.

For more details, write to the Law Society of Scotland with a 45p SAE – see Useful Addresses.

SELLING TIPS

Everyone knows a few tricks of the trade when it comes to making a house seem instantly more appealing to prospective purchasers. But there's more to it than simply putting out cut flowers in the sitting room and wafting the aroma of freshly brewed coffee around the house.

Do

- Tidy up any peeling wallpaper and repair damaged paintwork.
- Fix any dripping taps and replace broken light bulbs.
- Deal with sticking windows and doors.
- Keep halls and stairways clear.
- Kitchens and bathrooms sell houses more than any other rooms in the house. Keep them neat and clean.
- Tidy the airing cupboard, basement and attic.
- Clean windows.

Prior to a visit

- Keep the front of the house clean and tidy: lawns trimmed, flower beds cultivated and free of rubbish and clutter.
- In bad weather, be sure that paths and steps are free from snow and ice.
- Keep the driveway clear and the gates open with adequate room for the visitors to park easily.
- At night, turn on a porch or hall light to welcome them.
- Make sure the house number or name can be seen from the road, and if you have a doorbell, make sure it works.
- Keep pets under control and quiet, or out of the house.
- Turn off the radio, TV or stereo so buyers aren't distracted.
- If your buyer seems interested, offer to answer their questions but then let them look at their leisure.
- Have an idea of the latest gas/electricity/water bill, in case they ask.

Don't

- Have too many people present. Potential buyers always feel like intruders and wish to respect your privacy. Try not to hurry them through the house.
- Arouse suspicion with last-minute redecoration or telltale fresh paint smells.
- Apologise for your home. By doing so you might suggest problems which don't actually exist.

REMOVALS

Once you have exchanged contracts and been given a moving date, there's no time to lose in preparing for the big day.

PROFESSIONAL REMOVERS

If using a professional removal company, start selecting one well in advance. Ask friends and neighbours to recommend firms or contact the British Association of Removers (BAR, see Useful Addresses) for firms in your area. Alternatively, your local estate agent may well be able to recommend someone. You may stand a better chance of getting the firm you want on the day you want if you pick a day in the middle of the month, as this is when they are usually least busy.

Get two or three estimates based on a thorough inspection of your entire house, garden and belongings. Point out anything that may need special packing such as an antique clock, the freezer or built-in cupboards. Don't forget to include the loft, garage or shed in the grand tour, and remember to mention any items that need to be picked up from somewhere else. Also tell them what to expect in terms of access at the new house. (Break it to them gently if you moving into a fifth-floor flat with no lift.)

When you accept an estimate you are expected to give a firm date for the job. It's a good idea to confirm in writing any special packaging arangements. You'll also need to consider extending your insurance cover for the move. It's worth asking about the BAR Careline Guarantee which gives you up to £1,500 worth of protection against anything going wrong with the move, your car or even at your new home.

TIP Removal firms don't generally accept responsibility for damage to any items which have not been packed by them, and nor do their insurers. So check before you start packing. Watch out for the 'pairs and sets clause', which means that the insurers will not pay the costs of replacing any undamaged item forming part of a set such as a dinner service when replacements cannot be found.

DIY REMOVAL

It may be worth considering doing the removal yourself if you are a first-time buyer, or moving out of furnished rented accommodation, or simply have few heavy belongings and plenty of muscle to help. It will also be considerably cheaper. But don't attempt it otherwise, as the process can be totally exhausting, even with a removal firm who can pack more carefully and move furniture much more quickly than you.

You'll need to hire a large van for the duration of the move. You can drive up to a 7½-ton vehicle with a standard driving licence, but you have to be over 23 years to satisfy most hire firms. Choose a hire company that is a member of the British Vehicle Rental and Leasing Association (see Useful Addresses). Once you know the capacity of the van, you will need to estimate what loads it will take and therefore how many journeys you will have to make. Check whether you can hire it just one way.

If you are doing the removing yourself, allow plenty of time in advance for packing. You will need packing cases, rope or webbing to secure items in the van, and blankets or other protection for polished surfaces.

Many firms don't include contents insurance for the moving of your goods and

PACKING HINTS

- You may be able to hire packing cases along with a van. If not, collect some heavy-duty boxes from the local supermarket: arrange to call when they have had an unpacking session. Alternatively, a local removal firm may be prepared to sell you some cartons.
- Collect old newspapers for packing.
- For moving TVs and computers, etc, ask a local electrical retailer if they have any cartons with left-over polystyrene shavings.
- Don't fill boxes too full otherwise they become impossible to lift. Boxes of books should be no more than half full if you intend to lift them off the ground.
- Packing china and glass: make a thick bottom layer of crumpled newspaper. Put heavier items at the bottom. Wrap large items individually and put other items round them with plenty of crumpled newspaper.
- Label boxes as you pack by content, by room and with any other useful details such as non-essentials, or in order of unpacking.
- Remember that the order in which you load the van will be the reverse of how you unload it. Items you will want to unpack first, eg carpets, should go in last.
- Lift heavy items with your knees bent and your back straight to avoid strain.

chattels. Those that do usually offer two thresholds: £5,000 or £10,000. Otherwise it may be sensible to organise your own.

STORAGE

If you cannot move straight into your new home, you may have to put your belongings into storage for a while. Many removal firms have their own storage facilities. Look in the telephone directory or ask the British Association of Removers (see Useful Addresses) for a list of its members. Always get more than one estimate, and compare costs. Storage firms accept the whole contents of a house with the exception of perishable or flammable goods. Non-perishable food items will be accepted if they are packed carefully, in order to discourage attack by vermin.

Stored goods are usually packed into sealed containers at your home and the containers are stored untouched in a warehouse until you need them again. This way there is less risk of damage in transit or warehousing, there is greater protection from dirt, and a lower possibility of loss.

The storage firm or your own household insurers can arrange cover for house contents during storage. Make sure it is a sufficient sum and covers all risks.

It is expensive to retrieve items once they are in storage. Attach 'keep forward labels' to items you may want in advance so they can be kept reasonably accessible.

STORAGE COSTS

The British Association of Removers estimates that it costs about £10 for a 250cu ft/7cu m wooden storage container. Use the following as a guide for containers:

2-bedroom semi or terrace =
2–3 containers
3-bedroom semi or terrace =
3–4 containers
3 bedroom detached = 4–6 containers

TIP Storage firms recommend that you clean your carpets before putting them into store. Damage from moths can be a problem during storage. Wash then treat woollen clothes and blankets with a moth-deterrent spray.

PREPARING TO MOVE

UP TO A MONTH IN ADVANCE

1 Get removal firms' estimates and/or quotations for van-hire charges. Choose the firm, or van company, and confirm arrangements in writing with payment.

TIP Check the quotation. Usually, your mover will take down curtains/blinds and lift carpets if asked – but will not put them up again or lay fitted carpeting.

2 If doing the move yourself, book strong friends and family early for help with the packing, cleaning and moving.
3 Services: Arrange for electricity, gas (and if applicable, water) meters to be read at your old address. At the same time, arrange for the cooker, washing machine and dishwasher to be disconnected.
4 About two weeks before moving in, contact the various services – electricity, gas, and water – about your moving date so that they can connect supplies. Ask the previous owner not to disconnect the services when they leave.
5 Telephone: Arrange for a final bill to be made up to the day on which you move out of the old property. If new occupants don't want the phone, arrange for disconnection.

Make sure that the line to your new home is not disconnected, or if a new line is required, arrange for installation as early as possible since there may be a delay. Now's the time to think about also getting extra sockets installed.

TIP If you are moving to a new address within the same telephone exchange area, it is usually possible to take your existing number with you, but there will be a charge for doing so.

6 Arrange for carpets to be laid.
7 Get change-of-address cards, and fill in a mail redirection form, available from any post office. The postal service can redirect your mail for up to a year after the move, but you must give seven days' notice before the date you want the redirection to start.

The same form contains a section for you to complete for notifying the National TV Licence Records Office in Bristol of your change of address.
8 You may want to transfer your bank account to your new area. The bank may require a formal letter, or a new form, asking for the transfer to be made on a certain date.
9 Hired goods: If you hire appliances such as a TV, video recorder or washing machine, check with the rental firm whether you can take them with you to your new home. This is worth doing if you have been paying a reduced rent for an older appliance. Otherwise turn it in and take out a new contract locally.
10 Arrange buildings and contents insurance at the new house from the date of moving, and contents insurance during removal.
11 Locate your nearest household refuse site and start sorting and throwing things out. Buy plenty of strong black sacks, and check with charity shops exactly what they will and won't take. Then tackle hoarding places, such as a loft or garage, as early as posssible.
12 If doing your own removal, arrange to use boxes from a local supermarket.
13 Book overnight accommodation for the night after the move, if necessary.
14 Arrange for children and pets to stay with friends or relatives during the move.

ONE WEEK AHEAD

1 Plan in advance roughly where the furniture – or at least the heavier items – will be placed. Better still, make a room-by-room plan and mark the furniture with coloured stickers to represent different rooms. This will help you work out if you have room for everything, and will give you something to pass on to the removal men on the day.

2 Send off change-of-address cards, and let the following people know about the change of address:

- AA, RAC
- Bank/building society
- Children's schools
- Credit and charge-card companies
- Doctor/dentist/optician
- Employer
- Current employer and previous employer's pension fund
- Hire-purchase/TV rental company
- Inland revenue (notify Inspector of Taxes)
- Insurance company for policies on car, house, life, private health, etc
- Magazine subscriptions
- National insurance (notify DSS)
- Pension/benefit book (notify DSS)
- Professional bodies
- TV-licence records office (via post offfice)
- Vehicle registration and driving licence (notify DVLC, Swansea)
- Vet.

3 Cancel milk, newspapers, etc, at old address and settle accounts. Rearrange at new house.

4 Put valuables and documents in a safe place.

5 Tell police about the move and if necessary ask about getting the space outside your house coned off until the removal lorry has arrived. You need about 50ft/15m of parking for one large moving truck.

6 Check self-drive van arrangements.

7 Double check the arrangements and timings for meter readings, disconnection and connection of electricity and gas.

8 Double check with seller or buyer about leaving off or on electricity, water and heating, plus where to leave old keys and collect new.

9 To make life easier for the removers, put crockery and glass ready on a level surface ready for packing; and leave drawers as they are but unlocked.

10 Dismantle modular furniture (which isn't usually covered by insurance). Remember that your insurance will not cover items you have packed yourself so think carefully about what you should leave to the removal men.

11 Run down food stocks in your deep freeze so that as little as possible is left. (The removal men are not responsible for the contents.)

THE DAY BEFORE

1 To ensure your move out of the old and into the new house runs smoothly, it's a good idea to prepare two boxes of useful items, to take directly with you:

Box one for the kitchen, containing: kettle, tea-bags, coffee, milk, sugar, cold drinks (if summer), biscuits, mugs, spoons, plates, knives, cleaning cloth, towel, can opener, toilet paper, pain killers, plasters, antiseptic wipes, note-pad and pen, corkscrew and change.

Box two for the car: emergency tool-kit, screwdrivers, pliers, adjustable spanner, nails, hammer, screws, fuses, fuse wire, tape, string, light bulbs, plugs, adaptors and torch.

2 Pack overnight case if necessary.

3 Defrost fridge.

4 Get supply of cash for tips and meals.

5 Leave out vacuum cleaner, broom, cleaning equipment and plenty of black sacks for last-minute rubbish.

6 Keep the phone numbers for the service companies handy in case of problems.

COMPLETION AND HANDOVER OF KEYS

Your solicitor or conveyancer will have dealt with the legal and financial side of completion. Normally, the keys are not released until the purchase money has reached the seller's solicitor. The seller should give keys to the solicitor, who will give them to your solicitor and then to you. It may be more convenient for the keys to be handed over by the estate agent. The seller's solicitor will authorise this as soon as completion has taken place.

MOVING DAY

1 Don't leave your handbag, wallet or any valuables lying around either house on moving day. Keep cheque book and bank card handy.
2 Strip and pack bedding in labelled sacks.
3 Clear kitchen of foodstuffs.
4 The meters should be read and services disconnected.
5 When the removal company arrives, show the foreman around and explain your labelling system. Check that any special requests have been noted. If the men are doing all the packaging and loading keep out of their way.
6 Check that the heating system and mains water has been left on or off, depending on the arrangements made with the new owner.
7 Leave all the keys labelled.
8 Make sure the removal men know exactly where they are taking your belongings. Ideally, give them a map and a contact phone number.
9 Send someone on ahead to let the removal men in and start directing the proceedings.

AT THE NEW HOME

1 Stick your plan for rooms, if you have one, in a prominent place. Alternatively, you may prefer to stand there yourself and direct the men as they unload each item of furniture.
2 After all your possessions have been unloaded and the job finished, the removal men will expect a tip (about £5 per man is usual). If you aren't satisfied, say so now, otherwise any claim you make later may prove to be a problem. You may be asked to sign a discharge document that the job is completed. Write on this any reservations you have about the work. If you have not yet inspected your belongings, sign as 'unexamined'.
3 Make up beds and find towels and soap.
4 Ring the local council to find out the day for refuse collection, and the location of your nearest household waste site. (There's bound to be rubbish when unpacking is finished.)
5 You may want to have a good clean of the house before you unpack. But be warned, the time limit within which a claim for removal damage must be made, in writing, both to the insurers and the removal company, may be as little as three days after delivery.

Nevertheless, on the removal day, don't attempt to unpack everything immediately. Just sort out the essentials, and celebrate being in your new home.

AFTER THE MOVE

- Have locks of outer doors changed.
- Fit key-operated window locks if they are not already in place.
- Check if your insurer recommends specific types of lock or offers any discounts if certain brands are installed. In general, when buying new locks, look for the British Standards Kitemark on the front face of the lock or on the packaging. For further advice on security see Home Security, page 421.

EQUIPPING YOUR HOME

EQUIPPING A KITCHEN

The kitchen is one of the most hard-working areas in the house, and therefore its planning needs careful attention.

KITCHEN PLANNING

When planning a new kitchen, even if you are using a professional, it is wise to do a plan yourself. Although a professional kitchen planner is very experienced, only you know how you will use your kitchen. If you are not involved, minor details may be overlooked which will be irritating and make your kitchen less easy to work in.

However, if you decide not to do your own plan you will still need to spend time thinking about your new kitchen because a professional plan will only be as good as your briefing.

Starting points

- Be prepared to take some time to get the kitchen right.
- Think about how you use your current kitchen.
- Make a list of its good and bad features.
- Ask friends for their experiences and any grievances.

AREAS TO CONSIDER

- How much can you afford?
- What activities do you use your kitchen for? For example, cooking only, eating in, socialising, laundry, or supervising children while cooking?
- Will the kitchen be used for any specialised cooking such as stir-frying in a wok, or large-scale preserving?
- How many people will use the kitchen? One person, two adults, or a large family with young children?
- Do you want to eat in the kitchen? Will you include a breakfast bar or table (fold-away if space is tight) and do you want to obscure the food preparation area from the dining area?
- What is the maximum number of seats required, and what is the minimum (in a small area) that will be satisfactory?
- Which appliances do you want to include and will you be keeping any existing appliances?
- How much storage space do you need? For example: food that is chilled, frozen, dry, bought in bulk; cleaning products in lockable cupboards away from children; china and glass; rubbish disposal.

DRAWING A SCALE PLAN

The first step is to draw an accurate scale plan of your existing kitchen. Use graph paper and a scale of 1:20, so that 1.2in/30mm represents 2ft/600mm, which is the depth of many kitchen units.

Include all permanent features such as windows and sills, doors (mark the swing areas), chimney breast (external and recess dimensions), mains water supplies and stopcocks, waste outlets and soil pipes, boiler and controls, pipework, radiators and valves, and power points. Note which walls are internal and which are external. Include the ceiling height.

Measuring the kitchen

It is important to measure your kitchen accurately, as even the smallest inaccuracies at this stage will be vital when it comes to installation. You will need two people to do a proper job and it may take a few hours, depending on the size of the room. **It is very important to measure everything in metric, as**

kitchen units and components are always sold in metric sizes. Do not try to convert inches into metric later.

Measuring tips

- Use a metal tape measure.
- Measure walls at floor and ceiling level, and at work-top height.
- Watch out for uneven flooring and corners.
- Double check all measurements.
- Take overall wall dimensions, then step dimensions, then compare to plus or minus 10mm.

STRUCTURAL CHANGES

If you are short of space you may decide to change the shape of the kitchen. You will need to weigh up the inconvenience of leaving the kitchen as it is with the cost of carrying out the alterations. Relatively easy jobs include raising a window-sill or knocking out a larder.

Moving walls is more costly, but could make all the difference. You may have to apply for approval for alterations under the Building Regulations, depending on the type of alteration (minor or major). Contact your local authority for advice. For a booklet explaining the Building Regulations contact the Department of the Environment: see Useful Addresses. If a professional is carrying out structural work for you, ask if they have obtained the correct permission, because ultimately you will be responsible.

Plumbing, wiring and drainage should conform to regulations. If worried about these, contact The Royal Institute of Chartered Surveyors (see Useful Addresses), who will put you in touch with a building surveyor in your area. They will survey the kitchen and highlight any problems. Surveyors usually charge an hourly fee and a kitchen survey usually takes about two hours.

DESIGNING THE LAYOUT

Once you have the basic shape of your kitchen on paper you can work on the layout. Templates of the standard kitchen units and components on a scale of 1:20 are printed below. Photocopy, and use them to help plan the layout. Alternatively, use card shapes (drawn to scale) of the appliances and furniture you want to include. By moving the shapes around the plan it is possible to assess the pros and cons of different layouts. Aim to create maximum storage space and to position the largest area of work surface between the cooker and sink. Allow for swing areas of doors and windows and the door openings of storage units.

Work triangle

The three main activity areas in a kitchen are food storage (fridge and food cupboards), preparation (sink and work-tops) and cooking (oven or hob, depending on what you use most frequently).

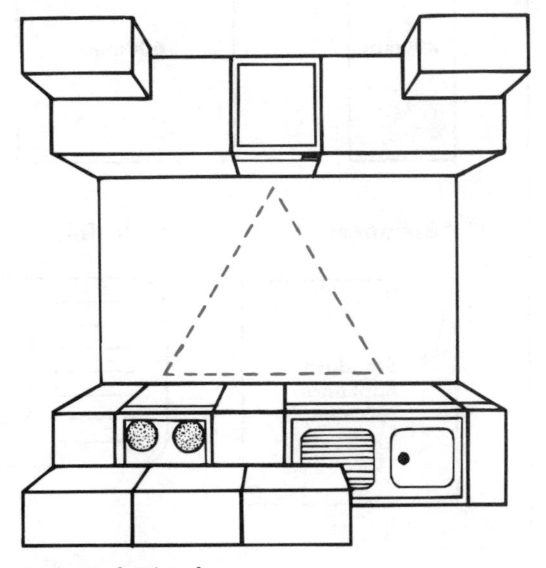

Basic Work Triangle

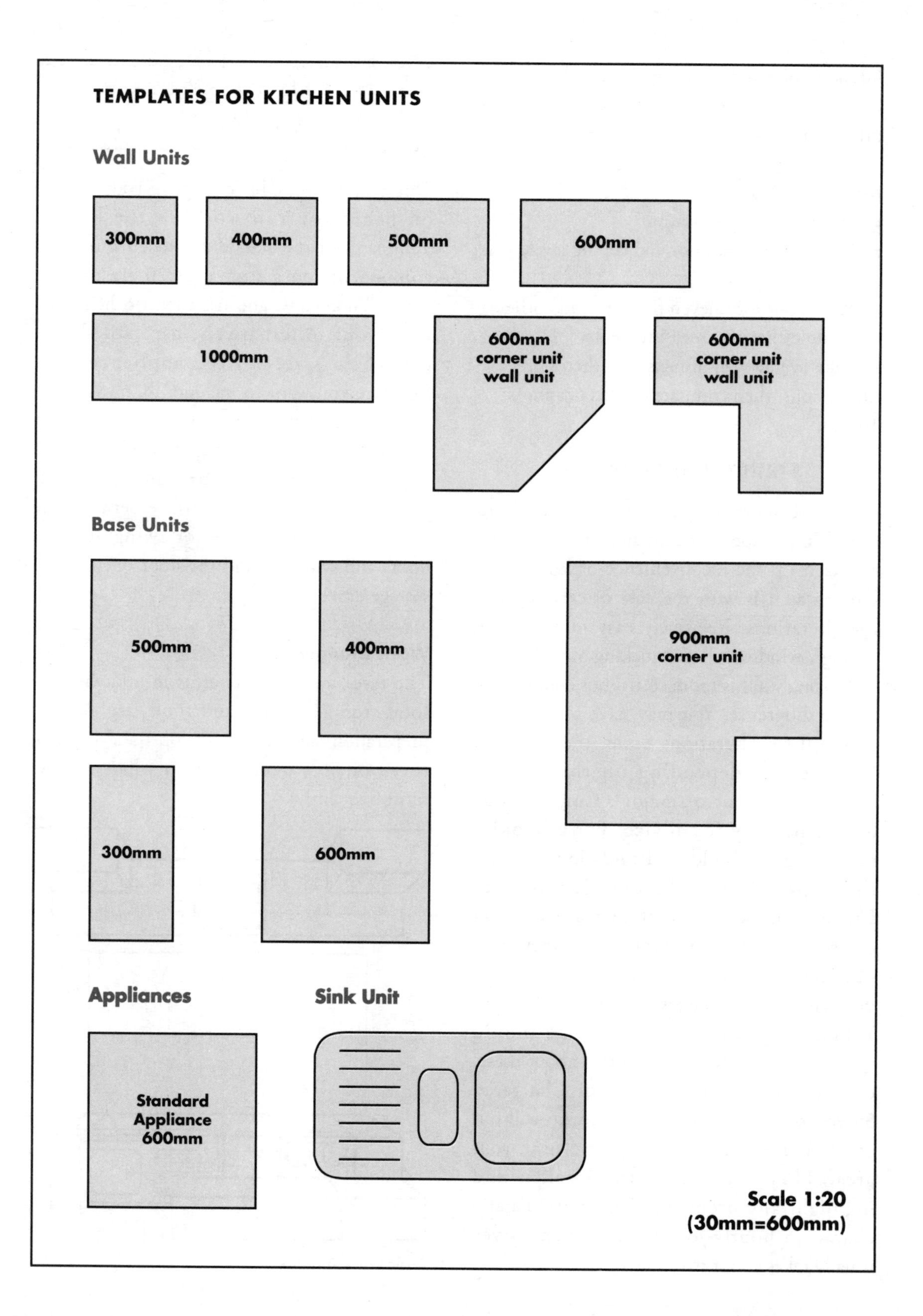
TEMPLATES FOR KITCHEN UNITS
Wall Units
300mm
400mm
500mm
600mm
1000mm
600mm corner unit wall unit
600mm corner unit wall unit
Base Units
500mm
400mm
900mm corner unit
300mm
600mm
Appliances
Sink Unit
Standard Appliance 600mm
Scale 1:20
(30mm=600mm)

Start your plan by positioning the fridge, sink and oven and draw a line in the shape of a triangle between them. The total sum of the three sides of the triangle should be between 4yd/3.6m and 7¼yd/6.6m. If too long you will find yourself doing tiresome legwork, but if too short it will be cramped. The cooking and sink points should be connected by an unbroken work-top, even if this turns a corner.

In a modern kitchen there is often more than one triangle in operation: for example, if you use a microwave as well as your cooker, or two people use the kitchen at the same time.

BASIC KITCHEN SHAPES

Kitchens are available in many shapes and sizes but there are only five practical layouts which will provide maximum working efficiency. You should be able to match one of these layouts to your own kitchen.

Single galley layout

In a single galley kitchen, the units and appliances are lined up against one wall. Most suitable for one or two people, it can be fitted into a very narrow space, but it will need a 3yd/3m run of interrupted wall space. The room should be at least 2yd/1.8m wide to allow space for two people to pass each other.

The sink should be placed in the middle with the fridge and cooker at either end with, ideally, the doors of each opening away from the sink for easy access. Allocate as much work-top space as possible. Choose built-under appliances so you do not lose any of the limited work-top space.

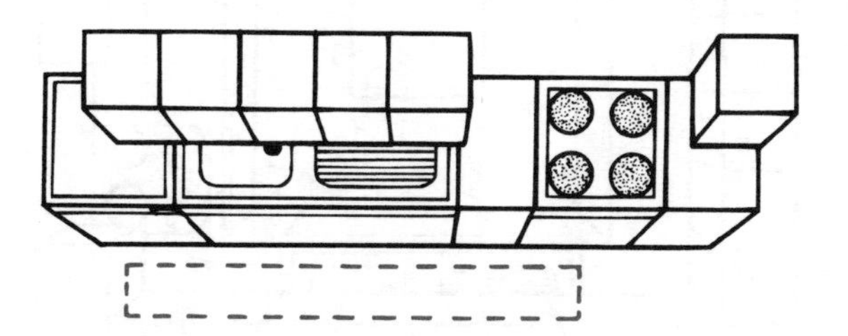

Eating usually has to take place elsewhere, unless a pull-out or flap-down dining table can be included on the wall facing the main run of kitchen units.

Double galley layout

In a double galley kitchen the units and appliances are lined along facing walls. Most

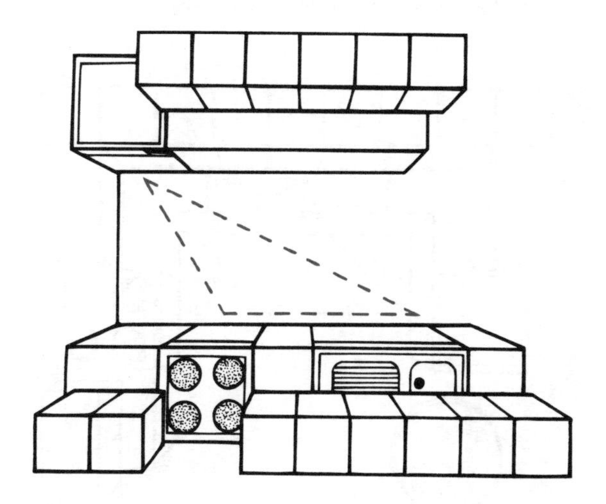

layouts will be dictated by the position of existing doors and windows but, ideally, the sink and cooker/hob should be on one side with the fridge and the main storage area opposite. This is an easy layout for one or two people to work in, although traffic through the kitchen can be a problem if there are doors at both ends.

There needs to be at least 4ft/1.2m between facing units, otherwise it will be difficult to bend down to get something from a low-level cupboard. Use 20in/500mm-deep units instead of the standard 24in/600mm.

It's possible to create a feeling of more space by using glass-fronted cabinets instead of those with solid doors.

U-shaped layout

In a U-shaped kitchen, units and appliances are positioned along three walls. It is the most flexible layout and works well in both a small and a large kitchen. There needs to be at least 4ft/1.2m of space between the legs of the U-shape, but in a larger kitchen make sure you keep to the dimensions of the work triangle to prevent unnecessary walking.

This layout can often incorporate a dining area or breakfast bar. This is probably the best layout for both working and safety.

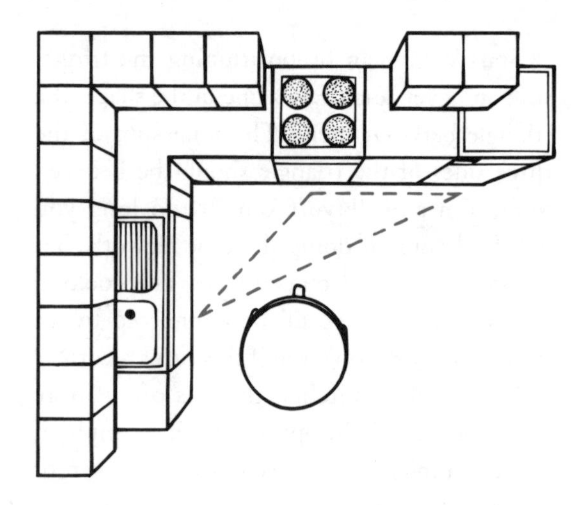

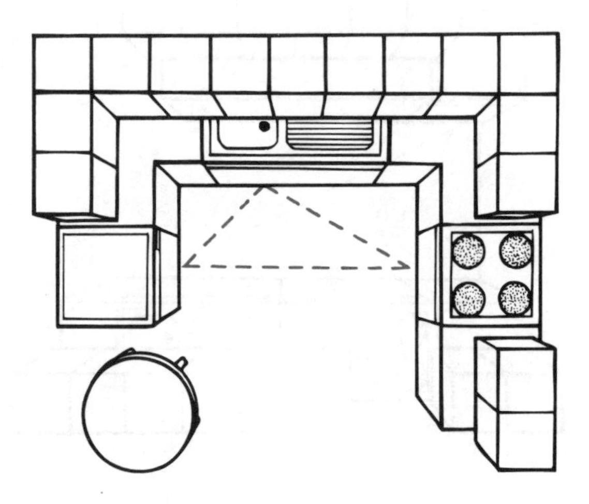

L-shaped layout

In an L-shaped kitchen the units and appliances are arranged on two adjacent walls. It is suitable for most rooms, except very narrow rooms or rooms with lots of doors. It is a good choice for an awkwardly shaped room because the sides of the L can be adapted to suit most shapes. The work triangle will not be interrupted by through traffic.

It is important to make sure the corner is used effectively, so use a carousel unit or consider a corner sink. Separate the sink, cooker/hob and fridge with stretches of work-top to avoid the three areas of activity becoming congested.

This layout is ideal for incorporating an eating area. It should be able to accommodate two cooks without them constantly getting in each other's way.

Island layout

An island layout is usually a U-shaped or L-shaped kitchen with an island of units in the centre. This layout is only suitable for large kitchens. The island can be used for a hob, but the necessary services (gas or electricity) and cooker-hood ducting will have to be brought to the centre of the room and this is costly. The space between the hob and sink must be a working area only and not a general

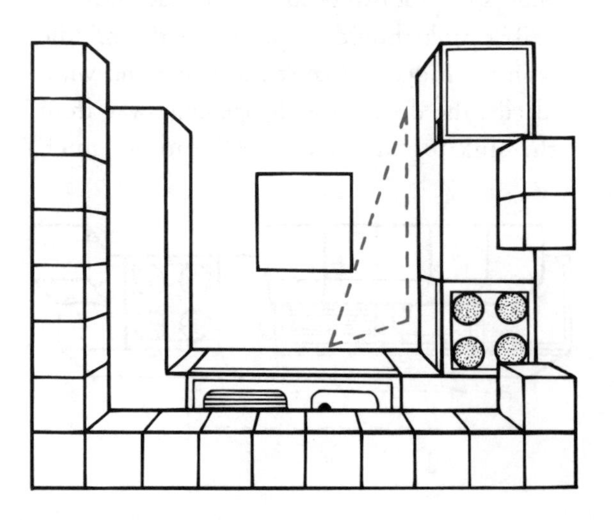

thoroughfare. It is usually used as an additional work surface, which can be positioned at a different working height.

To add definition to the island think about what will be placed above it. If the island houses a hob, a cooker hood is ideal, or place a light source or decorative rack for cooking pans or dried flowers above it.

Careful planning is needed to avoid wasteful journeys around the island.

POSITIONING COMPONENTS AND APPLIANCES

Storage units

Do

- Keep food storage near the preparation area.
- Provide accessible storage for commonly used items.
- Use the ends of base and wall units to store jars and cookery books.

Don't

- Position storage cupboards too high.
- Interrupt the work triangle with tall units. Tall storage for brooms and cleaning materials should not interrupt work surface runs. Keep tall units together.

Sink

Do

- Position with work surface either side for stacking dishes.
- Allow room for a second person to stand on the drainer side.
- Position within a feasible reach of a waste outlet or internal soil pipe.

Don't

- Think you have to position it under the window if you want to use the view for another purpose.
- Position opposite a hob.

Oven/freestanding cooker

Do

- Position with work surface on one side for putting down pans.

Don't

- Position in a corner.
- Position near or adjacent to a door.
- Position under a window.

Hob

Do

- Position with work surface either side for putting down pans.
- Position near deep cupboards or drawers for pan storage.

Don't

- Position in a corner, unless at an angle across it.
- Position near a window.
- Position under wall units without a cooker hood or extractor fan.
- Position near the eating area because children can reach across and touch the rings.
- Position too close to tall units or walls or at the end of a run of units.
- Position opposite the sink in an access way.

Fridges and freezers

Do

- Allow room for the door to open fully, in order to remove shelves.
- Position large fridge/freezers with work surface on one side to put down food.

Don't

- Position next to the cooker unless suitably insulated.

Dishwasher

Do

- Position near the sink for plumbing.
- Position near the crockery cupboard, for easy unloading.

Don't

- Position in a corner.

Washing machine or washer drier

Do

- Position near sink for plumbing.

Don't

- Position in the work triangle.

Plug points

- For each large, fixed appliance, have a fused switch control fitted above work-top level with a cable outlet box behind the appliance to suit.
- Fit at least four double plugs at around 8in/200mm above the work-top height.

Further information

For further information and guidelines for measurements look in specialist books. There is a good selection at The Building Book Shop at The Building Centre (see Useful Addresses).

SAFETY

See Home Safety, Kitchen, page 408

Safety planning considerations

- Avoid people using the kitchen work triangle as a passageway through to the cloakroom or garden.
- Avoid changes in floor level between kitchen and dining areas, to avoid tripping when carrying hot food.
- Avoid fixing units directly above a table.

THE HUMAN FACTOR

If you have children you may want to situate the hob so you can watch what is cooking and still keep an eye on the children in an adjoining room. This arrangement may mean you have to walk further to the fridge, but it is the most practical solution for you.

The average work-top height is up to 35½in/ 910mm, but if you are tall or short you may find this height uncomfortable. To change the working height, the base plinth can be adjusted at the fitting stage, or place timber on top of the base units before fitting the work top. Choose the timber to match the units.

FILLING IN THE GAPS

When designing a kitchen there are often gaps that are the wrong length to accommodate a unit, which is an irritating waste of space. Use the gap to house trays, or buy a custom-made fitting to fill the space, such as a telescopic towel rail. If the gap is large, fit shelves.

Gaps around a free-standing cooker collect crumbs and food spills so it is a good idea to fill them with a work surface. If you have a large gap, and cannot afford to fit more units, consider fitting a breakfast bar.

LIGHTING

See Lighting, Kitchen, page 180

VENTILATION

See Cooker Hoods, page 94

TIP When you have decided on your plan, use masking tape on the floor and walls to check that the layout works.

BUYING KITCHEN COMPONENTS

WHICH KITCHEN?

Where you buy your kitchen from depends on how much you have to spend and how much work you are prepared to do yourself. The more you do, the cheaper it will be, although savings on installation may not be as significant as they first appear.

Installing it yourself

Only consider installing a kitchen if you are a competent DIYer. This is the cheapest option but takes the most effort on your part. It will take longer than an experienced fitter and cause greater inconvenience, and you may need to take time off work.

Consider the cost of hiring tools, such as a jigsaw, if you don't have them already. It may be a more cost effective option to reduce your budget on the units so that you can hire a professional fitter.

Employing your own fitters

The responsibility for installing the kitchen is handed over to one or more fitters, whom you can supervise. This option usually works out cheaper than employing the supplier's installation service.

It is better to employ one fitter for the entire job, but check he is qualified to install both gas and electricity. If you employ more than one fitter, have an initial meeting with all the parties involved to sort out any problems before they occur.

You can buy kitchens for installation from builders' merchants, DIY stores, furniture stores and some kitchen specialists. These retailers will still offer a planning service but the complexity of the layout drawn up varies. Kitchen specialists and retailers offer computer-aided design with perspective 3D drawings. Remember the plan can only be as good as the measurements you have taken.

Installation using the supplier's fitters

This is the easiest but most expensive option.

Once a basic plan has been agreed using your measurements, the responsibility for checking the measurements and installation is taken on by the supplier. This option is available from DIY and furniture stores and kitchen specialists.

Using a fitting service from the supplier allows greater tailoring of the kitchen to suit your needs. Cupboards can be specifically made or tailored to exact measurements. Contact the Kitchen Specialists Association (see Useful Addresses) for independent kitchen specialists in your area.

Direct sales companies do not have high-street showrooms. Their costs should be less because they do not have high overheads. However, you do not have the same opportunity to see a fitted example unless they can provide a previous customer for you to visit. It is very unwise to buy a kitchen without visiting a fitted example first. You may feel pressurised having had the firm round for planning in your home.

If you do not choose the supplier's fitters, always check the guarantee. Some are invalidated if you arrange installation.

CHOOSING A KITCHEN SUPPLIER

- Ask contacts for recommendations.
- Visit a showroom or ask for recent customers who you can visit, to judge the quality of the materials and fitting.
- Take your measurements and scale drawing with you.
- Get more than one quote.

CHOOSING THE UNITS

You may have firm ideas on the final look of your kitchen, but do not overlook the quality of the units you are choosing.

FLAT PACK OR RIGID?

The first choice to make is between self-assembly, flat-pack units or factory-assembled, rigid units. Flat-pack units tend to be cheaper than rigid because of mass production. Over the past five years the quality of flat-pack has greatly improved, making it more sturdy than some rigid furniture.

Flat-pack units are joined together either with screw and dowel, or a cam and dowel fitting. A cam and dowel fitting is the easiest to assemble: you just fit the two parts together and only have to turn with a screwdriver once. With a screw and dowel you have to do all the work with a screwdriver. All units should be attached to the walls. The screw should penetrate at least 1in/25mm into the brickwork of the wall.

TIP It's worth investing in a rechargeable screwdriver if assembling the units yourself.

SIZES

Wall and floor units start at 8in/200mm wide (although 12in/300mm is more common) and usually increase in 4in/100mm steps to 24in/600mm wide for single cupboards and 48in/1,200mm wide for double units. With some of the most basic flat-pack units there is less flexibility in size; with expensive units there is more.

Wall units are usually 12in/300mm deep, but the Continental depth is 14in/350mm. Wall units can go up to the ceiling, but these taller units are generally more expensive than standard units.

The standard depth for most base units is 21½–22in/550–560mm which, with the door thickness and work-top overhang, brings the base run depth up to 24in/600mm. A few manufacturers have a 20in/500mm depth option, but many will offer wall units (12–14in/300–350mm deep) as base units. You can space base units out from the wall to achieve any intermediate depth.

UNEVEN FLOORS AND WALLS

When installing a kitchen, one of the biggest problems is uneven floors and walls, so adjustable fittings on units are useful. Look for adjustable hinges, to make alignment easier. Wall units should have adjustable brackets which will allow you to alter the wall unit height slightly. Adjustable legs compensate for changes in floor level.

QUALITY

For both flat-pack and rigid units, and other kitchen components such as work surfaces, look out for the following quality assurance schemes:

British Standards Institution Kitemark

The units have been tested by the British Standards Institution and have passed stringent tests for fitness for purpose, quality and workmanship. The majority of units have passed this standard, so be wary if the units you are buying are not covered. You may come across the equivalent Continental standard.

FIRA Gold Award

The Furniture Industry and Research Association (FIRA) has been commissioned by the manufacturer to test the units and they

have passed the BSI test. They also carry out additional tests for quality and sturdiness, ease of assembly, and how well they withstand staining and cleaning. This is not as widely used as the BSI Kitemark.

Qualitas

The units are not tested, but information is provided in the showroom on the materials used and how to care for them. A limited number of kitchen companies are members of the Qualitas Furnishing Standards Scheme.

Self checks

It is important to judge the quality of the kitchen in the showroom, and there are a number of checks you can do.

- The carcass of units is often made from melamine-faced chipboard. The chipboard is available in two thicknesses. Quality depends on density as well as thickness. Look inside the

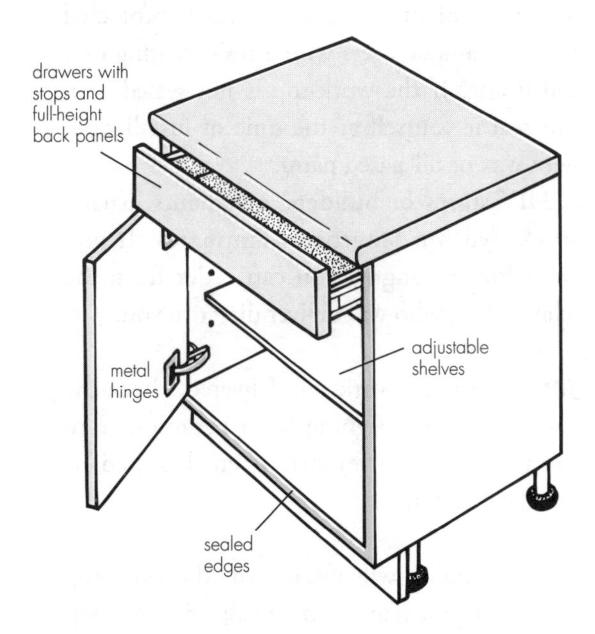

units and check that all exposed edges are sealed. If not the chipboard can be weakened by moisture.
- Door hinges should be metal, as plastic is not strong enough.
- Doors should open fully.
- For maximum versatility, the shelves in units should be adjustable.
- Drawer units should have full-height back panels to stop things falling down the back.
- Drawers should be fitted with stops so they will not fall out of the unit when opened fully.
- Drawers should run smoothly with a weight inside. Try placing something inside.
- Runners with ball bearings will run more smoothly than basic runners. Runners need to be metal and not plastic.
- Glass fronts of units should be safety (laminated) glass.

DOORS

When buying a kitchen, many people spend the most time choosing the doors. Although they give the kitchen its overall look, they do not have to withstand as much wear and tear as the other components.

The main choice is between coloured and wood effect, wood veneer or solid wood. Look for continuity in colour. Look for child-resistant locks, or doors which can be opened by a removable, lockable magnetic key from Alno (see Useful Addresses).

Coloured/wood effect

Medium-density fibreboard (MDF) or chipboard is covered with laminate, PVC or melamine. MDF is a smoother base than chipboard. A wide range of colours and patterns are available in both matt and high gloss. More and more manufacturers are introducing bright colours into their ranges. These doors are available in a wide price range.

Wood veneer

MDF or chipboard is covered with a thin layer of wood. This sort of door gives the look of solid wood and is generally less expensive and more environmentally friendly (if from sustainable farmed sources). There is often less variation than with solid wood, so they give a more standard look.

Solid wood

Popular solid-wood doors are oak and limed woods, while others are hand painted. They are the most expensive option, but cheaper ones can change colour, swell or shrink with increasing age.

Most companies are aware of environmental concerns, but make sure the wood comes from sustainable farmed sources.

Integrated appliance doors

Some manufacturers make integrated appliances which have special fixings so they can be fitted with a door to give a uniform finish. The doors are available as a full door or an appliance door which leaves the control panel exposed. Integrated appliances usually cost more and are not as widely available as standard appliances.

WORK SURFACES

The work surface gets the most wear and tear in a kitchen, so buy the best quality you can afford. Work surfaces are usually 24in/600mm deep, but most manufacturers make deeper ones for eating areas or peninsula units. If you have the room and want extra work surface area, set floor units away from the wall and use a deeper work-top.

The average height of a work-top is up to 35½in/910mm, but if you do not find this comfortable it can sometimes be raised or lowered accordingly.

Laminates

These are the most popular option and are available in a wide range of colours, finishes and textures. Laminate work-tops consist of a thin sheet of laminate on a chipboard base. There is a great difference between the top and bottom ranges in price and quality and, basically, you get what you pay for.

Most laminates will withstand temperatures of up to 355°F/180°C. High-pressure laminates such as Resopal or Duropal are heat resistant to 450°F/230°C. Some cheaper ranges will not withstand high temperatures and may become quickly damaged.

The chipboard used varies in quality depending on the thickness and density. The thickness of laminate work-tops varies from 1in/25mm to 1½in/40mm. Always choose the thickest you can afford. The weight of a good-quality work-top is an indication of the chipboard density.

The underside of a work-top can be water damaged if appliances, such as a dishwasher, are placed underneath. To prevent this the underside of most work surfaces is protected by the manufacturers with a resin coating or a foil lining. If the work-top is not sealed, you can seal it yourself at the time of installation, with wax or oil-based paint.

DIY stores or builders' merchants usually stock 3yd/3m lengths of laminates. If you want longer lengths you can order from the wholesalers, who will deliver direct to you.

TIP If having a work-top delivered, check the condition before signing for it because due to their large size they are often dropped or knocked in transit.

The supplier will usually cut the work-top to the size you require. If cutting the work-top yourself, use a circular saw and cut from the underside. Have a practise on an offcut first to check the effect on the laminate, because some blades are unsuitable.

The front of the work-top can be square edged or rounded (post-formed). A rounded edge is less likely to chip but is more difficult to join at the internal corners.

TIP It is usually worth having work-tops fitted professionally even if you are fitting everything else yourself.

Ceramic tiles

Ceramic tiles are available in a matt or glazed finish. The quality of tiles varies, so check the tiles you choose are suitable for work surfaces. They will not necessarily be thicker than wall tiles but will have a stronger glaze.

Tiles can be prone to scratching. Another problem is that the grouting between the tiles can become dirty. The work surface will be uneven so is not suitable for rolling dough.

Ceramic tiles are reasonably easy to fit yourself. A lip around the edge is needed. Use an epoxy resin grout.

Man-made solid surfaces (Corian)

Consist of a composite material which is the same colour and texture throughout. A variety of colours is available and the work-top can be shaped, carved or inlaid. Joints are virtually invisible, so it gives a smooth and seamless finish. However, this sort of work surface is expensive.

It is not possible to buy a solid surface and fit it yourself. They are sold by approved dealers who use fabricators to fit them. When the base units in the kitchen are fitted the fabricator will come and measure the area and make a template. This specification will then be sent to the factory and the work-top will be made to fit. This takes about a working week. It will then take about a day to be installed.

Installation will be a dusty process but the fabricators should come prepared with dust sheets and very often a commercial extraction system which they will have running during the job to remove dust particles.

Natural solid surfaces (granite)

A natural, solid surface will look good but it will not be very practical. Because of this it is often used for just one of the work surfaces in the kitchen. It will be cool to touch and is excellent for making pastry.

It is not possible to have as many inlays or carved features as with a man-made solid surface and joints will show. The surface is prone to scratches and chips. Natural solid surfaces are expensive.

It is possible to fit a natural solid work surface yourself, or the supplier will do it. If you are doing the fitting make sure you measure the area carefully. It is a good idea to make a template out of hardboard or plywood, not paper, which will not be as accurate. Some suppliers will come to your house and measure the area for you and then supply you with the work surface so you can fit it. Fix it in place dry first before using any adhesives, to check it is the correct size.

Care and cleaning

See Kitchen Surfaces, page 303

SINKS

Sizes

Sink units are usually about 3ft/1m wide, although other widths such as 24in/600mm and 48in/1,200mm are available. Sinks are generally 20in/500mm deep in order to fit in to a 24in/600mm-deep work surface.

The size of the bowl varies from small round bowls which are about 15in/380mm in diameter to large, rectangular bowls about 18in/450mm wide. In order to be practical for washing up a bowl needs to be at least 6–7in/ 160–180mm deep.

TIP If you think the sink bowl is too small take a large roasting dish with you and see if it fits in.

Sink options

- Inset sinks are the most popular type as they fit in a hole in the work surface. They offer the widest choice of shapes and sizes.
- Sit-on sinks are placed on a base unit and have no work surface about them.
- Corner sinks are designed to fit in the corner of a room and use space effectively.
- Choose the number of bowls (single, double or one and a half) and the combination of bowl and drainer. Composite sinks are available with a wide range of bowl sizes, including one and a quarter and one and a fifth. Blanco (see Useful Addresses) supply a sink with a bowl which is wider at the front so large pans will fit in. If you have a dishwasher you may find a single bowl is sufficient. Additional bowls provide useful extra sink space and, if used with a strainer basket, are suitable for draining or defrosting food.
- Sinks are available without draining boards. Draining boards are available in a range of sizes and can be sited on the left- or right-hand side of the sink bowl. When buying, check the position of the tap hole, which must be at the back. Reversible sinks have a hole at the front and the back, and the hole that is not used is used for pop-up waste control. Pop-up waste control allows you to activate the plug by turning a knob. This is useful because you do not have to get your hands wet. On some plastic sinks you may have to drill the hole for the tap yourself.

Accessories

Sinks can incorporate strainer baskets, draining racks and chopping boards, and these are usually sold as extras. If you decide not to have a draining board, a drainer basket in a second bowl can be used instead. Many sinks can be fitted with a waste-disposal unit. See Waste Disposal and Recycling, page 74.

Installation

Most sinks come with a cardboard template to use when cutting the work surface, and fitting instructions. Some sinks come in a complete pack with taps and a plumbing kit – which tends to be a cost-effective way of purchasing.

Care and cleaning

See Kitchen Surfaces, Sinks, page 304

Stainless steel

This is the most popular material for sinks. It is resistant to high temperatures and is durable and easy to clean, but it can dull and scratch easily. You will probably find that when new, the scratches will show up on the shiny surface, but with some wear they will become less obvious.

Stainless steel is available in different grades (which relate to the amount of nickel and chrome it contains). The majority of sinks are 18/10 grade, which is strong enough not to flex or distort.

A stainless-steel sink can be noisy to use so choose a sink with a vibration damper underneath. This will either be sprayed or stuck on.

Coloured sinks

Coloured sinks are becoming increasingly popular. They are available in a range of colours, usually creams and browns. They are quieter in use than a stainless steel sink but are not as easy to clean.

The quality of coloured sinks varies depending on the material used. Choose the most expensive you can afford because you tend to get what you pay for.

Polycarbonate or plastic sinks

Includes Prima and Riva by Astracast and Resan by Resopal. They are the least expensive, and are the least heat resistant and durable.

Blended composites

Includes Franke Fraquartz, MFI Quartzite, and Astracast Supersinks. A mix of an acrylic substance with minerals such as silica, quartz or granite. Choose a sink that contains granite for the most hard-wearing material, such as Carron Phoenix, Granite, Franke Fragranite or Blanco Silgranit.

Man-made solid surfaces

Includes Du Pont's Corian, Silkstone and Avonite. The most expensive, and very hard wearing and durable. There is more flexibility with shape and they can be fitted as a continuation of the work surface (integrated sink and work-top).

Enamel

This is usually enamelled cast iron or mild-steel and has a glass-like finish. They are available with a matt or gloss finish, and in a range of colours, usually white or brown. They can be vulnerable to chips and scratches so care must be taken when cleaning.

TAPS

Taps do not automatically fit all sinks so check that they are the correct size and reach for the sink bowl. If you choose a shallow sink, buy tall taps to give clearance for filling buckets. It is often possible to buy the taps as part of a complete pack with the sink.

All water fittings and their installation must satisfy your local water supplier's by-laws, so check before installing them.

Check that the taps and the sink are a good match before you buy. Coloured taps may not be exactly the same colour as a coloured sink, so compare carefully. Chrome taps are the most popular type of metal tap in the kitchen. Gold and brass finishes are available but they are not very practical for a sink that is frequently used because they can discolour.

For more than one bowl choose swivelling mixer taps that can reach all the bowls.

Taps are available with a pull-out spray. These are ideal for filling large containers with water, for cleaning large items and cleaning the sink itself.

FLOORS

See Flooring, page 195

APPLIANCES

See Large Kitchen Appliances, page 89

TIP If buying appliances as part of a kitchen package, check appliance and fitting prices at a local department store. Some special offers are not the great saving they seem!

PURCHASING THE KITCHEN

Check that the contract includes:

- Total price.
- Dates that payments are to be made. (A deposit of up to 25 per cent is reasonable, with the final payment when work is completed.)
- Exactly what is included in the price.
- Dates that work will start and finish. (Stipulate that 'time is of the essence' to help prevent major delays.)

TIP If you are shopping about, make sure the different companies are aware of the competition, as they may be prepared to offer a discount.

GUARANTEES

Expect a guarantee of five years to cover cabinets and work-tops against problems arising from faulty materials and manufacture.

Members of the Kitchen Specialists Association (see Useful Addresses) operate an insurance-backed deposit-protection scheme called KSA ConsumerCare. This protects deposits of up to 25 per cent of the total contract value.

Check if the guarantee is valid for installation you do yourself.

APPLIANCES

See Large Kitchen Appliances, page 89

INSTALLATION

Bad installation is the cause of most problems in a kitchen. Ask for a written quotation of how long it will take: usually a working week. Sometimes new jobs will come to light during the installation, such as moving a pipe, so be prepared to pay extra.

Before installation, make sure you are definitely happy with your plan, as changing your mind any later will be expensive.

If the units are flat-pack you can either collect them yourself from the store (many rent out roof racks) or have the units delivered.

INSTALLATION TIPS

- Allocate space for short-term storage of kitchen items.
- Empty cupboards, remove curtains and unscrew kitchen accessories.
- Keep doors shut to reduce dust spreading.
- Allocate parking space for the fitter's van.

If you are required to sign an acceptance form after installation make sure you thoroughly check the work first, and that the acceptance is subject to a reassessment after an appropriate period of normal use.

DIY

Only consider installing a kitchen yourself if you are competent at DIY. To give an idea on equipment, you will need an electric jigsaw, a spirit level, a power drill, plane, work bench, screwdrivers, electric glue gun, plumber's wrench, hacksaw, plumber's tape, wire strippers, electric cable and cable clips.

All gas appliances must be fitted by a member of the Council for Registered Gas Installers (CORGI, see Useful Addresses).

COMPLAINTS

See Problems with Building Work, page 458

CHOOSING COOKWARE

Before buying a new pan, it's important to consider your hob. Likewise, you may have to consider changing your pans when buying a new hob. Manufacturers' leaflets or even symbols on the pan base should tell you for which hob types a pan is suitable. But if you follow these general criteria you shouldn't be caught out.

CHOOSING PANS TO MATCH A HOB

CERAMIC AND HALOGEN HOBS

Avoid using copper and glass-ceramic pans.

Cast-iron pans

A word of caution is needed about cast-iron pans. Traditional cast-iron pans have rough bases, but as long as you are careful not to drag them across the glass there are no reasons why you can't use them on a ceramic hob. Some cast-iron pans have an enamel-coated base to reduce the risk of scratching the glass hob.

Cast-iron pans, particularly when full of food, can be extremely heavy. Don't drop them on to the glass hob.

Glass-ceramic pans

It's important to remember that glass retains heat. If you do use glass pans on ceramic-glass hobs, cook on a medium to low heat. If the heat is too high, the hob will get too hot and the thermal limiter may cut out more often, reducing cooking efficiency.

Copper pans

Never use copper or stainless-steel pans with an exposed single layer of copper on the base. Copper can distort when hot so you won't get that vital good contact between pan and hob. In addition, as copper is soft, flecks can rub off on the glass hob and cause scratching.

Copper is usually only suitable inside a sandwich base. However, there are copper-based pans that are suitable for glass-topped hobs due to their sandwich-base construction. If in doubt, check with manufacturers' details.

BRIEF GUIDE: WHICH PAN FOR WHICH HOB?

Ceramic hob

All pans except copper, stainless steel with exposed single-layer copper base, and glass ceramic.

Electric radiant

All pans except copper, and stainless steel with a base made of an exposed single layer of copper.

Gas

All pans.

Halogen

All pans except copper, stainless steel with exposed single-layer copper base, glass ceramic and pans with reflective bases.

Induction

The *only* suitable pans are ones made with a magnetic material in the base.

Sealed plate

All pans except copper, stainless steel with exposed single-layer copper base.

ELECTRIC-RADIANT AND SEALED-PLATE HOBS

All pans are suitable, except copper or stainless steel with an exposed single layer of copper on the base. This is for the same reasons given for ceramic and halogen, although scratching is not as much of a problem.

GAS

There are no limitations on what type of pan you can use. Lightweight pans are better for gas since they will use the controllability of gas to its full potential. Heavy-based pans, such as cast-iron, will be slow to heat up, but because they retain their heat, they will allow you to cook at low temperatures.

INDUCTION

You can only use pans made with a ferrous material such as enamelled steel, and cast iron. Stainless steel is not suitable unless it has a magnetic sandwich base.

RANGE COOKERS

Includes Aga, Rayburn. Check with the cooker manufacturer's details. Aga make their own range of pans. As a general guide, choose heavy-based pans to provide optimum contact with the hob.

TYPES OF PAN

Now you know which types of pan are suitable for your hob, you can check which type of material most suits your needs. Each material has its pros and cons.

ALUMINIUM

Plain, uncoated aluminium is no longer widely available. Over the past few years the scare from the alleged link between aluminium and Alzheimer's Disease has caused a dramatic decline in the demand for aluminium cookware. However, it is still widely sold in catering equipment shops because of its very good energy efficiency qualities.

Aluminium pans are either:

- Non-stick coated.
- Enamel coated, usually on the exterior with a non-stick coating inside.
- Hard-anodised.
- Cast aluminium, which has the appearance of cast iron but the weight and good heat conductivity of aluminium.

ALUMINIUM AND FOOD

Research has shown that the transfer of aluminium from plain uncoated aluminum pans into food is usually negligible. Slightly higher levels transfer when cooking very acidic foods, such as rhubarb, but this level is still insignificant when compared with that occurring naturally in food and tap water.

If you are concerned, it may be prudent to cook very acidic foods in a non-aluminium pan, especially if you are pregnant or have kidney problems.

CAST IRON

Cast iron heats up slowly, but once hot it retains heat well, so it's good for long, even cooking at a low heat. Cast iron rusts easily on its own, so you'll usually find it with either a non-stick interior coating or a thin layer of vitreous enamel to protect it. Uncoated cast iron is not dishwasher safe. Being magnetic, it's suitable for induction hobs.

COPPER

In terms of heat conduction, you can't beat

copper cookware. Good copper pans are very expensive, but should last a lifetime.

As copper reacts with certain foods, the pans are normally lined with tin or stainless steel to act as a barrier. For this reason, keep unlined copper pans for display only.

Copper pans will have to be cleaned periodically with a proprietary copper polish. Don't use on glass-topped hobs unless they have a sandwich base (see Choosing Pans to Match a Hob, page 61).

ENAMEL COATING

Enamel is usually applied to aluminium, cast-iron or steel pans.

Enamelled pans are inexpensive to buy. Other benefits are that they won't pit, scratch easily or react with food. But be warned, they can chip if knocked about.

Heat distribution can be a problem with some enamel pans. If the coating is too thin, there may be a problem with food sticking and burning, so avoid very lightweight pans.

GLASS-CERAMIC

These retain heat well, but they are also slow to cool, which means sticking can be a problem. They will withstand extremes of heat, so can be taken from the freezer straight to the hob, or even into a microwave (provided there are no metal components).

Transparent glass-ceramic pans also allow food to be watched while cooking without lifting the lid.

HARD-ANODISED ALUMINIUM

These are distinguished by their steely grey or black colour. The surface has been electrochemically treated to produce a hard finish so it won't chip, crack or peel. You can use metal utensils (but don't be too boisterous as it has been known for the metal utensils to leave marks on the surface of the pan).

The pans are not dishwasher safe but the surface is stick resistant. Some pans also have a non-stick coating to further improve cleaning. Hard-anodised pans are lightweight and heat up rapidly, eliminating hotspots. They are expensive but they perform and last well.

NON-STICK

Non-stick pans are a boon for frying, making sauces, etc. A non-stick coating stops food sticking, reduces the need for additional fat and is easy to clean, but there's little point in buying a non-stick pan for boiling vegetables.

They do need to be treated with respect so don't use metal utensils or abrasive scourers.

Non-stick coatings are applied to most types of cookware from aluminium and steel to cast iron and stainless steel. The coatings themselves have become far more durable over the last ten years and many now come with a five-, ten-year or even lifetime guarantee. But it is important to choose the non-stick coating carefully since quality does differ. Look out for branded non-stick coatings that come with their own guarantee.

STAINLESS STEEL

Good-quality stainless-steel pans should last a lifetime, but they can be expensive. As stainless steel is a poor conductor of heat and is liable to have hot-spots, a number of different materials are usually incorporated into the base to improve heat conductivity, such as copper or aluminium. This is sandwiched between two layers of stainless steel. Cooking on a medium to low heat will also help.

Stainless steel is dishwasher safe and food doesn't react with it. Overheating and minerals in water may cause a 'rainbow effect', but a proprietary stainless-steel cleaner will remove these. Satin-finish pans mark less.

BUYING TIPS FOR PANS

Check for:

- The manufacturer's details to ensure the pan is suitable for your hob.
- Stay-cool and heatproof handles and knobs. Handles should be a good length and not too narrow.
- Dishwasher safe: if you own a dishwasher, check that the pans are suitable. Reputable brands come with literature on care and use, so check this before buying.

As a general rule, pans with plastic or stainless-steel handles or knobs are dishwasher safe. Most pans with wooden handles and knobs are not, unless they have been specially treated.

All types of aluminium pans, whether coated or hard-anodised, are not dishwasher safe. The aluminium reacts with the strong alkaline detergent and the surface will tarnish.

- Pouring lips: both sides are useful if there are left-handers in the household.
- Well-fitting lids: but check they are free enough to allow steam to escape if there are no steam vents.
- Weight: is it going to be too heavy when full of food or water?
- For solid-plate hobs such as Agas choose heavy pans with substantial flat bases.
- For energy-efficient cooking, buy pans that are similar in size to the hob ring. If the pan is too small, it's not only wasteful of heat, but it may cause the thermal limiter to cut off the heat to stop the hob getting too hot. The glare from halogen hobs can also be very harsh on the eyes.

PAN BASES

Last but not least, it is very important to consider the pan base, particularly if you have a glass-topped hob.

Unless you're cooking on gas, choose pans with fairly thick bases (⅛in/3.5mm minimum) for good heat transference. Lightweight pans are only suitable for gas as they can distort over high heat.

GLASS-TOPPED HOBS

Includes ceramic, halogen and induction hobs.

Flat base

It's important to choose a pan with a smooth, flat base to provide the best possible contact between the hob and the pan. A medium-weight pan is best. Take a ruler with you when buying a pan to check the base is flat. It is necessary to have a small concave dip across the base to allow for slight expansion when cooking, so you will see some light showing through between the base and the ruler.

If the base is too concave or convex, pockets

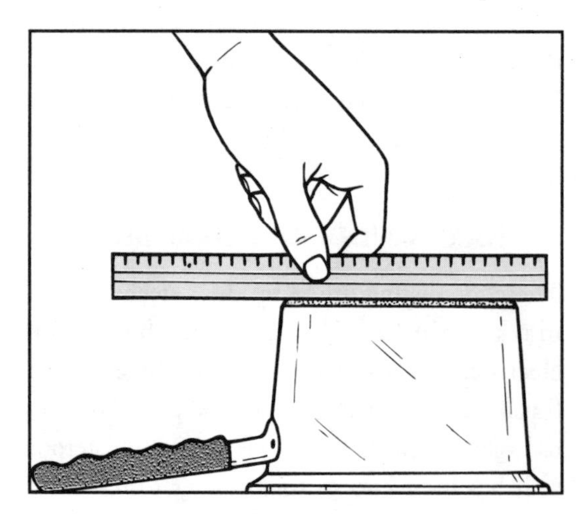

of air will be trapped between the pan and hob causing uneven heating. The hob's thermostat (thermal limiter) will cut the heat out until the hob has cooled down, in order to protect the glass from getting too hot and being damaged. (This is known as thermal cut-out.)

Any serious dents may have this effect, although small manufacturing indentations don't tend to cause any problems. Some pans have specialist bases designed specifically for glass-topped hobs. If you are in any doubt, check with the manufacturer's details.

Smooth base

Any blip on the base of the pan that stands proud could scratch a glass-topped hob. Run your hand over the base of the pan before you buy it to check for any roughness. Check the centre of the base for any little blips caused during manufacture.

Non-reflective base

With halogen hobs, it's important to choose pans that have dull or dark bases. The halogen lamps beneath the glass surface heat the pan partly by infra-red light and partly by conduction. If the base is too bright and shiny, the infra-red light will be reflected away from the pan and may cause the thermal limiter to cut out to prevent the glass overheating. This means it will take longer to finish cooking.

ELECTRIC-RADIANT AND SEALED-PLATE

Choose a flat, medium or heavy-based pan to provide optimum contact with the surface of the hob.

GAS

For gas hobs, it is not critical to choose a smooth, flat-based pan. There are few restrictions; almost anything goes. Lightweight pans are best.

RANGE COOKERS

For Agas and Rayburns choose flat, heavy-based pans to provide optimum contact with the hob.

PRESSURE COOKERS

A pressure cooker cooks more quickly than an ordinary saucepan and is useful for making stock, cooking root vegetables and pulses and tenderising tough cuts of meat. The pan is sealed and a weight is added to stop the steam escaping, so the water boils at a higher temperature, so reducing cooking time.

Stainless-steel pressure cookers are the most expensive, but they are hard wearing. Aluminium cookers are cheaper but they can discolour badly and are not dishwasher safe. Both sorts can be used on all types of hob, except induction, unless they have a special magnetic base.

Hi-dome pressure cookers tend to be aluminium and their extra height makes them especially suitable for making jams and pickles. Recently, mini or half-size pressure cookers have been introduced, which are ideal for small quantities.

COOKING FOOD BY STEAM PRESSURE

This principle has been known since about 1679 when Denis Papin, a French physician, invented the Papin Digester or 'Papin Pot'. This was a saucepan made of iron with a screw-on airtight lid and safety valve.

The first domestic pressure cooker was invented at the turn of the century in the USA, but they were not manufactured in the UK until 1947.

All pressure cookers have a safety valve that allows excess pressure to be released should the control valve become blocked. The valve is either pushed out or melted, but this should not happen if the cooker is used properly and the control valve is kept clear. This explains why such foods as dumplings should never be cooked in a pressure cooker, as the dough will rise and could block the safety outlets. Pressure cookers also have locking lugs that prevent the lid being removed when the cooker is being used under pressure.

Pressure cookers usually have three pressure weights for a choice in cooking control: 5lb/2.25kg for blanching and steaming puddings, 10lb/4.5kg for jam making and 15lb/7kg for everyday, general cooking. Some models, however, have fixed pressure controls instead of individual weights.

All pressure cookers come with a trivet and a separator basket so you can cook different foods at the same time using the divider.

Some models have an automatic steam release which works in conjunction with a timer. The timer is set according to the length of cooking and then releases the steam automatically at the end of the cooking time. De-pressurising the cooker can either be done quickly or slowly depending on the type of food being cooked.

Some models also have a useful 'rise and time' indicator or pressure-ready indicator to show that the cooker has reached the correct cooking temperature and that the temperature is being maintained. This helps to save energy and ensure consistent results.

Coloured pressure cookers are also available. These are made from aluminium with a painted exterior. You can now even get pressure cookers with a non-stick interior for easier cleaning.

WOKS

When selecting a wok, as with saucepans, you must consider the type of hob you have. All woks can be used on gas, but for glass-topped hobs, you must look for a smooth, flat base to provide good contact with the hob, as opposed to the traditional rounded base.

Traditional woks are made from uncoated carbon steel. Wash in warm water (without detergent), dry and then brush with a thin layer of vegetable oil to help to prevent rusting, as well as to season the wok.

If you don't feel you have the time or inclination for the preparation and maintenance needed with traditional carbon steel, choose a wok with a non-stick interior. These do not appeal to purists but they are easier to maintain.

Woks are now available in a variety of materials including enamel on steel or aluminium, and stainless steel. For details on which pan type best suits your needs, see Choosing Cookware, page 61.

KITCHEN ESSENTIALS AND TABLEWARE

A well-equipped kitchen is one in which every item earns its keep on a regular or infrequent but essential basis, and does not stay unused. There is masses of choice in kitchen equipment, utensils and bakeware, so ask yourself the following points before buying:

- Do I need it?
- Will I use it?
- Is it easy to clean/will it go in the dishwasher?
- Is it easy to store?

Below is a checklist, depending upon how much you cook and how often you entertain. For most people, entertaining is a small part of life, so it is better to have good-quality everyday items. There are four areas: cooking equipment, preparing, serving/entertaining and storage.

When choosing look for

- Quality and durability
- Comfort in use
- Ease of cleaning
- Ease of storage
- Cost.

KITCHEN BASICS CHECKLIST

COOKING EQUIPMENT

- Steamer
- Saucepans (see page 62)
- Large and small frying pans with lids
- Selection of casseroles with lids
- Roasting tin (with trivet) may be supplied as oven accessory
- Yorkshire pudding tin
- Flan tins

TIP Tins give a crisper pastry base than china flan dishes.

- Pie dishes
- Pudding basins
- Loaf tins
- Cake tins

TIP Choose non-stick bakeware for easier release.

- Baking sheets
- Ramekins
- Wire cooling racks
- Pan stands (to protect work surfaces from hot pans)
- Wooden spoons
- Fish slice
- Wooden spatulas
- Wok (see page 66)
- Skewers, wooden and metal

PREPARING

- Knives (see page 69)
- Knife sharpener (see page 70)
- Colander
- Sieves

TIP Metal sieves are more durable than nylon.

- Chopping boards (see page 68)
- Kitchen scales (see page 71)
- Measuring spoons
- Measuring jugs

TIP Buy a double-sided measuring jug for right- and left-hand users.

- Can opener

TIP Electrically operated can openers are useful for those who find it difficult to grip the manual type.

- Mixing bowls

- Cheese grater

TIP Choose a sturdy box type that has fine and coarse graters, and can also be used for citrus fruit.

- Pastry brush
- Rolling pin
- Ceramic baking beans (for baking pastry)
- Pastry cutters
- Garlic press
- Balloon whisk
- Potato peeler

TIP The Y-shaped peelers are easier to use and remove less flesh.

- Kitchen scissors
- Kitchen tongs
- Palette knife
- Ladle
- Basting pipette

TIP Also good for separating meat juices from fat.

- Slotted spoon
- Potato masher
- Flexible spatula
- Lemon squeezer
- Meat mallet

TIP Choose one with a metal head for better food hygiene.

- Funnel
- Minute timer
- Piping bag and nozzles

TIP Choose large nylon or fabric icing bags and metal nozzles. Plastic nozzles are not very durable.

- Food processor
- Hand-held mixer

TIP Better at incorporating air than a food processor: use for making cakes, whipping egg whites and cream.

- Mini chopper

TIP Useful for chopping small amounts of foods, such as nuts, vegetables and herbs, more quickly than by hand. They can also blend small amounts of liquids. Ideal if you don't want the hassle of cleaning or setting up your food processor.

SERVING AND ENTERTAINING

- Ice-cube trays
- Corkscrew
- Bottle opener
- Wine stoppers
- Wine cooler

TIP Vacu Vin's Rapid Ice is great for chilling a bottle of wine fast (10 minutes). Keep in the freezer then slip over bottle when needed. (See Useful Addresses.)

- Heat-resistant plate mats
- Serving dishes and plates
- Glass dessert bowl for fruit salads and trifles, etc.
- Citrus zester
- Hot tray
- Serving spoons
- Salad bowl and servers
- Bread basket
- Cream jugs
- Carving dish, knife and fork (with finger guard
- Water jug

STORAGE

- Freezer bags and ties
- Freezer labels and pen
- Airtight containers for fridge/freezer
- Airtight containers for dried foods
- Airtight tins for cakes/biscuits

CHOPPING BOARDS

PLASTIC

There are two types of plastic which are used for chopping boards, polypropylene (PP) and polyethylene (HDPE).

It's best to choose a polypropylene board. They are more expensive than polyethylene but are more robust, more resistant to staining and less likely to crack under stress. They can also withstand higher washing temperatures so they are dishwasher safe – the most hygienic method of cleaning.

WOOD

Choose boards made from either beech, or other hardwoods such as maple, sycamore or rubber wood, as these are more hard wearing than other wood types.

Ordinary wooden chopping boards are usually made in sections that are glued together, for extra stability.

End-grain chopping boards or blocks, although quite expensive, are very hard wearing and robust. They are made from hefty blocks of wood that have been glued together with the grain uppermost. These are traditionally used by butchers for heavy-duty cutting and chopping.

PLASTIC VERSUS WOOD

There are divided views on how hygienic wooden chopping boards are compared to plastic. Although wooden boards mustn't be soaked, as long as they are cleaned thoroughly and regularly and occasionally wiped over with a sterilising solution, they are not problematic. This also applies to plastic chopping boards.

Bear in mind that polypropylene boards can be washed in the dishwasher, where the higher temperatures ensure thorough cleaning.

Always replace a cracked, severely scored or stained board, whether its made of wood or plastic.

CHOOSING A CHOPPING BOARD

- The larger it is, the more convenient it is to work on.
- Buy a board that can be used on both sides, and keep one side for strong-smelling foods such as onions and garlic.
- Buy colour-coded chopping boards to use for specific foods to prevent cross contamination during the preparation.

MARBLE AND GLASS

These can be rather unyielding and will blunt cutting blades very quickly. They are also noisy to chop on. Marble and glass slabs are more suitable as a cool surface for pastry making.

KITCHEN KNIVES AND SHARPENERS

No matter how many knives you have, there will be one or two favourites that you usually use for almost every task. What you choose depends upon whether you are prepared to sharpen knives. Generally, most professional knives need regular re-sharpening. So if you want a knife that stays sharp for years you may have to compromise on the quality of cutting.

Carbon or stainless steel?

Most knives today are made of stainless steel, which is resistant to rusting and harder than carbon steel, although purists swear by carbon steel, which can be easier to sharpen.

Dishwasher safe?

Reputable brands come with care and use instructions. Generally, knives with plastic handles are dishwasher safe and knives with wooden handles are not, unless they have been

WHAT TO LOOK FOR IN A KNIFE

- A full tang – where the blade continues inside the handle to the end.

- A smooth heel to the blade, for safety.
- Evenly balanced weight between handle and blade. A good way to check this is to rest the knife across your fingers: it should remain level.
- The weight of the knife is a personal decision but professional cooks tend to prefer them heavier.
- Substantial handle with good grip.
- Don't assume that if a knife says Sabatier it will automatically be top quality. The Sabatier name is used by several different French manufacturers who produce knives of similar design and styling. Judge the knife on its own merits, not just by its name.

specially treated for dishwasher use.

Don't leave knives in the dishwasher on a rinse-and-hold programme.

Don't put wooden-handled knives in the dishwasher.

THE RIGHT KNIFE FOR THE TASK

You don't need a drawer full of knives for different food preparation tasks, but a basic set should include at least these four:

- Paring knife: for trimming, paring and decorating vegetables.
- Cook's knife (8–10in/20–25cm): versatile knife for chopping and slicing. The bigger it is the more control you have over cutting.
- Bread knife: serrated to slice bread without tearing.
- Serrated knife: suitable for slicing fruit.

Using knives

- Store knives separately, either in a divided cutlery tray or a knife block. Magnetic knife racks should be placed well out of range of young children.
- Don't leave knives soaking in the bottom of the washing-up bowl. It's easy to forget they are there – and it could damage the knife.
- Dry knives immediately after washing them.
- Choose tough, polyethylene chopping boards that can be washed at high temperature for better food hygiene.
- Use separate boards and knives for preparing raw and cooked foods.
- Be warned: cutting on to hard, unyielding surfaces like ceramic tiles or marble may be more hygienic than soft plastics or wood, but they blunt the blades more quickly.

KNIFE SHARPENERS

If you're going to invest in good knives it's vital that you keep them well sharpened. Get into the habit of sharpening them before use. The best way to sharpen a knife is to use a steel, but it requires practice to achieve the correct sharpening angle.

There are several ways of using a steel; find the most comfortable way for you. If you are right handed, hold the steel horizontally in your left hand with the tip pointing slightly down. Holding the knife in your right hand, place the heel of the blade at the top of the

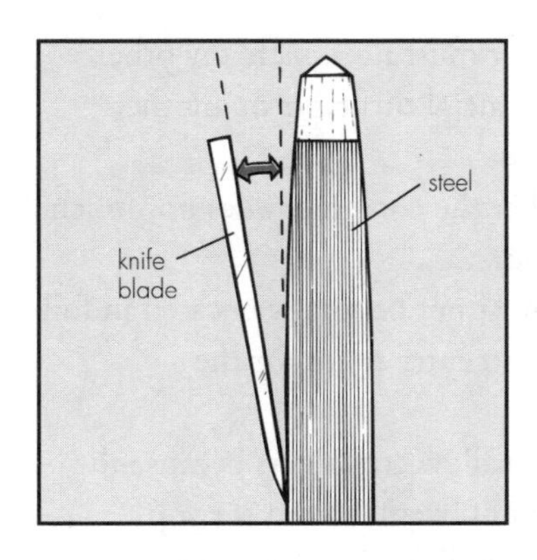

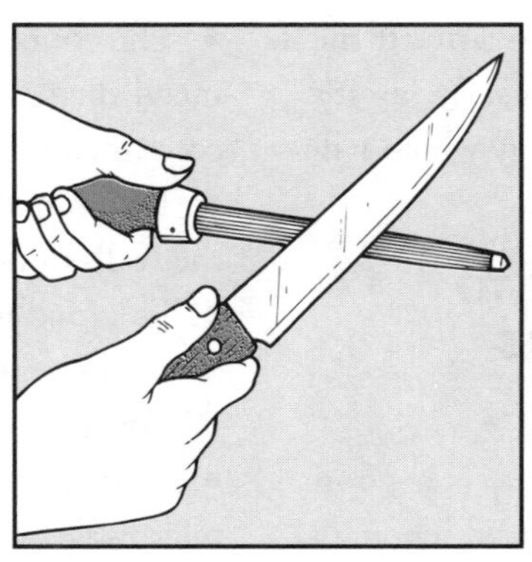

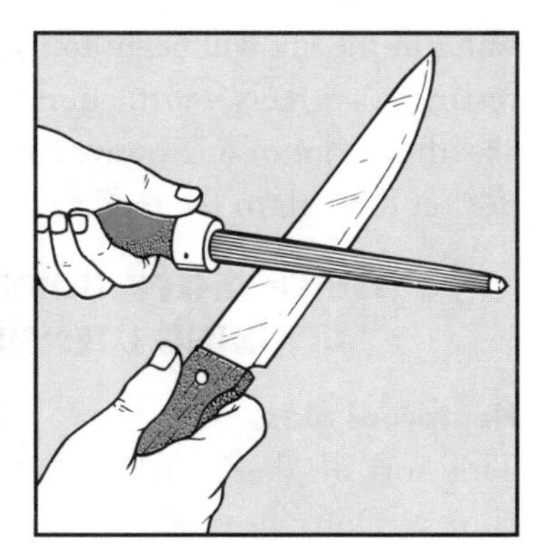

steel at an angle of about 20 to 30°. Draw the knife down the steel, gradually pulling the knife away so that the tip of the knife ends at the tip of the steel. Repeat with the knife blade under the steel to sharpen the other side.

If you find that you tend to blunt a knife rather than sharpen it, you may find it easier to use a sharpener which has angled slots to ensure the blade is always held at the correct angle. However, these gadgets tend to wear out the knife blade faster and give a coarser edge compared to a steel.

KITCHEN SCALES

There are three types of kitchen scales.

Traditional balance

Usually made of cast iron with separate weights. Limited weight range.

Mechanical

Numbered dial, usually in imperial and metric. Some types have a rotating weight gauge which can be reset to zero enabling precise amounts of different ingredients to be added in an add-and-weigh style.

Electronic/electro-mechanical

Electromechanical scales are no more accurate than their mechanical counterparts but have a digital readout. Fully electronic scales use a microchip and sensor to give a much more precise reading.

Most electronic scales have a versatile weight range and allow you to convert imperial to metric at the touch of a button. Others have memory facilities, automatic switch-off or a screen-save feature that switches the scales off if they're not touched for a couple of minutes, storing the weight in the memory until switched on again. The more sophisticated models provide calorie values or even enable you to break down individual foods into fats, carbohydrates, fibre and proteins. You do this by referring to a special chart and entering the code for that particular food.

MICROWAVE COOKWARE

It is not necessary to buy special microwave cookware. Many dishes in your kitchen cupboard are suitable for cooking and re-heating.

To test their suitability, fill a heat- resistant measuring jug with ½ pint/300ml of cold water. Place it on the turntable alongside the dish to be tested. If the dish is large, stand the jug on top of the empty dish. Heat on full power for 1 minute. If the dish is suitable for the microwave, it will remain cool, whilst the water in the jug will begin to feel warm. If the testing dish feels warm, don't use it, as it's absorbing a lot of microwave energy which will not get through to the food.

QUICK CHECK GUIDE TO COOKING UTENSILS

Heatproof glass

This sort of glass, such as Pyrex, is a good choice. Don't use delicate glass which may crack with the heat from the food.

China and ceramic

These vary in their ability to allow microwaves to pass through. Everyday, glazed-china plates, bowls, mugs and cups can be used if they are heat resistant. Porcelain and ceramic are also ideal. If in doubt, do the water test.

Fine bone china should only be used for reheating for short periods, otherwise the change in temperature may crack the dish or craze the finish. Don't use dishes with a metallic trim as this can cause 'arcing', a distortion of microwave patterns which can damage the magnetron.

Pottery, earthenware and stoneware

If completely glazed these dishes are suitable. Don't use if partially glazed or unglazed, since they absorb water which absorbs microwave energy. This makes the container very hot and slows down the cooking time.

Foil and metal containers

Metal containers should not be used in microwave-only ovens or microwaves with grills. They can be used in combination models, but check first with the manufacturer. Foil containers can be used in a microwave successfully if you follow certain guidelines:

- Always check with the manufacturer first.
- The container must not touch any other metal such as a metal turntable or another container.
- Take care that the container does not touch the walls or door.
- The food must not be totally encased in foil or else there is no entry point for the microwaves.
- Always use shallow containers because the microwaves can only enter from the top.
- Food may take slightly longer to cook. Check it is hot throughout before serving.
- Use foil to shield thin areas on joints of meat during defrosting and cooking. Because microwaves cannot pass through the foil, it prevents these areas from over-cooking or defrosting too fast.

Plastics

Different types vary in their ability to cope with use in microwaves. Most rigid plastics are satisfactory; flexible plastics tend not to be. Don't use cream or margarine cartons or yoghurt pots, as these will distort with the heat from the food; and in general, avoid using plastics to cook foods with a high fat or sugar content, as these substances get very hot and may melt or distort the plastic. Some plastic containers are designed specifically for use in a microwave and instructions will be given on their packaging.

Plastic freezer bags can be used for short periods of defrosting but be careful of plastic ties containing metal wire.

Cling film

This can be used for covering containers but it must be pricked to allow steam to escape. Don't let the film come into direct contact with the food for long cooking times. Check the packaging, as not all types are suitable for use in the microwave.

Paper

Is useful in a microwave to prevent fatty foods spattering, and to stop foods like bread and pastries from becoming soggy, but it is suitable for short cooking times only. Both greaseproof paper and absorbent kitchen paper work well.

Don't use waxed and plastic-coated cups and plates in a microwave as the coating can melt into the food.

Wicker and wood baskets

Wicker can be used for quick heating of items such as bread rolls, but because of their moisture content they will dry out and crack if used too often, or given a long exposure. Check the basket doesn't contain metal staples. Don't use wooden dishes.

WATER FILTERS

If you are concerned about what's in your tap water you should contact your water supplier and ask for written details. (They are legally obliged to tell you.) The information you receive will tell you how much of particular substances are in your water and how much is permitted under EC regulations. Your water should meet certain regulations about what it may and may not contain, and in what quantities. It may be that there is nothing to worry about, in which case you don't need to buy a filter at all.

JUG FILTERS

If you are simply not happy about the taste or colour of your water, or fed up with having a scaled-up kettle or a layer of scum on tea and coffee, it may be worth buying a jug water filter (for about £12 from your local chemist or housewares store).

Jug filters have ion exchange units which reduce water hardness as well as activated carbon filters to help improve the taste and appearance of the water.

JUG FILTER TIPS

- Make sure you buy a jug filter that can fit easily into your fridge. Once the water has been filtered of chlorine it has no defence against bacteria.
- Never keep filtered water for longer than a day.
- Always follow manufacturers' instructions for use, and change the filter regularly, otherwise you may be putting back into the water precisely what you intended to remove – and in far greater quantities.
- Most filter cartridges only last for 100–180 pints/60–100 litres (about a month, depending on the size of your family).

PLUMBED-IN FILTERS

If you find a jug filter too fiddly for your needs, and would prefer a more permanent solution, you may wish to consider a plumbed-in water filter. This is usually sited beneath the kitchen sink, and must have its own tap and a non-return valve to stop the filtered water getting back into the mains supply. There are numerous water filters on the market which could cost anything from £30 to £500. The main types you are likely to find in the shops are:

Granular Activated Carbon (GAC)

This will improve the taste, odour, colour and appearance of the water. It removes chlorine and some of the substances producing unpleasant tastes and odours. These filters may also remove nitrates, lead, aluminium and copper when new but, British Water (an organisation serving the water industry worldwide) feels that after a short time the filter ceases to be effective in this way.

Some companies claim a lifetime of three years for their filters; others only three months. They don't reduce water hardness.

Ceramic filter/ultra-violet disinfection unit
If removal of bacteria from a private water supply is considered necessary, consider a ceramic filter or ultra-violet disinfection unit. Mains water supplies should be free from harmful bacteria.

Reverse-osmosis unit
If other contaminants are present in the water, you can buy a reverse-osmosis unit. Be warned, this is an expensive option with units costing £400 or more.

The unit reduces the concentration of nitrates, lead, aluminium, copper and sodium chloride (salt). (This method has been used for years to produce high-quality water for use in kidney dialysis machines.)

For information on companies who supply water treatment devices contact British Water (see Useful Addresses).

WASTE DISPOSAL AND RECYCLING

A waste-disposal unit is a very fast and convenient way to get rid of kitchen rubbish. It will deal with biodegradable matter such as vegetable peelings, tea bags and food leftovers which together amount to about a quarter of household waste.

Waste disposal units are installed under the sink. With the cold tap running, the waste is fed into a grinding chamber. Here it is thrown outwards, by centrifugal power, against a shredder attached to the inside wall of the chamber. The small particles of waste are then, with the aid of water, discharged into the sewage system.

A unit requires two connections to the plumbing system. The grinder receives the food waste through an opening in the bottom of the kitchen sink. The ground particles are discharged from the grinder, via a tail pipe, connected to the household drainage system. The electrical connection needed to power the unit is via a switch to an earthed outlet alongside the sink.

If you don't have a one-and-a-half sink, you may have to pay for a fitter to cut your existing sink and install the unit.

As well as being convenient, a waste disposer is also very hygienic, getting rid of food which would normally begin to decompose and smell in an ordinary kitchen bin. It also helps to reduce the amount of rubbish in your own home. On the negative side, they do require quite a lot of water to work efficiently.

WASTE DISPOSAL METHODS

There are two types of waste disposer: batch feed and continuous feed. The difference between them is the way the waste is fed and processed in the machine.

WASTE DISPOSER TIPS

- Be careful when emptying food into the waste disposal unit. It's easy for a spoon or other cutlery to accidentally fall in. This then jams the unit and damages the blades. If this does happen, it is *essential* that you turn the appliance off at the mains before you attempt to take the obstruction out.
- To avoid putting your hands in the plug hole, use a pair of long-handled pliers and a torch so you can see what you are doing.
- Even when all the food has been ground up, it is essential that you still keep the tap running for a few minutes. If you don't run sufficient water through, the pipes may become blocked.

Batch feed

The unit is filled with waste, and the grinders will only start when the sink plug is put into place. The unit is therefore sealed, so there is no danger of getting fingers caught while in operation. You have to wait for the waste to be ground and flushed away before reloading. Batch-feed disposers cost about £100 more than continuous feed.

Continuous feed

The waste is fed in as and when you need to, which is ideal for larger families. You don't have to wait for the waste to be ground and flushed away before reloading. The main disadvantage, however, is that there is no cover on the unit, which could be dangerous, especially if inquisitive children are around.

Reverse unit

To reduce wear and tear it is worth investing in a fully automatic reverse unit. This feature is available on both types of waste disposer. Unlike a single-direction model, it grinds in alternate directions each time it is used.

WASTE COMPACTORS

Unlike waste-disposal units, compactors can deal with practically all household waste and

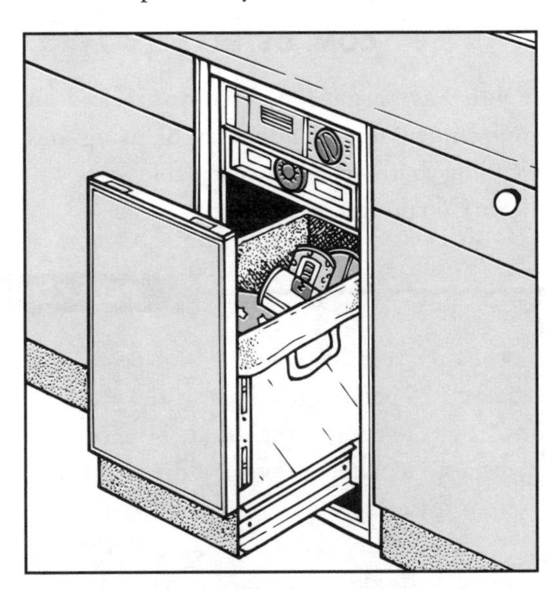

require no special installation or wiring. They work by crushing waste, using an electrically powered ram inside the rubbish drawer. This lowers on to the rubbish, then returns to a raised position and shuts off automatically.

This type of waste storage reduces household rubbish to one-twelfth of its original volume, saving space in the kitchen and numerous trips to the dustbin.

BIN SEPARATORS

A series of tough plastic boxes that are designed to be stacked on top of each other. They are an ideal way of storing rubbish suitable for recycling, such as glass, plastic, paper and metal.

Free-standing separator systems can be stored anywhere in the house, or outdoors.

Alternatively, built-in systems such as those made by Blanco (see Useful Addresses) are installed under the sink unit (see right). This is a more expensive option but it keeps the bins out of sight and saves space.

To save you time, find out if a local authority, charity or Scout group collect paper, or other recyclable waste, from your home.

COMPOSTERS

If you have a garden, a composter is an environmentally friendly way of using and recycling your kitchen biodegradable waste.

See Composters, page 212.

RECYCLING RUBBISH

- By the year 2000, we will be expected to recycle 25 per cent of all household waste. Changes to the way rubbish is collected and disposed of will be essential if the target is to be reached.
- Find out from your local council if they run a kerb-side collection scheme or if you have to go to a recycling centre yourself.
- Separate your rubbish into glass, paper, metal and plastic. Food waste (apart from meat) can then be put on the compost heap.
- Wash food and drink containers thoroughly to avoid any unpleasant smells developing and make processing easier.
- Remove caps of plastic bottles.
- Compared with glass and paper, plastic recycling is still relatively new. To identify different types of plastics look for these symbols on the bottom of containers and packaging. The initials refer to the type of plastic used in their manufacture.
- For details of recycling projects in your area contact Waste Watch (see Useful Addresses) or your local council.

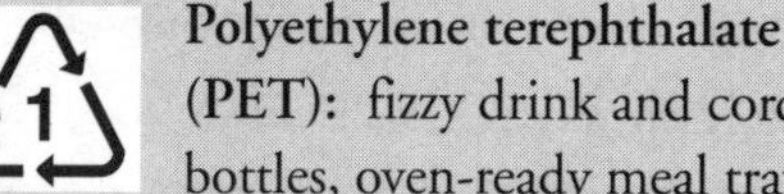

Polyethylene terephthalate (PET): fizzy drink and cordial bottles, oven-ready meal trays

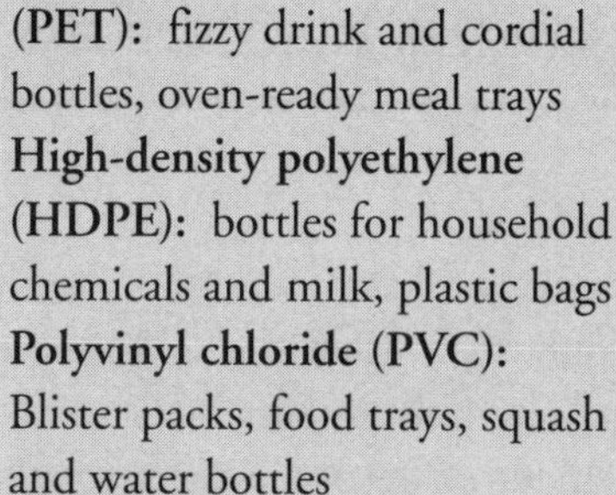

High-density polyethylene (HDPE): bottles for household chemicals and milk, plastic bags

Polyvinyl chloride (PVC): Blister packs, food trays, squash and water bottles

Low-density polyethylene (LDPE): sacks, bin liners and squeezy bottles

Polypropylene (PP): Margarine tubs, crisp packets, packaging film.

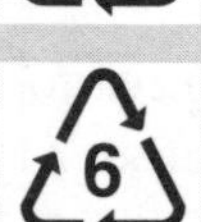

Polystyrene (PS): Egg cartons, yoghurt pots, cups for vending machines

- Don't just collect green glass. In terms of recycling, clear and amber glass is more valuable. Avoid Pyrex and light bulbs. Although they are made from glass, their composition makes them unsuitable for recycling.

HOUSEHOLD CLEANING APPLIANCES

The array of modern appliances can be bewildering, with models and features forever changing. Here is a guide to the basic appliances that will help keep your home in pristine condition.

VACUUM CLEANERS

The latest vacuum cleaners are more efficient and compact than ever, and a far cry from the huge early models delivered by horse and cart.

A carpet can hold up to three times its own weight in dust and grit. Carpets and upholstery wear because the dirt and grit trapped within them cuts through the fibres and destroys them. Choosing a good cleaner will make your furnishings last much longer.

There are two main types of vacuum cleaner to choose from: cylinders and uprights. Some people find cylinders hard work, especially if they've always been used to an upright.

Upright cleaners are generally recommended if you have large areas of carpet, and are a good choice for the elderly or people who suffer from a bad back as there is less stooping involved. However, uprights tend to be heavier to use and carry.

Cylinder cleaners are better on hard floors and short-pile carpets so are a good choice if you have a mixture of both.

In recent tests, GHI found cylinder cleaners to be more efficient generally than upright cleaners.

CYLINDER CLEANERS

Rely on suction power only to pick up dirt and therefore have a higher wattage (ranging from 800–1,500 watts) than an upright.

- Easier to use for stair cleaning and more convenient for carrying.
- Light to use because only the cleaning head and hose are hand held.
- More manoeuvrable than an upright and easier for cleaning under beds and furniture.
- Most have on-board storage for attachments.
- Better on hard floors and short-pile carpets.
- Generally better than uprights at cleaning right up to the skirting board.
- Automatic cord rewind and bag full indicators are sometimes standard.
- The smaller the cylinder cleaner the more often you will have to change the bag.
- Useful as a second cleaner for upstairs.
- Useful for rooms congested with furniture.

Points to consider when choosing

- Good manoeuvrability of cylinder with wheels that swivel.
- 360° swivel hose to prevent hose kinking.
- Anti-crush hose.
- Variable power control for different floor types and for upholstery, curtains and rugs.
- Tools on board for cleaning curtains, upholstery and crevices.
- Easy-to-use well-placed controls.
- Automatic flex rewind.
- Bag-full indicator.
- A parking-clip system for securing the hose when not in use.
- Telescopic extension tubes that allow you to adjust the height to suit.
- Metal tubes are more durable than plastic.
- Carpet beater (turbo brush) for heavy-duty cleaning.
- Filter-change indicator.

UPRIGHT CLEANERS

Use a combination of suction and the beating action of a rotating, motorised brush to loosen and remove dirt. The beater 'grooms' and helps to lift the carpet pile.

- Range up to 1,000 watts.
- Especially suitable for heavy traffic areas, where the beater helps to loosen deeply embedded grit and dirt that collects in the carpet pile.
- Heavier to use than a cylinder cleaner.
- Most have carpet-pile adjustment, some of which adjust automatically, and bag-full indicators.
- Many have tools on board, including the hose, so are slightly heavier to push around.
- Generally not as good as a cylinder for cleaning right up to the skirting board so you may have to clean edges with the crevice tool.

Points to consider when choosing

- Comfortable handle.
- Variable power control.
- On-board tool storage.
- Accessible fan belt.
- Carpet height setting which can be adjusted to suit different carpet piles.
- Edge-to-edge cleaning.
- Easy-to-replace dust bag and filters.
- Bag-full indicator.
- Automatic flex rewind.

WATTAGE

Don't be deluded into thinking that the higher the wattage the more efficient the cleaner. This isn't necessarily the case. The amount of dust and dirt a cleaner picks up depends not only on its wattage rating, but also on the air flow through the cleaner. Imagine trying to pick up a piece of paper with a drinking straw – it's fairly easy. But if the straw is kinked, it becomes much more difficult. So if the design of the piping inside the cleaner is poor, the cleaner can't utilise the wattage fully, no matter how high. Unfortunately, manufacturers don't quote airflow details so you have no way of knowing how well the cleaner will perform.

HIGH-EFFICIENCY CLEANERS

Allergic asthma can be triggered by a variety of irritants such as pollen, mould spores, animal fur and feathers. But doctors now believe that around 80 per cent of allergic asthma is irritated by house-dust mites, or their droppings, to be correct. These microscopic creatures live on the dead skin cells that make up 80 per cent of household dust. While you'll find them in carpets, upholstery and curtains, 90 per cent of them live in beds and bedding. Here they can be sure to find plenty of dead skin cells, so choose a cleaner with an upholstery nozzle and a crevice tool for vacuuming the mattress regularly, particularly around seamed sections and buttons.

If you're allergic to either dust, dust-mite droppings or pollen, a high-efficiency vacuum cleaner is worth considering. The cleaners have three or four filters to trap these small particles to give a filter efficiency of between 95 and 99 per cent. Expect to pay more than for a conventional cleaner. The majority of high-efficiency cleaners are only available direct from the manufacturer. These include: Nilfisk Allergy Vac, BVC-bivac CV7 NPF and Miele White Pearl (see Useful Addresses).

FILTERS

Filters help to trap dust and prevent it from being blown back into the room through the cleaner's exhaust. How much dust is retained depends on the cleaner's filtration system.

Over the last five years, conventional vacuum cleaners have improved greatly with more manufacturers incorporating extra filters to help improve filter efficiency. Conventional vacuum cleaners have a filter efficiency of between 70 and 90 per cent.

Cylinder cleaners tend to have a higher filtration than upright cleaners as they usually have more filters that are more substantial. Some models have electrostatically charged filters that attract dust, and others have a filter that inhibits mould growth.

The mainstream manufacturers are improving their products constantly. More and more conventional vacuum cleaners are claiming to have a filter efficiency of 99 per cent. Some can be upgraded to increase filter efficiency if you buy an extra, optional filter. These offer a cheaper alternative to the high-efficiency cleaners but check the manufacturer's claims, carefully. High-efficiency cleaners should be able to retain dust particles down to 0.3 micron (one-thousandth of a millimetre).

WHAT'S NEW IN VACUUM CLEANERS?

No dust bags

A recent development, although a return to earlier models, is the upright vacuum cleaner that doesn't use a dust bag. Instead, they have a canister to collect the dust which can be then emptied straight into the dustbin. This saves money otherwise spent on dust bags, but it can be messy to empty, and more immediate contact with the collected dust does not help those with allergies.

Sensors

Some vacuum cleaners have sensors to detect the amount of dirt in your carpet and adjust the power accordingly. Others can automatically adjust the suction power of the cleaner depending on the floor type. A useful feature if you have different depths of carpet pile and hard floor.

BUILT-IN VACUUM SYSTEMS

The central power unit and dust collection bin are hidden away in a cupboard, garage or utility room. Connected to this is a series of suction pipes that carry the dust and grit to the bin, for emptying a couple of times a year. The pipes can be concealed under floorboards, run through the attic, concealed inside cupboards or under stairs, and emerge at convenient inlets on the walls (the discreet sockets look like electric points). A three- or four-bedroomed house might need only two. An extra-long flexible hose and cleaning tools connect to these inlets and are used like a conventional vacuum cleaner.

Advantages

- There's only a light hose and cleaning heads to carry around and store.
- Cleaning the stairs is easier and there's no flex to trip over.
- Cleaning is quieter as the motor unit is tucked away.
- Sufferers of dust-related allergies could benefit. The central vacuum system is more powerful than a conventional vacuum cleaner, and as the exhaust air is passed outside the living area, there tends to be less dust in the atmosphere.

Disadvantages

- A central vacuum system will be more costly: anything from £500 (DIY price), and installation may be extra.

- The system should last for at least 20 years, but if you move, you can't take the system with you.
- Mess and disruption due to installation caused by drilling and brick dust.

Installation

You can ask a professional builder to install the system for you, although some manufacturers sell DIY systems.

The power unit should exhaust through an outside wall. In a garage, the installation has to comply with fire regulations. The power unit can be noisy when it's switched on, so the further away from the living area you can site it, the better.

Manufacturers in this market are: Beam and Univac (see Useful Addresses).

THREE-IN-ONE CLEANERS

These are predominantly cylinder cleaners, but there is one upright version available. They offer three functions:

- Conventional vacuum cleaning.
- Shampooing carpets.
- Wet pick-up: for mopping up floods and large spills.

There are three types to choose from.

Gravity

Relies on gravity to force the shampoo solution to the cleaning head. Not suitable for stairs or upholstery since the water pressure can't be maintained if the cleaning head is raised above the machine: water can't run up hill unless pumped.

Pump

A motorised pump forces the shampoo solution to the cleaning head and maintains water pressure. Suitable for carpet, upholstery and stair cleaning. More expensive, but worth paying extra for the added versatility.

Air injection

A cross between the gravity and pump types. The cleaner's exhaust air is used to force shampoo cleaning solution to the cleaning head. A cheaper alternative to a pump type, but not as good at maintaining pressure for stair cleaning.

Points to consider when choosing

- Good manoeuvrability – important when shampooing because it does become heavy when full of water.
- Separate nozzle for upholstery.
- Facility to store flex.
- Easy to change to various functions.
- Easy to change dust bag and filter.
- If you want to be able to shampoo stairs, curtains and upholstery, choose a pump type.
- Easy to grip handles on either side for ease of filling and emptying.

SHAMPOOING TIPS

- Always test your carpet in an inconspicuous area before cleaning to make sure that it is colourfast to the shampoo solution.
- Open windows for faster drying.
- Don't over-wet. Each stroke will leave about 5 per cent moisture behind, so don't go over an area more than is necessary.
- For carpet cleaning, clear as much furniture out of the room as possible. Clean in convenient sections, working towards the door
- Avoid walking on the carpet until it's thoroughly dry as the moisture in the fibres attracts dirt.

- Large filling hole on the water tank.
- Trigger spray to control shampoo solution: reduces the risk of over-wetting the carpet.

HAND-HELD CLEANERS

Lightweight cleaners which are usually rechargeable. Range from 40 to 150 watts. Ideal for spot cleaning, stair cleaning and for cleaning car interiors. Some models are suitable for wet and dry jobs and can cope with small spills.

Rechargeable cleaners are useful for cleaning areas away from a mains socket. They need to be charged for a number of hours initially, and usually provide about 20 minutes' operating time before needing to be recharged.

Some models are designed specifically for the car and operate from the car's battery by plugging into the cigarette lighter. Attachments are usually provided.

Mains-operated cleaners are more powerful and usually have a rotating motorised brush to loosen and remove dirt. A good choice for cleaning stairs.

FLOOR POLISHERS

If you want to polish parquet flooring, an electric floor polisher can save a lot of hard work and do an efficient job. Some models are suitable for scrubbing floors as well as shampooing carpets.

A polisher has two or three rotary heads driven by an electric motor. Depending on the purpose, sets of stiff-bristled brushes, softer brushes or polishing buffers can be clipped on to the heads.

The floor should be brushed or vacuumed first to remove loose dirt and dust. Then clean the floor with a proprietary floor cleaner, preferably one that doesn't need to be rinsed. Some models have a tank to apply the cleaning solution automatically: a trigger releases the cleaning solution when required.

Use the stiff brushes to scrub the floor. A liquid wax should then be applied to the floor and polishing brushes work the wax into the floor. Depending on the degree of gloss you prefer, felt polishing or buffing pads are used to give shine.

Some polishers have a detergent tank that is fixed to the handle to convert the machine into a carpet shampooer.

FLOOR SAFETY

WAXED AND POLISHED FLOORS CAN BE VERY SLIPPERY. NEVER USE RUGS ON THEM.

WASHING MACHINES

The most common type of washing machine has a porthole door at the front. This type can wash a maximum cotton load of 11lb/5kg, or 5½lb/2.5kg of synthetics (one set of double bed linen).

Standard dimensions to fit under a kitchen work-top measure 33½in/850mm high, 24in/600mm wide and 24in/600mm deep.

Slimline models are the same height but not as deep:18in/450mm or 13in/320mm.

WASH PROGRAMMES

The main programme dial selects the wash cycle, which is set to correspond to wash care labels on clothes (see International Textile Care Labelling, page 320). Some machines automatically set the temperature while others have a separate temperature control. This gives greater flexibility to use lower temperatures with different wash cycles.

Spin speeds are automatically set, depending

upon the programme selected. Full agitation cotton washes have a maximum spin (between 900 and 1,400 rpm), while the easy-care and wool programmes with less agitation use a lower spin (500 to 900 rpm). Spin speeds can often be lowered using an option button.

A lower spin speed (eg 900 rpm) does not necessarily mean that the spin is not as thorough as a high speed spin (eg 1,100 rpm); the machine may spin for longer to compensate.

A rinse-and-hold option (also called delay spin or Creaseguard) stops the machine during the final rinse when the easy-care programmes are used. This holds the clothes in the water and the machine will not spin until it is reset. This reduces creasing, as clothes can be removed from the drum immediately after spinning rather than left sitting wet in the drum at the end of a wash.

On some models this happens automatically while on others the rinse hold will only come into play if the option button has been used.

SOAK OR SPRAY?

Automatic washing machines work in one of two ways. Most manufacturers sell both types.

Traditionally, automatic machines take in a predetermined amount of water and the clothes are rolled around in the drum with the water and detergent solution.

More recent machines use a sensor-spray system, which is more economical on water. There are two stages in this system.

First, the drum is filled with an amount of water that depends upon the amount of clothes, using a minimum requirement of water. This saves on the amount of electricity used to heat the water.

Second, the water is circulated and sprayed back on to the clothes by being either scooped up by paddles on the drum or re-pumped from the bottom and showered in at the top of the drum. The latter has the advantage of using all the detergent that may otherwise be trapped in the washing machine's pipework.

Different manufacturers adopt different names for the shower system: Hotpoint, Aquarius; Candy, Aquamix; Zanussi, Jetsystem; and they tend to be more expensive than the traditional machines.

There are a few models that also have the sensor system on the rinses for even greater water savings.

OTHER FEATURES

- Ball Valve (also described with trade names such as Eco-lock) is positioned in the bottom of the drum and prevents detergent falling straight into the pipework and being wasted.
- Imbalance spin protector regulates the speed and length of the spin. If clothes are unevenly distributed in the drum this will prevent the bearings being unnecessarily strained. Some machines operate short spins to try to even out the load before spinning.
- Bio-enzyme phase (or bio-phase). To take full advantage of the enzymes in biological detergents the water temperature is held at around 100–120°F/40–50°C so that stains can be broken down.

PROGRAMME OPTIONS

Half load cuts down (but does not halve) the amount of water used in the main wash on traditional (soaking) machines. Reduces the rinse water used in sensor-spray machines.

Delay timer allows you to set the machine to wash when you want. The wash can be set to finish when you will be able to sort it, or you can take advantage of Economy 7 electricity. (If you intend to make use of this facility, a smoke alarm fitted in the kitchen is recommended.)

Quick wash is designed to freshen up lightly soiled items, this option may be a separate, cooler wash programme selected on the dial (takes about 30 minutes). Some machines have a limited maximum load for this programme and may also reduce the number of rinses.

Economy option may be similar to a quick-wash option by reducing the wash temperature or the length of the programme. Alternatively, it may reduce the temperature and extend the programme time to compensate. Check that you get a machine with the type of programme you want, and don't confuse a quick and an economy wash.

USEFUL FEATURES

- An extra rinse button allows you to increase the number of rinses. Useful for those with sensitive skin.
- Stage of wash indicators allow you to see how far the wash has progressed, at a glance.
- Rinse and spin programmes are useful for finishing off hand washing.
- If you frequently use different programmes, separate wash temperature and programme controls give you greater versatility.
- Accessible filters at the front of the machine (a small, square door which hinges open) save items like buttons from collecting in the pump, so reducing the necessity to call out a service engineer. Some machines don't have this access to the filter but claim to have a self-cleaning filter.

LESS-USUAL MACHINE TYPES

Automatic top loaders

These are designed to sit level with an adjacent work-top. The controls may protrude higher, and space is needed to open the lid. (Height from 33½in/850mm plus lid; width from about 16in/400mm to 24in/600mm; depth 24in/600mm.) The plumbing needed is the same as for an automatic washing machine (cold and hot water supply and a drain hose).

This type of machine will wash a maximum load of about 10lb/4.5kg of cottons and 6lb/2.7kg of synthetics.

The wash programmes are the same as for front-loading machines, corresponding to clothes care labels, but extra features and options will be less sophisticated.

Twin tub

These are not automatic and are filled from the kitchen taps, so need to be pulled out for use. They will slot under a work-top for storage when not in use.

There are two compartments, one for washing and rinsing and one for spinning. Clothes are agitated in the water either by a central spindle-mounted paddle or an agitator on the back of the compartment. The clothes are moved manually over to the second drum for spinning.

Twin tubs are good for households with small washes which can be finished quickly.

Height 30in/750mm; width 30in/760mm; depth 18in/460mm. Twin tubs will wash a maximum load of about 6½lb/3kg of cottons, and 4½lb/2kg of synthetics.

TUMBLE-DRIERS

There are two types, vented or condenser. Vented driers are more common.

The basic operation of tumble-driers is simple: you set the drying time according to the amount of clothes. Suggested drying times are usually given on the machine. All programmes have a cool-down period just before the end of the drying cycle.

VENTED

As the name suggests, the damp air from the drier is vented outside via a hose. The vent hose is connected to the front, back, or side of the tumble-drier and can be connected permanently through a window or wall. You will need special fixtures and probably a builder to install them. If a permanent fixture is not possible a flexible hose can be put out of a window, but you will need to keep the window open when drying.

CONDENSER

These do not need venting or plumbing. The damp air is cooled and the condensed water collected in a reservoir. The water is emptied from the drawer or can be piped away. (It is suitable for using in steam irons.) This makes the positioning of the drier less restrictive.

Look for condenser driers that have a warning light to remind you to empty the water drawer.

Condenser driers are more expensive than vented driers.

SIZES

Standard

Both models are available in standard size: height 33½in/850mm, width 24in/600mm and depth 24in/600mm. They are the same size as full-size automatic washing machines and can be stacked on top to save space. Permanent stacking kits are available but you must have the same brand of washing machine and tumble-drier.

Standard driers will dry a 9–11lb/4–5kg load of cotton items (a normal maximum wash load).

Compact

Only vented models are available as a compact size (height 26in/670mm, width 19in/490mm). They are a convenient size to sit on top of a work-top or hang on the wall.

Compact driers will dry about 6½lb/3kg of cottons at one time.

POINTS TO CONSIDER WHEN CHOOSING

- Basic machines have two heat settings, for cotton and synthetics. Some models may also have a cool setting for airing dried clothes.
- Reverse tumbling action changes the direction of the drum during drying to reduce tangling and assist drying.
- An intermittent tumble after the drying cycle has finished helps to minimise the creasing until you can put the clothes away.
- More sophisticated models have sensors: some lower the heat as the load dries to reduce creasing and prevent over-drying.
- Moisture-sensitive models are programmable and switch off when the clothes are dry. They can be set to switch off when the clothes are 'iron dry' or 'cupboard dry'.

Filters

- All tumble-driers have filters that need clearing of fluff. Some models have indicator lights to remind you. Check to see that the filter is easily accessible: one at the front of the drum is more convenient to clean than one on the back wall of the drum.

WASHER-DRIERS

These look just like automatic washing machines but are also able to tumble-dry in the same drum.

They are convenient, carrying out both operations where space is limited. The machine has to be plumbed in where a washing machine would normally fit. The washing capacities are similar to full-sized washing machines but you can only dry half the maximum load, 5½lb/2.5kg cotton, so you must remove half the load after washing.

For drying, the water is condensed using

cold water and is pumped away down the washing-machine piping. As the drum is the same size as a washing machine rather than a tumble-drier, there is less room for the clothes to tumble and the result is not as good.

POINTS TO CONSIDER WHEN CHOOSING

- Washing programmes and features are generally the same as for washing machines, but because a drier is also incorporated there are generally fewer extra options.
- The drying cycles have two temperatures to correspond to fabric types.
- All washer-driers can carry out a continuous operation, washing followed by drying, provided you halve the capacity for washing.
- They can also be used as a washing machine only or a drier only.

IRONS

We spend a staggering 12 months of our lives ironing so it's worth choosing the best iron you can afford. However, with the huge range available, with increasingly sophisticated features, the choice can be bewildering.

DRY IRONS

Choice is limited because these are the least popular type. Although cheaper and lighter than steam irons, they are less effective on heavy-duty fabrics such as denim and thick cotton, and badly creased items.

They have basic, variable temperature selection only, for ironing different fabrics.

TIP If the laundry is very creased, iron with a damp cloth or spray the clothes first.

Soleplate

Usually aluminium.

STEAM IRONS

These are the most versatile because they can be used as a dry or steam iron. They help take the drudgery out of ironing because they help remove creases quickly and more easily.

The greater the steam output, the more efficient the crease removal. If stated on the packaging look for at least 15g per minute.

Steam irons can be either corded or cordless. A cordless iron fits on to a mains-powered base. Some models offer an option to iron with or without a mains lead attached to the iron (combination corded/cordless).

Cordless irons are light, easy to use and safer because there are no trailing flexes. Ironing detailed and fiddly items such as frills and pin-tucks is easier. However, they must be returned to the power base frequently to ensure the temperature of the soleplate is maintained. If the iron cools below steam temperature, water may drip from the soleplate, which could watermark delicate fabrics. A cordless model can be more bulky to store than a corded model because of the separate base. If space is limited, choose a combination corded/cordless which can be wall mounted.

TIP A flex holder keeps the flex off the board if you are using a corded model, and it costs only a few pounds. You can fix it on to the edge of your board.

Soleplate

Originally chrome or aluminium, but many now have special finishes designed to reduce friction and speed up ironing.

- Nickel alloy polished with sapphires to strengthen the surface is one of the toughest and most scratch-resistant soleplates.
- Stainless steel: hard-wearing and glides easily.

• Aluminium flecked with titanium: glides easily.
• Ceramic-coated metal: ribbed to improve crease removal, scratch and stain resistance.
• Non-stick finishes (such as SilverStone) are easy to clean, but need extra care to avoid scratching the surface.

POINTS TO CONSIDER WHEN CHOOSING

With the exception of safety features, all the extras make ironing easier and, in most cases, faster. Decide which ones are the most important to your style and type of ironing and consider if they are worth paying more for.
• Water spray: most steam irons incorporate this feature. A fine mist or spray jet of water dampens the fabric just in front of the iron. Useful for very dry items, along seams and on stubborn creases.
• Boost of steam for dry or steam ironing: the iron will emit an extra surge of steam which will penetrate deeper into the fabric. Useful when pressing dry items, pleats and creases.

ANTI-SCALE FEATURES

Some models have anti-scale systems to combat the hard water salts from tap water. These include:
• Removable valves which take out the scale before it reaches the steam chamber. Can be cleaned by immersing in a weak acid solution such as vinegar, or a limescale remover.
• Removable anti-scale cassettes which filter mineral deposits from the water. When the crystals in the cassette change colour they should be replaced.
• Self-cleaning systems which clear the chamber and vents with a blast of steam.

This can cause water to drip from the soleplate and will use up the water tank more quickly. Continuous use will also lower the temperature of the soleplate.
• Variable steam control: the output of steam can be adjusted from slight to maximum, according to the fabric type and temperature selected on the iron. Useful for steaming delicate fabrics such as silk.
• Constant steam output: ensures a constant steam production and consistently good results until the tank is empty. Steam output decreases as the water level drops in the tank in irons without this feature.
• Safety features: range from non-fray flex to devices that switch the iron off:

All irons have a thermal cut-out that operates if the iron overheats when in use. Automatic cut-out turns the power off after a few minutes if the iron is left unattended; some will even bleep.

Plastic flex, or flex that's attached by a ball joint for easy movement, to prevent wear and fraying.
• Descaling: scaling-up of the element is the most common cause of failure. Even if the manufacturer states tap water can be used, it's worth using demineralised water (check instructions first) or distilled water (but not the distilled water used for car batteries, which may contain traces of acid).

TIP Make your own distilled water with one of the special bottles sold for about £2 in department stores. Called demineraliser bottles, they contain crystals which take the calcium ions out of hard water. It's easy to tell when the bottle needs replacing as the crystals change colour.

Always empty your iron after use to prevent scale build-up and check instructions before attempting any descaling procedure.

- Large water tanks are useful to minimise refilling, but they do add to the weight of the iron. Remember the size of the water tank doesn't necessarily relate to the ironing time. The frequency with which the tank must be refilled depends on the steam output, the frequency of using the boost-of-steam feature, the frequency of using the water spray on the front of the iron, the size of tank and the steam setting.
- A central flex entry is the most convenient for right- and left-handed users. Most irons now have this feature.

IRONING SYSTEMS

The more professional types of ironing systems have always been more popular in Europe, particularly in France and Italy. In the UK cost is the prohibiting factor, although they are becoming more popular.

Irons with separate steam generators

The iron is connected via a thick cord to a separate water reservoir, which plugs into mains electricity. Although more expensive than normal steam irons, they have a longer life because the element is not in contact with water, so limescale is reduced. Steam generation is greater because the water is heated in a separate container.

They can be used for both vertical and horizontal ironing.

This sort of system is worth considering if you iron several laundry loads a week and if you live in a hard water area.

- Place the reservoir on the floor or a nearby work-top to keep the ironing board clear.
- When ironing vertically, move the iron from top to bottom, keeping the steam button constantly depressed.
- Don't over-steam knitwear: a few seconds on a light steam setting is sufficient.

Rotary ironers

A rotary ironer has a roller and heating plate, which meet when a foot pedal is depressed. It does not replace an iron and board: ironing a shirt is possible but time consuming. These machines are designed for pressing bedding and table linen, and are recommended for guesthouses and similar businesses. The roller rotates to a vertical position for storage.

These can be used while seated and are less tiring on the arms. However, they are expensive and you will also need a normal iron for garments.

- Use the whole length of the roller where possible; for small items, use the ends of the roller, alternating between them for equal wear and tear.
- Buttons should be ironed face down on the roller, pressed into the padded surface; poppers should be fastened.
- Folded items should be fed into the machine fold first.
- Save smaller items until the end, turn off heat and iron using the residual heat.
- Make sure your chair is the correct height for working. A height-adjustable chair with castors is a good idea.

Ironing presses

Items are sandwiched between a padded board and a heated plate, which becomes extremely hot. The press is placed on a table or work surface allowing you to use it when seated. Some models have built-in water sprays and sleeve arms. Like rotary irons these are better suited to flat uncomplicated items like bedding and linen and are expensive as you will need an iron as well.

- To avoid creasing, make full use of the pressing cushion for awkward areas such as darts, sleeves and curved seams.
- When pressing large items, position fabric

in the storage area behind the ironing board. Place the first section on top of the board. Press, pull fabric towards you, and repeat the process.

Heated board and iron combined

This system combines a light cordless iron with a heated board.

The ironing system uses microprocessor technology in what looks like a standard ironing board. The ironing table houses sealed-in heating elements and a socket connection for the plug-in curly lead that connects it to the mains. The conventional iron rest is replaced with a control centre and iron station or dock. An electronic touch pad regulates the temperature of board and iron.

The iron, which can be dry or steam, is heated by slotting it into the dock and selecting the setting being used. If the iron is left unattended in the dock for over five minutes it reverts to standby.

As with all cordless irons this one has to be recharged during use, but because of continual contact with the heated board this takes very little time.

The board becomes hot during use but not uncomfortably so; maximum heat is generated when the board and iron are in contact with the fabric between them.

A typical machine is the Gemini Ironing System (see Useful Addresses).

- To iron sheets faster, fold and iron on one side only.
- Fold shirts and trousers at the seam; iron on one side only.

IRONING BOARDS

The quality and performance of an ironing board is very price dependent. Lower-priced models tend to be smaller and less sturdy.

POINTS TO CONSIDER WHEN CHOOSING

- Height is an important consideration, particularly for the elderly or those with back problems. Ideally the board should be adjustable between 31in/78cm and 35in/90cm. Set the height so that the iron handle is level with your elbow, or slightly below it. Alternatively, choose a board with angled legs, allowing room for a chair, so you can iron comfortably while seated.
- Longer boards are more convenient, so select one at least 5ft/150cm long.
- Ensure the board cover fits well and is easy to remove. Ill-fitting covers soon wrinkle and impair ironing performance. Look for covers with sturdy ties or preferably elastic. Covers can be either padded cotton or metallic (milium). The metallic type will reflect the heat back into the fabric but become quite hot during use.
- An iron rest is a useful feature as it offers greater stability for siting the iron and reduces the temptation to rest the iron face down on the fabric cover. It is either fixed at the end of the board or is retractable.
- The shape of the board is an important consideration. A pointed end makes it easier to iron trousers but a wide tip speeds up ironing because of the larger surface area.
- To stop the board slipping, look for rubber covers on the end of the feet. Levelling feet may be useful if your floors are particularly uneven.
- If you use a powerful steam iron, choose a board with a metal mesh top. This allows steam to pass through the board and helps keep the ironing surface dry.
- A laundry rack attachment allows you to hang garments once they have been ironed.
- Detachable sleeve board.

UNUSUAL IRONING BOARDS

The Shirtmaster (see Useful Addresses) is shaped like a double bass and has an extra-wide ironing area. The contours are ideal for fitting a shirt around and speed up the ironing process because you don't need to move the garment as much.

FRZ from Austin White (see Useful Addresses) retail an Ironing Centre which includes a variable ironing surface which can be adjusted from a broad to a narrow tip. There is a swivel iron rest, clothes rack, hanging rail, integral foldaway sleeve board, flex holder, angled legs and a levelling device for uneven floors.

LARGE KITCHEN APPLIANCES

Kitchen appliances such as cookers, dishwashers and fridges are some of the most expensive items bought for the home. As well, they are used with such frequency that an informed choice can make all the difference to the enjoyment of using the kitchen.

COOKERS

Cookers run on gas, electricity or dual fuel.

Their design can be:

- Free-standing.
- Slot-in: fits flush with your work surface and cupboards to give a built-in appearance.
- Built-in: the oven and hob are separate, with the oven built into a special housing usually around waist height, and the hob sited in the work surface. You can mix and match fuels, and you can position them exactly where you want.

HOBS

Hob cooking has become more popular recently. We are steaming and stir-frying more, reflecting healthy eating trends.

ELECTRIC HOBS

These provide a much wider choice than with gas. They are sealed plate, radiant or ceramic, glass-topped.

Built-in hobs

Most models fit into a standard 24in/600mm-deep work-top. If the hole is pre-cut, check measurements before purchasing the hob. A laminated work surface can be cut using a jigsaw, but make a template first. For other work-top material get the hole professionally cut. Electric hobs can be fitted by any qualified electrician.

Radiant

The traditional coiled radiant ring hob is only available on free-standing cookers. Compared with sealed plates, this type is slightly faster to heat up and cool down, but can be difficult to clean. At high temperatures the rings glow red.

Sealed plate

This type has always been popular in Europe, and is now replacing the traditional radiant ring in the UK. It is inexpensive and relatively easy to install.

As the heat source is a radiant ring covered by a cast-iron plate, the response rate is poor. Compared with other electric hobs it is slow to heat up and it is difficult to maintain a low temperature for simmering. When switched off cooling is slow.

To maintain appearance and condition re-blacken the plates with 4 Hob (see Sealed Plates, page 300 and Useful Addresses). This will help avoid rusting.

Some models have red dots in the centre of one or two plates. These have a higher rating relative to the diameter of the sealed plate and therefore a faster boiling time.

A pan sensor is sometimes fitted to one of the plates. This automatically turns the plate down to a simmer once the contents of the pan have come to the boil, and helps prevent liquids boiling over if not watching them.

CERAMIC GLASS-TOPPED HOBS

The heating systems are hidden beneath the tough ceramic-glass surface. Patterned zones on the glass surface indicate the size and position of the heat source. All have a safety device which prevents the ceramic-glass from overheating.

There are several types:

Ceramic

Radiant elements are housed under the glass surface. They are coiled like a radiant ring hob, or split and arranged in a series of lines or a star shape. Split elements heat up more quickly than the single coiled ones. Trade names for split elements include Solarglo, Speedglow and Quicklight.

Ceramic hobs are easy to keep clean, provided the manufacturer's instructions are followed properly.

> **SAFETY**
>
> Ceramic glass-topped hobs retain heat a lot longer than gas, so even when the hob has been turned off it can remain dangerously hot. To avoid accidents, look for models with hob-hot warning lights, particularly if you have young children.

Halogen

Heated by halogen lamps under the glass, which glow when the hob is switched on. This type offers the same benefits as ceramic hobs, plus it is slightly quicker to heat up.

The halogen light glows bright red so put your pan in position first to protect your eyes.

Easy to keep clean provided the manufacturer's instructions are followed.

Due to the cost it is rare to find a hob with four halogen heating zones. Instead this heat source tends to be combined with radiant ceramic zones.

INDUCTION HOBS

These are rare domestically in the UK because of cost, but are used widely in commercial situations. A four-zone hob is about four times the price of halogen.

They are the fastest reacting of the electric hobs, and are comparable with gas.

Induction cooking differs from normal cooking by heating the pan directly rather than by conducting heat through the hob surface. A spiral copper coil beneath the glass transfers energy directly to the pan by a process known as electromagnetic induction. This process means that no energy is delivered from the coil until a ferrous or iron-based magnetic pan is placed directly over it, and in contact with it, to activate the magnetic field. This makes it much more energy efficient

> **COOKWARE CHOICE**
>
> To check if your pans are suitable for an induction hob, place a magnet on the base. If it sticks then you can use it. There is a greater variety of pans available than you might at first imagine, such as enamelled pans with an iron base, stainless steel with an appropriate sandwich base and cast-iron pans.
>
> The correct choice of pan is critical for electric hobs. Good contact is essential, so avoid pans with dents or rough surfaces.
>
> (For further details on materials see Choosing Cookware, page 61.)

than other electric heat sources, and it is safer because the hob only gets hot where it is in contact with the pan.

GAS HOBS

Any gas appliance, by law, must be installed by a gas fitter registered by CORGI, the Council for Registered Gas Installers (see Useful Addresses).

Gas is a popular choice for hobs, being more responsive than electric ones: quick to heat up and reduce to a simmer. They can take any type of pan, but are awkward to clean. Look for easily removable pan supports.

Look for differently rated burners. This can usually be detected by their size. Large is for fast boiling and the small, less powerful one is for simmering. Some hobs may have identical-sized burners which can be confusing, so check the power ratings before you buy.

Ensure the burners are well spaced so all pans fit comfortably, and that the pan supports are well balanced and stable.

For ease of cleaning look for models with easily removable spillage wells.

POINTS TO LOOK FOR ON ALL HOBS

- Hot warning lights on glass-topped hobs.
- Easy-to-use controls with clear markings.
- At least one higher-powered cooking zone for fast boiling on electric hobs.
- Larger cooking zones for big saucepans.
- Drop-down lid on gas hobs to keep kitchen tidy and hob clean, but not intended to be used as a work-top.
- Automatic cut-out systems to cut off gas when the lid is lowered.
- Removable controls for easy cleaning.

OVENS AND GRILLS

Electric is the most popular fuel type. Choose from:

CONVENTIONAL (STATIC)

Found in basic models. Electric elements are in the sides or top and bottom of the oven. These have zoned heating: the top of the oven is hotter than the bottom. Some top and bottom elements work independently, which is ideal for base crisping, or browning the surface of some foods.

Good for traditional cooking: roasts, fruit cakes and bread.

FAN OVENS

Most electric cookers now incorporate a fan to circulate the heat more evenly, so the temperature is the same throughout the oven.

In 'fan-assisted' types, the air is heated by electric elements in the oven sides, while in convection ovens the element is wrapped around the fan. The advantages are:

- Cooking is quicker.
- Colour is even, but usually paler and less glossy than on food cooked in a conventional oven.

CHANGING OVEN TYPES

Changing from a static to a fan oven takes some adjustment.

Always follow manufacturers' instructions for cooking times and temperatures, or if you are trying an old favourite recipe reduce the heat by about 50°F/10°C and the time by 10 to 15 minutes. You can always return the dish for further cooking.

Leave space around dishes and at the sides to allow the air currents to circulate.

Check whether the manufacturer recommends grilling with the oven door open or closed.

- Pre-heating is usually unnecessary.
- Repositioning shelves is unnecessary, as is swapping trays half-way through cooking.
- Good for batch baking (cooking on more than one shelf) because of the even heat distribution.
- Cooking times and temperatures are always reduced from those of traditional ovens but by variable amounts depending on the make of cooker. So follow the manufacturer's instructions carefully.
- The food surface may be drier and less crisp.

MULTI-FUNCTION

This type of oven is a combination of a fan and a conventional oven. It therefore provides the user with the maximum versatility. Each option can be used separately or together depending on the type of food you are cooking and the grill can be used with the fan, giving a similar effect to a rotisserie.

A multi-function oven is ideal for batch baking and traditional cooking.

GAS OVENS

Conventional (British) gas ovens

The temperature in the middle of the oven relates to the selected gas mark. The top shelf is slightly hotter, lower shelf slightly cooler and the base cooler still. 'Zoned heat' is ideal for cooking complete meals, where dishes require different temperatures.

Gas is a much moister form of heat than electric, particularly noticeable in baking. It results in food with a glossy appearance on the outside and a moist texture inside.

Brand names for zoned heat are Gyroflo and Cycloheat.

Imported gas ovens

Many built-in gas cookers sold in the UK are of European origin. The burners are concealed under the base of the oven, so food is crisped from underneath. They are ideal for pizzas and pastries, but you must avoid using the base plate of the oven as a shelf.

Heat distribution differs from that in a conventional gas oven, so always follow the manufacturer's instructions carefully. Cooking techniques are similar to fan cooking, and heat is more evenly distributed throughout the oven, so you will have to reduce cooking times and temperatures. The amount of reduction does vary depending on the make of cooker, so again, always follow the manufacturer's instructions carefully.

GRILLS

Grilling is done by intense radiant heat at close range. It is quick, and provides even browning over the whole heated area.

Depending on the type of cooker, there is a grill either at the top of the main oven cavity, in the small oven, in both ovens, or in a separate grill cavity.

Electric grills

Most cookers and microwaves with grills use radiant elements which require about 5 minutes of pre-heating. On the more expensive cookers, grills are faster and more efficient and require little or no pre-heating. The more up-to-date models are using a finer heating element wound around a central core. To make cleaning easier this can either be behind a glass sheet or encased in glass tubing.

Trade names include Quick Grill Ceramic, Ultra Grill, Solar and Quartz Grill.

Gas grills

Sometimes separate or in the main oven cavity. There are three types to choose from:

Fret burners are situated either at the back or in the middle of the grill cavity. They require no pre-heating, but browning can be uneven, especially when the grill pan is at full capacity.

Surface combustion burners are concealed behind mesh. This provides a more even heat distribution, resulting in even browning.

Ceramic grill is situated behind a heat-resistant glass panel giving a very even heat distribution. It is easy to clean but it does take longer than a normal gas grill to heat up. Once it is pre-heated, grilling is very fast.

Halogen grills are only found in microwave ovens. (See Microwave Ovens, page 103.)

POINTS TO LOOK FOR ON ALL OVENS AND GRILLS

- If you batch bake and cook traditional foods, opt for a multi-function oven. If you only cook traditional foods choose a static type; otherwise a fan oven is better for batch baking, quick cooking (reheating ready meals) and defrosting.
- Double ovens offer more versatility and are good for families. Electric cookers, where the main oven is fan or multi-function, will have a smaller, traditional second oven. Make sure you can fit some of your popular weekday cookware in it; some second ovens tend to be very shallow.
- Alternatively, look for a separate grill and main oven for versatility and convenience.
- Check for cool-touch oven doors, especially useful if you have young children. Even on a high temperature the oven door will remain warm only.
- Eye-level grills are the most convenient to use. Otherwise, check that a grill below the hob is comfortable for you to use.
- To save money and energy choose a half-grill facility for small batches of grilling.
- Check the oven is at a comfortable height for loading.
- Choose side-opening or drop-down doors to suit your needs.
- Clearly marked and easy-to-use controls. Some are illuminated for easier use.
- On gas appliances look for safety and flame-failure devices.
- BSI/BEAB approval or equivalent European standards.
- Storage drawer and plate-warming racks. Grill can double for plate warming.
- Reversible door hanging to fit in with your kitchen layout.
- Stay-clean liners make cleaning easier. They may need replacing during the lifetime of the cooker. Normal linings are less expensive and may be cleaned with an oven cleaner.
- Minute minders may be useful.
- An oven light and clear door viewing panel.
- Automatic timers which will switch the oven on when you are out.
- Child-proof controls.

INSTALLING OVENS AND GRILLS

Built-in/under

These have become increasingly popular as more people opt for fitted kitchens. Compared with free-standing or slot-in models they can be installed at the most convenient height and position.

Fuels can be combined offering maximum versatility.

Before choosing, decide whether you want built-in or built-under. With a built-in, the oven is set into a column-style housing unit, so a cupboard and work-top space is lost.

If space is limited choose a built-under unit which slots under the work-top. Remember you will have to bend to use the oven and grill.

Built-in ovens come in standard sizes. A single model will fit into a space 24in/600mm wide, deep and high, and a double oven will fit into a space 24in/600mm wide and deep, and 36in/900mm high.

Electric double ovens require a special cooker socket, but single ovens use an ordinary 13-amp socket.

There is a greater choice of electric ovens than gas for built-in positions.

The small oven can be used for cooking, grilling, plate warming.

Free-standing

More traditional in design because they can have an eye-level grill. This is normally available on gas cookers only.

Most electric models have fan or fan-assisted ovens, while only the more expensive models have multi-function ovens. Check the oven is a comfortable height. Some models have a storage drawer which raises the oven above ground level.

The hob is usually the less expensive radiant, sealed plate or gas.

Slot-in

Gives a built-in look. It is streamlined because the cooker is the same height as the adjoining work surface. Unlike a built-in cooker, you can take it with you when you move.

Grills are low level, situated in the main oven cavity or in the second smaller oven. Some manufacturers recommend grilling with the door open, others with the door closed. Consider this if you have children around.

The type of hob depends on the price. Top of the range have either ceramic, halogen or a combination. Some cookers have a gas hob and an electric oven, ie, dual fuel.

COOKER HOODS

These can be installed above built-under or free-standing slot-in cookers to draw grease, odours and steam from the air. There are two types available: recirculating and ducted, and both require some sort of grease filter. Hoods come in two widths, 24in/600mm or 36in/900mm. Because hoods rely on moving air in order to operate, they can be noisy when used.

If you are fitting a hood above a gas hob there should be a minimum space of 30in/750mm between the two appliances. There is no specified distance for electric hoods, so follow the manufacturer's recommendations.

RECIRCULATING

The most popular type and the cheapest. It requires no external ducting so it can be sited on an internal wall. It has a grease filter and a charcoal filter for absorbing smells before recirculating clean air back into the room.

DUCTED

If your hob is on an outside wall, choose a ducted hood. They are more expensive than recirculating but performance is superior.

Stale air is ducted through pipes to the outside, so no charcoal filter is necessary. For the most efficient air flow make sure the pipework to the outside wall is as short as possible. A grease filter is necessary.

FILTER TYPES

Whether your cooker hood is of the ducted or recirculating type, it will have a grease filter. There are three types available: metal mesh, foam and paper.

The metal mesh found in expensive models is permanent so only requires cleaning. (See Cooker Hoods, page 286.) Foam filters can also be washed in hot soapy water but will need replacing once a year. Paper filters are found on the less expensive cooker hoods, and should be replaced every two to three months as they quickly become saturated with grease.

Charcoal filters are found only in recirculating hoods and can't be washed so will need replacing every six months.

POINTS TO CONSIDER WHEN CHOOSING

- Before you buy, check the extraction rate of the hood. On average this should be 450cu yd/350cu m per hour.
- There are four main hood designs available: canopy, telescopic, integrated and traditional. All are available in ducted or recirculating models.

If you want a basic, reasonably priced cooker hood choose a traditional design. Telescopic models are the most slim-line design: the hood pulls out of the cupboard in which it is sited so you don't lose any valuable cupboard space. A canopy model is designed to be the focal point in the kitchen and can be sited independently or between a run of wall units. Integrated cooker hoods take a furniture panel, swing out when in use and push back when not required. This type blends in with the kitchen units.

- An integrated light makes it easier to see when cooking on the hob.

TIP The cooker hood is only as effective as the filters are clean.

DISHWASHERS

Dishwashers are being regarded more and more as an essential rather than a luxury appliance. Ask any dishwasher owner and they will tell you that they wouldn't be without it, and that they certainly wouldn't revert back to washing-up by hand.

Dishwashers are more hygienic than washing-up by hand. In fact, new research on behalf of the Electricity Association reveals that washing-up by hand increases the presence of germs on dishes by as much as seven times, compared to those washed in a dishwasher. The dishwasher's high wash temperatures – hotter than your hands can bear – and efficiency of the dishwasher detergents play an important role in this result. And when you consider that the average dirty dish cloth can contain up to a million micro-organisms – more than the average kitchen pedal-bin – the contrast in hygiene becomes easier to understand.

DID YOU KNOW?

- A dishwasher saves time – washing up for an average family can take up to 1½ hours a day, which works out to a staggering three weeks per year.
- Dishwashers are cheap to run, costing 15p per load.

CHOOSING A DISHWASHER

Dishwashers are available in a wide range of sizes and capacities, from four to fourteen-place settings. The size of dishwasher that you buy will be determined by:

- space available in your kitchen
- number of people in your household
- how often you entertain.

It makes sense to go for the biggest dishwasher you can fit in if you have a family or entertain regularly. If space is limited, slimline models are a good option, and slot-in models are useful if floor space is at a premium. Generally, you tend to sacrifice wash and dry performance with compact/studio dishwashers compared with full-size models. So go for the largest you can accommodate.

SIZES

Full-size

- Width 24in/600mm.
- Majority will wash up to 12 place settings, although a few models will wash up to 14.
- Free standing; fits under a work-top.
- For easy plumbing, put adjacent to the sink.

Slimline

- Width 18in/450mm.
- Will wash up to eight place settings.
- Free standing; fits under a work-top.
- For easy plumbing, put adjacent to the sink.

Slot-in

- Width 20in/500mm.
- Will wash up to eight place settings.
- Designed to fit in a kitchen cupboard without having to pull the kitchen fitments apart.
- Height and depth is reduced so all the pipework fits behind the machine and the cupboard plinth is kept in place.
- For easy plumbing, put under the sink.

Compact/Studio

- Sits on the work-top, or some can be built-in. Some models are designed to fit inside a kitchen cupboard.
- Will wash up to four place settings.
- Models that sit on the work-top are about the size of a combination microwave.
- Wash and dry performance generally inferior to full-size models.

WASH PROGRAMMES

Most dishwashers take in cold water only (cold fill) and offer a range of wash programmes to allow you to select the one suitable to the degree of soiling and type of load.

Some dishwashers offer an array of programmes.

Main programmes

Normal: usually at 150°F/65°C. For general use, suitable for most loads, including normal to heavily soiled china and saucepans.

Intensive: a longer wash, usually at 150°F/65°C with pre-wash and extra rinses. For heavily soiled china, saucepans and bakeware.

Economy: the temperature is usually between 120–130°F/50–55°C. For light soiling and delicate items, eg, glasses and plastic ware.

Other programmes

Gentle and quick washes: useful for washing lightly soiled crockery and delicate items. Some quick washes are for half-loads only.

Rinse-and-hold cycle or pre-wash: loosens food to prevent it drying on to items if you are waiting to wash a full load.

Plate-warming cycle: utilises the drying cycle to heat items in the dishwasher, but is uneconomical.

Half-load washes: you load only one basket.

Tend to be uneconomical as they use more than half the water and electricity needed for a full load.

Freshen up: rinses loads that have been stored for some time.

Drying cycle

Full-sized dishwashers usually have a drying cycle. There are two different methods used:

Hot air drying (element): most effective drying method but uses slightly more electricity. An element heats the air to dry items in the dishwasher.

Residual heat (hot rinse): uses the residual heat from the final rinse to dry the load.

POINTS TO CONSIDER WHEN CHOOSING

In general you get what you pay for in terms of performance and quality. So it is worth trying to spend as much as you can afford as you should get a machine that will last longer.

- As a general rule, the more expensive the machine the better the insulation and the quieter it will be during the wash cycle.
- Good range of economy programmes.
- If you have an economy-7 meter a delay timer will allow you to make use of cheap-rate electricity.
- Anti-flood device.
- Hot air drying (element) rather than by residual heat (hot rinse).
- If you have plenty of excess hot water (for example, if your water is heated by a Rayburn) look for a hot-fill model.
- Stage of wash indicator.
- Door that will stay open at a right angle to make loading easier.
- Sturdy, smooth running baskets that pull out fully.

SAVE WATER AND ENERGY

Dishwashers are wrongly labelled as water guzzlers. Increasingly, they use less water. The latest machines use as little as 4 gallons/18 litres of water (equal to two washing-up bowls) to wash 12 place settings on a normal wash programme. Washing by hand uses more than two washing-up bowlfuls, and most water of all is wasted by rinsing off one or two items under a running tap.

With the introduction of concentrated dishwasher powders, dishwashers are becoming more energy efficient. This is because the enzymes in these detergents work at their maximum efficiency at 100–120°F/40–50°C, allowing dishwashers to use lower wash temperatures without sacrificing performance, and to therefore reduce energy consumption. Dishwashers are beginning to offer 'Bio-phase programming' designed to maximise the benefits of these enzyme-based detergents by extending the period the wash water is held above 100°F/40°C and below 120°F/50°C. Bio-phase programming claims to give washing performance as good as using a 150°F/65°C programme, but obviously using less energy.

Heat-exchange systems are another development in dishwasher technology. These work by a heat exchanger, within the dishwasher, taking heat from the main wash water and using it in the subsequent rinses. This feature claims to reduce energy consumption by 13 per cent, water usage by 5 per cent and programme time by 7 per cent, compared with a normally heated standard wash.

• Easy-to-clean filters. Blocked filters will impair the washing process.
• Refill indicators for rinse aid and salt. You need rinse aid to avoid streaking and improve drying, and salt works with the water softener in the machine to help prevent the build-up of scale.
• Good supports in the top basket for glasses and small items.
• Adjustable upper basket heights so you can fit in large dishes and tall glasses. With some dishwashers this can be done when the basket is fully loaded. Compact machines don't have adjustable baskets.

WHAT CAN OR CAN'T GO IN A DISHWASHER?

Most items can be washed, but some objects, because of their material or their construction, are not suitable. Once you have bought a dishwasher, you will need to consider whether pans and china are dishwasher safe before buying. If in doubt, check with the manufacturer's details: some items are labelled dishwasher 'proof' or 'safe'.

Items unsuitable for dishwashers

• Lead crystal: susceptible to damage by hot water, and may crack or dull in appearance.
• Antique or hand-painted china: colours on the china are not normally permanently fired to the china so they will fade, even with hand washing.
• Wooden items, unless specially treated, as wood tends to swell and crack.
• Cutlery with handles of bone, wood, pearl or plastic, unless recommended by the cutlery manufacturer. The glue used to secure the handle is often not heat or waterproof, and in time may soften, causing the handle to become loose.
• Uncoated cast-iron pans: these will rust. Even when hand washing care must be taken to dry them thoroughly.
• Some plastics. Rigid plastics are satisfactory although flexible plastic such as storage boxes can distort.
• Aluminium pans (including hard-anodised, non-stick coated and cast aluminium) react with the alkalinity of the detergent and can discolour.

SIZES

When comparing capacities of fridge and freezer compartments, use the net capacity figure, which is the usable space rather than the gross figure.

100 litres = 3.5cu ft
This is roughly equivalent to three shelves or drawers.

1cu ft = 28.6 litres

TIP Silver and silver-plated cutlery is dishwasher safe, but don't mix silver and stainless steel cutlery as it will cause the silver to turn black.

REFRIGERATORS

Refrigerators are available in a range of sizes to fit on table tops (2.9cu ft/82 litres), under work-tops and full kitchen height (13.6cu ft/384.5 litres).

To fit flush with work units they tend to be 24in/600mm deep and between 20–24in/500–600mm wide.

The majority of fridges and freezers work on a condensation mechanism. The coolant draws heat from the cabinet as it is circulated by a condenser motor.

There are a few small fridge units

(maximum capacity of 2cu ft/57 litres) which operate by an absorption mechanism. Because the unit is so small there is no compressor motor. These fridges have a very small ice box and are ideal for locations such as dining rooms because they are virtually silent and vibration free.

There are two main types of fridge construction: larder, and those with an ice box.

LARDER FRIDGES

These don't have an ice box so all the space can be used for storing food. They are also the cheapest to run.

The cabinet is coldest at the bottom, just above the salad box, because cold air sinks.

FRIDGES WITH AN ICE BOX

As well as the fridge compartment there is a compartment at the top for storing commercially frozen food and making ice cubes. The ice box will have a star rating to indicate how long food can be safely kept in it (see box, right).

The fridge is coldest at the top, adjacent to the ice box.

POINTS TO CONSIDER WHEN CHOOSING

Size

Factors will be the size of your kitchen and the storage space required. If you have a separate freezer you won't need a fridge with an ice box unless you need a lot of ice cubes.

Shelves and Storage

- Fridges with adjustable and folding shelves are more convenient for storing bottles and large containers. Removable door shelves give flexibility for fitting items and are easier to clean than moulded fittings.
- Shelves are usually plastic-coated metal or glass. A variety of shelf positions gives flexibility of storage.
- A solid surface like glass prevents items tipping and can easily be wiped clean.
- Some salad compartments have humidity control to retain the moisture around salad vegetables. Two separate salad compartments are useful for separating different types of food.

Controls

- May be inside the fridge or along the top edge. Higher external controls will be more child proof but inconvenient if you are small.
- Built-in thermometers and temperature displays are useful for at-a-glance assurance that everything is working properly, but for accurate measurements a separate thermometer inside is advisable.

STAR RATINGS AND STORAGE TIMES

Commercially frozen foods can be stored in an ice box or freezer compartment depending upon its rating, as follows:

1 week Compartment at 20°F/–6 °C

1 month Compartment at 10°F/–12°C

3 months Compartment at 0°F/–18°C

Compartments with the above star rating cannot be used for freezing down fresh food.

6 months (depending upon food type; refer to manufacturer's instruction book) Compartment at 0°F/–18°C

Door hanging

- Most fridges have reversible doors so that the hinge can be moved from one side to the other to make it hang on the right or left. Check before buying.

Other features

- A grille that encloses the condenser (the wires across the back of the fridge) reduces the operating noise and is also cleaner as it can't trap dust.
- Inside will also be easier to clean if the fridge has an enclosed evaporator plate behind the back wall, rather than protruding into the storage space.
- Both types of fridge are available with an auto-defrost system (see page 102).

FREEZERS

There are two main types, upright and chest freezers. Choosing the type depends upon where the freezer is to be situated and the space available.

UPRIGHT FREEZERS

Upright freezers vary in size between small table-top models (1.7cu ft/49 litres) holding 35lb/16kg of food; to full kitchen-unit height (about 5ft 9in/1,750mm) holding 197lb/89kg of food (11.1cu ft/317 litres).

They generally measure 18in/450mm to 24in/600mm wide and are about 24in/600mm deep.

Food is stacked on shelves and in pull-out drawers giving convenient and accessible storage. This type of arrangement suits storage of regular-shaped packets rather than large bulky items.

Upright freezers are usually designed to complement fridges. They have reversible doors to match.

POINTS TO CONSIDER WHEN CHOOSING

Storage

- The drawers are either plastic-coated wire mesh or solid plastic with solid fronts. Look for easy-to-grip recess handles with easy-glide drawers, especially considering that they will be heavy with food. Stops on the drawers stop them tipping out when opened.
- Drawers are easier to sort through than shelves.
- Extra features may include a twist-and-serve ice maker. Once the cubes are made they can be tipped out into a small drawer. They take up valuable storage space.

Controls

- Like fridges, some models have thermometers and temperature read-outs.
- Audible alarms and indicator lights are a good idea to ensure a rise in temperature (from power failure or door left open) doesn't go unnoticed.
- Indicator lights for the fast-freeze operation (see page 101) are also a useful reminder.

Defrosting

A flip-out defrost spout is useful to drain the melted water from the freezer.

CHEST FREEZERS

These are available in a range of capacities from 4cu ft/114 litres) to 17.2cu ft (492 litres).

Food is stacked in to the chest and hanging, removable baskets. Chest freezers cater for more awkwardly shaped items that may jam in the drawers of an upright freezer. They are usually about the same height (34in/855mm) and slightly deeper (26in/665mm) than a work-top and can be from 21in/540mm up to 52in/1,325mm wide.

POINTS TO CONSIDER WHEN CHOOSING

- The design of the chest freezer means that the cold air is kept around the food, as opposed to an upright freezer where the cold air can flow out of the bottom when the door is opened. They therefore retain the temperature well when opened and therefore use less electricity.
- The food is not as accessible as in an upright freezer. Some packets of food may need to be moved to get to food underneath. Short people may also have difficulty reaching food at the bottom of the cabinet.
- A self-supporting lid helps access.
- If a chest freezer is to be kept in a garage or out-house, look for one with a built-in skin condenser to prevent condensation which otherwise encourages rust formation.

Defrosting

- Chest freezers normally need defrosting once a year unless they are low-frost (see Chest freezers: low frost, page 103).
- A drainage spout is recommended to help clean out the bottom of the freezer.

FAST-FREEZE FUNCTIONS

Most freezers have an area for fast freezing. In uprights it is usually the top shelf; for chests a partitioned area at one end.

Manufacturers recommend that the fast-freeze setting is switched on 24 hours before fresh food is added to the freezer and left on for another 24 hours. This increases the operation of the condenser and takes the freezer temperature down to –14°F/–26°C. Before buying, check the maximum recommended quantity of food that can be frozen down at once. This may be important if you tend to freeze a lot of fresh-picked fruit or bulk-bought meat.

Some freezers don't have a fast-freeze option. This may be because they have frost-free systems or the manufacturer suggests just turning up the control to the maximum cold temperature for 24 hours.

Fast-freeze trays may be useful for open-freezing soft fruit or vegetables.

FRIDGE FREEZERS

These are upright units which combine fridge and freezer cabinets. These are put usually one above the other. As a general rule, the freezer is at the bottom unless it is less than about 3cu ft (86 litres) in size.

American-style units may have the fridge and freezer side by side with separate doors, or stacked with double doors for each compartment. They are therefore wider than conventional, upright fridge freezers. Extra features are incorporated, such as drinks dispensers, accessible from the outside.

Under work-top fridge freezers are also available but the freezer space is limited.

Some three-door models are also made The smaller, middle compartment can be set to operate as a fridge, as a zero-degree compartment, or as a freezer giving additional storage depending upon demands. The zero-degree setting is designed for safe storage of ready-cooked meals, meat and fish.

Fridge freezers are available with equal capacities, or one larger than the other.

Controls

The two compartments may be controlled by a single compressor or two separate compressors. Separate compressors give greater flexibility to maintain the separate compartments at their best temperatures. It also means that the freezer can be switched off independently for

RECOMMENDED OPERATING TEMPERATURES

Fridge: 32–41°F/0°C–5°C

Zero/Chiller Compartment: 32–37°F/0°C–3°C

Freezer: 0°F/–18°C

To check the fridge temperature, immerse a thermometer in a bowl of water. Leave in position for several hours and read without withdrawing the thermometer. It is not satisfactory to place a thermometer on the shelves. This will measure air temperature, not the temperature of the food.

defrosting on manual defrost models, or the fridge only switched off if you go away for a period of time, such as a holiday.

TIP If there is only one compressor, check the fast-freeze operation. If the manufacturer suggests just turning up the control this may also over-chill the fridge compartment.

ELECTRICITY CONSUMPTION

Fridges and freezers carry a label stating the energy consumption figures (as from January 1995). The appliances are given a rating between A and G (A being the most economical) for energy use and state how much electricity will be used over a year (this is stated in kWh: 1 kWh = 1 unit of electricity).

INSTALLATION

Free standing

For efficient and safe operation, fridges and freezers should have a gap of at least 1¼in/3cm around the sides and top of the unit. (Check with manufacturer for exact details.)

The position of the fridge or freezer can affect the efficiency during use. In a hot room it will obviously have to work harder. Never position one right next to a cooker or heater.

Built-in

Built-in fridges and freezers are fitted into the kitchen units, often with a matching door. The fitting is usually secure at the top with height adjustments made at the base.

TYPES OF DEFROST SYSTEMS

Fridges: auto-defrost

In traditional fridges, ice and frost build up on the evaporator plate on the back inside wall and must be defrosted manually every few months, by switching off the fridge. This is not very common nowadays.

Auto-defrost fridges will do this automatically. The temperature rises slightly to melt the frost. The water automatically drains to the rear of the appliance, where it evaporates naturally. However, if there is an ice-box this must be defrosted manually.

Upright freezers: frost free

Frost-free freezers need no defrosting as there is no build-up of frost.

A fan circulates cool, dry air throughout the cabinet. There is no water vapour to form frost around the walls or on the food. Because there is no frost the freezer is always running at maximum efficiency and returns to temperature quickly after the door has been opened. Although they are more expensive to buy they are more convenient to use. As well as needing no defrosting, the drawers run smoothly, the food packages do not frost up so they do not stick together and labels are clear.

Some storage space is lost due to the fan housing, and running costs are higher (from 20 per cent more) because the fan is constantly running, but the freezer itself is always running at optimum efficiency.

The frost-free feature is only found on freezers or fridge freezers with a larger capacity.

Fridge freezers: auto-defrost/frost-free

Combined fridge freezers may have one of three systems:

Auto-defrost fridge only: the fridge automatically clears any frost build-up but the freezer compartment will need manual defrosting.

Auto-defrost fridge and frost-free freezer: both compartments need no defrosting. The fridge automatically defrosts and the freezer, being frost-free, has no frost build-up.

Frost-free fridge and freezer: the air that circulates in the freezer to keep it frost free also circulates into the fridge. Manufacturers claim the drier atmosphere in the fridge, as well as the freezer, extends the storage of food as the conditions are even less favourable to bacteria and moulds.

Chest freezers: low frost

Chest freezers need defrosting once a year. A low-frost chest freezer reduces the frost build-up by about 80 per cent, so defrosting can be left for five years. Running costs should be reduced because the freezer is running more efficiently than conventional models.

Once conventional freezers have reached the correct temperature the compressor switches off. The air in the freezer then gradually warms and, as it does, expands slightly. The excess volume of air is pushed out between the door seal. The compressor then cuts back in, to prevent the freezer from warming. It cools the air, which shrinks it again, and moist air is sucked back into the compartment. This is a continuous process and moist air is always being introduced, which builds up as frost.

The low-frost freezers have a separate compartment which acts as a 'lung'. The expanded warming air is pushed into this space and drawn back in as the air shrinks. No new moist air is introduced except when the freezer is opened.

MICROWAVE OVENS

HOW THEY WORK

A microwave cooker works by generating electromagnetic waves. They are produced by a device within the oven called a magnetron.

Microwaves are attracted by water and will enter the food on all its exposed surfaces to a depth of 1¼in/3cm, causing the molecules to vibrate. In foods which are thicker than this, cooking takes place by conductivity: heat produced by the vibrating molecules gradually moves through the food. Unlike conventional cooking there is no external heat, which is why food does not brown.

Microwave energy travels through the air but no heat is generated until it is absorbed by the food. That is why it works so fast, because no energy is wasted. Microwaves can pass through certain substances without harming them, such as plastic, china, paper and glass. They will not pass through metal, but are reflected by it.

Microwave ovens work more quickly than conventional cookers and use one-quarter of the energy of a conventional cooker depending on what you are cooking. Cooking tends to be clean and there is less washing up as food can be cooked in the serving dish.

TYPES OF MICROWAVE

There are three main types, depending on the type of cooking you want to do.

Microwave only: the most basic option. It will

cook, re-heat and defrost.
Microwave and grill: will also brown food.
Combination oven: combines microwaves, grill and convection cooking (like a normal electric oven) and is the most versatile.

MICROWAVE ONLY

A microwave will re-heat, cook and defrost food. It is a boon to the cook in a hurry and a useful back-up to a conventional oven. It is most useful for re-heating foods which do not need to be browned such as pre-cooked meals and liquids. If you have a freezer, it is ideal for defrosting food quickly.

TIP In an 800-watt microwave it takes 10 to 12 minutes to defrost four pork chops and 4 to 5 minutes to re-heat a plated adult-size meal.

Most useful for

- Re-heating pre-cooked ready meals.
- Re-heating plated meals.
- Re-heating liquids such as soups or beverages.
- Cooking vegetables.
- Cooking fish.
- Defrosting bread, meat and poultry.
- Making jam.

MICROWAVE AND GRILL

These have a grill sited in the ceiling and are slightly more expensive than a microwave only. They are the most popular option because they will also brown the surface of foods. You can use the microwave only, the grill only and usually both together.

However, the grills are not suitable for cooking thicker cuts of meat all the way through because they are not as powerful as a conventional grill: ratings are about 1.3kW compared to 3kW. Even so, these machines have an advantage in that they can be plugged into an ordinary 13-amp socket. Instead, use grill and microwave together or microwave followed by grill.

Most useful for

- Grilling breaded products.
- Grilling meat products such as sausages and chops.
- Re-heating and browning ready meals.
- Re-heating foods with a cheese or potato topping.

Grill types

There are three types of grill used in a microwave and grill. They vary in performance, ease of cleaning and cost. Grilling is generally carried out with the door shut. Check the kW rating, which determines how powerful it is. They are usually around 1.3kW.

Radiant Similar to a conventional cooker grill element but smaller. It is the cheapest option but takes the longest time to brown because you need to pre-heat the elements for eight to ten minutes. Because grilling takes longer food can dry out more than when conventional grilling. After cooking fatty foods the element can be difficult to clean. Some ovens allow you to grill with the door open, which is useful, if you want to cook high-fat foods, to prevent excessive splashing.

Quartz Consists of a ceramic tube encasing fine elements, sited at the top of the oven behind a mesh. Heat is instant so there is no need to pre-heat. This grill is the quickest and tends to give the most even results. It is sited behind the ceiling panel so is easy to clean. Some quartz grills have variable power settings, but these have limited use because, for the majority of foods, high power is needed.

Halogen Has halogen bulbs set at the top of the oven, behind a mesh. The heat is instant, but a halogen grill browns only slightly quicker than a radiant element grill. It is sited behind the ceiling panel so is easy to clean. These tend to be the most expensive.

COMBINATION MICROWAVES

These are more expensive than microwave and grills. They combine a microwave, grill and convection oven, and allow you to cook by microwave only, grill only and convection only (roast and bake); microwave and convection together (combination cooking); and usually microwave and grill together. Some models allow you to use convection and grill together, which is useful for more rapid browning.

With all these options, combination microwaves are very versatile and can be used in place of a standard cooker. They are ideal for one or two people because they are smaller to heat, saving energy, take up less space, and can be positioned at a convenient height for the user.

In an 800W combination microwave it takes about 36 minutes to cook a 4lb/1.8kg chicken compared to 1 hour 40 minutes in a conventional oven. Four baked apples will take about 7 minutes, compared to an hour in a conventional oven.

Most suitable for

- Roasting meat and vegetables.
- Baking pastry and bread.
- Baking cakes.
- Baking jacket potatoes.

Grill types

The types available are the same as in microwave and grills.

Additionally, some models have a hot-air grill. Air from the convection fan is used, but this type of grill does not tend to brown very quickly or evenly.

POINTS TO CONSIDER WHEN CHOOSING

Type of controls

Choose between dial or key-pad.

- Models with dial control usually have fewer programmes and are cheaper. It is not very easy to set times accurately using dial control so check that the calibrations for the first five minutes (most frequently used) are clearly marked.
- Models with key-pad control use a digital display and enable you to set a more accurate cooking time. With microwave cooking this is important because seconds are critical. They tend to have a range of programmes. A key-pad is easier to clean.

Power levels

- When cooking by microwave the most frequently used power settings are high, medium and low, and it is unnecessary to have nine or ten power levels.
- Whatever the wattage of your microwave, the High/Full setting will always be 100 per cent of the power output.
- Some combination ovens only have pre-set programmes for combination cooking. This means the microwave power level and convection temperature is pre-set, eg medium microwave and 350°F/180°C. These can limit your choice if you want to use recipes other than just those in the instruction manual. A model which allows you to select your own settings is the most versatile.
- Make sure the oven has a full range of temperatures available for convection cooking.

PROGRAMMES/FEATURES

Basic ovens have a timer and a range of power settings. More complex models have a range of additional programmes and features. Not all are useful so think carefully before choosing them. For example, do you need a dough-warming facility for making bread, which may cost you more?

Auto-defrost

Some models allow you to specify the food type, such as meat, fish or bread, and after you have keyed in the weight, the oven will calculate the defrosting time.

On more sophisticated models there is a crystal beneath the turntable which monitors the deflection produced by the weight of food put on top of it, and causes a voltage change which triggers the correct defrosting time. It may or may not include standing time.

Auto cook/re-heat or sensor cook/re-heat

This allows you to cook or re-heat specified foods without having to select the power level and cooking time. You choose the food type and enter the weight, and the oven calculates the correct programme. Sensor cook/re-heat calculates cooking time using humidity sensors (to measure the amount of steam being released by the food) or infra-red sensors (to measure the surface temperature of the food). However, this is not always successful and you may have to increase the cooking time. Some models have more or fewer key-pads which allow you to adjust the cooking time.

Auto minute

Allows you to cook on high power for one minute. Quick and convenient because it's a single operation. Useful if you want to re-heat beverages or give a boost of heat at the end of re-heating.

Multi-sequence cooking

Allows you to programme in a series of power settings and times, at the start of cooking, should a recipe use different levels. Can also be used to programme different functions such as ten minutes' defrost, followed by five minutes on high power and five minutes on grill. It can save time but it is difficult to use unless you are sure of the cooking times you require. As cooking in the microwave is so fast, pre-programming is not particularly useful.

Auto repeat

The oven remembers the last programme you used so you can re-use it by touching the key-pad. Useful if you cook large quantities which will not fit in the oven in one go. Otherwise it is often easier to re-programme the oven.

Auto/delay start

Allows you to delay cooking for up to 12 hours. This is not a great advantage because cooking times are so short. It isn't very practical for hygiene reasons: it is not a good idea to leave uncooked foods in a microwave for long periods, particularly in warm weather.

Instant action

This is similar to auto re-heat. Allows you to cook set portions of specified foods, such as one jacket potato, by touching the key-pad. It is only useful if you cook the foods often in the quantities the oven is programmed for.

Jet start/rapid re-heat

Similar to auto minute. Allows you to cook with high bursts of energy for a short time. Useful if you often re-heat drinks.

Memory

Allows you to store the programmes you most frequently use so you can activate them by touching the key-pad. Saves time if, for example, you regularly defrost a loaf of bread or cook four jacket potatoes.

Minute minder
This is a separate timer to the clock. It is good for sequence cooking when the cooking time is not always displayed, or for calculating standing time.

Pause/stand time
Allows you to set a rest period during sequence cooking or at the end of cooking. Food will continue to cook by convection during pause or stand time from the residual heat. If the recipe requires a standing period this is important and should not be ignored.

Guides
Some ovens will guide you through programming procedures by displaying instructions on the digital readout; generally on family-sized models only. It is useful when you are first familiarising yourself with the oven or if the instruction booklet is not close at hand.

Calorie counter
This calculates the number of calories in the food you are cooking. You key in the weight and food category. It also acts as a calculator by allowing you to add up the calories you consume in a day.

Turntable deactivator
Some microwaves have the facility to stop the turntable rotating during cooking. This can be useful if you want to fit a large dish in the cavity, but you must stir or turn the food for even re-heating.

SIZES

All three types of microwave are available in different sizes, either compact which range from 0.4 to 0.8cu ft or family size which are around 0.9 to 1.13cu ft. Combination microwaves tend to be large family-size units of up to 1.4cu ft, although compact versions of 0.6cu ft are also available.

Compact microwaves are a popular choice because they lose most of their size in the height of the cavity, not turntable size. (For cooking plated meals, for example, height is not an important factor.) It's the turntable size that is important.

When buying a microwave look inside the cavity and think what you will want to fit inside it. If necessary, take a favourite dish to the shop and see whether it will fit in the oven and rotate on the turntable. Large rectangular or oblong dishes may impede rotation.

WHERE TO SITE A MICROWAVE

Microwaves are usually sited on a work surface. They need to be placed with a gap of about 6in/15cm above and behind for ventilation. This is particularly important for a combination oven, because a lot of air is dispelled when using the dual function.

Microwave ovens can be hung on the wall using special brackets to save space. If a microwave is built into a kitchen you will need a ventilation kit, available from the manufacturer.

WATTAGES

The wattage of a microwave indicates the maximum power output of the oven and relates to how fast it will work. The higher the wattage the quicker the microwave will re-heat. It is important to know the wattage of your microwave so you can calculate cooking and re-heating times.

The optimum wattage is about 750 watts. Lower wattages, such as 600 watts, are not as fast, whereas higher wattages, such as 1,000 watts, may heat food too rapidly and result in drying and uneven cooking.

Prior to 1991 there was no standard test for measuring the power output of microwaves, so microwaves rated at 800 watts from different manufacturers were not automatically the same. This led to confusion over the re-heating times required for foods. The Ministry of Agriculture, Fisheries and Food (MAFF) introduced a standard test for microwave power outputs (IEC 705), and now all microwaves are tested to it. The power output is displayed on a small label on the front of the oven. The oven is also given a heating category, A, B, C, D, or E, based on its ability to heat small food packs.

A B C D E

more heating time — less heating time

If your oven is category B it will heat up small portions of food faster than a category A oven but not as fast as a category C oven.

Most packaged foods suitable for microwave cooking are also marked with a heating category. To work out the heating time needed, match the information on the food packet with the heating category of your oven.

MICROWAVE INSTRUCTIONS	Column 1		Column 2
	Heating Category B	D	Power Rating 650W
Cook on full power	6 mins	4 mins	5 mins

For example, if you have a category D oven, heat the food for four minutes. If you have an E oven heat for three and a half minutes, and a C oven for five and a half minutes.

For further information on microwave labelling contact the Food Safety Advisory Centre (see Useful Addresses).

How to determine wattage

If your microwave oven does not have a MAFF label on the front, look in the instruction booklet or on the rating plate on the back panel of the oven for the power output. Do not get this confused with the power input of the oven, which is also given.

The cooking times given in recipe books or on food packaging is usually given for 650 watts. If your oven is a different wattage it is easy to calculate the correct time required.

WATTAGE CONVERTER

Power output in recipe/on pack (watts)
multiplied by
Cooking/reheating time (minutes)
divided by
Stated oven power output
= Number of minutes to heat for.

For example, if you have a 500-watt oven and the instructions say cook for 4.5 minutes in a 650-watt oven:

650 watts x 4.5 minutes,
divided by 500 watts
= 5.85 minutes

Always round down, so cook for 5½ minutes. You can always return it to the oven.

MICROWAVE COOKWARE

See Microwave Cookware, page 71

ACCESSORIES

Basic

- To ensure even cooking, food must be turned. If your microwave has a turntable (as do most models) this will be done automatically. With a turntable, re-heating is more even, and there is no need to keep interrupting the programme and turning the dish during cooking.

- A defrosting rack is useful because it raises the food off the oven floor or turntable allowing the food to be defrosted from below as well as from above.

Microwave and grill/combination oven

- Cooking racks are useful to raise the food nearer to the grill element to speed up the browning process. You will need a high rack for grilling small items such as sausages and a low rack so you can fit in larger cooking dishes such as a dish of cauliflower cheese.
- A drip pan is useful to catch fat and make cleaning easier. Some ovens have splash guards which are placed over the drip tray to prevent the fat splashing up into the oven.
- It can be difficult to remove a high rack with food balanced on it from a hot oven. To get around this some ovens have built-in shelves which make removing the food easier. Turn the food to ensure even re-heating.

MICROWAVE COOKING TIPS

After heating, always check food is piping hot throughout. If you have a food thermometer check it reaches 160°F/70°C in the centre. Feel the middle underside of the container: it should be hot.

The outer edges of food will cook first in a microwave oven. Place thicker parts of food at the outside of the cooking container and thinner parts at the centre. Stir food or rotate dishes during cooking to ensure even heating.

The cooking time needed depends on the density of the food, its starting temperature and the quantity being cooked.

Where a recipe specifies standing time it is important to follow it exactly. The heat within the food continues to cook it even when it has been removed from the oven and the standing time is calculated to take account of this.

MICROWAVE SAFETY

Microwave ovens are safe appliances. They will only work if the door is firmly shut. A microwave door has at least two switches, which will cut off the power if the door is not shut properly. Keep the oven door and hinges clean and inspect regularly for corrosion.

If you are worried about microwave leakage, contact the manufacturer, who will send a service engineer to check the oven with accurate equipment.

Microwave leakage detectors are available from electrical stores, but they are not always completely accurate.

SMALL KITCHEN APPLIANCES

ELECTRIC KETTLES

There are two basic designs to choose from: The jug style which is available as a full size, compact or travel model, and the traditional shape. Then there is also the option of corded or cordless kettles.

Most kettles are rated between 1,800 and 2,200 watts, so boiling times do not vary greatly between the designs. If you want a faster kettle, however, 2,600-watt models are available. If you like a co-ordinated look, manufacturers produce kettles and other small electrical appliances such as toasters with matching patterns. Russell Hobbs, in particular, have a co-ordinated range.

Traditional kettles

Available in chrome, stainless steel or polypropylene. They have a maximum capacity of 3 pints/1.7 litres.

They are very stable in use. The handle is positioned on the top of the kettle, making it much easier to balance when full. It is therefore a good choice for elderly people or those with weak wrists.

Jug kettles

The majority of jug-style kettles are made from polypropylene. They have a minimum capacity of ½ pint/250ml, which means you can boil less water than a traditional kettle (ideal if you often make just one cup) although the maximum capacity is the same.

Compact kettles

Suitable for a smaller householder if space is particularly limited.

They are less powerful – about 900 watts – and can hold a maximum of about 800ml of water (four cups).

Travel kettles

Can be universal/multi-voltage for using when abroad. Usually, mugs are provided with the kettle, and fit inside it for compactness during travelling.

POINTS TO CONSIDER WHEN CHOOSING

- On/off light.
- On cordless kettles, look for a cord-storage facility on the power base. Only a minimal amount of cord needs to be visible between the power base and the wall, because the kettle is removed from the base once it has boiled.
- Corded models should either have a short or coiled flex. This will ensure the flex never hangs over the work surfaces to cause accidents.
- Other safety features to look for are a locking lid, cool-touch walls and an automatic thermal cut-out device to prevent the kettle boiling dry. A cool exterior is achieved on some models by using a double skin.
- For extra stability, look for rubber feet on the base of the kettle or power base, which also makes it harder to pull along the work surface.
- For ease of use, choose a model with a wide spout so it can be filled from the tap without removing the lid.
- A clear water-gauge down both sides enables both right- and left-handed users to see at a glance how full it is.
- If you live in a hard water area, you may want to spend a little extra on a kettle with an integral filter. This acts like a tea strainer within the spout, stopping water scale being poured into your drink along with the water.

This is increasingly important with more people making hot drinks directly in their mug rather than in a pot. It does not, however, stop limescale from developing.

- To maintain efficiency it is still important to descale your kettle (see Kettles, page 302).

NON-ELECTRIC KETTLES

These are enjoying a revival. They are not significantly slower in use than the electric ones, whether boiling a mug or a large volume of water. However, they do not have as many of the safety features of the electric variety such as locking lids, automatic switch-off and stay-cool walls.

POINTS TO CONSIDER WHEN CHOOSING

- Does it fill through spout as well as the lid? Important when the kettle has just been boiled and needs refilling.
- Check whether it has a whistle.
- Check that the lid is secure and does not fall off when the kettle is held in the pouring position.
- Does it feel safe and secure to handle, with a lid that is easy to remove?
- Check that it has a stay-cool knob, handle and whistle.
- Are there good safety instructions?
- Check it's not too heavy.
- For an Aga buy one with a thick, heavy, flat base.
- For ceramic/halogen hobs buy one with a non-reflective base.

TOASTERS

Toasters are quicker and cheaper to use than the grill on your cooker.

There are three types available:

Two-slot, two slice: suitable for small households.

Single, long-slot, two slice: good for differing thicknesses of breads, eg doorsteps through to pitta bread.

Two-slot, four slice: good for families.

POINTS TO CONSIDER WHEN CHOOSING

- Electronic temperature sensors: although toasters with this feature may cost a little more money, they give consistently even results when toasting batches of bread. The sensors automatically adjust the browning time, preventing the bread from burning by taking into account the state of the bread, eg if it's frozen or stale.

TIP Traditional models' toasting controls are based on different units of time depending on the degree of browning selected. So the elements get hotter if the toaster is on for any length of time, which means it progressively grills more quickly, producing darker toast.

TOASTING TIPS

- Before buying, try the lever (that lowers the bread into the toaster) to see how sturdy it is, as this is generally one of the first parts of a toaster to break.
- If you eat only one or two slices at a time, choose a long-slot or traditional two-slot toaster. A better choice for family breakfasts would be a two-slot four-slice toaster.
- For safety, don't place your toaster under a cupboard or near curtains.
- Remove crumbs from the bottom of the toaster regularly. A build-up can catch fire.

- Cool walls: an air gap around the sides of the toaster makes them cooler to touch (about 25 to 30°C). A useful safety feature.
- Variable thickness bread slot: handy for toasting muffins, rolls, thickly sliced bread, etc. Well worth having.
- One-sided toasting: good for burger baps or the soft side of French bread as you can toast one side whilst warming the other. Rather specialised, its usefulness depends how much of this type of food you cook.
- Frozen bread setting: this is handy if you frequently toast bread taken straight from the freezer.
- Re-heat setting, designed to warm up your toast if it's gone cold. A rather gimmicky feature as it tends to dry the toast.
- Mid-cycle cancel button. This is handy if you suddenly decide you want your toast less crispy or it's burning.
- Removable crumb tray: very useful for easier cleaning.
- Keep-warm system: designed to keep toasted slices warm until you take them out. A rather gimmicky feature which tends to dry the toast.
- Flex storage.
- Non-slip feet.
- Easy-to-use controls (dial or slider).
- High-rise facility: makes it easier to remove small items of bread or muffins without burning your fingers, and to remove slices that have become caught in the machine.

FOOD PROCESSORS, MIXERS AND KITCHEN MACHINES

All of this type of labour-saving kitchen equipment frees you from the time-consuming and repetitive tasks such as beating, whisking, puréeing and chopping.

FOOD PROCESSORS

Their primary function is to chop, slice, grate, blend and purée.

Their secondary function is to mix cakes, knead bread, whisk egg whites and whip cream. Food processors are generally quite poor at tasks like mixing cakes and whisking egg whites as they are unable to incorporate air into the mixture very well.

Liquidising in the main bowl is poor. It is better if there is a separate liquidiser attachment, which is fairly commonplace now. Most machines are supplied with a large bowl, grating and slicing discs (fine and coarse), a metal blade for chopping, a whisk for mixing and a spatula.

In general, the more you pay, the larger the capacity and more attachments you will get such as a dough tool and juice extractor.

KITCHEN MACHINES

These are a good choice for mixing/whisking large quantities because the bowls have a larger capacity than a food processor.

They also have greater versatility than a food processor or mixer alone. However, they are expensive, so you have to be sure of using all the functions, and a considerable storage area is required.

The machines' performance for each task is not superior to each of the products individually. Results are comparable to a food processor, but they are not equal to a mixer, especially when whisking, which produces less volume and is less stable.

Points to consider when choosing

- A special mixing attachment, without sharp edges which tend to cut through the mixture and knock out the air.
- A separate liquidiser for a smoother result

than puréeing in the main bowl.

- Different feed-tube sizes: a double feed tube is useful for different-sized foods and a wide semicircular feed tube is good for large items such as cabbage.
- A variable-speed setting is preferable for slicing softer foods like cucumber. Faster speeds can produce mushy results. Three speeds are sufficient.
- A pulse (a short burst of high speed) to give you finite control over mixing.
- Measurements on feed tube and bowl.
- Some purpose-made or integral storage for attachments, especially discs which are sharp.
- Finger holes on discs to protect your fingers.
- Reversible discs, which save on storage space.
- Drip feed in the feed tube which allows liquids to be added to the bowl slowly. Useful when making mayonnaise.
- Mini chopping bowls for chopping small quantities of herbs, nuts and baby food.
- If you have a dishwasher look for dishwasher-safe attachments.
- Non-slip feet.
- Flex storage.

FREE-STANDING FOOD MIXER

This sort of machine is excellent for both mixing and whisking, and is a good choice for those cooks who do large amounts of home baking.

The optional mincer attachment performs better than a food processor.

To do chopping and grating, it is necessary to buy optional extras costing about £56. They don't perform as well as a food processor and are bulky and difficult to use.

If you are going to use all the attachments equivalent to those offered by a food processor costs will escalate by £140, so it is better to spend your money on a mixer and a separate food processor or a kitchen machine. There are hand mixers available for about £20, which will mix and whisk well.

COFFEE MAKERS

There are many different types of domestic coffee-making equipment, and the choice depends on the type of coffee you prefer. Espresso, cappuccino and filter coffee can all be made successfully at home, and you can even grind your own coffee beans at home for the best flavour.

ESPRESSO/CAPPUCCINO MAKERS

Espresso is strong, dark and slightly bitter black coffee served in small-sized cups called demitasse. Cappuccino is espresso coffee to which milk, heated and aerated by steam, has been added. Often it has chocolate powder sprinkled on the top for a touch of added sweetness and flavour.

Finely ground coffee is recommended to achieve the required strength. To make an authentic espresso with a 'crème' on the surface (a cream-coloured head) hot water has to be pushed through the finely ground coffee under high pressure.

This sort of coffee can be made in simple pots that are put on the hob, or in more complicated electrically powered pump-action machines. Models without the pump rely on steam pressure. They are half the price of pump-action machines but the coffee has less flavour and is more like filter coffee. The combination of steam and pressure extracts flavour that is left behind with a filter.

Pump-action espresso machines

Machines which have a pump produce the best results, but they are expensive.

Points to consider when choosing

- All pump-action espresso machines are quick to use, but most only make two small cups at a time. The maximum is four.
- You have to refill the machine with fresh coffee after each round and froth the milk for cappuccino, so it is only suitable for two people rather than a large gathering.
- Make sure the platform where the cups collect the coffee has sufficient clearance for the height of your cups.
- A water-level indicator on the water tank.
- Most of these machines have an integral milk frother. Frothers work by bubbling a jet of steam through cold milk. This both heats and froths the milk.

Hob espresso machines

Work on the pressure principle, using the hob to heat the water into steam. Water in the lower section of the pot is heated until it escapes as steam through the grounds trapped in the central filter. Coffee is then poured out from the top half of the pot.

If you have a coffee maker that doesn't froth milk or you want frothy milk for hot chocolate, you can buy machines which only froth milk.

Points to consider when choosing

- A hob espresso is ideal if you just want espresso, rather than cappuccino, since they cannot froth the milk.
- Less expensive than the electric machines.
- Comes in 2- to 12-cup sizes. They must be used at full capacity, so make sure you choose the right size.
- They can be used on all hob types, but once the coffee has been made it can't be heated up again. This is because all the water from the lower section of the maker has bubbled up through the coffee.

CAFETIERES

You don't need to invest in elaborate hardware to make real coffee. The simplest way is to use a heat-resistant jug and make it in the same way as you'd make a pot of tea, pouring it through a strainer into cups. This is the principle of the cafetière method.

Using a cafetière is the easiest way of making delicious fresh coffee. It is a glass jug

TIPS FOR USING ESPRESSO MACHINES

- Never pack the grounds tightly into the filter holder, otherwise the water won't be able to penetrate. Simply press gently, either with the tamper provided with the machine or with the back of a teaspoon.
- To get the strong, characteristic flavour, choose a rich blend of coffee where some of the beans have been roasted for longer than average.
- Once the espresso has filtered into the cups, the water can be heated to produce the steam required for cappuccino.
- For the best froth, use low-fat milk in a tall, straight-sided jug. A metal jug is ideal because it is a good conductor of heat.
- Only froth about 1½in/4cm of milk at a time, using a circular motion and keeping the head of the nozzle just under the surface of the milk.
- Always clean the nozzle as soon as you have finished, as the heat solidifies the milk residue, reducing performance, blocking the nozzle, and making later cleaning difficult. (See Coffee Makers, page 284.)

TIPS FOR USING CAFETIERES

- Before making coffee, warm the glass jug with boiling water.
- To keep the coffee hot, wrap a cafetière warmer around the glass jug. Available from department stores.
- It's important to pre-rinse the filter with boiling water and take the filter apart and clean it after use. This improves the flavour.

with a metal plunger which incorporates a stainless-steel mesh filter. This separates the grounds from the liquid as you push down the plunger. They come in a range of sizes with metal or plastic finishes.

Choose a good-quality medium-ground coffee for use in cafetières.

Points to consider when choosing

- There are many makes and designs on the market. Cafetières with plastic holders are the cheapest option but are not as stable as metal ones.
- Sizes vary from 2- to 8-cup capacity.

ELECTRIC, FILTER COFFEE MAKERS

Filter coffee isn't as strong as espresso. An electric element heats the water before passing it through a filter containing the ground coffee. The liquid then drips into a jug, keeping warm on a hotplate.

Filter machines use paper filters or permanent filters made from nylon, stainless steel or a metal mesh. As most standard-sized jugs can hold up to ten cups, and the hotplate keeps the coffee warm, filter machines are ideal for dinner parties, offices or occasions where larger quantities are required.

Use medium-ground coffee.

Points to consider when choosing

- An anti-drip device stops drips when the jug is removed.
- A filter holder that swivels out, making it easier to remove the filter and coffee grounds.
- A clear water-level indicator, so you know how many cups you are making. This is usually stated in small, demitasse cup sizes.
- Some filter machines have replaced the hotplate with a thermal jug to keep the coffee hot. A good idea if you want to serve your coffee away from the machine.

AND FINALLY...

With all coffee making at home use only freshly roasted and ground coffee. Once the packet has been opened keep it in an air-tight container, ideally in the fridge or freezer and in the dark, as otherwise the flavour is soon lost.

Alternatively use an electric coffee grinder. Choose a model with a variable grind. You can

TIPS FOR USING ELECTRIC FILTERS

- If you add cold milk, the temperature of coffee needs to be about 175–185°F/80–85°C to stay hot enough to drink. Look for a machine that claims to keep coffee above 175°F/80°C.
- Coffee made hotter than 195°F/90°C is more likely to lose its flavour.
- Keep your machine clean, particularly if it has a permanent filter (see Coffee Makers, page 284). The oils in coffee go rancid. If remains are left in the filter they will impair the flavour.
- If you make coffee regularly you will have to descale the machine every few months so that it will work efficiently (see Coffee Makers, page 285).

then make coffee for espresso (very fine) or filter machines and cafetières (medium).

TIP Always clean coffee grinders after use as rancid oil will taint the flavour.

ELECTRIC DEEP-FAT FRYERS

Because deep-fat frying heats oil to a very high temperature, safety is paramount when using this cooking method. An electric deep-fat fryer is safer and more convenient than a chip pan on the hob because it has a built-in thermostat, and frying with the lid on is cleaner because it prevents grease-laden steam and smells escaping. (Despite manufacturers' efforts, however, odours and grease still escape from fryers.)

SIZES

Most family-size fryers take 4½ pints/2.5 litres of vegetable oil and can cook up to three large or four medium-size portions of frozen chips. About the size of freestanding mixers; they take up a significant amount of work-top and cupboard space. Compact fryers use 2½ pints/1.5 litres of oil and can cook up to one to two portions of chips.

TIP In general, fryers with a rounded basket have a larger capacity than a rectangular basket, though the latter is better for cooking fish fillets.

POINTS TO CONSIDER WHEN CHOOSING

- Ease of cleaning.
- Odour control.
- To minimise the amount of airborne grease that escapes from the fryer with the steam, some manufacturers incorporate filters. The simplest of these are metal slats inside the lid.

Other methods include:

Charcoal filters in the form of a cartridge which must be removed before washing.

Charcoal/foam filter, which must be removed with a screwdriver if you want to put it in the dishwasher, but can be left in place if washed in soapy water. Having to use a screwdriver is inconvenient.

Linked in with some of these methods, the filters change colour when they need replacing (about every 30 uses).

- To make washing up easier, lids are detachable and some can go in the dishwasher.

CHANGING THE OIL

This needs to be done about every six uses, depending on the food you fry.

High-protein foods, such as meat and fish, will taint the oil faster. After frying, pour the oil through a filter to remove debris such as pieces of batter and crumbs. This can be quite difficult since fryers are unwieldy and heavy. If you are weak wristed look for a lighter-weight model. Other features to make emptying easier include a drain pipe or a removable reservoir, which makes lifting easier.

Look for a fryer with handles, as these are easier to lift. For convenience, some have a separate filter in the reservoir, which you can lift out, taking the crumbs with it.

OTHER FEATURES

Draining food

With today's emphasis on healthier cooking, it is important that food is left to drain thoroughly. Make sure that you give it a good shake. Some models have a special shake facility, although this is not strictly necessary.

Timers

Most models have a bell that sounds at the end of the cooking time – a useful feature. Some models ring once; others sound until switched off. A basket that is raised automatically once cooking is complete is useful.

Safety

All the fryers should have:

- Basket handles designed to lie flat when the fryer is in use, to prevent accidents.
- Cool walls, so the outside does not burn you if you touch it accidentally, even though it reaches a temperature of 122°F/50°C.
- Locking lids so that the fryer cannot be opened during frying or storage unless the open button is used. Oil can leak out if they are tipped over, but the mechanism will prevent a heavy spill. The better the seal, the longer the oil is likely to keep: about six uses.

Viewing window

A useful feature, as it allows you to see cooking in progress without having to take the lid off, which could be dangerous. Although the viewing window tends to get partially covered with condensation while in use, it's preferable to having no window at all.

ICE-CREAM MAKERS

Ice-cream makers allow you to concoct your own flavours and be sure the ice-cream is additive-free. These machines make ice-cream that is less fluffy than shop-bought varieties, but it has an equally good texture and consistency, and sometimes a far better flavour.

There are two types of ice-cream maker: those you put in the freezer before use, and those that have their own electrically powered built-in chilling unit.

FREEZE-FIRST

These have an electrically powered paddle and a bowl with walls that contain a refrigerant.

TIPS FOR USING ICE-CREAM MAKERS

- For best results, chill the ingredients before use.
- Switch on the paddles before pouring in the ice-cream mix.
- Mixtures containing a high percentage of alcohol, fat, gelatine or sugar take longer to freeze and remain softer.
- Use plastic or wooden utensils only when removing the ice-cream mixture from the bowl.
- Clean the machine after use as bacteria grow rapidly in ice-cream mix.
- Ice-cream tastes best on the day it's made, but you can freeze it for up to a month.

The bowl is put in the freezer for 8 to 18 hours before use, depending on the size. Although the insulated bowl keeps the refrigerant cold, it starts to defrost during mixing, so the ice-cream becomes fairly soft and may need further freezing.

These machines are fairly cheap: about £50. Their main disadvantage is that the bowl needs to be re-frozen after each use so, for the more professional cook, it takes a long time to make a large quantity.

SELF-CHILLING

Use a built-in chilling unit. You switch the machine on for five to ten minutes to chill the container before pouring in the mixture. Ice-cream can be made in the built-in bowl and in the removable inner bowl, which is useful as it can be put straight into the freezer. To keep the removable bowl cold, you have to use your own cooling solution such as brine.

These machines cost over £200, so are for the real enthusiast.

BREAD MAKERS

Automatic bread makers will mix, knead, wait while the dough rises, then knead again, leave to rise, then bake. All you do is put in the ingredients and set the controls, so it takes out all the guesswork. They also allow you to delay the start, so that you can set up the machine before going to bed and have freshly baked bread for breakfast.

POINTS TO CONSIDER WHEN CHOOSING

- They take longer to cook using a conventional oven, but you don't have to attend to the machine during use; it does everything automatically.
- They produce only one small loaf at a time. If you want to use the kneaded dough to make pizzas, rolls, etc, you have to shape the dough, leave it to rise again then cook in an oven, not the bread maker.
- Bread makers can use less electricity per loaf than an electric oven.
- They can make white, wholemeal and fruit loaves. Ideally, the recipe should be given in the recipe book supplied, since it is difficult to adapt your own.
- The bread pan and mixing blade are sometimes non-stick.
- Check whether it is dishwasher safe.

JUICERS

Freshly squeezed fruit and vegetable juices are not only a rich source of vitamins, minerals and enzymes, but they are also deliciously refreshing. In comparison, bought juices taste flat and uninteresting.

Juicing is quick; few fruits and vegetables need peeling; it's cheaper; and it's more flexible, combining unusual fruits. It allows you to make the maximum use of the whole fruit including the pulp, which is high in fibre and can be used in cooking.

JUICE EXTRACTORS

Cost about £45 and process hard fruit and vegetables as well as citrus fruit. They don't work with soft fruit such as bananas and canned fruit.

They are more complex machines than electric citrus presses, and are about the size of a food processor. The juice is extracted by centrifugal force (similar to a spin drier extracting water) and is filtered into a jug, while pulp, skin and pips are collected separately.

Advantages

- Can be used for a wide range of fruit and vegetables.
- Preparation is minimal.
- Juicers can process up to ten oranges without the pulp container being emptied.

TIPS FOR JUICING

- Juicing is a good way of using up a glut of summer fruit or vegetables from your garden.
- To produce a tumbler of either orange, apple or pear juice, you'll need at least two of each fruit.
- Store fruit at room temperature prior to juicing. More juice is extracted than from chilled fruit.
- Wash fruit and vegetables well since the whole fruit will be used.
- Pulp is rich in fibre and can be used in a variety of dishes, such as cakes, desserts and sauces.

Disadvantages

Cleaning is the greatest drawback. Although most parts are dishwasher safe there are a lot of pieces to dismantle.

Points to consider when choosing

- A juice separator and an extra sieving system in the jug gives clearer juice. You may however prefer juice with more flesh. The extra bulk is filling and useful for those on a diet.
- Two speeds: a slower speed intended for softer fruit and a higher speed for harder varieties. Not strictly necessary.

ELECTRIC CITRUS PRESSES

These cost about £15 and squeeze citrus fruits only. Juice is extracted by pushing a cut half on a revolving cone. (With a manual press you turn the fruit.)

Advantages

- Speed.
- An electric juicer extracts up to 50 per cent more juice than a manual one.

Disadvantages

- Limited to citrus fruits only.

APPLIANCE SERVICING AND GUARANTEES

Sales assistants often ask whether you would like to take out a service contract or extended guarantee. These policies prolong the free twelve-month cover provided by manufacturers but they are often an expensive way of covering an appliance, so consider some other options.

EXTENDED GUARANTEES

Bought at the time of purchase or within a specified time limit. Taking out an additional four-year guarantee for parts or parts and labour is the norm, giving you a total of five years' cover. All manufacturers and most electrical retailers sell extended guarantees. There are large variations in price between brands from £85 to £200. Insuring the same product but with different parties varies too: compare store costs with the manufacturer.

SO WHY THE DIFFERENCE?

- What's covered? Study the small print in the cover. Manufacturers tend to be more specific in what they cover than the retailers. Some retailers will include accidental damage, such as knobs knocked off and, for example with

IS IT WORTH INSURING APPLIANCES?

- Washing machines are far more likely to go wrong than fridge freezers and microwaves.
- Encouragingly, appliances are getting more reliable. It's in the manufacturers' interests, as any design faults will become apparent in the first year when the machine is under guarantee.

washing machines, items like coins from pockets and boning in bras getting outside the drum and stuck in the pump. They also offer same-day service, and new-for-old facilities if the machine is past redemption during its five-year life.

Others sidestep the issue claiming that accidental damage is covered by household insurance.

- Who does the work? Retailers may subcontract the work, whereas manufacturers have their own engineers.
- Cost of spares. Manufacturers' spare parts are made in their own factory, and supplied at cost to their own service engineers. Retailers are buying spare parts with a mark-up.
- Settling costs. With some store schemes you have to settle charges with the engineer and reclaim money from the insurers.
- Check you can take a guarantee or agreement with you if you move.

TIP Don't fill in your extended warranty at the counter. Take it home and study the small print. Go with the manufacturer's or retailer's schemes depending on whether you are a careful user or need to cover every eventuality.

SERVICE AGREEMENTS

These are an expensive way of buying peace of mind if you compare the costs, quoted per annum, with a one-off call-out repair cost or extended guarantee. They can be taken out on older appliances, but you will probably have to undergo an initial inspection visit first to have any necessary repairs carried out.

Service agreements usually include an annual maintenance inspection; when if something was seen to be amiss it would theoretically be put right.

Check the small print. If you are paying for this service, there should always be a machine provided for your use.

Normally bought as a one-year renewal option, so they are easier to budget for. Manufacturers often see them as an opportunity for a repeat purchase.

IF IT GOES WRONG

If the machine is still under guarantee when it goes wrong, it's quickest to contact the manufacturer's central office (given in instruction booklet), who will give you details of your local service centre.

If it's an own-brand machine, go back to the retailer for help.

SERVICING AN APPLIANCE

If you have not taken out extended cover or a service agreement there are several ways to get the appliance fixed.

LOCAL INDEPENDENT AGENT

Probably the least expensive option, because the repairers are within easy reach.

Independent agents tend to be more flexible with early and late appointments. The labour and call-out charge are usually charged together in a single fee.

Approach an agent who deals with a maximum of four manufacturers. It is more likely that he will be familiar with your appliance, that he will have attended the training sessions, will have the service manuals and carry the spare parts.

There are one or two points you need to watch:

- Check the small print from your manufacturer. The 5-year parts guarantee is only valid if repairs have been undertaken by its recognised service engineers.

BEFORE CALLING OUT HELP

It's worth going back to the instruction book. Suggestions for maintenance include cleaning the inlet filters and the main pump filter on a washing machine; filters and spray arms on a dishwasher; and bag full, blockages in extension pipes and broken belts on vacuum cleaners. Following these simple steps may save you a considerable amount of money.

- Cost of parts is at the discretion of the agent. A washing machine door seal and pump can be easily pirated. Bogus parts may wear more quickly, although you may be charged full price for them.
- A manufacturer or retailer carrying out the repair will guarantee workmanship and parts. An independent may go out of business, so any guarantee given on repair will be useless. Some spare parts, like those made by AEG, Bosch and Miele, are more difficult to source and so an independent will have to send off for them to the relevant company's head office. Hoover spare parts are more readily available and are priced very competitively.

Independent agents won't usually deal with own-brand appliances.

MANUFACTURES' ENGINEERS

Manufacturers' labour is charged in time slots: for example, for six minutes' work. Therefore a more complicated job may work out more expensive than using either a local independent retailer, or a service company where call-out and labour are combined in a single fee.

Servicing charged in narrower time bands will keep your costs down more than that in wider bands, such as half an hour.

RETURN TO RETAILER

This will be necessary with own-brand machines. Retailers like Comet have established a full service back-up, since they are sole importers and the manufacturer has no manufacturing base in this country.

Most retailers refer a main-brand service back to the manufacturer.

NATIONWIDE SERVICE COMPANIES

Typical companies include National Homecare for Servis and Currys; Appliance Care for Bosch, Siemens, Neff manufacturing group; electricity companies who have their own service fleet for each electricity region.

Companies such as Appliance Care may be the exclusive repairers for some brands. Others such as National Homecare mainly work on Servis but also guarantee work for other appliance brands.

With companies like these you don't get familiarity and loyalty, because they are dealing with lots of brands. Check how many brands the engineers are servicing. It's impossible to carry all the spares needed and the customer ultimately pays for two visits.

TIP When calling out a service person, give some idea of the symptoms so that the engineer can bring appropriate spare parts.

RENTING

Finally, if you'd prefer to do without the worry of repair and servicing charges, consider renting an appliance. For example, with appliances rented from Radio Rentals you can take out equipment insurance against accidental damage and theft, etc, as well as payment protection in the event of sickness, unemployment and redundancy.

BATHROOM FIXTURES AND FITTINGS

A new bathroom adds an extra personal touch to your home. Consider the choice of colours, materials, fittings and positions in the room.

The main limiting factors are permanent fittings such as windows, doors and plumbing connections. Some piping can be fairly easily moved or extended, but probably the greatest influence is the position of the toilet soil pipe.

PLANNING A BATHROOM

First, consider the space available and the fittings required. Measure the room and mark the plan out on graph paper. **NB: work in metric, as this is how bathroom fittings are always sold.**

Remember to allow for manoeuvring, or the 'activity space', around the fitting (see illustration below). Space is needed for bending over fittings such as a basin, and climbing in and out of baths. Access for cleaning should also be considered. Some activity spaces can overlap (see right), as fittings are unlikely to be used at the same time.

Siting the toilet, bidet, basin and bath in line is an efficient way to run water pipes.

The final decision to make is the actual style and colour for the fittings. Light, pale shades and co-ordinates will give an illusion of space in small rooms. Dark colours give the impression of intimacy and warmth but show dirt easily.

Lighting should also be considered at this stage as artificial or natural light will affect the look of a bathroom.

Built-in units can be used to fill spaces. They provide useful storage space and help to tidy up corners that may be difficult to clean.

BATHS

Acrylic

Lightweight, and the most common type of bath. They are warm to the touch, less slippery than metal and stain resistant, but will scratch easily. Light scratches can be removed using metal polish. Deep scratches may be removed by the manufacturer. The moulded acrylic is reinforced with fibreglass and mounted on a galvanised steel frame to give strength. A variety of shapes are available.

Enamelled

Pressed steel baths are coated with vitreous enamel and fired to give the hard finish. Cast-iron baths have a porcelain enamel. Both types of enamel can be damaged by abrasive cleaners and some limescale removers.

RECOMMENDED ACTIVITY SPACES

Bath: 28in/700mm-wide standing area along the side.

Basin: 40in/1,000mm-wide area extending 28in/700mm from the front of the basin. Remember to allow space above for bending down over it. Don't fit a shelf or cupboard above a basin unit so that people using it will bang their head, or drop things into the sink.

Toilet and Bidet: allow a total width of 32in/800mm each, extending 24in/600mm back from the front edge of each. Less space is needed at the sides if they are placed next to each other. Bidets are designed to be used facing the taps, so knee room at the sides must be allowed.

Shower: 28in/700mm standing space in front of the opening.

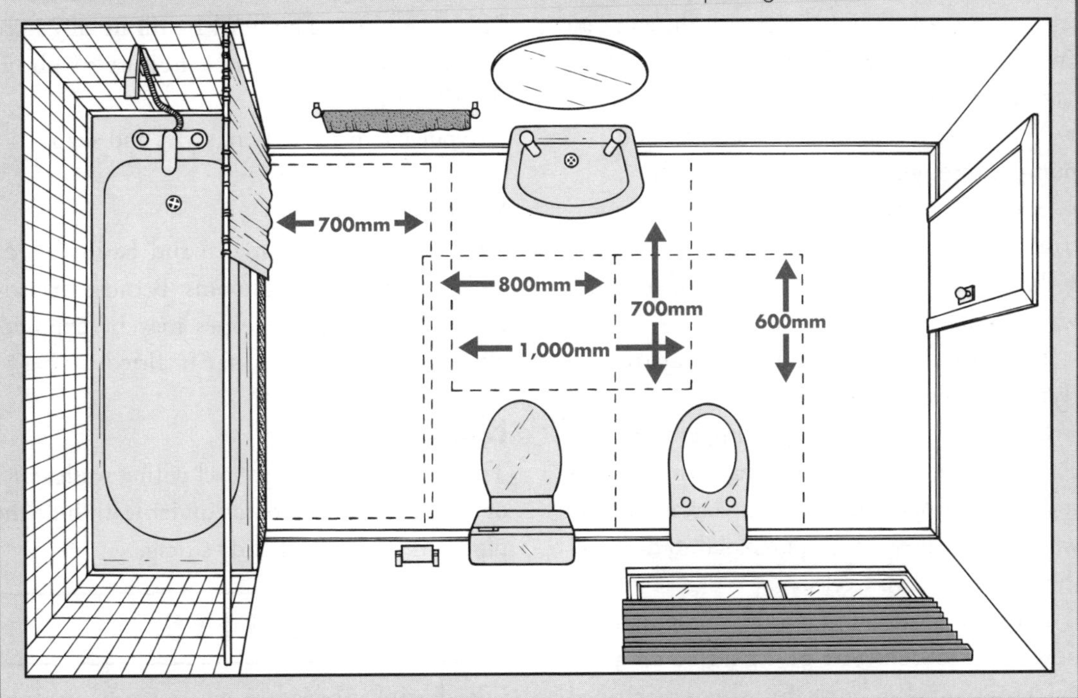

SIZES AND SHAPES

The standard size for a bath is 5ft 6in/1,700mm long x 28in/700mm wide. The average height is 20–24in/500–550mm. Alternative sizes available are smaller baths, starting at about 47in/1,200mm long, and unusually shaped styles, such as corner units. Contoured baths, usually made from acrylic, are shaped to trace the outline of the body, and are slightly more economical on water needed.

All these baths have a rectangular outer frame which usually has panels down the sides and ends. An embossed surface improves the grip and is safer, especially if the bath is to be used with a shower attachment.

Traditional Victorian-shaped baths are free-standing with feet and can still be obtained in cast iron.

A bath usually has taps positioned at the end of the bath, but some designs have them on the side or in the corner.

WHIRLPOOL BATHS

May also be called spa baths or jacuzzis, and are the most expensive types of baths. The jets and movement of the water massage the body, and can give relief to arthritic or rheumatic joints. Medical advice should always be sought before use if you are pregnant, or if you have a kidney complaint.

The number and position of the underwater jets can be varied, and along with different air and water pressures, different sorts of effects can be achieved. There are various options:

- Whirlpool jets recirculate the water and pump it through outlets along the bath.
- Spa baths pump air through holes in the base and back of the bath.
- Whirlpool spas pump a mixture of air and water round the bath.

Look out for self-draining features on recirculating water systems.

Some have a built-in sterilising system with a reservoir of cleaning chemicals which needs to be kept topped up. Alternatively, a separate whirlpool cleaner can be purchased to disinfect the bath every two weeks.

Baths fitted as whirlpools can be purchased new, or a system can be installed in your existing acrylic bath by the whirlpool manufacturer. The bath needs to be taken away to the factory for installation, but the only stipulation on design is that the bath needs to have a flat surface in which to fit the jet controls.

Before buying any type of whirlpool ask to listen to the pump working, as they can sometimes be noisy.

Check that the appliance is electrically safe and conforms to BS 3456. It should be protected by a residual current device (RCD) outside the bathroom.

WASH BASINS

Made from vitreous china, kiln fired and glazed. Like normal china, the finish is smooth with a high gloss and hard wearing but will crack or chip if treated roughly.

SIZES AND SHAPES

Pedestal

As well as supporting the bowl the pedestal hides the pipes. The bowl is still usually fixed to the wall, so it is at a height of about 32in/800mm.

Available in a variety of styles and shapes.

Wall mounted

Vary from large to small hand basins which will fit into small cloakrooms. Because they are fixed to the wall the pipes may be exposed, although half pedestals may be fitted.

Counter top

The bowl is sunk to sit level with a wash stand or vanity unit. Cupboards underneath hide the pipework and provide tidy storage.

TOILETS

Like basins, these are made from vitreous china. They consist of two main parts, the pan and the cistern.

TYPES OF FLUSHING SYSTEM

Wash-down: the most common type of mechanism where water washes down from the cistern through the pan.

Syphonic: a quiet and efficient method where the water from the pan is drawn out by a syphoning action.

Shredding and pumping unit: this enables the toilet to be installed almost anywhere in the house. The discharge is shredded so that it can be pumped through a narrower pipe. Being smaller, the discharge pipe can be run behind the wall. An electrical connection is needed to operate the pump.

They are an option for an additional toilet in the house. Permission must be obtained from the local authority before installation.

SIZES AND SHAPES

Close-couple

The cistern sits on the pan to give the look of a single unit. The pan sits on a pedestal (floor standing), but this can leave a space behind the toilet that is difficult to clean.

Low-level

The cistern is mounted a small way (about 37in/935mm) above the pan, connected with a small flush pipe.

High-level

The cistern is fixed on the wall high above the pan with a joining pipe. The cistern has a pull chain to flush the toilet.

Back-to-the-wall

Floor standing, but completely encloses the pipe work so that it is flush with the wall behind. It has a neat appearance and a smooth finish for cleaning.

Wall-hung

The pan and piping are enclosed and supported against the wall. The floor below is clear and easier to clean.

Concealed cistern

The cistern is positioned with a unit or behind the wall with only the flush handle protruding. It may be fitted with a back-to-the-wall or wall-hung toilet pan.

TOILET SEATS

Some manufacturers offer seats with different heights, particularly suitable for the disabled. They fit on to standard toilet-seat fittings.

BIDETS

A low-level wash basin made of vitreous china, like toilets and basins. Originally designed for personal hygiene, they are also used as a foot bath in Britain.

There are two main types, and they both need good, balanced water pressures in order to work effectively.

Over-the-rim

A mixer tap fills the bidet with hot and cold water, like a basin. The tap may have a swivel head to give directional water sprays.

The over-the-rim is the most common type made by UK manufacturers.

Below-the-rim/Box rim

More expensive, and looks more like a toilet. It is filled from under the rim.

Either type of bidet may also have an ascending spray or douche supply. The inlet nozzle is set in the base of the bowl giving an upward spray. High water pressure is needed for this type of bidet to be effective.

Before buying a bidet, check that it conforms to your local water regulations. It may need special installation to meet backflow prevention requirements specified by the water company. Consulting a qualified plumber is recommended.

Like toilets, bidets may be wall hung or floor standing. They are usually the same height as a toilet, and should be positioned as close to the toilet as possible.

TAPS

A variety of materials are used for taps and bathroom fittings. The most common are chrome or a gold-effect coating. Brass and coloured taps are also available coated with a coloured plastic finish.

The size, position and type of taps for baths, basins and bidets are restricted by the size and number of fitting holes.

Look for taps that comply to BS 5412/3 or EN 200, as this ensures that the tap allows water to pass through at an acceptable and practical rate. Taps to this standard should also satisfy water by-laws against wastage and contamination.

Pillar

These come as pairs for hot and cold water. The water enters the tap vertically, so they must be mounted on a level surface. They are generally small and neat with a twist top. Traditional styles have a cross-shaped handle.

Mixer

Water is supplied via a central tap (see illustration, page 249).

A dual mixer supplies the hot and cold together but keeps the two separate within the tap. A true mixer combines the water as it goes through the tap and needs equal water pressures to be controlled accurately.

Mixer taps may consist of a single unit with the taps connected on the same base as the spout.

A three-piece unit has the controls and taps mounted on to the basin or bath separately.

A bath/shower mixer has a diverter to send water to the attached shower head.

For bidets, look for taps with a swivel head to give a directional spray.

Single lever

As the name suggests, the tap is a single unit with a rotating control and lever. The flow of water is controlled by raising or lowering the lever, while the temperature is varied by rotating the control.

This tap style requires only one fitting hole.

PLUGS

Modern mixer taps often incorporate the plug control. Pop up plugs are operated by a lever. There is no plug chain connected to the bath overflow.

Alternatively, a twisting plug control may be mounted on the side of a bath.

SHOWERS

The main factor affecting a choice of shower will be the type of water system in your house. If you're not sure which type of system you have, ask a plumber to investigate for you: see Fitting a Shower, below.

If your hot and cold water are both supplied from a hot-water cylinder (in the airing cupboard) or a cold-water tank (in the loft) you can choose between a mixer shower (preferably thermostatic) or a power shower (a mixer shower with an extra pressure boost).

If your house does not have a hot-water cylinder or constant hot water, you need an instantaneous electric shower. The cold water supply, direct from the mains, is heated by the shower as it is needed.

An exception is for combination gas boilers (with gas-heated mains-pressure water), when you need a mixer shower. However, check first with your local gas company.

FITTING A SHOWER

The base of the cold-water tank needs to be at least 39in/1m above the shower head for a mixer shower. This is described as a 'head of pressure' and the greater the distance, the greater the shower flow. If there isn't sufficient head of pressure – perhaps if you live in a flat – you will have to install a booster pump (see Power Shower, page 128). With an electric shower (supplied direct from the mains), the only way to increase the pressure is to buy one with a higher wattage, or a power shower.

Check that your water supply can cope with the type of shower you are considering. Showers with a high flow rate must not drain the water-storage system too quickly.

Foreign imported brands may not fit British plumbing systems. Check that the shower you are considering will fit, and complies with UK water regulations.

Professional advice

Advice on your water system and appropriate installations can be obtained from a qualified plumber. Suitable local contacts can be obtained from the Institute of Plumbing (see Useful Addresses).

For advice on electrical work and a local electrician contact the National Inspection Council for Electrical Installation Contracting (NICEIC).

All gas appliances and connection must be carried out by a plumber who is CORGI-registered (Council for Registered Gas Installers).

Running costs and water consumption

It is a common belief that a shower uses less water and is more than economical than taking a bath. However, with high flow rates from modern showers such as power showers, the consumption may be similar. If you are concerned about water use, but want a power shower, look for one where you can turn the flow rate down while soaping yourself.

Mixer and instantaneous showers use the least water.

Sealing

Make sure that the area around a bath where a shower is to be installed is suitably sealed. Traditional grout is not durable enough against constant sprays of water. Use a silicon sealer; colours to match fittings are available.

TYPES OF SHOWERS

All types of showers can be installed over the bath, or in a separate shower cubicle, except bath/shower mixers.

Bath/shower mixer

The cheapest and easiest to install. Water is diverted from the hot and cold bath taps using a shower mixer which fits over existing taps. Alternatively, a new tap which mixes the water and includes a shower head can be used to replace the individual taps.

Adaptors that fit over the taps come as two types. The simplest only takes water from the taps, and has to be removed to fill the bath. A slightly more complex system clips permanently over the taps but has a diverter which switches the water from the shower through a tap into the bath. Some of this type may also have a temperature control for the shower, that is separate from and independent of the two taps.

No plumbing is needed (except if fitting a new mixer tap), but you still need an adequate head of water (see Fitting a Shower, above) and preferably equal pressure from the hot and cold water supply.

This type of system is likely to suffer from draw-off. Water drawn elsewhere in the house, such as flushing a toilet or filling a basin, will cause the shower to run hot.

Look for an automatic diverter which sends

water back into the bath if the supply pressure drops too low.

Mixer shower

A wall-mounted shower which draws water from the hot water cylinder and cold water tank. Some have separate temperature and flow controls. There are three types.

- Manual: as with taps, you mix hot and cold water. The shower is gravity fed and needs at least 39in/1m head of pressure. These can also suffer from draw-off (see above) so are best fitted with separate hot and cold supply pipes.

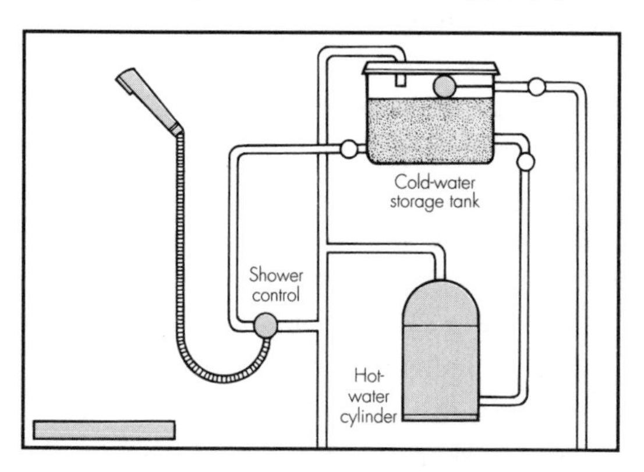

- Thermostatic: the temperature control has a build-in stabiliser so that water stays at the same temperature. It can't run too hot, and shouldn't be affected when water is drawn off elsewhere. Some can even be locked within a certain temperature range for safety.
- Pressure balance: balances the water supply pressures.

Instantaneous shower

The shower draws water from the rising cold-water mains only and heats it using electricity or gas. The shower is instantly hot and can be taken any time because the supply is not dependent on the stored hot water that may run out. They are a good choice if you don't have a lot of stored hot water.

Electric showers must be fitted with a

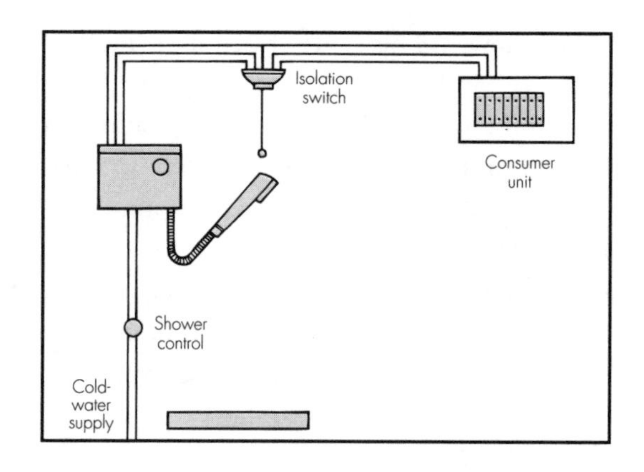

separate power switch for safety. It can be a cord-pull switch in the bathroom or a switch outside to isolate the power. If in doubt, check with a qualified electrician. For a local electrician contact the National Inspection Council for Electrical Contracting. (see Useful Addresses)

Usually, the water temperature is manually controlled, but some have a temperature stabiliser so they aren't affected by draw-off from other taps. The flow rate depends upon the shower's ability to raise the cold-water temperature, particularly in winter. Look for a shower with a power rating of at least 8kW.

The rate of flow may be reduced as the temperature is adjusted: more water can go through if it doesn't need heating, whereas colder water requires more heating, so the flow is slower.

Power shower

To achieve a power shower you can fit:

- A mixer shower with an integral pump to increase the water flow. The temperature is manually controlled, like a normal mixer shower taking water from the cold water tank and hot water cylinder.

They can be fitted where there would otherwise be an insufficient head of water, requiring only 3in/7.6cm head of pressure.

- An additional electric booster pump on an

existing mixer shower system. This allows thermostatic control and can be fitted somewhere out of the way, such as in the airing cupboard next to the water cylinder, where the

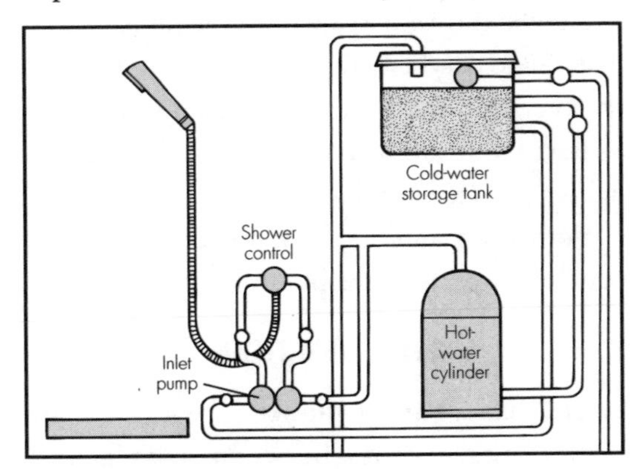

noise of the pump won't be so apparent.
A power shower is ideal if you suffer from low water pressure or water flow. A power pump can achieve as much pressure as 30–90ft/9–27m head of pressure. The pressure and type of flow from the shower head can be varied to give effects such as a needle jet or soft foam-effect spray.

The higher the wattage the greater the flow

POINTS TO CONSIDER WHEN CHOOSING

- A separate on/off switch, independent from the temperature control so that the temperature stays set where you prefer it.
- Some kind of marking, such as LED lights, to help you select your chosen temperature.
- Maximum temperature cut-out to prevent scalding.
- BS 3456 and BEAB approval for electric showers.

SHOWER HEADS

Fixed wall mounted

- The hose to the shower head is concealed behind the wall. Only the actual head is fixed to the wall, but it can be pivoted to change the direction of the spray. Traditional fixed heads have a large circular head connected by rigid exposed pipes. You are not able to adjust the height of the shower.
- The support for the shower head is fixed in one position on the wall. The wall bracket cannot be adjusted in height but the shower head can be unclipped from the bracket for use. The water hose hangs freely from the shower head.

Slide rail

The shower support is fitted on a wall-mounted slide rail, so that the height can be varied and the head can also be unclipped.

Spray variations

The actual head will also affect the power and effect from the shower. They can give a variety of spray types. The greatest variation is on power showers, where a jet of water, a soft spray or a normal shower effect can be achieved.

Self-cleaning

- Look for a shower head that is self-draining, so that no water is left in it to form limescale.
- Self-cleaning heads have internal plastic pins which will protrude through the spray holes when not in use and keep them free from scale.

Individual shower heads offering the designs above can often be bought as replacements compatible with current fittings.

BODY-SPRAY SHOWERS

In addition to an overhead shower, shower jets that spray water horizontally can be fitted on to the walls of the shower cubicle. They need to be fitted with a power shower, or a mixer shower with a pump, to have enough pressure to work.

Body sprays can be like small fixed shower heads, or be direct jets from a vertical rail with holes along it.

A diverter must be fitted to change the water between the shower and the body sprays.

SHOWER ENCLOSURES

Surfaces need to be cleaned easily to prevent the build-up of limescale or mould. Whichever type you choose, the area around the shower needs to be protected from the water spray.

Shower cubicles

- These may be built into a corner or alcove in the bathroom or other room, using two or three walls as part of the shower enclosure.
- Free-standing cubicles don't rely on any interior walls as frames but will need a wall to support the plumbing. The unit has its own four side panels and sometimes a top to contain water vapour.
- Usually they can be purchased as complete kits, including the shower tray.

Shapes and sizes

- Square shower trays are between 28in/700mm and 36in/900mm square.
- Rectangular trays are usually 47in/1,200mm long by 24in/600mm wide.

Different shaped trays, such as curved or triangular, can be purchased to fit into corners. For a neat edge with a tiled wall, look for a tray with a special tiling lip.

Look for slip-resistant trays, but bear in mind that if the base is too rough it may be difficult to keep a clean appearance.

Construction

Shower trays are usually available in colours to match existing bathroom furniture.

- Ceramic shower trays are the most durable and most expensive. They are made from fireclay, which is stronger than the ceramics used for basins and toilets, but is still cold to the touch.
- Acrylic trays are made from the same material as acrylic baths, are warmer to touch than ceramic and are the cheapest option.
- Resin trays are stronger than acrylic, but lighter and cheaper than ceramic.

Both resin and acrylic have removable side panels for access to the plumbing beneath.

SHOWER TUBS

Larger than a regular shower cubicle, these are rather like a cross between a bath and rectangular shower tray 47in/1,200mm x 29½in/750mm x 21½in/545mm. As well as a standing area under the shower there is a raised area for sitting towards the back of the tub.

SHOWER CURTAINS

The cheapest and simplest screening to put along a bath/shower, and can easily be pulled out of the way when the bath itself is needed.

For a simple rail between two walls look for a spring-loaded telescopic rail. A curtain rail fitted with brackets can be fitted between two walls, or in an L-shape or U-shape around a bath. The rail normally comes with the rings or fittings for the curtain. Glider rails have concealed fasteners.

Mildew and a build-up of soapy deposits in the folds are the main problems associated with shower curtains. Look for PVC, which can be wiped clean, or washable nylon, polyester or cotton. Mildew-resistant curtains are sold impregnated with a fungicide.

If you want a curtain to match the other furnishing in the bathroom, it can be hung with a waterproof curtain on the inside. Eyelets to use on home-made curtains are available from haberdashery stores.

BATH SCREENS

Usually made from toughened plastic or rigid glass, these are a more permanent arrangement than a curtain.

- A single-panel fixed screen can fit to reach halfway along the side of the bath and may be fixed or hinged for easy access.
- Screens made of several hinged panels will fold flat to be kept out of the way, making getting in and out of the bath easier.
- To create an enclosed shower cubicle round the bath, look for a screen with a hinged end panel, so that it swings round to fit across the width of the bath.
- For a completely enclosed bath, sliding panels on runners can be installed around all edges of the bath (or hinged along the bath length). For a rounded corner bath with a shower, curved screens are available with curved sliding panels.

Check that the screen will make a good seal with the bath before purchasing, and bear in mind how practical it will be to keep clean: a smooth plastic inside and smooth seals between the screen and bath will make cleaning easier.

BATHROOM ACCESSORIES

Wall brackets (grab rails)

Give extra support to the less stable. Can be mounted in shower cubicles, above baths, and can be incorporated into toilet-roll holders or towel rails.

Heated towel rails

There two main types which can be installed in bathrooms. Before buying, consider the facilities for connecting to a water supply or electricity as necessary. Heated rails are primarily designed to dry and air towels, but if they are large enough, they can both dry towels and give off room heat.

Electric towel rails: operated from an isolated switch positioned outside the bathroom.

Hot-water towel rails: connected to the central heating so they come on when the bathroom is likely to be used. They are more efficient to run compared to an electric rail, as they automatically go on and off with the house heating.

Multi-rail styles are the most popular, and are efficient for heating as well as drying.

Steel-panel styles are incorporated on to a radiator.

Tubular rails (sometimes brass) may be fitted to the central heating or the hot water system so that they come on when the water is being heated for use.

Shower and bath accessories

- Fold-down seat, for extra support and comfort for old and young.
- Shower tidy: self-draining sets of shelves fixed to the wall or on to the slide rail.
- Gel/shampoo dispenser: fitted on to the slide rail.
- Non-slip bath mats: plastic mats with suckers to improve grip in the bath. Always check that the mat is well suctioned on to the bath base or the whole mat may aquaplane.

Stick-on grips can also be purchased as a permanent solution.

BATHROOM VENTILATION

The requirements of domestic ventilation are specified in the Building Regulations. For rooms such as bathrooms, adequate ventilation must be installed in all new properties or extensions, but it is advisable to install ventilation in existing bath/shower rooms and toilets to prevent condensation and damp problems.

For good ventilation, a bathroom needs six to eight air changes an hour. If the minimum requirements set by the building regulations are to be achieved a fan should be installed which will extract at least 15 litres/second (54 m^3/hour) intermittently.

TYPES OF EXTRACTOR FAN

There are two main types of fans, to suit different installation circumstances:

Axial fans should be fitted through a window or wall, because they are designed to move air over only short distances. To reach through a cavity wall, telescopic tubing is usually attached.

Centrifugal fans will move air over distances greater than 6ft 6in/2m. They can be fitted with flexible ducting to extract to the outside via the roof cavity, but remember that the greater the distance of the ducting, the less efficient the fan will be. A condensation trap may also be needed (see page 133).

HOW TO CALCULATE SIZE OF EXTRACTOR FAN

To determine the size of extractor fan needed, the size of room must be considered.

1 Measure the size of the room in metres: length x width x height = volume in m^3.

2 Multiply the volume by the recommended air changes per hour (6 to 10 for bathrooms and toilets) = extract performance of the fan required (m^3/hr)

3 Look for a fan with a performance as close to this as possible.

If there is any doubt as to which sort of extractor fan is needed, the centrifugal type is the safest bet.

Ceiling fans, specially designed to fit above showers or baths, are recommended to remove steam directly from the source.

All fans require electrical connection to drive them, and supervision of a qualified electrician may be required.

POINTS TO CONSIDER WHEN CHOOSING

- Size of room and fan: see box below.
- Humidistat which automatically operates fan when humidity reaches a set level.
- Adjustable time selector for overrun (usually up to 20 minutes). The fan is connected to the light switch and will stay on for a set period of time after the light has been switched off.
- Back-draught shutters on the outside grill.
- Easy to clean parts, preferably removable grills.
- Pull cord to switch on and off.
- Dual speed for large bathrooms. The fan operates at full speed when the room is in use and a low speed during overrun on the timer.
- On small units, a manual boost speed facility.

FITTING AN EXTRACTOR FAN

To achieve the best efficiency the fan should be sited at the furthermost point from the source of replacement air, such as opposite the internal doorway.

To comply with wiring regulations a bathroom fan must not be situated where it can be switched on or off by a person using a bath or shower. A pull cord switch is the safest option and the fan is often wired into the light pull-cord switch. For additional safety, an isolation switch outside the bathroom is also recommended.

Warning

The extraction pipe must not be connected to a flue used for any other appliances other than electrically operated.

Window fitting

A hole must be cut for the fan. It is advisable to have this cut in a new piece of glass by a professional glazier. If you have a hole put in an existing pane the stresses may crack it.

Check with the glazier that the weight of glass is appropriate to take the fan.

The fan will need to be fitted with a waterproof seal around the hole in the glass, following the manufacturer's instructions.

Wall fitting

As well as the fan, a kit may be needed to fit the fan through the wall. Check that the selected position has no buried pipes or wires, or obstructions on the outside of the wall.

Ceiling fitting

Ventilation ducting will be needed to carry the air to the exterior via the roof cavity and an exterior grill.

If it is possible that condensation could run back towards the fan a condensation trap will be needed. The formation of condensation can be reduced by insulating the ducting in the roof space.

Check that the location and route of the ducting is not obscured.

Electrical work

Extractor fans are relatively easy to install by an experienced DIYer, but for electrical connections an electrician should always be consulted.

For advice on electrical work and a local electrician contact the National Inspection Council for Electrical Installation Contracting (see Useful Addresses).

BUYING A BED

In an ideal world, beds should be changed every ten years, but in reality it's more likely to be every fifteen to twenty years. For a piece of furniture that's expected to give over 36,000 hours of support to the entire body it's essential to choose a bed that matches your requirements exactly.

If we could see inside an old bed we'd never settle for a second-hand one. A sagging mattress with a stained and badly frayed cover, warped or bent slats or springs you can feel through flattened fillings is a sure sign that it's past its prime. Most importantly, if it feels less comfortable than it used to and you're getting more nights of disturbed sleep than before, it's probable that the springs have weakened, giving less support. This can give rise to back problems and continual loss of sleep. If you're not convinced of this, in a survey by the National Bed Federation (see Useful Addresses), 97 per cent of GPs questioned agreed that a new bed could help to alleviate back problems.

BUYING GUIDE

Never judge a book by its cover: don't be tempted to buy on the look of the ticking!

- Try it out. At the end of the day it's up to you to decide whether it's comfortable. Lie on the bed, with your partner if it's a double, and stay there for as long as possible. Ask for a pillow so it is totally representative of the way you will sleep on it.

A good department store will have arranged the floor so the beds are away from the main thoroughfare, to save embarrassment.

- Check the firmness of the bed by sliding your hand into the small of your back. If your hand becomes lodged the bed is too soft and if there is a distinct gap it's too hard. Make sure you can turn on to your side easily and that it isn't too hard on your shoulders and hips.

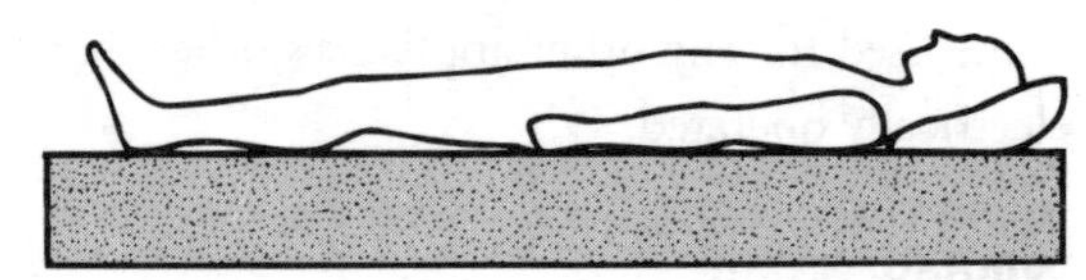

Too hard

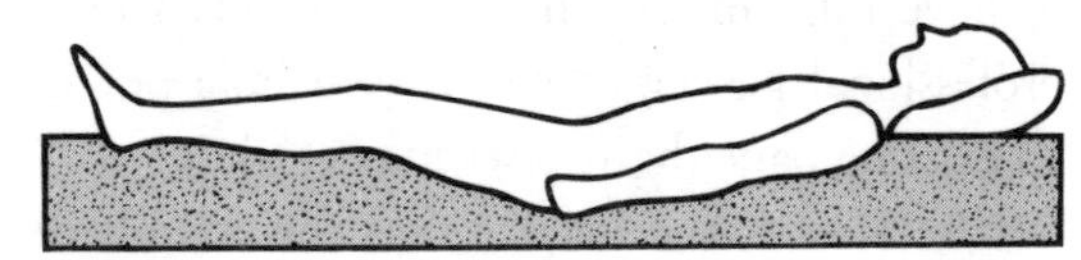

Too soft

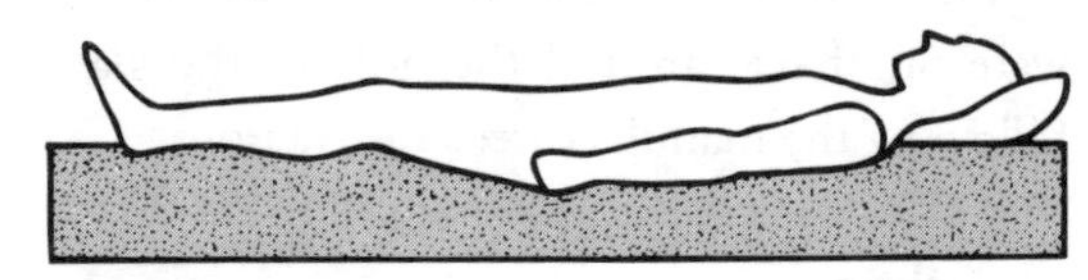

Correct

TIP Avoid shopping for beds when you are tired: everything feels good then!

- Read the labels carefully. You may be surprised how informative these can be. They'll detail the types of filling used for the mattress and the base.
- All beds made after 1988 must comply with the 1988 Furniture and Furnishings Fire Safety regulations. It is illegal for a retailer to sell a bed that doesn't conform, but there is no one to check private sales, so avoid second-hand beds because they may be pre-1988.
- Spend as much as you can afford. There is no such thing as a cheap bed, only a lower-quality one. It's worth paying more for strong, durable springs, better stitching, hand tufting and firm handles, all of which contribute to longer-lasting performance. Sale buys are good value, but avoid discount stores unless selling well-known genuinely labelled branded beds.

• A new bed will feel strange for a while; it will probably take about three weeks before you're used to it properly.

SIZES

Buying the right size of bed in terms of length and width is important for comfort and a good night's sleep. Check the bed is at least 6in/15cm longer than the tallest occupant. If the bed is not long enough, the body will automatically move across the bed to sleep diagonally. Work out the ideal width by laying flat with your hands behind your head. Elbows should not touch the sides or your partner.

Several specialist companies offer a made-to-measure service. Beds can be made up to 7ft 4in/224cm wide or long, or circular; but they can be expensive.

STANDARD BED SIZES

Compact Single
2ft 6in x 6ft 3in/75 x 190cm
Popular Single
3ft x 6ft 3in/90 x 190cm
Standard Double
4ft x 6ft 3in/120 x 190cm
Popular Double
4ft 6in x 6ft 3in/135 x 190cm
Queen Size
5ft x 6ft 6in/150 x 200cm
King Size
6ft x 6ft 6in/180 x 200cm

Manufacturers are at last recognising that the population is becoming taller and producing more beds up to 6ft 6in/200cm long.

Average bed height is
26–28in/66–70cm.

In general, a bed for two adults will be more comfortable if it is queen size or larger.

MATTRESSES

Choose between sprung interiors or foam.

SPRING INTERIOR

This is the most popular type in the UK. Springs form the central core of the mattress and are the main support layer. The thickness of the wire and the number of springs determine the firmness of a mattress. A spring made from a 12-gauge wire is harder than a 15-gauge one. A pocketed-spring bed tends to use 15-gauge or higher because there are so many more springs offering extra support. Orthopaedic beds, on the other hand, use 12- to 14-gauge springs.

In a top-of-the-range bed the number of springs used will be included in the sales literature or the cover label. A cheap, popular double will probably contain around 300 springs, whereas a bed at the luxury end of the market will contain over 2,500.

There are three main types of spring mattress.

Open springing

The most common, and generally cheaper than pocket springs. Found in cheap to mid-priced beds. They consist of rows of waisted spring coils joined to adjacent springs by a continuous small-diameter spiral spring known as a helical spring. The edge of the spring unit is strengthened by a heavy-gauge border rod at the top and bottom.

Continuous springing

A development of open-springing with one length of wire forming all the coils in the mattress, producing a three-dimensional

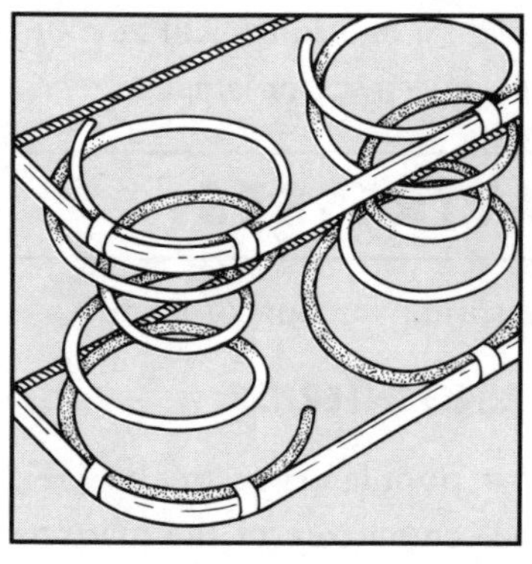
Open spring

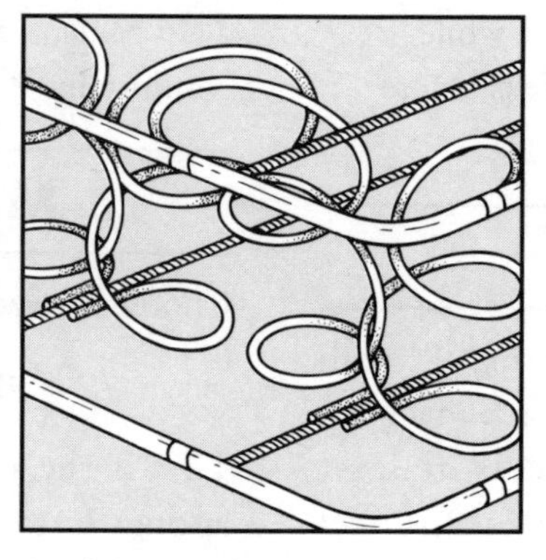
Continuous spring

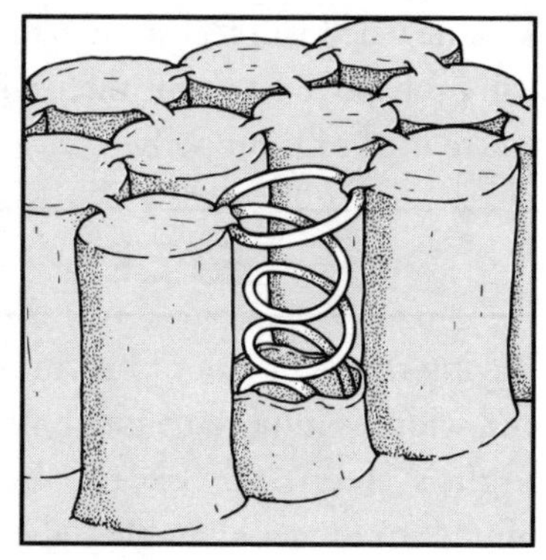
Pocket spring

knitted effect. The coiled unit is attached to helical wire springs and held within a metal border at the top and bottom.

These tend to be in the middle price range.

Pocketed springing

Has cylindrical coils individually enclosed in fabric pockets made from calico, viscose or polyester. These are generally in the middle to top end of the price range. The rows of springs can be joined in different ways.

Clipped pocketed springs are used fewer per bed than other types. Each encased spring is wire-clipped to its adjacent springs at four points, top and bottom.

Honeyc6mb pocketed springs have smaller coils and are crammed tightly into the frame. (There are over a thousand in a double mattress.) The coils are tied into position.

Independent pocketed springs have coils which are neither clipped nor tied so they act independently when pressure is applied. An ideal choice for a double bed where the occupants are very different in weight (see Special Requirements, page 138).

FOAM

The degree of support is determined by the density of the foam. Unfortunately this is difficult to determine, so always go to a reputable dealer where the beds are well labelled. Pay as much as you can afford: at least £600 for a popular double.

As a general rule, the heavier the mattress the better the comfort will be.

Look for latex foam, made from rubber, which is superior and more expensive than polyurethane. For cost reasons, most are a combination of both: an upper layer of latex for comfort and a lower layer of polyurethane for support.

Foam mattresses are worth considering if you are an allergy sufferer because they do not contain animal-derived fillings and are bacteria static, which means they cannot support germs or mildew. They should always be well ventilated to allow them to 'breathe'. Compared to typical spring interior mattresses, they are light in weight, warm and don't need turning, so are often recommended for the elderly or disabled.

FIBRE

This is quite a new development. Instead of springs or foam, the mattress is filled with hollow fibres which are curled up like tiny springs. The mattress is usually made up of several layers, having a firm central core for support, with several softer outer layers for maximum comfort.

INSIDE STORY

Although hidden, the upholstery filling contributes considerably to the comfort and support offered by the bed. Good-quality sprung mattresses will contain a number of layers (cotton felt, wool, coir, sisal or hair) on each side of the springs.

The layers are built up, finishing with the comfort layer, which is generally polyester fibre, cotton or wool. Each have different advantages: polyester is non-allergenic, cotton is cool for summer while wool is warm for winter. Top-quality mattresses can contain up to 33lb/15kg of pure new lamb's wool.

Basic materials include:

- Cotton felt, used for comfort and spring insulation.
- Wool: should be pure new wool, and is the luxury comfort ingredient.
- Coir or sisal, usually worked into a jute or polypropylene mesh for easier handling.
- Hair: has a big role to play in the upholstery of a mattress. The curled hairs act like springs and are very strong when matted together forming a good resilient layer.

COVERS

Manufacturers choose the cover, or mattress ticking, with care. There is no doubt that this 'packaging' influences people's choice, which is strange since it is never seen once the bed is in use. Tickings for expensive mattresses include woven damask, while other cheaper options include printed non-woven cloths or lightweight, strong, knitted nylon fabrics.

- Look for closely woven ticking, especially on a tufted mattress (see right) where the cover must be tight to hold the tufts securely.
- Check that handles are strong and securely fixed. These bear the brunt of the weight when the mattress is turned.

The mattress should be well finished off. Finishing methods include:

Tufted: the traditional method of finishing. Often found on top-quality mattresses. The mattress is punched through with cotton tapes or waxed threads with a tag left at each end. These are guarded by a cotton or wool-felt washer to prevent the tags pulling back into the mattress.

Deep-stitch quilting (diamond shaped): produces a smooth sleeping surface by stitching the top filling layers to the ticking. The quilted layer is then attached to the core of springs.

Micro or multi-quilting: involves stitching or quilting the ticking to a thin layer of foam or polyester fibre. The stitch pattern stretches over the whole area of the cover. Under the quilted ticking the primary insulating upholstery is attached to the springs. This extends right to the edges of the mattress.

Smooth top: usually found on the cheaper ranges. Here the ticking is pulled tightly over the filling and there is no stitching to hold the filling layers in place. Over time, this is bound to move around.

BACK TO BASE

Never mix and match mattresses and bases. They should always be bought together. An old base may look in reasonable condition but it's likely to have retained the sleeping pattern of the original mattress, so will not support the new one evenly.

In some cases, unless the correct mattress and base are used together, you invalidate the guarantee.

There are four types of bases:

Sprung-edge bases

Offer comfort right to the edge, and provide a

luxurious sleeping area. They consist of an open coil sprung-mattress unit which sits on top of a wooden platform. This acts as a giant shock absorber for a mattress, supporting it all over and increasing its durability.

Often found on drawer-divan bases and with pocketed spring mattresses.

Firm-edge bases

Lower than sprung edge. The support springs are held in the 'box' construction and held in place by webbing running from side to side, covered by upholstery. These are usually sold with an open-coil-type mattress, and nowadays most common on divans with legs. Because the edges are hard you tend to sleep towards the middle and this is where it will give first. It also reduces your sleeping area.

Solid-top bases

Have no springs, so are solid and firm with little give. They should be used with a specially constructed mattress; foam may be used rather than springs. The mattress and base must be ventilated to prevent the build-up of moisture from the mattress. These are the cheapest type of bed base, but make the mattress do all the work, thereby reducing its eventual durability.

Slatted bases

Also very firm, and becoming increasingly popular especially with the current fashion for pine furniture. (Wood frames help the bed look more like a piece of bedroom furniture with integrated head and foot boards.) The bases consist of wooden slats, generally about 4in/10cm apart, held over parallel support rails. Top of the range slatted bases have flexible fixings for extra 'give' compared with fixed slats. Initially a more expensive option, especially with adjustable sections. They don't wear like springs, so you only replace the mattress, unless the slats are badly bent.

It is important to choose the correct mattress for a slatted base as recommended by its manufacturer. Foam or latex is preferred with slats in Europe.

SPECIAL REQUIREMENTS

DOUBLE BEDS

- Choose a bed which is both wide and long enough for the tallest person. A double for two people should be at least 5ft/150cm. The standard double, 4ft 6in/135cm only allows you 27in/68cm of space for each person – about the size of a baby's cot.
- Weight is also important. If your weight differs by more than 66lb/30kg or more, it is worth opting for a zip-and-link type bed, so you can select the right support for each person. The two mattresses are joined together by a heavy-duty zip along the centre, and the bases are locked together securely at the head and foot of the bed.
- Alternatively, choose a king size, individually pocketed, sprung mattress on a sprung edge base.

ORTHOPAEDIC BEDS

These don't contain any miracle ingredients other than being firm. They will not cure a bad back. There is no standard definition of an orthopaedic bed, but it's generally accepted that such a bed is firmer than normal.

The right bed should support your spine correctly, but also be comfortable. Your size and weight will determine what's best. Often, just getting a good new bed makes all the difference. Check first that it's not too firm for you, bearing in mind we toss and turn over 70 times in the night.

If your doctor has suggested an orthopaedic bed, go to a good department store. Be wary of advertisements that claim to make beds for individuals. This is highly unlikely, and could be costly.

A short-term solution, if you feel your bed is past its best, is to buy a bed board. This is placed under the mattress. They could, however, shorten the mattress's life because it provides an unyielding base.

MULTI-MECHANISM BEDS

These have adjustable head and leg sections, and are good for sufferers of high blood pressure or rheumatism, or for people who are bedridden; but they are expensive. They can be manually or automatically operated, and are easier for the less mobile to get in and out of.

BEDS FOR BABIES

A small baby can sleep in a crib, Moses basket, carry cot or a cot. (Babies should not sleep in a baby nest. They can suffocate or get too hot.)

A crib is a small cot and may rock on a frame. Make sure the stand for the crib is firm.

A Moses basket is a woven basket, lined with fabric. They should conform to BS 7551 1992. The lining should be secure with no loose folds which could smother the baby. Handles should be long enough to meet together above the basket. Do not use these once the baby can move unaided.

COTS

When your baby gets older – about four months – he/she can sleep in a cot or cot bed. Look for British Standard BS 1753 when choosing a cot to ensure it's safe.

Buying tips for cots

- When buying, check it's deep enough, so your baby can't climb out while still young. Most have bases which can be lowered as the child gets older. Initially, start on the highest setting (this saves bending). There should be at least 20in/49.5cm between the top of the mattress and the top of the cot. The overall size is about 48in/120cm x 24in/60cm.
- There should be no footholds in the sides or cut-outs where the baby could put feet, or trap arms, legs or head.
- Spaces between the bars should be between 1in/2.5cm and 2½in/6cm so that the baby cannot trap his/her head.
- If the cot has drop-down sides check the mechanism is secure and the baby should not be able to open it. Choose one where the sides do not come away completely, because if accidentally left down a child could roll off.
- If it has castors, check they are lockable.
- If you want extra storage space, some cots have roll-under drawers.
- Second-hand: make sure the fastening mechanism and the slats of the mattress base are all in good condition. Check side bars are not loose.

If repainting, make sure the new paint used is unleaded.

- The mattress should fit properly. Check it conforms to BS 1877 for safety, comfort and hygiene. The right side should be marked on the mattress or in the instructions. Often they have fabric on one side and PVC on the other.

There shouldn't be a gap of more than 1½in/4cm anywhere round the mattress.

Types include foam with ventilation holes which ensures a constant flow of air; natural fibre (often have a core of coconut fibres coated with waterproof latex and wrapped in cotton felt); springs are less common.

- Cot toys should not have strings longer than 12in/30cm, so they do not trap or strangle your baby. They should be firmly tied in position.

Once the baby can pull himself up, remove toys which are strung across the cot as they could strangle him.

- A cot bed, which converts from cot to first bed by removing the sides, will last a child up to the age of six. They are useful for bridging the gap between cot and first proper bed.

TIP Don't position a cot near curtains or anything that might help your baby climb out. Keep away from blinds that could strangle.

CHILDREN'S BEDS

- They need proper support for a growing spine so don't be tempted to give them a second-hand bed which is already imprinted with someone else's sleeping pattern. However, it is not worth spending a lot because they should be changed more frequently than an adult's bed, ideally every four to five years.

When the child is ready to leave the cot she should be bought a new bed.

- After a cot, a normal single may seem huge and frightening at first. Site the bed in a corner and position a bookcase down the other side for added security.
- Stacker beds, where one bed folds under the other, are useful when children have friends to stay. Choose a good-quality brand, even though only one is in constant use.
- Novelty beds are fun, but you may find you are paying for the gimmick rather than support and comfort. Remember they'll soon outgrow them.

BUNK BEDS

- A good choice if your child is over five.
- Safety must be one of the prime considerations. Check they conform to the European Standard EN 747.
- The top of the mattress should be at least 4in/10cm below the guard rail for safety.
- There should be two guards on the top bunk.
- There should be no gaps in their structure more than 3in/7.5cm wide, except of course for access between the guards to the top bunk, which should be between 12–16in/30–40cm wide. It's illegal for anyone to sell new or second-hand bunks with gaps wider than this.
- There should not be any rough or sharp edges or points.
- The frame must be robust because children will use it as a climbing frame.
- The ladder should be firmly fixed and capable of supporting an adult's weight. Flat rungs are more comfortable to climb than rounded ones.
- A slatted base ensures that the bed maker doesn't get hair trapped in the wire mesh.

BEDS FOR ELDERLY PEOPLE

Don't be guided into thinking it's not worth paying much because it doesn't need to last! It's important to choose a good-quality bed that's supportive with comfortable upholstery; wool would be the ideal.

- A firm bed is easier to sit up on than a soft one.
- Higher beds are easier to get in and out of.
- A firm-edged base may be more practical because they are often used for sitting on when dressing.

BEDS AND STORAGE

If you need extra cupboard space, storage divans are a good option. Choose between:

- Top-of-the-range models that have divan bases with springs. Different levels of support are available.

• Solid platform or slatted bases are more common. Use the manufacturer's recommended mattress.
• Ottoman-type storage beds hinge and open along one side or at the headboard end. A good solution if you haven't the space to pull out the drawers.

WATERBEDS

Modern waterbeds are a great improvement on the early models, but are still generally mistrusted and bear the brunt of many a joke.

Surprisingly, they have a very long history, dating back some 3,500 years. During the Second World War they were widely used for treating badly burned patients. They offer a number of other benefits:

• The body sleeps in weightless suspension.
• The displacement of water takes up the shape of the body.
• There are no pressure points so sleep is less disturbed.
• The bed won't harbour dust mites: a typical bed can house over two million.
• Heated models are relaxing and particularly good for those suffering from rheumatism and arthritis. The gentle application of heat can help relax muscles and spine.
• They don't sag or 'age' in the way a conventional bed does.
• Because of their support they are recommended for those with back problems and pregnant women.
• Don't need turning.

MATTRESS

A waterbed consists of a vinyl mattress, like an envelope or series of cylinders filled with water. The degree of firmness depends on the amount of water and water motion controls within the mattress. The motion controls depend on the type of mattress you choose. These vary according to the type of obstructions, reducing the energy movement of the water, or movement inhibitors included in the mattress.

Full flotation

Free flow with no control. Purely an envelope of water. Moves the most.

Semi-motionless and motionless

Movement is inhibited in various ways:

• A linked-chamber system, with chambers of water linked together but free to move inside the mattress, just like a duvet in a cover
• A captive coil, where the vinyl chambers are welded in position to the outer surfaces of the mattress.
• Incorporation of internal stabilisers, special synthetic fibres which prevent the water from moving about.
• Sausage-shaped vinyl cylinders that lay lengthways in the bed. Movement is more up and down
• In full-size models a dual mattress system is available to suit different requirements.

Water

Contains special softeners which keep the vinyl soft, and prevent the water from going sour by killing bacteria. This should be added every six months. You only need to change the water if you move house.

Separate mattresses

The British Waterbed Company (see Useful Addresses) manufactures a separate mattress which is designed to fit most types of bed frames or divan bases, and a portable Hydropad which fits on top of a regular mattress. These mattresses can be either hard sided or soft sided.

Hard sided: has a rigid frame, usually made of medium-density fibreboard or wood, into which the vinyl mattress fits. The advantage of this is that the frame can match your bedroom decor. The frame usually rests on a deck and plinth that supports the whole bed.
Soft sided: a new type that has fabric-covered foam sides so it looks more like a conventional divan set. It is also easier to get in and out of, and bedding is easy to fit.

Both types have an internal safety liner attached to the inside of the frame round the mattress. Under this is a low-wattage heater mat containing a thermostat which will maintain the water temperature at blood heat. The heater stays on for about two to three hours a day and uses the same amount of electricity as a 40-watt light bulb.

Some tube beds don't have heaters because they have extra insulation between the vinyl of the mattress and the person sleeping on it.

The frame sits on a pedestal which lifts the bed to a convenient height, approximately 21in/53cm.

INSTALLATION

Most water beds are installed by the manufacturer or retailer *in situ*. However, because they come flat packed and are reasonably straightforward to put together, you could tackle this yourself.

Filling the mattress can take time, particularly if your water pressure is low. If installed by professionals, they will bring along a pump to transfer water from your bath to the mattress at the correct temperature. If you do this yourself with a hosepipe from the sink then you need to alternate between hot and cold water.

DISPELLING WATERBED MYTHS

- A waterbed won't burst or leak even if the filler cap comes off. This is because it is a pressureless system. It is very rare for a waterbed to leak unless deliberately damaged.
- Even is the mattress is punctured the water will only leach out slowly into the bedding. The corners are reinforced and seams are strong. Mattresses are surrounded by a safety liner so spillages are held in this.
- Don't expect a waterbed to enhance your sex life! Sadly, it won't make any difference.
- It won't go crashing through the ceiling below, although heavier than a conventional bed. A double will be similar to eight people seated around a laden dining table. The tube beds are the lightest, and largest hard-sided beds are the heaviest. Most floors will take this weight because it is distributed over the whole area, not just on castors or legs.
- You won't feel seasick because the bed will only move when you do. There are no direct pressure points when you are sleeping, so you should find you turn over less.
- A waterbed isn't noisy, once all the air has been eliminated when installed. Like a radiator, some types may need 'bleeding' occasionally to remove the build-up of oxygen.
- Normal bedding can be used. If there is no mattress pad, a stitched-in quilted layer in addition to the mattress cover, use a blanket under the bottom sheet for comfort to absorb perspiration. Because the bed is heated to body temperature you will probably get away with a thinner duvet.

FUTONS

These have been the traditional form of bedding in Japan for centuries, used on the floor, then rolled up and stored during the day. In fact futon literally means a bed roll.

A futon is a light-weight mattress, originally filled with cotton and very thin, about

3in/8cm thick. They need to be thin so the air can circulate properly, which in turn is the reason for their springiness.

They can be used directly on the floor, but generally in the UK they are used with slatted bases. Often they are a good space-saving idea, used as a sofabed on a stacking slatted wood base, but are lower than conventional beds.

Normal bedding can be used.

FILLINGS

Cotton

Pure cotton is the usual filling, as:

- It's the firmest support.
- It allows the skin to breathe, offers good heat retention properties in the winter and keeps you cool in the summer.
- It is naturally resilient.

The cotton is carded and carefully inserted into the cotton weave case in three layers. This ensures that the cotton does not bunch up or become lumpy. The three layers are held in place by hand tufting with cotton thread. The futon should not be washed or dry cleaned.

Wool/cotton

Usually composed of 30 per cent wool and 70 per cent cotton. Compared to 100 per cent cotton it is:

- Softer to lie on.
- Lighter in weight and springier.
- More expensive.

Like cotton, this mixture should not be washed or dry cleaned.

Polyester

Futons made of 100 per cent polyester are soft, non-allergenic and washable.

SIZES

Different manufacturers have differing sizing systems but most are similar to standard bed sizes (see page 135). Most specialist manufacturers will make individual orders.

CHOOSING A FUTON

A futon will feel very firm at first.

Choose one in the same way you would a normal bed: lie on it and see if your back feels well supported. Check you can lie on your side comfortably without too many pressure points. Pay as much as you can afford if it is to be a permanent sleeping arrangement.

CARE

Futons should last as long as a conventional divan bed, as long as you follow the manufacturer's instructions.

Air it regularly, as the futon will absorb body moisture during the night. Airing will ensure the filling remains fluffy. Occasionally, air it outside, or draped over two chairs in front of an open window. Turn the futon weekly, to prevent the filling from compacting.

Only polyester-filled futons can be washed.

Treat spills immediately: isolate the area and use a spot remover treatment on the cover. It's worth buying a removable cover for the futon, which can be laundered.

CHOOSING BEDDING

There is a choice of bedding for every taste: from traditional blankets to high-tog duvets. Making an informed choice may help you achieve sweet dreams.

SHEETS AND PILLOWCASES

Bed linen can be made of a variety of different fibres, each of which have their pros and cons.

Linen

Cool and smooth to the touch, and durable, but you pay for the privilege. They are often finished off with a corded hem or hem stitch. An equally strong but cheaper alternative is linen union, 60 per cent linen blended with 40 per cent cotton. Be warned: they are hard work to iron.

Cotton

Tightly woven Egyptian cotton and cotton percale are the most common. Percale is in fact combed cotton, silky smooth and a similar weight to poplin. Cotton twill is a strong herringbone weave and slightly coarser.

Flannelette sheets are still available. Although they have an old-fashioned image their soft, fluffy surface can be comforting and warm in winter, as the raised surface traps air. Unlike cotton or poly-cotton they do not have a cold surface, so are pleasant to get in to on a cold night.

Polyester cotton

Usually a 50/50 blend, and probably the most popular type of bedding available, mainly due to its easy-care properties. If hung straight from the machine you don't really need to iron them. Poly-cotton percale costs about 20 per cent more, but uses combed cotton for a silkier finish. Cotton-rich blends, 80 per cent cotton to 20 per cent polyester, came into vogue with the recent trend back to natural fibres, but sacrifice some of the easy-care convenience.

BUYING GUIDE

- Look for a strong tight weave. Hold a single layer up to the light to check its density.
- Matching sets work out cheaper than buying separate items.
- Check sheet sizes. Make sure there is enough to cover the mattress, its sides plus another 8in/20cm to tuck in.
- It's worth paying more for top-quality bedding – for comfort. All fabrics will pill (tiny balls of fibres appear on the surface, due to rubbing when you toss and turn) but it is less noticeable with pure natural fibres. The pill drops off during wear and laundering and you won't notice it. Pilling is more noticeable (and uncomfortable) on poly-cotton bedding: the cotton bobble is held on by the stronger synthetic fibre.
- There's nothing worse than sheets that don't quite tuck in, and wrinkled sheets can lead to a disturbed night's sleep. Several companies (see below and Useful Addresses) offer made-to-measure bed linen, or supply sheeting so that you can make your own.

Acton & Acton supplies coloured cotton, poly-cotton and super percale poly-cotton including fitted sheets for round and oval beds. Will also use customer's own fabric.

Givan's Irish Linen Store supplies Irish linen sheeting in king-size widths to hem yourself.

Janet Turner Fine Linens specialises in hand hemstitched white or coloured Irish linen.

Keys of Clacton supply poly-cotton and super percale poly-cotton to include round and oval beds; also long valances and traditional candlewick bedspreads.

Limerick Linens supplies special-sized bed linen, and sheeting by the metre.

TIPS FOR USING BED LINEN

- Protect pillows from greasy hair by using cotton under-pillowslips and lightly starching the top pillowslip.
- Fold straight from the tumble drier or clothes line to cut down on ironing.
- Gently pull side edges while evenly damp to help pressing.
- Rotate clean bed linen.
- The airing cupboard isn't the best place for long-term storage, as constant warmth marks and discolours the fabrics. Instead, use strong polythene or blanket bags and keep in a cool, dry, well-ventilated place.

BLANKETS

Blankets are made in wool, cotton, cashmere, acrylic or thermolactyl chloride fibre, or a combination of these. Wool is the warmest.

Blankets offer an advantage over duvets in that they can be removed or added to a bed as demanded by the temperature. On the other hand, they are less convenient when bed making and soon look a mess.

Tog values are not given for blankets, but three good-quality blankets are roughly equivalent to a tog value of 13.5. Three blankets are needed on average, a combination of two cellular (open weave) and one solid (close weave) or vice versa. Cellular blankets are warmer than solid ones because air is easily trapped in the holes. Also, they are lighter than solid ones, giving more warmth for less weight.

Blankets are good sale bargains, but check the finish and the correct size for your bed. Choose a reputable manufacturer.

UNDERBLANKETS

Although your mattress may be quite warm in itself, a greater feeling of all-round warmth and comfort can be achieved by putting a conventional blanket or underblanket on the mattress, under the bottom sheet. Make sure it is fixed securely to avoid rucking or wrinkling during the night.

If you use a duvet and find you need to add extra bedding on top use a blanket underneath the duvet instead. This prevents the duvet filling from compacting and does not impede air circulation.

ELECTRIC BLANKETS

When buying a new blanket check it is BEAB approved (British Electrotechnical Approvals Board) and conforms to the British Standard BS 3456. It is illegal to sell an electric blanket without an over-heating protection system. Follow the manufacturer's instructions for use.

Most electric blankets have a thermostatic control which permits safe night use. They should be returned to the manufacturer every three years for servicing. (See Electric Blankets, page 337.)

Overblankets

As a general rule, when using an overblanket, you shouldn't need other bed clothes apart from a light covering such as a bedspread. Do not put duvets or blankets over the top.

Underblankets

These should not be used folded or creased, and must be tied securely to the mattress. On double beds, differing warmth levels can be obtained on each half of the bed to suit sleepers' requirements. Always switch off and unplug before getting into bed.

DUVETS

Blankets are now generally out of favour, with 70 per cent of British people owning at least one duvet.

Duvets provide warmth and comfort without being restrictive, and are more dust free than blankets. Early quilts were simply an envelope of fabric filled with a stuffing, but they had a major disadvantage in that the filling was free to wander, leaving cold patches in one place and over-filled ones in another. Now a more sophisticated type of construction uses channels or pockets which follow the way the body lies to keep the filling evenly distributed at all times.

Look out for the label indicating that the duvet complies with BS 5335: this means it reaches set standards in both manufacture and performance.

TOG RATINGS

Duvets are rated in togs which is a measurement for warmth, not weight. The higher the tog rating, the warmer the duvet is; but it is not necessarily of a higher quality – or value for money.

If you live in a centrally heated house you'll probably find a 10.5 to 12 tog-rated duvet is fine. However, if you don't have central heating or live in a cold climate, look for a 13.5-tog duvet. Fifteen-tog duvets are available but are far too hot for most people.

TOG RATINGS

Summer 4.5, 6.0, 7.5

Mid-Season 9.0, 10.5

Winter 12.0, 13.5, 15.0

SIZE

Always measure your bed before you actually buy a duvet.

The duvet should be wider by 14in/35cm for a single, 26in/65cm for a double, and 30in/75cm for a king-size bed.

The length shouldn't be less than the length of the bed, and if you're taller than 6ft/1.8m, look for a 7ft 2in/220cm duvet.

FILLINGS

The important part of a duvet is the air inside it and how the filling traps it. This air, and moisture, control the temperature, as well as the duvet's softness.

When choosing a filling you need to consider how quickly it compresses; how resilient and durable it is; how good is its insulating efficiency and breathability. The ideal duvet has a light and fluffy filling which traps warm air.

In general, the better the quality of the duvet the less filling is required, which means it has a light weight to volume ratio. For example, a 13.5-tog goose-down duvet (best quality) is not as heavy as a 10.5-tog polyester-filled one.

Down can absorb 11.5 per cent moisture given off by the body during the night; feathers can absorb 12.5 per cent, and wool 14 per cent.

This moisture is slowly evaporated off so there is no excessive or rapid loss of warmth from the body, leaving it feeling cold. However, with polyester, although the latest fibres have improved, there is a quick evaporation of moisture which may lead to the body feeling chilly. As well, polyester quilts do not hug the body as effectively as natural fillings, so allow warm air to escape and cold draughts to enter.

Down

This is taken from ducks or geese, or is a mixture of the two. Down is a spherical plumule of thousands of soft fibres. Unlike feathers, which are used for flying, down traps the air at high altitude and low temperature with a minimum of weight.

The colour of the down (the feathers) doesn't make any difference to the quality, although white is usually marketed as a premium product. Duck down or feathers are a lower-priced alternative to goose down and feathers. As a general rule, the greater the proportion of feathers the cheaper and heavier the duvet will be. Always check the label carefully because the percentage of down to feathers does vary.

Choose pure down if you want a warm, light-weight duvet with excellent draping properties. However, it is expensive, because only ½oz/13g of down can be collected from each bird.

Down duvets are very durable: they will last up to four times longer than a polyester one.

Down and Feather

These mustn't contain less than 51 per cent down. This is a good alternative if you can't stretch to an all-down duvet. Still extremely light and warm.

Down and feathers cost more than synthetic fillings, but should last longer.

Feather and Down

These must contain a minimum of 15 per cent down. They will feel heavier than down and feather duvets so will suit you if you prefer a heavier weight of bed covering. However, they may also feel stiffer, depending on the type of feathers used. Some lower-quality duvets may contain chicken feathers which can be uncomfortably scratchy.

Other natural fillings

Wool is becoming more common and other luxurious fillings include silk and cashmere. Wool tends to be slightly heavier and firmer than the others. Brinkhaus (see Useful Addresses) manufacture luxury silk and wool-filled duvets.

Synthetic fillings

Usually made from layers of polyester fibres. They will not feel as light as natural fillings and don't mould round the body as well. However, they are quite fluffy and springy although they could compress slightly after being washed.

They are generally cheaper than natural fillings and make a good choice for children because they are easily washable. Also, they are suitable for people who have an allergy to down and feathers.

Different qualities are available: the more you pay the better. Fillings are split into solid polyester fibres, and hollow fibres which are a better quality. As the name implies, there is a gap in the middle of the fibres which holds air making a lighter filling without sacrificing any of the warmth.

Look for branded fillings such as Du Pont, Quallofil, ICI, etc. Avoid packaging which does not specify the type of filling.

Top-quality polyester fibres are siliconised, giving them the softest feel, and best imitating the softness of down.

ALL-SEASONS DUVETS

If your duvet is just right for winter but you find yourself too hot in summer it's worth considering an all-seasons duvet. This gives you three options depending on the weather. They consist of a thick (around 9 tog) and thin (4.5 tog) duvet which can be used separately or joined together for extra warmth.

CASINGS

Casings for naturally filled duvets must have a tight weave to prevent feathers and down from escaping. The fabric must also be able to breathe and allow free air circulation. Most are 100 per cent cotton and should be able to withstand washing without shrinking. Top-quality casings are made from fine Egyptian cotton. If you choose a polyester-cotton cover, it will shrink less, but will not be as absorbent, and therefore breathe as well.

CONSTRUCTION

Methods of construction vary depending on the quality and type of filling used.

Stitched-through channels: generally used for synthetic duvets, it's the simplest and cheapest method. The cover is sewn all the way through the layers to hold the filling in place. However, this has the disadvantage that cold spots can occur along the lines of stitching.

Intermittent stitching: patterns are stitched at regular intervals. If there is too much stitching there will be many cold spots, but insufficient stitching means the filling can move around.

Double construction: duvets are made from two layers of channelled polyester, enclosed within the cover and stitched through only around the edges. This eliminates the danger of cold areas.

Walled channels: often used with natural fillings. Inner walls are sewn between the two sides to form the channels. Unfortunately, the filling is free to move around and it tends to travel down the duvet. However, a useful feature in summer because you can shake the filling down.

Walled pockets: the duvet is divided into cassette or pocket-shaped sections which keep the filling in place without thin cold spots. Often used for top-quality duvets.

PILLOWS

However good your mattress, you still need support for your head.

A quick test to check if your pillow needs replacing is to lay it across your hand. If it droops over each side it is time to think about a new one.

Quality is determined by the speed at which a pillow regains its original shape after being depressed. When purchasing, test natural-filled pillows by laying them flat on a surface and pressing firmly in the centre. When pressure is removed the dent should fill out quickly, regaining at least half of its original shape.

The degree of firmness is a personal choice and depends on the way you sleep. If you sleep on your side, choose a firm one; if on your back choose a medium one, and if on your stomach, a very soft pillow.

WHICH FILLING?

As a general rule, natural-filled pillows will mould to the shape of your head better than synthetic ones. Synthetic ones tend to give firmer support.

- Unbranded foam rubber or crumb fillings are the cheapest, but don't expect them to last more than two to three years.
- Latex is more resilient, retains its shape well, can be moulded to fit the contours of the head and is non-allergenic.
- Polyester filled, also non-allergenic, vary in quality and support. Give a firmer, flatter pillow.
- Some pillows contain hollow-fibre polyester which is fluffier than the ordinary type. Look for branded polyester such as Dacron Hollofil, Quallofil or Aerelle.
- A relatively new type of polyester, Comforel, consists of millions of polyester

balls which allow good air circulation and recovery after use. Depending on the quality, a branded polyester pillow will last from five to ten years.

- Duck down and feather pillows offer the best support and recovery. Avoid poultry feathers as these are the least comfortable, although usually the cheapest.
- An all-down pillow would be too soft for most people.

COVERS

Coverings for natural-filled pillows are usually downproof sateen twill or cotton cambric. Synthetic fillings are usually enclosed in cotton or polyester-cotton covers.

Check for strong seams.

TIPS FOR USING PILLOWS

- Plump up your pillows frequently to avoid the filling compacting.
- Follow care instructions. Laundering should be kept to a minimum as it can reduce the life of a pillow.
- Wash the pillow occasionally. Never dry clean, because of the fumes from the solvents used during the dry-cleaning process.
- Natural fillings tend to wash better than synthetic ones, which can become lumpy.

NON-ALLERGENIC BEDS AND BEDDING

Doctors believe that 80 per cent of allergic asthma is irritated by house-dust mites. These microscopic creatures live on dead skin cells that make up 80 per cent of household dust. Obviously, they live in carpets and upholstery, but the vast majority thrive in beds and bedding, which provide the perfect habitat with plenty of dead skin cells and moisture. The older the bed obviously the more dust mites there are. In fact, medical evidence leans to the possibility that a child's first allergic attack may be triggered by dustmites hidden in the bed.

For non-allergenic beds choose a foam or polyester-fibre mattress. Alternatively, if you prefer natural materials, latex foam is a good choice. Waterbeds are also worth considering.

A tenth of the weight of your comfy old pillow could be dead skin cells, mould, dead mites and mite droppings. Unfortunately it's impossible to achieve a totally dust-free bedroom, but you could try encasing the mattress and pillow with a special microporous cover. This allows perspiration through but keeps mites and dropping out.

Covers should preferably be used on a new mattress. Otherwise, air the mattress and pillow thoroughly first.

Brands to look for (see Useful Addresses) include:

- Intervent: Allergen Exclusion Bedding System, which wipes clean. Mattress System includes pillow, mattress and duvet interliner, available from Boots.
- Banamite Anti-Allergy Bedding, machine washable at 140°F/60°C. Complete bedding kit includes pillow, mattress cover and duvet, from Medivac.
- Allerayde cotton/poly-cotton covers washable at 140°F/60°C. Bed kit includes pillowcase, mattress and duvet covers.
- Alprotec covers, machine washable at 140°F/60°C. Bed kit includes pillowcase, mattress, duvet covers, from Advanced Allergy Technologies.
- Medibed Anti-Allergy Bedding, machine washable at 140°F/60°C. Can be made to measure. Bed pack includes pillows, mattress barrier and duvet.
- Holden Medical One-in-Four Protector and Protector Plus complete bedding system

(pillow, mattress, duvet covers for all bed sizes and cots). Hand washable at 100°F/40°C. All available from Holden Medical Ltd.

TIPS TO COMBAT ALLERGIES

- Keep the bedroom well ventilated to keep the humidity down.
- Air the bed daily and wash bedding frequently at temperatures over 130°F/55°C.
- Vacuum your bed regularly using the upholstery nozzle, remembering to keep the window open when cleaning.

BEDDING FOR BABIES

Don't assume that babies are more susceptible to cold than they really are. It's just as dangerous to overdress them as to underdress. They do need to be warmly dressed in their first few weeks, but after this they are very good at keeping themselves warm. A young baby cannot kick off the covers if they are too hot. Feeling the baby's tummy is a good guide to how warm he is, even though the hands and feet may be cold.

Research has shown than too a high a temperature may be one of the contributory causes of cot death or Sudden Infant Death Syndrome (SIDS). Obviously, the bedding you use will affect your baby's temperature.

Blankets and sheets

These are best, because you can vary the combinations according to the baby's temperature (not the room temperature).

Use a sheet to cover the mattress and one between the baby and blankets. Combine cellular and solid blankets according to the baby's needs. Avoid open-weave blankets as they can trap the baby's fingers.

Cot duvets

Use on their own with a duvet cover. These are marked with a tog rating, which is a measure of their insulating properties. A cot-size duvet is not recommended for babies under 12 months as they could suffocate.

Cot quilts

Unlike duvets, these don't need a separate cover and are designed for use with sheets and blankets. Use as many layers or combinations as are appropriate for your baby.

Pillows

Not recommended for babies under twelve months because of the dangers of suffocation.

Cot bumpers

Useful to avoid draughts and bumps. Ensure they conform to BS 1877 and do not use once your baby can sit unaided as it could be used as a foothold to climb out of the cot. Ties should not be longer than 10in/25cm, should not fray, and must be securely sewn to the bumper and attached to the cot. Try to avoid your baby sleeping with his head against the bumper as this may prevent natural heat loss.

Baby nests

Babies should not be allowed to sleep in these, but they are useful for carrying babies inside and out up to the age of five months. Check it conforms to BS 6595.

Do not leave your baby unattended in a baby nest.

SOFT FURNISHINGS

Creating your individual style with soft furnishings can be an exciting process of experimentation: looking at different ways to combine colour, texture and form. Fabrics can be combined to create stunning effects, and often the simplest is the most dramatic.

For visual appeal, try plain fabrics with striped borders; look at different light effects; layer translucent fabrics with opaques; and try combining different weights and weaves. You can even design your own fabrics by making use of fabric paints and stencils on muslin or plain cotton lawn.

FURNISHING FABRICS

When choosing fabrics, price and design are not the only factors you need to bear in mind. Consider:

- Which room they are to go in. Is it a feminine bedroom, an all-purpose family room or a utilitarian kitchen? Does the room face north/east, with little sun or south/west, with plenty of sun?
- How hard wearing the fabric needs to be.
- Draping characteristics.
- Resistance to fading and mildew.
- Ease of cleaning. Some areas (such as the kitchen) will require more frequent cleaning than others, so opt for washable fabric rather than dry clean only.

BUYING FABRIC

- Have with you a sample of your wallpaper, plus colour charts and upholstery swatches for colour matching.
- Patterned fabric:

Check the pattern is printed correctly throughout the length you require.

A pattern woven into the fabric rather than printed on is more likely to resist fading.

Small or random patterning works out cheaper because you waste less matching pattern repeats.

Indian or hand-printed patterns are more irregular.

Allow one pattern repeat for each drop or length.

- Always try draping the fabric in the shop: you get a better idea of texture and effects of light on colours and patterns, and how translucent the fabric is.
- If the fabric is washable, allow for 10 per cent shrinkage, and wash the fabric at least twice before making up. Some fabrics may have been treated with a shrink-resistant finish. Check at point of purchase. Ready-made curtains include 5 per cent extra for shrinkage.
- Check the fabric is fade resistant. Curtains, for example, are constantly exposed to sunlight.

TIPS FOR USING PATTERNED FABRIC

- Centre the pattern for each width of curtain.
- Match up across the width.
- Parallel or horizontal lines need to be aligned with the walls and ceiling rather than furniture.
- To check the direction of the pattern, look at the selvedge. There may be directional arrows to guide you; otherwise, in the case of flowers, think about the natural way they would grow.
- Even random patterning may have some order. Stand well back and check all the lines of the pattern.

- Buy all the fabric you need for matching cushions, etc, at the same time as your curtain fabric, as batch colours may vary.
- Don't skimp on the amount of fabric because this can spoil the draping effect.
- Traditionally, curtains have been full length (drop to ½in/1cm above the floor) or sill length (leave ½in/1cm short of the window sill to avoid dust and condensation). Currently, it's quite fashionable to have long curtains that trail on the ground by about 4in/10cm, for an opulent feel.

FABRIC WEIGHT

Lightweights (cotton and poly-cottons) suit bathrooms and kitchens. In living rooms and bedrooms, use lining and interlining to improve the curtains' drape, insulation and light exclusion.

Hem weights help the curtains to hang properly. Sew weights into mitred corners and hem, or lay lead tape into the hem fold and secure it at intervals.

Heavier-weight fabrics and tighter weaves offer better insulation, but can be heavy to hang if lined. Check your curtain rail will support the weight.

TYPES OF FABRIC

Brocade

Woven with an embroidered, textured look. Made of silk, viscose or synthetic fibres.

Chintz

Tightly woven cotton with a shiny chemical glaze that drapes well. Don't hang in areas prone to dirt because the finish may wash off and fade. Once the glaze goes it cannot be replaced. Some companies will clean, re-build existing chintz finish and re-hang. Contact the Dry Cleaning Information Bureau for details (see Useful Addresses).

Cotton

Closer weaves are more hard wearing and crisp. Most cottons drape well, but fade and shrink unless specially treated. Cottons can almost always be washed, but may lose some body and colour.

Treatments for crease resistance, flame proofing and stain repellency are often applied to cotton.

Dupion

Generally made from synthetic fibres, and because of its slubbed appearance, looks like wild silk. It frays badly, so allow extra for seams and hems and overlock raw edges soon after cutting.

Gingham

Identical on both sides so saves on lining, unless of course you want to add extra weight to improve the drape. Will shrink.

Linen

Can be glazed or printed. Linen creases badly but can be treated to minimise this.

Tapestry

Lightweight tapestries drape better than heavy weights. Need regular vacuuming as they trap dust easily.

Velvet

Synthetic (Dralon) and cotton. Hang so that the pile runs down the length both to avoid the build-up of dust and to show off the sheen.

The denser the pile the more durable they will be. They crease at first but will hang out after several weeks; do not hem until after this initial period.

Dralon, unlike cotton velvet, is colourfast to light and moisture, but it should never be ironed or the pile will be ruined.

TIP When sewing velvet seams, sandwich tissue paper between the two pile surfaces to prevent slipping.

LININGS

These help the drape and general appearance of the main curtain fabric. They can be permanent or detachable. If they are stitched permanently in position it's wise to dry clean the curtains. Otherwise the top fabric may shrink at a different rate than the lining, causing puckering.

Lining also protects a curtain from sunlight, which can fade and rot the fabric; dust and dirt; and condensation, which can cause brown staining.

Cotton sateen is the most common fabric, in cream or white, for deflecting the heat of sunlight. It is tightly woven and keeps its shape. Contrasting, fade-resistant coloured linings are available. These add depth of colour to the main curtain.

Don't line curtains that will need to be washed, such as those in kitchens and bathrooms, and nets and sheers.

WARMING WAYS

With up to a quarter of heat escaping through the window it's surprising that most of us don't make the most of our curtains.

THERMAL LINING

A pair of thick or thermally lined curtains can be as effective as double glazing. All thermal linings work by reflecting heat back into a room, saving up to 17 per cent more heat than unlined curtains, and on the same principle keep the room cool in the summer. The reflective/coated side should be hung away from the window, with the reflective side facing into the room.

Pros
- Protect fabric and upholstery from fading.
- Dim the light coming into the room, but do not provide complete blackout.
- Provide heat insulation.

Cons
- Some types can be seen through lightweight and coarse-weave curtaining. Milium, for example, gives off a grey hue.

Types of thermal lining

Aluminium backed Also known as Milium, consists of tiny aluminium particles which are coated onto a sateen or plain cotton fabric.

WARMING TIPS

- Make your curtains long, to rest on the floor or sill to create a seal. Place lead weights in the hem to keep the curtain anchored.
- Make your curtains at least two widths of window.
- Hang so the sides touch the wall. If possible, use adhesive Velcro to attach them to the wall.
- Interline the curtain, or use a thermal lining.
- Make linings detachable so they can be removed in the summer.
- Beware of using net curtains on south-facing windows as they can deflect sunlight which would be a valuable addition to your heating.
- To preserve heat, close the curtains at night, an hour before it gets dark (even in unheated rooms).
- In winter, keep curtains closed in rooms you do not use and that do not get the sun.

The silver shield is very effective in reflecting both heat and light. In certain circumstances some fabrics of this type will provide up to 57 per cent reduction in heat loss compared with a bare window.

Should be dry cleaned only.

Available from specialist curtain shops and department stores.

TIP Use a sharp needle when sewing as the yarns tend to separate where threads are pulled through.

Acrylic/Polyester Cotton, or blends of polyester and cotton, which have been flocked with a dense compound of acrylic or polyester. These coatings are very supple and have a velvety feel. The properties are similar to milium, but it is not quite as effective an insulator.

Available in neutral shades such as white, ivory and cream.

Should be mostly dry cleaned, but some are washable, so check on purchase.

TIP Use a sharp needle when sewing to avoid holes forming.

BLACK-OUT LININGS

These have all the properties of thermal linings but are also impermeable to light. They are ideal for darkening children's rooms during light evenings in the summer, or for shift workers. They also act as a noise buffer, which is useful if you live near a railway or main road. They are very heavy and do not drape as well as thermal linings because of their plastic-like feel.

Black-out linings are similar to acrylic thermal linings, but have more layers, technically known as 'passes'. To be termed a black-out the fabric must have at least three passes. Some brands are also treated with a flame-retardant finish.

Most must be dry cleaned.

TIP Black-out linings are easy to sew by machine and do not fray readily. They are very thick fabrics, so if you are sewing them by hand, make sure your needle goes all the way through the layers.

INTERLINING

This must be used between the main curtain and the normal lining. It gives body to the curtain, and makes it hang better, especially with very thin fabrics such as satin and silk. For insulation, interlining is comparable to thermal lining, but it is not opaque enough to act as a black-out.

If a curtain is interlined it must be dry cleaned, even if the main fabric is washable.

There are various types and weights:

Bump

Coarsely woven brushed-cotton fabric similar in appearance to a blanket. It is very thick to sew, particularly at the top where the heading tape is sewn on.

TIP Check that your curtain track or pole can take the weight of curtains that have been interlined with bump.

Domette

Pure, brushed cotton, similar in appearance to a flannelette sheet. Is thinner than bump, so is easier to handle and sew.

Raised interlining

A bonded fabric made from 90 per cent viscose and 10 per cent polyamide. It has all the advantages of the other two types but it is thinner, so much easier to handle.

STAIN-RESISTANT TREATMENTS

To help keep your soft furnishings in top condition it's worth having the fabrics specially treated for stain resistance, or to buy pre-treated upholstery or fabric.

HOW THEY WORK

Stain-resistant treatments act like an invisible shield by preventing spilt liquids being absorbed before you've time to mop them up. You do still have to remove spills, but if you act quickly enough, permanent staining will be prevented. You'll also find the general grime from normal use is slower to build up.

When buying this sort of treatment, check the warranty being offered: some include the services of a professional cleaner. Before employing a cleaning firm or retailer offering this treatment, check they have undergone specialist training.

You can have existing furniture treated, but the protection will not be generally as good as when new fabrics are treated.

Two methods of treatment to look for:

Fluorochemicals

Form a protective layer that resists both oil and water-based stains. Spilt liquid forms droplets on the surface, giving you time to mop them up: about 10 minutes. The fabric is treated during manufacture, or in your home by a licensed applicator. Pre-treated fabric offers better protection than most treatments *in situ.*

Brands to look for (see Useful Addresses):

Pre-treated Fabrics: Crowguard from Crowson, Teflon from Du Pont, Scotchgard Protector from 3M.

In situ: Guardian from Service Master; Scotchgard from Scotchcare.

Copolymer resin

This coats or penetrates the fabric fibres, preventing spills from being absorbed. The resin is sprayed on to the finished fabric either in the shop or by a licensed cleaner in your home. Any spilt liquid is not absorbed for about 10 minutes.

Brands to look for (see Useful Addresses): Guardsman from Safeclean.

CHOOSING A SEWING MACHINE

The latest machines bear little resemblance to Isaac Singer's traditional black and gold machine of the 1800s. Computer technology has brought the sewing machine industry back to life and unearthed myriad home-sewing possibilities.

Today's machines have sophisticated functions which are easy to use, allowing you to concentrate on the work, not on the controls. They are becoming more user-friendly, with built-in sewing advice, and the operating manual is becoming more of a design handbook than an instructor.

TYPES OF MACHINE

Utility/basic machines

Will produce all the commonly used stitches such as straight stitch, zigzag, buttonhole, blind hemming and several stretch stitches.

Automatic machines

Can produce a variety of automatic embroidery patterns.

In early models, cams were inserted to extend the range of patterns available; most are now built in. They will generally include a selection of utility stitches, decorative stitches and an automatic buttonhole.

Good features include a range of stretch

stitches, variable needle positions, extra-wide needle swing and easily changed, clip-on feet.

Overlockers

Operated like conventional machines but will overcast, seam and trim raw edges, in one operation, to provide a neat professional finish.

They will not replace a conventional machine, but are ideal for basic stitches for seams and seam finishes, stitching seams with built-in stretch (such as on knit fabrics), rolled hems and decorative flat-lock stitches.

Threading can be complicated as they can take from two to five threads, so an initial demonstration is essential.

Electronic machines

Include speed control, to give jerk-free starting, greater needle penetration power and greater stitch control. The electronics will allow you to maintain a constant sewing speed whatever the fabric thickness.

Some machines will stop automatically with the needle in and out of the work. Several models have push button controls and digital displays for depicting the stitch size and width that has been selected.

Computer machines

Controlled by a microprocessor or chip which governs stitch selection, programming and memory functions, buttonhole formation and tension control. Stitches or patterns are selected either by:

- Push buttons and LED indication beside an image on the display panel.
- Numerical, digital selection by push button.
- Sensorised touch control panel.

Computerised machines have similar functions to traditional machines with some interesting extras. These include mirror-imaging (pattern can be turned over or reversed), visual stitch displays, memory banks, and the ability to elongate patterns. Stitch sequences can be built into a pattern and stored until recalled. The trend is towards total creativity: your own designs can be scanned into the machine's memory.

Stitch selection is simplified because width, length and tension are automatically chosen.

POINTS TO CONSIDER WHEN CHOOSING

- Good selection of basic stitches and range of stitch lengths and widths. If you are a keen sewer pre-set widths or lengths can be restrictive unless they have a manual override.
- Look for clear colour-coded controls for easy selection of stitch, width and length.
- Most machines have a free-arm sewing area for cuffs and sleeves plus an extension to convert to a flat-bed sewing area, useful when sewing large items such as curtains.
- An integral accessory box within the body of the machine. These are getting more and more ingenious and handy.
- Good range of presser feet for buttonholing, overcasting, zips and hemming. Easy to clip on or press on. Many others are available as optional extras, for example 'walking feet' for sewing difficult fabrics such as velvet, which creeps, and sheer fabrics that slip. A walking foot or Teflon-coated foot will feed both top and bottom layers of material through the machine together, eliminating this problem. Some machines have this facility built in (eg dual-feed from Pfaff).
- If you are a keen dressmaker, a good buttonhole mechanism is essential.

With the more basic machines you turn a control for each step of the buttonhole, whereas computer models will do this in one step; you don't have to turn the garment around half-way through the buttonhole.

The size of the hole needed for the button can be programmed into the machine's memory to obtain a series of identical holes.

Some machines will do differently shaped buttonholes, eg square or rounded ends.

- Auto-stop bobbin rewind is common to most machines to prevent the bobbin from over-filling.
- With some machines you can refill the bobbin without unthreading the machine.
- Transparent bobbin covers are useful so you can check how much bottom thread you have left, useful if you are about to start a long seam or intricate top-stitching.
- Check the machine has good height on the presser-foot lever, to give a little extra lift for fitting bulky fabric under or manoeuvring over thick seams.
- A range of needle positions ensures that the needle can be moved to various positions for straight stitching, stretch stitching, top stitching, etc.
- Needle stop up/down. Useful to have needle which stops in down position for embroidery, appliqué top stitching.
- Auto lock-off automatically finishes off.
- Easy threading systems.
- Full rotary hook ensures smooth and jam-proof sewing.

BUYING TACTICS

- Shop around. Mail-order and cash and carry may be cheaper, but remember you cannot try out the machines and after-sales service is more difficult to organise. Department stores and dealers will give you the best advice and after-sales service. All dealers who are members of the Sewing Machine Trade Association (SMTA, see Useful Addresses) will give the machine a pre-purchase check.
- Consider the type of sewing you do. There is no point buying a hi-tech computer model just for occasional mending.
- Consider weight and size. How portable do you want the machine to be? Compact machines are much lighter but will have smaller dials and controls. They offer a smaller sewing area and may not be as stable when sewing heavier-weight fabrics.
- Try out several different machines. Take some fabric along with you (heavyweight and sheer). Make sure you feel comfortable with the controls.
- Examine the stitch formation carefully, particularly the underside. Try satin stitching and buttonholes, often the most difficult to perfect.
- Check type of after-sales service available and the location of repair outlets.
- Some manufacturers run sewing schools – it's worth having instruction if buying a computer model or overlocker.
- It may be worth buying a better-quality second-hand model rather than a cheap new one, but check the guarantees as these vary from dealer to dealer. Look out for older top-of-the-range models which keen sewers are replacing with new computerised models. Buy from a recognised dealer. (The SMTA will give you a list.)

WINDOW TREATMENTS

Keep the dressing sympathetic to the period of the house and other decor in the room.

- Tall windows can be elegant and generous. Curtains should be floor length with a pelmet.
- Smaller windows should be simple; treatments like swags would be too overpowering.
- Curtains hung within a recessed window will block out valuable light. Fit blinds instead.

- If the window abuts a wall or furniture, blinds let in more light than curtains. Alternatively, opt for a single drape, tied back at one side. If there is space for a pair of curtains have the finial at one side only.
- If there is a radiator beneath a window do not block it with heavy curtains. Fit a blind and fixed dress curtains on either side.
- Pivot windows open horizontally or vertically. For privacy, attach net rods at both ends of the frame. The surround can be dressed using any style.
- Sloping windows: use a roller blind with a side-winding mechanism, and anchor it at the lower edge. Alternatively, have wooden poles at both top and bottom of the window. Head the curtains at the top and the bottom and attach them to the poles.
- A third of homes have bay or bow windows (see Curtain Poles and Tracks, page 404).
- For fixed curtains on arched windows, try using Rufflette's Press 'n Drape: an adhesive tape sticks to the wall or a wooden batten so you don't need to fix a track or pole (see Useful Addresses). The heading, sewn on to the curtain, is then pressed on to the wall tape. The curtain can be held back with tie-backs.

HOW TO MAKE CURTAINS

FABRIC QUANTITY

1 Measure the width of the curtain track.
2 Multiply the width by the figure below that corresponds to the type of heading tape:

Standard gathered:	1½
Pencil pleats:	2½
Pinch Pleats:	2–2½
Triple Pleats:	2–2½
Smocked, goblet, Tudor ruff, box pleat:	2– 2¼

3 Divide this figure by the width of the fabric and this will give you the number of widths of fabric required.
4 Measure the length required.
Sill-length curtains: either add 2–4in/5–10cm, or if the sill protrudes, deduct ¾in/1.5cm so that they stop just above the sill.
Radiator-length curtains: measure to the top of the radiator and deduct ¾in/1.5cm so the curtain will not touch the hot radiator.
Floor-length curtains: measure from the top of the track to the floor and deduct ¾in/1.5cm to stop the curtain from dragging and the hem from wearing.
Hem and top turning: add an extra 6in/15cm to each length: this allows for 2in/5cm at the top and a double 2in/5cm hem at the bottom.
Patterned fabric: measure the repeat and add this amount to each length, except the first, to allow for matching.
5 Multiply this by the number of widths and you'll have the total length of fabric required.

PREPARING THE FABRIC

1 Straighten the raw edges along the grain of the fabric: snip about 1in/2.5cm into the selvedge at right angles to the edge. Tear or pull out a loose weft (widthways) thread from the snip to the opposite edge and cut along the resulting line.
2 Check the grain is straight by pulling on the bias until the fabric is smooth and flat and all the corners form right angles.
3 Press the fabric.

CUTTING OUT

Plain
Measure the length first, keeping the tape measure parallel to the selvedge. Mark the cutting line or pull a thread. Cut along the marked line.

Cut all the lengths in the same way.

Patterned

Mark the bottom of the pattern with tailor's chalk. Make sure that after allowing for hem turnings the bottom of the pattern will lie on the hem edge. Trim off surplus fabric, then cut out as above.

Reposition the uncut fabric next to the previous cut lengths so that the two match exactly. Repeat until all lengths are cut.

To cut half widths, fold one length in half lengthways, pinning selvedge to selvedge. Cut along the fold with sharp scissors.

TIP Half widths should be attached to curtain on the outer edges.

UNLINED CURTAINS

You will need

- Curtain fabric
- Heading tape
- Curtain hooks
- Sharp scissors
- Pins, needles and thread
- Tape measure

1 Cut away the selvedge at each side of all the widths. A tightly woven selvedge left attached to the material will cause the seams to pucker when the curtain is finished.

2 **Plain fabrics:** with right sides together, align two lengths, matching the raw edges. Pin and tack down one long side, allowing ⅝in/1.5cm seam allowance.

Patterned fabrics: the pattern must match exactly before stitching. Work from the right side of the fabric, and tack the widths together.

3 Using matching thread, stitch all the tacked seams using flat seams

TIP Support the fabric on a large table when sewing.

4 Turn in the side edges about ¾in/2cm and press. Turn up the hem about 2in/5cm and

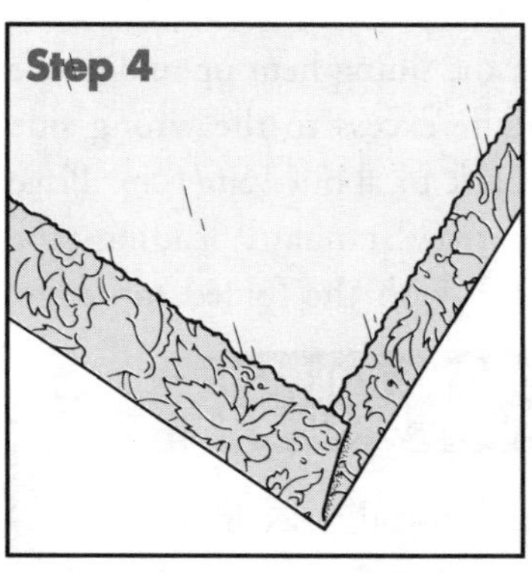

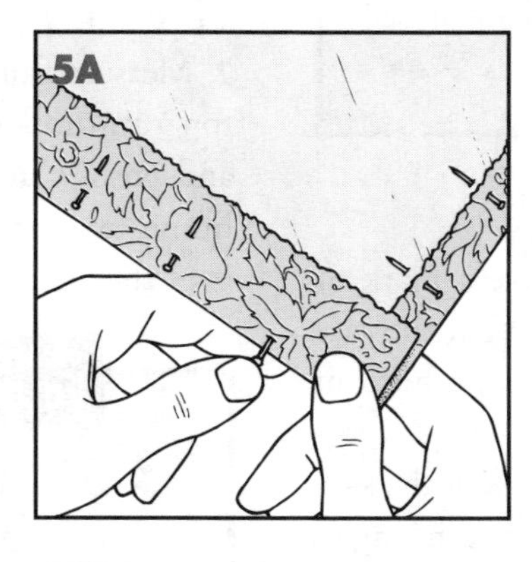

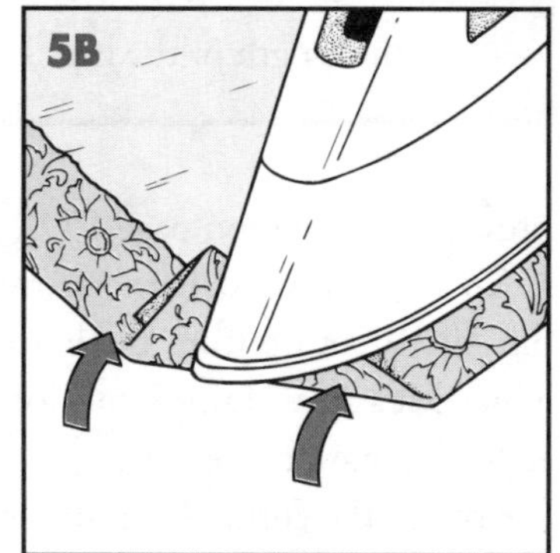

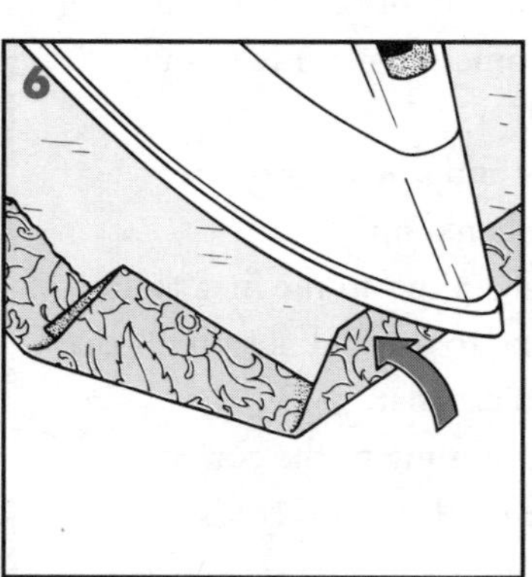

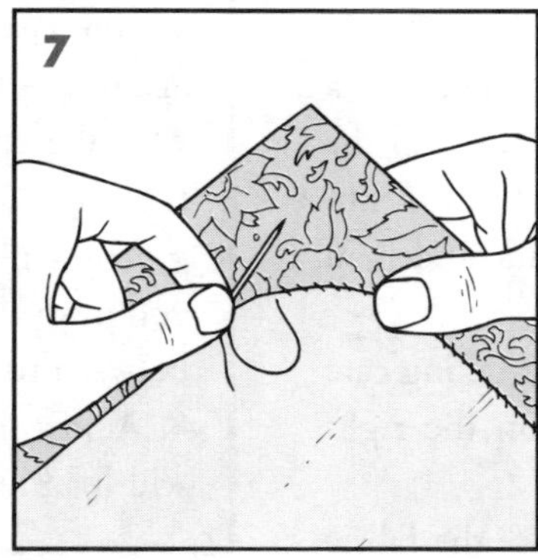

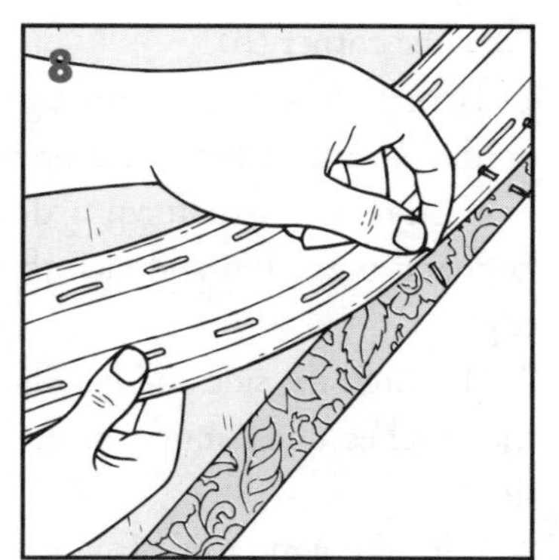

SEWING HEADING TAPE

- Always sew the top and bottom edges of the tape in the same direction, to avoid puckering.
- Always buy a little more tape than you need to allow for position of pleats.
- When buying deep heading tape, choose ones with 3 or 4 cords for pulling up, as this is easier and gives a more even result.
- When you've pulled up the cords, don't cut off the ends. Use a cord tidy, available from curtain shops or haberdashery departments, or wind up the excess, or make a cleat. You need to let out the cords when cleaning the curtain.
- Use five hooks to every 12in/30cm of tape for good support.
- To add body to sheer fabric insert Vilene or non-woven interfacing material along the length of the heading.

press (see illustration page 159).

5 **To make mitred corners:** make a mark or pin 4in/10cm up from the bottom, at the side edge. Measure 1½in/4cm along the bottom edge and mark or pin (A).

Fold in the corner from the mark at the side and bottom edge to form an uneven angle. Press the corner (B).

6 Turn in the side seam again to form a double ¾in/2cm hem, and press. Turn up the hem edge again to form a double 2in/5cm hem and press. Pin and tack the side and hem edges.

7 Slipstitch the side and base hems taking care the stitches don't show through on the right side.

8 With the wrong side facing, place the fabric flat and measure the length up from the hem edge. Turn over the excess at the top and press flat. Trim back to around 1¼in/3cm. On the wrong side, position the curtain tape on the folded top edge. Pin and tack.

DETACHABLE LINING

You will need

- Lining fabric
- Heading tape
- Press studs and ¼in/5mm-wide tape

or

- Tape and touch-and-close (Velcro) fastening
- Scissors, thread, pins, tape measure, etc

Calculate the quantity of fabric as for unlined curtains (see Fabric Quantity, page 158), but deduct about 1in/2.5cm from the length.

The lining should be 1½ to 2 times the curtain track length.

1 Make as for unlined curtains, steps 1 to 7: see page 159.

2 Measure from the lining hem up and at the top turn under the excess to the wrong side and press. Cut back to about ½in/1cm. Place lining tape or narrow standard heading tape over the top, flush with the folded top edge.

HOW TO PULL UP CURTAIN HEADINGS

- Knot the ends together securely.
- Anchor over a door handle or table leg so you have something sturdy to pull against.
- Pull evenly and slowly until the heading is gathered up.
- Triple pleats: pleat up the first pleat, and push along to the end, keeping space between the pleats flat.
- Adjust the heading to the correct width and tie up the excess cords.

Pin, tack and sew in position.

3 To hold detachable linings in place either:

- Stitch a 1in/2.5cm length of ¼in/5mm-wide tape every 12in/30cm along the seam and inside edge of lining. Stitch a press stud to the free end of the tape. Stitch the opposite half of the stud to the top curtain.
- Alternatively, stitch a length of touch-and-close fastening to the tape and the curtain.

LINED CURTAINS

You will need

- Curtain fabric
- Lining fabric
- Curtain weights (optional)
- Heading tape
- Curtain hooks
- Scissors, thread, pins, tape measure, etc

To calculate how much lining you need, measure as for unlined curtains and deduct 4in/10cm per fabric width.

1 Cut out curtain and lining as for unlined curtains, page 158, deducting 4in/10cm from the drop of the lining. Stitch the curtain widths together with flat seams taking ⅝in/1.5cm seam allowance. Repeat for the lining widths.

2 Main fabric: turn in 2½in/6.5cm down each side and press. Turn up 5in/13cm hem and press. Unfold. Mitre the corners (see below) making only single turnings.

3 If the fabric is very light, add curtain weights inside the hem. Slipstitch across mitres at each corner. Herringbone stitch down the sides and along the bottom hems.

4 With the wrong side of the curtain facing, lay it flat, and mark down the centre with pins. Draw in the centre line using tailor's chalk.

5 With wrong sides together, centre the lining over the main curtain material, with the raw edge of the lining level with the curtain top

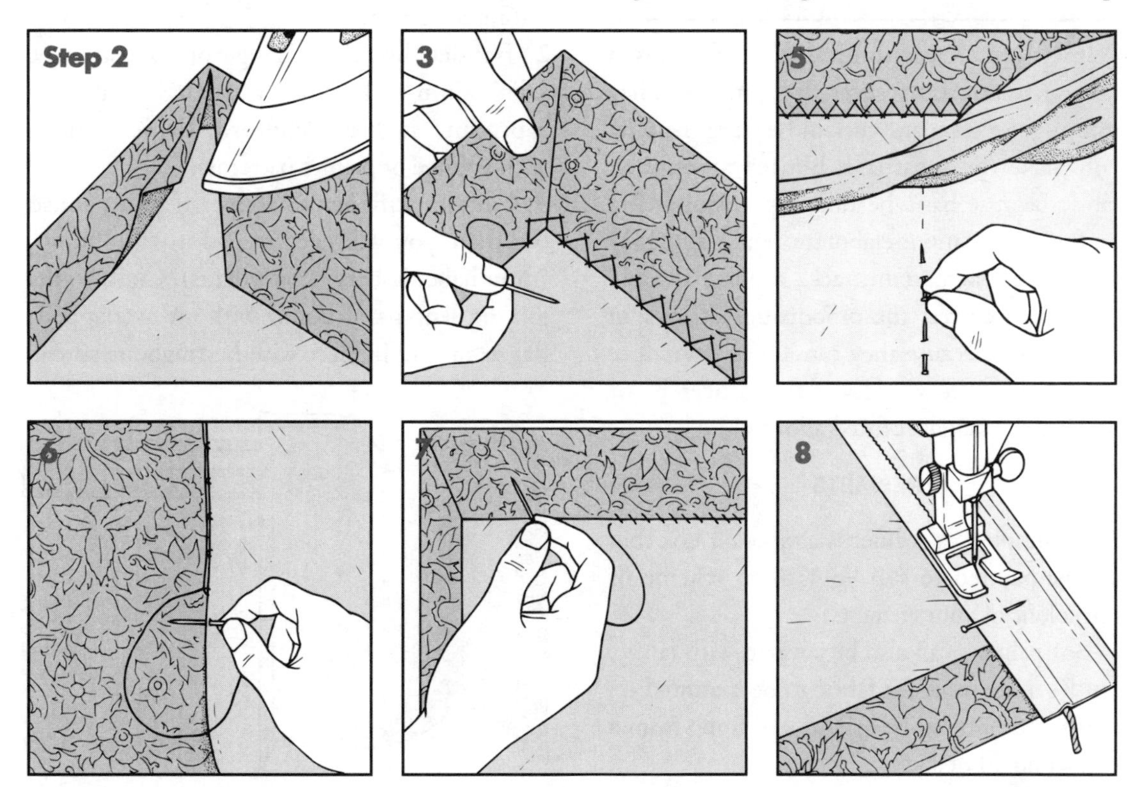

and bottom. Pin fabric and lining together along the centre line.
6 Using thread to match the curtain fabric lock stitch the fabrics together carefully. Begin at the top edge and end just above the curtain hem. Only pick up one thread from the main fabric so the stitches don't show through on the right side.
7 Tack the lining to the curtain at the top. Trim lining level with curtain at the sides. Turn in lining side edges by ¾in/2cm, and turn up the base hem by 1¼in/3cm. Press and slipstitch the lining to the curtain along the sides and hem.
8 Turn in both top edges by ¾in/2cm. Press. Position heading tape on the curtain top, and stitch in place through all thicknesses. Pull up cords evenly and knot together.

PELMETS AND VALANCES

Pelmets are an economical way of giving a decorative flourish to everyday curtains. They can disguise standard curtain heading, helping you make the most of a limited amount of fabric because basic heading tape requires less material than more elaborate types; and they can cover basic curtain track. You can also use pelmets to correct the proportions of a room or window, because they can appear to reduce the height of a window if fitted over it, or increase the height if fitted above it.

PELMETS

At its simplest, a pelmet is a wooden box that can be painted to suit your room scheme or the colour of your curtains.

Box pelmets can also be covered with fabric, but it's more usual for fabric to be mounted on a stiffened backing (see right) and hung from a pelmet board or shelf.

TIP Pelmets look best when their length (drop) is about one-sixth the total length of the curtains.

PELMETS STEP BY STEP

You will need

- Dressmaker's graph paper
- Fabric and lining
- Pelmet board fixed in place
- Iron-on buckram and bump interlining, or Pelmform
- Tape measure
- Touch-and-close (Velcro) fastener, same length as the pelmet board, or large drawing pins, or upholstery tacks

1 Make a paper pattern for the pelmet by drawing the design on to dressmaker's graph paper, remembering to include the width of the pelmet board, or 'returns', on each side: 4–6in/10–15cm.
2 Transfer the pelmet design on to a stiffener such as iron-on buckram which is washable, or a product such as Pelmform (which comes with a range of pelmet patterns).
3 Cut the stiffener to shape. If you choose buckram, you will need to pad it with 'bump' (from haberdashery departments). Cut it to fit, joining lengths of bump with an overlapped, flat seam held in place with herringbone stitch.

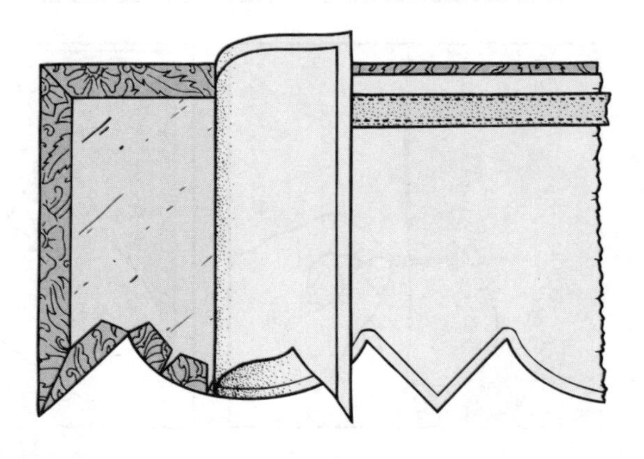

4 Transfer the design to the fabric and lining and cut to shape, allowing a 1in/2.5cm margin all round. Notch any curves to ease the fabric.

TIP If you have to join widths, attach the extra fabric each side of a central panel, to avoid an obvious centre seam.

5 Sew the edges of the lining under so that the lining is ¼in/5mm smaller all round than the pelmet stiffener.

6 If using Pelmform, fix the wrong side of the fabric to it. If using buckram and padding, lock-stitch the bump to the wrong side of the fabric. Then iron the buckram on to the padding. Iron the overlap of the fabric into place on the wrong side of the buckram or Pelmform.

7 Attach the soft side of the Velcro to the right side of the lining fabric along the top. Slipstitch the lining to the fabric overlap, so that it hides the raw edge.

8 Stitch, tack or glue any braid or fringing into place.

9 Tack or glue the hooked side of the Velcro to the top edge of the pelmet board, and attach the pelmet, making sure the two strips of Velcro line up and the pelmet is quite level.

TIP If the pelmet is large or heavy, you may need to use large drawing pins or upholstery tacks to keep it in place.

VALANCES STEP BY STEP

Valances are fabric ruffles, made with gathering tape or a shirred heading. They are hung from curtain track fixed to a pelmet board, or a valance rail attached to the curtain track, which projects so the valance hangs clear of the curtains (see above). You can also simply tack the valance on to a pelmet board and hide the fixings with ribbon or braid.

You will need

- Fabric, domette interlining and lining

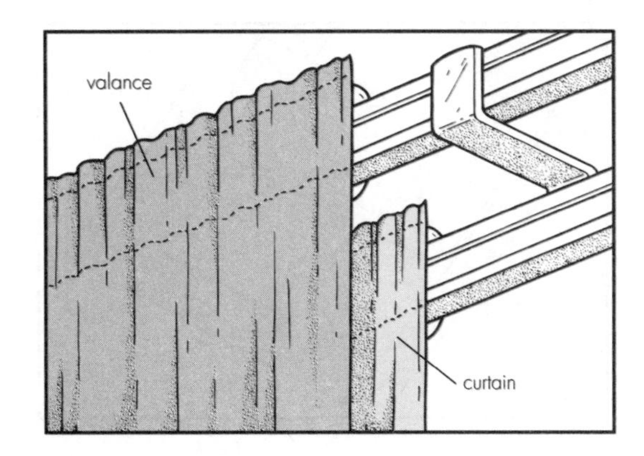

- Pelmet board or valance rail
- Pencil-pleat gathering tape 3in/8cm wide and 2½ times the length of the pelmet board or valance rail

1 Cut the number of widths of fabric required, allowing 2½ times the width of the pelmet board or valance rail, plus an extra

DESIGN IDEAS

- Thread a length of fabric through brass pelmet rings for a softly draped pelmet.
- For an asymmetrical look, swathe 6½yd/6m of fabric along a curtain pole and down one side of a window.
- Drape a length of fabric each side of the window and swathe it over a pole, holding it in place at the corners with ribbon.
- Knot three 1yd/1m-long pieces of fabric at each end and in the centre of a curtain pole.
- Use a swag of sheer or lace fabric to filter the light.
- An arched valance gives a formal finish but admits plenty of light.
- Stepped or zigzag pelmets give maximum visual impact.

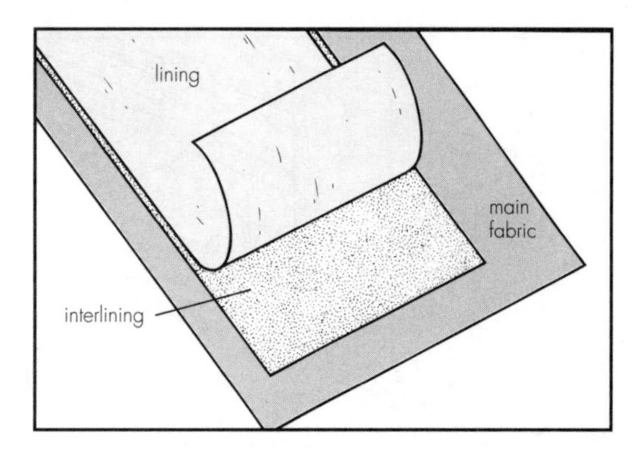

2in/5cm for side hems and ⅝in/1.5cm for each seam. Add ¾in/2cm to the length for the hem, and a minimum of 1½in/4cm for the heading. Join widths with an open seam.

2 Cut the lining to the finished size, allowing ⅝in/1.5cm for each seam. Join widths with an open seam.

3 Cut the interlining to the valance's finished size, joining any necessary seams flat and overlapped with a herringbone stitch.

4 Put the main fabric, interlining and lining together, and tack the layers in place.

5 Pin the side and bottom hems in place, and slipstitch to the lining.

6 Turn over the top edge of the valance and sew on the heading tape. Pull up the cords to the desired length, then space the pleats and insert the curtain hooks.

BLINDS

Blinds can be as elaborate as you choose, yet cost less than lined curtains.

Not all blinds block out the light so check carefully when purchasing or choosing fabric.

Most soft blinds are easy to make and kits are available. Venetian blinds are generally bought ready made, or made to measure. Roman and louvre blinds are not generally ready made because they must fit exactly. Other blinds can usually be adjusted by altering the gathers or cutting the roller.

Choose between:

Roller blinds

Simple blinds which operate by means of a spring-loaded roller. Popular on windows which require shading from the sun. For a more elaborate effect use with front curtains in a sheer or delicate fabric.

Roman blinds

These resemble roller blinds when hanging to their full drop but when raised, by a system of vertical cords at the back, they pleat into a series of neat horizontal folds.

Austrian blinds

These look like a curtain but are pulled up from the bottom by a series of vertical cords. They are made longer than the required drop of the window, and this extra fabric ruches up from the bottom to form a swag-like effect.

Festoon blinds

Similar to Austrian blinds, but use more fabric because they are ruched all along the complete drop. Suitable fabrics include lace, voile or other soft fabrics to achieve the correct draping effect.

Venetian blinds

A series of horizontal slats which can be made of plastic, wood or metal. They are operated by a cord system at the sides which raises or lowers the slats. They can be totally raised to the top of the window in the day time. Good for providing shade. Simple but effective.

Vertical louvre blinds

Similar to Venetian blinds, but the slats are vertical. Can be drawn to one side like curtains. Often used in conservatories.

BUYING FURNITURE

Don't be seduced just by the look of the furniture: appearances can be deceptive. Performance, durability, construction, safety and value for money are all equally important factors to consider when choosing. It's worth waiting until you find exactly the right piece rather than buying something to 'make do' until you can afford something better.

THREE-PIECE SUITES

A suite is likely to be one of the major investments for your house or flat. It must look good, be comfortable, practical and hard wearing. Choose wisely; don't just be tempted by the colours and pattern. Consider:

Size

Is it right for your room? Too small and it will look lost, but too large and it will dominate the room and nothing else will fit in. In a large room a three-seater looks best, although the middle position is usually the last to be filled. Put a two-seater in a smaller room, so it won't dominate. With a two-seater you may have room for two sofas and a chair or one sofa and two chairs.

There should be about a 3ft/1m clearance at the front and sides of armchairs and settees. Although it seems obvious, check it will fit through the relevant doorways.

Comfort

Sit in it for at least ten minutes. It should support your back and head and be easy to get in and out of.

The degree of firmness depends on the filling used. A foam cushion will be resilient and keep its shape, whereas a feather one will be very soft and need plumping up regularly. Modern furniture generally uses different layers of foam and polyester. Traditional fillings are hair, combined with spring seats and backs, and tend to be more expensive.

Back height and angle are important. Seating with a low back looks better in a small room, or if you want to position it away from walls, while high backs look grand in large living rooms.

Check you have good support for the base of your spine. It's personal preference whether you prefer to sit upright on a firm high back and head rest, or curled up on a squashy, low-backed sofa. However, you should be able to get out of the chair without having to use the arms for support.

Seat height

You should be able to rest your feet flat on the floor while sitting back in the chair. If the seat is too high your legs will dangle, putting pressure on the underside of your thighs. Too low and its difficult to get out of the seat. If the depth of the seat is too great it will put pressure on your calves and restrict circulation to your legs. You will also find you have to climb out of the seat, and you may tend to sit on the edge instead, therefore losing back support.

Style and design

Does it fit in with the other style of furniture in the room? Modern and period furniture don't mix. Remember gimmicky or trendy furniture will date within a few years.

Avoid buying unusual shapes because they will date more quickly. Bold and fussy patterns can be tiring and restrict your choice of other soft furnishings and decor. They can also make your room look smaller.

Ease of cleaning

If you have children or pets it should be easy to clean. Alternatively, consider loose or permanent covers.

Arm rests

It's useful to have one chair without arms, especially if you enjoy knitting, etc.

Modular

Not as popular now as in the 1980s, when individual middle and end sections were employed for greater flexibility, especially for seating a lot of people. Makes full use of corners, and useful if you move house, because it can be rearranged to suit.

Fabric type

A huge range is available, including both natural and synthetic fabrics. Check with the retailer as to the suitability for the purpose. The choice of fabric will affect the feel, look, durability and resistance to staining. The most expensive fabrics may not be the most durable, but will look and feel good.

Look at the weave. Textured fabric will snag more easily than a smooth, dense pile. A closely woven fabric should wear the best. Dark and patterned fabrics will show dirt less.

The fibre content of fabrics on furniture must be included, by law; check labels. Most are blends so it can be difficult to assess their wear. Check there is a high proportion of hard-wearing fabric, especially if textured. It might be worth buying one which has stain protection; discuss with your retailer.

Wool wears well but is quite expensive. Somewhat limited in style and colours. However, resists most staining well and is inherently flame and crease resistant.

Cotton is quite durable but depends on the weave; opt for a closely woven cotton. Will show stains and burn marks. Can get cotton pile fabrics such as velvet and corduroy.

Linen union is a blend of cotton and linen, and is good for printed patterns. Linen, however, is not very resistant to abrasion.

Dralon, other acrylics and modacrylics (flame-retardant versions) are crease resistant. Choose the denser piles for greater durability. However, they show the dirt easily. Wide range of colours, patterns and textures.

Viscose is quite durable but it does crease badly and shows dirt and stains.

Polypropylene wears well and resists dirt and is easy to clean. It will melt if burnt.

Polyamide is crease resistant and resilient but shows the dirt.

Polyester is similar to polyamide but is not as hard wearing.

Quality

Look for good craftsmanship.

Price

Pay as much as you can afford. Choose reputable dealers and brands. Shop around to see what's on offer.

Durability

The frame should be robust. It should have a little give, but a lot of movement indicates poor workmanship and cheap, ill-fitting components.

Padding

Usually foam. Modern suites have to conform to fire regulations, but secondhand pieces might have been made before the new rules came into effect.

The thicker and denser the foam, the more resilient it will be. Check by feeling the cushions: they should be resilient and heavy.

The cover should fit tightly without being

over-stretched. Seams should be straight without any puckering.

IN-STORE CHECKS

- Bounce lightly on the seat. You shouldn't be able to feel the support layer.
- Lean heavily against the back. You shouldn't be able to feel the springs or frame.
- Sit on the front edge of the seat. Again, you shouldn't be able to feel any part of the frame.
- Look at the overall finish, including in the hidden sections.
- Feel the cushions. Loose cushions should not flop when balanced across your palm. If too deeply padded, surfaces of the fabric will rub against each other when buckled under a person's weight. Constant abrasion will cause the pile to rub away.
- Put hands down the sides of cushions. There should be no hard lumps or bits of wood which will rub against the fabric and wear down the pile.
- Check buttoning, and that they don't irritate you when seated. Check that there are no large holes underneath the buttons.
- Ask sales staff about colour fastness to light. Bright prints and patterns can fade in the sun.
- If buying leather, check on the swatches that the colour on the wrong side matches the top surface. There is a transparent finish, or lacquer, on leather, which is often coloured. The natural leather beneath may be a different colour, so if it gets scratched or worn a different colour may show through.
- If the wooden frames are on show check there are no knots, splits or cracks visible; joints smooth and a good fit; corner supports in the leg joints, especially the rear ones, as these take the most strain; well finished off.
- Check the flexibility of the frame by sitting on one end of the settee and get someone else to lean on the back of the settee at the other end. There should only be a slight 'give'.
- The back should be softer than the seat.
- If covers are too tight, wear will be more rapid. Bulky, softer styles with cushioning in areas of maximum body contact will last longer.
- Piping at ends of arms will probably wear quickly.
- Look out for the Qualitas logo. The Qualitas Furnishing Standards Organisation was set up to promote good standards throughout the furniture and floor- covering industries. A Qualitas charter exists as a guarantee of strict quality standards.

HOW TO MAKE A LOOSE COVER

The fastest way to revitalise a chair or sofa is to buy a throw over, but a loose cover is a more permanent solution, and ideal if you move house and need to blend old furniture with new decor.

Loose covers tend to be made of printed fabrics with a plain or basket weave; made in linen-union fabrics and cottons of a strong, smooth, regular yarn. If you have basic sewing skills, you can easily make one yourself, but you do need patience, time and space.

TIPS FOR LOOSE COVERS

- A good fit is essential to keep creasing to a minimum.
- Seams should be strong for maximum durability. It's worth reinforcing seams with a second row of stitching. Overlock the edges to prevent fraying.
- Check washable fabrics are pre-shrunk, otherwise wash it several times before you start.
- Always wash or dry-clean all the sections at the same time to avoid differential fading.

- When sewing several layers together, always machine sew very slowly, helping to feed the fabric through, or finish by hand if necessary.
- When calculating the quantity of fabric required allow for pattern repeats. Remember that inside arms, outside arms and arm strips should be symmetrical. Motifs should be centred on cushions.
- Piping the seams is a great way to add the professional touch and to strengthen seams. It also disguises mismatched patterned sections. For greater emphasis, apply piping in contrasting fabric (making sure it's roughly the same weight and texture as the main fabric).

CHOOSING FABRIC

- Avoid loosely woven fabrics which wear and snag easily.
- Expect to join up to eight layers in some places. This can be tricky with heavy fabrics.
- Check for colourfastness: stretch a white hanky over your fingers and rub the fabric. If lots of dye comes off don't buy, but a trace of colour is acceptable.
- Synthetic fabrics are more hard wearing than naturals but don't have the same feel. They often need more regular cleaning.
- Fabric must be flame retardant. Check with the retailer. Follow laundry instructions precisely, to avoid damaging the finish.

INSTRUCTIONS FOR A BOX-SHAPED TWO-SEATER SOFA

You will need

- Fabric: see below to calculate length needed
- Thread: 4 x 273yd/250m reels
- Piping cord
- Touch-and-close fastener (Velcro) or hooks and eyes
- Four zips

TIP Wash cotton piping first, as it can shrink up to 25 per cent when washed. Alternatively, use polyester piping, which doesn't shrink.

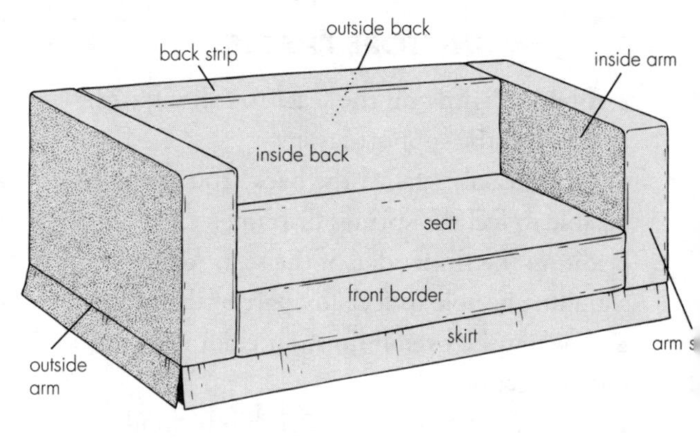

Measuring up: cover

1 Sketch the shape of your sofa (see above). Measure the width and length of each section.
2 List the measurements of each section, adding 1¼in/3cm to each measurement for ⅝in/1.5cm seam allowances. For tuck-ins, add a further 4in/10cm to: bottom and both sides of inside back; back and both sides of seat, back and bottom of inside arms. On the finished cover, the tuck-ins will be pushed into the corners of the sofa until the cover fits snugly. They will help to secure the cover and allow some give.
3 Decide on the style of skirt you want – these instructions apply to a tailored style, but you could substitute a frill. Measure the length of the sides, the back and front of the sofa, adding 7in/18cm to each length for pleats and seams. The depth of the skirt should be 6in/15cm plus 1¼in/3cm for seam allowances. You will need 1½ x 7in/4 x 18cm square inserts for the corner pleats.

Measuring up: cushions

4 Measure panels: top, bottom and gusset sections. Add ⅝in/1.5cm for each seam allowance. For zip openings, one gusset panel of each cushion must be cut into two equal sections, with an extra ⅝in/1.5cm seam

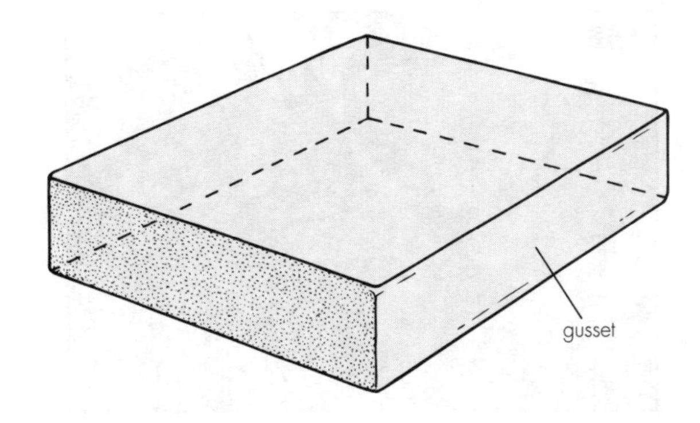

allowance added to each.

On the seat cushions, zips will face the back, while on back cushions zips will face downwards.

TIP You may want to match the pattern on the front cushion gusset to the front border, and the back cushion to the inside arms.

Calculating fabric requirements

5 Using scaled-down measurements draw and cut out each section on graph paper. Mark the direction of the grain (on a sofa it should run top to bottom). Position pieces.

6 Taking pattern repeats and motifs into account, position each piece on a second piece of graph paper cut to the scaled-down width of the fabric, with the grain of the fabric running in the same direction.

7 If the cover is to be piped, you will need 2in/5cm-wide bias strips (cut on the cross) to cover the piping cord.

TIP It's possible to cut about 33yd/30m of strips from 1⅔yd/1.5m of 55in/140cm-wide fabric.

8 Convert the length covered on paper back to scale, to calculate the total length of fabric needed for the cover.

Cutting out

9 Lay out the fabric in a single layer on the floor. Cut out the pieces to the measurements you made earlier. (You could make full-size paper patterns first, but if the pieces are all rectangular it's as easy just to measure and mark the sections with tailor's chalk.) Label each section, marking top and bottom and centre lines.

10 To cut bias strips for piping, fold over a corner of a raw edge so that the fold lies at 45° to the selvedge. Cut strips parallel to the fold.

Cover: pinning together

TIP When pinning, always leave ⅝in/1.5cm seam allowance on all edges.

11 With tailor's chalk, mark on the base upholstery the centre back (inside and outside), seat and front border.

12 With right sides out, position and pin the section to the sofa, matching centres, in the following order: outside back (A), inside back, back strip, inside and outside arms (B). For a taut finish pin down the centre lines

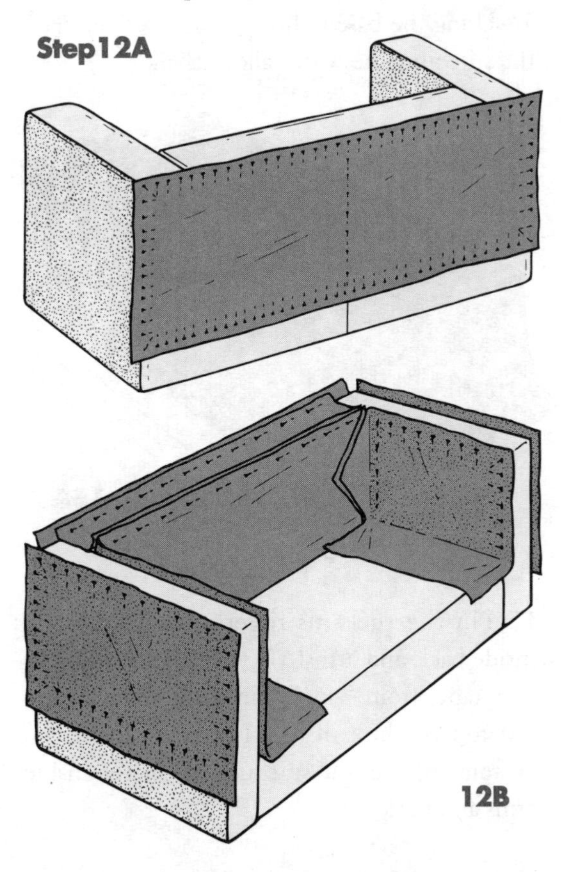

(previously marked) and smooth the fabric out to the sides, pulling slightly.

13 Pin pieces together in this order: outside back to right outside arm, arm strips to outside and inside arms and to ends of back strip. Pin seat to sofa. Pin left outside arm to back, leaving three-quarters of length open for fastenings.

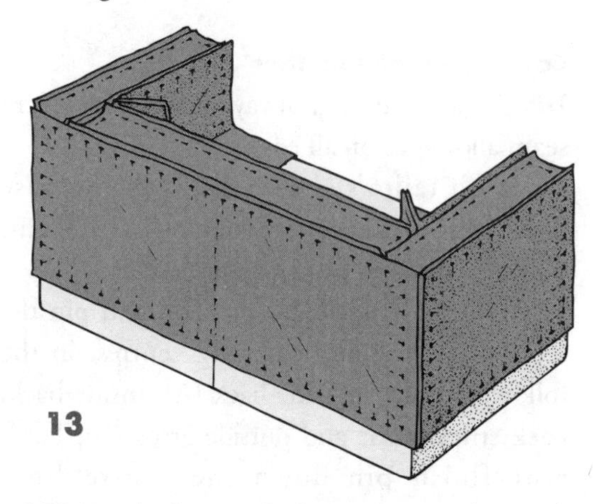

14 Using the base upholstery as a guide, mark the stitching lines with tailor's chalk.

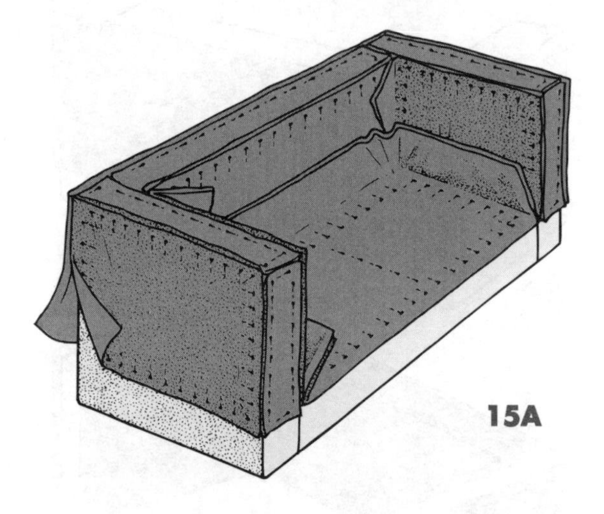

15 Pin the tuck-ins together between the inside back and arms(A). Trim the tuck-ins so they taper from ⅝in/1.5cm seam allowance at the top to the full 4in/10cm width at the bottom (B). Pin the seat tuck-ins to the inside arms and back.

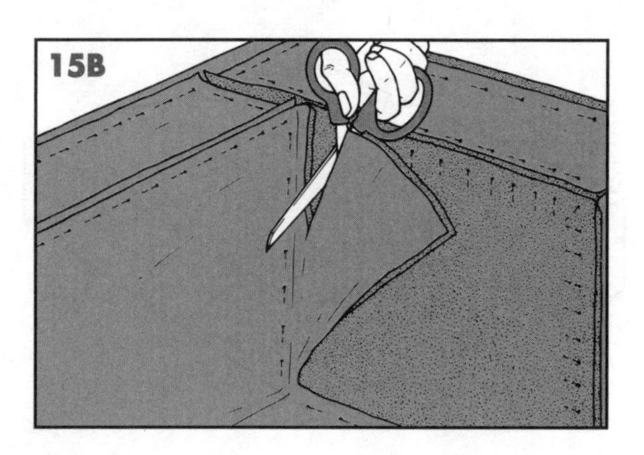

16 Unpin the cover.

Piping cover

17 Pin and sew bias strips for piping together into a long strip. Join by marking seam lines ¼in/5mm in from the short raw edge of the two strips. These should meet exactly, leaving triangular corners. Press seams open and trim the corners.

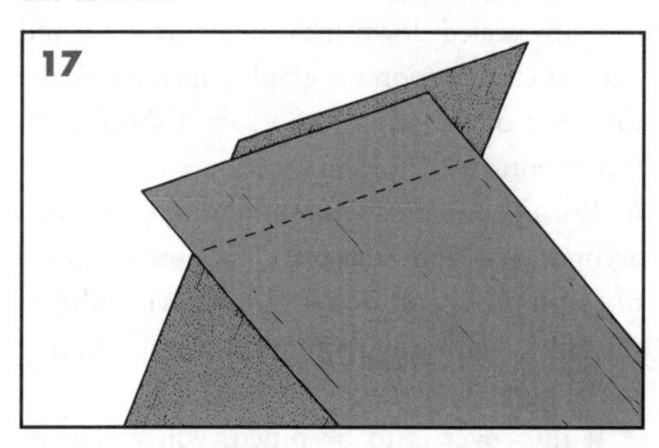

18 Place piping cord on the centre of the wrong side of strip. Fold the strip in half, enclosing the cord. Using the zipper foot on the sewing machine, stitch close to the cord down the length of the strip.

19 With raw edges together and still using the zipper foot, pin and stitch the piping to the right side of the front edge of the back strip and inside edges of the arm strips.

20 Join the arm strips to the back strip following the stitching lines.

21 Stitch a continuous piece of piping to the outer edge of the strip.

TIP For neat joins of two piped sections, cut ⅝in/1.5cm of piping cord from the casing of one section where the piping meets.

22 Pin and stitch piping to the seat front along stitching lines.

Stitching together

TIP It is worth taking the time to tack all the pieces together first, then check fit and make any adjustments.

23 Stitch pieces together with right sides together, in the order marked on the diagram, following previously marked seam lines. Sew as close to the piping as possible.

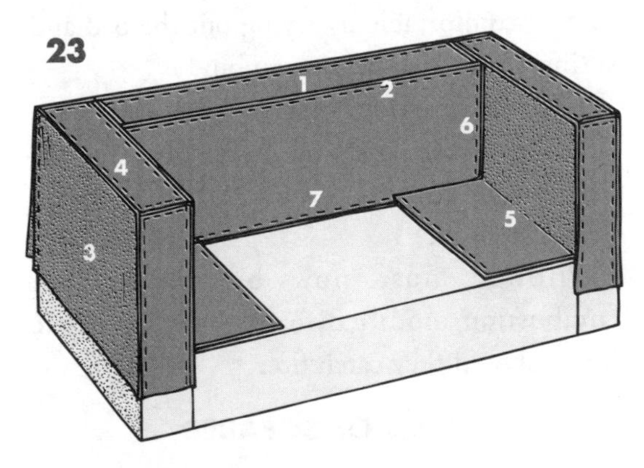

24 Trim seams if necessary, and finish edges.

25 Re-fit cover on sofa, right side out, and fit around the seat.

TIP To get a neater finish, trim the tuck-in to fit the sofa.

26 Pin the front panel to seat and arm pieces, mark in stitching lines as before.

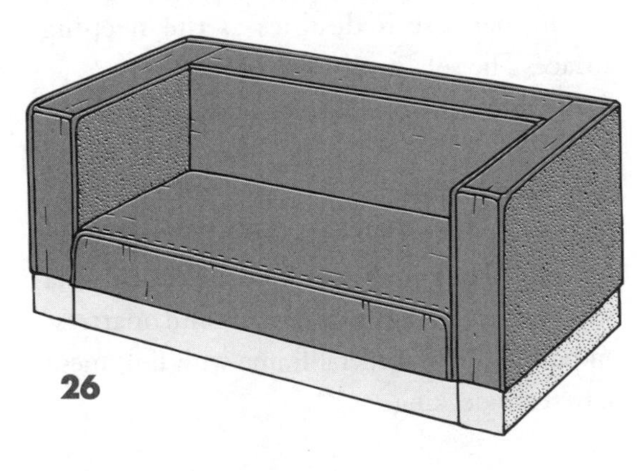

27 Check the base edge all the way round for length. This should finish 5⅓in/13.5cm from the floor. Remove the cover, tack and stitch the front border in place.

Back opening

28 To make a facing for the back opening, cut a strip of fabric twice the length of the opening (excluding the skirt) and 3in/7.5cm wide. Hem one long edge.

29 With the right sides together, stitch the raw edge of the strip around the opening. Turn facing to inside. Hand stitch the hemmed edge of the facing to the seam line on the wrong side, encasing the seam.

Skirt

30 With the right sides together, pin and stitch skirt pieces together in this order: outside back, insert, outside arm, insert, front, insert, outside arm, insert. Hem along the bottom edge.

31 Fold each insert to make an inverted pleat and tack across the top edges to secure. Press pleats flat.

32 Pin and stitch the skirt to cover with right sides together, matching pleats to corners.

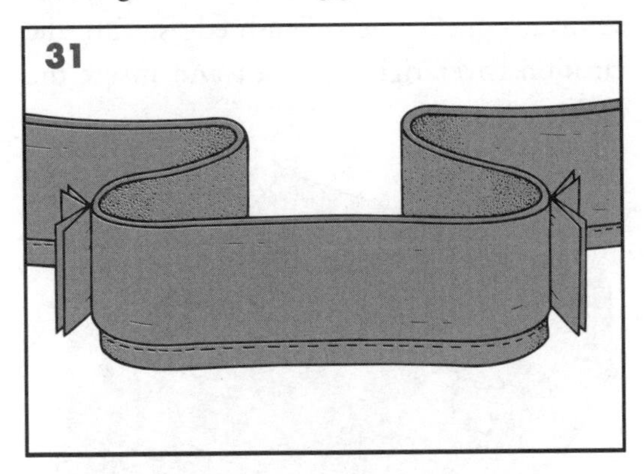

33 Place cover over sofa and fold in edges of opening. Mark positions of hooks and eyes, placing last pair just below the seam line of the skirt (see page 172). Stitch fastenings in place.

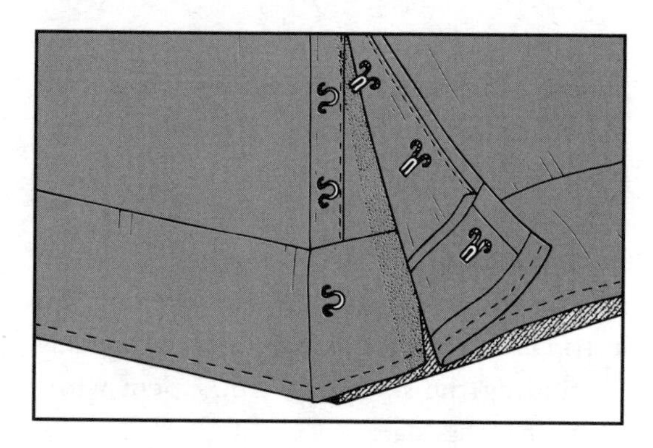

TIP If it's a tight fit, Velcro will give a firmer finish.

Cushions: fitting zip

TIP For easy removal of cushion pads, the zip should run the full length of the gusset.

34 Tack together the two halves of gusset, and position the zip with the teeth centred behind the tacked seam. Pin, tack and stitch the zip in place. Remove tacking.

Assembling cushions

35 Pin and stitch gusset pieces together, leaving ⅝in/1.5cm open at each end of seam.

36 Add piping as previously to top and bottom panels.

37 Attach gusset to panels, matching gusset seams to panel corners. Finish edges. Turn the cushion cover right side out and insert the cushion pad.

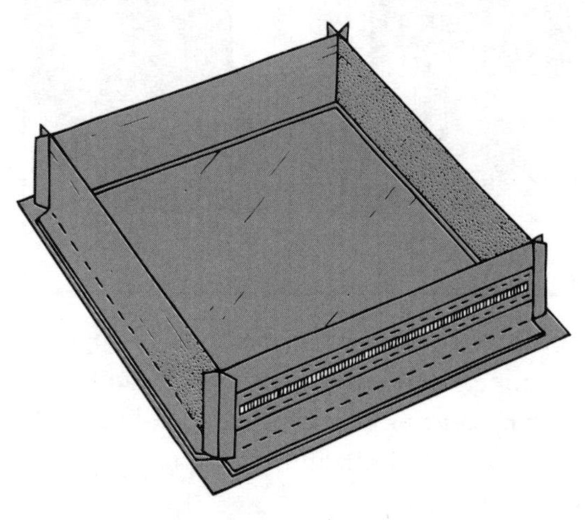

CHOOSING A SOFABED

These can be invaluable, especially at Christmas and big family events. However, you need to consider how much use it will have as a sofa, and as a bed. If it is for serious sitting and regular use as a bed it's worth spending as much as you can afford. If it's mainly tucked away in a study or spare room, and slept on occasionally, you can get away with a cheaper model.

A sofabed may look attractive, but do make sure its comfortable by trying out the bed and sitting on the sofa before you buy.

Check for good instructions and care labelling. Often, opening instructions for the bed are inadequate, so ask for a thorough demonstration.

Fillings must now be made from combustion modified foam to reduce toxic fumes should they catch fire.

TYPES OF SOFABED

Foam or French bed

This is the simplest type, with a folding system of foam cushions. The seats and sometimes the back unfold to lie on the floor in front of the carcass of the sofa. Easy to change to the bed position, but the mattress sits on the floor, so is very low. You may find it too firm for seating because it doubles as the sleeping surface. The sofa is very low.

Suitable only for occasional use.

Fully convertible

These can be either three-fold or two-fold pull-out. They look like a conventional sofa but have a spring mechanism and mattress support made of a metal frame with link-mesh polyweave decking.

Two-fold types have an interior-sprung mattress about 4in/10cm thick. Alternatively, the three-fold mattress is thinner and made of foam. The two-fold are more expensive and a better choice for frequent use.

Pull-out drawer

The bed pulls out of a drawer at the bottom of the sofa. It is easy to open, but the bed is quite low. Often has a slatted wooden bed support. More common in Europe than the UK.

Reasonable as a sofa, and for occasional use as a bed. Foam on slats can be for more frequent use.

Lengthways fold

Good if it's mainly used for a bed. The back of the sofa folds down to make a double bed. Easy to operate. Mattresses are usually quite thick, so offer good support. Sprung ones are available. Each side of the bed has a separately sprung wooden-slatted base so good for partners of differing weights. Covers can double up as a duvet, but check that they are securely attached or else they will move around when you sit on them.

A-frame

Pulls out to form a bed and folds into three when it's up as a sofa. Mattress is reasonably firm but can be heavy and awkward to change. Quite low.

BUYING GUIDE

- Try the opening mechanism in the shop before you buy. See how easy it is to trap fingers and how much effort is needed. It should operate smoothly and shouldn't rub against the fabric.
- Check that cushions fit well and there are no gaps between the cushions and the arms and back.
- Padding should be even and secure. You should not be able to feel the frame beneath.
- Frame should be durable and very robust to withstand use as a bed.
- Check that it is stable when sitting and lying on it. Try tossing and turning. Sit on the bottom in the middle to see if the middle legs lift off the floor. Should be well supported.
- Check that the depth of the seat suits you. Short people may find depth a problem, and the back should give good support.
- Buy the thickest mattress you can afford: sprung if possible.
- Check height, width and length: the bed and sofa should be able to hold two people comfortably.
- Removable covers are useful, or choose fabrics treated with stain protector.

WOODEN FURNITURE

The most popular woods are ash, oak, yew, beech, pine, rosewood, mahogany, teak, maple and walnut. All these woods can be stained darker, or given various opaque stains such as black, white, grey and even hints of pinks, blues and greens.

Solid timber has been considered to be better than a veneer, but that's not always the case. Cabinets and tables can be made completely of solid wood, but they are very expensive, and unless the quality is excellent there is always the danger of the wood cracking or splitting and twisting. Solid wood can change in an unstable environment, such as frequent changes in humidity, causing problems such as warping and loose-fitting drawers. Colours can change if exposed to excess sunlight. Chair and table frames are usually made of solid timber for strength, while panelling is another way of using solid timber, particularly for doors.

For horizontal surfaces, veneers – thin layers of wood peeled from logs and laid on a base of robust and stable chipboard or fibreboard – are the best and most common option. On top-quality furniture, edges are often lipped with strips of solid timber for extra protection.

With the huge range of finishes available, it's often difficult to distinguish between imitations and the real thing.

As well as wood, surface finishes include laminates, melamines, PVC, and paper foils. Because of advancements in printing techniques, paper foils are no longer the cheap nasties of the 1970s. Other hard surfaces for furniture include metal, glass and marble.

The development of fibreboard (such as MDF), which is finer than chipboard and easier to cut, has brought many new shapes into furniture and also encouraged more painted and lacquered finishes.

DINING TABLES

- Round tables are more sociable and seat more people without table legs getting in the way. However, they do reduce usable space by 25 per cent and work best in square rooms.
- Rectangular tables look more formal and are a better choice for a long, narrow room. Allow about 20–24in/50–60cm of table edge per person. You also need about 3ft/1m all around the table for chair space, but you may get away with 18in/45cm at the least.
- Choose an extending table to cater for different occasions. Gate-leg tables can fold down to a width below 12in/30cm and drop-flap tables can be as much as halved in size. Extension leaves can be added to round or square tables to make them oval or rectangular.
- Occasional tables: look for nesting ones to save space. Check that the finish matches the main furniture.
- Kitchen tables tend to be simpler but more robust because they take a lot of hard use. Ash is good because it is tough; pine is very popular; beech is good because it has a tight grain texture, and can double as a chopping board – but keep it scrupulously clean.

In-store check

- Look for tables with good edge protection.
- Check stability: lean on the table and push it gently to see if there is movement.
- Easy to operate: any extensions should be well hidden.
- Pedestal tables should be very firm.

DINING CHAIRS

Pay as much as you can afford; you'll find that chairs without arms are cheaper.

Chairs with arms may not go under the table and so take up more space. Check there is enough leg room: there should be about 10–12in/25–30cm between the chair seat and table top. Chairs with upright legs will save on space. Check they are a comfortable height for the table and offer good back support. Benches are good for rectangular tables. They take up less room in depth, and seat more people. Junk shops often have old church pews which are great for adding character to a room.

In-store check

- Check flexibility of the frame by pushing the arms of the chair downwards and outwards; and kneeling on the seat and pushing the back of the chair gently. Also kneel on the front rail or edge.
- Check they're right for the table: table legs don't get in the way.
- Check arms don't restrict movement and don't stop you getting close to the table.
- If upholstered, the back should be sloping slightly, allowing you to sit back into it with the backrest supporting you adequately.

CABINETS AND UNITS

There is more to choose from than just a sideboard or wall units. As well, you must choose between free-standing pieces of furniture or fitted, modular systems. If furnishing a small room it may be more practical to opt for lots of flexible wall systems to house the stereo, TV, computers and children's play things, as well as glassware and ornaments.

Modular units are extremely versatile with various depths and widths of shelving and cupboards. However, solid walls of shelving and units will make your room look smaller and can be oppressive. Counteract this by including glass-fronted units and open shelving.

Take care if mixing traditional and modern styles of furniture.

In-store check

- Close-fitting drawers and doors: important for easy operation, strength and durability.
- Good joins.
- Smooth finish.
- Good lacquered finish for better heat and scratch resistance. Check there is no flecking.
- Ensure they fit flush into the wall: some are recessed at the back to allow for skirting boards.
- Front recesses are useful to guard against feet kicking the furniture.
- Drawer stops to avoid drawers being opened too far.
- Good-quality handles and knobs: must look good and be easy to grip.

BEDROOM FURNITURE

Furniture for bedrooms has advanced dramatically over the last decade, and because it is not generally on show, allows you to express your own individuality. Streamlined, fully fitted bedrooms or pine country style are the most common.

Fitted bedrooms can be full of ingenious storage areas like the kitchen, but remember you can't take them with you if you move. Free-standing ranges now have the fitted look, and are movable.

- Bedroom furniture should be multi-functional, so choose built-in or free-standing modular units to maximise storage space.
- Look out for fold-away furniture such as fold-down desks and tables.
- Inexpensive white-wood furniture is ideal for children's rooms, and you can paint or stencil your own styles. Cover white melamine furniture with borders or stencils.
- Small bedrooms can look cluttered with free-standing furniture.
- Professionally fitted units can be expensive, but if you are a reasonably competent DIYer, try installing them yourself. You could just buy floor and ceiling tracks and slide the doors between them: the bedroom walls act as sides and back of the cupboard.
- To make the most of space, fit cupboards over the entire height of the wall.
- Free-standing furniture looks best in older houses with high ceilings and old mouldings.

BUYING FURNITURE SECOND-HAND

Buy either through an auction, an antique shop or local paper.

BUYING CHECKS

- Test joints by pushing from the back.
- Check table and chair legs to see if they have been repaired: a trick is to repair any breaks quickly with metal brackets.

- Line up sets of chairs to see if they are the same height, and identical.
- Look for signs of woodworm: tiny holes which could be hidden under the rails and upholstery.
- Mahogany is the least expensive wood, then comes walnut, and rosewood is the most expensive.
- Sets of chairs are more valuable if they include a carver.
- Tables: check that the top and bottom go together and that the top is not warped.
- Buy an old chest of drawers and paint it.

ARRANGING A ROOM

- Don't cram too much in.
- If there's no fireplace, create another focal point: often the TV, unfortunately.
- Make a plan to help you make the most of all available space in the room.
- A conventional settee may overwhelm a small sitting room so single chairs would look better.
- As a general rule, there should be 3ft/90cm around each piece of furniture for walking around, etc.
- Traffic flow in a room is important. The more furniture, the less accessible.
- Break up large rooms by dividing into sitting and working areas using a bookcase, screen, etc.
- If symmetrical, it's best to follow that formality and arrange the room accordingly.
- Use furniture to disguise defects; eg put a bookcase over a door that's never used.

LIGHTING

Lighting is a necessity in the home, and used creatively it can enhance your decor considerably. Good lighting gives a feeling of space, enhances decor and highlights areas of interest such as paintings and alcoves; and is essential for many practical activities.

The most effective artificial lighting combines three forms, called general, accent and task.

General

Good background lighting is necessary for efficiency and safety, and can be supplemented by directional lighting, used as required.

Accent

This provides highlights and shadows which make the room more interesting. It is also sometimes called 'mood' lighting.

Low-voltage fittings are suitable and unobtrusive, especially if recessed.

Task

Task lighting needs to be bright enough for the job in hand, such as work at a desk, needlework or chopping food, but it must not provide any glare.

Working with inadequate light may lead to eye strain, and the older we get the more light we need. Visually-demanding tasks can be carried out by a window during the day, but an additional light source is often necessary at night.

Daylight-simulation bulbs

Daylight-simulation bulbs are useful for task lighting. These blue bulbs give out less of the yellow light given out by ordinary tungsten bulbs. They show colours more correctly, and are therefore good for hobbies such as needlecraft and art. Available as tungsten, (bayonet and screw fittings) fluorescent and spotlights. Available from needlecraft and art shops, or by mail order from Daylight Studios (see Useful Addresses).

QUALIFIED ELECTRICIANS

In the UK electrical contractors do not have to comply with any of the official regulations. This means that anyone can carry out electrical work, so it is important to choose someone who will work properly and safely. The trade association for electrical contractors is the Electrical Contractors' Association; they will provide details of members (see Useful Addresses). The National Inspection Council for Electrical Installation Contracting is a consumer safety organisation. It carries out detailed inspections of electrical contractors and specifies compliance with national regulations. Contact for details of local Approved Contractors (see Useful Addresses).

TYPE OF LIGHT FITTINGS

Select fittings for their light quality, and then their appearance.

CEILING LIGHTS

Gives all-round lighting but needs accent and task lighting to enhance them. The shape and size of the shade determines the direction and spread of light. (A, see page 178.)

PENDANTS

A variation of ceiling lighting with a rise-and-fall facility. Especially useful for people who can't climb to change a light bulb.

The amount of light depends on the height

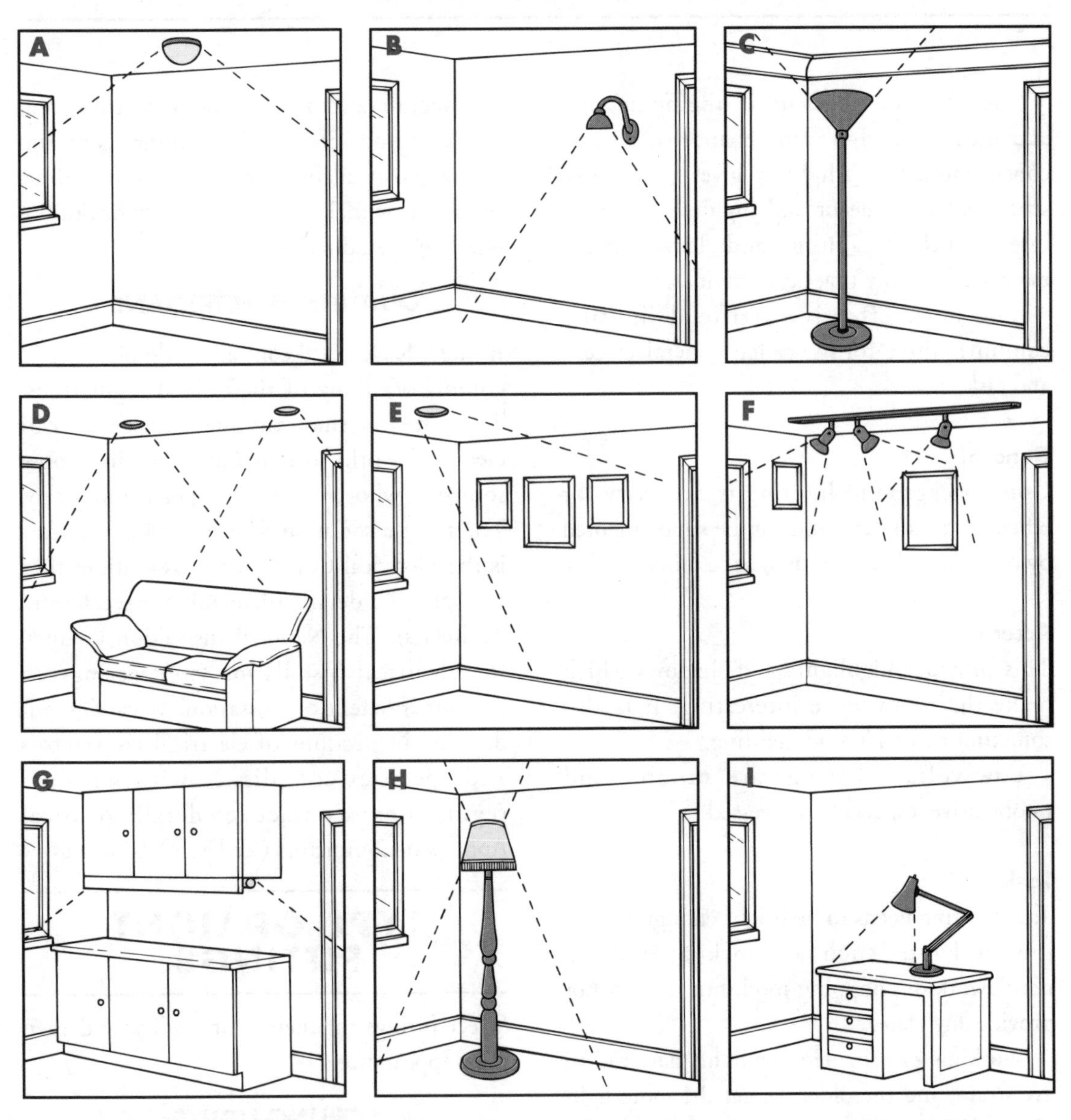

at which the pendant is hung, the type of bulb and the shade. A pendant should relate to the room size.

WALL LIGHTS

Give a decorative effect. They contribute to general lighting but also help illuminate particular objects. (B)

UPLIGHTERS

Light the ceiling, and this light is then reflected back to provide soft gentle illumination. They are really a way to achieve accent lighting. (C)

Uplighters are only suitable if the ceiling is in good condition, of a reasonable height and a pale colour. Don't use them if the ceiling is low or dark, as it will absorb the light, not reflect it. Ideal ceilings for uplighters are period ceilings, with wonderful, original mouldings or cornices.

Uplighters may be wall mounted, free

standing, or suspended on a stem from the ceiling. They can be placed on the floor for a dramatic effect, behind large, bushy plants or in corners.

DOWNLIGHTS

Illuminate the carpet and furniture, and are usually recessed or semi-recessed into the ceilings. They achieve a clean, unfussy look and are useful for emphasising particular areas of a room. (D)

Give thought to the reflector you choose: a gold reflector is wonderful for earthy tones and wood but not for pastel shades.

Make sure the beams of the downlights merge into each other so that you don't get pools of light. This will be dictated by the bulb and housing. For example, a halogen bulb in a recessed fitting will be more concentrated than a tungsten bulb in a surface fitting.

WALL WASHERS

Provide light like a downlight, but directional, to accent a wall or picture. (E)

SPOTLIGHTS

Provide adjustable, directional lighting, with a dramatic effect. (F)

Not all spotlights require a track mounting; they can be fixed directly on to the wall and ceiling or clipped on to shelves to accent areas or objects.

While most fittings obscure the bulb, some don't, so choose them carefully.

STRIP LIGHTING

Used a lot in kitchens. It contributes to general, accent and task lighting. The source of light is usually concealed. (G)

STANDARD LAMP

A free-standing floor lamp that provides general or directional light depending on the shape of the shade. Provides a flexible source of light as it can be moved around. Standard lamps tend to be used in traditional settings, but there are modern equivalents. (H)

TABLE LAMPS

Provide accent lighting and contribute to general lighting in a small area. Their light tends to be multi-directional.

DESK LAMPS

The ultimate task lamps. They provide concentrated light in a particular area. An adjustable head, such as Anglepoise, allows you to alter the angle. (I)

TIP If table or standard lamps provide general lighting, have them wired on the same electrical circuit. They can then be switched on together or dimmed simultaneously.

PLANNING LIGHTING

Consider the following:

1 Practicalities: eg, can fittings be recessed into the ceiling?

2 Space and mood: how is the area used, what is its ambience; or is it multi-functional, so the lighting needs to be flexible?

3 Design and colour schemes: textures, walls, ceilings and curtains.

4 Any special features: eg, fireplaces, paintings and alcoves.

5 Would the installation of dual switches and dimmers be useful?

6 Quality of light required in a specific area, the type of fixture which will provide this, and whether it will look aesthetically pleasing.

7 Location of sockets and switches: traditionally, sockets are 18in/46cm and switches are 51in/1.3m above the floor.

LIGHTING ROOM BY ROOM

SITTING ROOM

Usually multi-functional, so flexibility is essential and you will probably need to combine the three types of lighting.

- Is it used mainly for entertaining, or as a family room?
- Are there formal paintings to be displayed or is it informal, for watching TV and reading?
- Any areas that need to be highlighted, such as the fireplace?

For general lighting, ceiling and table lamps are popular, but you could use track-mounted spotlights for a high-tech look, or recessed downlights and uplighters combined with dimmer switches.

TIP Watching TV in the dark tires your eyes so ensure there is low-level lighting behind the TV to soften the contrast.

Table lamps provide a warm atmosphere and concentrated light, although for task lighting, such as reading or sewing, you will need a standard lamp or an angled table lamp. Don't forget to use accent lighting to highlight pictures or ornaments, by using uplighters or fluorescent lamps concealed behind pelmets or shelves.

DINING ROOM

Requires subtle yet plentiful lighting. You may wish to create different moods, such as a children's party versus dinner for two.

A pendant with a rise-and-fall mechanism is popular. You can raise it to lay the table and lower it for eating.

TIP A pendant should hang just above the head level of diners. With a large table you may need one in the centre and one at each end, possibly on different lighting circuits so that they can be used independently. If you are using several, fit them with dimmers.

To add interest elsewhere, such as the fireplace or for necessity at the serving area, use spotlights, a downlight, or wall lights.

KITCHEN

Lighting needs to be functional and directed where it's needed to ensure safety and comfort.

There are three main work areas: the main work surface, the cooker and the sink. All can be lit by task lighting, ideally controlled independently so that you can darken and hide clutter in the sink area while you eat.

Use spotlights, on tracks or otherwise, to provide lighting. This means that light can be directed on to the cooker and work surfaces or into cupboards, and eyeball downlighters can be rotated to direct light exactly where it is needed as well as bouncing light off the ceiling for overall illumination. Ceiling-mounted lights should be placed above the edge of any horizontal surface so that cabinets, shelves and the cook do not cast shadows on to the work surface.

Work surfaces need localised task lighting. Fluorescent lights produce a bright light, do

SAFETY TIPS

- Never work in your own shadow.
- Make sure all work surfaces are well lit.
- Avoid positioning lights where they may dazzle.
- Don't trail flexes over work-tops or near water.

not cast shadows and are cheaper than tungsten lighting. Work surfaces can be reflective, so minimise glare by placing the light towards the front of the cabinet or shelf, using a baffle or cornice to cover the bulb, so that it does not shine directly on to the work surface or into your eyes.

HALL

An area where you can be adventurous because you are not living in it. Wall or ceiling fittings are more practical than table lamps. Create an even level of gentle light, although you want to aim for some contrast otherwise it can be uniformly dull. For example, highlight a table of ornaments with a spotlight.

Don't forget you will probably need extra light by the phone.

STAIRS

Safety is a priority. Aim for an even light, as contrasting brightness and darkness can be a hazard. The light above the stairs must be brighter than the hall light below so that the stair treads are well defined, and the risers are in the shadow.

If you have any dark corners, or a half landing, consider a downward-directed light to emphasise the change of level. Make sure the light does not shine into the eyes of someone using the stairs as this could be hazardous.

LANDING

Aim to provide an adequate light level while avoiding glare for those coming upstairs. A dimmer switch is useful when using the bathroom at night.

BEDROOM

General lighting should be soft and gentle to create a relaxing atmosphere, but extra light is needed for reading and putting on make-up.

Ensure there is good lighting near mirrors. For this a pair of lights placed about 3ft/1m apart is ideal.

Bedside and dressing tables need extra thought. Choose wall lights or mini spots for bedside lights as they don't take up space on the bedside table. They should be set above head level so that you can read easily but the light doesn't annoy your partner.

At the dressing table, the light needs to be in front of you to throw light on to your face. Put lights above the mirror, at either side, or ideally around three sides.

Light wardrobes and cupboards with a fluorescent tube placed inside the door so that light shines on the contents. A switch fitted to the door hinge brings the light on when the door opens and turns it off when closed.

BATHROOM

As well as general lighting, task lighting is needed for shaving and applying make-up.

The mirror is often sited above the

BATHROOM SAFETY TIPS

- It should not be possible to touch any piece of electrical equipment while using the bath or shower.
- In Britain, only pull-cord switches are allowed inside the bathroom, and if a dimmer switch is used it has to be wired outside the door.
- The high level of moisture means that fittings have to be approved for damp locations, which inevitably limits the choice available.
- All bathroom light fittings should be either double insulated with no metal parts that can be touched, or properly earthed.

washbasin. Ideally, it should be lit on three sides with long incandescent tubes or lots of small low-wattage pearl bulbs, or for a strong clear light install a fluorescent fitting with a diffuser, behind a valance or pelmet.

TYPES OF LIGHT BULB

TIP When talking to professional electricians it may help to know that what we commonly call a bulb is called a lamp in the trade.

In the UK, light bulbs come with either bayonet or screw fittings, in standard and small sizes. They cannot be interchanged, so make sure you buy the correct one.

To achieve the desired lighting effect the correct bulb must be chosen to go with the light fitting. The types available are tungsten, tungsten halogen, fluorescent or compact fluorescent or ESB.

TUNGSTEN FILAMENT

Most common type of bulb, available in various wattages, as clear or pearl. Pearl gives a diffuse light, clear adds sparkle to glass fittings.

Electricity heats the filament, a thin coiled tungsten wire, until it glows white hot. This is an inefficient means of lighting because most of the electricity goes into producing heat rather than light. This is why it is very important to use only the wattage recommended by the manufacturer of the shade, to avoid risk of melting or fire.

These bulbs cast a warm, slightly yellow light in all directions, although ultimately their direction is controlled by the shade or fitting.

Softone and pastel

These are tungsten bulbs, internally coated with a layer of colour to reduce glare and produce a soft, slightly coloured light.

Decorative bulbs

A variety of shapes such as candle, globe and mushroom can complement the style of a fitting. They are attractive when unlit and are often used without a shade. Available in several sizes and wattages.

Spotlight or downlight reflector

A tungsten filament bulb with a silver or aluminium reflector coating. It directs light into a narrowed beam for accent lighting. Available for most light fittings.

TUNGSTEN HALOGEN

These combine a tungsten filament with a halogen gas. They produce a brilliant white light rather than the warmer light given out by simpler filament bulbs. The glass is closer to the filament so the bulbs are smaller, and the fittings are more compact.

Initially expensive they have, however, two to three times the life of a conventional bulb, and they are efficient to use. There are two types: mains voltage or low voltage.

Mains-voltage halogen lamp

The most popular, and easy to use. They are a direct replacement for ordinary bulbs of the same wattage, running at 240 volts, so they do not require a transformer.

Give a particularly bright light, so choose one where the fitting keeps the bulb hidden. Ideal for display lighting with wall washers and downlights.

Low-voltage halogen lamp

The low voltage requires a transformer to convert it to 6, 12 or 24 volts. This means that you have to call in an electrician to hide the transformer, perhaps behind a wall or table.

The bulbs are filled with a combination of tungsten and halogen gases giving a very white light, much closer to real daylight than the more yellow tungsten lights.

This sort of bulb is ideal for spotlights because they give a really concentrated beam, and better sparkle in and around the light than the mains voltage type.

FLUORESCENT

These are high-efficiency tubes, and are inexpensive to run. They give less shadow than tungsten because they are a more diffuse source of light. Ideal for kitchens, garages and work rooms.

In these tubes the electric current passes through an inert gas (such as neon) inside the glass tube, and makes a coating on the inside of the tube glow brightly, or fluoresce. This is more efficient than tungsten so it lasts longer. The light given out is usually bluer and harsher than tungsten, but the tube is cool to the touch.

COMPACT FLUORESCENT

These are scaled-down versions of ordinary fluorescent tubes. Called energy-saving bulbs (ESBs) they are even less expensive to run. They come in a wide range of shapes and sizes.

How they work

The bulbs look totally different to normal fluorescent lights because the glass tube has been narrowed and bent in half and sometimes in half again, so that they can look like four pencils put together; or they can be doubled into a circular shape. Available also as a globe design to be used without a shade in kitchens and bathrooms. Sometimes the bulb is covered by a glass dome, although this tends to be an older design.

The lamp's electronics are housed in an adaptor which fits into an ordinary bulb holder. With more economical designs just the tube can be replaced; with others the whole unit, including the adaptor, has to be replaced (which costs about twice the price).

The harsh white light associated with conventional fluorescents has been replaced by a warm white light more akin to tungsten bulbs. ESBs give a more diffuse light because they have eliminated the dazzling centre of conventional bulbs.

What are the savings?

Lighting uses about 10 % of all the energy in our homes. With an ESB you are making savings in two ways.

1 Running costs are reduced. A 20-watt ESB is equivalent to a 100-watt ordinary bulb, therefore giving an 80 per cent energy saving.

2 It has a longer life. Outlasts a normal bulb by eight times.

So, although ESBs cost more to buy, over one year you can save a considerable amount and also help the environment because you are using less electricity.

Where to use them

So that they pay for themselves as soon as possible, site them where bulbs are on for a long period of time: eg halls, kitchen, porch, but not the downstairs toilet. If you consistently have a bulb on for more than four hours a day then switch to an energy-saving bulb. Another good reason for using them where they will be left on for long periods is that they take a few minutes to reach full brightness, and they may flicker briefly when you turn them on.

These bulbs emit little heat so they are a good choice for paper or delicate fabric shades or where children might touch them, such as a table lamp. They are also a good choice in areas where it's difficult to reach to change the bulb, for example the light fitting at the top of a high stair well.

ESBs are getting progressively smaller and lighter, but some lampshades and fittings won't be able to take them, and they can't be used with dimmer switches.

Availability

They are on sale in most DIY outlets, supermarkets and high-street stores. For much more information and a mail order service, contact Green Light (see Useful Addresses).

TYPES OF SWITCHES

STANDARD SWITCHES

These vary according to design and application. Standard, plate switches are available in white with various sizes of rocker control, or in decorative brass or metal. Architrave plate switches can be mounted on narrow door architraves

Ceiling-mounted switches operated by a pull cord are usually used in bathrooms for safety, because wet hands could cause an electric shock.

DIMMER SWITCHES

These work by reducing the voltage passing through a bulb. This will not only cut down on the amount of electricity used, but also prolong the bulb's life. They are inexpensive to buy and provide an easy means of changing the mood of the room at the turn of a dial.

They are easy to install (see How to Fit a Dimmer Switch, page 224). It is possible to wire them to all kinds of fittings from floor and table lights to ceiling and wall lights, but do not use dimmers with fluorescent fittings.

ONE- AND TWO-WAY SWITCHING

A one-way switch means that the lights linked to the switch are controlled only from one switch position. A two-way switch is linked to a second switch to control the light. In most homes the commonest use of this is on the staircase, so lights can be switched on or off from either the bottom or top of the staircase, and on bedside wall lights.

GARDEN LIGHTING

With the advent of outdoor entertaining this form of lighting has become more in demand. Installing just a few lights will have a dramatic effect outside as a little light goes a long way. Look for appropriate IEC standards.

Illumination

Use indoor mains-wired floodlights to cast a bright, even light over drives and lawns and deter burglars. The higher the position of the light the wider the beam.

Effect

Outline shrubs and trees by using spotlights at ground level. For best effect, the light should be placed the same distance from the feature as the feature is high.

Entertaining

Strings of lights with weatherproof cable provide a party atmosphere. Available from hire shops such as HSS, see Useful Addresses. For instant light, use flares and candles.

Safety

Guide the way down steps with post-mounted lights along the way.

Security

Use an infra-red detector light which switches on when it detects body heat within its range. See Outdoor Security Lights, page 427.

TYPES OF EXTERIOR LIGHTING

Low-voltage lights

These are clipped to waterproof cable which is attached to a transformer. This converts mains voltage (240 volts) to 12 or 24 volts so that if you accidentally cut through the cable with a mower, you will come to no harm. The advantages of this type are that the cable need not be buried and it can be installed by a competent DIYer.

Mains lighting

Permanent garden lighting should have a separate circuit. It should have waterproof sockets, a PVC cable encased in a plastic conduit buried at least 20in/50cm deep, a current breaker (RCD) and a fuse. It should be installed either by a qualified electrician or an expert DIYer.

The advantage of mains lighting systems is that you can have much more lighting than on a low-voltage system, for practical rather than decorative use.

LIGHTING AND THE ENVIRONMENT

If every household in the UK bought just one energy-saving light bulb (for use where light is needed for long periods each day), this country would save power equal to the output of one large power station. This would help cut down on carbon dioxide emissions, and so the use of these bulbs helps to reduce the threat of global warming.

Solar lighting

Solar panels absorb sunshine and convert it into electricity, which is stored in a battery.

The advantage is that you have no installation or running costs, but they will only give a decorative glow and efficiency depends upon the amount of sunshine absorbed.

Security lighting

See Security Lighting, page 426.

STORAGE

It's not always possible to move to a larger house just when it suits. Sometimes it's necessary to use the existing space in your current home in a better way.

It's easy to miss out on potential space by being too rigid in the way we use rooms. Just because the dining room has been there since you moved in, it might be better, particularly if you always eat in the kitchen, to free the room for other uses and and replace it with a fold-away trestle and chairs.

Storage can nearly always be improved when required. Look for dead areas under beds, stairs, backs of doors, in alcoves, beneath the ceiling and under windows. Keep readily available only the things you use regularly; those 'might come in useful items' can go to the charity shop.

KITCHEN

Take a fresh look at your kitchen. There are usually several different ways of storing the same item: for example, by hanging, wall racks, shelves, cupboards above kitchen units, etc. Nowadays, even budget kitchen units offer a good choice of storage systems.

HANGING SPACE

- Fix items, wherever possible, above the work surface; remember you only use the front portion of the work-top for preparation. For example, magnetic knife racks, tools with a hanging hole in the handle, spice racks, extra narrow decorative shelves, racks and rails for mugs or spices can all be fixed to the wall.
- Hanging rails, butchers' hooks and clothes airers can all be used for suspending kitchen clutter. Traditional cast-iron and pine self-

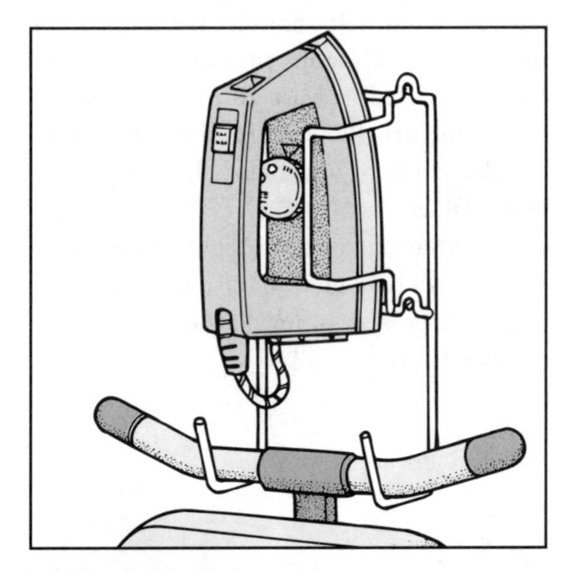

IDEAS TO GET YOU GOING

- Think about which way your doors hang. Would hanging it around the other way make it possible to fit more furniture in the room?
- Interior fitments storage systems can be tailored to fit your exact needs.
- To make space, use every square inch, adding shelves and cupboards to take the clutter.
- Make an old-fashioned plate shelf. Fix it round the room or hall at picture-rail level to display old china.
- Fix shelves across a dull window and cover with plants: they'll thrive in the sunlight.

For more information about putting up shelves, see All About Shelves, page 393.

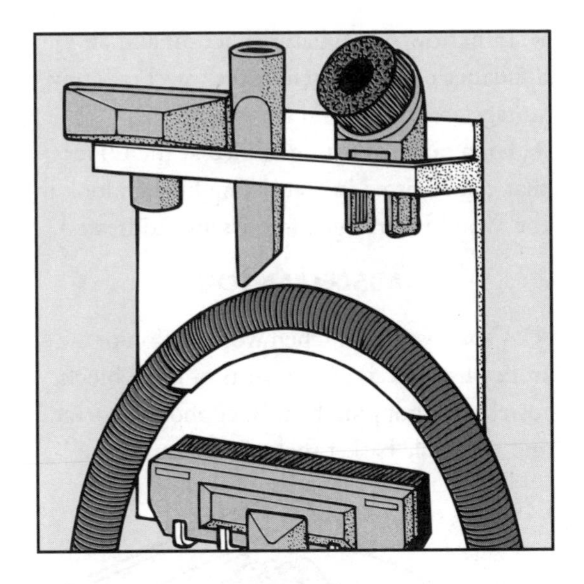

assembly clothes airers are available from The Domestic Paraphernalia Co (see Useful Addresses).

- An ironing organiser from Kleeneze (see Useful Addresses) hangs both an iron and board on the back of a door or wall (see page 186); or use a vacuum tool tidy (above).
- If work-top space is limited save space by wall mounting your microwave on brackets, available from DIY stores. Make sure you have a put-down area adjacent.

DRAWERS

- Use drawer space carefully. For example, a knife block on the work surface saves drawer space; invest in deep drawers with shallow sides for saucepans. Usually double width, they allow you to see and reach contents easily.
- Drawers can get filled up with wasteful clutter unless the inserts are carefully chosen for the cutlery and tools required.
- Huge lift-out baskets allow you to fit more awkward items into drawers.

PAPERWORK

- Keep pieces of paper on a pinboard rather than in drawers.
- Store appliance guarantees and instruction books in an accordion-style plastic wallet from Lakeland Plastics (see Useful Addresses).

CUPBOARDS

- Fit tall rather than standard wall units so that you have storage space right up to the ceiling.
- Fit cupboard interiors with wire racks that slide on and can hang suspended from the shelf above, so that you don't have to stack items too high.
- Utilise the backs of doors (whether kitchen, larder or cupboard) with shallow racks for small items such as spice racks, packets and tubes.
- Fix narrow shelves to the inside of kitchen cupboard doors or at the back of the larder or broom cupboard, for extra storage.
- Use screw-in hooks on the underside of shelves for hanging mugs and cups.
- Base unit space is wasted unless there are more than just one or two shelves. You can buy studs use in the pre-drilled holes. Use for melamine-faced chipboard for the shelf.
- Fit the corners with carousel units to use all available space.

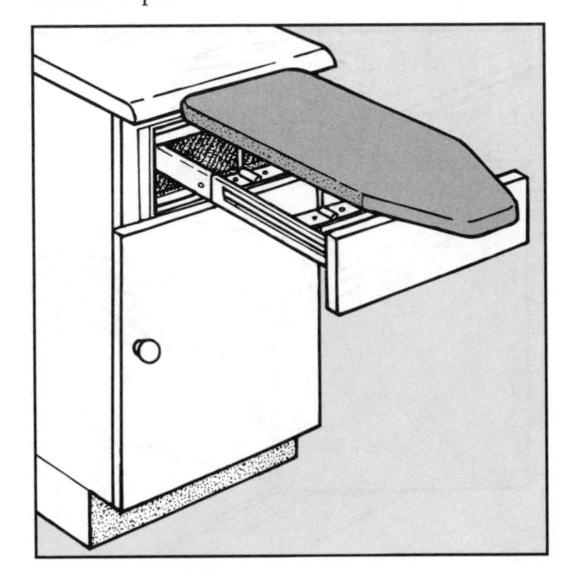

• Some units have extra drawers hidden in the plinth; others have folding steps stored there – invaluable if you have high cupboards.
• Waste bins swing out when a kitchen unit door is opened, leaving the lid behind.
• Use pull-out work-tops (see above), tables and ironing boards (left), which fold down or slide away under a work surface when not in use.
• Use mixer and food processor shelves which swing out (below).

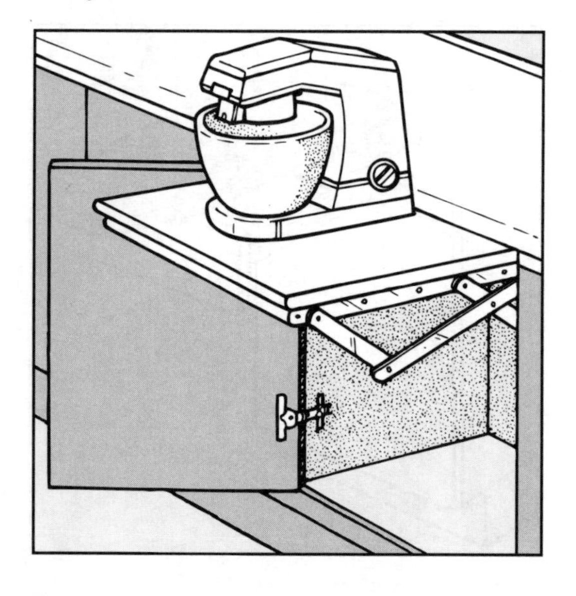

• In narrow spaces between a unit and an appliance consider a telescopic towel rail, tray storage area or built-in wine rack.
• For a range of fittings aimed at the DIYer that can be fitted in an existing kitchen look in the Woodfit catalogue (see Useful Addresses).

MISCELLANEOUS

• A space-saving kitchen work station or trolley has wheels and consists of knife block, towel rail, chopping boards, cupboard storage and vegetable basket (below). Examples are

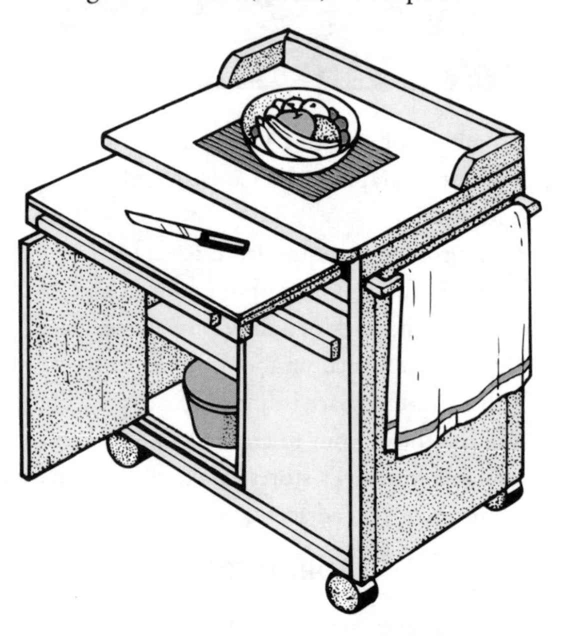

available from Lakeland Plastics, or a cheaper version with one chopping board and no knife block can be bought from Scotts of Stow (see Useful Addresses).
• Multi-pots and steamers are compact to store and can be used to cook many foods.
• Stackable cooling racks fold flat for easy storage (see page 189).
• Use tiered mobile vegetable baskets, or floor-standing pan stands.
• Use a four-bar radiator airer to make the most of radiators (see page 189).
• If the back door comes into the kitchen use

a shoe rack, available in numerous designs, wall mounted or with wheels, horizontal or vertical in shape.

- Maximise the storage potential of a galley kitchen by fitting extra-deep base units.
- Fit units with sliding doors which don't obstruct a narrow passage.
- If your kitchen doubles as a dining room, look for folding tables, chairs or stools.
- If you want to maximise your cupboard

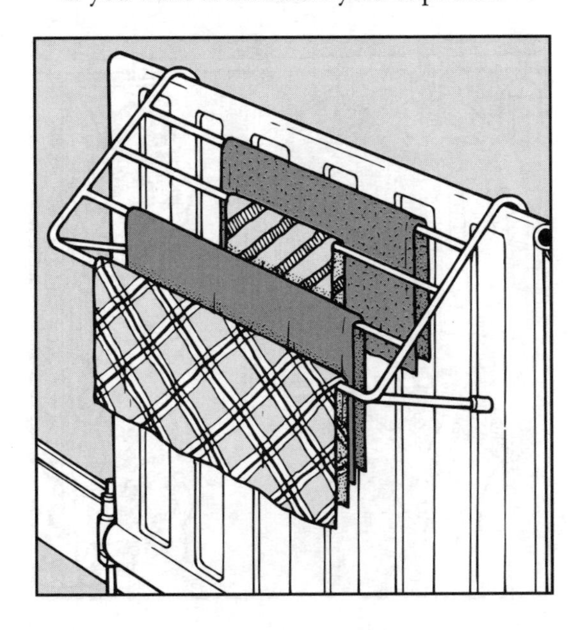

space, many appliance manufacturers make narrower space-saving equipment 18in/450 mm wide rather than the standard 24in/600 mm wide. This applies particularly to cookers, dishwashers, fridges and freezers and some washing equipment. (See Equipping a Kitchen, page 46 and Large Kitchen Appliances, page 89.) Some unit manufacturers, such as Paula Rosa, specialise in micro kitchens (see Useful Addresses).

HALLS

Old-fashioned cupboards under the stairs are fine for the vacuum cleaner but are not sufficiently organised for really efficient storage. Divide it into three separate cupboards, each with its own louvre door, for sports equipment, home office filing, outdoor shoes and wellies, small DIY equipment and spare light bulbs.

- Alternatively, open up the under-stairs space and fit the wall with shelves for books or games, or turn the area into a wine cellar with racks (see page 190).
- Consider a wall-hung telephone and notice board.
- Fix coat hooks and/or make a cloaks cupboard in the corner of the hall, behind the front door, if there is sufficient room. Sliding doors will save space.

LIVING ROOM

The first decision is whether you want individual pieces of furniture, wall mounted or free-standing storage systems. An integrated system can accommodate lots of different types of clutter.

- To save surface space mount your TV and speakers on brackets. They swivel to give adjustable angles and it prevents toddlers from

fiddling with the knobs. Available from catalogue shops.

- If you are short of a spare bedroom consider buying a sofabed for overnight guests.
- Choose a dining room table with drop-down leaves or extending flaps.

BEDROOMS

- Make the most of wardrobe space. There are numerous internal fitments to make better use of the space available. First, consider whether the clothes rail is unnecessarily high for your clothes, or are you more a separates person? Could you lower it and put shelves above or have two hanging rails?
- Use fixings on the backs of the doors, such as a tie bar.
- Add a bar hook over your existing rail to create additional space (see right).
- Invest in heavy-duty clothes-storage covers with an extra-wide gusset, for ball gowns.
- Invest in multiple hangers, so that you can hang several skirts and trousers on one hanger.
- Use a 16-pocket shoe caddy from Betterware (see Useful Addresses, and right), or a 12-pair shoe tower.
- A shelf at the bottom of the wardrobe can store shoes both on and underneath it.
- If you have too many cupboards and not enough drawers you can buy wire basket racking systems in a variety of shapes and sizes to fit exactly the space you need from Britannia Shelving Ltd. (see Useful Addresses).
- You can buy clothes and linen storage bags which are usually transparent. They slide under the bed and store bulky items like sweaters when not in use.

• Use galvanised zinc or tough cardboard boxes and free-standing drawer units, some with carrying handles and wheels. Zinc boxes are available from Muji (see Useful Addresses). Compact storage chests in black, white or silver steel, with matching slot-in wire baskets, are available from Aero (see Useful Addresses).
• Choose a bed with built-in storage drawers, for storing bulky items.
• Consider installing a wall bed from The London Wall Bed Company (see Useful Addresses).
• There is a new design concept from Strachan (see Useful Addresses) called Convert-a-Room. It forms two rooms in one, converting from a fitted study to a fitted bedroom using a folding bed and a swivel-action dressing table that changes into a desk or work station.

CHILDREN'S ROOMS

The number of children's belongings expands rapidly, so any storage systems need to be adjustable.
• Furniture needs to be adaptable so that you can rearrange and change it as necessary. Toys will give way to sports equipment, audio equipment or clothes.
• For a teenager it will become more of a bed-sitting room than a bedroom. A bed-length bolster and cushions can turn a bed into a daytime sofa.
• Colourful plastic boxes and baskets are useful for storing toys. Keep them on low-level shelving in the early years. They are more accessible than stacking boxes, and the shelves can be used for books and stereo as they grow older.
• Use broad, widely spaced shelves in children's rooms. Make sure they're too high to be climbed or sat on.
• A wide shelf with strong brackets can serve as a desk in a study/bedroom.
• Foldaway Plus brackets from DIY stores (above, left) can be used to create a desk surface at an angle of 45° and after use will fold away. Top with bookshelves.
• A computer trolley will hold all the essentials in the minimum space, and free the desk space for hand-written homework and other activities.
• Beds at a higher level above furniture saves space.
• Stacking beds, where one of the beds rolls away under the main bed, saves space.
• Foam beds fold into cube seating when not in use.

BATHROOMS

• Open shelving and hooks solve some storage problems. Organise shelves in the bathroom or cloakroom: narrow glass ones for toiletries, wide wood or melamine for extra supplies and clean towels.
• A built-in vanity unit, or, even better, full-length fully fitted units from wall to wall will give you somewhere to house toilet rolls and

AND FINALLY ...

If you are still short of space, remember that by carefully choosing your colour and lighting scheme you will be able to create an illusion of more space. See Painting and Decorating; Design Tips, page 367 and Lighting, page 177.

cleaning items.

- Utilise space underneath the bath for storing infrequently used items. It is relatively easy to fit a door or some kind of access on the bath panel.

ATTICS

By adding flooring, access and running a light up into the attic you can make a large and useful storage area for infrequently used items like Christmas decorations and suitcases.

Make sure that the ladder used to gain access to the loft is firmly fixed: see Ladder Safety, page 381.

GARAGES AND SHEDS

Storage efficiency outside the house can be easily improved.

- Use lots of racking systems and hooks suspended from the ceiling.
- To store bikes out of the way and save floor space there are special bike hinges by Mountain Ledge from cycle, sports shops and department stores.
- Fit shelves to hold tools and DIY equipment.
- For gardening, choose multi tools which save space because you have one handle to which you can fit several heads. A fold-away wheelbarrow is compact to store.

STORAGE OF VALUABLE ITEMS

If you inherit something of value and don't want to display it, it is important to consult a conservator to make sure that you store it properly.

FINDING EXPERT HELP

- Contact The Conservation Unit of the Museums & Galleries Commission (see Useful Addresses) for details of conservators of movable items such as paintings, stone, glass, metal, fabrics and furniture. For £5 they will put you in touch with five specialist

CAUSES OF DETERIORATION

Light is a source of energy and the chemical changes it causes cannot be reversed. Even weak light causes damage so lower the level by drawing curtains or covering items.

Humidity and temperature are closely related. We can take in drinks; objects can't. Central heating lowers the relative humidity. A humidity of 50 to 60 per cent is ideal for most objects. Too much humidity and you encourage mould growth; too little and paper becomes brittle and wood shrinks and cracks.

Condensation occurs when the temperature of a solid surface is lower than that of the air around it, so anything in contact with a surface like this will have water and dust deposited on it.

Lack of ventilation: insufficient air is the best way of promoting mould growth. To prevent it, allow plenty of fresh air to circulate.

conservators in your area, and provide information on training, previous work, security on the premises and references.

- The Institute for Conservation of Artistic and Historic Work (see Useful Addresses) is the professional body for conservators not accrediting and can provide you with names of specialists.
- Estimates for work and storage should be given free of charge.
- Contact your local art museum and ask for the conservation department or curator. He will put you in touch with those conservators that he uses.
- Look for a regional conservation centre in your area.
- There are specialist firms that store and transport valuable and precious pieces of fine art. Momart (see Useful Addresses) will keep the work of art wrapped and crated in a stable environment, which means controlling temperature, light and humidity. Each valuable object is different and requires different conditions. Ask about insurance and to see crated facilities.
- The Institute of Paper Conservation (see Useful Addresses) will put you in touch with conservators of paper items including watercolours, photographs, books and maps.

Questions to ask

- How are they qualified: in other words by apprenticeship or are they formally qualified?
- Do they have good references? Can you speak to other people who have used them?
- Can you see the studio?
- Are they adequately insured?
- Do they have a security system or alarm?

DIY STORAGE

Only consider this if you have a big house, with unused rooms. Do not push valuable items away in an attic or on top of the wardrobe.

You need a dry room with a low level of relative humidity: 50 to 55 per cent. It needs less heat than normal domestic heating, but it does need just a little so it's not damp.

You can buy a hair hygrometer from garden centres or from Conservation Resources (see Useful Addresses), who also provide a catalogue of items to help with conservation.

Storing paintings

Don't clean gilded frames and don't touch the painting itself.

If you have a painting in a frame, wrap and protect the whole thing. Don't wrap in household blankets and sheets; they are dusty. Buy some plastic sheet called Melinex from Conservation Resources. It is almost impervious to moisture, and if the item should be knocked it will keep all the pieces together. Tape Melinex to itself only. Don't use tape on the picture. Then wrap it in bubble wrap, and use heavy card as packing. Check its condition at least once a year.

If you don't use Melinex, then acid-free tissue paper, which is widely available, is the next best option.

Any damp in a room will manifest itself throughout the floors and walls, so keep away from these where possible.

If you hang a picture use cork spacers behind the picture to allow for ventilation by keeping the picture away from the wall. Make sure the cord is adequate. If you do anything to the picture, such as replace the cord, do it on a cushioned surface.

Storing carpets

It is essential that storage is dry and warm and not in a cold outhouse or shed.

Before storage make sure the carpet is dry to

prevent mildew. Roll carpets and rugs; do not fold them.

If the carpet is dirty have it professionally cleaned. Ask for a beating and cleaning treatment. Ensure that all dirt and foreign substances are removed from the base of the carpet, and ask for the carpet to be dried and wrapped. Contact the National Carpet Cleaners Association (see Useful Addresses).

If storing in an attic, wrap in a plastic sleeve, but leave both ends open to allow ventilation. Unroll periodically to check its condition.

Some cleaning firms or furniture removers will store carpets. Contact the National Carpet Cleaners Association.

Storing silver

See Silver; Storage tips, page 310.

Storing wedding dresses

See Wedding Dresses, page 348.

Storing books

Glass cabinets will protect books from dust and sunlight but adequate ventilation is still essential for preservation. Leaf through the books occasionally. Regular use stops books from smelling musty.

Books should be stored at a moderate temperature, 55–65°F/13–18°C, to prevent the paper drying out.

Store weighty tomes flat to stop the pages breaking away from the spine.

For professional help contact The Society of Bookbinders (see Useful Addresses).

Storing photographs

Buy albums or binders containing acid-free paper for photos you treasure.

Use detachable corners, not glue to fix the photos in place.

Store negatives and old prints out of sunlight, at an even temperature, in polyester covers to prevent the photograph adhering to the surface and avoid bleaching of colours. Clear polyester sleeves are available from Secol (see Useful Addresses). They also have a specialised storage system which can be used for photographs and negatives, documents and tickets.

Also contact The Royal Photographic Society (see Useful Addresses) for advice. They sell a booklet: *Caring for your Family Photographs at Home*, published by DPA (Documentary Photography Archive, see Useful Addresses).

Storing possessions when moving house

See Storage, page 40

FLOORING

Flooring is the most hard-working area in the home so it must be functional to withstand abrasion, weight and spills, yet still be decorative. As well, the colour, texture and finish must blend in with the rest of the decor.

Who doesn't admire the cool stone slabs or rich terracotta tiles of Mediterranean villas? But, when it comes to the crunch, most of us opt for foot-friendly carpets or inexpensive, easy-to-clean vinyl. However, there may be other alternatives worth considering.

THE SUB-FLOOR

Before you decide on the surface, think about what the flooring is to be laid over, that is, the sub-floor.

This greatly affects the wear and appearance of the covering. The sub-floor must be dry, level, and without cracks, bumps or protruding nails. If it is uneven, damp or not very rigid, it is essential to deal with the problem before laying the new covering. You will probably need to get specialist help for this. There are plenty of suitable professionals: look in the Yellow Pages under flooring, flooring services and contractors, and obtain several quotes.

Remove any residual bitumen backing or adhesive used for the previous flooring, because you could find that this works its way through the new flooring, particularly cork, linoleum or vinyl, causing discoloration.

WOODEN SUB-FLOORS

If it is uneven you may be able to sand out the bumps yourself with a floor sander, or better still cover with hardboard or plywood.

Use squares of hardboard (about 1/10in/2.5mm thick) which have been conditioned with water and stacked for 48 hours. Lay them textured side up. Alternatively, use sheets of ¼in/6mm-thick primed plywood.

Secure using 1in/25mm rustproof nails, set at 4in/10cm intervals around the edge and every 6in/15cm across the middle of the room. Take care to avoid any cables or water pipes under the floorboards.

Wood flooring needs a dry position and it is usual practice to lay it over a damp-proof membrane or polythene sheeting. Check with a flooring specialist.

Quarry, terracotta, brick, stone or ceramic tiled flooring should not be laid over a suspended wood sub-floor because their weight would be too great.

CONCRETE SUB-FLOORS

To level out an uneven concrete floor use a ready-mixed self-levelling compound or screed, about ⅛in/3mm thick.

LAYING A NEW FLOOR

Never lay new flooring on top of an old one, as tread and wear patterns would soon be transferred. Some types of flooring can be laid by a competent DIYer, following the manufacturer's instructions, particularly tiles, carpet, vinyl, linoleum and cork. Laying sheet linoleum can be a problem because it isn't very flexible, and even sheet vinyl can be awkward because of the size.

Always use the correct adhesive or grouting. Some vinyl does not need to be stuck down: check when purchasing.

Hard flooring such as terracotta, quarry stone and ceramic tiles should be professionally fitted: contact the National

Master Tile Fixers Association (see Useful Addresses) for details of recommended tilers.

TIP Plain, small patterns and light colours will give an effect of spaciousness.

TIP In a fitted kitchen, lay floor coverings once the units are in place.

HARD FLOORING

BRICK TERRACOTTA PAVING

Suitable for kitchens and dining areas, outhouses and conservatories.

This is warm and rustic, and available in many shades. Different patterns can be laid by positioning the bricks at different angles, eg herringbone style.

The York Handmade Brick Company (see Useful Addresses) has a good selection and will advise on installation and sealing.

Pros

- Can be laid directly on to the damp-proof course.
- Non-slip.
- Stain and grease resistant.
- Can be sealed.

Cons

- Hard.

CERAMIC TILES

Suitable for kitchens, bathrooms, hallways, and conservatories.

Should be floor strength and laid on to a solid floor which should be perfectly flat. The International Abrasion Resistance Grades include four ratings. Class III is suitable for kitchens and Class IV for bathrooms. Whether matt, glazed or unglazed, there's a huge range of colours, styles and patterns available.

Sizes vary from tiny mosaic tiles to 1ft/30cm square, and hexagonal, rectangular and interlocking shapes.

Pros

- Impervious to water and chemicals.
- Cool.
- Low maintenance.
- Chips and scratches are less noticeable in unglazed tiles because the colour is distributed throughout the tile.

Cons

- Dishes will crack if dropped on to them.
- Noisy.
- Can be tiring on the feet.
- Slippery when wet.
- Hygienic, but attract dust in a bathroom when damp, due to condensation.

MARBLE

Suitable for hallways, reception rooms.

Composed of limestone that has been compacted under natural pressure. It's expensive and can be overpowering if used all over, but is stunning for panels and inlays.

Pros

- Hard-wearing and impervious to water and staining.
- Built-in lustre, but can be polished after laying.
- Improves with age.

Cons

- Heavy, so the sub-floor must be sound and strong.
- Cold to the touch.
- Noisy.
- The polished surface can be slippery, especially when wet.

MOSAIC

Suitable for hallways, and as a border to other hard flooring.

Can be ceramic, glass and marble. The individual pieces should be no larger than an inch, and irregular. Sheets of mosaics with a peel-off backing are available, to make laying easier, but they are usually designed and laid by specialist craftsmen.

Pros
- Hard wearing.
- Cool.
- Look stunning.

Cons
- Rough to walk on.
- Need an absolutely flat sub-floor.
- Noisy and hard.

QUARRY AND TERRACOTTA TILES

Suitable for kitchens, halls, conservatories and porches.

Various different colours are achieved by the use of clays from different areas of the UK and the world, as well as the materials used to fire the kiln which bakes them. Gas-fired kilns make a plain, uniform-coloured tile, while the irregular-coloured Spanish or Mexican tiles vary from cream to deep russet from a fuel of almond or coconut shells.

Tile shapes vary: squares (4in/10cm or 16in/40cm), rectangles, hexagons, octagons and lozenge shapes, with clipstones or insets and borders.

Encaustic tiles are made from different-coloured clays. The overall effect can be similar to a geometric patterned or oriental rug with border, set into the floor.

Acrylic seals will maintain the natural colour of the tiles, while linseed oil will darken and change the colour during its life. Quarry tiles have a more regular appearance and are generally not sealed.

Pros
- Can improve in appearance with age.
- Hard wearing.
- Impervious to water.
- A little softer underfoot than ceramic tiles.

Cons
- Cold and noisy.
- Break if a hard object is dropped on them.

TIP If using glazed ceramic insets, sink these in ⅛in/3mm to minimise the wear of the glazed surface.

SLATE

Suitable for halls, porches, conservatories.

British slate is quarried in Wales and Cornwall; African and Chinese slate is richly coloured, but expensive. A good range of colours and finishes include diamond sawn with a smooth matt finish; riven, where the slate is naturally split leaving a textured surface; and fine rubbed with a light sheen.

Treat with a mixture of linseed oil and turps for extra lustre.

Pros
- Hard wearing.
- Easy to maintain.
- Impervious to water.

Cons
- Brittle and heavy to handle, so needs a strong sub-floor.
- Some types have an uneven surface.
- Will stain, but this will fade or blend in over time.
- Cold and noisy.

STONE

Suitable for kitchens, halls and utility areas.

Includes granite, sandstone, limestone, and York stone, which have a variable texture and colour. It is usually cut into simple shapes: square or oblong.

Pros

As slate.

Cons

As slate.

TERRAZZO

Suitable for halls, porches, kitchens and bathrooms.

Made from marble chippings and dust set into cement, and is mottled rather than veined like real marble. Takes its colour from whatever type of marble has been used; a large range of colours is available. It looks smooth and elegant but is very expensive.

Pros

As marble.

Cons

As marble.

WOOD

Suitable for throughout the house, with the exception of wet areas such as bathrooms.

There is a wide choice of woods and finishes available. Use clear grades of ash, beech and maple for cool modern interiors, and the more subtle tones of rustic grades to bring warmth to traditional rooms. Oak is available in a wide range of grades from rustic knotty to the clear straight-grained qualities found in the classic parquet floors of France and Italy. Ash, oak, beech and maple are all well-established hard-wearing woods suitable for a wide variety of areas, while cherry is quite new to flooring, bringing a feeling of softness and warmth.

Surfaces can be lacquered, oiled or waxed. Popular branded ranges include mainly lacquered finishes, but more oiled products are becoming available for heavy traffic areas. Oil is less shiny than lacquer, and brings out the grain and texture of the wood.

Strips and boards provide a good background to rugs and furniture. To create space, try laying the wood diagonally instead of vertically.

Blocks, battens and tiles can be used to create herringbone and other parquet patterns. If laying over floorboards, install a layer of plywood first.

Recent developments in adhesive and mechanical fixing systems allow easy installation over existing floorboards, concrete or any level base such as plywood, chipboard, etc. The thickness of the flooring is important. When nailing to joists or battens, do not use products under ¼in/19mm in thickness. Overlay flooring, which comes in thickness from 3⁄10in/8mm upwards, can be used where it is totally supported, for example over floorboards or concrete.

Solid and laminated branded ranges include Junckers, Kahrs, Tarkett, Vigers and Wicanders. Wicanders Wood-O-Cork has a cork core sandwiched beneath the wood, which is protected by a vinyl-wear layer on the surface. If buying non-branded products, check they have been properly kiln-dried and beware of reclaimed timber from derelict buildings where changes in humidity may well have affected the dimensional stability of the wood itself.

To see a wide selection of wooden floors, and for professional advice, visit Vigers' new showroom (see Useful Addresses).

Pros

- Durable and can improve with age.
- Warm and stylish.
- Easy-to-clean surface.

Cons

- Not waterproof, so avoid over-wetting.
- Can be dented by heels and castors.

RENOVATING OLD FLOORBOARDS

Renovating old wooden floors is only worth the effort if they are in good condition. Hammer down protruding nails, fill in nail holes or gaps, and remove sharp edges or splinters. These can then be sanded, stained darker or bleached a lighter colour, and sealed or varnished.

When sanding down, use the sander along the length of the board, never across. Remove all traces of dust, and then wipe over with white spirit. Bleach, stain or paint.

LIGHTENING WOOD

Scrub with domestic bleach and leave to dry. Repeat until the correct colour is achieved. Thoroughly wash the floor with water. Allow to dry. The wood grain may have expanded slightly due to the water: if so, sand it down before sealing.

STAINING

A good range of colours is available, and they can be combined with a varnish.

Choose either oil, water or spirit-based stains. Oil based tend to give a more even colour but are slower to dry.

Apply with a clean dry cloth, along the grain. It's easier to concentrate on one floorboard at a time. Repeat until the required depth of colour is achieved. Dry, and then seal.

SEALING

Use either wax or a polyurethane varnish.

Polyurethane varnish

Varnishes can darken and yellow the wood, but they are tough, water resistant and easy to maintain. Choose from gloss, satin and matt finishes. Gloss is the toughest, but shows up dust and marks easily.

Apply across the grain, finishing with long brush strokes down the grain. Apply at least three coats in areas of heavy wear. Sand in between each coat to give the next one something to grip on to.

Wax

Not as tough or as water resistant. Needs frequent re-treating. Seal the floor with a floor sealer to prevent dirt penetrating the wood. Apply wax thinly with a soft cloth, leave, and then buff up the surface with a floor polisher. Polish with a soft cloth.

SEMI-HARD FLOORING

CORK TILES

Suitable for kitchens, bathrooms and halls.

Made from natural cork mixed with binders and then baked. There is a large range of coloured corks available. When choosing the thickness make sure you don't choose wall tiles. For floors, 3⁄16in/5mm is average, but for the most durability, go as thick as possible: they must be thick enough to withstand sanding down if wear occurs. Choose around 1⁄4in/6mm if you are covering a solid floor.

Finishes

Unsealed: seal with four to six layers of polyurethane. It's worth spending time building up the seal. Colour unsealed tiles with wood varnish for unusual finishes.

Waxed finish: very warm and non-slip with a natural sheen. Good for bathrooms, bedrooms and lounge, but not designed for kitchen use.

Acrylic sealed: ready-sealed tiles are suitable for heavier wear areas including kitchens. An extra coat of sealant after installation gives a completely sealed surface, covering the joins. They can also be varnished to give an extra matt or high-gloss finish.

PVC surface: completely sealed. Impervious to dirt and spills, and are very good for kitchens and bathrooms.

Pros

- Warm and comfortable.
- Quiet with good insulating properties.
- Slip resistant, even when wet.
- Good resistance to abrasion and friction.
- Easy to lay.

Cons

- Will wear in high traffic areas but can be sanded down and resealed.

LINOLEUM

Suitable for kitchens, bathrooms, conservatories.

Currently enjoying a revival because of the designer patterns available and its natural image. It is processed from wood flour, cork, linseed oil and various resins baked together, rolled under pressure and pressed on to a strong jute backing.

Available in sheet or tile form. Sheet form should be professionally laid.

Pros

- Hard wearing.
- Quiet and warm.
- Springy underfoot.
- Designs with borders, motifs and patterns can be tailor-made, but have them professionally done.
- Does not indent as readily as vinyl – but protective cups should be used under castors.
- Improves with age as the linseed oil oxidises and destroys surface bacteria.
- Resistant to minor burns and fading.

Cons

- Over-wetting can damage the finish and cause rotting.

VINYL

Suitable for kitchens, bathrooms, playrooms, halls, porches.

Manufacturers have at last come up with stunning new ranges with more than a hint of the Continent about them: rustic reds, deep blues and grey flecks, symmetrical designs and bold borders and insets.

It's a flexible plastic surface available in

TIPS FOR FITTING VINYL

- If you are fitting it round a lot of awkward shapes in the bathroom for example, it's easier to lay tiles, but if it's a rectangular-shaped room, sheet vinyl will give a better result.
- Cut a little larger than the actual size because it does shrink slightly when laid. Trim to fit after several weeks.
- If you've chosen a geometric pattern, try and square it up with the line of the doorway so that it runs either at right angles or parallel.
- Leave the vinyl in the room in which it is to be laid for at least 24 hours beforehand, either opened up flat, or loosely rolled.

sheets (generally 2, 3 or 4yd/m widths) or tile form. It can be cushioned with expanded PVC foam sandwiched under the wear layer. A thickness of at least 0.06in/1.4mm is the best choice. Price varies according to thickness of wear layer (0.2 to 0.4mm) and the cushioning.

Sophisticated hard vinyls such as Amtico (see Useful Addresses) look realistically like wood, quarry tiles and marble. They should be professionally fitted.

Special safety flooring is available; good for bathrooms.

Pros

- Very versatile.
- Cushioned vinyl is very comfortable and warm.
- Tiles are very easy to fit because they are flexible. Some have self-adhesive backing.
- Waterproof and resistant to oil and most domestic cleaning agents.
- Easy to clean because of its smooth impervious surface.

Cons

- Cheap flooring can scuff so choose the thickest you can.
- Will burn and mark if something hot is placed on it.
- Dents, and can be damaged by dragging heavy appliances and furniture across the surface. Stand heavy equipment on hardboard or special discs.

CARPET

Thanks to advances in fibre technology, today's carpets are better value than ever before – a far cry from the 1950s when the choice available was restricted to either wool or nylon. In the UK, man-made carpets now account for 80 per cent of all sold.

CHOOSING A CARPET

There are several factors to consider when choosing a new carpet:

- Cost: the maximum you can realistically afford.
- Durability: how much wear and tear the carpet is likely to get.
- The purpose of the room it will go in.
- How long you want it to last.

This will give you some indication of the quality required, the type of fibre, the depth and the density of the pile.

COST

Pay as much as you can afford: cheap carpets are false economy.

Shop around, as prices vary considerably. Check what you are getting for your money: ask for a breakdown of fitting and accessory costs such as gripper rods, tape, etc. Check whether extra is charged for removing doors, etc. Check what widths the carpet is available in. Obtain several written quotes and compare cost breakdowns.

DURABILITY

This is determined by looking at the denseness of the pile and its resilience. Check this by pressing your hand on the pile and monitor how long it takes to spring back into shape; the faster the better. Short, dense piles are more durable than long shag piles.

Carpets are made in a variety of weights: light, medium and heavy. A combination of 80 per cent wool to 20 per cent nylon is probably one of the most durable blends, if the construction is good.

Synthetic carpets now look more like wool than they used to, and they have fewer problems with static electricity as the fibres are now treated to reduce it.

Carpets are either woven, tufted or bonded. Woven carpets tend to be the most expensive.

Woven carpets

Usually called Wilton or Axminster.

Axminster carpets are named after the loom on which they are woven. Many colours can be used in the weaving and so they are often patterned. They can be natural, synthetic or a blend of fibres, with a short cut or shag pile (or a mixture of both).

Wilton carpets also derive their name from the loom they are woven on. The loom weaves the yarn in a continuous strand so combination of colours is more limited. A maximum of five can be used. They have a close-textured pile which can be a smooth velvet finish or loops and twists. Can be natural, synthetic or a blend of fibres.

Brussel-type carpets are a Wilton with an uncut pile. They are very hard wearing but without the velvety appearance and sheen of a cut pile.

Tufted carpets

These are quicker to produce and constitute 80 per cent of the UK market.

Tufts are inserted into a pre-woven backing, anchored by latex or a polyvinyl compound and then another backing – usually hessian – is applied. Fibres are natural, synthetic or blended, which can be looped, cut or twisted. Available in a large range of widths, colours and textures.

Tufted carpets can have a secondary foam backing which acts as an underlay. This type of carpet is usually cheaper and less durable, and so is more suitable for bedrooms rather than heavy wear areas.

Bonded carpets

The carpet pile is held between two specially treated adhesive bases and is then sliced in two. This means that all the pile is on the carpet surface.

Density of pile is one of the most important factors in determining quality. The closer the tufts, the more hard wearing is the carpet.

Loop pile consists of a series of small loops. Low loop piles are very hard wearing.

Cut pile is cut off to form a flat, level surface to give its characteristic sheen and soft feel. Axminster carpets can only be cut pile.

Velvet is short, dense, cut pile which feels luxurious, but is susceptible to shading and shows up tread and furniture marks.

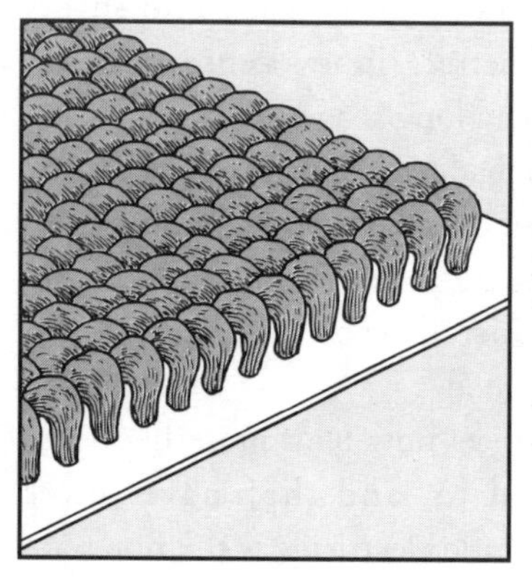

Loop pile

Cut pile

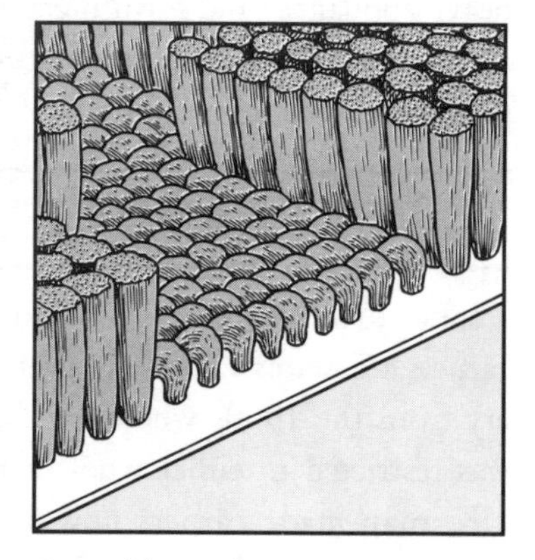

Cut and loop pile

Alternatively plush and saxony carpets have a slightly longer and less dense cut pile.
Shag is the longest cut pile.
Cut and loop pile is a combination of the two constructions, creating a textured, sculptured effect.
Berber can be either a cut or loop pile (although traditionally is a wool, loop pile carpet) which has flecks of contrasting colour throughout.
Twist pile is a tightly twisted cut pile. The greater the twist, the greater the durability and resistance to flattening.
Cord carpet is woven carpet made from a mixture of yarns and very low loops, like corduroy. Very hard wearing but can be harsh to the touch.

WHICH FIBRE?

Acrylic

Often blended with other fibres, it's particularly suitable for bedrooms and other low-duty areas. Not very common.

Pros

- Lightweight carpet with a wool-type texture.
- Does not absorb dirt and stains easily.

Cons

Not as durable as other fibres.

Polyamide/Nylon

About half of British-made tufted carpets have a nylon pile. Short-looped nylon pile is a good choice for kitchens, play areas and bathrooms. For heavy-wear areas, look for a twisted-pile nylon carpet.

Pros

- Very strong fibre.
- Durable, and if the pile is dense will resist crushing.
- Keeps its colour well.
- Good economy choice.
- Rot resistant.

Cons

- Doesn't maintain its appearance well in low-density carpets (fewer tufts per square inch).
- The pile, once flattened, is difficult to restore.
- Cheap, untreated types can cause static shock.

Polyester

A suitable choice for bedrooms.

Pros

- Reasonable resistance to abrasion.
- Does not fade easily.
- Warm feel.

Cons

- Cheap versions which haven't been treated are prone to soiling.
- Once the pile has been flattened it's difficult to restore.

Polypropylene

Suitable for kitchens and bathrooms. About a quarter of British tufted carpets have a polypropylene pile or one that is blended with other fibres. Blends of 50 per cent wool and polypropylene are very popular, and if they have a good proportion of wool it helps to prevent the pile from flattening permanently.

Pros

- Good value.
- Non-absorbent and easy to clean.
- Withstands abrasion well.
- Colourfast.
- Low in static.

Cons

- Traditionally harsh textured, but new ranges are softer.
- Will flatten more easily than wool so polypropylene is often used in low loop pile constructions (so the pile does not crush as easily).

Wool

Generally blended with 20 per cent nylon for greater resilience and durability.

Suitable for heavy-duty areas. For maximum durability look for a short, dense pile.

Pros

- Inherently good resistance to soiling and wear.
- Soft and comfortable.
- Good insulation properties.
- Does not burn readily.
- The pile does not easily flatten so retains its appearance well.

Cons

- Can rot if left wet.
- All wool is expensive, but you get what you pay for. A better option is to go for an 80/20 wool/nylon mix.

CARPET WEIGHT

Look for the British Carpet Manufacturers Association (BCMA) label and grading scheme on British carpets (see Useful Addresses). It gives details of pile fibre, construction, cleaning and room suitability. Their grading system specifies:

Class 1: Light use, such as bedrooms.

Class 2: Medium general use, such as dining areas.

Class 3: Heavy use in halls, living rooms and on stairs.

Class 4 : Extra-heavy use.

However, some manufacturers use their own labelling system and this may not be as stringent as the BCMA requirements, so look for their logo.

FITTING CARPETS

Even if you are refitting a second-hand carpet, it's worth paying for professional fitting. According to the National Institute of Carpet Fitters: 'Anyone can lay a carpet but it takes a professional to fit one.'

A good fitter will ensure that the floor is properly prepared, that patterns and seams are correctly matched, that the pile is laid in the right direction, and that carpets are wrinkle-free and snug fitting. (Pieces of carpets should not run at right angles to each other.)

For a recommended carpet fitter in your area, contact the National Institute of Carpet Fitters (see Useful Addresses).

Carpet tiles

Carpet tiles are easy to lay yourself.

- Don't lay on to carpet, underlay or vinyl flooring.
- Always start in the centre of the room.
- Make sure the pile runs in the same direction.
- Stick every third row of tiles with spray adhesive or double-sided sticky tape.
- For cutting, use a sharp Stanley knife or strong scissors and cut from the wrong side.

Underlay

Never underestimate the importance of a good underlay. Not only does it prolong the life of your carpet and prevent the penetration of dust from the floorboards, it also adds comfort and offers sound and heat insulation.

There are several different types available:

Rubber: different thicknesses and weights are

available, from light domestic to top-quality heavyweight. Generally, they have a waffle construction.

Rubber crumb: made from reconditioned rubber. Top-quality is hard wearing and dense so is a good insulator, although it is not as springy as the waffle type.

Felt: made from matted fibres. Top-quality ones will discourage indentations caused by furniture. Recommended to be used under seamed carpets.

Tips for underlay include:

- A good quality underlay is particularly important in heavy traffic areas such as halls and stairs.
- Never use old underlay with a new carpet. It's false economy. An old underlay will carry the tread patterns of the previous covering.
- Latex and plastic-foam underlays, and foam-backed carpets should be laid over a strong paper first, to stop them from sticking to the floor.
- Avoid foam-backed carpets in heavy traffic areas or if you intend to take carpets with you when you move.

COLOUR AND DESIGN

- Ideally, choose your carpet before your other soft furnishings as it is the most expensive item and takes the most wear. Unfortunately, most of us choose it last and have to go for plain colours. Patterns disguise wear and soiling.
- Light colours make a room appear larger and more spacious, whereas dark colours can be oppressive. Choose warm colours for dull rooms with little light.
- Large patterns can dominate the room making the floor area seem smaller. Combine them with plain or textured fabrics for curtains and upholstery to balance the busy design. With directional patterns, it should be the right way up if you look at it from the door.
- Stripes can make a hall look longer and more narrow if laid lengthways.
- Primary-coloured rooms are hard to match with a carpet: use a contrast.
- When choosing your carpet shade, check against the colour of floor-length curtains, the door, and any strong colours showing from other rooms.
- If you have a pet, it's wise to choose a neutral shade, similar to your pet's coat.
- For a really elegant look, choose a carpet with a border. These are becoming increasingly popular, and you can mix and match styles. Borders give definition and detail to a room lacking any focal point. They are most effective if there is no furniture around the edge of the room, emphasising details like the fireplace, alcove or bay window.

STAIN PROTECTORS

These are mainly applied to synthetic carpets because wool carpets have greater inherent stain-retarding properties.

Carpets can be treated in two ways:

1 An overall soil-retardant finish acts as a shield to retard penetration of dirt and liquids.

2 A stain-resistant finish reacts as stains occur and prevents the stains from being absorbed. Stain-resistant treatments do not provide total protection but they do give you time to blot up spills and thus help to prevent any permanent staining on the carpet.

Try to use a combination of both types of treatments. They can be applied *in situ* but they last longer if applied during manufacture. To check that a carpet has good stain protection, look out for the National Carpet Cleaners' Association (NCCA) logo, which can be found on the carpet itself, or on the point-of-sale literature.

CARPET PROBLEMS

Fluffing or shedding

With the exception of loop pile, all new carpets tend to 'fluff' because of the short fibres left in the pile when the yarn was cut. These will disappear after several weeks.

Sprouting

Occurs if a heel or pet's claw pulls a loop so that the next one is pulled flat. Rectify using a tapestry needle.

Shading

Occurs when the tufts lean in different directions so the light reflects in different ways, creating light and dark effects on the carpet. It's more noticeable on new, plain velvets or with small motifs on a plain background.

This effect can be temporary and rectified by brushing the pile in the same direction.

Watermarking or pooling

This is permanent shading that cannot be brushed away. Manufacturers find it difficult to explain away, especially if the carpet left the factory in perfect condition. It can be caused by contraction and expansion of the backing material; changes in temperature and humidity; changes in direction of traffic, etc.

Tracking

Most noticeable in plain carpets, this is the compression of the pile where foot traffic is restricted to certain areas: between furniture, in front of fireplaces and in doorways. Wherever possible, furniture should be re-arranged to minimise differences in wear.

Help with carpet faults

If you have a problem with a newly bought carpet, the British Carpet Technical Centre (BCTC) (see Useful Addresses) runs an arbitration scheme, dealing with alleged manufacturing faults. Its service is free.

Qualitas Furnishing Standards (see Useful Addresses), set up by some retailers and manufacturers, runs a complaints service for disputes against its members. Look for the Qualitas logo (see page 55).

NATURAL-FIBRE FLOOR COVERINGS

Suitable for all dry areas.

These traditional coverings have been around since the days of the Ancient Egyptians but have become more popular in recent years as they provide a warm, muted background for many styles of room, contemporary or period. They provide a good range of rich colours and interesting weaves; are hard wearing; and do not suffer from static.

Choose natural-fibre flooring with a latex backing for a total fitted look. The backing helps it to stay flat and keep its shape. Extra underlay will increase their comfort and insulation. It can be fitted or loose.

Contact Crucial Trading for details (see Useful Addresses).

COIR

Thick, rough fibre which protects the inner section of the coconut from the casing. Coir matting has become more sophisticated in recent years, and can be combined with sisal or other natural materials which can be dyed exciting shades. Often backed with latex or vinyl, to prevent the dust from penetrating through and improve its durability.

Pros

- Relatively cheap and hard-wearing (although not as durable as sisal or seagrass).

Cons

- Uncomfortable on bare feet.
- Needs to be tightly fitted or it waves, looking untidy and becoming a hazard.
- Lengths need to be stitched together.

SEAGRASS AND RUSH

Woven into plaits and herringbones which look great in old rooms, especially with stone.

Pros

- Much tougher and smoother than coir.
- Warm underfoot.
- Inexpensive.
- Good stain-resistance.

Cons

- Can be slippery, so if using on stairs lay the grain parallel to the stair tread.

SISAL

A fibre produced from the leaves of the plant, *Agave sisalana* by a special spinning process. Types of weave include herringbone, plaid, bouclé and panama.

Pros

- Soft and hard wearing.
- Inexpensive.
- Dyes well, so good range of colours.

Cons

- Porous: stains can be hard to remove.

FLOORING ROOM BY ROOM

KITCHENS

Needs to be easy to clean, waterproof, tough, grease and spill resistant, non-slip and comfortable. Vinyl and lino are a good choice.

LOUNGE/LIVING AREAS

Comfort and appearance are important. Flooring needs to be hard wearing, especially in areas in front of chairs and sofas.

HALL/LANDING

A very heavy wear area so if using carpet look for the corresponding BCMA label. To help prolong its life use scraper mats outside exterior doors and door mats inside.

STAIRS

Very heavy wear area, especially the first step or two. Risers are kicked and edges scuffed over time. Flooring must be safe and durable.

If using carpet, avoid a pattern that disguises the stair edges: it may confuse young children and the elderly.

Foam-backed carpets wear quickly on stairs. Chunky, low-density loop-pile carpets are not the right choice either as the backing is exposed between the carpet tufts as it covers the nose (edge) of the tread.

BEDROOMS

As we often walk about in bare feet, carpet is the best choice for comfort. A longer, more luxurious pile is suitable, but in children's rooms you want tough stain-resistant carpets.

BATHROOMS

Flooring should be non-slip, rot resistant, comfortable and hygienic. Use cork with non-slip bath mats. Ceramic tiles look good but are cold, slippery and the grouting traps dirt; unglazed textured tiles are safer. Cushioned vinyl or Amtico are a good choice.

Special bathroom carpet is available with a synthetic or foam backing and a short pile. Avoid wool carpets, as they can rot if wet for prolonged periods. Nylon is a good choice.

GARDEN EQUIPMENT

Garden tools and furniture must cope with damp, the sun, the stresses of digging, etc. A well-informed choice is therefore very important

GARDEN FURNITURE

CAST AND WROUGHT IRON

Cast and wrought iron are made from the same basic materials, but where cast iron is shaped using a mould, wrought iron is hammered into shape.

Painted cast-iron furniture is usually based on traditional Victorian designs with table and chair sets (now copied in cast aluminium). The style of the furniture makes it quite rigid and not suitable for lounging in. It is usually painted white, green or black, and the paintwork will need annual maintenance.

Cast iron is an expensive and rather impractical option for garden furniture and is hence not seen as frequently as other types. Unless you have your heart set on the real thing, it's more practical to look at cast-aluminium copies (see below).

Wrought and cast iron are also used for the end supports of wooden benches. Look for durable hardwood slats as the bench is likely to be left out in all weathers.

Iron is very heavy, so consider where the furniture will be positioned. It won't be appropriate if you want furniture you can move about, or if there is no firm surface to stand it on. The weight does, however, make it less likely to be lifted by a thief.

CAST ALUMINIUM

This looks like cast iron in traditional designs, but is much lighter and doesn't rust. It is also cheaper. Like cast iron, the designs are rigid and not comfortable for lounging.

SOLID WOOD

Durability and weather resistance varies depending on the type of wood used: Oak, Sweet Chestnut and Western Red Cedar are naturally resistant to rot, but prolonged damp spells will eventually lead to discoloration.

Furniture from non-durable woods such as Ash, Beech, Elm, European Redwood, Pine and Spruce will need preserving and re-treatment regularly. Similarly, painted wood will require regular maintenance to keep it in good condition.

TIP To reduce the risk of rotting, site furniture on concrete or gravel.

Consider where the furniture will be positioned as solid wood can be heavy. For more portable wooden furniture consider folding slated pine furniture, or casual seating such as directors' or deck-chairs.

SYNTHETIC RESIN/ INJECTION-MOULDED PLASTIC

Lightweight, durable and available in a variety of styles, synthetic resin is practical and comfortable. Good-quality furniture of this type is very resistant to moisture and deterioration due to chemicals.

It is usually made in white, so look for UV-stabilised resin that shouldn't fade in the sun. Cheaper furniture will contain more chalk and yellow in the sunlight more quickly. Coloured styles will be less likely to show stains and signs of ageing.

For convenience of moving or storage look for folding or stackable styles.

TUBULAR METAL

A practical, portable option. Its folding styles make storage simple.

The tubular steel is either coated with zinc to prevent rusting or more commonly with polyester or epoxy resin (white or green). This feels like a plastic coating, is chip resistant and preserves the metal. The furniture should still be kept indoors to prevent the rivets rusting and making it look shabby.

Choose between woven plastic or cloth seats and cushions.

CANE/WICKER

More suitable for attractive conservatory furniture that can be moved into the garden occasionally, rather than for heavy garden use. Available in cane, rattan, willow and bamboo.

Look for makes that have been varnished or sealed, as they will then only need vacuuming and wiping with a damp cloth to remove dust.

GARDEN TOOLS

There is a mammoth difference between having the right tool for the job, and just making do. The more comfortable and easier it is to do the job, the more likely you are to do it and the more pleasurable it will be. In reality, it changes keeping the garden under control from a chore to working at leisure.

DIGGING TOOLS

When choosing a conventional spade look for a head made from one piece of metal. Known as solid forged, this type is stronger than pressed steel, which is more likely to have weak joints. A longer socket also adds strength to a spade because it houses the weak point where the metal and wooden handle join.

Digging for a long period can cause backache. To avoid this, choose the weight of your spade carefully. The material used to make a spade will determine its weight.

The length of the shaft can vary by about 8in/20cm on different spades. Longer shafts mean less bending.

Spade handles can be D or T shaped; the choice is down to personal preference.

AVOIDING BACK STRAIN WHEN DIGGING

- 200,000 people suffer from backache due to gardening.
- Try to dig on a fine day. If the soil is wet it can be twice as heavy.
- Wear a good pair of boots with treads.
- Always keep warm.
- Do some loosening-up exercises before starting.
- Change jobs frequently.
- Don't dig for too long.
- Keep you back straight and bend at the knees.

STAINLESS-STEEL SPADES

Most tools are made from carbon steel, which is often coated to prolong its life. The coating wears off and so pitting and rusting occur, which impairs performance.

For a heavy clay soil, a stainless steel tool makes digging much easier. The soil adheres less to the polished surface, so the spade does not get as heavy. The quality of the stainless steel can vary but generally these spades are much more expensive than those made of carbon steel.

TIP When buying a spade, make sure it is quite comfortable when you are wearing gardening gloves.

Ergonomic tools

There are also ergonomically designed spades and other digging tools available which do not look like conventional spades. They have been specially designed with a bend in the handle, so that the spade bends rather than your back.

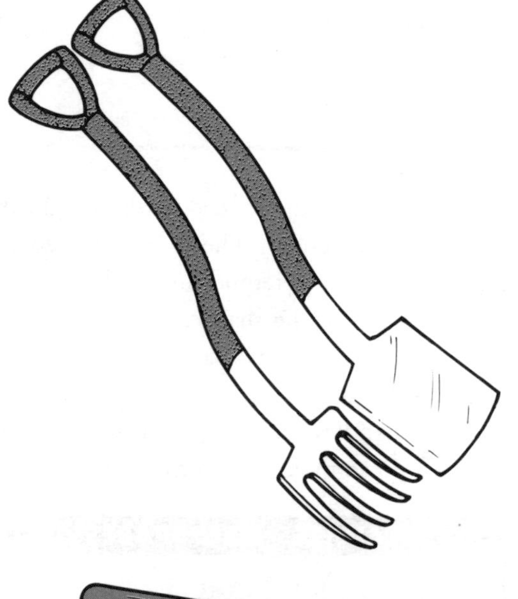

This gives more momentum when lifting. The handles are often longer.

HAND TOOLS

If you are buying hand tools for the first time choose multi-system tools, which use interchangeable heads with a choice of handles of different lengths. There is a range of telescopic handles: those for use while standing, or short handles.

Although they cost more than conventional tools initially, because of the multi-purpose function you only buy the handles once and then add whichever tool head you need. The essentials are a trowel and a three-pronged cultivator. They are also useful when storage space is limited.

Choose one with a firm click-fit attachment (like a seat belt) rather than a screw fitting. The screw fittings are fiddly and if soil gets into the fixing, locking the two pieces together could be a problem.

Short-handled tools are useful if working on rockeries or raised beds, or gardening from a seated or kneeling position rather than standing. They represent better value for children than some flimsy children's tools.

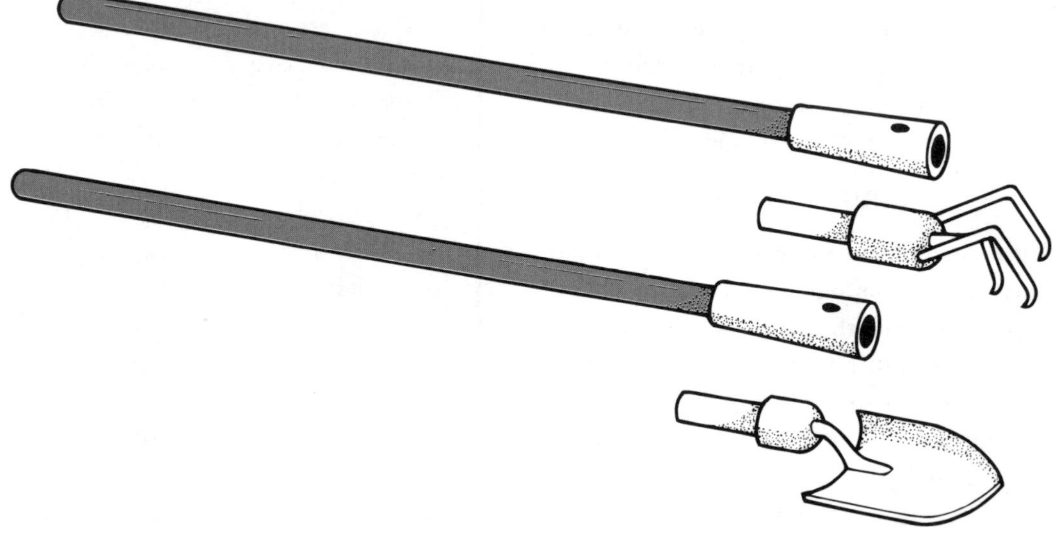

ELECTRIC TOOLS

In a large garden, electric tools are ideal for cutting a big expanse of lawn or pruning a long hedge.

At first, electrically powered tools had to be connected with a flex to a power point. In recent years, however, rechargeable battery-powered tools have become very popular. As they have no leads you can use the tools at the bottom of the garden away from a power point, and there is no danger of cutting through an electric flex. Battery-powered tools also tend to be quieter and lighter to hold. Most will operate for about 20 minutes before they need to be recharged. Lawn-mowers, grass shears and hedge trimmers are all available as battery-powered models.

Safety and performance of electric tools have improved significantly in recent years. Before buying, always check for safety features. This is particularly important for hedge trimmers. All models should incorporate a lock-off switch with a two-step starting procedure, and a hand guard. When not in use always place a plastic cover over the blades.

PRUNING TOOLS

Secateurs

There are two types of cutting action available: anvil and by-pass.

By-pass use an action like scissors, and should be used for delicate pruning.

Anvil are designed for heavier pruning. These work like a ratchet, cutting in two stages. First they grip and then they cut.

Points to consider when choosing

- A smooth action is essential. This is controlled by a spring, and buffers on the handle ends to stop jarring. These features become obvious after long periods of work.
- Some manufacturers make right- and left-handed versions.
- Some models have a rolling top handle so that as you squeeze the secateurs it rotates in the palm of your hand. This shifts the pressure around the palm of your hand, reducing the risk of blisters.
- Secateurs usually have brightly coloured handles, to avoid losing them amongst cuttings or bushes.

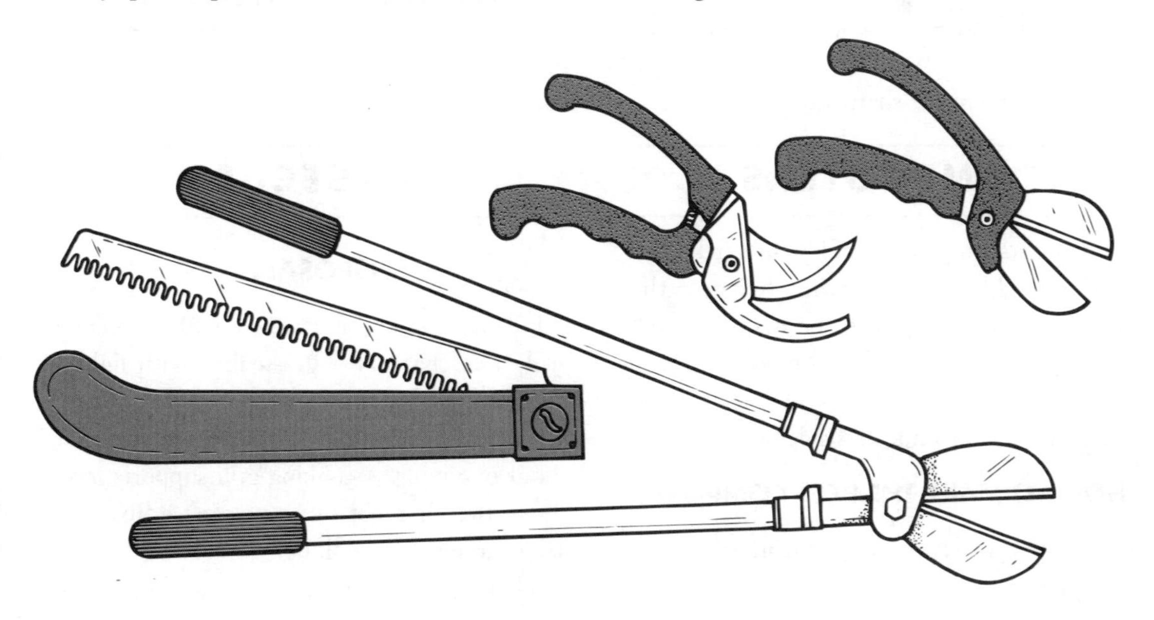

Loppers

Use these for thicker branches. They are similar to secateurs but have longer handles, giving you much greater leverage and reach.

Points to consider when choosing

• Like secateurs, these are available as by-pass or anvil construction.
• Weight is an important consideration because loppers are usually used at shoulder level.
• Loppers vary in length, so choose according to your height.

Pruning saws

Suitable for even heavier pruning work, they are a better choice for thicker branches with less intricate work.

They fold in half with a hinge in the centre and the sharp teeth enclosed.

Points to consider when choosing

• Check the balance and ease of opening.
• Check the length of the blade, because it will be used for wood over 1¼in/3cm thick. With a shorter blade you have greater control, but a longer blade gets the job done more quickly.
• These saws are self-sharpening.

COMPOSTERS

If buying a composter, make sure it is well insulated. This is important because the bacteria which break down the matter require heat to work effectively. As compost can take two to three months to produce, it's a good idea to have two composters side by side.

HOW TO MAKE THE BEST COMPOST

• Start with a layer of tougher material to help drainage.
• Use a mix of tougher fibrous material, such as garden cuttings or prunings, and softer, wetter material such as garden waste and lawn mowings. Try to balance quantities of each or you'll get an uneven slow rot or a soggy mess. Add tougher material such as shredded cardboard if you have a lot of soft material.
• Don't use kitchen waste containing meat or bones, it will attract vermin.
• Keep a square of old carpet on top, as well as the lid, until you've finished building up the compost heap. This helps to keep heat in.
• Water occasionally to keep the heat moist.
• Turn after four weeks, when the heap has cooled, to speed up and even out the rot.
• Complete composting should take about two to three months if the tough material has first been shredded, otherwise the rotting down will take about six months. Speed it up by adding nitrogen-rich material (animal waste) or proprietary compost accelerator.

For more information on composting contact the Henry Doubleday Research Association (see Useful Addresses).

GARDEN SAFETY

See The Garden, page 419, and Barbecues, page 420

BARBECUES

DISPOSABLE

A foil tray containing charcoal with a cooking grill. The charcoal is pre-soaked with lighter fluid to light instantly, and is ready to cook on in 10 to 15 minutes. The barbecue lasts for about one hour. A cooking grill supports food above the charcoal but you can't adjust the height to regulate cooking.

They are fun for picnics, but cooking space

is limited, and you can't add extra charcoal to extend the cooking time. Care is needed in siting the barbecue and moving it after cooking, as it gets hot underneath.

PORTABLE

Small, and ideal for beginners. They tend to lack extras such as a wind shield, so are best used in a sheltered place.

Portables come in all sorts of shapes and sizes. Features to look for include a wind shield (some are a suitcase style with a lid), a grate to allow air flow under the coals, and folding legs. Without legs they are difficult to site. If there is no wall or similar structure nearby you could find yourself cooking on the ground.

The Hibachi style is compact and designed with a good air flow underneath the grate, and adjustable brackets for the food racks.

Consider how much you will be moving the barbecue. Look for a lightweight one made of aluminium as opposed to cast iron, if you will be carrying it far. Also consider how practical it is to carry around. Suitcase styles may appear convenient but are messy when you have to pack the legs back in with the greasy grill rack.

OPEN/BRAZIER

Larger, open-sided barbecues, usually with a windshield into which the grill rack slots.

Check these can have their height adjusted easily, so that food can be moved away from the hot coals for gentler cooking. Some barbecues have a spit or rotisserie, which also slots into the sides.

KETTLE/COVERED

Similar in size and variety to open barbecues, but with a dome to cover the food during cooking. Good for the more adventurous chef as they have more sophisticated options.

The dome concentrates the heat and keeps

LIGHTING TIPS

- Always site on a level base. Some ventilation is needed to draw the fire and heat, so choose a spot which is neither too exposed nor too sheltered.
- Line the ash tray with aluminium foil, shiny side up, to reflect the heat and make the ashes easy to remove, but make small holes to allow ventilation.
- Pile a small quantity of charcoal in a pyramid shape, inserting a few fire lighters, or spray with barbecue lighter fluid or paste. *Never* use petrol, paraffin, methylated spirits or other flammable fluids.
- Light this pile, and as the heat begins to spread add more charcoal to the sides and top. Keep the pile small and to one side if you are only cooking for two.
- Light the fire about an hour before you intend to cook, to pre-heat the coals. Coals become covered with a grey ash which may glow red in the dark. When the coals are fully covered with this ash and look cool, the cooking temperature has been reached. If you start cooking too soon, before the flames have subsided, you will end up with food that is over-cooked on the outside, and uncooked in the centre.
- If the fire goes out, remove coals with tongs to a metal bucket and start everything afresh.
- Always have some means of extinguishing a fire at hand, such as a domestic fire extinguisher or fire blanket. Even sand will suffice.

TIPS FOR CHARCOAL BARBECUES

- Choose lumpwood charcoal for quickly cooked foods such as sausages and burgers. Briquets are better for longer, hotter cooking such as roasting.
- A 6½lb/3kg bag of charcoal should be sufficient for at least two full barbecues based on a 17in/43cm diameter barbecue.

the moisture in the food. With the lid closed, large joints of meat can be oven roasted because the heat accumulates in the closed unit and enters the food from all sides. They can also be used open to barbecue food in the normal way.

Temperature is regulated by opening vents in the lid and fire bowl. Some have useful viewing windows.

Useful features are levers to adjust the height of the cooking racks, a motor-operated rotisserie, wheels, and racks for food at the sides or underneath.

GAS

Range in size from large trolley styles to portable (but remember you'll need to carry the gas cylinder).

Contain lava rocks that are heated from beneath by gas burners. The heat is radiated from the hot rocks to give the same effect as burning coals. The gas allows easy control of the heat. They usually have a lid, and are on a trolley with wooden shelves.

Gas barbecues are easy to light and heat up in only a couple of minutes.

They tend to be cleaner to maintain than other types because the rocks burn off the fats (rather like stay-clean oven liners) and don't need replacing for about five years. (*See* Gas Barbecues, page 279.)

BUILD YOUR OWN

For a permanent barbecue look for a kit which includes an ash-pan, grate and cooking racks.

Alternatively, make your own with an old cooking tray or similar for an ash-pan, and an oven shelf for the grill. Remember to measure the ash-pan and grill before laying any bricks.

Choose a design with good ventilation from underneath, for example an open brick design.

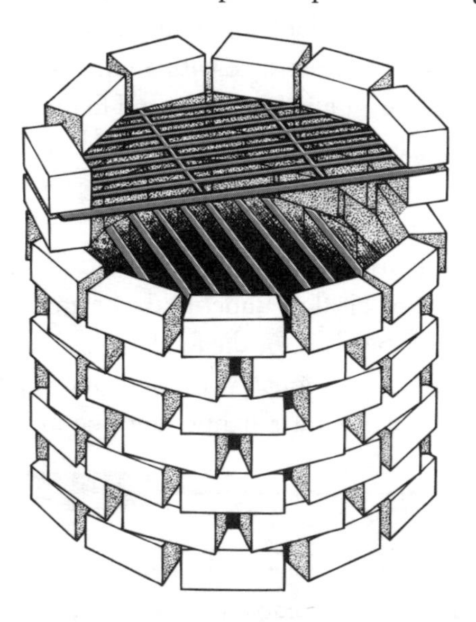

ELECTRIC BARBECUES AND GRILLS

These use electric elements under a griddle. The same types of foods can be cooked, but they don't take on the same smoky flavour.

Check ease of cleaning: most can't be immersed in water because it would damage the electric elements.

POINTS TO CONSIDER WHEN CHOOSING ALL BARBECUES

- Ease of assembly.
- Wheels for mobility.
- Shelves and side racks for food.
- Variety of grilling heights.
- Tools supplied for cooking.
- Storage space required when out of use.

COOKING ON BARBECUES

- Brush grills with vegetable oil before cooking, to reduce food sticking to them, and make cleaning easier afterwards.
- For added flavour, marinate the meat, or scatter herbs or aromatic wood chips over the coals while cooking.
- To avoid charring the food on the outside, lift the grilling racks and cook for longer, or spread the coals further apart.
- Always use long-handled implements and barbecue gloves when cooking.
- A fine water spray is useful to damp down flames that flare up from dripping fat.

AFTER COOKING

- Before storing or leaving the barbecue overnight make sure it is completely out and cold by extinguishing with water from a spray or covering with sand.
- Before storing for the winter, wipe clean metal parts with vegetable oil to prevent rust.
- Cover a permanently built barbecue with a plastic sheet to protect it from severe weather.
- Turn the gas supply off at the cylinder and store both the barbecue and cylinder outdoors in a well-ventilated garage or shed. Use a plug or cap to seal off the valve outlet of the gas cylinder, and make sure it is away from heat or ignition sources and combustible materials.

CARE & MAINTENANCE

HOW THE HOUSE WORKS

Before you can check that your house is running smoothly, you'll need to know how the systems inside it are designed and how they operate.

PLUMBING AND WATER HEATING

COLD-WATER SUPPLY

Cold water comes into the house via a high-pressure mains pipe. The supply is controlled by a stopcock, now called a stoptap, belonging to the water authority. You'll find it two or three feet underneath a square metal flap somewhere outside the house, usually in the front garden. If your home is very old, this may be the only stoptap, and in an emergency, you'll need to turn the water off here. Because it's so deep, a special tool is required.

TIP The water board is responsible for the mains pipe on its side of the exterior stoptap; the house owner is responsible for anything to do with the plumbing that happens on the other side.

Most homes have an internal stoptap as well, which can be used to shut off the water if a pipe bursts or the cistern overflows. This is usually in the kitchen, or a downstairs toilet or bathroom, close to where the mains supply enters the house, although occasionally you'll find it located in the airing cupboard.

Direct plumbing systems

This type of system supplies all the cold taps in the house with water from the rising main, a continuation of the mains pipe. This goes all the way up the house to the cold-water storage cistern, a rectangular, open-top tank at the highest point of the house: in the roof space, loft or attic. As water is drawn from the cistern and the level drops, water from the rising main tops it up, and a float valve cuts off the incoming supply when the correct level is reached. Because all the cold taps in the house are connected to the rising main, the cold-water tank only supplies water to the hot-water cylinder.

TIP If the cistern is uncovered, it should be checked regularly to make sure it's not contaminated by birds, insects or other debris. It's worth covering it with a plastic top to make sure the water is clean and to stop particles damaging taps, valves and other components, but make sure the lid doesn't exclude air as well.

Indirect plumbing systems

Found in most houses. Only one cold tap, usually the one that supplies the kitchen sink, is connected directly to the mains. Drinking water should be drawn from this tap, because

HOW TO CURE AN AIRLOCK

Air trapped in the pipes can interrupt the hot water supply or bring it to a stop altogether. You can cure it, using pressure from the mains. Use a piece of hosepipe to connect the tap without water to the mains pipe, usually the cold-water tap at the kitchen sink. Turn both taps on and leave for a few minutes. Remove the hose from the affected tap and try it: it should run freely. If it doesn't, try the procedure again.

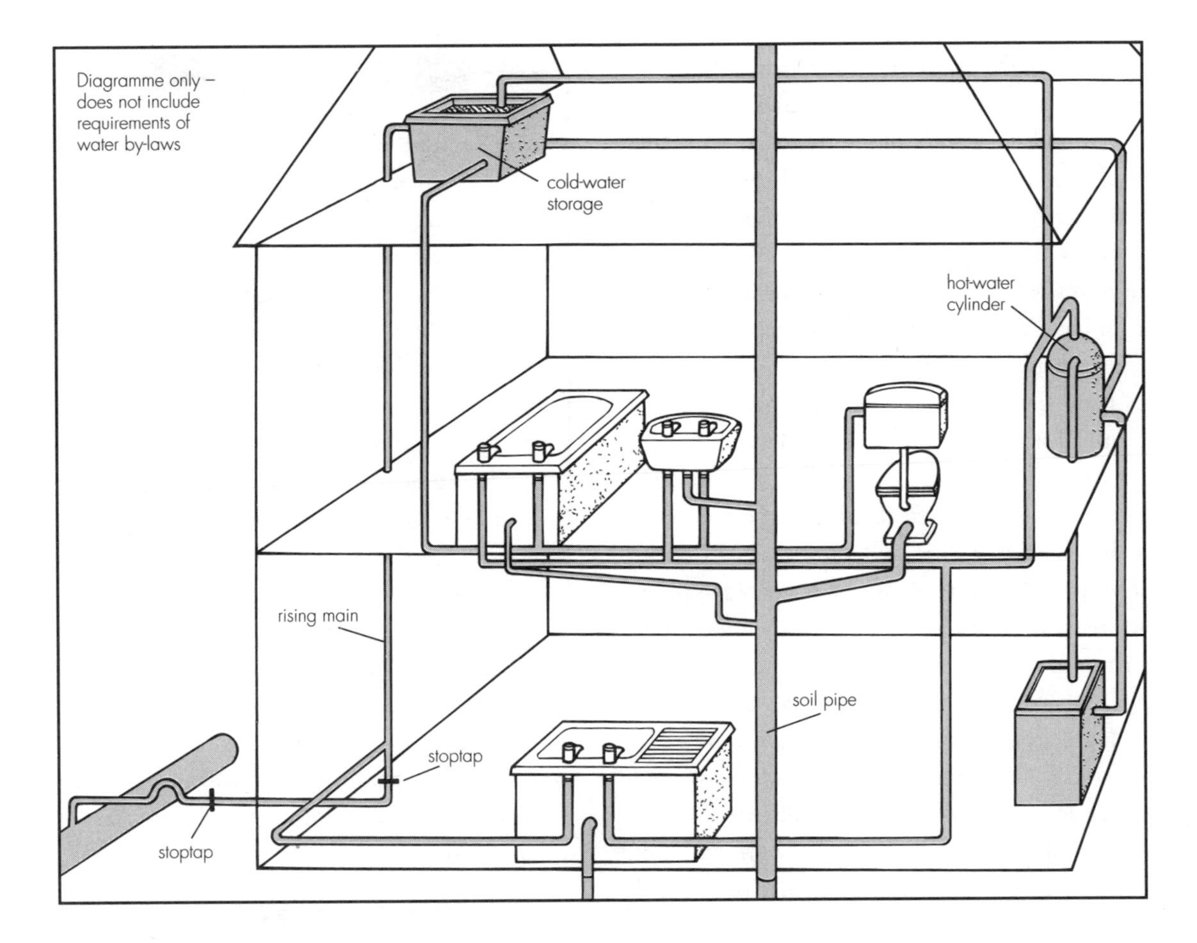

other taps, and toilets, will be fed with water from the cold-water storage cistern, which also sends water to the hot-water cylinder.

There are three pipes leading from the cistern in an indirect plumbing system; two if the plumbing is direct.

1 The overflow pipe prevents flooding if the cistern float valve fails, by directing water outside the house. Dripping from this pipe is a visible warning that the valve needs attention (see Dripping Overflow, page 271).

TIP Most modern cisterns' float valves have plastic floats that are virtually trouble-free. Older houses may still have copper balls for floats, which can spring a leak, and it's well worth replacing these with plastic ones before they give trouble.

2 In indirect plumbing systems, another pipe serves the other cold taps in the house, lavatory cisterns, and appliances such as power showers and bidets.

3 The third pipe feeds the hot-water cylinder, usually located in the airing cupboard.

The cold-water system also incorporates wheeled gate valves, which can be turned off to isolate the supply in an emergency. If you find that a stoptap or gate valve has seized, it's worth using some form of penetrating oil to free it. Don't use force if it won't budge, as this could fracture the capstan or wheel head, or even worse, break the valve.

TIP Lubricate stoptaps and gate valves with a thin oil and turn them off and on from time to time, to make sure they work if you need to cut off the supply in an emergency.

Most water pipes are made from plastic or copper, but you may also find stainless or galvanized steel. Very old houses may still have lead plumbing, which can be a health hazard. Contact your local water board for advice, and meanwhile, run the cold tap for several minutes before using the water for drinking or cooking. Additionally, consider using a water filter whenever possible.

Pipe sizes are now metric: 15mm (½in), 22mm (¾in) and 28mm (1in). Because metric pipes are measured externally and imperial plumbing is measured internally, there may be a discrepancy in size, and problems can occur if you need to extend or repair an old system. Metric adaptors are available to make sure joints are tight, and you will need special adaptors when joining plastic pipes to metal.

It's a good idea to inspect all pipework regularly. Though it's not possible to see concealed pipes, a quick check of the joints of those you can see is well worth the effort. Look for tell-tale signs such as moisture round joints, or discolouration of the pipework, walls or floors.

TIP Buy a roll of waterproof mastic tape to keep for emergency plumbing repairs.

Although you're allowed to carry out straightforward repairs yourself, you must comply with water and electricity company requirements and building regulations when extending or installing a plumbing system. Contact your local authority building control officer for information.

HOW TO FIX NOISY PIPES

Loud 'water hammer' noises indicate that plumbing components, in the tap or cistern, need replacing. In hard water areas, a knocking noise may also be caused by a build-up of limescale in the pipes. Consider a water softener to solve the problem, or try padding the pipe with a piece of foam until you can find the source of the trouble.

SAVING WATER

More and more houses, especially new ones, are being fitted with water meters, which means you pay for the amount you use. Make sure taps don't leak (see How to Mend Leaking Taps, page 249) and turn them off properly. If you wish, you can have push taps fitted in cloakrooms or utility rooms, which turn themselves off after a pre-determined interval. Modern toilet cisterns have a much reduced water capacity, making them just as efficient, but more economical.

HOT-WATER SYSTEMS

Water heated by a boiler or immersion heater is stored in a hot-water cylinder, which usually ranges in size from 25–50 gallons/114–227 litres, though larger capacities are available. Cylinders need a thick lagging jacket made to BS 5615 (see Improving Energy Efficiency, page 243). If you're replacing a hot-water cylinder, it's possible to buy one with a polyurethane shell for better insulation.

Indirect hot-water systems

Have a heat exchanger, or coiled pipe, inside the hot-water cylinder. Hot water from the boiler circulates inside the heat exchanger, which heats the cold water that surrounds it. The heat exchanger has its own small water tank in the loft, and a vent pipe which takes steam and hot air back to this cistern.

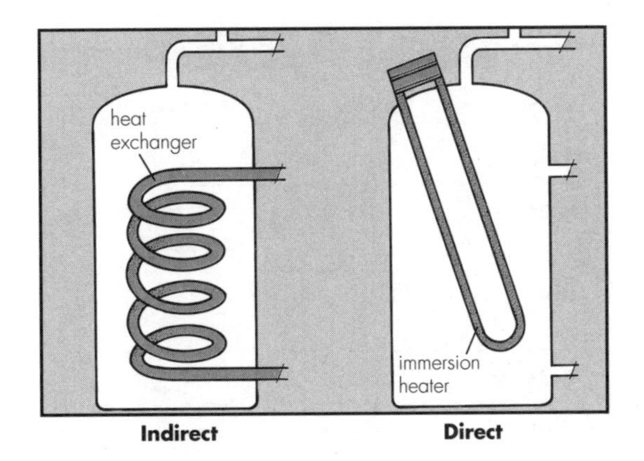

Direct hot-water systems
Usually supplied by an electric immersion heater. Cheaper and easier to install than indirect hot-water systems, but won't supply central-heating radiators.

Other forms of water heating

- Back boilers, are so called because they are incorporated into the back of a gas or coal fire. Their advantage is that they supply water to the hot-water cylinder, so you get hot water at the same time, but coal-fired models cannot supply hot water without lighting the fire.
- Combination boilers provide both hot water and central heating, diverting water from the radiators when ther's a demand for hot water. The advantage is that water is heated as required, so no hot water tank is needed; the disadvantage is that the boiler may not be able to supply sufficient warmth and hot water simultaneously for a large family.
- Gas, coal, oil, or wood-fuelled cooking ranges, like those by Aga/Rayburn, can provide hot water as well as central heating and cooking facilities.
- Immersion heaters can be fitted to the hot-water cylinder, where there is no boiler, or for use when the boiler is turned off or if it breaks down. Immersion heaters are powered by electricity and work on the same principle as an element in an electric kettle.
- Instantaneous water heaters, connected directly to the rising main, heat water as you use it, so you are spared the expense of keeping it warm until it's needed. Powered by either gas or electricity, they can be fitted directly over a sink, but are only suitable for producing relatively small amounts of hot water. Gas heaters must *not* be fitted in bathrooms unless they have a balanced flue to make sure that harmful gases are extracted. Regular maintenance is also essential.

Electric heaters are available in 3kW sizes for basins; 7–9kW for showers. They must be carefully sited and installed to prevent any possibility of wet hands coming into contact with the electricity supply, which could cause an electric shock.

DRAINAGE SYSTEMS

Rainwater always drains into downpipes outside the house so that the drains will not be flooded if there is a storm, but waste water and sewage may be taken away separately or together.

- Two-pipe systems are found in older houses. Waste water from sinks, baths and basins is taken by pipes outside the house to a gully at ground level. This has a U bend to prevent smells and an underground pipe that empties into the main drain. Waste from toilets uses a separate soil pipe, connected directly to the

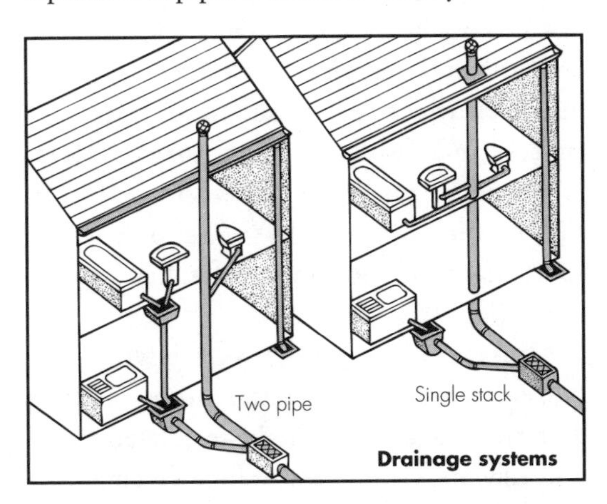

Drainage systems

drains.

- Single-stack systems have been standard for the past 40 years. With the possible exception of the kitchen sink, which may send water down a separate gully, and a downstairs toilet, which may have its own drain leading to a manhole (also called an inspection chamber), all waste water and sewage drains into a single soil pipe, which is often inside the house.

Houses in towns are linked to mains drainage systems, but in the country, waste may be stored in a cesspit or a septic tank. Cesspits need emptying regularly, but septic tanks use bacteria to break down the sewage and disperse the waste underground. All the waste must be siphoned off via a filter system to drain on to the property.

TIP If you are thinking of a house that's not on mains drainage, have the cesspit or septic tank professionaly checked to make sure it is in good order and that it is big enough for your family. It should be able to cope with about 25

ELECTRIC CIRCUITS

Electricity comes into the house via an armoured cable connected to a sealed fuse board, and like the meter it supplies, it is installed by the local electricity company. The domestic 'consumer unit' (still often called the fuse box), which incorporates a master on/off switch and fuses, or the more modern miniature circuit breakers, is also wired from the meter. Modern systems may have additional protection from a residual current device (RCD).

Miniature circuit breakers have a trip switch, which cuts off the supply if it is overloaded, and which can be reset later. There is usually one circuit breaker for each circuit.

WHICH FUSE?

Colour	power	purpose
White	5–6 amps	lighting
Grey	10 amps	light duty (eg lighting)
Blue	15–16 amps	standard immersion heater
Yellow	20 amps	storage heater
Red	30–32 amps	ring mains/ shower unit
Orange	40 amps	cooker
Green	45 amps	cooker

Fuses up to 55 amps are available if required.

Fuses are an intentionally 'weak link' in the system, designed to melt in the case of an overload and so protect the appliance and prevent any risk of fire. Fuses can be cartridges or one of three types of wired holder: a bridge type with a raised plinth, where the fuse wire is held in place by a screw at each side; an asbestos mat with a small piece of asbestos beneath the fuse wire; or a protected tube, where the wire is concealed inside the holder.

TIP If your system uses fuses, keep a supply of

MEASURING ELECTRICITY

Electricity system: measured in volts. The number of volts denotes the pressure at which the electricity is supplied: 240V in the UK (230V from 1995).

Appliances: measured in watts, which assess power. 1,000 watts = 1 kilowatt (kW).

Fuses: measured in amps, which indicate the amount of electricity in the circuit.

Ring main circuit

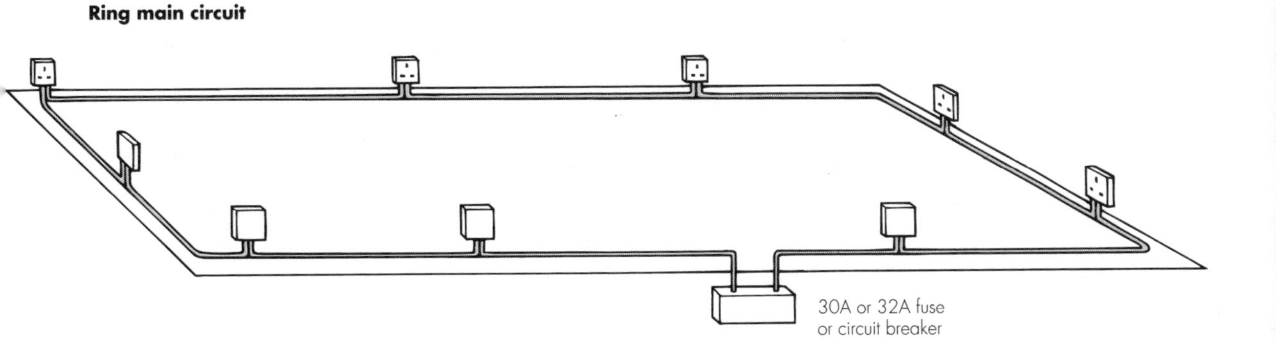

spare fuses or fuse wire and a torch handy, for emergency repairs.

WIRING SYSTEMS

There are two main types of wiring systems for appliances in Britain today: the old-fashioned radial type (also used for cookers and other powerful appliances), and the modern ring main system, which is now standard.

Radial systems

Are wired in series, one after the other, from the fusebox. Modern radial circuits are protected by a 20-amp fuse, for an area of up to 24sq yd/20sq m, or a 30-amp fuse, covering up to 60sq yd/50sq m.

Cookers and other appliances that make heavy demands on electricity, such as immersion heaters and power showers, will also have their own circuits and fuses.

Ring main circuits

This type of circuit has been standard since the late 1940s. A number of sockets – such as all those on one floor of a house – are linked in a central 'ring'. This ring can be broken into if you want to add extra sockets. There are usually two separate circuits on the ground floor, for the living rooms and for the kitchen. Each circuit covers up to 117sq yd/100sq m and supplies up to 7,000 watts.

LIGHTING CIRCUITS

Most houses have two lighting circuits, each supplying about ten lighting points. There are two types (see next page).

Junction box systems: found in older houses, and use more cable. Each ceiling fitting or 'rose', and switch, is wired into a junction box which is above the ceiling.

Loop-in or three-plate lighting: has one cable

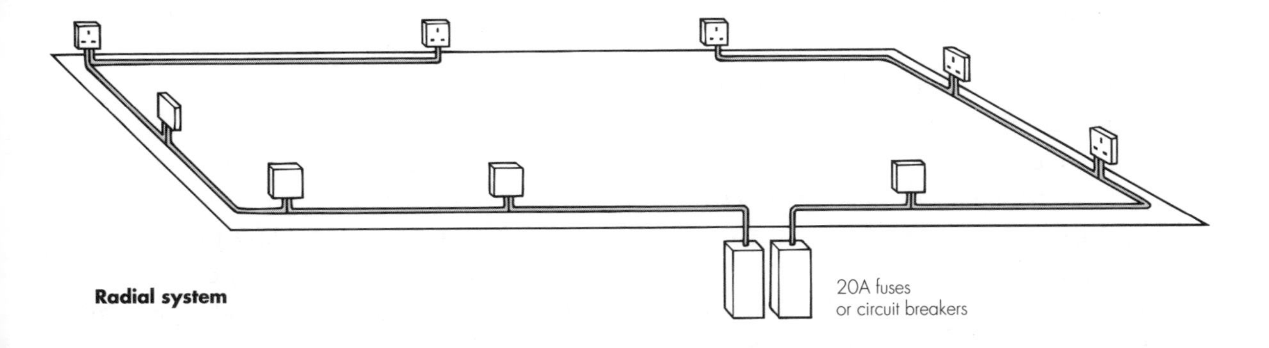

Radial system

Junction box

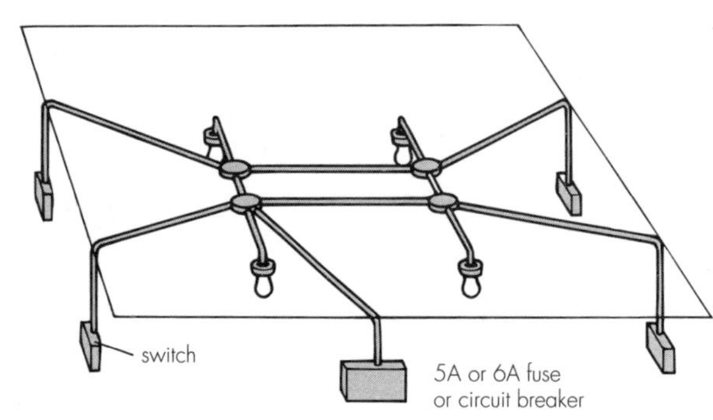

Loop-in

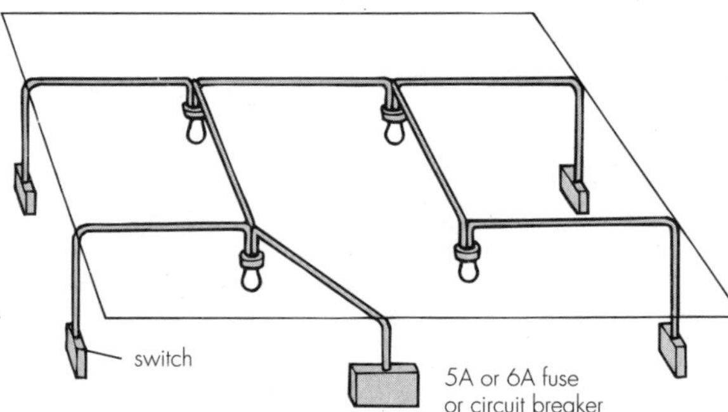

that supplies each ceiling rose. Switches are wired into the rose.

TIP Don't assume that if a light is turned off at the switch, the wires in the lamp holder will be dead. Always switch off the master switch at the mains before attempting any electrical repairs. To make absolutely certain that wires are not live it's also worth investing in an electrician's screwdriver, which has a current tester at the end.

HOW TO FIT A DIMMER SWITCH

1 Turn off the electricity at the mains and unscrew the switch's cover plate.
2 Loosen the screws inside the switch to free the wiring.
3 For maximum safety, cover the earth wire with green and yellow plastic sleeving if it is bare, leaving the tip uncovered, and wrap red insulating tape round the black wire, which is live.
4 Connect the wires to the dimmer switch terminals, following the manufacturer's instructions.
5 Screw the dimmer switch into place (it will probably be a tight fit) and turn on the electricity.

TIP Do not use a dimmer switch to control a fluorescent light or a low-voltage light fitting.

HOW TO WIRE A TELEPHONE EXTENSION

All the equipment you need is available in kit form, so you don't have to call in a professional to install a telephone extension. But the number of extensions you can have is limited by the distance from the master socket (maximum 55yd/50m) and the total of ringer equivalent numbers or RENs. Basically, this means that you can't have more than four telephones on one line – one at the master socket and three others – because phones are usually 1 REN each and the maximum number of RENs a line can support is four.

TIP If you want to run a fax or answering machine, check the REN rating, which may be higher than for a phone.

You will need

- Extension converter for the master socket
- Cable and fixings
- Extension socket

1 Fix the converter to the end of the cable if necessary and plug into the master socket. Fix the cable firmly in place on the wall with one of the cleats provided, close to the master socket. Then unplug the converter.
2 Fix the extension box in place, where required.

HOW SAFE IS YOUR WIRING?

Wiring that's older than 25 years may be dangerous because the rubber insulation that was used to protect the wiring until the 1960s may have perished. Signs of old wiring include:

- An old fuse box, or a number of fuse boxes governing individual circuits.
- Three-pin round sockets.
- Frayed or perished flex and wiring.
- Scorch marks around sockets and ceiling roses.
- Fuses that blow constantly.

If you spot any of these, contact your local electricity board or ring the National Inspection Council for Electrical Installation Contracting or the Electrical Contractors' Association (see Useful Addresses) for the name of an approved contractor. An inspection costs from about £50 and it's a good idea to have the system tested every ten years by a qualified electrician.

Modern 3-pin square sockets don't always mean that your wiring is safe.The system may have been only partially updated and the wiring may still be a hazard.

3 Run the cable from the master socket to the extension box, along the top of the skirting where it will be least noticeable, fixing in place at least every 1ft/30cm.

4 Strip back the plastic insulation covering each of the wires and connect them to the extension box, following the manufacturer's instructions.

5 Plug the converter back into the master socket and connect the new telephone to the extension socket.

TIP A junction box, served by cable from the master socket, can supply up to three telephone extensions.

GIVE YOUR HOUSE A CHECK-UP

You probably remember the last time your car was serviced, but do you recall the last time you gave your house a check-up? It's easy to ignore regular maintenance until things go wrong, and repairs can be expensive. That's why it's a good idea to keep an eye on the structure of the house and check it over twice a year, so you can cope with problems before they become emergencies. Look at it in late autumn before winter sets in, and again in the spring to check for damage done by bad weather. Here's what to do.

OUTSIDE

1 Step into the street and take a good look at the roof. Use binoculars if necessary, because it's difficult to see damage here. (If you're on friendly terms with your neighbours, ask to look at the roof from their upstairs windows.)

Look for any loose or missing tiles or slates; damaged ridge tiles and crumbling mortar; cracked or crooked chimneys, and faulty flashings which seal chimneys; problems with bay windows, and extensions to the main roof. Try to peer into the 'valleys' if your house has two roofs or is built on different levels, because these are where water tends to collect and leaks often occur.

If the chimney smokes, consider fitting a cowl to prevent downdraughts. If you don't use the chimney at all, have the chimney pot capped to keep the weather out. (Have an airbrick set in the chimney above the roof line.) If you decide to block up the fireplace, you'll need to fit an airbrick or ventilator to the wall to allow sufficient air to circulate, to prevent damp.

2 Walk round the house outside and make sure there's no earth piled against the damp-proof course, which runs round the walls about 6in/15cm above ground level; paths and terraces should be at least 6in/15cm below it. If it's obstructed, it won't work effectively and your home may be affected by damp.

Clean out the airbricks with a garden cane to make sure they're not blocked; they supply the ventilation beneath suspended floors which is vital to protect them from rot.

TIP Make sure the damp-proof course is clear all round your house, not just where the airbricks appear.

3 Look up and check that the gutters are secure and not broken or sagging. Patches of green slime may mean that there's a leaking downpipe, or that a blocked gutter needs attention (see Repairing Leaking Gutters and Downpipes, page 269). The mould can then be wiped or brushed away and the wall can be treated with bleach solution.

4 Check the walls. See if any rendering is cracked and in need of replacing. Use binoculars if necessary to check the mortar, to see if the walls need repointing. Large cracks need investigating, especially if you live on clay soil and they appear after a long, dry summer or a very wet winter, because they could be signs of subsidence. Tree roots can cause problems too. Look out for cracks near the corner of the house and diagonal cracks in the main walls running through the brick joints. Contact a chartered building surveyor or structural engineer, who will know if these are signs of normal movement or if subsidence could be the cause.

TIP If your house is affected by subsidence, it

may need underpinning and you may need to move out while work takes place. Check your buildings insurance policy to see if it covers the cost of renting a home elsewhere, as well as structural repairs.

5 Take a look at all the woodwork: the bargeboards beneath the eaves, window sills and frames, decorative timbers, and outside doors, including garage doors. Look for cracked and rotting wood. Test gently with a screwdriver if possible. If the wood splinters or crumbles away, it needs replacing with a new strip, or an entire board, door or window if the rot is extensive. If you check it regularly, the damage should be limited and you can often treat affected areas with an exterior grade of wood filler, as part of regular redecoration. See Exterior Painting, page 380.

6 Check the windows to make sure that they're weather-tight, making a note to replace any crumbling putty or cracked panes (see Mending a Broken Window, page 474). If the frames have shrunk away from the walls, scrape out the crumbling mortar with a screwdriver or filling knife and clean out with a brush. Dry the gap with a hot air gun, taking care not to melt the paintwork, and fill with exterior sealant when cool. Press into place and smooth down with a finger.

TIP Exterior sealant is available in a special 'gun', which allows you to force the filler deep down into the crack.

INSIDE

1 Go up into the loft and see if you can spot any obvious leaks or damage to the roof. It should be cool and airy. A gap of about ⅜in/10mm or airbricks at the eaves will allow the air to circulate. If there's insufficient ventilation, condensation may rot the timbers.

Make sure the storage cistern has adequate frost protection, and check for corrosion.

2 Check the interior woodwork for rot or pests, looking under the stairs and in cellars, where damage may go unnoticed.

Dry rot is a fungus that looks like cotton wool in its early stages and sprouts reddish brown growths as it advances. It eats into wood and can affect masonry too, causing serious structural damage. Specialist treatment is needed as soon as possible: contact the British Wood Preserving and Dampproofing Association (see Useful Addresses).

Woodworm leaves small holes or heaps or trails of powdery dust. Small areas can be treated with woodworm fluid but serious infestation needs professional treatment.

TIP Check all second-hand and antique furniture buys for woodworm before bringing them into the house. If they're left untreated, woodworm could spread from the furniture to the structural timbers.

3 Look out for damp. Penetrating damp, which seeps through the walls, usually appears in isolated patches, often well away from the floor. Rising damp can be detected by stains up to 3ft/90cm high on the walls, a tidemark of salts, and peeling wallpaper. The chief cause is a blocked or absent damp-proof course.

TIP If you need a new damp-proof course, check that the company is a member of the British Wood Preserving and Damp Proofing Association, and find out what safeguards there are if the firm goes out of business.

4 Consider the wiring. Mains wiring needs testing every 10 years (see box How Safe is your Wiring? page 225).

5 Subsidence can also be spotted inside the house. Cracks that occur inside as well as outside may be especially serious, but you should also look for walls that are out of true, tops of internal doors that are not level, and doors that stick. Contact a surveyor for advice.

IS THIS YOUR HOUSE?

PRE-1830

If your house is more than 200 years old, you need specialist advice about repairs and renovation. Your house may be a listed building, or it may be in a conservation area, both of which limit any alterations. What's more, the materials and building methods used may differ radically from those used today. There may be lath and plaster walls inside, and stone walls up to 1ft/30cm thick outside; even the glass in the windows may be handmade and far thinner than that used today. Though it may be difficult – or not advisable – to install a damp-proof course that works effectively, or a central-heating system that won't dry out old timbers, you'll know that your house was built to last – and you'll have the pleasure of knowing that you're caring for part of the country's heritage.

For advice on looking after a period home, contact English Heritage, Welsh Historic Monuments or Historic Scotland, or the Society for the Protection of Ancient Buildings, which has a range of technical leaflets. (See Useful Addresses.) Your local authority may also be able to give advice about local materials and style. You could also join a special interest group such as The Georgian Group (see Useful Addresses). Another source of information is the Building Conservation Directory and the Salvo Directory (see Useful Addresses), often available in libraries.

VICTORIAN

More houses were built in Victorian times than in all previous times put together, from back-to-back terraces for workers to impressive Gothic mansions for the rich.

Decoration was considered important and even modest terraced houses are likely to have fanlights over the door and richly patterned tiles round the fireplace. By the end of the century, these started to give way to plainer Arts and Crafts designs, based on an idealised version of the traditional cottage.

- Roofs are usually made from slates.
Replacing these can be expensive, but cheaper reconstituted slate is available.
- Walls are usually 9in/23cm solid brick.
Check for crumbling mortar, or rain may seep through if the wall becomes saturated during a storm. Contact The Building Employers' Confederation (see Useful Addresses) which offers a guarantee scheme for repairs and extensions.) Damp-proof courses were installed in houses built after 1875. These may need attention if it has cracked or the level of the ground has risen as the house has settled.
- Windows are usually sash (double-hung) designs. Old sash windows often stick or slam shut unexpectedly, and may fail to work at all if the sash cords are broken or have been over-painted. The window can be renovated, or replaced by one in an identical style if it is too far gone to repair, by a skilled joiner.

TIP If you want to install double glazing, you can opt for secondary glazing fitted inside the original window, to keep the character of your house.

- Floors were usually a mixture of suspended timber floors and quarry tiled or stone floors. These hard floors can cope with a certain amount of damp and shouldn't be covered with vinyl, which prevents moisture from evaporating. If you want to replace them you may need to take them up, repair the sub-floor and lay a sheet of heavy-duty (1,000 gauge) polythene, as a damp-proof membrane.
- Architectural details include picture rails and deep skirtings, plaster friezes and cornices, elaborate ceiling decorations and tiled or

marble fireplaces. Some of these – especially mouldings and tiles – may still be in production today. If timber mouldings are broken, take a piece to your local timber merchant and ask if it can be copied. Architectural salvage companies can provide original doors, door furniture and fireplaces to suit the style of your house. See magazine small ads or under Architectural Antiques in the Yellow Pages.

If you are interested in period restoration you could join The Victorian Society (see Useful Addresses).

1920s

The country cottage inspired many houses built during the 1920s, but though simple in style, the houses are often spacious and comfortable. Half-timbered gables, tile-hung bays, windows with brick mullions and stained-glass country scenes all emphasise the rural theme. But, at the time, there were few controls on building, and standards of construction vary. Statistics show that owners of inter-war houses carry out the most repairs.

- Roofs are often covered with clay tiles, which should be replaced by tiles in a similar colour if they are cracked or delaminated.
- Walls may be cavity walls, about 12in/30cm thick. Look out for regular horizontal cracks along the mortar joints, which may mean that the metal ties that join the exterior and interior walls are rusting. Repair can be costly, because it involves drilling through the brickwork and fixing new ties to the inner wall. Rendering and pebble dash may drop off in patches and should be filled: hanging tiles also need to be checked and any missing tiles replaced.
- Windows continued in the country style. Leaded lights were popular at the time, as were curved 'eyebrow' dormers and stained-glass panels. Specialist restoration may be needed for some of these individual windows; contact The Conservation Unit of the Museums and Galleries Commission (see Useful Addresses) for stained-glass restorers.

ART DECO

These 'modern movement' homes associated with the 1930s were designed to make the most of light and space. Although they often contain art deco motifs, lights, and stylish chrome bathroom fittings, most thirties homes turned their backs on decoration. The style is continental in spirit, with white, concrete-rendered walls, wrap-around metal-framed bay windows and roofs, covered with green or turquoise tiles.

- Walls were mostly made from brick, which was then rendered and painted, because the use of reinforced concrete was not widespread. (Rendering should stop short of the damp-proof course, which cannot work if it is covered). If water is trapped behind the rendering, it can freeze and expand, and chunks of rendering may fall off. To prevent this, repair cracks as soon as they appear and keep the surface watertight by repainting with masonry paint every few years.
- Windows were often made from metal. If it's inadequately galvanized, it may rust and corrode.
- Roofs were often flat or low-pitched. The glazed, continental-style roof tiles popular at the time can be hard to replace. Try architectural salvage depots.
- Architectural details include chrome fixtures and fittings and tiled fireplaces with Art Deco details, which should be renovated or replaced by similar styles if possible. Contact the Twentieth Century Society for advice on this style and others up until the present day (see Useful Addresses).

POST-WAR

Strict limits on the size of buildings mean that space in many post-war houses is at a premium. Building materials were effectively in such short supply that they were sometimes recycled from bomb-damaged buildings. Houses destroyed in the war had to be replaced by exact copies, so there was little innovation until the 1950s, when American-style ranch houses with large picture windows and fitted kitchens became fashionable.

- Roofs may be of clay tiles or, by the 1950s, concrete tiles.
- Walls should be checked to see if the wall ties have been bridged, or need replacing, which can lead to damp; contact a chartered building surveyor. A more serious problem affects many houses that were system-built using prefabricated concrete. In time, some of these homes were found to be defective because the reinforcement had corroded. You should be able to get a grant for repairs from your local authority, under the Housing Defects Act.
- Floors should be checked if you find your home is affected by rising damp. Some early plastic tiles were stuck directly on to concrete and relied on the adhesive to provide a damp-proof membrane, which was rarely satisfactory.

1960s–70s

Airy and light, homes were influenced by a popular Scandinavian style, with weather-boarding, balconies, wide windows and patio doors. Wood preservation treatments didn't become widespread until the 1970s, so all the timber – window frames, doors, cladding and structural timbers – should be checked carefully for signs of rot and woodworm. As fuel was cheap at the time, standards of insulation were low, and there's usually scope for improvement to make sixties homes more energy efficient.

- Roofs are often flat or have a shallow pitch. Flat roofs should be checked each year and any splits repaired. Felt-covered roofs are often covered with stone chips for protection, and these shouldn't be removed. If you need to replace a felt-covered roof, you can now choose high-performance materials that should last for about 30 years.
- Walls were often clad with aluminium, plastic or wood. This cladding should be checked to make sure it's sound and won't break off in high winds. Lack of building land meant that some houses were built on land reclaimed from gravel extraction, or sloping sites, so look for signs of movement such as cracks and doors sticking in their frames, and contact a structural surveyor if you find them.
- Windows may be single-glazed, however large in size. Double-glazing may reduce noise and improve insulation.

AFTER THE 1980s

Most housing developments have featured cottage-style houses with dark, stained timbers or neo-Georgian styles, rather than innovative designs. But there has been a revolution in the use of low-maintenance materials, and a recognition that most house-buyers want their homes to last: houses built under the National House Building Council's Buildmark Scheme are now covered by a 10-year warranty, which protects against structural defects. Modern houses are well insulated to keep fuel bills down, but this may sometimes cause condensation. Adequate ventilation, installing an extractor fan or dehumidifier if necessary, should cure the problem.

- Roofs are usually covered with modern concrete tiles for durability, designed to resemble traditional clay tiles.

- Walls on new houses often have white salts showing on the surface (efflorescence) as they dry out. Outside walls can be cleaned with a wire brush. Don't use water, which will only bring more salts to the surface. Inside walls can be wiped with a soft brush or cloth. Any problem that lasts more than two years should be reported to your builder.
- Plaster inevitably shrinks as it dries out and leaves hairline cracks, especially between walls and ceiling. You can keep this to a minimum by using heat sparingly when the house is new, so it has a chance to dry out naturally. Don't decorate with wallpaper or a solvent-based paint, which traps moisture in the walls, for the first year.
- Windows may have frames made from uPVC, which doesn't need painting, or stained timber. New wood absorbs paint or stain quickly, so it's worth redecorating exterior timbers when the house is two years old and every four years from then on.

WHO CAN HELP?

National societies may give restoration grants in exceptional cases; special interest groups can give detailed advice. To find out more, see Useful Addresses.

COPING WITH PROBLEMS

Your house is designed to keep the weather out and warmth in, but to make sure it does so efficiently, you need to watch for the insidious damage caused by damp, woodworm and rot. Here's how to detect and treat them.

DAMP

Damp is a problem that affects more homes than almost any other; it's estimated that about 15 per cent of homes are damaged by it to some extent. As well as causing extensive harm to both the structure and furnishings, the mould it encourages can aggravate health problems such as asthma, so it's important to keep it under control.

The main causes of damp are penetrating damp which seeps through the walls, rising damp from the ground, and condensation caused by warm, moist air inside the house, but don't forget that faults in the roof, or fractured pipes and water tanks can cause damp patches too. Stains on the ceiling that gradually increase in size may be traced to one of these, so it's worth searching for obvious causes before you investigate further.

You'll usually know if your home has a major problem with damp, but if you want to assess its extent precisely, you can buy a battery-operated damp meter from a DIY store. You can also contact a specialist damp-proofing company, but remember that it will have a vested interest in the problem.

DAMP THROUGH WALLS

Penetrating damp means that the windows or walls of your house are not watertight, perhaps because you live in a very exposed part of the country in the north or west, or by the coast, where gales and heavy rain are frequent. Traditionally, many houses in these areas were low or single-storey designs, with small windows and thick, rendered walls for extra protection against bad weather.

Even if you don't live in the wilds, it's worth checking north and west-facing walls to make sure that the mortar or rendering is sound. Solid walls are more likely to be affected than cavity walls, which have the extra protection given by the double skin. Check the mortar first to see if the walls need repointing (see Repointing Bricks, page 270); if not, you can try applying a proprietary damp-proofing liquid – during dry weather – to see if that will cure the problem.

Cladding, rendering, and masonry paint certainly repel damp but they will also radically change the appearance of your house and need regular maintenance. Don't be tempted to use a completely water-resistant finish or a solvent-based paint, because any water trapped in the bricks will be forced inside the house itself and may then cause structural damage.

TIP If a damp patch is caused by penetrating damp, it will usually be worse after heavy rain. To make sure that's the cause, soak the area with water from a garden hose, and then go inside to see if the damp patch enlarges.

Other reasons for penetrating damp are:

- Cavity walls, where the ties between the inner and outer skin have been bridged, allowing damp to seep between the two. Ask a builder to investigate by removing a few bricks from the outer wall near the damp patch. Alternatively, contact a chartered building surveyor, who can use a special, less disruptive boroscope to investigate the problem. If mortar has dropped on to the ties, extensive repairs may be needed, but a single blockage can be cleared relatively easily.
- Cracked rendering, which allows rain to penetrate but not evaporate. Isolated cracks can be stopped with an exterior filler but larger patches need professional treatment.
- Leaking gutters and downpipes (see Repairing Leaking Gutters and Downpipes, page 269).
- Window sills without a drip channel underneath to stop water running down the walls. A blocked channel can cause similar problems (see Leaking Windows, page 273).
- Cracks between the window frame and the wall. To repair these, see Give Your House a Check-Up, Outside (page 226).

DAMP FROM THE GROUND

The damp-proof course is your first defence against rising damp, which is why it is so important to make sure it's kept clear. One sign of rising damp is a tide-mark up to 3ft/90cm from the ground, caused by salts carried by moisture that rises up the walls. Older houses are more likely to be affected, because the mortar used in their construction is more permeable.

The only way to cure rising damp is to make sure you have an effective damp-proof course, but it can be kept at bay by treating the interior walls: dry lining them with plasterboard, for example. The battens to which the plasterboard is attached should be treated with preservative and both wall and plasterboard treated with fungicide to prevent rot. Thermal plasterboard should be used, or sheets of polythene stapled to the battens. This will not stop rising damp, but it will prevent it from ruining your decor and furnishings. (You will need to provide ventilation between the wall and the plaster board.)

TIP If you have rising damp, examine the wall inside as well as out by removing the skirting by the damp patch. Check that the plaster stops short of the damp-proof course – it shouldn't cover it.

CONDENSATION

The average family produces 5 gallons/20 litres of moisture a day by washing, cooking and simply by breathing. As home comforts, especially insulation and home heating, have steadily improved, this water vapour is trapped inside the house. The most obvious sign of condensation can be seen any winter morning on streaming mirrors and glass, but it does more than mist up windows. If condensation is extensive, it can lead to mould and damp, which ruin furnishings and cause structural damage, so prompt action is vital.

Condensation occurs when there's an imbalance between humidity, ventilation, and the temperature of the air and the surrounding surfaces. When warm, moist air comes into contact with a cold window or wall, it cools, and the water vapour condenses into drops on the surface. Unless the room is well-ventilated, this moisture can build up and cause rot. Older houses with open fires that create currents of air, and which also have high ceilings and low standards of insulation, may have frightening fuel bills but are rarely affected by condensation unless they're allowed to become too cold. It's more of a problem in modern, energy-aware houses.

TIP To find out if damp is caused by condensation, dry the damp patch with a hair-dryer or fan heater and then stick foil to the wall with adhesive tape. Leave it for a week. If there's moisture on the back, it's probably caused by penetrating or rising damp. If it's wet on the surface, it's due to condensation.

Preventing condensation

1 Make sure that walls are as well-insulated as possible. Solid walls are colder than cavity walls because they lack an inner 'skin', so consider covering them with expanded polystyrene, cork or panelling, or dry-lining them with thermal plasterboard (see Damp From the Ground, page 232) if condensation is a real problem. Cavity walls can be professionally insulated with material inserted between the two brick layers, or dry-lined with ordinary plasterboard.

TIP Try to avoid fitting cupboards, especially wardrobes, against a solid outside wall, or condensation may build up and you could find mould on your clothes. If this is the only practical site for a wardrobe, consider fitting louvre doors, which will allow the air to circulate in and out of it.

Sometimes only small areas of wall are affected by condensation, often because a solid lintel or column forms a 'cold bridge' in an otherwise well-insulated wall. Although in theory you can deal with this by insulating the patch concerned, you will usually need to treat the whole wall if the result is to look acceptable.

TIP If condensation is slight, try painting the wall with anti-condensation paint, which contains insulating particles.

2 Consider double glazing to improve insulation at the windows. Double glazing with sealed units rather than secondary double glazing can drastically cut condensation on windows, but choose a naturally warm material for the frames, such as wood, uPVC, anodised aluminium or aluminium frames that contain a thermal 'break', to prevent moisture condensing when it comes into contact with a cold surround.

TIP If you decide to install double glazing, make sure the rest of the room is well insulated too, or the condensation may simply be moved on from the windows to the walls.

3 Check the roof to make sure that the loft space is free from condensation, which can

cause considerable damage here. Every surface on the floor of the loft should be insulated, including the loft hatch, and gaps round pipes except for the base of the cold-water tank. Ventilation spaces, or ventilators under the eaves, will encourage air circulation.
4 Keep the house warm and don't allow the temperature to drop dramatically – a common cause of condensation. Turn the heating to low, rather than off, if the nights are very cold or if you go away during the winter, so the structure doesn't cool down completely. This can prevent pipes freezing, too.
5 Keep moisture production to a minimum, by closing kitchen and bathroom doors when you're washing up or running a bath, and covering saucepans when cooking. Try to leave a window ajar if you have to dry clothes indoors and make sure your tumble dryer door is well sealed and that the dryer is vented to the outside.
6 Improve ventilation: each living room should have at least three changes of air every hour. Install a ducted cooker hood, which takes smells and steam outdoors, or an extractor fan in the kitchen. Fit an extractor fan in the bathroom too, especially if you have a shower, which creates a lot of steam. Some fans will come on automatically when humidity reaches a certain level.
TIP Make sure the fan is the right capacity for the room and is sited in the right place. Kitchens need about 15 changes of air an hour, bathrooms about six (see Bathroom Ventilation, page 131). The fan should be high on the wall, opposite the door if possible.

Check that any airbricks are clear and that a fireplace, if blocked off, is fitted with an airbrick to prevent condensation in the flue.
TIP Efficient ventilation is essential for safety if you have gas or solid-fuel heating. To check, ask your Gas Board or branch of the Solid Fuel Association (see Useful Addresses).

If condensation is an intractable problem – in a holiday home, or a cellar or scullery for example – consider using a dehumidifier, which extracts moisture from the air and collects it in a container, which has to be emptied periodically. Though dehumidifiers cost several hundred pounds to buy, running costs are low and they are very effective.

PROBLEMS WITH ROT

DRY ROT

Dry rot is a fungus that flourishes in damp, poorly ventilated places that are often hidden from view. Look under stairs and floors, in cellars, beneath floorboards and behind skirting boards, though it can occur in other places too. It has long cottony strands, but as it proceeds, it can put out reddish-brown mushroom-like growths. These produce spores that look like brick dust, have a musty odour and crumbling, cube-like wood.

Don't close your eyes to them, because dry rot affects masonry as well as timber and is a serious structural threat. Contact the British Wood Preserving and Dampproofing Association (see Useful Addresses) for professional help.

All dry rot must be removed from brickwork and plaster; affected wood should be removed beyond any sign of infestation; and all wood treated with an approved fungicide. Contaminated bricks should be safely disposed of to prevent the rot spreading.

TIP An early sign of dry rot is cracked paintwork by window frames and skirtings or distorted skirting boards. Push a knife blade down and if the wood crumbles, call in a professional.

WET ROT

As its name suggests, wet rot attacks wood that's wet rather than damp. Like dry rot, it's a fungal infestation, but it's much easier to spot: look for dark, rotten wood that's split along the grain. Wet rot usually occurs outside, on fences, window sills, window frames and doors, all of which tend to rot at the base.

Regular decorating will keep wet rot at bay. If it occurs, cut away the damaged part and replace with timber treated with preservative. For small areas, you can use a wood repair system. The rot is removed and the wood treated with hardener, before being built up with filler. Preservative tablets are inserted to keep the wood sound.

HOUSEHOLD PESTS

Most household pests are destructive or unhygienic or both, and a few, such as woodworm, may pose a serious threat to the structure of your house.

Others, however, can affect your health: asthma or rhinitis may be irritated by the house dust mite; wasp or bee stings can cause serious reactions; food poisoning is caused by contamination from house flies or mice. Each year 56,000 people receive hospital treatment for accidents involving insects alone, so it's well worth making sure that they don't take refuge in your home.

As for larger pests, it's your legal duty as a householder to keep your home free from vermin and to contact the local authority's environmental health officer if the problem gets out of hand.

TIP Local authorities may not charge to rid you of rats or other pests which could cause a major threat to public health (a large-scale infestation of mice or cockroaches for example). If you decide to use a commercial company, ring round for estimates before you commit yourself. Contact The British Pest Control Association, (see Useful Addresses) and ask for a list of their members.

HOW TO PREVENT PESTS

- Keep food covered, preferably in sealed containers, or in the fridge.
- Wrap rubbish well and dispose of it in sealed sacks and animal-proof bins if possible, kept well away from windows.
- Clean sink wastes and drains regularly.
- Stop up cracks and holes where pests may emerge, especially round pipes.
- Clean up spills and crumbs as soon as they occur.
- Vacuum carpets, mattresses and upholstery and move the furniture frequently.
- Clean up after your pets.
- Look behind and inside cupboards, lofts and sheds regularly so pests can't breed undisturbed.
- Turn out lofts, larders and other kitchen cupboards from time to time, to get rid of stale food and unwanted papers and textiles.
- Keep gutters and chimneys clear to prevent birds nesting and insects breeding.

TIP Pesticides for home use have been strictly controlled since 1986, so you may need professional help to control infestation.

ANTS

Ants love sweet, sugary things, so keep food covered, bottles wiped, and plates and glasses rinsed clean. Don't ignore the problem, or you may find your home is overrun when the ants grow wings and swarm in late summer.

If you can find the nest, you may be able to solve the problem temporarily by pouring boiling water over it, but you'll need to use insecticide for a permanent solution.

Try to trace the ants to their source, and lay liquid bait, which the worker ants take back to the nest. For safety, if you have small children or animals, use a sealed tin trap, or use powders, spray or gel along the ant runs. An 'ant pen', used to draw a barrier round the house, can be a very helpful deterrent.

TIP For a traditional alternative to insecticides, you could try using cayenne pepper, cedar oil, or a mixture of one part borax to two parts sugar. To repel ants, plant strongly scented lavender, chives, spearmint and African marigolds by the back door.

BOOKLICE

Booklice need damp to survive because they live on the mould that grows on the glue of bookbindings, damp cardboard, damp starchy food, and moist plaster, leather or wood. To remove them, thoroughly dry and ventilate the surrounding area, discard affected food, and wipe away all signs of mould. A powder or aerosol insecticide for crawling insects will destroy any remaining booklice.

CARPET BEETLES

Carpet beetle grubs, called 'woolly bears', are furry little bugs that thrive in centrally heated homes. They damage all woollen fabrics, from carpets to clothing, leaving holes similar to those made by clothes' moths.

Because the source of infestation is often an undiscovered birds' nest or feathers, it's worth searching the loft for signs of these before you try to eliminate grubs that have moved further down. Look for traces of damage in airing cupboards, wardrobes and chests where clothes and blankets are stored as well as under carpets and rugs.

Clean thoroughly if you spot signs of carpet beetle, taking care to remove any fluff, and launder or dry-clean any affected items. Vacuum carpets thoroughly and spray floorboards, cracks and the corners of cupboards with mothproofer or special carpet-beetle insecticide.

CAT FLEAS

Cat fleas are the most troublesome type of flea, because they're the ones most likely to transfer to humans and dogs. True dog fleas are comparatively rare; though dogs may well have fleas, they are usually cat fleas, which account for four out of five infestations.

Cat fleas multiply fast in a hot summer (August and September are peak biting times) and they can survive for some time in carpets and furnishings.

To get rid of them, treat your cat or dog with a veterinary flea powder or shampoo. Wash pets' beds and burn old pet bedding, and launder any washable furnishings, such as cushions or bedding, they may have sat on. Vacuum carpets, mattresses and upholstery thoroughly and spray with flea killer; if this doesn't do the trick, you may have to shampoo furnishings too. It may be worth banning pets from bedrooms (and keeping the doors closed) to prevent fleas infesting beds and bedding if your pet is affected. Pet flea collars can help keep the problem at bay: ask your vet.

TIP If you are bitten, stand in the bath to undress and then soak or spray your clothes. The fleas are unlikely to be able to scale the bath's shiny sides.

COCKROACHES

Cockroaches cause food poisoning so they should be eradicated as quickly as possible. They like warm, moist and often dirty places: behind boilers, by hot-water pipes and under sinks, and emerge at night in search of food, which they soil as they eat.

Clean out any areas where they may breed and treat with an insecticide for crawling insects. If they persist, call your local authority environmental health department, or a commercial pest-control company.

FLIES

'Follow a fly for a day and you won't eat for a week' is a saying that still holds true today. House flies breed in rotting organic matter and the maggots hatch in about 24 hours, turning into adult flies within a week in high summer, when the life cycle starts all over again. Blowflies (blue or green-bottles) lay their eggs on meat and take slightly longer to mature but are even more unpleasant.

Because flies transfer bacteria from their breeding ground to food, they are responsible for many cases of food poisoning. The easiest way to prevent them is to destroy any potential breeding sites, making sure rubbish is well covered and bins kept clean, taking care to clean up after pets, and covering food.

TIP Cluster flies are small flies that hibernate in roofs and attics, and they may return every year. Call in a professional contractor.

If you've no control over the source of infestation, keep windows on the sunny side of the house closed or fit fly screens to them. Fly papers impregnated with insecticide can help. Reserve fly spray for individual flies, as it should be used sparingly and not over exposed food or fish tanks. Hanging bunches of mint or basil and growing strongly-scented flowers such as marigolds and perlagoniums at the doors or window sills are all 'green' ways to deter flies.

TIP To stop flies buzzing at the windows, rub the panes with a little liquid paraffin.

HOUSE-DUST MITES

The house-dust mite is a major factor in allergies such as rhinitis and allergic asthma, and it's thought to aggravate eczema too. You can't eliminate it from your house because this microscopic creature is found in all textiles, especially pillows, mattresses and upholstery, where it lives on flakes of human skin and produces droppings, no bigger than a grain of pollen, that contain the cause of the problem. If affected, the first step may be to replace your mattress and pillow. Most mattresses are about 15 years old and many pillows about 12, so mould, mites and skin cells could account for one-tenth of their weight. It's also an idea to keep soft furnishings to a minimum, choosing synthetic fibres where possible, and fabrics (including bedding) that can be laundered at 135°F/58°C, which is hot enough to kill mites. If textiles are not washable, vacuum them regularly – mattresses, curtains and upholstery as well as carpets – preferably with a high-efficiency vacuum cleaner or one that offers an extra filter for maximum dust collection, like those by Miele or Medivac.

TIP Use a damp cloth when dusting to keep airborne dust to a minimum.

Because beds often harbour house mites, it may be worth investing in covers for pillowcases, mattresses and duvets made from a special, microporous fabric that keeps house-mite debris in but still allows your body to breathe. See Non-allergenic Beds and Bedding, page 149.

Other approaches include sprays to eradicate the mites, available from pharmacies or by mail order. Sprays can also be applied professionally, by Servicemaster for example (see Useful Addresses), and several companies offer liquid nitrogen treatment for textiles, which reduces surface temperatures to minus 320°F/196°C, so mites are killed by the cold. (See Useful Addresses.)

TIP Asthma sufferers may be exempt from VAT on some products: check with the retailer or maker, and ask your pharmacist for an exemption form. You may need a doctor's certificate when ordering products by mail order.

Good Housekeeping publishes a fact sheet on allergic asthma, which lists products that may help: see Useful Addresses. For further information, contact the National Asthma Campaign), or send a large SAE to the British Allergy Foundation (see Useful Addresses).

MICE

The mice that invade your home may be resident (House Mice) or merely taking refuge from hunger and cold (Field Mice), but both have the same unhygienic habits which spread disease. Because mice urinate to mark their territory, they contaminate food and can cause outbreaks of food poisoning; and because they are rodents they need to chew constantly, and are responsible for many fires when they bite through cables and wiring. Small dark droppings, shredded packaging, nests of paper, and a sour smell are all signs of mice, and you may also hear them scuttling around at night.

Lay traps, baited with chocolate, cereal, nuts or dried fruit if necessary (cheese is not very successful), or buy a cat. Both of these measures will kill individual mice, but though they will keep mice at bay, they will not rid your house of them.

TIP Mice run alongside the walls, so place traps here for the best chance of success.

TIP Traditional deterrents include newspaper balls, or corks soaked in turpentine or eucalyptus oil to block holes, and cayenne pepper scattered along mouse runs.

To control mice completely, buy poisoned bait, based on either warfarin, which prevents blood clotting (though many rodents are now be resistant to this), or chemicals that interfere with body temperature or calcium balance. If these fail to work, contact your local authority's environmental health officer, or a commercial pest-control contractor.

TIP Fill mouse holes with a mix of wire wool in cement, and seal gaps around pipes to prevent mice emerging from or returning to their nests.

MOSQUITOES

In Britain, the damage mosquitoes cause is limited to an unpleasant bite, though in other parts of the world, mosquitoes carry malaria and other tropical diseases. They cause most trouble at dusk and at night, so you should wear insect repellent and cover arms and ankles outside after dark.

Mosquitoes hibernate in dark, still sites such as sheds and hollow trees and breed in stagnant water. Cover water butts and consider adding a fountain to create movement in ornamental ponds. You also need to keep drains and gutters clear so they empty swiftly, and renew the water in bird baths regularly.

TIP A few drops of paraffin on the surface of still water will stop mosquitoes breeding, by sealing the surface and depriving the mosquito larvae of oxygen.

Indoors, you can fit screens to windows or burn impregnated mosquito coils. These measures should be enough to cope with most cases of gnats and midges as well as mosquitoes, but if mosquitoes from marshland or rivers are a serious problem, contact your environmental health officer for professional help.

TIP A traditional way to repel mosquitoes is to add a few drops of citronella oil to a saucer of water.

MOTHS

House and clothes moths can damage woollens and blankets, especially those that are stored for some time, because their larvae feed on wool and fur. House moths may attack cork and leather too.

New or perfectly clean fabrics are rarely affected because the moths are attracted to food and perspiration stains, so always dry clean or launder woollen clothes or bedding before you put them away. Store them in sealed polythene bags, and hang moth repellent in cupboards and wardrobes as an extra deterrent; the latest type no longer smells pungently of camphor. To protect furnishings, vacuum well from time to time along the edge of fitted carpet, inside sofas and armchairs, and beneath heavy furniture before spraying with mothproofing spray.

TIP These days carpet beetles actually cause more damage to fabrics than moths, so take care to check for their 'woolly bear' grubs if you spot holes in carpets or clothes.

RATS

One in five homes in Britain is now plagued by rats, which carry a range of diseases from salmonella and Weil's disease (a water-borne bacterial infection that can cause liver damage) to fires and floods, caused as rats chew their way through pipes and wiring.

Rats are a public health priority, so your local council will often deal with them free of charge: contact the environmental health officer. Rats stick to traditional 'runs', which makes them relatively easy to trace once you know that they're about, but they're nocturnal, so you're unlikely to see them until they are well established. Look for large, dark droppings and smears made as they pass along walls, as well as obvious pilfering of food.

Once they have been eradicated, block up all possible entry holes and remove or block areas of shelter, such as wood piles and spaces beneath shed and outhouse floors. Don't throw out scraps for the birds, which will attract rats; use a bird table or hang food in a net instead.

If you have been bothered by rats, it's worth keeping a supply of bait to use promptly if you spot them near their runs again. It's highly poisonous, so keep it locked away from children and pets.

SILVERFISH

These tiny grey insects like damp conditions. They feed on starch, but the damage they do is minimal and is usually limited to paper, books and wallpaper, though they may occasionally invade the larder too. A powder insecticide for crawling insects should cope with them, but wipe away any mould and eliminate the source of the damp to prevent silverfish returning.

WASPS

A particular nuisance in late summer, when the workers emerge from the nest. Each nest can produce up to 30,000 wasps, and they will fly several miles in search of sweet food. Foraging wasps can be kept at bay by fitting fly screens to windows, backed up with a wasp or flying-insect spray to kill those that find their way inside. Outdoors, it may be worth making a wasp trap by putting soft drink or a spoonful of jam, plus a little detergent, in a jam-jar of water, and partially covering the opening with paper to stop the wasps from getting out again. (Place it some distance away from where you are sitting, or they will be attracted to any food you eat and drink.)

Wasps' nests often need professional attention, especially if they are close to the house. Never try to remove a wasps' nest inside the house by yourself; call in your council or a commercial pest control company instead. You can buy proprietary wasp nest killer to deal with any nests that are further away, but take great care to protect yourself. Treat the nest at dusk when the wasps are inside, and cover yourself from head to foot, wearing a hat, gloves, boots, and a scarf round your face. Leave the area as soon as you've applied the wasp killer; don't stay around to see what happens.

If you're stung by a wasp, you can soothe the sting with vinegar, essential oil of lavender (an aromatherapy oil), or 1 per cent hydrocortisone cream, available from pharmacies. Minor swelling can be treated with over-the-counter antihistamines, but you should call a doctor immediately if you are stung by a number of wasps, if you have ever had a severe reaction before, or if you begin to have symptoms that affect other parts of your body – such as hives ('nettle rash'), shortness of breath, redness or severe swelling – because wasp stings can sometimes cause life-threatening anaphylactic shock.

WOODWORM

Woodworm is, in fact, infestation by any of three different insects: the furniture beetle, which is the most common and feeds on softwoods and adhesives, the death-watch beetle, which infests old timbers, and the house longhorn beetle, which is restricted to parts of south-east England.

Woodworm thrive in untreated wood, so preservative, varnish, paint and polish all act as a deterrent. The grubs cause most problems, by tunnelling through the wood as they feed, and you can often tell if your house is affected by active woodworm by looking for the powdery trails they leave, generally in spring and summer. Tiny, round exit holes are made in wood by the adult beetles when they fly away, which remain after the infestation has been treated.

To prevent woodworm, check all second-hand furniture buys for signs of infestation before bringing them into the house, looking at the back and in the corners of drawers as well as at wood that is easily visible. Woodworm in furniture can be treated with a proprietary solution or aerosol, available from hardware shops, but specialist treatment is needed if the structural timbers in your home have been affected. Contact the British Wood Preserving and Dampproofing Association (see Useful Addresses) for the address of an approved firm.

WAYS TO KEEP WARM

CENTRAL HEATING

There are two main types of central heating system: 'wet' or radiator systems, which are the most popular, and 'dry' warm-air systems.

WET CENTRAL HEATING

Uses a boiler to heat water, which is pumped through pipes to radiators or heaters and returns to the boiler where it is heated again. The advantages of wet central heating are that it can be linked to a hot-water heating system and run by almost any fuel: gas, oil, liquefied petroleum gas (LPG), solid fuel, or electricity.

TIP Make sure a corrosion inhibitor is added to the system, to prevent rust and scale and help stop leaks.

Boilers

The size of the boiler depends on the number of radiators it supplies, the standard of insulation in your home, and the size and construction of your house. Electrically heated boilers don't need to be vented outside, but solid fuel boilers must have a chimney. (If you rely on wood, the chimney should be swept monthly.) Gas, oil, or LPG boilers should be connected to a chimney or have a balanced flue, which draws in air and passes waste gases back through an outside wall. Gas and solid fuel can also be used with a back boiler which is located behind an open fire or room heater.

All boilers should be approved by the relevant organisation – British Gas, the Heating Equipment Testing Approvals Scheme (HETAS), the Electricity Board or the Solid Fuel Association – and serviced annually. All gas appliances must be installed and serviced by British Gas or a firm approved by the Council for Registered Gas Installers (CORGI). It's illegal to do it yourself.

Radiators

Radiators are usually made from pressed steel

HOW TO BLEED A RADIATOR

If a radiator is colder at the top than the bottom or drums loudly when the heating comes on, air in the system may be the problem. In conventional central heating systems, you can remove it by 'bleeding' the radiator with the radiator key supplied when the central heating was installed. If you've lost it, you can buy another from a DIY or hardware shop.

This can't be done if you have a sealed system, where water is not automatically topped up, so you'll need to call in a plumber.

1 Turn off the pump and boiler.
2 Find the square-shaped bleed valve at the top corner of the radiator and insert the key.
3 Holding a jar or bowl underneath the valve to catch any water, turn the key cautiously anti-clockwise, about 90 degrees. (Don't turn it any more than this or water will flood out.)
4 The air will hiss as it escapes. As soon as it stops, and water starts to spill out, turn the key clockwise to close the valve.

TIP Bleed radiators once or twice a year, because air can cause corrosion.

although some, very rarely, are alloy, and older systems may have cast iron radiators. Pressed steel has the advantage of being cheaper, lighter and quicker to heat up, but will rust more quickly than cast iron, so leaks are more common. Cast iron takes a long time (and a lot of fuel) to heat up, but retains the heat better.

Radiators can be single panels; double-panel designs, which give more heat and allow heat to circulate between the two panels as well as the surface; or panels with fins at the back for greater efficiency.

Convector heaters

Convector heaters produce warm air rather than radiant heat. They contain two copper pipes, (one flow and one return), surrounded by fins inside a casing which has a grille at the top and bottom for warm air to pass through.They're available as skirting board fixtures or as fan-assisted heaters, often fitted in draughty hallways.

WARM-AIR HEATING

Usually runs on electricity, though some systems are still oil or gas-fired. Most electric heating uses off-peak electricity, which accumulates overnight and is stored in an iron or other heat-retaining block. It's programmed to give out heat later in the day, and usually incorporates a convector heater running on full-price electricity to top it up during the day. Heating is either from separate storage heaters or, in flats and small houses, a single, central storage unit, with ducts or vents leading from it to the main rooms.

The chief problems are the lack of control – the heating is either on or off – and the fact that 'dry' heating systems cannot be used to heat water.

Electric under-floor heating, which used to be commonly fitted in flats, has fallen from favour because it is so expensive to run. It requires good insulation and to be effective, needs your neighbours to use it too.

Ducted warm-air heating, popular in the 1960s when energy was cheap, uses a conventional oil or gas boiler to heat the air and a blower or fan to push it along ducts in the floor and ceiling.

TIP Make sure the ducting and fan are cleaned regularly.

CENTRAL-HEATING CONTROLS

Hot-water controls include thermostats or sensors connected to the hot-water cylinder, and boiler thermostats. Immersion heaters usually have a thermostat that can be altered to lower the water temperature, if you would like to cut costs.

Thermostats switch the boiler on and off to maintain the chosen temperature. They can be fitted on walls, usually in the living room or the hall, or as thermostatic radiator valves (TRVs) connected to individual radiators.

Room thermostats are relatively inflexible, because they can only react to the temperature where they are sited. Bedrooms ,may become unbearably hot as the boiler struggles to maintain the temperature set in the draughty hall, or you find yourself shivering, because a thermostat by a sunny window has switched the boiler off.

In contrast, TRVs adjust the heat given out by each radiator, so you can fine tune the system to provide the heat you require in each room. At least one radiator in the house should have a manual control or a bypass pipe, not a TRV, which should be left open when the heating is on, so the boiler and pump are not put under strain if heat to the other radiators is shut off.

WHICH FUEL?

FUEL	AVAILABILITY	PROS	CONS
Gas	Towns/suburbs	Versatile	Needs chimney/flue
Electricity	Almost everywhere	Clean; easy to install	Expensive for heating
LPG	Anywhere	Portable form of gas	Costly; needs flue/storage
Oil	Anywhere	Versatile	Needs flue and storage
Solid fuel	Anywhere	Open fires	Needs flue/storage/attention; may need to be smokeless

Time switches and programmers control gas or oil-fired boilers, switching them on and off at pre-set intervals. The simplest versions switch on water and central heating together, twice a day, though you can override the setting manually if you want to. Modern devices allow you to control heating and hot water separately, while with electronic controls, you can programme the system on a day-to-day basis. For example, you can turn it off until 6pm from Monday to Thursday if you're at work, then on at Friday lunchtime if you always shop that morning, and on all day at weekends.

TIP Look for a battery back-up, so the timer won't need to be reset after a power cut.

Zone controls use thermostats linked to motorised valves which divert heat along particular pipes, so different parts of the house – such as upstairs or downstairs – can be heated separately.

INSULATION

Now that there's VAT on fuel in Britain, effective insulation is more important than ever. Here's what you can do to keep the heat high and fuel bills low.

IMPROVING ENERGY EFFICIENCY

Insulate hot-water cylinder and pipes
This is one of the most cost-effective steps you can take and one that's good for the environment too, because all insulation reduces power requirements and so helps reduce the carbon dioxide emissions that can damage the ozone layer.

A lagging jacket costs only a few pounds but because it can cut heating costs by £10 to £15

IS YOUR HOME ENERGY EFFICIENT?

You can have your home assessed for energy efficiency, and get valuable advice on how to cut fuel bills with the government-approved Standard Assessment Procedure. This calculates the cost of heating your home and providing hot water, plus the heat systems and construction of the house, and comes up with an efficiency score of between 1 and 100; the average is between 35 and 49. Assessments are offered by MVM Starpoint and the National Energy Foundation (see Useful Addresses), from about £50 for a written report.

a year, it should soon pay for itself. Look for a jacket made to BS 5615. It should be at least 3in/80mm thick, so if you have one thinner than this, it's well worth buying another to put on top. You can also fit a thermostat to regulate the temperature of the water in the cylinder.

TIP If you need a new hot-water cylinder, find that the jacket is constantly slipping, or want more space in the airing cupboard, consider buying a cylinder complete with pre-formed foam insulation.

Wrap up your hot-water pipes too, because they also lose precious heat. Concentrate on the hottest pipes and those in the coldest places, especially the pipes connecting the boiler and hot-water cylinder and those leading from the cylinder to the hot taps, even if it's just the first yard or metre. This will help you save money on water if it's metered too, because you won't have to wait so long for the hot water to come through. Materials to use include polyurethane foam, split rubber tubing, mineral wool or felt-strip, which are available in narrow-width rolls.

Draught-proof doors and windows

It's important to distinguish between draughts and fresh air, because adequate ventilation is vital for health as well as comfort, especially if you use fuel-burning appliances such as a boiler or a gas or open fire. Unless they have a balanced flue, which means air is drawn in and vented outside the house, they need an air supply to burn effectively (remember the experiments with candles and oxygen at school?) and to take away the harmful gases that are the by-products of combustion. For safety, there should be a permanent source of air, such as an airbrick, in the room.

TIP To prevent condensation, don't draught-proof kitchen and bathroom windows. Instead, make sure the interior doors are well-sealed and keep them closed, to prevent damp air causing problems elsewhere in the house.

Draughts provide fresh air where you don't want it. To exclude them, fit compressible draught excluders – brush strip, rubber, or silicone rubber tubing – to window frames, and brush strip to internal doors. External doors need tough, weather-resistant materials. Choose a brush type for outward opening doors; narrow if it fits close to the floor, longer bristles if the floor is uneven or worn.

TIP Brush draught excluder in an aluminium

WHICH DRAUGHT EXCLUDER?

- Brush pile seal is often self-adhesive but needs a clean surface or it can be difficult to fix firmly. Look for brush seal in a holder that can be nailed in place, for warped wood.
- Compressible rubber can be ribbed or tubular in shape. Most is self-adhesive but some tubular seal comes in a holder that's nailed into place.
- Foam strip is self-adhesive and easy to apply but it's not very durable and can quickly become grimy. Look for PVC or polyurethane foam with a wipe-clean finish to minimize these problems.
- Sealant from a tube is excellent for filling gaps permanently but won't help where you need to stop draughts around opening windows and doors.
- Silicone rubber tubing may be self-adhesive or fixed with sealant. Very durable.

or plastic holder is best if the door is warped.

You can also use brush draught excluder if the door opens inwards and there's a step up to it. If an inward-opening door is flush with the floor but the floor is uneven, look for a flexible flap that lifts when the door opens.

TIP Don't forget the letter box. Cover it with twin-brush draught excluder or a sprung flap.

Improve loft insulation

Twenty-five per cent of heat loss in houses occurs through the roof. Good loft insulation can cut heating costs by one-fifth and should pay for itself within three years. Even if you have some loft insulation, it may not be up to current standards, particularly if your home was built more than 20 years ago, so it's a good idea to check: a depth of 8in/20mm is now the recommended standard.

TIP Watch how long snow stays on your roof, and on your neighbours' houses. Poorly insulated roofs become snow-free first, because the heat inside the house rises to melt it.

If you don't want to do the job yourself, you can hire a professional contractor, but it's relatively easy, if laborious, to install mineral wool loft blanket or loose-fill loft insulation (useful if access is awkward or the joists are irregularly spaced) by yourself. Because the loft 'floor' is fragile and the materials used can irritate the lungs and skin, you need to take the following safety precautions.

- Wear clothes that cover you from head to toe, tucking trousers into socks and sleeves into gloves. (Choose smooth fabrics, not wool, so that fragments of insulation won't adhere to your clothes.) Wash these clothes separately from the rest of the laundry.
- Put on a mask that complies with BS 6016/EN 149, rubber gloves and safety goggles.
- If you use a stepladder make sure it's tied securely in place.
- Take up a torch and a board to stand on, wide enough to cover several joists.
- Never stand between the joists: you'll go straight through the ceiling.
- Open the bags of insulation in the loft, so particles don't spread outside.

To fit it, first fill any cracks between joists, and gaps where pipes or cables pierce the ceiling with silicone rubber or foam sealant, which will prevent warm, moist air from below causing condensation. Then unroll the loft blanket or spread the loose-fill insulation between the joists. It's important to insulate the water tank (but not beneath it, because warm air from below helps stop the water from freezing), using loft blanket or a lagging jacket, and the pipes, because the loft will be much colder once it's properly insulated. Make a cover for the water tank and insulate that too if you can, and don't forget to insulate the back of the loft hatch.

Make sure there's ventilation at the eaves, so that the roof timbers won't rot. You can use plastic eave ventilators or cut insulating blanket to a wedge shape at the ends. If you use loose-fill insulation, you may need to fit boards by the eaves to hold the insulating material in place.

TIP While you're in the loft, take the opportunity to examine the timbers and wiring to see if they need attention.

Special cases: flat roofs can be covered with pre-felted insulation slabs, topped with high quality roofing felt to create a 'warm roof deck'. Alternatively, you can call in a contractor to remove the ceiling or roof covering to install insulation underneath.

TIP Leave a 1in/2.5cm gap at the eaves when insulating a flat roof – more than you'd need for a sloping roof.

Loft conversions usually have ceilings attached directly to the rafters. Professional treatment is best, because it may be necessary to remove either the ceiling or the roof.

Insulating walls

More heat escapes through the walls than anywhere else in the house; up to half of the heat you pay for may be lost this way. Wall insulation can reduce this by two-thirds, but although you should notice an improvement in comfort immediately, it can take longer for fuel savings to cover the cost. Though cavity wall insulation may pay for itself in four years, it can take up to 15 years for solid wall insulation to recoup its cost.

Solid walls, standard in older houses, can be insulated inside, by plasterboard attached to battens, creating a gap that can be filled with mineral wool. (See Damp, page 231). Alternatively, use thermal board fixed directly to the walls. As you may have to remove all mouldings, skirting and electrical points, this may be best left to professionals.

External insulation – rendering or cladding – may need planning permission and should be carried out by a specialist. Contact the External Wall Insulation Association for a list of members (see Useful Addresses).

Cavity-wall insulation must be carried out professionally, using either chemical foam, mineral wool, or polystyrene beads. Make sure the contractor you employ is registered with the British Standards Institute (for Foam), or holds a British Board of Agrément certificate (mineral wool/ polystyrene beads).

ENERGY-SAVING TIPS

- Fix reflector foil behind radiators, to reflect heat back into the room.
- Turn the thermostat down 1 degree. This can save up to 8 per cent on fuel bills.
- Use a microwave instead of the hob for cooking vegetables. It saves money, and they often taste better too.
- Fill the oven completely, cooking an apple pie with the roast, batch baking, or cooking several casseroles at once, to make the most of the heat.
- Choose a water-saving washing machine that sprays, rather than soaks the clothes. Results are just as good.
- Use a pressure cooker to save time and energy.
- Keep your freezer full and defrost it regularly.
- Descale appliances conscientiously, to cut running costs.
- Use a shower rather than a bath.

Floor coverings

Fitted carpet helps stop the draughts that can account for 15 per cent of heat loss. Good quality underlay is important, especially if the floor beneath is made from concrete or tiles.

For a smooth floor, consider extra-thick cushioned vinyl, which contains a layer of foam, or cork tiles. If you're set on sanding the floorboards, fill gaps between boards with wedge-shaped offcuts of wood or papier-mâché, stained to match the surround, and stop the gaps that appear along the skirting and the floor with flexible filler, or wooden moulding, tacked in place with panel pins.

If you have large areas of exposed boards, it's possible to insulate them from below, if you have access (from a cellar, for example), using loft blanket secured with netting, or polystyrene boards, between the joists. You can also insulate floorboards from above, by lifting the boards. You'll need to take the same precautions as you do when laying loft insulation, and you should take care not to cover any airbricks, so that there's adequate ventilation to the floor.

Window insulation

Double glazing has other benefits besides improved insulation, because it can reduce noise and condensation too. It can halve heat loss through the windows, but it's expensive and may considerably alter your home's style.

TIP Employ a firm belonging to the Glass and Glazing Federation or the British Plastics Federation Windows Group (see Useful Addresses) which follows a code of practice, and ask three or more companies for a full quotation before committing yourself.

If you don't want to treat the whole house, concentrate on the rooms you use most and those with the largest windows. It's also worth considering replacing windows that are in poor condition with new sealed units (custom-made double-glazed windows).

HOW BIG A GAP?

Sealed unit
Made to BS 5713, ¾in/20mm gives the best heat savings.
Secondary glazing
8in/200mm provides the best sound insulation.

CALCULATING ELECTRICITY RUNNING COSTS

Appliance	Time per unit of electricity
Fan heater (2Kw)	30 mins
Food processor	5 hours
Freezer	9 hours
Immersion heater	20 mins
Iron	2 hours
Kettle	30 mins
Light (40 watt)	25 hours
Oven	20 mins
Fridge	10 hours
Towel rail	6 hours
Tumble drier	30 mins
TV (colour)	3 hours
Vacuum cleaner	4 hours
Washing machine	20 mins

TIP 'Low emissivity' coating reflects heat back into the room and can further reduce heat loss.

If you're good at DIY, you can install secondary glazing, which is used over existing windows. Kits contain frames made from aluminium or plastic, plus a draught-proof strip and glass.

Cheaper alternatives to glass include flexible plastic sheet, which is taped in place, rigid plastic panels fixed with magnetic strip, and plastic film, which is stretched across the pane and shrunk to fit using heat from a hairdryer. Though not lovely to look at, it shouldn't be noticeable when fixed properly and can also improve safety, because it will hold the glass together if the window breaks; worth considering if you have small children.

TIP Make sure that there is always one window in every room you could escape from, in case of fire.

A-Z OF HOUSEHOLD REPAIRS

Breakages and blockages don't need to spell disaster or expense. With a little basic knowledge, you can tackle minor repairs yourself without waiting for professional help.

BATHS, BASINS AND SINKS

COPING WITH BLOCKAGES

Grease, hair, peelings and tea leaves are all common causes of blockages. To keep the waste pipes clear, keep them free from rubbish and fat, and pour down a little neat bleach occasionally. Flush the pipe with boiling water and washing soda once a week, opening the windows first to dispel fumes. If, despite your efforts, a blockage occurs, here's what to do.

If there's a partial blockage, and the water drains away slowly:

1 Pour down a strong solution of washing soda (8oz/225g to 1½ gallons/7 litres of boiling water).

2 Use a plunger to suck away the blockage. Cover the overflow outlet with a cloth and add enough water to cover the base of the plunger before pumping it up and down.

TIP You can improvise with a sponge on a stick, tied in place with a dishcloth.

If these steps fail:

3 Use curtain wire to fish out hair and solid waste from the pipe.

4 Pour caustic soda or proprietary cleanser into the waste pipe, using as directed. See A–Z Cleaners, page 276)

TIP You can also try clearing the waste with a wet-and-dry vacuum cleaner.

If the waste is completely blocked or other measures don't work:

5 Undo the U-shaped trap beneath the sink and put a bowl or bucket beneath it to catch the dirty water. Plastic traps can usually be unscrewed by hand, but if you have copper piping, you'll need to insert a piece of wood in the U-bend to hold the pipes steady, and undo the plug at the bottom with a spanner, turning it carefully anti-clockwise. Be prepared to probe with curtain wire or a wire coathanger to remove the blockage.

DISGUISING CHIPS AND SCRATCHES

Chips in ceramic (china) basins and sinks can be repaired by sticking the piece back in place with epoxy resin adhesive, which is sold as separate tubes of glue and hardener.

Allow the sink or basin to dry out completely and wipe the broken edges with methylated spirits to remove any trace of dirt or grease. Brush on the adhesive as instructed and replace the chip. Remove any excess glue when dry, using a safety blade. Any joins can be disguised with enamel paint.

If the piece has fragmented or disappeared, apply layers of enamel paint, leaving each one to dry thoroughly before applying the next, building the paint up until it is level with the surrounding surface.

Enamel paint is also useful for hairline cracks and crazing but shouldn't be used to cover large cracks, where bacteria could collect. If the damage is substantial, you'll need to replace the sink or basin.

Scratches and burns on plastic baths can be gently rubbed out with metal polish. Make sure the bath is completely dry first and finish by buffing with a soft cloth.

HOW TO MEND LEAKING TAPS

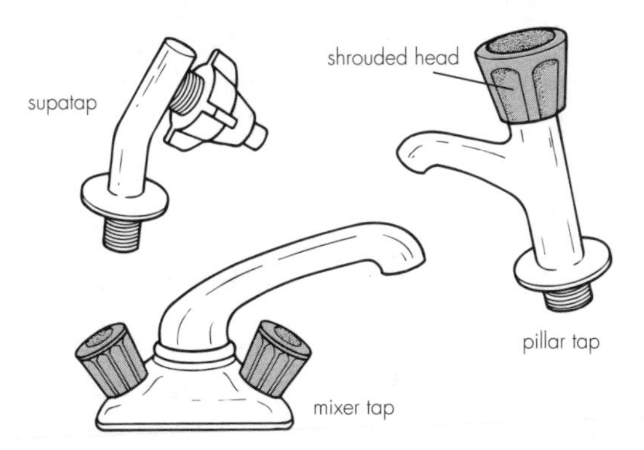

Dripping taps leave stains on baths and basins, and waste water.

If the tap is dripping from the spout, the leak is probably caused by a worn washer, which is relatively easy to replace.

1 Turn off the water supply to the tap, either at the stop valve on the pipe running to it, the gate valve in the loft or airing cupboard, or at the main stoptap. If you turn the water off at the stoptap, you'll need to drain the system before you start work, to stop water pouring out. That means turning all the taps on until they run dry and you may also have to switch off the immersion heater, or central-heating boiler (if you have a 'wet' central-heating system).

It isn't necessary to drain the system if:

- The tap you're working on is a Supatap (reverse pressure tap) which turns off the water internally when the tap casing is removed. These taps were popular in the 1960s and are still found in some homes.
- The tap is directly connected to the mains. This is usually (though not always) the cold-water tap in the kitchen.

TIP If a mixer tap is leaking, you'll need to replace the washers on each side.

2 If the tap has a standard (capstan) head, loosen the little screw in the side, if there is one, and unscrew the top part of the casing beneath by twisting it anti-clockwise to reveal the tap head. If the casing is very stiff, wrap the tap with a thick cloth to protect the chrome plating and use an adjustable wrench for extra power.

If the tap has a shrouded head, the head and casing form a single piece. There's no one way of removing it, so first look to see if there's a screw in the head (this is sometimes hidden by a flap that can be prised off). If there's no obvious way of removing the head, pull it to see if the head comes away. If it doesn't, turn the tap on full and carry on twisting to see if that works.

TIP Put the plug in before you dismantle the tap, to stop any tiny screws disappearing, and protect the the surface of the sink, bath or basin with an old towel.

3 Holding the tap firmly, unscrew the large nut inside with a spanner, turning it anti-

REPLACING A WASHER ON A SUPATAP

1 Turn the tap full on and unscrew the nut at the top of the tap with a spanner in an anti-clockwise direction.
2 Remove the nozzle (the water will stop flowing as you do so), then turn it upside down and tap gently on a hard surface. The ribbed anti-splash unit to which the washer is attached should fall out.
3 In Supataps, the jumper and washer are designed as one unit. Pull them out and replace.

clockwise (you may need to oil the nut first). This frees the 'headgear' that contains the washer.

TIP Some modern taps don't contain washers but use stainless steel or ceramic discs instead. If this is the case, you'll need to call out a plumber.

4 Detach the 'jumper' rod, which has a disc or nut at the base holding the washer in place. Prise off the disc to remove the washer, or oil the nut if necessary, and unscrew it with a spanner. Remove the old washer and examine it. If it's a conventional flat washer, you can use a standard replacement. If it has a special domed or curved shape, you may need to contact a specialist supplier. If you can't undo this nut, you can buy a new jumper complete with washer.

TIP Look or feel inside the base of the tap to see if the 'seat', which the washer fits into, is worn and needs replacing.

5 Fit the new tap washer. Standard sizes for sink and basin taps are ½in/15mm and ¾in/20mm, and 1in/25mm for bath taps.

6 Put the tap back together and turn on the water supply.

TIP While the tap's dismantled, check the small 'gland' nut and O ring at the top of the spindle in a capstan head tap, or on the headgear assembly on a shrouded head tap. If the O ring is worn, or the nut is loose, the tap is liable to leak from the top. Replace or tighten as necessary.

SEALING GAPS BY THE WALL

It's important to make sure there's a watertight seal between the bath, sink or basin and the wall behind it, because dripping water seeping through the gap can cause rot or damage ceilings.

If the gap is quite large, you can use curved pieces of ceramic tile called ceramic quadrants behind ceramic basins or pressed steel for cast iron baths. These are not suitable for plastic bathroom ware, which needs a flexible seal, such as plastic strip or extruded silicone. For small gaps, or to finish the strip along the bath when using ceramic quadrant, you will need silicone rubber sealant.

To apply it:

1 Make sure surfaces are clean and dry.
2 Protect the wall and bath, sink or basin with masking tape.
3 Apply silicone rubber sealant into the gap and press down with a wet spatula if necessary. Remove the masking tape within five minutes and leave until completely dry (about 24 hours).

BLINDS

HIDING STAINS

Roller blinds are ideal for use above sinks and basins, but may become spattered with use. Stains usually mark the lower part of the blind, and if the drop is longer than the window requires, you can salvage the blind by detaching the fabric and turning it round, provided it's plain or has a non-directional pattern. Simply take down the blind, unpin it from the roller and remove the batten at the base. Cut away the damaged area and tack the new end to the roller. Make a new slot for the batten, replace, and re-hang the blind.

TIGHTENING A LOOSE BLIND

If a roller blind is becoming difficult to rewind, you need to increase the tension. Pull the blind until partially closed, then unclip it and rewind by hand until fully wound. Replace, and repeat if necessary.

CHINA

HIDING CHIPS

You can repair chips in white china by mixing together epoxy resin and artists' powder paint, and coating with varnish to resemble glaze when dry. Alternatively, try building up the level with thin layers of enamel paint, allowing each to dry before you apply the next.

MENDING BROKEN CHINA

Even china that has broken into several pieces can be mended successfully if you take care to glue it piece by piece. Although you should leave precious or antique china to the experts, it's worth repairing other items at home. Use epoxy resin adhesive for crockery, and super glue for purely decorative china that won't be washed. Once repaired, china is best kept as an ornament or for occasional use, because dirt can lodge in fine cracks and very hot water (in a dishwasher for example) can soften the glue and make the piece disintegrate. Don't attempt to use a jug if you've mended the handle, because it may give way when lifted by the handle. Similarly don't try to mend anything used to contain hot liquids.

1 Clean the fragments with liquid detergent, to remove all traces of grease and dirt. Rinse and allow to dry completely.

2 Mix together the epoxy resin adhesive and hardener and brush sparingly along the broken edges of the two largest pieces. Press these together. Wipe the surface to remove excess adhesive. You can use a solvent such as methylated spirits or acetone, but avoid making contact with unglazed pottery.

You'll need to hold the china together as it dries, using elastic bands or masking tape, or by clamping it in a partly opened drawer. Ornaments and difficult shapes can be pressed into a piece of plasticine, or kept in place in a box of sand.

TIP Number the pieces lightly in pencil, in order of gluing, and have a trial run at fitting them together.

3 Glue and fix the other sections in place in the same way.

4 Leave for at least 24 hours to harden completely.

TIP Chips in glass can be ground down professionally, or mended if you've kept the broken piece, with a clear adhesive such as Loctite Glass Bond. Smooth down any sharp edges with DMT Crystal Saver (see Useful Addresses) which can also be used on china.

WHICH ADHESIVE?

General purpose glues

(eg Bostik All-Purpose Clear and Solvent-Free, Evo-Stik Household Adhesive, Evo-Stik Multi-Purpose Clear, Loctite Clear) make a good, invisible bond, but shouldn't be used where strength is important (for handles, for example). Allow about 20 minutes to dry. Any surplus can be removed with acetone or nail varnish remover.

Best for: leather, paper, plastic, textiles, wood.

Contact adhesives
(eg Bostik Contact Adhesive and Evo-Stik Impact, Impact 2 and Time-Bond) bond instantly and are heat and water resistant. Both solvent-based and solvent-free (water-based) types are available: choose solvent-based for metals, solvent-free for flexible plastic and polythene. Use in a well-ventilated room and remove solvent-based versions with oily nail varnish remover.
Best for: the same purposes as general purpose glues, plus pottery – but remember, the bond is instant.

Epoxy resin adhesives
(eg Araldite Rapide, Araldite Standard, Bostik Epoxy Adhesive, Loctite Tough Bond) consist of two parts that are mixed together to form a bond. They are very strong, but though they are heat and water resistant, they won't stand up to frequent washing.
Best for: bonding items that don't fit neatly together (though the join will be visible); gluing metals and rigid plastics.

Latex adhesives
(eg Copydex, Evo-Stik Fabric Adhesive) are rubber-based and will resist water, oil and steam. Special brands for children are also available. They take about 45 minutes to dry, after which any surplus glue can be removed with a knife.
Best for: flexible joins on carpets and textiles.

PVA (polyvinyl acetate) or wood adhesives
(eg Evo-Stik Wood Adhesive Resin 'W', Loctite Wood Bond Rapid, Unibond PVA). These are water-based adhesives that form a strong, permanent bond. Some can be stained or varnished and waterproof versions are available, but others should not be immersed in water. Remove any excess glue with methylated spirits.
Best for: carpet, cork, fabric, leather, paper, and wood.

Super glue or cyanoacrylate adhesives
(eg Bostik Super Glue 4, Evo-Stik and Loctite super glues, UHU Action and Multi-Purpose Extra Strong Glue.) Forms a very strong bond. Use gels for splintered surfaces, complex repairs, porous surfaces and working vertically as they are less likely to drip. Special releasing agents such as Bostik Skin Release Agent and Loctite Detach are available if the super glue adheres to the skin, but it's best to wear gloves when you use it to prevent this happening.
Best for: china, cork, fabric, jewellery, leather, metal and plastic.

CURTAINS

TEARS IN CURTAINS

Rips needn't ruin your curtains. It's well worth trying to patch them, especially if they're made from expensive fabric, before you decide to throw them away.

Light cottons, silks and synthetics
Bring the edges of the tear together as closely as you can without puckering the fabric and sew as neatly as possibly to a matching offcut of fabric used to reinforce the back of the curtain. (Take this from a hem or seam if you have to, and patch the hidden area with plain fabric.)

Sheer, unlined fabrics
Make a tiny seam to mend the tear. Re-hang the curtains, pulling up the gathering tape differently, if necessary, to hide the repair.

Lace, nets and loosely woven fabrics
Either remove a few strands from a hidden area, or buy thread as close in texture and colour to the curtain material as possible, and weave carefully into the damaged area, working from behind. If you have snipped the curtain seam or hem, reinforce it with a patch.

DOORS

DAMAGED DOORS

If the joints of a panelled door have come loose, you'll need to clamp and glue them back in place.
1 Take the door down and gently push the joints apart.
2 Glue the joints and fix back in place. Hire a sash clamp or bind tightly with rope, to keep the door together as it dries.
3 If necessary, strengthen the joints by drilling holes in the door at each joint and inserting small plugs of wood.
4 Sand and repaint.

If a door is very bowed, you can help correct it by fixing an extra hinge, or by inserting wedges between the door and frame and leaving it shut tight for at least a week. If the curve is most marked in the centre, try taking the door down and laying it across two chairs. Place bricks in the centre and leave for seven to ten days. Take care with all these methods, because if you use too much pressure, the wood will crack.

DOORS THAT WON'T CLOSE

Doors that have warped or moved may not close because the two parts of the latch don't connect. If the door fits fairly well in the frame, you can unscrew the striking plate and move it to a better position.

TIP Make sure you fill the old screw holes for extra strength, before you reposition the striking plate.

Sometimes, doors won't stay shut because they're 'hinge-bound', which means that the hinge is set too deeply in the frame, or that the screws project, forcing the door open. To remedy this, either unscrew the hinge plate and pack the recess with offcuts of wood until the hinge is flush with the frame, or re-fix the screws. You may have to use smaller screws, and pack out the screw holes to fit them.

DROPPED DOORS

Although doors often sag when the screws holding the hinges work loose, it's worth checking first to make sure that the hinges themselves are intact, or that there are sufficient hinges to support the door. If the existing hinges are suitable but need re-fixing, you'll need to fill the existing screw holes with wooden dowels and drill new holes, using longer screws if necessary to hold them firmly in place.

RATTLING DOORS

As long as the door still closes, you can often cure a rattling door by fixing a strip of wooden beading to the door frame, or using a draught-proofing strip. If the door frame itself has worked loose, you'll need to re-fix it to the wall using special frame-fixing wall plugs and screws, making sure you drill 2½in/6cm into the wall, using a masonry bit.

SQUEAKING DOORS

Ordinary hinges should be oiled from time to time to prevent doors sticking and squeaking.

TIP Move the door back and forth as you oil it so that the oil is worked into the hinge.

Rising butts, which lift the door over obstacles, can be lubricated with petroleum jelly. Remove the door before treating the hinge fixings.

STICKING DOORS

Wood swells when damp, which is why doors that open and close with ease in the summer may start to stick in autumn and winter.

1 Tighten the hinges, which can work loose with time.

2 If the door still sticks, rub the edges liberally with chalk, or slip carbon paper between the door and frame. Open and close the door several times. The places where the chalk rubs away the most, or the carbon paper leaves black marks, show where the problem occurs.

3 Rub the problem areas with a candle to lubricate them.

4 If this fails, sand or plane the door edge as necessary, leaving enough space to admit a knife blade all round.

TIP If the problem is at the bottom of the door, try opening and closing it over a piece of coarse sandpaper. This is easier than taking it off its hinges to treat it. Prime any bare wood; sand the edge lightly, then wipe with white spirit and repaint.

TIP If you use a plane, work towards the centre where the wood is strongest, to avoid damaging the corners.

ELECTRICAL APPLIANCES

When appliances such as the oven, washing machine or vacuum cleaner won't work, carry out a few elementary checks on them. Here are some simple tests you can do before calling out an electrician or service engineer.

COSMETIC REPAIRS

Touch up scratches on white appliances by wiping with white spirit and then painting with white enamel (such as Hammerite) applied with an artist's brush. Proprietary products are also available.

Use heat-resistant enamel for cookers and boilers.

Make sure that there is in fact a problem. Check that the appliance is switched on at the socket and that any taps (to a washing machine or dishwasher) are also turned on. Check its fuse and flex, and renew if necessary. If the appliance still fails, try it in a different socket before taking it for repair.

The following advice applies only to the UK: in some countries, it is illegal to attempt any electrical repair unless you are a qualified electrician. For safety, always switch off and unplug an appliance before you examine it, unless instructed otherwise.

Check the small print from your manufacturer. A five-year parts guarantee is often only valid if repairs have been undertaken by a recognised service engineer.

Make sure that electrical repairs are carried out correctly. Electricity used carelessly can kill, or at least result in a shock or burn.

DISHWASHER

Dishwashers work wonders but they aren't miracle machines and won't cope with burnt saucepans or dried-on leftovers. To make the most of your dishwasher, scrape plates clean before stacking them and use the rinse programme if you don't want to run a full wash for some time.

Make sure that spray arms can swing freely

and aren't impeded by tall or bulky dishes. From time to time, the spray arm may become clogged and the dishwasher won't operate properly. You can usually unscrew the arm and flush it clean under the tap

To avoid a build-up of scale that can damage the machine, renew the salt for the water softener when the warning light shows that the level is low. Clean the filter after every use and wipe the door seal after every load or it may perish and leak. For best cleaning results, use the detergents and rinse-aid products that are recommended, in the correct amounts.

TIP Before going away for any long period, clean out the dishwasher with proprietary dishwasher cleaner and leave its door slightly open so that air can circulate.

ELECTRIC BLANKET

Electric blankets should be serviced every second year and repaired or discarded if they become frayed, or if you detect scorch marks. To care for them:

- Examine the wiring inside by holding the blanket up to the light and making sure that the wires don't overlap.
- Check the flex and connections regularly.
- Clean in accordance with the manufacturer's instructions. Do not use an electric blanket that's damp. Dry naturally.
- Make sure the blanket lies flat and don't fold it for storage. Lay it flat under the mattress or on a spare bed, or roll if necessary.
- While an underblanket is switched on, don't sleep on it, let a pet lie on the bed, or put heavy weights on it.

ELECTRIC FIRE

Fan heaters often pick up fluff, which interferes with the air flow through the heater and can cause overheating, so keep the grille clean and dust-free. If it does stop working, you can unscrew the grille and clean inside very gently with a soft brush.

Radiant fires need to be kept sparkling clean so they reflect the maximum amount of heat, but take care not to knock the bars or the ceramic mounts when wiping the fireback.

FRIDGE/FREEZER

Fridges and freezers are among the most reliable kitchen appliances, partly because there's so little to go wrong in them. If a fridge or freezer suffers a major breakdown, the compressor may have stopped working, and you will have to decide whether it's worth repairing it or whether it's better to buy a new fridge or freezer. Don't attempt any repairs to the sealed unit yourself: call the service department or a refrigeration engineer.

TIP Connect your fridge or freezer to an inaccessible electric point where it's not likely to be switched off accidentally.

Improving efficiency

If the fridge or freezer is working but inefficient, try the following.

1 Don't allow ice to build up. Check that the thermostat's set correctly and defrost your freezer regularly. Most fridges are automatic defrost. If your fridge doesn't automatically defrost, even though it's supposed to, examine the hole at the back of the fridge and the channel where the water drains off to make sure they're not blocked. Clean out any debris.

Ice shouldn't build up to more than ¼in/6mm in the freezer compartment of a fridge or freezer. To defrost a fridge or freezer:

- Remove the fridge or freezer contents,

wrapping frozen food in thick layers of newspaper and storing them close together or storing them in a cool-bag or a neighbour's freezer.

• Switch off and unplug the fridge or freezer and leave the door open.

• Push towels around the bottom of the fridge or freezer and use baking trays to catch the water. To speed up defrosting, place bowls of hot water inside and prise away large chunks of ice with a plastic kitchen tool, not a knife.

• Wipe out the fridge or freezer and the shelves and compartments with dilute bicarbonate of soda (1 tbsp/15ml to 1.7 pints/1 litre of water), applied with a clean cloth, and dry thoroughly.

TIP Rub the freezer compartment or freezer with glycerine (from pharmacies) to prevent ice from sticking hard to the surface.

• Switch on or use the fast-freeze setting. Allow a freezer to run for at least an hour before filling it.

TIP Don't put warm food in the fridge. Cool it first by putting the container in a bowl of cold water.

2 Make sure there's sufficient ventilation at the back of the fridge or freezer and don't site either appliance next to a cooker or radiator as the heat will affect their efficiency. Allow an air gap of at least ¾in/2cm above the fridge or freezer, and at each side if they are beneath a work-top.

3 Clean the back of the fridge and dust the condenser. Dirt can prevent the motor running efficiently.

4 Check the seal round the door and replace if necessary. Warm air may lead to a buildup of ice as well as affecting temperature control.

TIP Insert a sheet of paper between the seal and the fridge and close the door, then move the paper to different points. If it falls out, the seal may be worn.

If your fridge or freezer is past repair, contact your local council to arrange disposal, as it may operate a CFC-recycling unit so that harmful gases aren't released into the atmosphere. Remove the door while you're waiting for it to be collected, to prevent young children from shutting themselves in and suffocating.

HAIR DRYER

Strands of hair that get into the fan will slow it down and make the hair dryer overheat, so examine the dryer and clean with a soft brush regularly. Check the flex for wear at the same time.

IRON

Steam irons often need demineralised water if they're to work efficiently, even if tap water is suitable in theory, because hard water affects many parts of the UK. You can buy demineralised water or crystals from hardware stores, so don't be tempted to use water for car batteries or from fridges or dehumidifiers which may contain particles that clog the iron. If you do use tap water, the iron will usually need descaling with a special descaling product or white wine vinegar to keep it free from residue.

For best results when ironing, you also need to keep the sole plate clean: see page 301.

It's also important to keep an eye on the flex and its connections to both plug and iron, not only for safety reasons. Fitting a flex guard prevents undue wear. The flex can be damaged if wound too tightly around the iron after use. The iron must be quite cool before winding the flex and storing the iron on its heel.

TIP Fill a steam iron before switching it on for safety and always empty it completely when finished to prevent the vents from clogging.

TIP It is always a good idea to begin with 'cool' fabrics and work up to hotter settings. An iron heats up more quickly than it cools down so working this way will save both time and electricity.

KETTLE

Kettles need regular descaling if they're to work efficiently and the water is to remain clear. Use a special descaling product – see page 302 – bring to the boil and leave overnight. Remember to rinse well and boil several times with clean water before using for food or drink.

Kettle elements are less likely to burn out now that so many designs switch off automatically once they've boiled, but it does happen. Electrical retailers sell replacement elements for many makes, so take note of the model number before you buy to make sure you get the right one.

TIP If the element does not come complete with new seals and washers, buy these and renew them at the same time.

To maintain your kettle in good working order do not unplug by pulling the cord.

On cordless kettles:

1 Never allow the inlet pins to become wet.
2 Don't use the kettle when the water level is below the minimum mark or above the maximum mark. It a kettle is overfilled there is a danger that boiling water may splash from the spout.
3 Always close the lid before switching on the appliance otherwise the kettle will nto switch off automatically.
4 Do not force the kettle on to the base.

A boil-dry protection is a safety device to protect the kettle should it boil dry. If the kettle is left unattended whilst switched on with insufficient water or without the lid properly closed the kettle will cycle on and off to protect if from overheating. If this happens, switch off at the mains, allow the kettle to cool down for approximately five minutes.

MICROWAVE

If your microwave is elderly or seems to take longer to heat food than it used to, it's worth carrying out a few simple checks. Do not attempt to carry out repairs yourself.

1 Clean the microwave thoroughly to rid it of food particles, which attract microwave energy and can block up the air vents.

TIP Several slices of lemon in a small bowl of cold water, cooked on full power for ten minutes, will soften food deposits so they're easily wiped away. Then wipe the interior dry.

2 Make sure the microwave is sited in a dry position, away from the sink or hob if possible, or steam may gradually corrode it.

There is no need for a routine service as long as your oven is functioning properly. If you wish to have your microwave or combination oven checked you should have this carried out every three to five years, although this will be at your expense.

There are a number of microwave checking devices available. The results can be variable as the readings obtained are not always accurate.

Before calling out an engineer, check the following questions.

1 Does the oven lamp work?
2 Does the cooling fan work? (Put your hand over the rear ventilating opening.)
3 Does the turntable rotate?
4 At the end of your trial cook time is there a signal and does the indicator light go out?
5 Is your trial sample of water in a cup hot?

If the answer is no to any of these questions check the wall socket and fuse before calling out an engineer.

OVEN

To keep the linings clean and prevent the build-up of soil, make sure you use higher temperatures, over 390°F/200°C, periodically.

Many oven doors can be removed for easier cleaning.

Clean the fan *in situ.* Wipe it gently using a cream cleaner. Do not exert pressure on the fan or you may damage it. If it becomes greasy you may have to remove the retaining nut to make cleaning easier.

If your oven goes wrong try the following:

1 If the clock goes dead but the oven works, get in touch with the manufacturer.

2 If the clock goes dead and neither oven seems to work, check the main fuse box.

3 If the main oven does not work check that the oven is not set on automatic.

4 If the main oven works but the small oven does not, check the the small oven has not been inadvertently put on to the grill symbol.

5 If the main oven works but the light does not, contact the manufacturer for heat replacement bulbs and instructions. Remember to turn the oven off at the mains before replacing the bulb.

TELEVISION

Poor picture reception can ruin your enjoyment of a TV programme. Here are a few simple checks that can help you identify any problems with picture quality.

1 Check all cables and connections. If they seem sound, turn the television on and lift the cable, running it slowly through your hands while you (or a helper) look at the screen. A sudden deterioration in picture quality may mean that the cable is faulty at that point and should be replaced.

2 Read your instruction book to make sure you have tuned in the channels correctly. With older sets, it's a matter of fiddling with the dial on the control panel and the pre-set buttons, but new televisions are more sophisticated. Simply call up the tuning command on the handset or switch the set to tune, select a number, and set the television to search until it finds a strong signal. When you're satisfied with the reception, store it in the memory against the number of your choice. For example, 1 for BBC1, 2 for BBC2, 3 for ITV and so on.

3 Look outside to check that the aerial (or satellite dish, if pictures from this are unsatisfactory) is still in place and has not been blown off, knocked out of position or obstructed in some way.

TIP Look at your neighbours' aerials to see the way yours should face.

4 If you live in a hilly or remote area, reception may be generally poor. You can write to the BBC Engineering Information Department, for advice and to check that you have the right aerial for the transmitter in your area (see Useful Addresses). As well, it might be worth buying a special amplifier from a DIY or electrical store, to improve your TV reception.

TOASTER

Trying to unjam a toaster with a knife while it's still switched on is a common cause of electrocution in the home, so never do this. It's rarely worth repairing a toaster, but treating it with care should make it last longer.

If your toaster sticks or won't work, turn off and unplug. Don't prod inside, which may damage the element: instead turn it upside down and shake out any debris or hook the blockage out carefully. A full crumb tray may prevent the toaster from working, so empty it regularly and don't wrap the lead round the toaster, especially when it's still warm.

TIP Clean the toaster casing with a damp cloth but don't allow water to seep inside.

TUMBLE DRYER

Cleaning the filter every time you use the dryer will keep drying times to a minimum and help save money.

Vented driers need an outlet through a window or cut in a wall to prevent steam collecting and condensation causing damage indoors. If you find the windows are steaming up, check that the hose hasn't split and that the connection is still secure.

If the load takes longer to dry than usual, make sure that the vent isn't blocked before you decide that the thermostat's at fault.

VACUUM CLEANER

Blockages make a vacuum cleaner slow to pick up and quick to overheat, and they're liable to occur when you are trying to clean up large amounts of dust or animal hair. To keep them to a minimum, change the bag or empty the cleaner when it is two-thirds full, and clean or replace any secondary filters.

TIP Make a temporary repair in a split hose with insulating tape.

If problems do occur, it helps to know how your style of vacuum cleaner works. In an upright, a belt links the motor to a roller which has brushes on it. The brushes beat the dust out of the carpet and it is then sucked past the motor into the dust bag. In a cylinder, air is sucked through the hose inlet into the dust bag. Filters ensure that dust is not expelled in the exhaust air. These cleaners rely on suction only.

Wet and dry and three-in-one cleaners are very robust but should always be cleaned thoroughly after being used for mucky jobs and you should take care to use the detergent recommended, to prevent foam from damaging the motor.

TIP Don't continue to use your vacuum cleaner if the sound it makes becomes noisier or high pitched. It's a warning that the brush roller may be stuck, the inlet blocked, or that the fan is vibrating.

If the blockage is near the inlet of an upright, you may need to take off the base plate to get at it. (You will also need to do this to remove the brush roll and replace the belt.) Check all the ducts and hoses at the same time, and clear if necessary, by fitting to the blowing end of the cleaner, or with a bent wire.

TIP Drop a coin through hose attachments to find out if there's a blockage.

Uprights and cylinder cleaners with power heads have, as well as suction, motorised brushes to sweep up hairs and threads. Keep an eye on the brush to make sure it doesn't become jammed, and cut (don't pull) any threads that prevent it rotating. If the brush becomes stuck and you continue to use the cleaner, the drive belt may burn through. This is very cheap and easy to replace, so it's well worth having a couple in stock.

To replace a drive belt:

1 Unclip the cover from the front and remove the belt from the drive shaft.
2 Unscrew the plate at the base of the cleaner and lift out the brush roller and drive belt.
3 Slip the new belt in place over the brush roller, replace the belt and refit the base plate.
4 Stand the cleaner up, twist the belt clockwise (or it will fall off in use) and slip it over the drive shaft.
5 Replace the front cover.

VIDEO RECORDER

Dirt and dust can damage your video recorder as well as the tapes you use in it: warning signs are a drop in sound and picture quality. To prevent problems, site the video recorder on a shelf or in a purpose-built unit, not on the floor, and regularly run a special cleaning cassette through the machine. Avoid using cheap video tapes, which can produce enough oxide dust to clog the video, and store tapes out of the sun, away from sources of magnetic energy, such as loudspeakers.

If the picture is poor, check that all the connections are sound and that cables aren't stretched, before calling in an engineer.

TIP You may need to adjust the tracking control for the best results with rented videos.

WASHING MACHINE

Heat, water and constant motion put washing machines under terrific strain, so it's not surprising that they are among the domestic appliances most likely to go wrong. In many cases, faults need expert attention, but regular checks can make major problems less likely. Here's what to do:

1 Check the hoses for kinks, which can affect drainage, and make sure the connections are sound.

2 Check the water pressure. On hot and cold fill machines, you can do this by switching to a hot wash (140°F/60°C or 195°F/95°C) programme. If the machine fails to fill or start washing within a few minutes, the water pressure may be inadequate.

3 Keep the dispenser drawer clean to prevent clogging with detergent or fabric conditioner.

4 Check the door seal regularly and replace it if it's split or perished.

TIP Wipe the inside of the door and the seal after using the machine to stop water collecting and leave the door open when the machine is not in use.

5 Check that the machine is stable and level if it vibrates when you're washing a normal load. Don't overload or unbalance by washing heavy items alone. Add several light or medium-weight articles for balance.

6 Empty pockets and close zips when washing clothes to prevent objects from damaging the drum. Check it from time to time.

If the machine fails to drain, it's worth looking for blockages before you take matters further. Empty the machine manually, check the outlet hose, filter and sump hose, if possible. Even a small item like a button can cause problems because it may act as a valve.

ELECTRICAL CONNECTIONS

Electricity can be dangerous, so don't attempt complex repairs unless you have expert knowledge. The following advice applies only to Great Britain: in some countries, it is illegal to attempt any electrical work unless you are a qualified electrician.

HOW TO WIRE A THREE-PIN PLUG

Although more and more appliances are now sold complete with plugs, it's often necessary to fit plugs to new electrical goods, or to replace them.

For safety, always buy plugs made to BS 1363, and look for reinforced shatter-resistant plugs if the appliance is constantly being plugged in and unplugged.

TIP If you're worried about fitting a plug, there's a new easy-to-wire model. There's no need to take the plug to pieces because it can

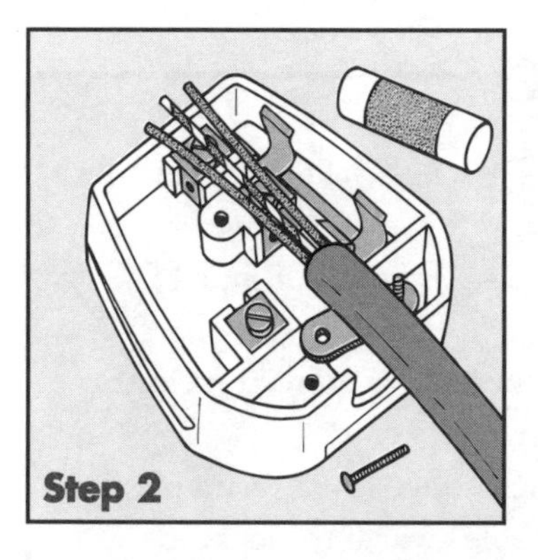

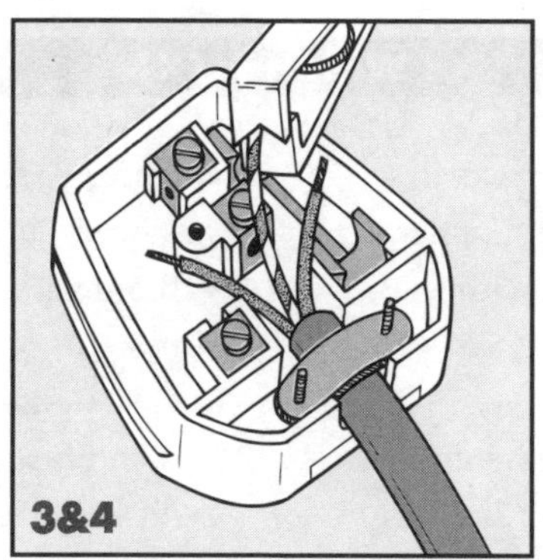

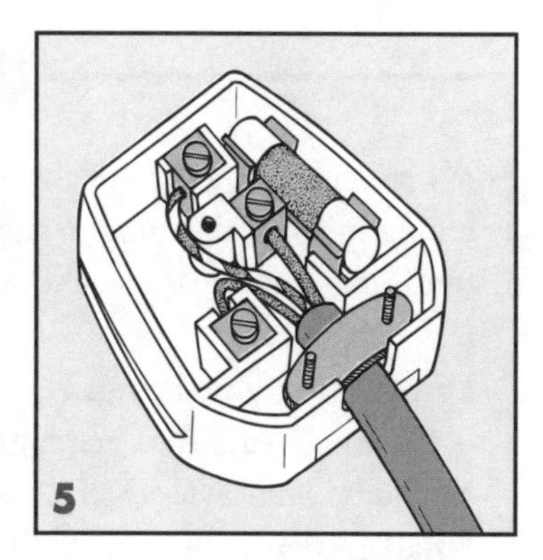

be wired via a panel whose lid contains the fuse. The lid flips open to reveal colour-coded channels for the wires and the cord grip rotates, twisting the wires securely in place.

1 Unless the wires are already prepared, you will need to cut back the outer flex casing with a trimming (Stanley) knife, to reveal about 2in/5cm of the insulation covering the three separate wires, taking care not to sever the wires. (Brown is live, blue neutral and the yellow/green wire is the earth.) If you damage this insulation, cut away the end of the flex, discard it, and start again.

2 Unscrew the back of the plug and remove the fuse if it's in the way of the wiring.

TIP You'll need to thread the back of some impact-resistant plugs on to the flex before you start; it can't be clipped on afterwards.

3 Push the flex between the grips or under the retaining bar through the main channel. Loosen the grips or bar first if necessary and make sure the flex casing, which protects the wires, passes underneath.

4 Adjust the wire strippers to the thickness required, press the handles closed to cut through the insulation covering each strand of wire, and strip it back to reveal about ½in/12mm of bare wire. Neaten the ends with pliers.

5 Remove the screws covering each terminal. Wrap the wires round the terminals in a clockwise direction until no bare wire is showing. If the terminals have holes, twist the strands of wire together and double the ends over before pushing into place. Connect the brown wire to L (Live), blue to N (neutral) and the green/yellow wire to E.

6 Replace the screws, the fuse if necessary, and the back of the plug.

REPLACING A FUSE IN A PLUG

A cartridge fuse in an electrical plug protects you from an electric shock, so it's important to

WHICH FUSE?

Details of the wattage should be inscribed on every electrical appliance. Although some appliances specify 2, 5 or 10-amp fuses, most use a 3-amp or 13-amp fuse.

- 3-amp fuses are for appliances under 720 watts: clock/radios, computers, electric blankets, fans, food mixers and processors, hair driers, radio and stereo systems, table lamps.
- 13-amp fuses are for appliances over 720 watts. These include dishwashers, electric fires, fan heaters, fridges and freezers, irons, kettles, toasters, tumble driers, vacuum cleaners and washing machines.

WHICH FLEX?

When replacing a flex it's always worth taking the original along to the supplier, but if that's not possible, check with the following table.

Lamps and light fittings:
0.5sq mm/3-amp flex. Pendant lights should be no heavier than 4½lb/2kg.
Small appliances (up to 1400 watts):
0.75sq mm flex.
Appliances between 1400–2400 watts:
1sq mm flex.
Appliances between 2400–3000 watts:
1.5sq mm flex.

• Three-core PVC insulated flex is suitable for general use.
• Braided, kink-resistant flex is best for irons.
• Heat-resistant flex is required for electric fires and heaters.
• Fit kettles and coffee makers with plastic-coated 'curly cable', which reduces the length of cable trailing across work-tops and therefore the chance of accidents.

Make sure you buy enough flex to use with the appliance. For example, about 2yd/2m is needed for an iron.

make sure you fit the right one. If a fuse blows, it's often a sign that's there's something wrong with either the appliance or the plug or flex, which needs attention. Unless this is seen to, the fuse will blow again as soon as it's replaced.

1 If the appliance just doesn't work, try another socket before you think about replacing the fuse.
2 If you hear a bang when you switch on an appliance, the fuse has blown. Turn the appliance off at the mains and pull out the plug. (If you smell burning, or see black round the plug that could indicate charring, don't attempt to replace the fuse, but take the appliance for repair.)
3 Take the back off the plug and take out the old fuse. Check to see if any wires have come adrift and make any necessary repairs before replacing the fuse.

TIP If you're not sure whether a fuse is working or not, try testing it on a metal torch. Unscrew the end and rest one end of the fuse on the casing and the other on the battery. If the fuse is working, the torch will light up.

4 If the fuse blows again when you've replaced it, there's an underlying problem. Take the appliance to a service centre or a qualified electrician for repair.

To replace a fuse in a main circuit, see Replacing a Fuse Wire, page 472.

REPLACING A WORN FLEX

Always replace damaged flex as soon as you can, because it's important to put sufficient insulation between you and the electricity-bearing wires. Flex soon wears through if it's rubbed or is constantly under strain, so it's worth checking small appliances, such as irons, hairdryers, and hand mixers, where the flex is pulled about, and fan heaters, which may be moved from room to room.

1 Unplug the appliance and remove the plate which covers the flex connection.
2 Carefully note which wire connects to which terminal.
3 Loosen the flex grip (a small retaining bar).
4 Connect the new flex, stripping the wires as for wiring a plug (see page 261). Be careful to replace any small fixings or heat-resisting sleeve.

5 Connect the other end of the flex to the plug.

TIP If the flex is in good repair but needs to be longer, you can add new flex, connecting it to the existing length via a flex connector, from hardware and electrical shops.

FLOORS

Most houses today have a solid ground floor, usually made from concrete, and suspended floors on the upper stories, made from floorboards or sheets of chipboard or plywood, on timber joists. Older houses, built before the middle of the century, may have suspended floors throughout the house, with the exception of the kitchen and scullery. Whatever they're made from, they need to be kept in good repair and free from rot and damp, because problems in the sub-floor can affect the covering you put on top.

DAMP FLOORS

Damp can seep through solid floors and affect the floor covering you lay above, so it's vital to treat it. Remove the floor covering first so you can examine the subfloor and see the extent of the damp: if it's severe, you'll need professional help. If the damp is limited, you can keep it at bay by installing a damp-proof membrane. The easiest way is to remove the skirting and seal the floor with dilute PVA adhesive, taken up the wall to the level of the damp-proof course; but you can also use bitumen, bituminous felt paper or adhesive, and polythene sheet, in the same way.

TIP Quarry tiles and flagstones can resist a little damp, so they're ideal for use in old houses, basements, cellars, utility rooms and conservatories, which are rarely completely dry.

LEVELLING CONCRETE FLOORS

Large faults

Hollows and dips in solid concrete floors are not only unsafe, but will cause extra wear on the floor covering laid on top, and thus ruin its appearance in a short time.

Large cracks and hollows are best filled with a mix of sharp sand and cement, available from builders' merchants.

1 To make a clean edge, tap round the damaged area with a hammer and chisel, wearing goggles to protect your eyes.

2 Clean out the crack or dip, and coat with dilute PVA adhesive for a better bond.

3 Apply the mortar with a filling knife or trowel and smooth level.

Small faults

Slopes, crazing and small dents can be treated with self-levelling compound.

1 Make sure the floor is perfectly clean and free from grease before you start. Sweep and wash it well and allow to dry. Remove any resistant oily patches with white spirit, rubbed on with wire wool.

2 Mix the self-levelling compound to a thick, creamy consistency.

3 Starting at the corner furthest from the door, pour it over the floor, spreading it on with a trowel or steel float. Work backwards until the floor is completely covered.

4 Leave to dry for about three hours.

LOOSE AND SQUEAKING FLOORBOARDS

Central heating is often the culprit here, because it makes timber dry out and shrink. Once gaps appear between floorboards, they may rub together and squeak.

- The simplest way to deal with the problem is to puff talcum powder (or a powder lubricant) between the boards.

- If only one or two boards are affected, try screwing the board to its neighbour, or to the nearest joist, taking care to avoid wires or pipes.
- Tiny gaps can be sealed with wood filler, and sanded level with the surround when dry.
- If there are numerous gaps, pack them with papier mâché (made from newspaper soaked in wallpaper paste and coloured to match the boards if they are stained or varnished), pushed well into the space between boards with a filling knife and sanded level when dry.
- Large gaps can be covered with wedges or fillets of wood coated with wood adhesive and coloured if necessary, then planed and sanded level with the floor.
- Use wood filler in the gaps formed where boards have shrunk away from the skirting. If there's a substantial gap, use quadrant (curved) moulding, attached to the skirting with panel pins every 6in/15cm.
- Very gappy boards need re-laying or covering with plywood or hardboard, laid rough side up so that the texture acts as a key for any adhesive. Condition the sheets by sprinkling them with water on the textured side and stacking them on edge, in the room where they're to be laid, for a few days.
- If the floorboards sag substantially, lift those most affected with a wide bolster chisel or a spade. (Place a wedge of wood underneath to prevent the board springing back into place.) Examine the joists, and if they are broken or rotten, call in a builder.

TIP Strengthen stairs and stop them squeaking by screwing wedges of wood underneath the staircase, where the tread and risers meet. If you can't get under the stairs, use countersunk screws (which won't protrude above the level of the stair) to fix the tread to the riser just behind the nose of the stair.

PATCHING VINYL FLOORS

It's always worth keeping a spare offcut of vinyl that has been used on a floor, in case the flooring is accidentally scorched or torn.

1 Place the piece of new flooring over the damaged area and cut through both pieces with a sharp trimming (Stanley) knife, following the outline of the design if there is a tile motif or similar regular pattern. Lift and discard the damaged section.

2 Clean the floor underneath thoroughly and allow it to dry.

3 Stick down a new patch of flooring to fit. Use double-sided heavy duty adhesive tape for loose-lay floors; or if the floor is stuck down, clean away any old adhesive and stick the patch in place with new adhesive.

TIP Scrub gently with detergent and a brush or very fine wire wool until the new patch matches the surrounding floor, to 'age' it and make it less conspicuous.

TIP Stop loose-lay vinyl flooring lifting by sticking the edges with double-sided tape or clear household adhesive. Put a weight on top until the glue dries.

TIP You can lift a damaged vinyl floor by pressing with a hot iron over aluminium foil. The heat should soften the adhesive.

FURNITURE

With a little work, a neglected piece of furniture or unpromising junk-shop buy can become a useful and attractive addition to your home. One advantage of rescuing old furniture is that it's very often made from solid wood, which is easier to restore and gives the best results. Badly damaged veneered pieces are rarely worth bothering with, unless they are intrinsically valuable.

First, examine the piece carefully. If you suspect you've bought a bargain-price antique, ask for a valuation and seek expert advice before doing more than dusting the piece. If you're confident that it's nothing special, check it for previous repairs, which may need replacing or removing.

Look for signs of woodworm: a powdery dust in drawers and corners, and pinholes in the wood itself. Treat the furniture with woodworm solution if necessary before you bring it indoors, or it may infest the rest of your home, which can be a serious hazard to the structural timbers.

Next, wipe the furniture with a detergent solution to remove the grime. If it has been treated with French polish or button polish the surface will almost inevitably be damaged and it's best to remove what's left by rubbing with methylated spirits.

If you want to remove old paint, try hand-sanding on small pieces or use a chemical stripper (gel or paste are best for intricate designs) before sanding with fine abrasive paper. Try not to use a hot air gun for this purpose because it may scorch the surface of the wood.

TIP A cabinet scraper (a flexible sheet of steel held in both hands) removes a very thin layer of wood. The smooth finish then means furniture needs only minimal sanding.

If there are only minor flaws, you can simply polish the piece, using a traditional wax polish, or varnish it. If it has been substantially patched and filled, it can be difficult to achieve a consistent finish and you may do better to stain it or give it a coat of paint.

For further details, see Paints for Woodwork, page 368.

FIRST AID FOR FURNITURE

Blisters in veneer

Can sometimes be flattened by covering with a cotton tea-towel and ironing them. Leave for two days to see if there's an improvement; if not, slit with a safety blade and glue flat.

Broken mouldings

These may need replacing if the damage is extensive. For a perfect match, it's often possible to have simple patterns copied by a timber merchant.

Burns

Can be cut away with a safety blade. Sand the hollow with fine abrasive paper and if the damage is extensive, repair with wood filler stained to the colour you require. Otherwise, build up with several layers of varnish.

Cracks

Cracks in wood can be filled with wood filler and epoxy resin glue. Sand level with the surface when dry.

Dents

Can be filled, or drawn out by heat, if you're treating bare wood. Wrap a pad of cotton wool in a cotton tea-towel and soak in boiling water. Wearing rubber gloves, wring out the pad and press down on the dent for several minutes. The wood should swell and lift the dent, but the heat and moisture will bleach the surface, so sand and stain when dry.

Loose hinges

Caused by screw holes growing too large. Unscrew the hinge and replace with thicker screws, or make the holes smaller by packing with wall plugs before replacing the hinge with the original screws.

Loose or broken chair stretchers

Need repairing or replacing for stability. If the stretcher is loose, fill the original holes to make them smaller before gluing and clamping the old stretcher in place. If the stretcher is broken, try to replace with one in a similar style. Architectural salvage depots often have a selection. Remove the old stretcher and if the holes are too small, drill them out, then plane the ends of the new stretcher to fit. If the holes are too large, fill as required.

TIP Remove old glue from the stretcher holes before fitting the new stretcher. It's often animal glue, which is not compatible with modern adhesives and won't bond to them. Coat the ends of the stretcher and the holes with glue, fix in place and secure with clamps until dry.

Scratches and ring marks

Can be disguised with matching wax crayon or shoe polish. Treat individual scratches on

DESIGN TIPS FOR FURNITURE

If a piece of furniture is badly proportioned, try removing inessentials such as a top-heavy mirror on a chest or unwieldy legs beneath a wardrobe. They're usually relatively easy to unscrew, and removal can make all the difference to the look of the piece of furniture.

- Simple mouldings can be used for panels that will transform dull chests and doors. Mitre the corners as for picture framing (see page 397).
- Before you decide to varnish or polish natural wood, make sure there are no unsightly patches that will show through. Bleach or stain the wood first to a consistent colour and tint filler so that it matches the surround as nearly as possible.
- When varnishing, apply an initial coat thinned with 10 per cent white spirit. Sand with very fine abrasive paper between each coat and apply the varnish with a tapered varnish brush for the best results. Don't allow the varnish to dry out as you apply each coat or the joins will show.

TIP Use non-drip varnish for vertical pieces like chair and table legs and stand them in saucers, to catch the drips.

- Furniture that has a number of flaws may look better painted. Shiny paint mirrors defects, so choose a satin-effect eggshell finish. Alternatively, lime or colour-rub the wood to show the grain, or choose one of the colour treatments outlined on page 377, which will disguise a multitude of faults.
- Vinegar graining over an existing painted base is a quick and easy treatment that has a textured effect, to disguise flaws. Paint the piece the colour required if necessary, and allow to dry. Mix together half a cup of vinegar or brown ale, a large teaspoonful of sugar and a squeeze of washing-up liquid. Add a little of the mixture to three heaped tablespoons of poster paint, blend to a paste and add the rest of the liquid. (If it's too runny, add more paint.)

Wipe over the surface with vinegar or beer (whichever you've used) and brush the vinegar or beer mix on to the surface. Leave until tacky and then make a pattern in it with crumpled paper, plasticine or putty, corks, cardboard combs, leaves or even fingerprints. Allow to dry and then coat with polish or varnish to protect the surface and revive the colours.

French polished surfaces by brushing the damaged area with an artist's brush dipped in methylated spirits, to thin the coating. Build up with layers of shellac, and sand level with very fine abrasive paper. If you are renovating the furniture and working on bare wood, sand the scratches or rub with metal polish before staining or polishing. Deep scratches will need wood filler, stained to match the surround.

Sticking drawers
Often the result of damp, which makes the wood swell. Check the runners first to see if they are broken and need replacing. If they're intact, chalk the drawer edges, push the drawer shut as far as possible and then tug open. The areas rubbed clean of chalk will show you where it sticks. Sand or plane until the drawer closes easily, and spray the runners with furniture polish so the drawer opens and closes smoothly. Check the base of the drawer to see if it has split or warped and replace if necessary.

Unsteady tables and chairs
Often have loose joints, because the dowels that fix them have broken. Unscrew the block, drill out the holes and fit new dowels ¼in/6mm shorter than the hole size. Cut a groove along the dowel with a safety blade, fill with wood glue and put back on the block before refixing.

Wobbly chairs
Caused by uneven legs can be levelled by cutting the legs to the length of the shortest, or building up the short one to match the rest. Glue and screw the extra piece in place so it's perfectly stable.

REPAIRING CANE CHAIR SEATS

Sagging cane seats can often be shrunk back using plain water. Wrap the frame of the chair in clingfilm to protect it and thoroughly wet the chair seat with cold water. Allow to dry and it should spring back into shape.

TIP To make sure the seat is thoroughly wet, soak a towel in water and leave it on the seat for a few hours.

If a few strands of cane are broken, you can mend them with pieces of cane, available from craft shops. Soak the cane in cold water to make it supple before use. Study the broken strands to see how they are woven into the seat, and then remove one. Replace with a new strand, weaving it in to fit, and glue the ends in place under the frame. Repeat until all the broken strands have been replaced.

LOOSE CASTORS

Castors often become wobbly when the holes that house the screws that hold them on become enlarged. Try packing the screw holes with slivers of wood coated with woodworking glue, or move the castor so that it screws into an undamaged piece of wood. If the furniture legs are badly split, you may have to consider replacing the legs completely or shortening them to reach sound, solid wood, or you can try replacing all the castors with cup castors, which are screwed into the side rather than the base of the chair leg.

TORN UPHOLSTERY

Torn upholstery needs patching for strength as well as looks.

1 Carefully neaten the edges of the tear and remove loose threads.

2 Cut an offcut of fabric slightly larger than the tear.

3 Apply latex adhesive to the face of the patch and the underside of the torn fabric and leave until almost dry.

4 Slip the new patch underneath the tear, pulling the edges of the torn fabric together if possible. Press down and hold in place to form a firm bond.

TIP If you don't have an offcut of fabric, try looking in department stores for a close match and ask for a sample. If all else fails, take a piece from a hidden area, remembering to patch that too with another fabric for strength.

TIP When replacing buttons on deep buttoned upholstery, use a long mattress needle and keep the button in place with a knot.

GAS COOKERS

Repairs to gas cookers and fires should always be left to experts, but if your gas cooker won't light, check that the pilot light is still alight, or that the oven is not set to automatic. Erratic lighting may mean that the spark igniter or a burner is clogged and needs cleaning.

LIGHT FITTINGS

FLUORESCENT LIGHTS

Fluorescent light tubes last for years, but when they begin to flicker or blacken at the ends, they usually need replacing. To fit a new tube, pull one end of the tube away from the lampholder (you may need to turn it 45 degrees) so that the pins come away from the socket and repeat at the other end to disconnect it. Reverse the procedure to fit the new tube.

LAMPSHADES

If the binding that attaches the lampshade to the frame works loose, the shade will droop. This not only looks unattractive, but will continue to get worse as the weight of the shade exerts more pressure on what's left of the binding. Replace with new binding, glued into place with latex adhesive.

TIP If the lampshade fabric is torn, it may be worth making a new one, using the old covering as a pattern. Choose a lightweight but tightly woven, flame-resistant fabric and replace any lining at the same time.

OUTDOOR REPAIRS

CLEARING A BLOCKED DRAIN

If you've cleared the waste pipe of a sink or basin and the water still doesn't run away, if the toilet won't flush correctly or there's an unpleasant smell outside, it's likely that the drains outside are blocked. The drainage system in your house takes used water from baths and basins, and sewage, into pipes underground that can be examined via inspection chambers or manholes set along them at intervals.

Sometimes a blockage forms when leaves and debris clog up an open gully at the base of a pipe. This is usually easy to clear by lifting the grate and cleaning it, or by fishing out solid waste with a stick or bent wire.

If the blockage is in the underground pipes, you will need to lift the manhole cover to clear it. You will need a set of drainage rods from a hire shop, stout rubber gloves and a strong stomach, because this is not a pleasant job, though it can save both time and expense.

1 Find the manhole closest to where you've detected the blockage and raise the lid. If the inspection chamber is full, the blockage is beyond the manhole. If it's empty, the blockage will be in the pipes between the

manhole and the gulley close to the house.

TIP Manhole covers are heavy, so get help if possible. Scrape away impacted earth with a knife and tilt the cover backwards, using the grips provided.

2 If you can't find the blockage, examine all the manholes on your property in turn. If they are all clear but you still have problems, ring the local authority and ask them to examine the drainage system in the road.

3 Once you've located the blockage, assemble the drainage rods, and wearing rubber gloves, push the rods down the manhole and into the drain, turning them from left to right. (Don't turn them the other way or they'll unscrew and you'll lose them.) Hook out and remove any solid waste and flush the pipes with a garden hose. When the pipe is clear, replace the manhole cover.

TIP You can try shifting the blockage first with a burst from a garden hose turned on full, but don't persevere if it doesn't shift or flooding will add to your problems.

REPAIRING LEAKING GUTTERS AND DOWNPIPES

Blockages can make gutters sag and overflow. To prevent problems, check and clean the gutters annually, before winter sets in. Netting can be clipped over the guttering to prevent leaves or bird nests accumulating, but this will need checking too as anything that collects on the netting may make it sag into the gutter, causing the very sort of blockage it was intended to prevent.

If the gutter itself is sagging, check the brackets supporting it to see that there's sufficient slope: there should be a drop of at least 1½in/45mm towards the downpipe every 10ft/3m. If necessary, reposition the brackets.

For a quick repair, insert a small wedge of wood beneath the gutter, inside the bracket.

Clearing a blocked gutter

1 Block the downpipe with a rag so the debris doesn't cause a blockage in the pipe.

2 Brush plastic guttering clean with a stiff bristled brush; use a wire brush for cast iron gutters.

3 Using a trowel, decant waste into a bucket suspended from the ladder by an S hook. Follow ladder safety tips (see Exterior Painting, page 381) and if necessary use a ladder 'standoff' (which supports the ladder but holds it away from the roof) for better access to the gutter.

4 Remove the rag from the downpipe and flush the system with water.

If the gutter leaks, loose joints or cracks may be responsible. Plastic guttering should be unclipped to see if the foam gasket needs replacing. Check the neighbouring joints at the same time and replace any gaskets that look worn.

Cast iron guttering needs regular cleaning and painting to prevent rust, or it may crack. If leaks occur:

1 Clean the gutter thoroughly, blocking the downpipe with a rag to prevent blockages occurring further down.

2 Clean out the affected joint or crack with a screwdriver or a pointed trowel, and dry thoroughly.

3 Treat with a sealing compound, pressing it down well into the crack or joint.

If this doesn't solve the problem, call in a professional to replace a length of guttering or seal and re-bolt the joint, because cast iron is heavy to shift.

Clearing a blocked downpipe

Cover the drain with a cloth and work from the top down and the bottom up, using a bent wire (a wire coat hanger will do) to fish out the blockage. Flush through with a hosepipe when clear. If that fails, you can unclip plastic downpipes or hire a special clearing tool with a screw action.

Leaks in downpipes

These can be traced by looking for signs of green mould on the walls near them. Plastic downpipe may need to be clipped back into position or wrapped in a self-adhesive flashing strip. This can also be used for cast iron downpipes and painted to match the surround. Alternatively, coat cast iron pipes with sealing compound (such as epoxy repair paste) and wrap the pipe with a glass-fibre strip while the paste is still damp. Overcoat with a second layer of compound and allow to dry before painting.

REPOINTING BRICKS

When the mortar between the bricks becomes loose and flaky, rain and snow can penetrate the wall and cause problems with damp. Although repointing a whole wall is best left to professionals, there's no reason why you shouldn't tackle small areas yourself using ready-mixed mortar.

1 Clean out damaged mortar with a screwdriver or a hammer and chisel and clean the wall thoroughly with a wire brush.

2 Soak the bricks and existing mortar with water.

3 Mix the new mortar with water and push into the gaps with a pointing trowel, treating verticals before horizontals. Smooth away the excess.

4 Leave until it is almost dry, and brush thoroughly.

TIP New mortar can make the repointed area contrast with the surrounding brickwork. Try tinting the mortar with colouring, available from builders' merchants, before it is applied, to blend in with the rest of the wall.

REPAIRING A FLAT ROOF

Worn flat roofs often leak where rainwater collects in pools instead of draining away. A flat roof won't bear your weight, so cover it with boards or limit repairs to areas you can reach easily from a ladder or steps. (See Exterior Painting, ladder safety, page 381.) Don't work on anything higher than a garage or sun room unless you have scaffolding, professional spreader boards, and feel completely comfortable working at a considerable height.

1 Brush away the roof chippings and put to one side.

2 If the roofing felt is torn, clean out the crack. If it has bubbled, slit the bubble and pull back the flaps to let the interior dry out.

3 Apply a layer of felt 6in/150mm wide, losely over the split. Apply a second layer 12in/300mm wide on top and bond them together with bitumen.

4 Leave to dry and apply again after 48 hours. Then replace any chippings.

For further information on flat roofs, send an SAE to the British Flat Roofing Council (see Useful Addresses).

TEMPORARY REPAIR TO A CRACKED TILE OR SLATE

If rainwater is coming in through a cracked tile or slate and you can not get a replacement immediately, make a temporary repair to the slate itself, to reduce to a minimum the damage done by damp.

1 Raise the one or two tiles or slates that overlap on to the cracked one to give you better access. Prop them up with wooden wedges.

2 Use a wire brush to clean the surface round the crack.

3 Brush a coat of flashing-strip primer into and round the crack, painting a strip as wide as the flashing strip. The primer ensures a good bond between the tile or slate and the flashing strip.
4 Cut a piece of flashing strip with a sharp knife. Make it long enough to cover all of the crack.
5 Press the flashing strip into place and bed it well down into the primer. Run a small wallpaper seam roller to and fro over it to firm it down.
TIP For a fine crack, just seal it with bituminous sealant (in an applicator gun). Using wooden wedges, prop up the tiles or slates that overlap the cracked one, brush out the crack and then inject sealant.

ROOF SAFETY

- Set the ladder up at the correct angle: 3ft/1m away from the wall for every 4yd/4m up the wall (see page 381). The ladder should reach above the point where you are working.
- Always move the ladder along the wall to keep within easy reach of the point where you are working.
- Get someone to hold the ladder when you are ascending and descending and keep him/her within calling distance while you are working.
- Have a safe place to put your tools such as a sturdy apron or a purpose-made belt.
- Don't go on the roof without a roof ladder hooked over the ridge and reaching down to the eaves.
- Take care not to drop anything. Have a sack or bucket hooked on to the roof ladder. Lower it with a rope.

REPLACING A ROOF TILE

Slates and tiles that are nailed in place are difficult to replace, but most roof tiles have nibs at the back that slip over a retaining batten and so are relatively easy to move.
1 Carefully lift a few tiles in the course above the broken or missing tile and wedge them with offcuts of wood so that they stay raised.
2 With a large trowel, detach the broken tile from the batten that secures it to the roof, and remove it.
3 Push the new tile into place, making sure it hooks securely over the retaining batten. (A loose tile can be replaced in the same way.)
4 Remove wedges of wood beneath the top row of tiles.

TOILETS

DRIPPING OVERFLOW

A faulty ball valve or float can't control the flow of water from the tank to the lavatory cistern, and that means that water will drip through the overflow pipe. You can stop this temporarily by tying the float arm to a piece of wood laid across the top of the cistern, but you won't be able to flush the lavatory while this is in place. For a permanent repair, you'll need to replace the ball float, if this is worn, or repair the ball valve in the following way.
1 Turn off the water supply at the stop valve or main stoptap (see How to Mend Leaking Taps, page 249) and drain the system, flushing the toilet to empty the cistern.
2 Take off the end of the valve to remove the float arm, using pliers if necessary.
3 Take the plug out of a narrow Portsmouth valve, then unscrew and remove the washer, or take out the plastic diaphragm from the wider diaphragm valve.

4 Clean out the inside of the valve.
5 Replace the new washer or diaphragm and reassemble the valve.
TIP Smear a little petroleum jelly inside the thread before screwing the valve back together to make it easier to dismantle next time.
6 The water level in the cistern should be about 1in/2.5cm lower than the overflow. To allow more water in, you'll need to raise the float; to lower the water level, you'll need to lower it. You should be able to adjust it if the float arm is attached to a diaphragm valve, but if it's attached to a Portsmouth valve, you'll probably need to remove the float arm and bend it into shape.

UNBLOCKING A TOILET

See page 469

WALLS

PATCHING WALLPAPER

Ordinary wallpaper

Wallpaper is best repaired with an irregular patch of paper torn into shape which, perhaps suprisingly, makes a far more discreet repair than a neat offcut.
1 Carefully tear away the ripped or stained patch of wallpaper in an irregular shape.
2 Take an offcut of wallpaper to fit the pattern of the damaged area and tear into shape to soften the edges.
3 Coat the back with wallpaper paste and press into place.
4 Wipe away any excess adhesive and make sure the edges lie flat by pressing with a clean cloth or a wallpaper seam roller.

Vinyl wallpaper

If the patch is very difficult to match, or a vinyl wallcovering has been damaged, try the following method.
1 Place an offcut over the wall, covering the damaged area and matching the pattern.
2 Cut through both layers of wallpaper with a sharp trimming (Stanley) knife, to make an irregular shape.
3 Throw away the damaged piece and stick the new one into place.

LOOSE WALL FIXINGS

Shelves and curtain poles that are properly fixed should stay put almost indefinitely, but they may be pulled out of place if they're subjected to sudden pressure. Once the fixings have come loose, it's best to drill into a new area of wall if possible, because the filled patch may not be as strong. The existing holes can be filled and touched up with paint or patched with wallpaper.

If this is not possible, allow the filler to dry hard and drill more deeply, using longer wall plugs and screws than before. If the screws and plugs have merely worked loose, you can try packing the existing holes with some filling compound.

REPLACING CRACKED WALL TILES

To replace a cracked ceramic tile set in the middle of a wall or work-top:
1 Drill into the centre of the tile using a power drill fitted with a masonry bit.
TIP Wear safety glasses and gloves to protect yourself from tile chips.
2 Repeat until you have drilled several holes, then carefully chip away sections of the tile with a chisel and hammer, working outwards from the centre.
TIP Fix sticky tape over the spot you want to drill, to stop the drill skidding on the slippery surface (useful also when you want to drill screw holes for towel rails or shelves on tiles).
3 Chisel away the old adhesive in the gap left

by the old tile before spreading new adhesive on the back of the replacement tile. Press into place and re-grout.

4 Crumbling grout can be removed, using a stiff brush plus a chisel if necessary, and replaced with new grouting, applied with a small sponge and worked in well. Wipe the surface with a damp cloth or sponge, and polish when dry.

For ways to fill cracks and chips in walls, see How to Fill Cracks, page 371.

WINDOWS

LEAKING WINDOWS

Windows need regular maintenance to keep the weather out and heat in. As well as checking the frames and sills for rot, you need to replace crumbling putty around the glass panes, with the correct type for either timber or metal.

If the window sill is wood, it should have a drip groove so that rainwater runs off, away from the house. If this is missing, paint or stain a fillet of wood to match the sill and nail it to the underside of the sill, near the front, to keep the water away from the wall.

MENDING A BROKEN WINDOW

See page 474

FINDING PROFESSIONAL HELP

You'll need expert help for repairs that are too large or complicated to tackle yourself, but finding it isn't always easy. To make sure of a fair deal:

- Ask friends and neighbours whom they would recommend. (If you can't find a builder this way, contact the Building Guarantee Scheme UK – see Useful Addresses – which provides insurance-backed guarantees.)
- Ask to speak to two or three of the firm's former customers.
- Ring a professional body or trade association for an up-to-date list of members. If you pick a firm from a trade directory or Yellow Pages, check that membership is current and genuine.
- Look for trade associations with codes of conduct drawn up in association with the Office of Fair Trading, which guards consumers' interests.
- Ask for a written quotation, which should be binding, rather than an estimate of costs, which is not. Make sure estimates and quotations are put in writing on company letterhead and include a detailed breakdown of costs and VAT. Get two or three for major jobs.

TIP A very high estimate or quotation is often a way of saying that the company doesn't want the job.

- Ask your local authority if you need planning permission or building regulations approval before you give the go ahead for work to be done.
- Insist on a written contract, but think carefully about what you want done before you sign it. Changing your mind or asking for extras gives the firm a golden opportunity to inflate the bill. Make sure the work schedule specifies a completion date, costs and cancellation rights.
- Check if subcontractors are to be used, and who is responsible for the quality and timing of their work.
- Make it part of the contract that an agreed sum is not to be exceeded without your written permission.
- If the job is large, it's reasonable to agree to

IF THINGS GO WRONG

- Complain to the managing director of the company in writing as well as by phone. Send letters by recorded delivery and keep a copy of all correspondence. Make a note of all phone calls.
- Contact the Trading Standards or Consumer Protection Department at your local council.
- Check the trade association code of practice to see if it offers a conciliation procedure.
- If conciliation fails, the association may offer an arbitration procedure. You'll usually have to pay a token sum (approximately £30) towards this, which you forfeit if your claim is rejected. If you accept this arrangement, you may have to agree that the decision is binding and may not be able to take your complaint to court.
- Consider taking your complaint to the Small Claims Court if the total value is less than £1,000. Your local county court will have details of how to proceed. See Types of Court, page 452.

stage payments, but be suspicious of any company that asks for a sizeable deposit or money for materials: it may not have the funds to finish the job. Always obtain written receipts whenever money changes hands.
- Don't pay the bill in full until the work is completed to your satisfaction.
- If possible, pay by credit card if the bill is for £100 or more, because the finance company will have joint liability for any breach of contract.
- Check that the company has public liability insurance, and check that it covers all damage to your house.
- Try to ask for an appointment inside office hours, even if you need work done urgently, because rates should be more reasonable then. Always enquire about call-out rates, prices of parts and hourly charges, and make a note of them before asking a firm to call.
- Make sure you receive a written guarantee for parts and for the work done.

CLEANING IN THE HOME

A–Z CLEANERS

There is almost always a ready solution for any household cleaning problem, but before starting it is helpful to be aware of common cleaning materials and substances.

ABRASIVES

Any material used to rub or abrade surface. Available in differing degrees of fineness from metal polish cleaners to cream cleaners. You can feel how abrasive a material is between your thumb and forefinger. When using an abrasive cleaner, follow the grain of whatever you are rubbing.

SCOURERS

Metal
For the toughest jobs on hard surfaces. May be formed of a ball of metal coils, or look like wire wool.
(Include Vileda Heavy Duty Scouring Pad, Spontex Tough Scourer [stainless steel] Goldilocks [brass].)

Nylon
Traditionally made of green nylon. Gentler than metal, but will still scratch delicate surfaces. May be in thick squares, or bonded on to sponge cleaners.
(Include Vileda Super Scourers, Vileda Washmaids, Spontex Washups, Spontex 'Brisk', Minky Sponge Scourer.)

Non-stick nylon
Similar to above, but a softer nylon, traditionally white, and bonded on to sponge cloths. Good for rougher cleaning on delicate surfaces such as baths.
(Include Spontex 'Nonstick Brisk', Vileda Non Scratch Washmaids.)

SPECIAL CLEANERS

Non-stick: rough but not sharp surface
Vileda Scrunge looks like melted plastic on one side of a synthetic sponge, and is recommended for all household surfaces, including stainless steel, ceramics, enamel, glass and non-stick cookware.
Brillo Lite is similar to traditional Brillo, with soap pellets inside. The outer material is woven plastic over foam and must be wetted to make use of the soap. Recommended for all surfaces, including ceramics, microwaves, glass and non-stick surfaces.
Brillo metal scourers must be wetted to get the benefit of the soap pellets inside. Designed for tough cleaning, but will rust if kept for more than one job.

ACETIC ACID

This is a common acid; a dilute form is household vinegar.

ALCOHOL

Dissolves grease and evaporates quickly, although not as effective as dry-cleaning fluids. As a solvent it is excellent for cleaning glass because it removes oils and waxes. Most commonly used is methylated spirits and vodka (but not gin, which contains juniper berry stain, and not surgical spirit, which is composed of alcohol and castor oil).

ALKALIS

Household alkalis include ammonia and some soda compounds. They will harm certain materials, including wool, silk and aluminium.

Ammonia is an alkaline gas dissolved in water. For household use, its strength varies from 5 to 15 per cent. It is great at cutting through grease and removing dirt from floors and walls. Can be used for stain removal as it is a mild bleach. Be careful, however: ammonia is poisonous.

DRY-CLEANING FLUIDS

These are particularly effective for stains caused by grease, oil and adhesive tape. Most proprietary dry-cleaning stain removers contain a grease solvent and are sold under a variety of trade names, for example Dabitoff, K2r; and both as a liquid or a spray.

Dry cleaning solvents dissolve the grease which holds the stain on. Don't flood the fabric with cleaning fluid. Several applications are best. The spray variety contains the solvent to dissolve the grease and an absorption powder to take the grease away and control ring marks. Carefully follow the directions about the suggested distance for using the spray, and wait for the powder to dry completely before brushing it off.

HOUSEHOLD BLEACH

This is a strong chlorine bleach, with a strong swimming-pool smell, and is usually made from sodium hypochlorite. It can range in concentration from about 5 per cent and has detergents and perfumes added. It is sold under trade names such as Domestos, Parozone and Vortex.

Bleach should be used with great care because it can weaken fabrics and fade colours.

Milton is sodium hypochlorite, about 2 per cent concentration. For cleaning, it is used diluted 1 part to 4 parts water, and there is no need to rinse afterwards.

HYDROGEN PEROXIDE

A mild, slow-acting bleach safer for all fabrics. It has a different chemical composition to the hypochlorites. Its percentage strength varies. It is one of the slowest-acting bleaches and therefore the easiest to control. Available from chemists.

SILICONES

Used in furniture and floor polishes. They act by lubricating the polish, making it easier to spread, so that an even film reflects light and appears glossy.

Silicone textile finishes give resistance to wear, water, weathering and stains because they form a film that acts as a barrier to make the surface more durable.

SODIUM BICARBONATE

Baking soda or bicarbonate of soda. It removes stains from china, cleans your teeth, deodorises drains, cleans your fridge, eliminates stomach aches due to gas, and acts as a rising agent in biscuits and cakes. It also brings a sparkle to jewellery, neutralises bee stings (because it is an alkali), cleans glass, tiles and porcelain, and kills odours.

SODIUM CARBONATE

See Washing Soda, page 278

SOLVENTS

A substance used to dissolve another substance, such as grease, which attracts and holds dirt on to a surface.

Water is the safest and best solvent. Try it first on all washable materials.

Alternatively, to dissolve and remove grease-based substances you need to choose a grease-based solvent (such as dry-cleaning fluids).

TURPENTINE

An oil-based solvent that is obtained from pine and fir trees.

It is used in certain paints, varnishes and waxes, and as an ingredient of furniture polishes and waxes. It will remove paint stains and grease.

Turpentine is flammable and poisonous.

VINEGAR

About 5 per cent acetic acid. If using vinegar for stain removal, it is always best to use white vinegar because it is colourless.

WASHING SODA

Sodium carbonate. It is a cheap and effective cleaner, and is sold in most supermarkets: 2.2lb/1kg costs about 65p. Sometimes referred to as washing or soda crystals. Useful for cleaning drains, greasy pots and pans, and can also be used as a water softener.

HOW TO CLEAN SURFACES A–Z

BAMBOO

See Basketware, page 279

BARBECUES

Refer to the manufacturer's instructions if you have retained them.

ASH PAN

Line with aluminium foil to hold the coals and ash, and also reflect the heat towards the food. The foil and ashes can simply be lifted out when cold.

Don't line gas barbecues with foil; it will obscure the burners.

GRILLS

There are two main types: chrome-plated, like ordinary oven shelves, and porcelain-coated (which look black). Both types are easier to clean while still warm.

Use a solution of washing-up liquid in warm water. Abrasive cleaners or oven cleaners should be avoided as they will damage the coating. A brass-bristled brush will help remove food (brass is softer than steel and won't damage coatings). Avoid the bristles clogging with grease by first rubbing food remains off the grill with crumpled aluminium foil. Porcelain-coated grills can be washed in the dishwasher. (At GHI we find the chrome can be washed in a dishwasher too, but this may be at the user's discretion.)

TIP Before using, wipe cooking grills with cooking oil to prevent food sticking.

CASING

Usually made from aluminium, coated with a black paint or enamelled steel. Wipe clean with washing-up liquid to remove grease marks. Don't use abrasive cleaners. If the paintwork is looking shabby, touch up with a heat-resistant metal spray paint on the aluminium or enamel (eg Plasti-Kote Bar-B-Q Paint, see Useful Addresses). Paint after priming the area.

VIEWING WINDOWS

Some gas and kettle barbecues have glass windows which should be wiped over with a detergent solution. Use a ceramic hob scraper to remove burnt-on splashes.

FRAME

Check the legs and frame, as steel frames may be susceptible to rust. Use a rust-preventing metal paint to touch up if required.

Don't neglect any wood on the frame. About once a year, treat with preserving wood varnish after rubbing down the old finish with sandpaper.

GAS BARBECUES

Volcanic rocks

Fats and oils will be absorbed by the rocks and vaporised as the rocks are heated. To clean thoroughly at the end of cooking, close the lid and heat on high for five to ten minutes. Turn the rocks to expose the clean side before each use. Replace about every five years.

Gas burners

Disassemble and clean every two to three months, as insects may find the burner tubes cosy homes and cause flash backs. Check the manufacturer's details for disassembling the unit for cleaning.

Barbecue-cleaning kits are available that include a de-greaser, a wire brush and touch-up paint. (For example, B&Q Barbecue Cleaning Set or Thermos Clean-up Kit; see Useful Addresses.)

STORAGE

Before storing for the winter, wipe clean metal parts with vegetable oil to prevent damp corroding them.

Cover permanently built barbecues with plastic sheeting to protect from severe weather.

Gas barbecues should not be stored indoors with the cylinder attached. Disconnect, using a plug or cap to seal off the valve outlet. Store the barbecue indoors and the cylinder outdoors only, in a well-ventilated area.

BASKETWARE

Basketware may be made from one of many materials: bamboo, rattan, wicker or willow. It is used for furniture, ornamental baskets and hampers. Large items may come with care instructions, so follow these where possible.

CANE

Generally, imported baskets are made with split cane. They may have a light seal or varnish. For general cleaning wipe down with water. For heavier dirt you may need to use a solution of washing-up liquid, but anything harsher may break through the seal and damage the cane underneath.

WILLOW

Mainly used for hampers and similar baskets. Usually unsealed, so clean as above. Don't over-wet or leave basketware to soak.

If staining occurs and cannot be removed with normal washing it may respond to gentle bleaching. This is likely to whiten the cane. Varnish if you wish to re-colour.

TIP If a stain does not respond to bleaching, varnish the basket with a coloured polyurethane wood varnish to cover the stain.

BAMBOO

A hollow cane, often split for weaving. Wipe clean with a solution of washing-up liquid, then dry with a cloth.

BATHROOM SURFACES

If you know the manufacturer of your bathroom suite, contact them for cleaning advice. Follow all the cleaning-product recommendations carefully.

BATHS

Acrylic

Daily care: Rinsing and drying the bath after every use – if you have the time – will prevent water staining. Clean daily with an all-purpose bathroom cleaner endorsed by the British Bathroom Council (see Useful Addresses) to prevent build-up of dirt and scum. A product with a spray applicator is quick and easy to use, and just needs wiping with a damp cloth. For real convenience a bathroom cleaner mousse is simply sprayed on, left and then rinsed off. However, it will not remove heavy build-up of scum, and is expensive compared to conventional cleaning products.

Thorough care: Once a week, give the bath a thorough clean, paying particular attention to scum build-up. For stubborn marks, use a nylon bristle brush but not an abrasive cleaner. Look for the British Bathroom Council's logo on literature that comes with recommended products. In a hard-water area use a limescale cleaner. Pay particular attention to the area around the taps.

Maintenance: To remove fine scratches, rub gently with metal polish, and then clean the bath afterwards.

Vitreous enamel-coated cast iron or steel

Daily care: See Baths, Acrylic

Thorough care: Clean as for acrylic baths, but look for a product recommended by the Vitreous Enamel Development Council (see Useful Addresses).

Cleaning products with anti-limescale ingredients may cause enamel to dull, so are not recommended. To remove limescale try using a plastic scourer and neat concentrated washing-up liquid – this job requires lots of elbow grease. With enamelled surfaces avoiding limescale is down to prevention rather than cure.

Maintenance: For re-enamelling ask for advice from the VEDC (see Useful Addresses). This is only worthwhile if your bath is of some value, such as a Victorian cast-iron bath.

Whirlpool and spa baths

Although most are self-draining, it's important to clean out the scum left in the pipework.

About once a week fill the bath with warm water and add a cleaning agent: the manufacturer's proprietary product or a cupful of Milton. Allow to circulate for five minutes. Empty the bath, re-fill with clean water, and circulate for a further five minutes to rinse. Some whirlpool and spa baths will dose the pipework automatically with disinfectant.

BASINS

Clean daily with an all-purpose bathroom cleaner. Wipe with a damp cloth. Once a week, wipe over the outside and the pedestal.

TIP After cleaning, make sure the plug hole is thoroughly rinsed as bathroom cleaners can damage the coating. Brass or gold-plated plug holes should be buffed dry after use to prevent them from discolouring.

SEALANT

The sealant between baths or basins is difficult to clean effectively. Use a fungicidal spray to remove mould, and spray regularly to prevent re-growth. Once the sealant is discoloured the only solution is to replace it (see Sealing Gaps by the Wall, page 250).

TOILETS

Daily care: Clean every day to keep germs at bay. Wipe the rim of the bowl and the seat with a solution of washing-up liquid. Seats range from polyester to solid oak, but can all be cleaned in this way.

To clean the bowl, either use a bathroom cleaner with added disinfectant, or fit an in-cistern cleaner or a bowl cleaner, both of which will release cleaner or bleach into the bowl after every flush.

Thorough care: At least once a week, wipe the outside of the toilet bowl and the cistern with a solution of washing-up liquid or a bathroom cleaner.

To clean the bowl thoroughly, use a liquid or powder cleaner and a toilet brush, paying particular attention to under the rim. Keep the brush clean by rinsing in a flush of bleach after every use.

If you live in a hard-water area, regularly use a toilet cleaner with a built-in limescale remover. To remove limescale in the bowl use a limescale remover with a thick gel consistency so it can stick to the vertical bowl surface. For heavy deposits empty the water from the bowl first. Bail out the water by hand or, if the cistern is accessible, tie up the float-operated inlet valve (otherwise known as the ballcock) and flush the toilet. (This lowers the water and stops the cistern from filling it again.)

TIP Do not use two different toilet cleaners at the same time, even if one is bleach. When they mix, toxic gases can be released into the bathroom.

TIP Do not leave toilet cleaner in contact with the surface longer than recommended, or the cleaner will penetrate through worn areas or cracks in the glaze and cause the surface to discolour. Remember this if going on holiday.

SHOWERS

Daily care: Clean the shower tray with an all-purpose bathroom cleaner.

Thorough care: If you are in a hard-water area use a limescale cleaner once a week.

Clean shower screens with a solution of washing-up liquid. On folding shower screens pay particular attention to the hinging mechanism, which can get grubby.

Damp areas will be susceptible to mould, which appears as black spores. To remove it, spray with a fungicide. Regularly re-spray any susceptible areas to prevent further growth. Make sure you spray when everyone has finished in the bathroom so it is not immediately washed off.

To remove mould from shower curtains see Mildew, page 359.

Descale shower heads using a liquid descaler, available in conveniently measured sachets or in a bottle. An old toothbrush is useful to dislodge any particularly stubborn scaly deposits.

If grout between tiles is dirty and discoloured, apply a whitening product which also contains a fungicide. Tile Guard (see Useful Addresses) has a foam applicator that makes it easy to apply. Alternatively, you can use a solution of diluted household bleach (one part bleach to four parts water) and an old toothbrush, although this doesn't contain mould inhibitors.

TAPS

Includes chrome, plastic, gold and brass finishes.

Daily care: Many products used in the bathroom, such as denture creams, toothpaste and strong detergents, can damage the protective coating on taps, particularly those with a gold or brass finish. Ideally, after every use, wipe the taps free from such products and then buff dry. Clean regularly with a solution of washing-up liquid, rinse and dry. Do not use an abrasive cleaner.

Thorough care: To remove heavy limescale deposits soak a cloth in a proprietary descaler and wrap it around the tap. Do not leave for longer than the recommended time. Rinse thoroughly and dry.

WALLS

See Kitchen Surfaces, page 305

FLOORS

See Flooring, page 289

BOOKS

Valuable books should be stored correctly to avoid damage. Don't let them slump on partly filled shelves. Invest in some book ends. Large and heavy books such as atlases or the Bible should be kept flat.

Keep them in a cool room (about 60°F/15°C). Too much heat can damage leather bindings and make the adhesive brittle. Sunlight fades covers, and dampness will cause mildew and other moulds.

Dust books at least once a year. Do them one at a time using a fine paint or unused blusher brush. Holding the book closed, gently brush along the edges. Never bang the book as it will damage the bindings.

TIP Once a year, fan the pages of those books which are left undisturbed on your book shelf. This will help remove dust.

Valuable books may need professional treatment for bookworm, rust or mildew, in which case contact your local specialist bookseller, museum or The Institute of Paper Conservation (see Useful Addresses).

BRASS

See Metals

BRUSHES

See Paint Brushes

BROOMS AND CLEANING BRUSHES

These pick up a lot of dirt which should be removed regularly. Wear household gloves and pick out the larger particles by hand.

Nylon brushes are easier to wash than bristle brushes. They won't rot or go mouldy, and they are softer. Wash them in a warm, mild detergent solution with a final rinse in cold water to stiffen the bristles. Then hang them up to dry.

TIP Do not store brushes and brooms so that they rest on their bristles as this flattens them and destroys their effectiveness. Many come supplied with a hanging hook. If not, make one by screwing a hook into the top of the handle or lean the brush head end upwards.

CANE

See Basketware, page 279

CAR

BODY WORK

A neglected film of dirt discolours paintwork and holds moisture, which encourages corrosion in crevices.

Clean the paintwork once a week. It is important to use plenty of water as the dirt film contains tiny particles of grit which scratch the surface if they are removed with a dry cloth. Make sure all windows and doors are closed and use several buckets of water.

Always clean the car away from direct sunlight and when the bonnet is cool. Hot surfaces cause smearing. Use tepid water and car shampoo to wash the bodywork. (Washing-up liquid does clean but leaves smears and makes polishing difficult.)

Begin with the roof and work downwards so that dirt does not wash over areas just cleaned. Do not clean the windscreen with a shampoo containing wax as this will cause the wipers to smear. Use a soft brush dipped in car shampoo to clean dirt from between the grille and the wheel rims.

After cleaning, rinse with clean water. In winter, direct a powerful jet from the hose under the wheel arches and the underside of the car to flush away road salt and mud.

Buff the glass and bodywork to remove water spots. Polish using a proprietary car polish. Remove tar spots with white spirit. Retouch small areas of chipped paint with brush-on touch-up paint. Minor rust spots must be treated with a rust remover and repainted carefully before they grow any larger.

WINDOWS

Lift the wipers and wash the windscreen, using plenty of water to float off the dirt. Sponge clean the edges of the wiper blade rubbers. There are proprietary car-window cleaners, for example Autoglym or Decosol (see Useful Addresses), which are intended for both inside or outside use.

Plastic bumpers and exterior trim can be bleached by sunlight and trap dirt. Use a proprietary cleaner and conditioner such as Autoglym Bumper Finish.

INTERIOR

Empty the ashtrays and remove unwanted clutter from glove box, etc. Remove and shake rubber floor mats. Use the nozzle attachment on a vacuum cleaner to remove grit and dirt from the carpets, cloth-covered seats and boot. To remove stains on cloth-covered seats use a carpet and upholstery shampoo. Use a nail brush for bad stains.

To clean leather upholstery, wipe with a damp cloth. If it is dirty it can be occasionally sponged with a solution of washing-up liquid, worked up into thick suds. Rinse with a damp cloth and buff dry. To keep the leather really supple, treat it occasionally with a suitable hide dressing.

PVC trim panels, the fascia and steering column can be freshened up with a damp cloth. A 'cockpit shine' polish will restore a deep sheen, but avoid use on the steering wheel as it will make it slippery. Clean the inside of the windscreen using a solution containing 2 tablespoons of vinegar in a bucket of warm water or a car windscreen cleaner. On heated rear windows, take care not to accidentally break one of the elements.

Finally, check that the tool kit, jack and wheelbrace are in order and that the spare tyre has not lost pressure.

CARPETS

See Carpets, page 334

CERAMIC FLOOR TILES

See Flooring, page 289

CERAMIC WALL TILES

See Kitchen Surfaces, page 303

CHANDELIERS

Turn off the electricity before starting to clean. For thorough cleaning, remove as much of the chandelier as possible. It is easier with two people to keep the chandelier intact, if possible. Use a warm solution of washing-up liquid and pat dry with a lint free cloth.

For occasional cleaning use Antiquax Crystal & Chandelier Cleaner (see Useful Addresses). Clean *in situ* by spraying on and allowing the cleaner to run off along with the dirt. Remember to protect the floor underneath with a polythene sheet covered by an old towel and newspaper.

CHOPPING BOARDS

PLASTIC

There are two types: polythylene (HDPE) and polypropylene (PP). Polypropylene can withstand higher temperatures and therefore can be washed in the dishwasher, which is the most hygienic method. They are also more resistant to staining and less likely to stress crack. However, if not labelled, the two types of materials are difficult to distinguish. If in doubt, follow the manufacturer's instructions. Otherwise, clean in hot soapy water, dry thoroughly and wipe over with an anti-bacterial solution such as Dettox cleanser or Milton (one part to four parts water). There is no need to rinse.

If stained, soak overnight in a mild solution of bleach. Then wash in hot soapy water.

LAMINATED MELAMINE

This type often has a picture on one side. It is not dishwasher proof and should never be soaked. Wipe over with a solution of washing-up liquid and dry immediately.

WOOD

Hold the board under very hot water and occasionally wipe over with an anti-bacterial solution. Never soak as this will swell the wood, which cracks upon drying. Leave to dry naturally, resting on one long edge. Drying flat can cause warping and with all chopping boards the warm, moist conditions under the board speeds up the multiplication of bacteria.

COFFEE MAKERS

TIP Coffee beans are oily and any residue turns rancid and impairs the flavour of the next batch of coffee made.

PLUNGER POTS/CAFETIERES

Remove the plunger and unscrew the rod from the filter assembly. Wash the filter and the glass beaker in hot soapy water or the dishwasher if appropriate. Bicarbonate of soda will remove any stains on a bone china beaker. Buff brass or chrome frames with a soft cloth.

ELECTRIC FILTERS

Always unplug. Allow the machine to cool down before cleaning.

The filter holder and nylon filters should be washed by hand in warm soapy water. Glass jugs can be washed by hand or in the dishwasher. Wipe the body of the machine with a damp cloth.

Descale every eight to ten weeks in a hard-water area or every six months in areas of moderately hard water. Only use proprietary descalers that specifically state they are suitable for plastic kettles and/or coffee makers.

TIP If your coffee starts taking longer to filter through then the filter needs descaling.

ELECTRIC ESPRESSO/ CAPPUCCINO MACHINES

Descale in the same way as a filter machine but never try to force open the lid of the water tank. Immediately after use wait until the pressure has subsided and the lid comes off easily. Wash the filter very carefully as espresso grains are extremely fine.

Make sure you wash the steam/cappuccino nozzle thoroughly. Most are removable and should be washed by hand. If you haven't used the machine for a while it is a good idea to check the nozzle before you switch it on. If necessary, use a pin to unblock it.

COMBINATION OVENS

See Microwaves/Combination Ovens, page 311

COMPACT DISCS

See Stereo Equipment, page 315

COMPUTER EQUIPMENT

Wipe the screen and keyboard with a soft cloth. To remove any dirt or fingerprints always use a special computer cleaner.

For ingrained grease, dust or dirt on the exterior of equipment and keyboards, use Foamclene, an antistatic foam cleaner which neutralises the static charge. Spray on to the cloth, not directly on to the equipment. For cleaning the screen use Screenclens antistatic wipes (see Useful Addresses). Your instruction manual should recommend the best cleaners for your machine.

TIP Never place a computer in direct sunlight as this will cause discoloration. If it is not going to be used for a while, place a cover over it to avoid dust.

COOKERS

Prevent it from getting too dirty in the first place. Wipe up spills and splashes on the hob or in the oven as soon as it is practical, preferably while still warm so that the spill has not solidified. For major cleaning, switch the cooker off at the mains if the switch is accessible.

OVENS

Most modern cookers have stay-clean oven linings, otherwise called easy clean or catalytic. (The oven sides are rough to the touch.) Never attempt to clean these as it will damage the finish and render them useless. They work by vaporising the splashes from cooking at high temperatures during cooking.

TIP Self-cleaning ovens work at an optimum temperature of 390°F/200°C, but if you are a low-temperature cook, turn the oven to 425°F/220°C for 30 minutes each week to stop the linings clogging up and to keep them working efficiently.

If you have a cooker with pyrolytic cleaning you will have a special high-temperature dial. This reaches about 930°F/500°C, which carbonises any deposits in the cooker and leaves the inside really clean. Any remaining ash can be wiped away using a damp cloth.

To clean ordinary enamel linings and oven floor, use a proprietary liquid, paste, impregnated pad or aerosol oven cleaner approved by the Vitreous Enamel Development Council (see Useful Addresses). Make sure the oven cleaner doesn't come in contact with any stay-clean liners and always wear rubber gloves. Most oven cleaners contain corrosive chemicals that can damage the skin. You should also open a window and make sure the room is well ventilated.

TIP To make cleaning easier: before you begin, place a bowl of water in the oven and heat the oven on a high temperature for 20 minutes. The steam produced will help loosen the dirt and grease and make it easier to clean. To avoid diluting the oven cleaner wipe away condensation with cloth or a paper towel.

TIP After cleaning, use a cloth to smear a thin paste of bicarbonate of soda and water on enamel linings. It dries to leave a protective coating that absorbs greasy soiling and makes it easier to clean next time you clean the oven. It looks messy, but it is effective.

COMBINATION OVENS

See Microwaves/Combination Ovens, page 311

OVEN SHELVES

The easiest way to clean the oven shelves is to put them in the dishwasher. You may have to remove the top basket, and make sure the spray arms can rotate freely.

TIP You may find it easier to remove the racks before the drying cycle. Stubborn residue will chip off easily with the back of a knife.

If you do not have a dishwasher, soak off the soiling in a hot biological washing powder solution. Any remaining deposits can be removed with a mild, abrasive cream cleaner or impregnated pad. If you have to resort to an oven-cleaner, check it is suitable on chrome.

OVEN DOOR

Remove cooked-on deposits with a ceramic hob scraper. If the glass in the door is removable, soak in a solution of biological washing powder. If the door can't be removed, use an oven spray cleaner.

COOKER HOOD

Whether you have a ducted or recirculating cooker hood, it is important to clean and or replace the filters regularly. New filters are available from cooker manufacturers, kitchen specialist shops or department stores.

Charcoal filters Only found in recirculating hoods, and remove odours. They are not washable so will need replacing about every six months.

Grease filters are made from foam, metal or paper. Paper filters are not washable and need replacing every two months. Metal and foam can be cleaned in a hot solution of washing-up liquid, and should be soaked for a few hours if they are really greasy. Alternatively, metal filters can be washed in the dishwasher, but always check the manufacturer's instructions first. Although washable, foam filters will need replacing about every 6 to 12 months.

Filters are removed by unclipping the hood and sliding them out. The replacement is then simply clipped back into place. If you buy filters directly from the manufacturer then they will be cut to size. 'Universal' ones bought from a department store may need trimming.

COOL BOXES

Food and drink marks that have stained the inside of a box can be removed with a proprietary stain remover.

TIP To remove odours, use a solution of bicarbonate of soda. Before you store the box, wipe out with an anti-bacterial solution and leave the lid off, to allow air to circulate.

COPPER

See Metals, page 307

CROCKERY

Most china can be put in the dishwasher with the exception of hand-painted and antique pieces. Check it is labelled as dishwasher safe. Use a detergent recommended by the china manufacturer. Load the dishwasher so that pieces do not touch each other, to avoid risk of chipping.

HAND WASHING

Use a hot solution of washing-up liquid, and a soft brush, cloth or mop. Avoid scouring pads, harsh abrasives, bleach or soda which can damage the surface or dull patterns, especially gold and silver decoration. Use a plastic washing-up bowl to prevent knocking china on the sink itself. After washing, rinse each piece in clear, warm water, drain, then dry and polish with a soft tea towel. Do not stack wet pieces on top of each other because the footing is often unglazed and may scratch the piece underneath.

TIP If cups are stained use a proprietary stain remover. Alternatively, try soaking the china in a solution of biological washing powder.

TIP Bar Keepers Friend (see Useful Addresses) will help to remove pencil-type marks caused by minute deposits of metal from cutlery.

Use a soft brush to clean china with a raised pattern. China which is kept on display should also be wiped occasionally, first with a damp cloth and then with a dry one.

Earthenware and stoneware are much tougher than china so they are oven proof, dishwasher proof and can withstand boiling temperatures.

CUPBOARDS

See Kitchen Surfaces, page 303

CURTAINS

See Curtains, page 336

CUTLERY

See Silver, page 309

TIP Don't mix silver and stainless steel cutlery in a dishwasher as it will cause the silver to turn black. Don't allow dry dishwasher detergent to come into contact with silver items as it will cause black spots to appear. Remove and dry (if necessary) silver cutlery immediately at the end of the dishwasher cycle, as any salt residue which is not removed will cause staining and pitting.

STAINLESS STEEL

Check if it can be washed in the dishwasher. Occasionally polish with a proprietary stainless-steel cleaner to maintain the mirror finish. Wash thoroughly after cleaning.

Dishwasher tip

Always remove stainless-steel cutlery immediately at the end of the dishwasher cycle. The humid atmosphere inside the machine may cause 'rust' marks to appear, particularly on poorer-quality stainless steel. (The rust marks are corrosion pits, although the pits are barely visible.)

For the same reason, never use the rinse and hold cycle. If the dishwasher is not to be switched on for a while, rinse food deposits off by hand.

After refilling the salt container, make sure to run the dishwasher through the rinse programme before washing stainless-steel cutlery in the machine.

Staining

Although tough and relatively stain free, stainless steel still needs a certain amount of care. Permanent staining or etching on stainless steel is caused by contact with a dip-type silver cleaner.

Hot grease may leave a stubborn rainbow-coloured mark. Mineral salts in tap water can cause a white film if not dried off thoroughly and prolonged contact with acidic foods, such as vinegar, also causes staining. A proprietary stainless-steel cleaner will remove most marks. Wash the cutlery thoroughly after cleaning.

To remove tea stains from teaspoons use a proprietary stain remover and soak overnight. Rinse and wash thoroughly. For stubborn marks use Bar Keepers Friend (see Useful Addresses).

Dishwasher safe?

Wooden handles are not dishwasher safe since wood tends to swell and crack. Plain-coloured plastic-handled cutlery can be washed in the dishwasher, but patterned ones are not suitable since the pattern can lift off.

DECANTERS AND CARAFES

To remove port and sherry stains in the base of a decanter, fill it with a warm solution of biological washing powder and leave to soak. If the stain is stubborn, try adding two tablespoons of rice to the liquid and gently swirling it round. This will act as an abrasive and help loosen the dirt. After cleaning you should rinse the decanter thoroughly in warm (not hot) water.

If unsuccessful, use a stain remover.

To dry, stand upside down in a wide-necked jug to drain and become thoroughly dry before it is stored. If draining is not appropriate, the Manor House Decanter Drier, a gauze tube filled with moisture-absorbing crystals, can be hung inside (see Useful Addresses).

If the stopper is stuck, wrap a cotton cloth soaked in very hot water around the neck to expand the glass. Also dribble some warm oil around the edge of the stopper.

DEEP-FAT FRYERS

Modern electric deep-fat fryers incorporate filters to reduce airborne grease from escaping in the steam. To reduce odour, some models also have charcoal and paper filters. These need to be replaced. Apply to the manufacturer.

To make washing up easier, the lids of most fryers are detachable and some can even be put in the dishwasher, but always check the manufacturer's instructions first.

The inside of the fryer needs to be thoroughly cleaned every time the oil is changed – every six uses. Once the oil has been emptied clean the tank with a plastic scouring pad and washing-up liquid, taking care not to damage any non-stick coating. Wipe over the outside with a damp cloth and a non-abrasive cleaner. Always store the fryer with the lid slightly ajar to allow air to circulate, and wipe out before use.

DISHWASHERS

Switch off electricity supply. Clean the filters after each use. If they are blocked it will really impair the machine's performance.

The spray arms should be cleaned in a solution of washing-up liquid. Direct running water through the inlet of the spray arm to check that the water can escape through the holes and no grains of rice or food debris are blocking them.

Wipe the exterior of the machine with a damp cloth and a solution of washing-up liquid. If the machine is not going to be used for a long time, leave the door ajar to allow air to circulate inside.

TIP If the dishwasher is not performing well check that:

- the baskets are not overloaded
- the spray arms are not blocked
- the correct detergent and programme has been chosen
- the filter is clean.

There are some specialist cleaners on the market which will de-scale and freshen. Use them occasionally and always follow the manufacturer's instructions.

EXTRACTOR FANS

Unplug at the mains. Remove the outer cover and wash it in a warm solution of washing-up liquid; rinse and dry. Wipe the fan blades with a damp cloth wrung out in a solution of washing-up liquid. Avoid getting them wet and ensure that everything is dry before replacing the fan's cover.

FIREPLACES

Wherever possible, keep the fireplace manufacturer's cleaning instructions.

Made of either cast or wrought iron, both are the same material but shaped in a different way. Cast iron is produced in a mould and tends to be more brittle, whereas wrought iron is hammered into shape.

Before any cleaning, remove all rust using a wire brush or wire wool. Wear goggles to protect yourself from flaking particles. Severe cases may need treating with a chemical rust remover; always closely follow the manufacturer's instructions.

Re-blacken iron using a black grate polish (such as Liberon Iron Paste, Zebo Black Grate Polish; see Useful Addresses) or a heat-resistant paint such as a barbecue paint (Plasti-Kote Bar-B-Q Paint; see Useful Addresses).

FLOORING

Always use doormats to catch grit and mud trodden in from outside. Vacuum or sweep hard floors regularly to avoid surface scratching by grit.

Follow manufacturers' recommendations for sealants and polishes. Apply polish in thin coats. Use wax in liquid or solid form for wood or acrylic emulsion.

To remove build-up of polish, use a cloth moistened with white spirit. Remove stains with repeated gentle action, rather than a severe single treatment. Re-apply polish.

VINYL

A popular choice, and easy to maintain. Most vinyls have a clear wear layer on the top which consists of various forms of polyurethane. Simply sweep with a soft brush or vacuum, and wipe over with a damp cloth or sponge using a solution of detergent or floor cleaner. Follow by rinsing.

TIP It is advisable to rinse, otherwise a build-up of detergent occurs which can become smeary and sticky.

Remove scuff marks with a cloth dipped in neat washing-up liquid or white spirit. Then rinse off.

TIP If you have pets as well as children in the kitchen, you may want to use a disinfectant cleaner such as Dettox on the floor. Use diluted and then rinse off. These products are cleaners as well as disinfectants.

LINOLEUM

Sweep or vacuum the surface to remove grit and dust. Clean with a mop or cloth dampened with a solution of detergent or floor cleaner. Use water sparingly. Rinse after washing.

For stubborn marks rub lightly with a fine nylon pad, and neat detergent. Cigarette burns can be removed; they won't melt lino whereas they will vinyl.

Polishing isn't strictly necessary. Without it, the lino will have more of a satin, matt finish. Polishes give a glossier finish. Use an emulsion water-based polish, especially in kitchens and bathrooms, such as Johnson's Klear. Apply only a thin coat at a time and allow to dry completely before applying another one, otherwise you may get a milky appearance. Apply twice a year to give a natural shine and help protect the surface. Do not wax polish.

CERAMIC TILES

Scratching is less noticeable on unglazed tiles, which need minimal maintenance. Sweep

FLOOR POLISHES

There are three different types. You cannot mix them, ie solvent and water based. If you start with one you have to stay with it.

Solid wax polish Old-fashioned type, sold in a flat tin like shoe polish. Generally a wax, it is solvent based and suitable for unvarnished wooden floors and cork. Hard work to apply and has to be done by hand and buffed up to shine. The shine lasts a long time.
Liquid wax polish A solvent-based liquid, sold in a tin with a screw top opening. It can be applied with an electric floor polisher. Suitable for the same floors as the solid wax, and is easier to apply but may need more applications. Has to be polished well to give a good shine.

With both these polishes a good shine is not achieved by lots of polish but by hard buffing. The more buffing, the harder the finish, since the friction builds up heat which drives off the solvent leaving the wax gleaming.
Water-based emulsion polishes Generally silicone polishes. They are easy to apply because they are often self-shining. Simply apply them and leave to dry. They are reasonably long lasting and claim to make the floor easier to keep clean because the gloss repels dirt.

them, then wash with a mild detergent solution. Rinse with clear water, then buff with a soft cloth tied round a mop or broom head. Don't polish as they will become slippery and more difficult to clean. Remove stubborn stains on unglazed tiles with an abrasive cleaner such as Jif.

Terracotta tiles

These are porous and therefore need to be sealed. Use either a traditional linseed oil and beeswax-based seal, suitable for all terracotta tiles, or a synthetic water-based acrylic seal.

Check with your supplier that the acrylic seal you are intending to use is suitable for your tiles. Acrylic seals keep the natural colour of tiles; oils darken it initially, but the colour will fade again in time.

After sealing, build up a hard finish. Wax immediately with two or three coats of oil sealant, followed by more sealant once a week for four to six weeks; then only when worn patches start to appear. Wax acrylic-sealed floors once a week for four to six weeks; then as necessary.

For the first year after installation terracotta tiles mature in character. Most suppliers have their own special cleaner, sealant and polish so it is worth making enquiries at the point of sale and using recommended products.

WOOD

Wood flooring will be sealed with either a polyurethane or acrylic varnish, or left unsealed and waxed.

If you don't know what's on your floor, put two or three drops of water on the surface. If the surface turns white this indicates that the floor has a wax finish. (Don't worry, the white marks will disappear as it dries.) If the water beads on the surface, the flooring has been sealed with polyurethane or varnish.

Sealed wood

This is the most usual treatment for wooden floors. Sealed floors only need to be swept and damp mopped. Don't use too much water as wood swells.

It's not strictly necessary, but you can apply an emulsion polish, such as Johnson's Klear, on top of the varnish. This gives the surface shine and an extra wear layer which takes care of a lot of minor scratches. But after several applications, this will have to be removed using a proprietary wax remover or a floor cleaner with a little ammonia added.

TIP Don't be tempted to apply a wax, even if it is non-slip, on top of a sealed wooden floor. You will make it very slippery.

Unsealed and waxed

This type of finish is less common because it's harder work to maintain.

Sweep regularly and polish occasionally with wax polish. A new floor will take a long time to build up a traditional-looking finish. Too much wax will leave a tacky surface and attract dirt. Apply sparingly, infrequently and buff well. Polish occasionally when worn patches appear in the surface with a non-slip floor polish. Remove fruit, milk and coffee stains with a dilute solution of washing-up liquid.

TIP Don't be tempted to apply a varnish on top of a waxed floor. You will end up with a gooey mess as the varnish won't dry.

Removing wax

On waxed floors, polish and dirt builds up over time. The only way to clean them is to remove the wax and start again. To do this use a cloth moistened with white spirit. Let it soak in, and as the wax and dirt begin to dissolve wipe them off with crumpled newspaper. Scrub obstinate parts by hand or with abrasive pads on a floor polisher. When the polish is removed from the floor, finish by damp mopping with clean water. Allow the floor to dry completely before applying new polish. Work over small sections at a time.

CORK

Cork has the advantage of disguising dirt with its mottled appearance. It is an absorbent material so is normally sold sealed.

Factory-sealed cork tiles with a vinyl wear layer are simply wiped clean with a damp mop using a solution of washing-up liquid. If you wish to give an extra protective layer, especially in the kitchen or bathroom, apply an emulsion polish. Never over-wet, and take care not to damage the seal or wear layer by dragging appliances or furniture over it.

CERAMIC TILES

Wipe over with a solution of washing-up liquid. Rinse and wipe dry. Never polish ceramic tiles as they will be too slippery. Dirty grout can be tackled with a soft brush dipped in a mild solution of bleach. Rinse well.

QUARRY TILES

Quarry tiles are available in glazed or unglazed types. Glazed quarry tiles only need mopping with a solution of household cleaner. Unglazed can be treated with a liquid or solid wax polish, preferably the slip-resistant type, buffing well. Unglazed tiles are reasonably stain resistant due to a low surface porosity, but they are not stain proof.

Tackle stubborn marks with very fine steel wool dipped in white spirit. Then wash, rinse, dry and reapply polish, buffing well.

Quarry tiles are the same colour all the way through so wear patches are not apparent, although the surface can dull with excessive wear. Pigmented wax dressing or polish may help to enhance a very dull surface.

To restore faded colour, remove the polish with steel wool and white spirit, then wash and rinse them. When the tiles are dry, sparingly apply a pigmented wax polish, eg Cardinal Red Tile Polish (see Useful Addresses), and buff well.

When quarry tiles are first laid, white patches may appear on the surface. This is due to the lime content of the concrete sub-floor. Until the patchiness has faded, do not polish the tiles.

TERRAZZO

A mixture of cement and marble chips. It just needs damp mopping with a mild detergent solution.

STONE FLOORS

Include slate, flagstones, granite and marble. Damp mop with a mild detergent solution.

FLOWERS

Use a hair dryer on the cool setting or a feather duster to get rid of surface dust.

SILK AND POLYESTER

Don't immerse in water, since the stems may have a wire base which will rust. Wipe the leaves with a damp cloth, supporting them with the other hand.

DRIED

Look for a proprietary petal spray such as Petal Fresh (see Useful Addresses) which precipitates the dust, brings up the colours, and prevents the dried flower arrangement from shedding its leaves. Available from garden centres, some florists and gift shops.

FOOD MIXERS/ PROCESSORS

Disconnect from the electrical supply before cleaning. Pushers, lids and bowls are usually dishwasher proof, but always check manufacturer's instructions first. The blades should be cleaned in a hot solution of washing-up liquid using a kitchen brush, not a cloth; they may cut through this. Any food stains can be wiped away using a damp cloth and a very mild solution of bleach.

FREEZERS

DEFROSTING

Freezers need defrosting when the frost is about 1¼–1½in/3–4cm thick. Load the contents of your freezer in a basket or other suitable container, wrap the food in newspaper and then cover with an old blanket or duvet and put it in a cold place.

To speed up defrosting, place containers of hot but not boiling water in the cabinet. Ice can be scraped off using a wooden spoon or plastic scraper, but never use a knife or anything with a sharp edge as this could damage the cabinet interior. When all the ice has melted, wipe the freezer dry, replace the food and switch on again.

CLEANING

To clean and freshen the freezer, wash with a solution of warm water and bicarbonate of soda (1tbsp/15ml to 1.7 pints/1 litre). A solution of washing-up liquid might taint the plastic. On stains, use neat bicarbonate of soda on a damp cloth.

Clean the outside with a solution of washing-up liquid, rinse and wipe dry.

Lingering odours

If the freezer smells strongly, wash out as above then wipe the interior with a sterilising fluid or branded fridge-freezer cleaner. Dry with a soft cloth and leave the door open to allow air to circulate.

FURNITURE

There are many different types of wood finishes, but they can be roughly divided into three main areas:

French-polished The finish has been achieved by the repeated application of shellac (varnish) dissolved in spirit to give a satiny finish.

Lacquered This accounts for the majority of the furniture we buy. A hard-wearing finish that may be applied to solid wood, or on top of a veneer (either wood, paper foil or plastic).

WARNING ON WAXED FURNITURE

Don't be tempted to use furniture polishes with added silicones, or aerosol polishes. These give an instant shine and make the polish easier to buff, but the film does not fill scratches or other surface blemishes as a wax does. More importantly, the solvents can soften the underlying layers of wax. If used too frequently, the surface acquires a slight milky look for which there is no cure, short of stripping and resurfacing the furniture.

Furniture cream waxes present a similar problem. They contain a high percentage of solvents (used to make the wax easier to apply) that can also soften the lower layers of wax, to the extent that you can remove as much old wax as the new wax being applied.

A veneer is usually applied on top of chipboard or medium-density fibreboard (MDF), and then lacquered to seal the whole piece, and for protection against knocks and scratches.

Waxed Wax polish is built up by repeated rubbing with wax and turpentine to give a rich deep shine.

FRENCH-POLISHED FURNITURE

Treat as for waxed furniture.

Serious damage on valuable, French-polished pieces should be repaired professionally. Contact either the Association of Master Upholsterers or the British Antique Furniture Restorers' Association (see Useful Addresses) for companies that carry out furniture restoration.

LACQUERED FURNITURE

It's not necessary to polish lacquered furniture. The hard-wearing lacquer is designed to protect the wood against heat and moisture and so doesn't need additional protection. The polish won't be able to penetrate the lacquer – it just gives the surface a shine.

POLISH: WHAT IT DOES

The basic purpose of a polish is to assist in the removal of surface dirt and to help encourage the dust to stick to the duster. Polishes also provide surface protection and revive the shine, leaving a finish which is easier to dust than a dull one. For wooden furniture, polish also helps enhance the colour and grain.

Wipe over the furniture with a damp duster. Use a fine, water-mist spray directly on to the duster to avoid over-wetting the wood. The water will help the dust stick to the duster, preventing it from becoming airborne. Wipe dry and buff with a soft, dry duster.

To remove grease and fingermarks, use a damp cloth and a mild solution of soap flakes. Take care not to over-wet. Dry thoroughly with a soft cloth.

Use an occasional application of a good furniture polish to revive the shine when it starts to disappear.

WAX TIPS

- Don't apply wax over a build-up of dirty wax or on a dusty surface. You'll seal in the dirt. Dust and clean first.
- Apply wax polishes sparingly. If you put it on too thickly it will dry before you have finished polishing, leaving the surface smeary and making it difficult to buff up. If wax is applied too frequently or thickly, it will, over a period of time, build up, making the surface sticky and thereby attracting dirt. Check by running your finger across the surface. If it smears, it's an indication that too much polish has been used.

If the dye in the wax polish is darker than the wood, it will darken it. If you use a lighter coloured polish on dark wood, take care that no residue is left in the crevices because it will show up as the wax dries out.

Allow the wax to dry before buffing to achieve a better shine with less effort.

To remove a build-up of wax, soak a cloth in white spirit and wipe the wood, following the direction of the grain, until all the dirt has been removed. Allow to dry and then wipe over with a clean, dry cloth. Alternatively, use a proprietary product such as Rustin's Surface Cleaner. The surface is then ready for repolishing with a wax paste.

WAXED FURNITURE

Unsealed furniture doesn't have a protective lacquer, so it needs to be waxed from time to time to give it protection against damaging elements such as heat and moisture.

Dust waxed furniture regularly with a soft cloth to remove dust and to revive the shine. Remove sticky marks with a cloth wrung out in a warm, mild solution of soap flakes, taking care not to over-wet. Dry thoroughly with a soft cloth.

Occasionally, apply a wax polish – only once, or at most twice, a year. Solid wax, as opposed to creams, produces the best results but it requires lots of elbow grease.

REMOVING MARKS

Where furniture is antique or valuable it is best to have marks and dents removed professionally. Contact either the Association of Master Upholsterers or the British Antique Furniture Restorers' Association (see Useful Addresses) for companies who carry out furniture restoration.

TIP To minimise marks, stand flower vases, glasses or hot cups on mats, so that the heat or liquid doesn't damage the surface. Place self-adhesive felt pads underneath ornaments to prevent them from scratching the surface.

Heat marks

White marks caused by heat often indicate that the finish has been damaged. Before calling in a professional refinisher, try the following methods.

If the surface is not roughened you may be able to burnish out the mark with a cream metal polish rubbed briskly in the direction of the grain. Then polish lightly with a wax polish. Alternatively, use a proprietary product such as Mr Sheen Classic Topps Ringaway or Liberon Ring Remover (see Useful Addresses). Work in small sections at a time, wiping away the paste at frequent intervals to assess the progress made.

Where the surface has roughened, use very fine steel wool dipped in liquid wax polish. This method should be used with extreme care on veneered finishes.

Water marks

To remove ring marks caused by wet glasses, vases or plant pots follow the suggestions for heat marks.

Scratch marks

Light scratches can often be masked using a similar-coloured wax crayon or shoe polish. Apply, and leave for a while before buffing the area briskly.

Alternatively, use proprietary products such as Mr Sheen Classic Topps Scratch Cover, Rustins Scratch Cover or Liberon Retouch Crayon (see Useful Addresses). All are available for light, medium and dark wood, but test colour match in a hidden area first.

TREATING MARKS

The golden rule when treating marks on furniture is to go carefully. Start with the mildest method first. Repeated milder methods are far more effective than one, very harsh treatment.

Try home remedies before spending money on proprietary cleaners you may not use again. Read all instructions carefully, work in a well-ventilated place and keep children out of the way.

Test proprietary ring removers on a hidden area first.

Alcohol spots

Perfumes and alcoholic drinks cause damage because alcohol dissolves the finish. If spotting occurs, try burnishing out the mark with a cream metal polish rubbed briskly in the direction of the grain. Then polish lightly with a wax polish.

CLEANING BEHIND FURNITURE

At least once a year, lift furniture to clean behind it and the floor underneath it. Otherwise dust collects, providing a haven for carpet beetles and moths. You'll know if this has happened because there will be a series of small holes in the carpet. Treat (see Carpet Beetles, page 236) and replace the furniture slightly to one side since they don't like light.

TIP If drawers are not running smoothly and tend to stick, try rubbing a little wax or even a white candle along the runners.

TIPS ON LIFTING

- Empty drawers and wardrobes to make them lighter to move. Remove drawers and make sure doors are shut securely so that they cannot fall open and be damaged while the object is being moved.
- Always carry using the lowest load-bearing part.
- Separate the object into smaller units where practicable.
- Even if fitted with castors, lift, don't drag because this puts a strain on the framework. This can loosen joints or snap off a leg.
- To help move heavy furniture, use Glisdomes (available from department stores). Place under the furniture you wish to move and their non-stick surface glides over most surfaces, taking the strain off you. They will also prevent damage to floors and surfaces.

GARDEN FURNITURE

CAST ALUMINIUM

This looks like cast iron but is much lighter and doesn't rust. Wipe clean with a solution of washing-up liquid. Touch up chipped paint with enamel metal paint after rubbing off any loose paint with wire wool. (Check with the manufacturer who may supply a touch-up kit.)

GARDEN FURNITURE CARE

- Even a heavy dew or light drizzle could help establish mildew on cushions. For treatment see Mildew, page 359. Store indoors over winter.
- Lubricate hinged metal sections with household oil or WD-40 spray lubricant.

CAST AND WROUGHT IRON

Needs annual maintenance as painted cast iron can suffer from surface rust and discoloration. Rub down with wire wool and repaint with an appropriate anti-rust primer and exterior metal paint. If rust is severe, a wire brush or a rust-removing paint may be needed to shift flaking rust. Repaint as above. (Wear goggles to protect yourself from dust.)

TIP Sprinkle sand or earth around pieces to be painted to absorb splashes and drips. Remove after painting.

SOLID WOOD

Durability and weather resistance varies depending on the type of wood used: oak,

WHICH PRESERVATIVE?

Wood stains not only protect the wood but also provide a finish. Some have a paint-like consistency for easy application. It needs to be a type that will not rub off on to clothes, eg: Cuprinol High Performance Woodstain. It will give light protection against the elements and colour to wood. Re-coat every two to three years, rubbing down the previous coat with sandpaper.

Wood preservative is far more liquid and penetrates deeper into the wood but doesn't give a surface finish.

sweet chestnut and Western red cedar are naturally resistant to rot, but prolonged damp spells will eventually lead to discoloration.

Don't leave softwood furniture, such as pine, out in the rain unless well treated with a wood preservative.

TIP To reduce rotting, site furniture on concrete or gravel. Preferably, soak the feet in preservative annually for added protection.

WOOD RESTORATION

Before starting any work ensure that the wood is clean, smooth, dry and dust free.

Remove rot with a blunt knife. Rub down surface discoloration with sandpaper; don't use wire wool or you'll encourage rust impregnation.

If the wood is severely discoloured, wipe it with a solution of one part bleach to four parts water, or use a proprietary wood bleach.

Treat degraded areas with preservative wood hardener, then fill. Don't confuse a wood filler (for shallow dents, rough, open grain and fine cracks) with a wood stopper (for deep cracks, nail and screw holes).

Ensure the surface is free of oil, grease and wax by wiping with white spirit before applying any other treatments.

Preserved wood

Some modern wood may be impregnated with a preservative. To check this, ask your supplier.

If your furniture is made from durable wood such as teak, iroko, western red cedar, American mahogany, pitch pine or oak, it doesn't usually need preserving. Left to the

APPLICATION TIPS

- Protect yourself and the surrounding area with rubber gloves, overalls and newspaper.
- Products containing pesticides or fungicides must be used carefully. Always refer to precautions given on the container.
- Work in well-ventilated conditions.
- If you're applying wood stain to oily woods such as teak or iroko, they'll need cleaning first with white spirit or cellulose thinners.
- Preservatives are very liquid so be careful not to splash children, grass or plants. Apply quite liberally, starting from the top.
- Don't overlap areas when applying wood stain: the finished result will look streaky.
- When applying wood stain, paint or varnish, sand lightly between coats to provide a 'key' for it to adhere to, and remove the dust before applying the next coat.
- Apply thin, even coats rather than one thick one, to avoid a tacky finish.

elements these woods will weather naturally to a silver grey. (Simply wipe over with teak oil twice a year to help preserve the colour.)

Furniture made from non-durable woods such as ash, beech, elm, European redwood, pine and spruce does need preserving. Apply a proprietary wood preservative followed by a good varnish.

Painted and varnished wood

This requires regular maintenance: at least every year.

Rub down sound finishes with fine sandpaper and reapply the coating using an appropriate wood finish.

If you want to recolour the wood with a wood stain the wood will have to be completely stripped.

SYNTHETIC RESIN (INJECTION-MOULDED PLASTIC)

Good-quality resin furniture is very resistant to moisture and chemical attack. UV-stabilised resin shouldn't fade in the sun. Cheaper plastic furniture will contain more chalk, and yellow in the sunlight more quickly than higher-quality items.

Stains on plastic moulded furniture can be treated with a mild solution of household bleach and rinsed well.

TUBULAR METAL

This is usually coated. The coating is resistant to chipping and rusting but the furniture still needs to be kept indoors for most of the time, as the rivets can rust, making the pieces look rather shabby.

Plastic-coated tubular furniture can be washed down with a warm solution of washing-up liquid. A light application of wax polish on the plastic or enamel adds some protection from the elements.

CANE

Such furniture is made of cane, rattan, willow or bamboo. Don't ever leave outdoors, even just overnight. If cane gets saturated allow it to dry naturally away from direct heat; otherwise it will splinter.

Retain the manufacturer's instructions for cleaning. Most items have a varnish or sealer to protect the cane and only need vacuuming with an upholstery nozzle or a wipe with a damp cloth to remove the dust.

FABRICS ON GARDEN FURNITURE

Tubular metal and deck-chairs sometimes have canvas seating. Heavy canvas can be scrubbed with a nailbrush and household soap and rinsed by pouring water through the fabric. Dry naturally, supporting if necessary with a couple of chairs underneath.

Repair torn fabric as soon as possible. Cut a patch slightly larger than the damaged area. Use a rubber glue such as Copydex on the patch and the canvas, allowing it to dry before sticking the two pieces together.

If canvas needs replacing, the appropriate width for deck-chairs can be purchased from department stores. Take the old fabric along to compare the size.

Plastic weave on chairs can simply be wiped with a solution of washing-up liquid.

GLASSES

Avoid putting lead-crystal glasses in the dishwasher as the detergent will etch and dull the surface. Always wash in warm water, using washing-up liquid. Rinse in water of the same temperature, drain and dry with a soft cloth. Cotton tea-towels tend to leave fluff, so linen is preferable.

Do not store glasses stacked one inside the

WHY DOES ETCHING OCCUR IN THE DISHWASHER?

With time, glassware can start to etch due to the general wear and tear from everyday use. Different qualities of glass will etch at different rates. The etching attacks the glaze and causes the glass to develop very fine cracks and scratches on the surface.

These areas can attract calcium deposits from the dishwasher water. This then gives the glassware an unattractive milky appearance. If this happens to your glassware, top up your rinse aid, salt and detergent levels.

It is more likely that the cloudiness will be permanently etched on to the glass surface. Oversoftened hard water, high drying temperature, alkaline detergent solution and the components of the glass all contribute to the problem.

However, you can try washing the glasses in the dishwasher with citric acid crystals. Fill the detergent dispenser with the citric acid and run the glasses through a normal wash (don't add any detergent). The citric acid acts as a limescale remover and will, in fact, descale the dishwasher at the same time. So make sure you follow the dishwasher detergent manufacturer's recommended dosage.

It is also important to make sure that the salt regeneration unit is always topped up and is correctly adjusted to suit your local water supply.

Lead crystal is the most susceptible to damage and should not be washed in a dishwasher as it is too soft.

other as they may stick. Store the right way up as the top rim is the most delicate part and prone to chipping. Take care when drying wine glasses as the stems can easily snap.

GROUTING

See Bathrooms, Showers, page 281

HOBS

GLASS-TOPPED

Includes all ceramic, halogen and induction kitchen hobs.

Turn the hob off and make sure the surface is cool before cleaning. The only exception is sugar-based spills. With these, turn off the heat immediately, remove the pan and, with extreme care, wipe the glass before continuing cooking. If you leave the sugar, it will crystallise on to the glass surface during cooling, causing pitting.

TIP Do not use your current dishcloth wrung out in water. It will contain lots of sediment and greasy deposits that will smear and burn on when the hob is turned on again.

Light soiling can be easily removed with a paper towel or a clean damp cloth. It is important to use a specialist hob cleaner recommended by the hob manufacturer such as Easy-Do Cleaner Conditioner for ceramic hobs. These are less abrasive than general-purpose cream cleaners, so they won't damage the glass.

Really stubborn stains and cooked-on food deposits should be removed using a ceramic hob scraper. Don't use any other type of blade, as it may not be sharp or flexible enough and could damage the glass.

Conditioning

Once the hob is clean, use a conditioner to protect the glass. This may already be incorporated in the cleaner, come as a separate product, or alternatively you could wipe over with a conditioning cloth.

Remember to reseal the cloth after use to stop it from drying out.

To avoid scratches, always lift pans, never drag them when moving them around the hob. Check the base of the pan is clean, dry and dirt free.

SEALED PLATES

Sealed plates have now replaced radiant rings. Make sure they are turned off. To clean, use a scourer and cream cleaner, rubbing in a circular pattern following the grooves on the hob plates.

Conditioning

Involves polishing and blackening to avoid rusting and to maintain colour. There are proprietary products such as 4 Hobs (see Useful Addresses) and Minky Cloths to do this. Most contain oils and graphite, so wear rubber gloves when applying because they can be messy. Use a strong cloth as the steel plates have quite a rough texture.

Once the conditioner has been applied, the plates should be pre-heated, during which period a slight amount of smoke and smell will develop. This is quite normal.

TIP Don't lay saucepan lids face down on adjacent unused hobs while you are checking the cooking. The condensation in the lid will encourage rusting.

GAS

Pan supports and spillage wells make gas hobs more fiddly to clean. If you have a dishwasher, check to see if the parts are dishwasher safe. Otherwise use a cream cleaner, recommended by the Vitreous Enamel Development Council (see Useful Addresses) and a damp cloth.

Also remove the controls as dirt can build up behind them. Some just pull off.

Clean metal surround on hobs with a proprietary metal cleaner.

HOUSE-PLANTS

Like other household items, plants get dusty. Dust spoils the appearance of the foliage, blocks the leaf pores so that the plant can no longer breathe properly, and forms a light-blocking screen.

To remove it, you need to wash the leaves during the day so that they will be dry before nightfall. When the foliage is very dirty it should be dusted with a soft cloth before washing, otherwise when you do wash it a strongly adhesive mud forms upon drying.

Foliage tends to become tired and dull looking as it ages. Many plant-polishing products are available, as wipe-on liquids and aerosol sprays. Aerosols are simple and quick to apply, but are not usually suitable for repeat treatment at regular intervals.

TIP When cleaning and polishing the leaf support it in your hand and never press down on the surface. Wipe the top surface only of the leaves (not the under surface where the cell openings are). Do not wash or polish very young leaves.

Use ordinary milk, which produces a shine. Alternatively, use a Minky Leaf Cleaning Cloth.

Cacti, succulents and plants with hairy leaves should not be sprayed or washed. Use a soft brush to remove the dust.

ICE-CREAM MAKERS

Many ice-cream recipes use raw eggs so hygiene is essential to reduce the risk of salmonella. Models with a removable bowl are much easier to clean than those with a fixed one. In both cases, however, you should use a hot solution of washing-up liquid. Always dry thoroughly before use.

IRONS

The soleplates of modern irons vary. Most have an aluminium or chrome-plated base or a ceramic-coated aluminium soleplate. Check the manufacturer's instructions before starting to clean.

To remove burnt-on deposits on the soleplate, whether spray starch or melted deposit of synthetic fibre, try the gentlest treatment first.

Use a proprietary soleplate cleaner or an impregnated cloth from Minky.

Alternatively, heat the iron on a warm setting and rub at the edge of the board across a damp, loosely woven cloth or a coarse towel which is held taut over the edge of the ironing board.

Use a moistened plastic scouring pad gently to avoid scratching. Make sure the iron is plate down, as this will stop dirt falling into the steam holes and clogging them up.

Descaling

Limescale reduces efficiency, so regular descaling is necessary. Most irons take tap water, but if you live in a particularly hard area try using demineralised water. You can buy a bottle to demineralise tap water at home.

To descale an iron use a proprietary scale remover and always follow the manufacturer's instructions. Some models come with a built-in anti-scale device, either in the form of a valve or a removable section on the soleplate. These attract limescale and therefore require cleaning or replacing every few weeks.

JEWELLERY

Needs care if it is to remain in perfect condition and, if real, keep its value. A jeweller will ensure that the piece is not likely to break, has loose stones or damaged claws.

TIP Have jewellery revalued while it is being cleaned. The value of jewellery continues to grow and inadequate insurance might mean you are unable to replace a treasured piece.

TURQUOISE AND OPALS

These are porous stones so should never be immersed in water. Simply polish with a soft dry chamois leather and use a soft bristle brush to clean the claws.

PEARLS

Never wash in water. Oils from the skin help to maintain their gleam, so wear them as much as possible (but not while applying make-up, scent or hair spray). Rub them with a chamois leather from time to time.

MARCASITE

Never wash. Polish with a soft brush, then rub with a chamois leather.

AMETHYSTS, DIAMONDS, RUBIES AND SAPPHIRES

These are all hard stones so they can be cleaned in a solution of washing-up liquid, scrubbing gently with a soft toothbrush or an eyebrow brush. Rinse in lukewarm water and then dip quickly into surgical spirit to remove any remaining detergent film before draining on absorbent paper and buffing with a chamois leather.

These particular stones can also be cleaned by immersion in a proprietary jewellery care kit such as Goddard's Gold and Platinum Cleaning Liquid.

Although diamonds are extremely hard they have a grain, similar to that of wood, and a hard knock could split them. Diamonds may also scratch other diamonds if they are stored close together.

EMERALDS

Are softer than other precious stones and can chip easily. They can be cleaned, with care, in a warm solution of washing-up liquid.

TIP Always wash jewellery in a plastic bowl with an old towel or cloth in the base. This will prevent pieces getting damaged, or disappearing down the plug hole. Put the plug in just in case of an accident.

JUICERS

Juicers have many parts to clean. It should be done immediately after use to avoid the fruit and vegetable pulp sticking and staining.

Most juicer attachments are not dishwasher safe so check the manufacturer's instructions.

Using a kitchen brush or a specially provided cleaning brush and hot soapy water clean all the parts, taking care with the grating sieve, which has sharp edges. The motor housing may be wiped with a damp cloth, using a solution of washing-up liquid. If the plastic has stained use a damp cloth and a mild solution of bleach.

KETTLES

Over half of British people live in hard-water areas, so the build-up of limescale can be a considerable problem.

Chrome kettles get coated all over the interior as well as the element. Most plastic kettles are made of polypropylene, which doesn't attract scale, but their elements take on the excess.

Built-in filters stop pieces of limescale from being poured into your drink but do not stop limescale building up inside the kettle. They too need descaling.

There are a variety of different chemical descalers, some designed specifically for metal kettles, others for plastic models. Check carefully before you buy. These come in liquid or sachet form.

For very light scaling try covering the element with a solution of vinegar and water (equal parts of each). Bring to the boil and leave overnight.

TIPS FOR DESCALING

- Descale frequently: every four to eight weeks.
- Don't let scale build up as it will then be more difficult to remove.
- Expect to treat heavy deposits twice.
- Don't over-fill the kettle when descaling as the solution may effervesce over the side.
- Rinse the kettle thoroughly, and boil up with fresh water after treatment.
- Use a kettle protector: a stainless-steel wire ball which attracts deposit away from the element. Rinse and squeeze each month to clear the scale.

KITCHEN SURFACES

UNITS

Aim to clean the inside of food cupboards every few months. Remove all items and wipe the surfaces with a damp cloth using an anti-bacterial cleaner or a washing-up liquid solution. Do not rinse the surface. Replace items when the surfaces are thoroughly dry. Take care not to soak exposed chipboard and around hinge joints where water can seep through to chipboard.

DOORS

Coloured/wood effect

Wipe with a damp cloth and a washing-up liquid solution. Take care not to over-wet the surface. Stains can be rubbed carefully with a slightly abrasive cream cleaner (except glossy surfaces). High-gloss surfaces can easily be scratched, so use a soft cloth and make sure it is free from grit. Wipe thoroughly with a dry cloth to prevent smearing. Use a neat solution of washing-up liquid on stains and rub gently with a soft cloth.

Wood/wood veneer

Wipe with a damp cloth and a washing-up liquid solution. Use a neat solution of washing-up liquid on stains and rub along the grain with a soft cloth.

WORK SURFACES

Laminates

Include Formica and Duropal.

Daily care: After use wipe the surface with a washing-up liquid solution. Alternatively use an all-purpose cleaner with spray application for ease and speed. Choose one with an anti-bacterial agent and do not rinse.

Thorough care and stains: At least once a week remove all items from the work surface and clean with neat multi-surface liquid cleaner, or cream cleaner, using a damp cloth. Rinse with clean water and allow to dry. For stubborn stains use a slightly abrasive cream cleaner or diluted bleach. On textured surfaces use a nylon bristle brush to get into the grain.

Solvents will not damage laminates so stains such as felt-tip pen can be treated with methylated spirits, white spirit or nail polish remover.

Maintenance: Chips and scratches can be repaired with ColorFill (see Useful Addresses), a purpose-made laminate repairer and sealer. It requires patience because, like any filler, several thin layers are preferable to one thick layer.

Man-made solid surfaces

Include Corian, Silkstone and Avonite.

Daily care: See Laminates.

Thorough care and stains: See Laminates.

Maintenance: Solvents can damage the surface after prolonged contact but can be used on stains such as felt-tip pen if thoroughly rinsed after application. Stubborn stains can be rubbed gently with an abrasive cream cleaner.

Cuts and scratches can be sanded away using medium-grade sandpaper followed by fine-grade. This removes some of the surface so you need to buff well afterwards to restore the shine. For severe damage contact the manufacturer to sand down the area.

Natural, solid surfaces

Includes Granite.

Daily care: As for Laminates. Pay particular attention to any joins in the surface. Wipe thoroughly with a dry soft cloth.

Thorough care: At least once a week, remove items from the work surface and give the surface a thorough clean with a solution of

washing-up liquid. Buff with a soft cloth to maintain the shine. This sort of surface is difficult to stain and neat washing-up liquid should be sufficient to remove marks.
Maintenance: For severe damage contact the Stone Federation (see Useful Addresses) for details of a specialist who can repolish the surface. This may not be advisable because the colour of the surface may alter.

Ceramic tiles

Daily care: See Laminates.
Thorough care: See Laminates. For stains, use a slightly abrasive cream cleaner on work-surface tiles, which are matt finished and therefore less likely to show scratches than glazed tiles.
Maintenance: If grouting becomes dirty, clean with a solution of bleach (one part bleach to four parts water). Use an old toothbrush to get between the tiles. Wipe over with a damp cloth and allow to dry. Do not use a grouting whitener on matt tiles. Chipped tiles on work surfaces must be replaced.

SINKS

Many sink manufacturers sell their own cleaning products and will send you instructions for care of your sink.

Stainless steel

Daily care: Wipe with a damp cloth and a washing-up liquid solution or an anti-bacterial spray cleaner, but do not rinse.
Thorough care: Give the sink a thorough clean using a neat multi-purpose liquid or cream cleaner. Pay particular attention to the area near the taps. If you are in a hard water area use a limescale cleaner once a week.

Coloured sinks

Polycarbonates are less expensive to buy and less heat resistant than blended composite sinks (see below). Brand names include Prima and Riva by Astracast, and Resan by Resopal.
Daily care: See Stainless steel. Tea, coffee and fruit juices will stain the sink if they are left to dry, so clean it every day. Use neat multi-surface liquid or non-abrasive cream cleaner, rinse and dry.
Thorough care: See Stainless steel. Stubborn stains can be soaked with a solution of biological washing powder or well-diluted household bleach.

Blended composites

Mix an acrylic substance with minerals such as silica, quartz or granite for a very hard and heat-resistant finish. Brand names include Franke Fraquartz, MFI Quartzite, Carron Silquartz and Astracast Supersinks.
Daily care: See Polycarbonates.
Thorough care: See Polycarbonates.

Blended composites containing granite, such as Blanco Silgranit, Carron Phoenix Granite and Franke Fragranite, are more hard wearing and you can rub stains gently with an abrasive cleaner.

Du Pont's Corian, Silkstone and Avonite are even more hard wearing and you can use any cream cleaner, abrasive powder or scourer on hard-to-shift stains.

Enamel

Daily care: See Stainless steel.
Thorough care: As for Stainless steel. Look for a product with the Vitreous Enamel Development Council's logo (see page 280).

Limescale removers are not recommended for enamel. See Enamel Baths for how to deal with limescale.

TAPS

See Bathroom Surfaces, page 282

WALLS

Ceramic wall tiles

Wipe with a damp cloth and a solution of washing-up liquid. Buff dry. Stains can be rubbed with neat washing-up liquid.

Paintwork

As for ceramic wall tiles. For heavy soiling, wash with a solution of sugar soap and rinse with clean water.

Washable/vinyl wallpaper

Sponge over with a solution of washing-up liquid. Take care not to over-wet the surface. Remove grease marks immediately as they are more difficult to remove if left.

FLOORS

See Flooring, page 289

LAMINATED SURFACES

See Kitchen Surfaces, page 303

LAMPSHADES

FABRIC SHADES

Clean with a vacuum cleaner fitted with a dusting brush, but don't forget to reduce the strength of the suction if possible.

Treat spots with a solution of washing-up liquid at your own peril: it is possible to remove the surface finish and cause water marks, or to dissolve the glues holding the shade together.

GLASS/PLASTIC SHADES

Can feature delicate finishes and surface effects. Dust regularly or use a clean cloth and a solution of washing-up liquid.

PAPER/PARCHMENT SHADES

Brush often with a feather duster. When dirty, buy a replacement.

RAFFIA AND STRAW SHADES

Vacuum with adusting brush.

LAUNDRY BASKETS

See Basketware, page 279

LEATHER

For cleaning, see Leather furniture, page 340. If an item needs repair contact the British Antique Furniture Restorers Association (see Useful Addresses).

If you want to tackle leather desk-top repairs yourself contact Artisan Brighton Regency Leathers or Just Desks (see Useful Addresses).

LIMESCALE

See Bathroom Surfaces, page 280, Kitchen Surfaces, page 303 and Kettles, page 202.

Products to prevent and remove limescale vary in toxicity and formulation.

Limescale removers/general-purpose cleaners

For regular use:

- Oz Limescale Remover for Bathrooms and Kitchens (liquid).
- Oust Surface Limescale Remover (liquid).

For heavier deposits:

- Limelite Thick for Surfaces (gel).

For encrustations:

- Manger's Stainex (thick gel) applied with a brush. It is particularly suitable for vertical surfaces such as toilet bowls.
- Descalite Lift Off (liquid).

Appliance descalers

- Limelite for Kettles and other Appliances
- Descalite Kettle Scale Remover
- Oust All Purpose Descaler (in sachets)
- Oz Kettle Descaler and All Purpose Descaler Powder (sachets)
- Quickshine Descaler Bag. (Sachets like teabags that you drop in the kettle, see Useful Addresses,)

LLOYD LOOM

Lloyd loom furniture is made from twisted paper and wire and so is easily damaged. For general cleaning simply vacuum with a nozzle attachment. A small, stiff brush may help loosen dust. Wash down using a solution of washing-up liquid and a soft brush. Rinse and allow to dry out thoroughly. Take care not to over-wet. (Best done on a sunny day to allow natural drying out.)

Restoration

You may want to tackle simple restoration yourself. Repairs to the weave will require new materials. A Lloyd-loom repair kit is available from Lloyd Look Furniture (see Useful Addresses) which includes paper yarn, braid, tacks and paper-covered wire.

Alternatively, contact a specialist restorer such as Graham Mancha (see Useful Addresses).

Repainting

Weave clogged with paint is a sign that the furniture has not been painted correctly in the past. You may have to live with it, or have it professionally restored.

Never use paint stripper, as it will weaken the paper and could shred it completely. It may be possible to pick out some of the paint carefully with a small screwdriver. Flaking paint may respond to a stiff brush.

Never use decorating paints or a brush as they will clog between the weave. Touch up using a can of car spray paint. For large items use a car paint spray. The aim is to allow the paint to blow through the weave to obtain a satisfactory finish.

Use the appropriate undercoat spray paint first. It is wise to check the paint on an inconspicuous area. If the paint does not adhere it may be due to an oil-based paint that has been used previously. If this seems to be the case, seek professional help.

LUGGAGE

Includes travel, sports and handbags.

Leather

The natural oils will keep leather luggage in good condition at first but you will then need to occasionally apply hide food.

After use, loose dirt should be brushed off the luggage and the leather wiped over with a damp cloth which has been rubbed over a tablet of glycerine soap or wrung out in a warm soap-flake solution. Finish with a cloth wrung out in clear water and pat dry.

Cotton/cotton tapestry

Any marks or grease on cotton luggage can be removed with a solution of biological washing detergent, sponged on the affected area. This should then be dabbed with clean water to rinse it.

Synthetic

Many of today's suitcases are made from polypropylene, which is a hard, strong plastic. To clean, use a cloth and a warm solution of washing-up liquid. Wipe dry and then polish with a silicone cleaner.

TIP Cleaners used for plastic car bumpers and trim can also be used as this type of luggage has the same textured finish. Ensure the cleaner matches the colour of your suitcase.

Polyester sports bags and travel bags can be wiped with a cloth and a solution of washing-up liquid. Dry thoroughly before using again.

Handbags

If not being used, fill with screwed-up newspaper inside a paper bag to help it retain its shape.

If the bag is leather, keep it clean and supple with a leather shoe and bag polish. Plastic and vinyl bags can be wiped over with a solution of washing-up liquid. Alternatively, use a proprietary vinyl cleaner.

Any staining can be removed with a solution of washing powder, or a Vanish soap bar, sponged on to the affected area. Once the stain has been removed, wipe it over with clean water and dry.

MARBLE

Marble needs special care to prevent it from dulling. For regular cleaning, wipe over with a solution of washing-up liquid. Polish once or twice a year with a proprietary marble polish to bring back the shine. Be prepared to use elbow grease and repeat the process if necessary. Bell marble polish gives a matt finish whereas HG Marble Polish gives a high gloss (see Useful Addresses).

Treat stains with HG Marble Stain Colour Remover, available in an easy-to-use spray bottle, or Bell Special Marble Cleaner, which is mixed to a paste and left to dry on the marble. For severe chipping and marking call in a professional: contact the Stone Federation (see Useful Addresses).

METALS

COPPER AND BRASS

Brass is an alloy of copper and zinc. It's easier to polish if first washed in a warm solution of washing-up liquid. Brush gently with a soft brush (stiff bristles can scratch) then rinse and dry with a soft cloth.

Copper and brass polishes come in two forms and most include anti-tarnish agents.

Creams/liquids These quickly break down the grease and tarnish without hard rubbing and buff well to leave a good shine. The majority of creams/liquids are applied with a cloth and polished off before the polish has completely dried. Some polishes can be rinsed off with water and buffed dry to leave no residue.

CLEANING METALS

- Work in a well-ventilated room.
- Protect your work surface with newspaper as some cleaners can leave marks on laminates and stainless-steel surfaces.
- Wear cotton or rubber gloves to prevent your hands from getting messy, and to also prevent grease from hands getting on to the polished metal.
- Have plenty of soft cloths for buffing. They soil quickly.
- Use a soft, old toothbrush or cotton buds to get into and clean intricate areas. But if working on expensive silver, buy a silver-cleaning brush, which is much softer.
- After cleaning cutlery wash thoroughly before use.
- Follow the manufacturers' instructions.

BRASS AND COPPER AFTER-CARE

- After brass or copper has been cleaned, use a transparent lacquer, such as Rustin's Transparent Lacquer for Metal, to protect against re-tarnishing, especially on intricate items that are awkward to keep clean. Apply two coats to ensure the item is fully covered.
- For valuable pieces and a more durable finish it may be preferable to have lacquering done professionally. Contact the Metal Finishing Association (see Useful Addresses).

These are ideal for intricate pieces.

Wadding For heavier tarnishing, use copper or brass wadding impregnated with polish. It's easy to apply but messy to use and does require elbow grease. It moulds well into ornate sections but is quite abrasive so don't use too frequently.

TIP Reseal metal-cleaner containers firmly after use to stop them drying out. If polishing wadding dries out, it can be moistened again with white spirit.

Verdigris

For really heavy, green corrosion (verdigris) use Rustin's Rust Remover. Apply with a paintbrush and gently rub the surface with fine steel wool. Then clean with a proprietary metal polish.

DIY polish

If you only have one or two small pieces to clean and don't want to buy a proprietary cleaner, use the following DIY method. Rub the surface with half a lemon dipped in salt. The lemon cuts through the grease and the salt acts as a mild abrasive. Don't leave the mixture on too long as it will pit the surface. Rinse and buff dry with a soft cloth. This cleaning method tends to lighten copper and bring out the orange colour.

Lacquered brass and copper

Many copper and brass pieces are lacquered by the manufacturer, especially door furniture which will be touched a lot and pieces subject to weathering. Lacquered items only need dusting and occasional washing in a soapy, warm solution.

Over a period of time the lacquer can wear, usually unevenly, allowing the brass or copper underneath to tarnish. The lacquer should then be removed with a proprietary paint remover in order to clean the brass or copper underneath with a proprietary polish.

Either reapply the transparent lacquer or have the item professionally lacquered (see Brass and Copper After-care box, above). Unfortunately, lacquers you apply yourself are not as durable as those applied by manufacturers, and may need reapplying every 9 to 12 months.

PEWTER

Pewter is a grey-coloured alloy made almost entirely from pure tin. Small amounts of other metals give strength and harden the tin. It is a soft metal so should not be subjected to harsh polishes. Many people prefer their pewter to look quite dull, although it can be polished up like silver.

Wash in warm soapy water and dry well with a soft cloth about once a year. If your pewter is more heavily tarnished use a proprietary silver polish.

For cleaning antique pewter contact the Association of British Pewter Craftsmen (see Useful Addresses).

SILVER

Silver is the metal most prone to tarnishing. Tarnishing is caused by hydrogen sulphide present in the atmosphere acting on the surface of silver.

Several things encourage silver to tarnish including certain foods such as salt, eggs, peas (especially mushy), olives, salad dressings, fish, vinegar and fruit juices, mainly because of their acid content. Acid etches into the silver and can cause pit marks. Cutlery and salt cellars are particularly prone, so it is important to rinse and wash them as soon as possible after use.

To reduce cleaning keep silver away from open coal or gas fires.

Don't mix silver and stainless steel cutlery in a dishwasher as the silver will turn black. Also, don't allow dry dishwasher detergent to come in contact with silverware as it will cause black spots to appear.

Regular cleaning

Wash silver promptly after use, using a warm solution of washing-up liquid and a soft cloth. Rinse in hot water and dry. In between polishing and when dusting use an impregnated silver polishing cloths and mitts. Metal cleaning products come in five types and most include an anti-tarnish agent:

Creams/liquids These are the largest section. Allow them to dry to a fine powdery deposit, then buff with a dry cloth to bring up the shine. Some require rinsing in water so are ideal for ornate and engraved pieces and cutlery that will need to be washed after cleaning anyway. Manufacturers of fine silver services recommend this type of cleaner. They are good at cleaning medium tarnishing.

Foaming silver pastes These are a good choice for cleaning ornate and engraved pieces and for covering larger areas such as a platter. They are easy to use and require little effort. The paste is applied with a damp sponge and lathers to a foam. The item is then rinsed in water. Particularly good for cutlery, which has to be washed after cleaning anyway.

Sprays Liquid polish in a spray formulation. A good choice for covering larger areas such as a silver platter.

Wadding Thick cloth impregnated with polish. Use for items with heavier tarnishing. It's easy to apply but messy to use and requires a degree of elbow grease. It moulds well into

STERLING SILVER

Pure silver is rarely used as it is too soft so sterling silver is used instead. Sterling silver means that the metal contains at least one-quarter silver to three-quarters copper. The copper is added to give strength, making the silver more resistant to wear and to the effects of polishing. Unlike the different qualities of gold (where copper and zinc is added to 'dilute' the purity), sterling silver is not necessarily cheaper than pure silver.

CLEANING TIPS

Silver is a soft metal. A very fine layer of silver is removed every time tarnished items are cleaned, so keep polishing to a minimum. The abrasive action can, over a period of time, remove fine detail and wear silver plate.

Don't rub too hard since it can scratch the surface; use straight even strokes. Do not rub silver crosswise or with a rotary movement.

TIPS FOR PROPRIETARY AND DIY DIPS

- Don't leave items in the dip solution for too long, especially silver plate. Always follow the manufacturer's time limits.
- Avoid getting dip solution on stainless steel knife blades as it can stain or even etch the surface. Rinse off any drops immediately.
- Don't use dips on very heavily tarnished items. They can produce a dull white finish.
- Don't use on damaged silver-plate items.

ornate sections but is quite abrasive, so don't use too frequently.

Dips A less arduous method of cleaning as items are just immersed in the solution and buffed dry. The dip solution converts the film of tarnish (silver sulphide) back to silver by removing the sulphide and leaving the silver behind. Not recommended by experts as it leaves the silver duller with less lustre. Best for small items such as jewellery (do not use on pearls, corals or opals) and heavily embossed designs. Only suitable for light tarnish.

DIY dip

To make your own silver dip line a plastic washing-up bowl with aluminium foil. Fill with very hot water and add a handful of washing soda. Immerse the tarnished silver, making sure it is in contact with the foil.

This method of cleaning involves an electrochemical reaction by which the silver sulphide is removed from the silver and deposited on the aluminium foil.

If you have a large item that comes above the water line, turn it after five minutes. When the foil darkens, it has lost its effectiveness and needs replacing. Leave items in no longer than ten minutes.

Silver teapots

Remove tarnishing, water scale and tea stains using a silver dip. Pour the contents of the dip into the teapot and swirl around. The hydrochloric acid in the dip will dissolve the water scale and get rid of the tarnish. Rinse well before using.

Lacquered silver

See Lacquered brass and copper

Storage tips

- To store silver, wrap in acid-free tissue paper to protect against tarnishing. Don't use newspaper or brown paper as they will accelerate tarnishing. Press out the air as you wrap the silver and never secure any wrapping with rubber bands as the rubber will corrode the silver, even through several layers of cloth.
- Use cutlery rolls and storage bags impregnated with anti-tarnish agents.
- Use tarnish-inhibiting capsules in the back of a display cabinet, such as Tarnprufe's Carosils from department stores and jewellers.
- Cabinets and cutlery drawers should be lined with cotton felt. Woollen felt contains sulphur, which may tarnish silver.

Repairs

It is always best to seek professional advice before attempting to repair or restore silver yourself. Contact your local retail jewellers who are a member of the National Association of Goldsmiths (see Useful Addresses). For more specialist enquiries contact The Worshipful Company of Goldsmiths, who can suggest silver restorers (see Useful Addresses).

SILVER PLATE

Silver plate consists of a coating of silver applied on top of another metal, nickel, by a chemical process called electroplating. Hence silver plate is marked EPNS: electroplated nickel silver.

The majority of household silver items are silver plate which is more affordable than sterling silver. There are various qualities of silver plate, depending on the thickness of the silver coating. The thickness is measured in microns (one micron equals one-thousandth of a millimetre). Good-quality silver plate will be 30 microns plus.

Silver plate is cared for in exactly the same way as sterling silver. However, it should be polished with less vigour and without excessive pressure. This is because the plating is made from solid silver, which is a softer substance than sterling silver (see Sterling Silver box, page 309).

Cleaning precautions

- Don't use dip solutions to clean silver plate that is wearing in patches since they can attack the base metal.
- Never leave silver-plated items in the dip for more than ten seconds.
- Avoid using abrasive cleaners, such as wadding, too frequently.

Worn silver plate

If silver plate has worn, exposing the base metal, you can have items re-silvered.

This can be expensive. (Most companies will need to see the item in order to quote a price, so consider if the cost is justified by the value of the item.)

Contact the British Cutlery and Silverware Association for companies who offer a re-plating service (see Useful Addresses).

MICROWAVES/ COMBINATION OVENS

Always disconnect before cleaning.

Those with an acrylic interior should be wiped out with a cloth and a hot solution of washing-up liquid. Alternatively, use a branded microwave cleaner. Never use anything abrasive.

Some ovens with a stainless-steel interior can be cleaned with a normal oven spray-cleaner, but spray on to a cloth first to avoid spraying into the vents.

Spillages cook on to the glass plate, so this should be wiped after use and occasionally cleaned in a hot solution of washing-up liquid, or in the dishwasher.

To avoid spattering, particularly of fatty or liquid foods, cover while cooking with a paper towel, an upturned plate or special plate covers. Joints of meat can be cooked in roasting bags loosely tied with string and pierced so steam can escape.

TIP To clear lingering smells, switch off at the wall and leave the door open, particularly if you are going away on holiday. Alternatively, put several slices of lemon into a basin of cold water. Bring to the boil in the microwave, uncovered, then simmer for ten minutes so that the steam passes through the vents. Wipe the interior dry.

MIRRORS

Glass mirrors can be cleaned in the same way as windows, using a proprietary window cleaner according to the directions and buffing up with a soft cloth.

For bathroom and kitchen mirrors it is possible to reduce misting. Wipe the mirror with neat washing-up liquid and rub vigorously with kitchen paper, or use an anti-mist product such as Holts Anti-mist spray or cloth, obtainable from cycle and car accessory shops.

TIP Don't let any liquid run between the glass and the backing or under the frame as this could eventually cause spots on the silver surface, behind the glass.

OVENS

See Cookers, page 285

PAINTBRUSHES

Water-based paints need cleaning only in water, or in a warm solution of washing-up liquid and water.

Lacquer needs a lacquer thinner or acetone; oil-based paints, varnishes and enamels need a proprietary paintbrush cleaner.

Cleaning tips

- If soaking is required do not stand the brush directly on its bristles as this will splay the hairs and weaken them.
- To stop the hairs from splaying on small brushes, wrap the bristles in kitchen towel as they are left to dry naturally.
- If a brush has splayed out at the tip during cleaning, when storing slip a small elastic band over the tip to hold the bristles close together.
- If a brush has set hard with paint on it, soak it in a brush cleaner and restorer. When the paint has softened, scrape it out of the brush with an old kitchen knife.

PAINTED SURFACES

See Kitchen Surfaces, page 303

PICTURES AND PAINTINGS

If your paintings need cleaning or restoration this should always be carried out by a conservator. Contact the Institute of Paper Conservation (see Useful Addresses).

PORCELAIN

See Crockery, page 287

PRESSURE COOKERS

Available in aluminium or stainless steel (see Saucepans).

Care tips

- Remove food as soon as possible or pitting of the metal may occur.
- Never immerse the timer in water or put it in the dishwasher.
- Don't put trivets and separators in the dishwasher.

If food has boiled up and the inside of the lid is soiled, remove the gasket and wash the lid in a hot solution of washing-up liquid, then wipe the lid and gasket with a damp cloth. Wash the pressure control, and if blocked use a piece of wire or the end of a coat hanger to unblock it. Check that the Rise'N'Time and Ready to Serve indicators move freely.

RADIATORS

It is important to clean radiators, especially in the winter, as heat carries dust up and spreads it over the paint and wallpaper above.

To clean, use a duster or a vacuum-cleaner radiator brush or dusting head, then wipe over with a cloth wrung out in a solution of washing-up liquid. For bad soiling use a heavy-duty household cleaner.

Remember to cover the floor below the radiator while cleaning.

Rinse thoroughly and wipe dry.

REFRIGERATORS

Modern fridges have automatic defrost. They should be cleaned occasionally, however, to maintain their hygienic condition.

Wipe over all the inside surfaces except for the metal sections, and dry well with a soft cloth. Alternatively, use a branded fridge cleaner which removes grease and inhibits the growth of mould and algae.

Clean the outside with a solution of washing-up liquid. Wipe metal parts with a damp cloth.

Non-automatic fridges need to be defrosted and cleaned regularly. Use a bowl of hot water to help loosen the ice. Once it has all melted, empty the drip tray and wipe the frozen food compartment dry.

TIP If you intend to switch off the fridge and store it remember to leave the door ajar.

REMOVING ODOUR

To remove odour from the fridge, wipe with a solution of 1tbsp/15ml bicarbonate of soda to 1.7 pints/1 litre warm water. Alternatively, either buy a fridge deodoriser or put some bicarbonate of soda in an open container and leave in the fridge for six months approximately. Any stubborn deposits can be removed using baking powder and a damp cloth. This is a very light abrasive, but take care when applying.

SAUCEPANS

ALUMINIUM

Uncoated, plain aluminium cookware is best washed by hand. Never put in the dishwasher as the aluminium will react with the alkalinity of the detergent and will tarnish. If it develops a black tarnish this can be removed by boiling up acid foods such as rhubarb or a cut lemon in water. Then wash out the pan thoroughly.

Hard-anodised aluminium has a chemically treated surface to produce a hard finish. You can use metal utensils (but don't be too boisterous as it has been known for the metal from the utensils to leave marks on the surface of the pan). The hard-anodised surface itself is stick resistant so shouldn't be too difficult to clean in a hot solution of washing-up liquid. Some pans also have a non-stick coating to further enhance their cleanability.

Never put hard-anodised pans in the dishwasher. If a brownish film starts to develop on the surface, use a mild abrasive cleaner to remove it.

CAST IRON

Cast iron rusts easily on its own, so it usually has a non-stick interior coating or thin layer of vitreous enamel to protect it.

Wash uncoated cast iron in a hot solution of washing-up liquid and take care to dry it thoroughly. Brush with a thin layer of vegetable oil to prevent rusting. Never put uncoated cast-iron pans in a dishwasher as they will rust.

COPPER

Most copper pans are lined with another metal, usually tin or stainless steel, since unlined copper will react and discolour with certain foods such as eggs and vinegar due to

DISHWASHER SAFE?

As a general rule, pans with plastic or stainless-steel handles or knobs are dishwasher safe. Most pans with wooden handles and knobs are not, since the wood tends to swell and crack. Reputable brands come with literature on care and use; check this before buying.

their sulphur or acidic content. For this reason, keep unlined copper pans for display only. Wash in a hot solution of washing-up liquid. Remove tarnish with a proprietary metal polish, and then wash the pan thoroughly after cleaning.

ENAMELLED

Enamel is usually applied to steel, aluminium and cast-iron pans. Its main benefit is that it won't pit in reaction to foods or scratch easily. But, be warned, it can chip if knocked.

Wash in a hot solution of washing-up liquid and dry immediately to prevent a whitish film forming on the surface. If the enamel coating is very thin, you may experience problems with food sticking and burning, in which case simply soak the pan and use a nylon scourer to remove deposit. For severe burnt-on deposits, see Tip, below right.

Worn enamel may stain, particularly with curry-based foods. Marks can be removed with proprietary stain removers. Soak overnight and rinse thoroughly.

GLASS-CERAMIC

Glass-ceramic pans tend to retain heat well so can suffer from sticking and burning if used at too high a temperature. For burnt-on food, soak the pan in a warm solution of washing-up liquid before using a nylon scourer. For severe burning, see Tip below.

For general cleaning, wash in a hot solution of washing-up liquid.

NON-STICK COATINGS

Non-stick coatings are applied to most types of cookware these days from aluminium and steel to cast iron and stainless steel. The coatings themselves have become far more durable over the last ten years and many now come with a five- or ten-year guarantee.

Before using a new pan, wash, rinse and dry it. The non-stick coating may need to be lightly 'seasoned' by brushing the interior with a thin layer of vegetable oil. Don't forget to re-season after dishwashing.

Remove burnt-on food deposits with a scourer specifically for non-stick surfaces. Never use metal utensils or abrasive scourers.

STAINLESS STEEL

Stainless steel is very durable and is not prone to pitting or etching by acidic foods. Hot soapy water or dishwashing should suffice. For burnt-on deposits, see Tip below.

Over a period of time, stainless steel can develop rainbow markings inside. This is not a fault of the pan, just a chemical reaction with the minerals in the water. Marks are easy to remove with a proprietary stainless steel cleaner, or Bar Keepers Friend (see Useful Addresses), which is particularly good. Wash thoroughly after cleaning.

Pans which are subjected to too high a heat may develop brown marks on the exterior. These may come off with a proprietary cleaner.

TIP For severe burnt-on deposits try boiling, in the saucepan, a solution of biological washing powder (1tbsp/15ml powder to 2 pints/1.1 litres water). Boil for ten minutes, repeat if necessary then wash thoroughly.

SILVER

See Metals, page 309

SINKS

See Kitchen Surfaces, page 303

SHOES

See Shoes and Handbags, page 340

SHOWERS

See Bathroom Surfaces, page 280

SHOWER CURTAINS

See Shower Curtains, page 344

SLATE

See Flooring, page 289

SPORTS BAGS

See Luggage, page 306

STEREO EQUIPMENT

The exterior of a stereo should only be cleaned using a duster or damp cloth. Avoid using any type of polish as this will damage the casing. To remove finger marks, use a small amount of washing-up liquid diluted in water.

The internal workings of a cassette-tape recorder require regular cleaning (every 50 hours of play)to ensure good sound. There are a number of specialist tape cleaners, such as TDK, on the market. These look like normal tapes but clean the heads while they run. Alternatively, the heads can be cleaned using a cotton bud moistened with a little methylated spirits. Absorb any remaining moisture with the dry end of the bud.

As tapes are magnetic, the tape player should be de-magnetised. You can buy de-magnetising tapes for this job. To use, always switch off all the stereo apart from the tape player and run the de-magnetising tape according to instructions.

The stylus on a record player should be cleaned using a very fine paint brush and alcohol. To avoid damage always brush from back to front.

To keep compact discs clean avoid fingering them. Always hold them around the edge and put them back in their case after playing. If they do require cleaning use some felt and lightly wipe from the inside out, not in a circular motion.

SUEDE

See Suede, page 345

TAPS

See Bathroom Surfaces, page 282

TELEPHONES

Dust a telephone when doing other furniture. If it is really grimy clean with a damp cloth and a solution of washing-up liquid. To untangle the flex, hold in your hand with the receiver dangling down and leave it free to unwind.

TUMBLE DRIERS

The most important part to keep clean is the filter, which is removable and usually situated in the front of the appliance. A build-up of lint in the filter impairs efficiency so it must be cleaned after every use. The easiest way to do this is to moisten your fingers before collecting up the fluff into a ball.

If a condenser dryer is not plumbed in you must regularly empty the water drawer where the condensed water is collected.

Clean the exterior by wiping with a solution of washing-up liquid.

UPHOLSTERED FURNITURE

See Upholstery, page 347

VACUUM CLEANERS

Many vacuum cleaners have a plastic casing which can become statically charged and attract dust back on to the cleaner. To avoid this happening, use an antistatic polish.

Remove any hair or threads caught up in the brush head.

To ensure the best performance, filters should be changed frequently and the dust bag replaced when full. Follow manufacturers' instructions for clearing blockages.

VACUUM FLASKS

Clean the inside with hot water and washing-up liquid. Don't immerse in water as it may become trapped in the casing. To remove odours use a solution of bicarbonate of soda and rinse thoroughly. When storing, leave the top off to allow air to circulate. If stained by tea or coffee, use a proprietary stain remover.

VENEERED SURFACES

See Furniture, page 293

VASES

See Limescale page 305, and Decanters and Carafes, page 288

WASTE BINS

Use a disinfectant spray such as Dettox or a solution of Milton and a damp cloth for regular cleaning. If the bin is soiled and stained, wash out with a mild solution of bleach and rinse with clean water.

WICKER

See Basketware, page 279

WINDOWS

Take down net curtains and blinds as they could be damaged if they got wet. Remove any ornaments from the window sills.

Always clean the frames before cleaning the glass. Because of condensation, mildew grows on the frames. It can be cleaned off with an old rag dipped in a fungicide such as Polycell Mould Cleaner or Rentokil Mould Cure. This stops the black mould from growing back. Alternatively, try a solution of bleach.

Avoid cleaning windows on a sunny day. The heat from the sun dries the glass too quickly and causes it to smear. Make sure the window is dry before cleaning.

Proprietary window cleaners come as a liquid or a trigger-operated spray so are easy to apply. They are quite expensive, so an alternative is 2tbsp/30ml vinegar or methylated spirits to 7 pints/4 litres of water. For grimy exteriors of windows use the same dilution of ammonia.

Always use a lint-free cloth, or chamois

leather, to clean windows. For a really good shine, buff the dry window with a crumpled pad of newspaper: the printer's ink really gives the glass an extra sparkle. Alternatively, rub with a dry chamois leather or a soft cloth.

A window cleaner incorporating a rubber blade and a cleaning reservoir such as the Scoopy (see Useful Addresses) is a quick way of removing the water plus dirt on large panes of glass. Only use this on the exterior windows to avoid water dripping on to carpets. Wipe the blade after each stroke.

WOOD

See Furniture, page 293

WASHING MACHINES

Before cleaning the machine, always check the manufacturer's instructions.

The detergent dispenser drawer can get clogged up with unused detergent and fabric conditioner. Choose a powder or liquid that is used in a ball and placed directly in the drum on top of the clothes. Otherwise remove the drawer and rinse out in a bowl of warm water. Detergent can also accumulate inside the drawer recess so wipe out with a damp cloth. Once done, replace the drawer.

Always check the drain filter, usually on the front of the machine. This collects coins, buttons, cuff-links and other small objects left in the clothes. Make sure the machine is disconnected when emptying, and place a shallow bowl underneath to collect any water. Replace the filter securely after cleaning.

When the machine is not in use, keep the door open to allow air to circulate, but if you have a cat, check before switching on that it has not crept inside.

The outside of the machine can be cleaned with a warm solution of washing-up liquid. Wipe with clean water and dry.

WASTE DISPOSAL UNITS

Put a slice of lemon in the waste disposal unit to help reduce any odours, and avoid using any drain-cleaning chemicals as these are caustic and may damage the unit.

WATER FILTERS

Whether you have a jug water filter or a plumbed-in unit beneath the sink, it is essential to keep a check on how old the filter is as there is no way of telling when the filter cartridge has reached the end of its life. (Activated carbon filters are the most common type available.) Manufacturers suggest you watch out for a slower flow rate or an inferior water taste and change the filter in accordance with their recommendations.

Jug filter cartridges should be changed every 100–180 pints/60–100 litres, or roughly once a month. The frequency depends very much on how often you use the filter.

It's also a good idea to wash the filter jug and housing (not the cartridge) regularly in a warm solution of washing-up liquid. Rinse thoroughly, and drain.

The lifetime of plumbed-in filter cartridges varies considerably depending on the model: from six months up to three years, or a certain number of litres. As this is less easy to calculate over a longer period of time and easy to forget about, reputable manufacturers send out reminders when the filter needs changing. But it's still a good idea to make a note in your diary when it's due for a change. There is very little else you can do in the way of cleaning a plumbed-in unit as they are usually sealed.

WASH-DAY WISDOM

Laundry habits have changed dramatically over the past 20 years. Long gone is the tradition of washing on a Monday; wash-day blues can last all week with some of us washing around five loads. Not only do we wash much smaller loads, but with the increase in synthetic and man-made fabrics, gone is the boil wash and in many cases the pre-wash. As well, lower-temperature wash programmes are making new demands on detergents.

GETTING THE BEST OUT OF YOUR WASH

Whether washing by hand or machine, it's important to match the correct washing procedure to the type of fabric. Depending on how dirty your washing is, you need to consider water temperature, type of detergent, fabric and wash type; whether any special treatments are needed and how you are going to dry and iron afterwards.

WATER TEMPERATURE

It's vital to choose the correct water temperature because this can affect various aspects of successful washing:

Colour: too high a temperature will cause non-colourfast fabrics to fade.

WASHING-MACHINE PROGRAMMES

Even though the average washing machine has over fifteen programmes to choose from, as many as 23 per cent of us use only one programme; 35 per cent use two programmes; and 26 per cent use three programmes.

Creasing: some fabrics, such as polyester, will crease more at high temperatures.

Cleaning efficiency: too low a temperature will not remove some types of stains. With the increase in man-made fibres, 100°F/40°C and 120°F/50°C washes are the most popular. However, the colder the water the more difficult it is to get a really clean result because detergents traditionally work better at higher temperatures. The latest detergents have been specially formulated to include enzymes and bleaching systems which work effectively between 100–140°F/40–60°C.

Fabric finishes: easy-care finishes, for example, can be broken down by too high a temperature.

Fibre type and construction: delicates and synthetics generally prefer lower temperatures, whereas cotton and linen wash better at higher temperatures.

Energy consumption: in low-temperature washes less energy is required to heat the water, making them more economical. Most UK machines are hot and cold fill. It is often more economical to use water heated by the domestic boiler than by the heater in the machine.

WHICH DETERGENT?

Ten years ago, buying a washing powder or detergent was simply a matter of deciding between the brands and choosing a box size. Now you have to choose between shelves of different products after deciphering the descriptions on the packaging. From powders to liquids, micros to ultras, refill pouches to powders just for coloureds, it's not surprising that a trip to the supermarket can baffle the best of us.

Conventional powders
These are for machine or hand washing and can be biological and non-biological. Dispense through the detergent drawer.

Concentrated powders
Similar to conventional powders, but in a concentrated form and should be used with a dosing ball provided by the manufacturer.

They are worth considering because they:

- Use less packaging – an important environmental issue. Many brands also use recycled cardboard.
- Are more convenient to carry home.
- Are more free-flowing than conventional powders and so less likely to cake in the box.
- Are very slightly cheaper to use per wash than conventional powders.

Powders for coloureds
Use these for washing coloured items to reduce fading and dulling. Unlike standard powders they don't contain bleaches and fluorescers. However, once fading has occurred, colour cannot be restored.

Liquid detergents
When using in the machine dispense through the drawer (without the problems of clogging) or in a dosing ball.

Bottles are more practical to store and some brands use recycled plastic. To save money make full use of refill packs or pouches.

Concentrated liquids can also be used for pre-treating stains. If using in your machine dispense only via a dosing ball.

Environmentally-friendly detergents
These can be powders or liquids and usually do not contain phosphates, fluorescers or perfume. However, you may have to compromise on performance.

Soap flakes
More gentle products, specially formulated for hand washing delicate items and woollens, and should not be used in the machine.

Pre-wash detergents
Useful for removing heavy soiling. Use for pre-soak prior to machine or hand washing, or use with the pre-wash programme on your machine. Because they don't contain bleaches, use for whites, coloureds and most delicates – but always check the fabric can be soaked.

Fabric whiteners
If your whites are looking grey and dull, try a speciality product for whitening wool, cotton and some synthetics.

Fabric conditioners
After washing you'll find most fabrics begin to lose their natural softness and texture as the fibres become entangled and matted. Use a fabric conditioner to:

- Help untangle the fibres and restore some of the lost softness and texture.
- Coat the fibres to reduce creasing and make ironing easier.
- Reduce static which builds up, particularly after tumble drying.

In normal or concentrated forms, conditioners can be used in the washing machine or for hand rinsing. Follow the manufacturers' dosing instructions and always use in diluted form on fabrics.

Special impregnated sheets are available for use in tumble driers.

TIP Clean the fabric-conditioner drawer of the washing machine regularly to avoid clogging. If undiluted fabric conditioner does come into contact with fabric, rub the affected areas with soap and re-wash normally.

INTERNATIONAL TEXTILE CARE LABELLING

Always use the recommended care label advice to achieve the best results and help make your clothes look good and last longer.

Labels on clothes should correspond with programmes on your washing machine.

The wash-tub number shows the most effective washing temperature.

Cotton wash (no bar) Articles which will withstand normal (maximum) washing conditions at quoted tub temperature

Synthetic wash (single bar) Synthetic articles, easy-care cottons and blends which will withstand reduced (medium) washing conditions at quoted tub temperature

Wool wash (broken bar) Machine-washable wool and wool blends which require much reduced (minimum) washing conditions

Other symbols used outside the UK

Synthetic wash (single bar) White nylon and white polyester/cotton mixtures. Wash as for 50 (single bar)

Cool wash (single bar) Short cool wash often found on washing machines as a hand-wash option.

See manufacturer's manual for details. If your washing machine does not have this programme, cool hand wash gently

Hand wash only Do not machine wash

Bleaching

Chlorine bleach may be used

Tumble Drying

May be tumble dried

If dots appear:

Highest heat setting

Low heat setting

Ironing

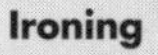

Hot iron: Cotton, Linen, Viscose

Warm iron: Polyester mixes, Silk, Wool

Cool iron: Acrylic, Nylon, Polyester

Dry Cleaning

May be dry cleaned. Where letters appear in the circle (eg, P)or it has a bar underneath, these are special instructions for the dry cleaner.

Any symbols appearing with a cross through them mean DO NOT (eg, do not iron).

As a general guide you can combine:

- All items without the bar symbol, and wash at the lowest quoted temperature.
- All items with the same bar symbol, and wash at the lowest quoted temperature.
- Wash labels with and without a bar, provided that you wash at the lowest temperature, but you must also reduce the washing action.

Always follow any special instructions shown on labels, particularly 'wash separately', which means what it says. Heavily soiled goods should be washed according to the care label, and not included in mixed loads.

Compiled by the Home Laundry Consultative Council

TIPS ON POWDERS

- For good, all-round stain removal and cleaning efficiency choose a biological powder.
- For a coloured wash load use one of the specially formulated coloured products.
- For delicates, hand washing and light soiling choose a non-biological formulation, or one specifically targeted at certain fabrics such as Woolite for wool.
- All-in-one detergent and fabric conditioners are available for extra convenience.

DECIPHERING THE PACKAGING

Biodegradable

This is a word we're always coming across with the increase in environmental awareness, but what does it have to do with detergents?

Basically, it's what happens when you rinse them away. They are broken down into harmless ingredients, naturally, by micro-organisms. When detergents first came into widespread use, they contained ingredients which were not very biodegradable, and were held responsible for widespread foaming on rivers. Now EC Regulations stipulate that detergents must be 80 per cent biodegradable. Most UK detergents are around 95 per cent.

Biological

These detergents contain enzymes that help improve wash performance at lower temperatures (100–140°F/40–60°C). This means we can wash using less energy.

Their job is to break down stains, namely proteins, fats and starch, commonly found on clothing. Once they have been broken down by the enzymes it's easier for the other ingredients in detergents to remove the dirt.

Some people with sensitive skin are allergic to certain enyzmes, so if a reaction occurs use a non-biological detergent.

TIP If you have a lot of greasy stains, look for a biological detergent which contains lipase. This enzyme, which works best at low temperatures, is good for tackling grease on collars and cuffs and helps prevent yellowing of whites.

Bleach

Bleaching agents in detergents help to keep fabrics looking bright and clean. They also remove stains caused by coloured foods and drink such as tea, coffee and wine. The most common is sodium perborate or oxygen bleach, but if you're concerned about their effects on the environment look out for sodium percarbonate. The latest bleaches work well at low temperatures, giving a boil wash hygiene at 100–120°F/40–50°C.

Builders

These ingredients hold the dirt in the water and stop hard-water salts forming scale.

Fluorescers

Also known as optical brightening agents, they have a whitening or brightening effect on fabrics. Whites appear whiter and coloureds brighter.

Phosphonates

A bleach alternative, generally found in liquid detergents and powders for coloureds.

Phosphates

Help soften water and prevent soiling from re-depositing on the clothes in the wash. More environmentally-friendly alternatives are zeolites, found in most concentrated powders.

Surfactants

These are the ingredients which do all the hard work to remove soiling.

CHOOSING THE CORRECT WASH

Always read garment labels thoroughly before washing. These have been included by the manufacturer to give you information about the fabric and how to care for it. The labels may not be immediately obvious, so look at the neck, hem or in a side seam. Furnishing fabrics often have the instructions printed on the selvedge, so keep a section back when sewing. If you find garments more comfortable without labels make sure you keep them safe so you can refer to them when necessary.

The label should include details of:

COUNTRY OF ORIGIN

This isn't a legal UK requirement but a manufacturer can be prosecuted under the Trades Description Act if he's deliberately set out to deceive the consumer. Country of origin refers to the country where the last major process in manufacturing the garment was carried out.

FIBRE CONTENT

This tells you exactly what the garment is made from – whether it's pure cotton or a blend, for example – and is a legal requirement. However, if there is less than 15 per cent of a fibre included it doesn't have to be listed as long as the bulk of fibres are. You may come across 'mixed fibres', which means mixed waste or reclaimed fibres have been used, which are difficult to analyse.

WASHING AND CARE INSTRUCTIONS

International Textile Care Labelling (ITCL): although only voluntary in the EC (compulsory in the USA), most garments in this country have washing instructions as promoted and recommended by the HLCC (Home Laundry Consultative Council); see the chart on page 320.

These instructions include washing recommendations, whether by hand or machine, suitability for certain treatments such as bleaching, plus drying and ironing procedures. Dry-cleaning instructions are also provided.

As a general rule, the wash-tub symbol represents washing, the triangle is about bleaching, the square is about drying, the iron about ironing and the circle about dry cleaning.

OTHER DETAILS

Information about sizing, distributor's or manufacturer's name, and flammability should be included.

PREPARING THE WASH LOAD

- Empty and turn all pockets outwards.
- Brush off any surplus mud, dust or fluff.
- Remove tissues from sleeves.
- Close zips and do up buttons.
- Make all repairs before you wash not after. Washing will make any damage worse.
- Turn pile fabrics, jeans and corduroy inside out.

SORTING THE LOAD

- Identify any items which must be washed separately.
- Sort out hand-wash only items.
- Group together items with the same wash symbol, but don't mix whites and non-colourfast fabrics.
- If you have to machine wash mixed loads, always wash them according to the instructions for the most delicate fabric.

Whites, however, will benefit from washing every few washes at their correct recommended temperature.

PRE-WASH SOAKING

- Use when items are very heavily soiled or stained.
- As a general rule, don't soak silk, wool, leather (including trimmings), elastanes, fabrics with special treatments such as flame retardancy, easy-care, non-colourfast dyes and items with metal fasteners.
- Soak in a plastic bucket or bath with plenty of water and check detergent is thoroughly dissolved before adding the clothes.
- Water should be cool for protein-based stains, such as egg, blood and milk; and hand hot for others.
- Leave to soak for several hours, or overnight for whites.
- For persistent marks, rub detergent or a stain-removal bar directly on to the stain.
- Treat collars and cuffs before washing. Dampen and rub soap along the marks. Leave for an hour and then scrub with an old toothbrush.
- To reduce colour run, soak the fabric in a solution of salt and water using 1tbsp/15ml of salt to 1pint/500ml of water.

MACHINE-WASHING TIPS

- Before loading, shake items out, and load one at a time to reduce tangling.
- Load evenly with small items, then large, taking care not to over-fill.
- Follow care label instructions and do not over-dose with detergent, especially if washing small loads.
- If colours do run place the dyed item back in the machine and re-wash.
- Wash tights and stockings in a pillowcase or cotton bag.
- Don't leave damp items in the machine or clothes basket as mildew can develop.
- To eliminate fluff, add 1 cup/7fl oz/190ml of white vinegar to the final rinse; or put some netting in the tumble dryer to catch the fluff.

HAND-WASHING TIPS

- Sort according to colour and temperature.
- Make sure the detergent is thoroughly dissolved.
- Rinse in cold water until free of scum. Add a little vinegar to the final rinse to remove all the scum.
- Don't rub wool or it will matt. Gently squeeze the water through the fabric.
- Do not lift items out of the water as they will stretch.

WASHING THE GREEN WAY

- Most manufacturers have at least one environmentally-friendly machine in their range (see Washing Machines, page 81). They may cost a little more to buy, but because they feature a range of energy-saving options, running costs can be less. Performance isn't sacrificed either.
- If you have to wash small loads use the half load option, which many machines now have. This uses less water, energy and detergent but not half the amount as you might expect, so always wash maximum loads if you can.
- Use a ball-dosing device if this is applicable to your type of detergent (see Which Detergent? page 318). This ensures all the detergent stays in the drum of the machine rather than escaping into the pipework.

TIP Look out for washing machines with

special devices or locks to prevent detergent escaping from the drum. Alternatively, some machines have detergent regeneration systems which recycle the detergent through the pipework back into the drum.

- Use lower temperatures for lightly soiled loads.
- Always rinse in cold water when hand washing.
- Make use of off-peak electricity if you have the option.
- Use high spin speeds before tumble drying (except for synthetic fabrics).
- Use refill packs of detergents and fabric conditioners. Use correct dosages, don't guess.
- Use concentrated products.

SPECIAL TREATMENTS

BLEACHING

- Always wear gloves.
- Bleaches, particularly chlorine, should be diluted or they will rot fabric.
- Do not bleach wool, silk, viscose, fabrics with special finishes, and deep colours.
- Check the care label and try on a hidden area first.
- Avoid bleaching damaged or discoloured items as they won't bleach evenly.
- Rinse thoroughly or residual bleach will damage the fabric.
- Check container you use is colourfast.

STARCHING

- Mostly used for stiffening cotton or linen.
- If you want a very stiff result, use a powdered starch. Vary the concentration depending on the application.
- Liquid starches such as Dip are easier to use.
- Use a basin or bucket for powdered starches, rather than the washing machine.
- Starch after washing, spin, and finally rinse to remove excess starch.
- Spray starches often contain silicones for easier ironing.

DYEING

Home dyeing is an inexpensive way of adding a new lease of life to sad-looking clothes. However, it's not suitable for all fabrics and there are a few basic rules to bear in mind and choices to make:

Machine dyes for natural fibres – cotton and linen – but not for silk, wool or viscose.

Hand dyes for natural fibres, including wool and silk.

Multipurpose/universal dyes for natural fibres and polyamide.

Cold water dyes for natural fibres, including wool and silk.

Remember you can't:

- Dye acrylics.
- Cover patterns with dye.
- Cover stains and marks with dye.
- Dye anything a perfect black.
- Remove colour from polyesters before dyeing them.

Ten golden rules for home dyeing

1 Wash and remove all stains so the fabrics will take the colour evenly.

2 You'll get better results if you remove the original colour first. Proprietary colour removers will strip non-colourfast dyes (natural fibres and some synthetics) to neutral.

3 Follow the manufacturer's recommended instructions carefully. Don't skimp on dye or else the colour won't match the colour card.

4 Wear gloves and wipe up spills immediately.

5 Machine dyeing will produce more even results than dyeing by hand, and is less messy.

6 Specialist machine dyes won't leave the drum of your machine dirty, but wipe any spills off the outside or window immediately. If using multi-purpose dyes in the machine you will need to dissolve the dye in a container beforehand and to clean the machine after use.
7 Smaller items, such as T-shirts and shirts, dye the best. Anything bulky or expensive should be professionally dyed.
8 If you have to dye over the original colour remember the basic rules: blue on yellow goes green, blue on pink equals mauve, red and yellow will make orange or red, etc. For best results, dye within the same colour spectrum from pale to dark, for example pale blue to navy or black over grey.
9 Use a proprietary colour fixer which helps to keep colours brighter after dyeing. Also stops dye bleeding on to other items.
10 Polyester does not dye well and blends containing this are pale and may be slightly mottled where the different fibres are. Obviously, the more polyester in the blend the paler the result will be.

TIP Add very dark blue dye to black dye to give a darker result.

DRYING TIPS

First spin dry the wash load, if possible, to remove any excess water.

When spinning delicates, such as tights and stockings, place them in a pillowcase first. Otherwise wring them gently or roll them carefully in a towel to soak up the water.

LINE DRYING

Do

- Wipe the line before use.
- Line dry whites: the sunlight will bleach and freshen them.
- Hang pleated garments on a hanger.
- Hang drip-dry skirts by the waistband.
- Turn coloureds inside out to prevent fading.
- Fold sheets in half and hang by the hem.
- Hang striped garments vertically.

Don't

- Dry silk, wool or polyamide outside because sunlight will cause them to yellow and weaken considerably.

FLAT DRYING

Do

- Flat dry knitted and jersey fabrics to avoid stretching.
- Pull into shape when damp.

Don't

- Dry near a direct heat source such as a fire or radiator.

TUMBLE DRYING

Do

- Make sure to always check care labels. Do not tumble dry wool, knits, delicates and elastanes.
- Choose the correct heat setting for the type of fabric. Synthetics must be dried using the cool cycle or else the fibres could melt, crease or shrink.
- Tumble dry harsh towels – it should soften them.
- Clean filters regularly.

Don't

- Over-load, or drying will be patchy and uneven.
- Dry very large and small items together or results will be uneven.
- Over-dry, as the fibres can become brittle, more difficult to iron – and it's also a waste of energy.

WASH-DAY BLUES: TROUBLESHOOTING

FABRIC HARSHNESS

This applies particularly to towels.

Cause

- Over-drying natural fibres.
- Continual under-dosing with detergent, allowing mineral salts to build up.
- Inadequate rinsing of the wash load.

Cure

For under-dosing, soak in a solution of water softener (eg Calgon) using 2tbsp/30ml of softener to 7 pints/4 litres of water. Also run the machine empty using the hottest programme with the recommended dose of detergent containing a bleaching agent to remove any calcium build-up within the washing machine.

For inadequate rinsing, wash the fabrics at as high a temperature as possible without any detergent. Add 1 cup/7fl oz/190ml of white vinegar to the drawer dispenser of the machine.

Prevention

Follow the manufacturer's pack recommendation for dosage. Increase this if the items are very heavily soiled.

If drying natural fibre garments on a radiator or in a tumble drier, remove them before they are fully dry to prevent removal of natural moisture within the fibres. Over-drying will lead to harsh and brittle fibres.

GREYING OF WHITE COTTONS

Cause

Dirt and soiling removed during washing has re-deposited on to the clothes as a very thin uniform layer making whites appear slightly grey and coloureds dull. It occurs if insufficient detergent is used to suspend the soiling in the water.

Cure

Re-wash using the maximum dose of detergent and wash temperature.

Prevention

Follow the manufacturer's recommended dosing instructions and wash programme. Don't overload the machine.

PATCHY COLOURS OR STAINING

Cause

Chemicals in the wash water. Light patches on bedding and nightwear can be caused by some skin creams and acne treatments; or neat, heavy-duty powders in direct contact with damp, non-colourfast fabric.

Cure

Re-washing may remove some types of staining. If the dyes have been affected the problem is permanent.

Prevention

Avoid fabrics touching offending chemicals or neat detergents.

DYE TRANSFER FROM OTHER GARMENTS

Cause

Non-colourfast items have been washed with paler items at too high a temperature. Excess dye from dark-coloured items has leached to other items in the wash load.

Cure

Re-wash in as hot a wash as possible. It may be

necessary to soak whites and colourfast items in a proprietary colour-removing product.

Prevention
Sort your load carefully and test for colourfastness (see Ten Golden Rules for Successful Stain Removal, page 350). Always wash dark colours separately at first and do not use too high a temperature for non-colourfast items. Do not mix whites and coloured items.

WHITE/GREY SPECKS OR STREAKS

Cause
Hard water deposits that are present in the local water supply.

Cure
Re-wash using maximum dosage of detergent. It may be necessary to soak the load in a water softener.

Prevention
Increase the dosage of detergent. In very hard-water areas, carry out an idle wash periodically with just detergent and no load, to help reduce scale build-up.

EXCESSIVE CREASING

Cause
Incorrect wash programme, over-drying or overloading machine.

Cure
Reduce temperature, or wash with smaller loads. Use the specific synthetics programmes which have reduced drum agitation and shorter spin cycles at lower speeds.

Prevention
Follow care labelling. Creasing of synthetics occurs if too high washing and drying temperatures are used.

SHRINKING AND FELTING OF WOOL

Cause
Too high wash temperatures, excessive agitation, and tumble drying.

Cure
None. It is irreversible.

Prevention
Only machine wash if the label states it is machine washable. If in doubt, hand wash. Never tumble dry wool.

CLINGING AND RIDING UP OF SLIPS AND SKIRT LININGS

Cause
Build-up of static electricity in synthetic fibres.

Cure
Use fabric conditioner in the final rinse. Alternatively, use an antistatic spray before or while wearing the garment.

Prevention
Wear a natural fibre garment between two synthetic ones, eg a cotton slip between a polyester skirt and polyamide tights.

BOBBLING ON COTTON AND SOME SYNTHETIC BLENDS

Cause
Abrasion of the fibres from normal wear.

Cure
Pick off the bobbles by hand or with sticky tape. Alternatively, use a safety razor or specific de-fuzzing gadget.

Prevention
Difficult to prevent, but try washing garments inside out and use a fabric conditioner.

RUCKING OF COLLARS AND SHIRT FRONTS

Cause

Collars and bands have facings with layers of different sorts of fabrics to stiffen them. These can shrink at different rates when washed, causing puckering of the top fabric. Alternatively, using cotton thread to sew synthetic fabrics can cause puckering as the cotton shrinks.

Cure

This rucking or puckering may be irreversible. However, try steam ironing the garment while it is damp and carefully pulling the offending layers into shape.

Prevention

Dry clean items or wash them in cool water to avoid any shrinkage. If home dressmaking, ensure you don't over-stretch the facings when fitting and sewing them. Always match the thread content to the fabric.

IRONING

All irons have at least three heat settings, each suitable for certain fabrics, depicted by one to three dots on the iron: • •• or •••. These dots relate to specific temperatures recommended by the HLCC (Home Laundry Consultative Council).

Cool: one dot • 250°F/120°C
Acrylic, Silk, Polyamide, Acetate, Polyester

Warm: 2 dots •• 320°F/160°C
Polyester blends, Wool

Hot: 3 dots ••• 410°F/210°C
Cotton, Linen, Viscose, Denim.

Most irons have a steam setting (see Irons, page 85).

TAKING THE STRESS OUT OF IRONING

• Always allow the iron to heat up thoroughly. This will give the thermostat time

IRONING TIPS

• Iron pile fabrics on the reverse side, on a thick cloth or towel, using minimum pressure.
• When ironing pleated items, tack the pleats down first; this will be quicker in the long run and will avoid double lines. Alternatively, hold pleats down with paper clips.
• If the fabric has a special finish, iron on the wrong side.
• To avoid shine, iron fabrics on the wrong side. Steam pressing with a damp cloth may remove slight shine.
• Don't iron over zips. Close the zip and iron lightly down each side of it, avoiding the teeth.
• Don't put clothes on immediately after ironing as it will encourage creasing.
• To remove bagginess, from skirt seats for example, lay the baggy area flat and work from the outer edge of the bagginess towards the centre, pressing it repeatedly with a damp cloth, on the right side, until it flattens. Remove the cloth, place a piece of brown paper on the area and iron all over. This will absorb the moisture from the cloth and the shape will therefore hold better. Allow to cool.

to settle down. Leave the iron for several minutes when changing temperatures as it does take time to adapt. This is particularly important when going from hot to cool.

- Start with the items needing the coolest settings, and work up to the hottest.
- If in doubt about temperature, start at the lowest and work your way up, ironing a small hidden area of the garment.
- When using a damp cloth you will need a higher temperature setting because the cloth will cool the soleplate.
- Move the garment away from you as you iron, supporting large items to avoid the fabric distorting.
- Use a plant sprayer to dampen really dry cottons and linen.
- Sleeves: avoid creasing down the sleeve by inserting a rolled-up towel and ironing gently.
- Shirts: start at the top and work down. Iron all the double sections first on the wrong side (collars, cuffs, front bands); then do shoulders and sleeves, back and front.
- Sheets: fold lengthwise twice.
- Trousers (with a centre crease): iron pockets, waist; fold trousers lengthways so seams are in the middle and creases at outside edges. Repeat with other leg.
- Gathers: press on the reverse side, working with the point of the iron towards the gathers.
- Belts: iron on the wrong side first.
- Hems: iron from the wrong side.
- Seams: press flat from the inside.

DRY CLEANING

WHY DRY CLEAN?

Always dry clean items:

- If specified on their care label.
- If instructions are not available.
- With leather trim, pleated skirts, tailored wool suits, wool, jersey, hand-painted silk.
- Anything old, valuable or delicate.

Either use a coin-operated dry cleaning machine or a professional dry cleaner.

Coin-op machines use a system similar to a professional cleaner, but you don't get the personal care, advice and finishing. However, it is cheaper, because several garments can be treated at once. These machines use different solvents so only use if the item is labelled with an A. Otherwise have it professionally treated. If you have any problems with such machines, write to the National Association of Launderette Industries (see Useful Addresses).

TIP Always air items thoroughly before wearing to remove any toxic fumes.

Professional cleaners have the edge on stain removal because they have a whole range of cleaning solvents which are not available on the domestic market. Choose a dry cleaner who is a member of the Textile Services Association. They should display a blue and white logo in their window with the current year's date on it (see below). These cleaners agree to observe a code of practice to guarantee high standards of service, and to protect you should anything go wrong.

Taking a garment to the cleaners

- Draw their attention to any specific stains or unusual fabrics.
- Avoid treating a stain yourself first, because this may fix it. However, if you have tried to remove it, inform the cleaner of the treatment.
- Remove unusual and ornate trimmings.
- Point out any dry-cleaning symbol which is underlined because this tells the dry-cleaner that a special treatment is required.

• You may find that some stains, such as colourless spills that contain sugar-lemonade or alcohol, only show up after dry cleaning because they have been brought out by the solvents used. These will need re treating.

IF THINGS GO WRONG

1 Make a formal complaint, in writing, to the manager of the company explaining the problem, keeping copies of all correspondence.
2 If you don't hear anything after ten days, or are not satisfied with the response, ask for help from your local Citizens' Advice Bureau or Trading Standards department.
3 If you don't seem to be getting anywhere, contact the Customer Adviser of the TSA (see Useful Addresses). If the cleaner is a member, the adviser will help sort out the problem. If the cleaner is not a member, the adviser will suggest your next step.
4 If the problem is difficult to resolve you may want to have the garments analysed by an independent test laboratory (see Useful Addresses). You will be charged for this service, but should the cleaner be found to be at fault you will be reimbursed and compensated.
5 If the cleaner is not a member, under the terms laid out by the Office of Fair Trading, they still have a legal duty 'to provide their service with reasonable care and skill and in a reasonable time'. If this is not followed you are entitled to part or all of your money back.

CARING FOR CLOTHES

A little time taken to care for clothes is time well spent. The suggestions below will help to prolong their life and keep them looking their best.

1 Always follow the care instructions found on clothes labels.
2 Before you put clothes away give them a good brush down to remove any loose hairs and dust. Never put them away dirty. Clothes with stains – especially wool – attract destructive clothes' moths.
3 Avoid wearing the same garment two days running. Fabrics need time to recover. Hang them up while still warm from the heat of the body, to help creases drop out.
4 To help garments keep their shape close all zips and fasten buttons and hang or fold them away carefully.
5 Don't fill the wardrobe too full, or clothes will crease and natural fibres cannot breathe. If you're short of space only hang those items you wear frequently.
6 Pack summer clothes away in winter and vice versa.
7 Wet clothes, such as swimsuits and sportswear, should be allowed to dry naturally before being put away.
8 Don't allow clothes to become over dirty; clean regularly.
9 Repair hems and replace buttons, etc, straight away.
10 Cover hanging garments that are only occasionally worn with a plastic bin liner or dry cleaning cover. This will protect them from dust and unwarranted creasing.
11 Don't leave silk items in direct sunlight as they could fade.
12 Line drawers with wallpaper or self-sticking plastic.

CLOTHES-CARE TIPS

- Swimsuits: After a swim don't just wring out your swimsuit. Rinse it thoroughly in tap water and then dry flat. Salt water, perspiration, suntan lotions or chlorine from swimming baths can rot the fibres. Wash by hand rather than the machine, and avoid wringing, tumble drying and ironing especially if it has bra cups. Never leave damp swimwear in a plastic bag, for even a short time, or the fabric may rot.
- Trousers should be folded along the vertical crease line and stored on a solid coathanger (not wire).

TIP To avoid getting a crease across the legs of trousers, place a piece of cardboard or foam rubber along the bar.

- Hang evening dresses inside out to keep them as clean as possible. Sew loops on the waist so hems do not trail.
- Hang skirts by loops on the waistband, or if storing don't fold pleated skirts. Instead, cut the feet and top off an old pair of tights, roll up the skirt lengthwise and pull it through. Store flat.
- Shirts: Hang up on a coathanger, if possible, or store in a drawer. When folding, after fastening all the buttons, lay it face down. Turn both sides to the middle, with sleeves lying flat down the back. Turn the tail up about three inches and then take the bottom fold up to the collar.
- Knitted/woollen items: Don't hang or they will stretch. Fold, and put in a drawer. To fold place face down, fold one side and arm to the middle. Fold the arm back on itself and repeat with the other side. Fold in two, taking the top down to the bottom.
- Jackets: Use a wooden coathanger which spans the width of the shoulder. Never hang by the loop as it will pull the shoulders out of shape.
- Shoes: Wipe wet shoes, stuff with newspaper or a shoe tree and dry away from direct heat.
- Hats: Stuff with tissue in boxes. Felt and velour hats need to be brushed, and if they become misshapen hold them in some steam, press them to shape again and let them cool supported by crumpled paper. Straw hats can be brushed and scrubbed with lemon juice and left in the sun if they become dingy.
- Ties: hang over expanded curtain wire, or a wire coathanger hung on the inside of the wardrobe door.
- Belts: hang by the buckles from hooks on the inside of the wardrobe door.
- Linens: rotate the use of sheets to prolong their life. Store duvets in a large bag, on top of a wardrobe or under the bed.
- Remove fluff or hair from clothes by dabbing with a piece of sticky tape. Wind a length round the back of your hand, sticky side out.
- Stop clothes falling off hangers by sticking a piece of foam rubber at each end.
- Store black items inside out to stop them from picking up fluff and dust.

MOTHPROOFING

Moths attack natural fibres, particularly wool. Synthetics are mothproof, but if blended with natural fibres they can be attacked.

When storing clothes at the end of the season, make sure they are washed; then pack in plastic-lined cases or boxes, or hang in mothproof bags.

Hang an insecticidal strip in the wardrobe or put moth-repellent crystals between blankets and woollens. Natural substances such as lavender and cedar wood are sometimes used to repel moths.

PACKING CLOTHES

When going away, first make a list of the things you need to take with you: clothes, cosmetics, first aid kit, etc.

- Collect together all items and discard non-essentials.
- Avoid over- and under-filling the case.
- Do up all fastenings on clothes before folding, and pack everything face down to minimise creasing.
- Place tissue paper between the folds.
- Place heavy items, such as shoes, books, etc, at the bottom and fill gaps with underwear and socks.
- Pack heavy garments next, followed by woollens and breakables.
- Lay trousers with the waistband at one end of the case and the legs overhanging at the other. Pack shirts, sweaters, etc, on top and then fold the legs over to reduce creasing.
- Finish off with dresses and blouses covered over with a towel or tissue paper. Fold dresses horizontally, as these folds drop out quicker than vertical ones.
- Unpack as soon as you can and hang creased garments in a steamy bathroom.

A – Z OF FABRIC CARE

These guidelines must not be used instead of care labels. Read the labels thoroughly and match up to the instructions to the symbols in the chart (see page 320). If there isn't a label, follow these guidelines, or dry clean only. When washing and ironing try on a small, hidden area first.

ACETATE

Man-made fibre which has a silky appearance so often made into synthetic silk-like fabrics such as satin, taffeta and brocades. Often used for linings, which can shrink.

- Wash in warm water using a delicates programme as hot water will soften and damage the fibres.
- Do not spin.
- Iron using a cool setting.
- Some acids and solvents can dissolve acetate, therefore avoid acetone (nail-varnish remover) and vinegar when removing stains.

ACRYLIC

Made from petrochemicals and solvents as an alternative to wool. Often used for knitwear because it is soft, warm, shrink resistant and inherently mothproof. However, it does not have the same warmth as wool.

- Use a warm wash using a synthetics programme with a short spin.
- Fabric conditioner in the last rinse will reduce static.
- Do not wring and use a cool iron, not the steam setting.
- Acrylic knitwear has a tendency to become baggy, so pull it back into shape when wet, and dry flat.
- Curtains and soft furnishings should be dry cleaned.
- Pile fabrics should be ironed carefully on the wrong side. Then brush the pile with a soft brush.

ANGORA

Soft rabbit wool used for jumpers, mohair fabrics and knitting yarns. Sometimes mixed with nylon.

- Always hand wash, and treat as for wool.
- To prevent moulting store in the fridge!

BLANKETS

Usually made from wool, but cotton and synthetics are available.

- Rest blankets periodically to help prolong their life.
- When not in use, wash, clean, air and store sealed in a polythene bag in a cool cupboard, and avoid crushing. If you've forgotten to wash them and they've become infested with moths, (see Moths page 239).
- Check the care label for cleaning details; most wool blankets should be dry cleaned. Some laundries and dry cleaners operate special blanket washing and cleaning services. Local addresses are available from the Textile Services Association (see Useful Addresses).
- Synthetic and cotton blankets can generally be machine washed but always check the label first. Make sure the dry blanket will fit in your washing machine. If hand washing, use the bath and remember the blanket will get heavier when wet and become bulky to handle.
- Dry naturally away from direct heat.

BLINDS

Austrian/Festoon

Vacuum with the upholstery tool. Occasionally wash or dry clean.

Roller

Vacuum with the upholstery tool or use a soft brush. If spongeable use an upholstery shampoo but avoid over-wetting. Alternatively, try a proprietary blind cleaner, available from department stores or specialist curtain shops.

Re-hang while still damp. If it doesn't wind properly, re-tension by pulling down the blind halfway. Remove from the brackets and rewind by hand. Pull down and repeat if necessary.

Venetian

Special brushes are available, or, alternatively, wearing cotton gloves, run your hands along both sides of the slats. Wash in the bath, avoiding immersing the operating mechanism, using a nylon scourer and a dilute detergent solution. Line the bath with a towel to prevent scratching. Rinse, shake off excess water and hang to dry.

BROCADE

Heavy, stiff fabric with a raised pattern on a plain background. Can be made from cotton, viscose, silk, acetate or a combination. Often used for soft furnishings and upholstery.

- Dry clean only.
- Iron on the reverse side with a cool iron.

BRODERIE ANGLAISE

Traditional open-work embroidered fabric or lace. Available in cotton or polyester cotton.

- Wash according to fabric type.
- Wash delicate pieces by hand or in a muslin bag in the machine to avoid other garments catching the embroidery.

CALICO

Plain, closely woven cotton. Generally unbleached and coarse.

- Wash as for cotton.

• To whiten unbleached calico, add a little white spirit to the first wash. Rinse thoroughly afterwards to remove the smell.

CAMBRIC

Traditionally a fine linen from France but now generally cotton. Often used for table linen and handkerchiefs.
• Wash as for cotton.
• To crispen its texture, use a spray starch when ironing or a liquid starch such as Dip, after washing.
• Easier to iron when damp; use the steam setting.

CANDLEWICK

Patterned, tufted fabric of cotton, nylon, polyester or viscose, used for bathmats, dressing gowns and bedspreads.
• Wash according to fibre type.
• Do not iron as this will flatten the pile.
• Shake frequently to maintain the appearance of the pile.

CANVAS

Stiff, coarse cotton used for strengthening tailored garments, and making tents, handbags and shoes.
• Sponge or scrub soiled areas with a stain-removal bar of household block soap. Rinse with cool water.

Shoes

Some will withstand washing in the machine. Use a low-temperature synthetics programme.
• If they become muddy, allow the mud to dry before brushing off.
• Use an upholstery shampoo or proprietary cleaner for fabric shoes.

CARPETS

(For specific stains look under the stain: see A–Z of Stain Removal, pages 352–363.)

Most carpets are now supplied with care instructions. If not, contact the National Carpet Cleaners' Association (see Useful Addresses) for advice.
• Vacuum regularly to remove embedded dust and grit which could damage the fibres, and keep the pile in good condition.
• Tackle stains and spills immediately.
• For spot cleaning use the lather from a solution of dry-foam shampoo, or use a carpet-spotting kit available from hardware and department stores.
• For all-over cleaning use:
– a carpet shampooer, manual or electric (can be hired) that dispenses dry-foam shampoo which forms a powder when dry, absorbing dirt. This is then vacuumed away.
– a steam cleaner (can be hired) that sprays hot water and a cleansing agent under pressure into the carpet and then extracts it immediately together with any dirt.
– a three-in-one-type cleaner. These will vacuum, shampoo and pick up water spills. Water and a cleansing agent are sprayed on to the carpet and immediately sucked back up together with any dirt. All these machines can be hard work to use and results are variable.
• For stubborn staining it's worth having a carpet professionally cleaned. Choose a cleaner who is a member of the National Carpet Cleaners' Association (NCCA) (see Useful Addresses). Members have training in all the different techniques of carpet cleaning and will advise on the best cleaning method for your problem. However, do get several quotes and compare advice.
If you have a problem with the cleaner, the

NCCA has an arbitration scheme. Contact the organisation and it will put you in touch with their Standards and Fair Trading Officer.

- Raise the pile of crushed carpet by covering the area with a damp cloth. Apply a hot iron carefully. When dry, brush up to lift the pile.

CASHMERE

Light, soft and warm wool made from the Kashmir goat.

- Always hand wash. Treat as for wool.

CHENILLE

Heavy fabric of cotton, viscose, wool or silk with soft velvety pile. Often used for furnishing.

- Wash according to fabric type or dry clean.

CHIFFON

Finely woven sheer fabric from cotton, silk or man-made fibres.

- Wash according to fibre type, or dry clean.
- Handle with care and do not wring or spin.
- Iron gently while damp using a cool iron.

CHINTZ

Tightly woven cotton, generally with a flowery design used for furnishing fabrics. Some chintzes have a chemical glazed finish.

- Avoid using glazed chintz in any areas very prone to dirt because continual cleaning will remove the glaze.
- Dry clean only. The finish can wash off and fade. Once this goes it cannot be re-built. Some companies offer special cleaning for chintz. Contact The Textile Services Association (see Useful Addresses) for details of cleaners offering this service.

COIR MATTING

Slightly hairy fibre from the coconut husk used for natural floor coverings. Some floor coverings can be treated with a stain inhibition treatment which slows down the penetration of spillages.

- Vacuum regularly with a suction-only-type cleaner (cylinder) to keep it dust free.
- Treat stains immediately. Spills on treated flooring can be mopped up with absorbent paper or a sponge, and wiped over with clean warm water.

CONTINENTAL QUILTS

See Duvets, page 337

CORDUROY

Includes needlecord and jumbocord.

Cotton or synthetic-mix woven ribbed fabric. Used for garments and upholstery.

- Wash using a synthetics programme with minimum spin.
- If washing garments such as trousers, turn inside out.
- Iron on the reverse side, while damp, using the steam setting.
- Brush up the pile gently.

CREPE DE CHINE

Lightweight, slippery fabric traditionally made from silk but now mostly from synthetics such as polyester.

- Hand wash according to fibre type. Cold rinse and roll in a towel to remove moisture.
- Iron on a cool setting.
- If washing pure silk, soak in cold water first.

CURTAINS

The type of cleaning and treatment required depends on the type of fabric. Some can be washed; others *must* be dry cleaned. Often, though, it's not just the fabric type but the weight and size which will make washing impossible. Remember that whatever the fabric, dirty curtains will eventually rot and need to be replaced.

- Brush down monthly using the upholstery nozzle of the vacuum cleaner or a soft, long-handled brush.
- Curtains should be thoroughly cleaned every few years.
- As a general rule the following fabrics should be dry cleaned only: velvet, velours, chenilles, tapestries and brocades, all fabrics containing wool or silk, and all interlined curtains.
- Remove all hooks and curtain weights and loosen the heading tape. Let down the hem if the fabric is likely to shrink. Shake them first to remove dust.
- Soak curtains made of washable fabrics in cold water first. Then wash carefully, according to the type of fabric. Make sure, if hand washing, that the detergent is thoroughly dissolved before putting the curtains in.
- Do not rub or wring. Rinse thoroughly. Squeeze out as much water as possible, or use a short spin.
- If machine washing, use a programme specifically for delicates.
- Iron the curtains while they are still damp. Work lengthways, on the wrong side, stretching the fabrics gently to avoid puckering of the seams.
- Clean curtain tracks, windows and sills before re-hanging.
- For care of net curtains, see Net, page 341.

DAMASK

Heavy woven fabric with shiny thread. Silk, cotton, viscose or a combination. Used for table linen, soft furnishings and upholstery.

- Wash according to fibre type.
- Dry clean heavier items.

DENIM

Hard-wearing, twilled cotton fabric.

- If not pre-shrunk, use a cool wash.
- Turn inside out and wash separately, as the colour runs even after several washes.
- Iron using the maximum or steam setting while still damp.

DRALON

Trade name for an acrylic-fibre, velvet-type, furnishing fabric.

- Brush or vacuum upholstery and soft furnishings regularly. Brush against the lay of the pile to raise it, then in the other direction.
- Curtains should be dry cleaned at temperatures below 120°F/50°C. Do not iron, but hang immediately to avoid creasing.
- Do not over-wet Dralon upholstery, because this is often woven on to a cotton or cotton/synthetic backing which could shrink and distort the surface.
- Clean using a dry-foam upholstery shampoo.
- Remove water-based stains by immediate and thorough blotting, followed by sponging with a weak solution of biological detergent. Work in the pile direction. Rinse and blot dry.
- For other stains, try acetone applied with cotton wool.
- If in doubt, have it professionally treated.
- Do not apply heat as the fibres will melt.

DUVETS

These can have natural feather and down fillings, or polyester, eg hollowfibre.

- Should not require frequent cleaning.
- Air frequently in order to keep the filling fluffy and dry.
- Shake occasionally to redistribute the filling.
- Store in a cool place; on a spare bed is ideal, but if it must be put away, fold it loosely.
- Mop up spills immediately to avoid them soaking through the filling. If the casing has become stained, ease the filling away from that area and tie it off from the rest of the cover with an elastic band or string. Sponge this area first with cold water and then with a mild detergent solution. For stubborn marks, soak in a biological detergent solution.
- Unless specified, washing is recommended over dry cleaning, whatever the filling. Before washing, check there are no holes or weak points in the casing. Repair and patch the casing where necessary.
- Use a launderette machine, as domestic ones are too small even for single duvets. Dose with one-third the usual amount of detergent.
- Wash children's smaller duvets using a wool programme with a short spin. Line dry or dry in a launderette-sized tumble drier on the cool setting.
- Dry thoroughly and leave to air for a day.
- For companies offering commercial cleaning of duvets contact the Textile Services Association (see Useful Addresses).

ELASTANES/LYCRA

These are a synthetic alternative to rubber. They keep their elasticity well and resist attack from perspiration and suntan lotions. Often in blends with other fabrics, between 2 per cent and 20 per cent.

- Machine wash at low temperatures using a delicates programme.
- Alternatively, hand wash in warm water, rinse, and use a short spin or roll in a towel.
- Do not iron or tumble dry.

ELECTRIC BLANKETS

There are only a few companies who still manufacture under- and over-blankets. They carry out servicing and may offer cleaning services.

- Always check the manufacturer's instructions first.
- Some may be washable. Use a little washing-up liquid and water on a sponge, avoiding over-wetting.
- Dry completely. To freshen up, use a little talcum powder and then brush it away with a clothes brush. Never re-use the blanket until completely dry.
- Never have them dry cleaned. The internal wires may be disturbed.
- Clean and service every three years.
- Dreamland Appliances Ltd (see Useful Addresses) service and repair their own models of blanket only.
- Warmabed Ltd (see Useful Addresses) service and clean their own and other manufacturers' models (under-blankets only).
- Warmalux (see Useful Addresses) service and repair their own under-blankets only.
- Johnson and Calverley (*see* Useful Addresses) will repair and service any make of over- or under-blanket and electric duvet.

EMBROIDERY

- Silks and wools used for this type of work are frequently not colourfast. Check by pressing a wad of white cotton fabric against the stitches and ironing over it gently, in a hidden area.

- Dry clean if not colourfast, otherwise hand wash and treat as wool.
- If the piece is valuable, contact the Royal School of Needlework (see Useful Addresses), who offer a restoration service.

FELT

Thick, non-woven material made from matted wool fibres.

- Dry clean, as it shrinks and is not always colourfast.

FLANNEL

Woven wool or wool and cotton blend. Mainly used for suitings.

- Dry clean tailored and expensive garments. Otherwise, treat as wool.

FUR

Includes natural and synthetic.

Natural

- Have cleaned regularly by a professional.
- Put expensive furs into cold storage during warm weather.
- Do not cover in polythene: store in a cotton bag in the wardrobe.
- Hangers should be padded.
- Allow air to circulate between the fur and other garments in the wardrobe.
- Shake before wearing.

Synthetic

Made from polyamide, viscose, cotton, acrylic or polyester.

- Cotton and viscose should be dry cleaned.
- Wash others as polyamide, and shake well before allowing to dry naturally.
- For light soiling, sponge the area with a warm solution of non-biological washing powder, rinse and towel dry.
- Brush straight-pile fabric while it is still damp. Curly pile should never be brushed while damp.
- Between washings, brush the pile with a medium to hard brush.

GABERDINE

Made from wool, cotton or either of these, blended with man-made fibres. The woven fabric has fine diagonal ribs.

Often used for suits, coats, trousers, etc.

- Dry clean only.

GEORGETTE

Fine, sheer fabric from cotton, silk, wool or man-made fibres.

- Dry clean natural fabrics.
- Wash man-made fabrics according to fabric type.

GINGHAM

Checked or striped fabric typically made in bright colours and white, from cotton or polyester-cotton.

- Wash according to fibre type after testing for colour fastness.
- Steam iron while damp.

GOATSKIN

Rugs should always be professionally cleaned because the hairs become brittle and break away from the base if washed. Coats are specially treated to avoid this.

GROSGRAIN

Fine, ribbed fabric of silk or man-made blends.
- Wash according to fibre type, or dry clean.

JERSEY

Stretchy knitted fabric of wool, silk, cotton or man-made fibres.
- Wash according to fibre type or dry clean.
- Short spin.
- Dry flat and pull to shape while wet.
- Steam iron on the reverse side to avoid the surface becoming shiny.

LACE

Cotton, polyester, polyamide or a combination.
- Wash according to fibre type.
- Use a gentle non-biological powder.
- If washing in a machine, first place in a muslin bag or a pillowcase.
- Iron while damp, on the wrong side, pulling to shape.

Antique lace

- Wash by hand, using a mild detergent which does not contain fluorescers, and dry flat.
- Delicate pieces should be pinned on to a padded board covered with cotton sheeting, sponged with a mild detergent solution and then rinsed with cold water.
- Precious items should be dry cleaned; or consult the Royal School of Needlework (see Useful Addresses).

LAMBSWOOL

See Wool, page 349

LEATHER

Chamois

- Hand wash in a warm soap-flake solution and squeeze in the water to release the dirt.
- Rinse once in a warm water solution to which 1tsp/5ml of olive oil has been added, to retain a soft texture.
- Squeeze out moisture and pull to shape.
- Hang to dry, away from direct heat. Scrunch up the leather during drying to maintain its flexibility.
- Store damp in a polythene bag.

Leather clothing

Leather clothing described as washable can only be sponged, so do not immerse it in water.
- New or newly cleaned clothes should be treated with a waterproof spray such as Meltonian Protector.
- A scarf around the neck will prevent grease marks on leather collars.
- All leather clothing should be professionally cleaned every three to four years, including re-tinting and re-oiling. Contact the Textile Care Association for details (see Useful Addresses).
- Skins are stretched during manufacture so will contract with cleaning. These should stretch out when worn again but don't buy a very tight-fitting garment just in case.
- If it does get wet wipe over with a clean cloth and allow to dry naturally.
- Remove surface soiling from washable leathers with a soapy sponge (use glycerine soap or soap flakes). Then wipe with a clean damp cloth and hang to dry.
- When not in use store in a cotton cover, not plastic, in a cupboard, using a padded hanger.
- Treat the garment occasionally with an application of hide food.

Leather furniture

Always check manufacturers' care instructions first because some leather should not be wetted.

Dust leather furniture regularly and give it an accasional application of hide food (available from specialist outlets or department stores) to prevent the leather from drying out and to protect against stains. Try to site furniture away from direct heat, such as radiators, which can encourage cracking. Remove all-over grime by wiping over with a soft damp cloth. For obvious staining have the item professionally cleaned.

Leather gloves

- Wash in a warm soap-flake solution whilst on your hands. Rub together gently. Remove and allow to dry naturally.
- When nearly dry, pop them back on to restore their shape.
- Do not rinse doeskin gloves as the soap keeps them supple. After washing, press between two towels to remove excess moisture and dry naturally.

Reptile skin

- Dust shoes and handbags regularly.
- Occasionally, apply a special reptile dressing or hide food, rubbing it in the direction of the scales.

Shoes and handbags

- When new, apply a waterproof protector spray.
- Before polishing, wipe the leather over with Mars Oil NonScratch Cleaning sponge (see Useful Addresses).
- Clean shoes regularly with recommended shoe polishes which will clean and maintain the dye colour. They will also cover scuff marks.
- If shoes get really wet, allow them to dry out at room temperature in a well-ventilated spot. Stuff them with paper to help retain the shape or use a shoe tree. Never dry in front of a radiator as it could crack the leather.
- Handbags need similar care, but less often. Do not use pigmented polishes as they will rub off on to clothing.
- To remove grease and oils from speciality leathers use a rubber adhesive which will absorb the grease. Coat the stain with a thin layer and leave on for 24 hours, then roll the adhesive off. Treat with hide food. Alternatively, try Meltonians Grease and Tar Remover (see Useful Addresses).

Patent leather

- If patent leather becomes very cold it will crack.
- Dust with a soft cloth and apply patent-leather dressing when looking dull and lifeless.
- If the item is only used occasionally, apply a thin layer of petroleum jelly or Vaseline all over and wipe off before use.
- Always use shoe trees or stuff with a wedge of paper.

LINEN

Woven fabric from flax fibres. The sign of good linen is creasing.

- Hot wash and spin dry. Hang drying is preferable because it will remove some of the creasing.
- Some garments have special finishes applied to minimise creasing, and these should be dry cleaned.
- Iron while still damp on the reverse side, to prevent shining. Use a hot steam iron.
- Stored table linen can become soiled along the crease marks. Rub a stain-removal bar along the dampened lines before washing.

LYCRA

See Elastanes

MATTRESSES

It's worth buying separate mattress covers which are removed for washing.

Spring interior

- Turn over or swing round to reverse head and foot frequently when new, then quarterly after several months. This helps the filling to settle.
- Occasionally, brush the mattress and base to remove fluff and dust. Don't vacuum or it may dislodge the filling.

Foam

- Foam mattresses with a layered construction should never be turned.
- Single-layered mattresses should be turned monthly.
- Use the crevice tool on the vacuum cleaner.

METALLIC YARN

Includes lamé and woven brocade-type fabrics which contain a metallic thread.

- Dry clean.

MICROFIBRES

These are fabrics made from ultrafine polyester or polyamide yarns. Air pockets become trapped between the fibres making the fabrics soft with good draping characteristics.

- Follow care-label instructions.
- Machine wash using a 100°F/40°C wash programme. Minimum spin.
- Warm or steam iron.

MILIUM

Metallic-coated fabric used for its insulating properties, particularly in curtain linings and ironing boards. If making curtains the metallic side should face inwards.

- Dry clean.

MOHAIR

Light woven fabric made from hair of the Angora goat, often mixed with other fibres.

- Hand wash and treat as wool.

MOIRE

Traditionally made from silk, but now often from synthetics. Heavy weights are used for furnishings and lighter weights for ball gowns.

- Watermarked surface is easily damaged by water, so dry clean only.
- Do not use a steam iron.

MUSLIN

Open weave, loosely woven, sheer cotton.

- Hand wash in warm water.
- Do not spin and dry flat.
- Iron carefully while damp with a medium setting.

NET

Loosely woven mesh fabric made from a variety of fibres such as polyester, cotton and polyamide. Mostly used for curtaining or underskirts.

- Wash net curtains frequently because they tend to hold on to dirt once soiled.
- Wash separately in hot water (but do not exceed the recommended washing and drying

temperatures or they will become permanently creased), followed by a cold rinse.
- Use a proprietary whitener, for greying polyester, available from department or hardwear stores. Alternatively, try soaking in biological detergent.
- Hand wash dress net in warm water. Rinse, drip dry and iron with a cool iron.

NUBUCK

Made from cow leather like suede but is buffed to a finer velvet pile.
- Use specialist nubuck and calf-leather cleaners which are solvent based, eliminating the need to brush as they evaporate.
- Do not use suede shampoos (which are water based) or brushes as they will damage the pile.

NYLON

See Polyamide, below right

PATENT LEATHER

See Leather, page 340

PERCALE

A finely woven cotton or cotton-polyester blend, often used in bedding. Can be glazed.
- Wash according to fibre type.

PILLOWS

Natural filling
- Air regularly outside in summer.
- Do not have them dry cleaned as it is difficult to remove all the toxic fumes from them.
- Can be washed in a washing machine. Check first that the machine will take the weight as pillows can be heavy when wet. Must be spin dried to remove as much moisture as possible.
- Dry thoroughly, or the pillow will start to smell and the feathers will be damaged. Hang outside and shake occasionally. It may take several days to dry.
- Air thoroughly before re-using.
- If possible, have them professionally cleaned. The feathers are removed and sterilised with ultraviolet light and the old pillowcase is replaced with a new one.

Polyester/Hollowfibre
- Machine wash using the wool programme and about a third of the normal quantity of detergent.
- Spin, then tumble dry.

Foam
- Sponge in warm soapy water, about once a year.
- Rinse well and remove excess water with absorbent towel.
- Do not wring, and dry away from direct heat and sunlight.

POLYAMIDE

Usedto be known as nylon.

Lightweight and non-absorbent man-made fibre; elastic and strong even when wet; flame resistant.
- Wash in hand hot water, or 100°F/40°C delicates programme; cold rinse, short spin and drip dry.
- It absorbs dye very easily so wash separately from coloureds if possible.
- Whites become grey quickly, particularly if washed in water that is too hot.
- Wash pleated and delicate items after each

use because once soiling occurs it is difficult to remove.
- Use fabric conditioner to reduce static.
- Do not bleach or expose to direct heat or sunlight.
- Inherently crease resistant, but if it does need ironing use a cool setting. Do not iron pleated nylon.

POLYESTER

Versatile synthetic fibre. Will not shrink, stretch, fade or crease. Often combined with cotton because of its easy-care properties.
- Wash using the 100°F/40 or 120°F/50°C synthetics programme with a short spin.
- Can be tumble dried.
- Prone to static, so use a fabric conditioner in the final rinse.
- Grease stains are very difficult to remove from polyester so treat immediately by soaking in a biological powder.
- Do not wash over 120°F/50°C as it will crease badly when plunged into cold water.
- Whites have a tendency to grey or yellow.
- Cannot be home dyed successfully, but can be professionally treated.
- Hand wash pleated items and drip dry.

POPLIN

Closely woven cotton, viscose, silk or wool.
- Wash according to fibre type.

PVC

Polyvinylchloride: a strong plastic material or coating. Used for upholstery, tablecloths, shower curtains, etc.
- Sponge marks off upholstery with warm water. Use a dilute solution of washing-up liquid for all-over soiling.
- Where applicable, hand wash in warm water and drip dry.
- Do not apply heat as it will soften and melt.
- Do not dry clean.
- Shoes should be wiped clean and dried away from direct heat.

QUILTS

See Duvets, page 337

RAINWEAR

Includes garments that are completely impermeable to slightly showerproof cotton coats.
- Check care label as some items can be machine washed.
- Bulky items and those with protective finishes should be dry cleaned only. Some dry cleaners offer a re-proofing service: contact the Textile Services Association (see Useful Addresses).
- Rubberised macs such as riding coats should be scrubbed with a soft brush and detergent solution. Wipe with a damp cloth and dry with a towel.

RUSH MATTING

Hand-plaited strips of rush which are sewn together.
- Vacuum as regularly as carpet.
- Treat stains with a solution of warm water and washing soda. Occasionally scrub over the matting with soap and warm water.
- Lift occasionally and vacuum underneath.

SATIN

Lustrous, smooth fabric with a short nap made from silk, cotton, polyester, polyamide or

acetate. Used for dress fabrics, linings and lingerie.
- Wash lightweight satins according to the fibre type.
- Iron while still damp until dry, on the reverse side.
- Acetate satin will spot if sprinkled with water so do not dry clean.
- Dry clean heavier weights.

SEAGRASS MATTING

Seagrass is grown in paddy-like fields and needs a flooding of seawater during the crop cycle. It is spun into strands. It is naturally stain resistant and dye resistant so excellent for tough natural floor coverings.
- Vacuum regularly.
- Sponge up any spills.

SHANTUNG

Originally a term for slubbed Chinese silk; now also made from acetate or polyamide.
- Wash according to fabric type.

SHEEPSKIN

Coats

- Have professionally cleaned regularly.
- When new, or just after cleaning, apply a protective spray to help prevent marking.
- Wear a scarf around the neck to prevent grease marks. If these do occur the wool side can be freshened by using a dry shampoo for hair.
- To clean small areas of the skin use a suede cleaner. Test first.

Rugs

- Can be washed at home if the wool pile is quite short.

SHETLAND WOOL

See Wool, page 349

SHOWER CURTAINS

- To prevent the build-up of soap deposits, clean down after use by spraying with water.
- Leave the curtains drawn so air can circulate freely.
- If machine washable use the wool programme, adding detergent and bleach. Bulk out the load using old white towels.
- Add one cup of white vinegar to the final rinse water.
- Do not spin or iron.
- To remove mildew, see Mildew, page 359.

SILK

Lightweight, resilient, luxury fibre made from the cocoon of the silk worm. Weakened by sunlight and perspiration.
- Dry clean taffetas and brocades.
- Avoid biological detergents, heat and washing soda, which can damage silk fibres. Preferably, use a mild liquid detergent designed for hand washing.
- Do not rub or wring the fabric or the fibres break and produce a white, chalky effect.
- Wash garments after each wear or perspiration stains may become impossible to remove.
- Have other stains professionally removed. However, for fatty stains try a detergent designed for coloureds which contains lipase.
- Iron while still damp with a warm iron. Do not use a steam iron on silks as the water will leave marks.
- Silk is not very colourfast so after washing coloureds, to preserve the colour, soak the item

in a solution of 2tsp/10ml vinegar to 5 pints/3 litres water after the final rinse. Leave for three minutes. Dry.

- Use the special detergents for coloureds with care because they weaken silk fibres.
- Printed silks should be dry cleaned.
- Never hand wash a garment labelled dry clean only. Some silks have a resin applied to give texture and body which may watermark if hand washed.
- Two-piece garments should be cleaned or washed together to avoid differential fading.
- Use a fabric conditioner in the final rinse to add softness.
- After rinsing, roll up in a clean dry towel and squeeze lightly to remove surplus water before ironing.

SISAL MATTING

Sisal is a fibre produced from the leaves of the *Agave sisalana* bush. It is soft and tough and available in a range of different weaves.

- Vacuum regularly except when wet or muddy.
- Lift occasionally to clean underneath.
- If necessary, clean very occasionally with a dry-foam shampoo, avoiding over-wetting.
- Dry naturally.
- Treat stains immediately as dried stains are difficult to remove. Some manufacturers will pre-treat with a stain inhibitor.

SOFT TOYS

- Wash frequently to avoid permanent soiling.
- Hand wash using a mild detergent solution. Rinse thoroughly.
- Wrap in a towel to soak up excess moisture, but avoid squeezing, to keep their shape.
- Hang by the feet to dry and air.

SUEDE

Clothes

- Washable suede does exist but is more expensive than ordinary suede.
- New or newly cleaned suede should be treated with a waterproof spray to prevent the colour rubbing off, and to provide a protective coating. Test first.
- Dirty or rain-spotted suede should be wiped over with a clean damp cloth and allowed to dry naturally.
- Brush up frequently with a wire brush or suede block.
- Proprietary suede cleaning cloths or blocks are useful for removing soiling along wear creases.
- For serious discoloration have the item professionally cleaned to restore both colour and oil.

Shoes

- Treat new shoes with a protective suede spray.
- Fading can be improved with an overall application of coloured suede dressing, generally available only in brown, navy, black and neutral.
- When necessary, clean with a nailbrush and clean soapy water. Rinse and blot dry.
- Proprietary cleaning products work well, but follow instructions carefully.
- If they get wet allow them to dry naturally, then use a rubber or nylon suede brush to remove dust and raise the pile.
- Scrape off mud while still wet and blot with a damp cloth.

TACTEL

See Microfibres, page 341

TAFFETA

Crisp, closely woven shiny material, made from a variety of fibres, including silk, acetate, viscose, polyester or polyamide.

- Dry clean.
- Iron on the reverse side.

TAPESTRY

- The Royal School of Needlework (see Useful Addresses) will restore valuable tapestry. Ring them for an appointment. Otherwise try the textile department of a museum.

TIES

Most are polyester, wool or silk.

- Stains on these fabrics are quite difficult to remove without leaving a ring mark, so spray new ties with a fabric protector. Try on the back first and leave to dry before doing the front.
- If stains do occur try a dry-cleaning spray, otherwise get professionally cleaned as laundering is rarely successful.
- To iron, position the tie wrong side up on the ironing board. Make sure the interlining is lying flat.
- Slip a cardboard shape inside the wide end of the tie so you press it without causing an imprint of the seam on the right side. Press over a damp cloth to avoid scorching.

TOWELLING

Looped pile fabric, usually made from cotton.

- Machine wash using a cotton programme.
- Dark colours should be washed separately.
- Nappies should be washed on a very hot wash. Add fabric conditioner to the final rinse.

TRAINERS

These are made from a multitude of materials, including plastic, leather, latex, canvas and other synthetic fabrics.

- After use, check the sole for thorns and grit, which could penetrate and damage the mid-sole.
- Rinse off mud after use, using the back of an old knife in the tread. Pack with newspaper and let them dry naturally at room temperature.
- Clean according to the manufacturer's advice; only machine wash if specifically recommended. Most should only be wiped over with a soft cloth soaked in a detergent solution.
- Don't leave shoes in bright sunshine or keep damp shoes in a bag.
- Occasionally, remove the in-sock and wash it in warm soapy water. Rinse and dry naturally.

TREVIRA

Trade name for polyester fabric.

TULLE

Fine, sheer net-like fabric of silk, cotton, viscose, polyamide or other fibres. Used on evening and bridal wear.

- Dry clean silk.
- For other fibres, hand wash following the instructions for fibre type.
- If cotton tulle becomes limp, starch it in a weak starch solution, such as Dip, or use spray starch when ironing.
- Nylon and viscose tulle can be stiffened with a gum arabic solution available from health food stores.

TWEED

A woven woollen fabric available in different weights. Imitations are also made in polyester and acrylic.

- Dry clean.

UPHOLSTERY

- All upholstery should be thoroughly dusted every week, using the brush attachment (on pile fabrics) and crevice tool of the vacuum cleaner.
- Upholstery should be positioned away from sunlight to avoid fading.
- Removable cushions should be turned weekly to ensure they get even wear and soiling.
- Clean all upholstery before it becomes heavily soiled, following the manufacturer's advice.
- Loose covers should be washed or dry cleaned according to the fabric type. Take care because they often shrink.
- If washed, place them back on the furniture before completely dry to re-shape and prevent shrinkage.
- Iron while they are in position, using a cool iron on foam furniture.
- If covers cannot be removed, have them professionally cleaned or clean them with an upholstery shampoo and spotting kit. Try on hidden areas first.
- Avoid over-wetting, particularly on Dralon (see Dralon, page 336).
- Always dry clean chenilles, tapestries, velours, velvets and fabrics containing silk, wool or viscose.

Leather

See Leather Furniture, page 340.

VELOUR

Pile fabric similar to velvet usually made of acrylic but may be other man-made fibres, cotton or silk.

- Dry clean or wash according to the fibre type.
- Iron with a cool iron on the reverse side of the fabric.

VELVET

Originally a silk or cotton cut-pile fabric. Now many velvets are made from viscose, polyamide, polyester, etc.

- Treat according to the fibre, or dry clean.
- Curtains, particularly cotton velvet, should be lined as they fade readily in sunlight.
- Dry clean curtains.
- Shake periodically while drying and smooth the pile with a soft cloth or velvet brush to restore the pile.
- Use steam to remove between-wear creases, eg hang over bath of steamy water.
- Iron velvet with pile face down on a soft cloth or towel.

VISCOSE

Also known as rayon, this is a cellulosic fibre made from the pulp of eucalyptus and spruce wood which is reacted with certain chemicals. It is used on its own, or in blends. Drapes well but creases easily so is sometimes treated with an easy-care finish.

- Wash with care at low temperatures because fibres are weak when wet. High temperatures will affect finish.
- To discourage creasing, use a short spin when washing, and do not wring.
- Iron on the steam setting while damp.

VIYELLA

Brand name for lightweight wool-and-cotton blend fabric.

- Hand wash in hand-hot water.
- Do not spin; remove water by squeezing gently or rolling in a towel.
- Warm iron on the reverse side while damp.

WAXED JACKETS

- Some brands can be cleaned by specialist companies, eg Nikwax (see Useful Addresses). They will clean and re-wax jackets, trousers, hoods and waistcoats.
- Barbour branded jackets can be re-waxed, repaired and re-proofed by the manufacturer, J Barbour (see Useful Addresses). Barbour does not recommend dry cleaning.

WEDDING DRESSES

This information also applies to accessories such as the veil and other special, occasional clothes such as christening gowns.

A wedding dress should be professionally dry cleaned before storing. Contact the Dry Cleaning Information Bureau (see Useful Addresses), who can give you specialist dry cleaners in your area. This should be done, even if the gown is not visibly dirty, since colourless stains such as alcohol, perfume and perspiration can develop and discolour as they react with the air. The discoloration cannot be removed.

FOLDING A WEDDING DRESS

- If practical, detach bulky or stiff underskirts and store separately.
- Line the base and sides of the box with overlapping layers of acid-free tissue.
- Start from the hem and work upwards.
- Fold in a concertina fashion, interleaving with layers of acid-free tissue.
- Place rolled layers of tissue along each of the folds.
- Insert tissue inside bodice, sleeves, shoulders and inside any bows.
- Finish with layers of tissue and cover with lid.

WARNING!

Never use ordinary plastic bags, PVC zip covers or cardboard boxes to store a wedding dress. Chemicals within these packaging materials can leach out over a period of time and cause the fabric to discolour. This reaction is accelerated if there is little air movement. Storing the dress in a wooden chest of drawers can have a similar effect. The yellow discoloration is permanent and cannot be removed.

For long-term storage, use an acid-reduced cardboard box and interleave the dress with acid-free tissue. These are available from Harry Berger (see Useful Addresses), although acid-free tissue is sold by department stores. Unlike conventional tissue or cardboard, the acid-free has been specially treated and doesn't contain harmful chemicals.

Don't be tempted to use an ordinary cardboard box with acid-free tissue paper since the chemicals from the cardboard can still leach through the tissue.

Place the box in a cool cupboard, away from damp, indirect heat or sunlight. Inspect the gown every 18 months to two years, re-folding the dress along slightly different lines to help prevent permanent creasing.

Vacuum packing: Another option is to have the dress vacuum packed. Jeeves of Belgravia (see Useful Addresses) offer a vacuum-packing service. The process involves storing the gown in a polythene bag which has had all the air removed and replaced with nitrogen, a bit like shrink wrapping ham. This prevents the oxidisation of stains and discoloration. Vacuum packing should 'preserve' the gown for at least 25 years.

However, bear in mind that you won't be able to remove the dress, since once the seal is broken, the preserving properties will be lost. The other disadvantage is that leaving the dress in a fixed position for so long can cause permanent creasing.

WOOL

Natural, versatile fibre used to manufacture woven fabrics and knitting yarns.

- Wash with care as it is easily spoiled. Wool has a coating of scales which work against each other if rubbed while wet, causing the fibres to shrink and felt. It stretches when wet but will never unfelt.
- Only machine wash if the label specifies that the item is machine washable wool. If so, use the special woollens programme, which has reduced agitation and a very short spin.
- Hand wash in warm water using a gentle detergent. Do not rub, wring or twist. If your washing machine has the option for washing woollens, a very short spin will not harm the fabric.
- Dry flat between two towels. Pull gently to the correct shape while still damp.
- Never tumble dry wool.
- Oiled wool such as Guernsey sweaters should be washed in warm water using well dissolved soap flakes as detergents will remove the oil. They can be re-oiled. Check with the manufacturer.
- If you have washed a woollen garment and it has shrunk, sometimes a gentle wash in hair shampoo will soften the fibres and allow you to pull it back to shape.

HOW TO TREAT STAINS

In these days of sophisticated cleaning substances, stains need not be an insoluble problem. With prompt and careful attention – detailed in the following pages – they can usually be readily removed.

TYPES OF STAINS

ABSORBED STAINS

These include liquid spillages such as tea, coffee, milk or beer which have been absorbed into a surface. Fresh stains can generally be removed from washable fabrics by rinsing out with warm water and washing as normal. If you can't wash immediately, leave to soak. Treat stubborn stains with a proprietary stain remover or bleach.

Sponge non-washable fabrics with warm water and blot dry.

BUILT-UP STAINS

Such as grease, nail varnish and paint. They do not normally penetrate the surface. Treat immediately to remove as much deposit as possible and then according to type.

COMPOUND STAINS

These penetrate the surface *and* leave a deposit, such as blood. Treat first as a built-up and then an absorbed stain. These sorts of stains will require a final laundering.

TEN GOLDEN RULES FOR SUCCESSFUL STAIN REMOVAL

1 Use stain-removal products with care and always read the instructions thoroughly. Wear rubber gloves if you have sensitive skin.

2 Before using any solvent or cleaner, check on a hidden area first. This is particularly necessary on synthetic fibres.

3 Test fabric for colourfastness by rubbing a white damp cloth repeatedly on a hidden area of the fabric. If the dye rubs on to the white fabric it is not colourfast, and should be treated with care.

4 Some fabrics react better to stain removal than others. Wool, for example, is very absorbent, so marks can become embedded and difficult to remove. Polyester, on the other hand, does not dye readily so colours from stains do not penetrate the fabric.

Delicate fabrics should always be professionally treated.

5 If you can't launder at once, try interim measures:

- Sprinkle talc on fresh, greasy stains.
- Sprinkle salt on coffee, fruit, wine and beetroot, to absorb the colour and moisture (but not on carpets).
- Rinse non-greasy stains with cold water.

6 Washable fabrics should be machine washed using as high a temperature as the fabric will allow.

7 Protein stains should be soaked in cool water first to avoid setting the stain.

8 Small repeated applications work better than totally saturating the stain.

9 If coloured traces remain after treating a stain, dab with methylated spirits (except on acetate fabrics) until clear.

10 Dry clean-only fabrics should be professionally treated, or for small areas follow the directions for upholstery.

TREATING STAINS

Whatever the stain, act quickly to prevent permanent staining and odour. Blot up any excess, using absorbent paper, or scrape off with a palette knife.

Work from the outside inwards to avoid spreading the stain, holding white absorbent paper on the top side. Dab rather than rub, using a white cloth or cotton wool.

Several small applications are better than totally soaking the stain.

SOLVENT SAFETY

- Wear rubber gloves.
- Always ensure solvents are kept away from children because many of the substances are toxic and highly flammable.
- Never smoke or use solvents in a room where an open fire or radiant heater is burning. Turn off any pilot lights.
- When using solvents, always open a window if possible or leave the door open, because some give off toxic fumes.

STAIN-REMOVAL KIT

It's worth keeping a few essential remedies at the ready. Label clearly and do not decant into different containers, such as squash bottles, which could encourage children to open them.

The following are the most useful items to help with stain removal. Most are available from chemists, hardware or department stores.

Absorbent materials

Include a selection of clean white cotton cloth, cotton wool, paper towels, cotton wool buds, soft brush and sponge.

Ammonia

Will remove certain water-based stains and neutralise acid marks. Always use diluted with cold water, and in a well-ventilated room. Test on coloured fabrics because dyes can bleed.

Biological detergent

These contain enzymes which break down specific stains such as protein (blood, egg, milk, etc) and fat. They have improved so much in recent years that many stains will be removed just by normal washing.

Use as a pre-wash for soaking heavy stains. Ensure detergent is thoroughly dissolved before immersing fabrics.

Do not use on protein fibres such as wool and silk, or on non-colourfast or flame-resistant fabrics.

Glycerine

Used for lubricating and softening stains, making it easier to remove. Dilute with equal parts warm water and rub into the fabric. Leave for about an hour and then rinse or sponge with warm water.

Hydrogen peroxide

Mild oxidising bleach. For fabric stain removal use the 20-vol strength and dilute this with one part to six parts of cold water. Soak fabrics for around 30 minutes.

It will fade coloured fabrics. Do not use on polyamide or flame-resistant fabrics.

Methylated spirits

Used for removing oil-based stains and dyes. Use neat, dabbed on to the area with cotton wool. If using on coloured fabrics always try on a hidden area first.

Not recommended for use on acetates, but check first.

Other solvents

For grease use a spirit, eg vodka, surgical spirits, turpentine, lighter fluid or white spirit.

For water-based stains use caustic soda, sodium bicarbonate, Milton, or dilute hydrochloric acid.

Pre-wash products

These proprietary products are designed to be used on heavily soiled and stained areas, on washable white and colourfast fabric. They either break down or soften soiling ready for washing, and eliminate the need for pre-soaking and scrubbing.

They are most effective on grease stains but less so on protein- and dye-based stains.

Proprietary stain removers

These can be general or very specific. Always follow the manufacturers' instructions very closely. Recommended brands include Stain Devils, Mykal DeSolvit, Dabitoff and The Stain Slayer.

Spotting kits, available for upholstery and carpets, include a selection of chemicals for removing different stains.

White vinegar or acetic acid

Good for removing water-based stains. Always wash out thoroughly after applying.

A – Z OF STAIN REMOVAL

ADHESIVES

Work quickly and scrape off any excess deposit. Stain-removal advice is generally given on the packaging, or contact the manufacturer direct. Several of the manufacturers have specific products for removing their glues.

ALL-PURPOSE HOUSEHOLD

Carpets and Fabrics

Dab area with acetone until glue is dissolved. Launder where possible.

CONTACT ADHESIVE

These harden on contact so speed is essential. Treat as all-purpose adhesives.

EPOXY RESIN

These consist of two parts: a glue and a hardener, and once mixed and hardened they are nearly impossible to remove. Before they set, use acetone or methylated spirits to remove any residue.

Carpets and fabrics

Before it dries, dab with cellulose thinners, methylated spirits, or lighter fuel on synthetic fibres. Once dry the glue cannot be removed except by cutting away the pile.

PAPER ADHESIVE AND LATEX

Carpets

Pick off any residue before treating. Dab area with a dilute detergent solution, and avoid over-wetting if possible. Rinse and dab dry.

Fabrics

Remove as much residue as possible. Dried adhesive will wash out as normal. If any greasy marks remain try Stain Devils Glue and Chewing Gum Stain Remover.

SUPER GLUE

Skin
Use special remover from manufacturer, eg Bostik's Skin Release Agent or Loctite's Detach, or immerse in hot soapy water to soften it.

Carpets and fabrics
Try dabbing with acetone or use one of the proprietary glue removers as above.

WATER-SOLUBLE ANIMAL AND FISH GLUES

Carpets and Fabrics
Usually soluble in cold water. If not, try dabbing with household ammonia. Rinse thoroughly. If not removed, apply liquid detergent and rinse.

ANIMAL STAINS

BLOOD

See Blood

EXCRETA, VOMIT AND URINE

Carpets
Scrape away or blot up excess carefully to avoid spreading further. Flush the area with a solution of sodium bicarbonate or sponge with warm water. Blot dry. Clean and deodorise the area with a proprietary pet stain remover such as Bissell 'Not on the Carpet' Accident Cleaner, Secto Enz Stain (available from hardware and pet stores, or see Useful Addresses), Shaws Pet Stain Remover (pet stores and mail order, see Useful Addresses). Shampoo the carpet if necessary and blot dry.

Fabrics and upholstery
Scrape away any deposit and blot dry. If it is not possible to remove the area, isolate and gather up the area by tying string tightly around it. Rinse under cold running water or treat with a pet stain remover such as Shaws Pet Stain Remover or Secto Enz Stain (see below left).

BALLPOINT PEN

Fabrics and upholstery
Dab gently with cotton wool moistened with hydrogen peroxide solution (one part 20-vol peroxide to six parts cold water). Machine wash if possible. If it is unsuccessful contact the manufacturer for advice, or dry clean.

Suede
Rub gently with abrasive paper or a suede-cleaning block such as Swade Aid. Alternatively, seek professional advice.

Vinyl upholstery, wall coverings and bags
Must be treated immediately or cannot be removed. Scrub with warm detergent solution using an old nail brush.

BEER

Carpets
Clean with proprietary carpet shampoo or carpet spotting kit available from department stores. Alternatively, try a proprietary stain remover such as Carpet Devils No 3 followed by a carpet shampoo. On old stains try dabbing with methylated spirits.

Washable fabrics
Should be removed by machine washing with a biological detergent. For dried stains soak in a warm washing soda or a proprietary pre-wash detergent solution. Wash as normal using as hot a wash as possible.

Upholstery and non-washable fabrics

Blot and wipe with warm water. Dried stains can be treated with a white vinegar solution (one part vinegar to five parts water) and then with clear water. Blot to dry.

BEETROOT

Table linen

Sponge immediately with cold water and soak overnight if possible. Then wash using a biological detergent. For stubborn dried stains try Stain Devils Fruit and Wine Stain Remover or Mykal DeSolvIt 2.

BIRD DROPPINGS

Washing on the line

Scrape off the deposit and then wash the items again, as normal.

If stains persist on white or colourfast fabrics (not polyamide) immerse all the items in a hydrogen peroxide solution (one part 20-vol peroxide to six parts cold water). Wash and then rinse thoroughly.

Canvas and awnings

Allow to dry thoroughly and then brush off with a stiff brush. If marks remain, dip brush in a biological detergent solution and rub area. Hose down and rinse well.

BLACKCURRANT JUICE

Also applies to other dark berry fruits.

Carpets

Blot up as much as possible, while still wet, with absorbent paper. Rub with a stain-removing bar and shampoo the area. Remove any remaining stain with Carpet Devils No 3 and then shampoo.

Fabrics

Rinse under cold water. Pre-soak in a solution of washing soda followed by machine washing at 120°F/50°C using a biological detergent. Treat dried stains with Stain Devils Fruit and Wine Stain Remover followed by washing. If stubborn stains persist on whites, try bleaching with dilute household bleach. Rinse thoroughly.

Upholstery

Sponge with cold water and blot dry. Dab dark, dried stains with a hydrogen peroxide solution (one part 20-vol peroxide to six parts water).

BLEACH

Carpets and fabrics

Neutralise with soapy water. Blot up excess with a sponge, and rinse. Blot dry. Wash if possible.

BLOOD

Carpets

Sponge fresh stains with cold water and blot dry. If staining remains, shampoo the area. Dried stains will need professional treatment: contact the National Carpet Cleaners' Association (see Useful Addresses) for recommended cleaners in your area.

Bedding and washable fabrics

Sponge with cold salt water. Machine wash using a biological detergent and a wash temperature of at least 120°F/50°C. Pre-soak dried stains using a pre-wash detergent or washing soda followed by washing as above.

Mattresses

Dried stains are difficult to remove. Tip the mattress on its side to prevent penetration and sponge with cold salt water. Blot thoroughly.

Treat with the foam from a carpet or upholstery shampoo. Rinse and blot dry.

Non-washable fabrics and upholstery

Brush away surface deposit and sponge with cold water. Rinse and blot to dry. For stubborn stains try an upholstery spotting kit or have professionally cleaned.

CANDLE WAX

Carpets

Scrape off excess deposit. Remove the remainder by placing a sheet of brown or absorbent kitchen paper over the area and iron gently. Do not let the iron touch the pile as it may scorch and melt. Continue until all the wax has been absorbed. Keep moving the paper around for maximum absorption. Clear any remaining colour or stain using methylated spirits or Carpet Devils No 1.

Table linen and washable fabrics

Scrape away surface deposit using the back of a blunt knife. Place clean absorbent paper on both sides of the stain and melt out remaining wax using a warm iron. Launder as normal using a hot wash if possible.

Upholstery

Melt out using a moderately hot iron and white absorbent paper. Remove any remaining colour by dabbing with methylated spirits. On pile fabrics try removing the deposit by rubbing lightly with a cloth, or melt out by placing the absorbent paper on the pile and ironing the reverse side if possible.

Wooden surfaces

Chip away at the wax, when hard, using a fingernail or plastic spatula. Remove remaining film with a duster and polish as normal. If heat marking has occurred rub along the grain with a metal polish.

CHEWING GUM

Carpets

Hold a plastic bag of ice cubes on the area to harden the gum. Pick off as much deposit as possible. Remove any remaining marks using a proprietary stain remover such as Mykal DeSolvIt 1 or The Stain Slayer.

Fabrics

Harden the deposit as above or place in the freezer and pick off the deposit. Remove any remains with The Stain Slayer, rubbing in gently until the stain dissolves.

Upholstery

Remove excess deposit and treat with Stain Devils Glue and Chewing Gum Stain Remover. If a greasy residue remains, try Dabitoff.

CHOCOLATE AND COCOA

Carpets

Blot or scrape up any excess deposit using a blunt knife. Treat the stained area with carpet shampoo or a carpet spotting kit.

Treat any remaining stain with a proprietary stain remover such as Dabitoff or Carpet Devils No 2. Follow by shampooing the carpet in the normal way.

Fabrics

Scrape off excess deposit using the back of a knife blade. Soak in a solution of washing soda or proprietary pre-wash detergent, followed by machine washing at 120°F/50°C using a biological detergent.

Upholstery
Blot or scrape up any deposit with the back of a knife. Use a proprietary stain remover such as Carpet Devils No 2, rinse and blot to dry.

COFFEE

Carpets
Flush fresh stains with cold water and blot well to dry. Dried stains should be treated with Bissell Carpet Shampoo or Mykal De-Solv-It 2.

Fabrics
Soak in a warm solution of washing soda or pre-wash detergent followed by washing at 120°F/50°C using a biological detergent.

Upholstery
Sponge with cold water followed by treating with Carpet Devils No 4 or 1001 carpet spray, and then shampoo.

CURRY

Carpets
Small areas can be treated with Carpet Devils No 1 followed by shampooing. Large stains should be professionally cleaned.

Fabrics
Fresh stains will respond to sponging with a detergent solution before and after dabbing with Dabitoff. Machine wash. Treat dried stains on white and colourfast fabrics with a hydrogen peroxide solution (one part 20-vol peroxide to six parts water). Machine wash. Non-washable fabrics should be dry cleaned.

Upholstery
Dampen the stain and treat with a stain-removing soap bar. Alternatively, have professionally treated.

DYES

Carpets, upholstery, non-washable fabrics
Should be professionally treated.

Washable Fabrics
Soak in a cold-water solution of washing soda or proprietary pre-wash detergent to avoid setting in the dye. Machine wash using a biological detergent. Alternatively, on whites, try Beckmann Colour Run Remover or Dylon Colour Run Remover (also suitable for colourfast fabrics). Beckmann In-wash Colour Run Remover can be used in a washing machine on a 140°F/60°C wash and therefore eliminates soaking.

EGG

Carpets
Scrape to remove as much deposit as possible. Treat with Carpet Devils No 2 followed by shampooing.

Fabrics
Rinse through with cold salt water. Soak and wash using a biological detergent.

Upholstery
Scrape off surface deposit and sponge with cold salt water, then clear water. Blot dry. Treat with Stain Devils Blood and Milk Stain Remover.

FATS, GREASE AND OIL

Carpets
First, using an iron, blot up as much as

possible. Treat with a stain remover such as Mykal De-Solv-It 1 or Carpet Devils No 1 followed by shampooing.

Fabrics
Wash in as hot a wash if possible using a biological detergent containing lipase. If a hot wash cannot be used, try Mykal De-Solv-It 1 followed by washing.

Upholstery
Spread French Chalk or talcum powder over small marks on pale fabrics. Leave for several hours and then brush off. If marks remain, try Mykal De-Solv-It 1. Sponge with water and blot dry.

FELT-TIP PEN

Fabrics and upholstery
Blot up as much as possible while still wet with absorbent paper. Treat with Stain Devils Felt Tip Pen Stain Remover followed by washing or sponging.

FOUNDATION CREAM

Fabrics
Clear away any surface deposit. Soak using a pre-wash detergent and then machine wash at 120°F/50°C with a biological powder containing lipase. Stain Devils Grease and Oil Stain Remover will remove light markings. For stubborn stains wash in a detergent solution, treat with Dabitoff and re-wash.

Upholstery
Wipe away wet deposits or brush away dried stains. Sponge with a detergent solution and treat with Dabitoff. Finish by sponging again with the detergent solution and rinse with clear water. Blot well to dry.

GRASS

Fabrics
Before washing treat with Stain Devils Grass Stain Remover then machine wash using a biological detergent. Use as high a temperature as possible. Dry clean non-washable fabrics.

GRAVY

Fabrics
Pre-wash or soak using a proprietary product and machine wash using a biological detergent. Use a hot wash if possible.

Upholstery
Treat as for Foundation Cream.

ICE-CREAM

Carpets
Scrape away deposit and wipe up as much excess as possible. Shampoo area. If any staining remains use Carpet Devils No 2 followed by a carpet shampoo.

Fabrics
Soak and then wash in a biological detergent using as hot a wash as possible.

Upholstery
Sponge with warm water and then treat with The Stain Slayer or a hydrogen peroxide solution (one part 20-vol peroxide to six parts cold water). Rinse and blot dry.

INK (WASHABLE)

Carpets
Tackle immediately. Remove as much ink as possible by dabbing with absorbent paper

soaked in cold water. Keep blotting to avoid over-wetting. Soak a clean pad in soap solution and leave for 15 minutes. Repeat until clear, blotting between applications. If stains remain, try a carpet spotting kit or have professionally treated. It might be worth contacting the ink manufacturer for further advice.

Fabrics and upholstery

Ink is easier to remove from some fabrics such as polyester-cotton but more persistent in pure cotton. Act quickly! Sponge or hold under cold running water until excess ink is removed. Machine wash if possible using a high temperature and a biological detergent.

If staining remains, rub area with lemon juice and rinse thoroughly. Keep repeating until clear. Or soak in a hydrogen peroxide solution (one part 20-vol peroxide to six parts cold water), followed by laundering. Treat dried stains on white cotton and linen with a dilute solution of household bleach. Other whites and coloureds may respond to Stain Devils Mould and Ink Stain Remover. Non-washable fabrics should be professionally cleaned.

Treat upholstery with an upholstery spotting kit or upholstery shampoo.

IRON MOULD

Fabrics

Rub with lemon juice, cover with salt and leave for at least an hour. Rinse and wash as normal. Treat stubborn stains with a proprietary stain remover such as Stain Devils Rust and Iron Mould Stain Remover.

KETCHUP AND BOTTLED SAUCES

Carpets

Carefully remove excess, taking care not to spread the stain further, or soften dried stains by rubbing in a glycerine solution. Sponge gently with warm water and blot to avoid over-wetting.

Apply foam from a carpet shampoo or spray such as 1001. Alternatively, treat with Carpet Devils No 2. Rinse and dry thoroughly.

Fabrics

Pre-soak followed by washing with a biological detergent.

Upholstery

Sponge the affected piece with cold water followed by a detergent solution. Rinse well and blot dry.

If marks persist use Mykal De-Solv-It 2 followed by rinsing.

LIPSTICK

Carpet

Scrape away any deposit, then treat with a stain remover such as Stain Devils Grease and Oil Stain Remover, or Carpet Devils No 1, followed by shampooing.

Fabrics

Difficult to remove on natural fabrics. Soak in a detergent solution then dab with Dabitoff. Wash off with a detergent solution followed by ordinary laundering.

Upholstery

Have professionally treated.

MAYONNAISE

Fabrics

Sponge with warm water (avoid hot water as this will set the stain). Soak and wash in a biological detergent.

Upholstery

Remove excess, taking care not to spread the stain. Treat with Mykal De-Solv-It 1 or Stain Devils Grease and Oil Stain Remover. Rinse and blot dry.

MILDEW

Upholstery

Brush away spores and spray with a proprietary fungicide to kill the bacteria. Dab marks with Milton, and be prepared to be persistent. Sponge with cold water to rinse. Mattresses also respond well to treating with Milton. Start with a dilute solution and then get more concentrated until it is cleared.

Before treating items of value consult the Victoria and Albert Museum (see Useful Addresses).

Plastic shower curtains

To prevent mildew growth see page 344.

Soak in a solution of bleach (one part bleach to four parts water). Rinse thoroughly by hand, or if possible, wash in a washing machine to prevent the fabric from being damaged by bleach residue. However, bleach will not inhibit future mould growth, so after bleaching apply a mould killer or inhibitor such as Cuprinol Interior Mould Killer, Rentokil Mould Cure or Fungo.

Walls

Wash down with a mild detergent solution followed by wiping over with a mould killer or inhibitor as above.

Fabrics

Fresh mildew marking should be removed by normal washing procedures. For old stains on whites, cotton and linen, soak in a solution of household bleach. Treat white and colourfast fabrics (except acetates) with Stain Devils Mould and Ink Stain Remover. Regular washing will reduce marks.

MILK

Carpets

Treat quickly to stop penetration and drying, as the smell lingers. Flush the area with warm water and blot to dry. Use a carpet stain remover such as Carpet Devils No 2 or 1001 carpet spray.

If any odour persists try Neutradol Carpet Deodorizer (see Useful Addresses), which neutralises smells rather than masking them with a perfume.

Fabrics

Rinse through in lukewarm water and then wash as normal. You may need to soak dried stains first in a biological detergent solution.If any odour persists try XO (see Useful Addresses). This product can be sprayed directly on to fabrics.

Upholstery

Sponge with lukewarm water and blot dry. If a stain remains, use a spray stain remover or Dabitoff. If any odour persists try XO as above.

MUD

Carpets

When the mud is completely dry, brush and then vacuum. Use a carpet spot cleaner or shampoo.

Fabrics

Quite difficult to remove dried-on stains. Pre-wash in a biological detergent solution or pre-treat with a stain-removal bar.

Upholstery

Lightly brush when mud is completely dry. Sponge remaining marks with a warm, mild detergent solution. Sponge with clear water to rinse and blot dry.

NAIL VARNISH

Carpets

Treat with Carpet Devils No 1 followed by shampooing. If marks remain, have them professionally cleaned.

Fabrics

Treating with acetone will fade the mark, but probably not totally remove it. Dry cleaning may be effective but, if not, try to disguise the mark by adding a motif or brooch.

Upholstery

Have professionally treated.

PAINTS

WATER BASED

For example, emulsion: rinse out or flush fresh marks with cold water followed by laundering. Dried marks are difficult to remove. Treating with Stain Devils Tar and Paint Stain Remover may fade it, but don't expect total removal.

OIL BASED

For example, gloss: marking is usually permanent. Dabbing with turpentine may help fade it. Professional cleaning may help.

PERFUME

Non-washable fabrics

Lubricate with a glycerine solution (equal parts glycerine and water), leave for up to an hour and then sponge clean, avoiding over-wetting. Blot dry. Expensive items and silk should be dry cleaned.

Washable fabrics

Rinse through immediately. Lubricate dried stains as above or use Stain Devils Fruit and Wine Stain Remover before washing as normal.

PERSPIRATION

Non-washable fabrics

Dry clean heavily stained areas, particularly on tailored items. On lightly soiled areas try a solution of white vinegar (using 1 tbsp/15ml vinegar to 250ml warm water) to clean and deodorise the area.

Washable fabrics

To tackle a build-up of staining on shirts use Beckmann Stain Salts. Immerse colourfast items and soak overnight. Scrub affected areas with a nail brush and then wash with a biological detergent. For stubborn stains try White Wizard (see Useful Addresses).

POLLEN

Fabrics

Treat stain with Stain Devils Grass Stain Remover. Wash as normal.

SALT AND WATER MARKS

Leather and suede shoes

White tide marks occur when water leaches out of the salt used to preserve the leather (involved in the tanning process) or when leather comes into contact with sea water or salt used to grit roads. Try moistening the stain and rubbing with a soft cloth, or try a proprietary product such as Meltonian Stain Remover and Cleaner (see Useful Addresses). After treating, spray shoes with a water-repellant spray protector to help prevent further stains.

Nubuck

Cow leather similar to suede but with a finer velvet pile. Use special nubuck and calf-leather cleaners which are solvent based and evaporate (no brushing required). Do not use suede cleaners or brushes as they will flatten the pile.

SCORCH MARKS

Carpets

These cannot be removed, but if it's only a small mark, trim the tufts or loosen any fibres using a stiff-bristled brush. Some carpet manufacturers will re-tuft or patch a small area but it is expensive. Contact the British Carpet Manufacturers' Association (see Useful Addresses) or look in your local Thomson Directory for companies who offer this service.

Fabrics

Impossible to remove heavily scorched marks because the fibres, particularly synthetics, will be permanently damaged. You may be able to fade but not remove light marks by soaking in Beckmann Stain Salts. If possible, try disguising the offending area with motifs or brooches.

SHOE POLISH

Carpets

Carefully scrape away excess, avoiding spreading deposit further. Dab with Carpet Devils No 1 followed by carpet shampoo to dissolve remaining residue.

Upholstery

Scrape away the deposit. Sponge the upholstery with warm water to rinse and blot dry. Sponge with biological detergent, avoiding over-wetting and scuffing the surface. Rinse and blot dry.

Fabrics

Scrape away any deposit and treat with Mykal De-solv-It 1 before rinsing and laundering.

SOOT

Carpet

Do not brush as this will spread the mark. Use the nozzle attachment of your vacuum cleaner to pick up any residue. Try absorbing the stain with talcum powder. Rub in lightly and then vacuum away the deposit.

If stains remain, try Carpet Devils No 1 followed by shampooing.

Fabrics

Vacuum up the residue to avoid spreading it further. Washing will gradually fade the stain.

SOY SAUCE

Fabrics

Launder using a biological detergent.

Upholstery

Sponge with cold water and then with a biological detergent solution. Rinse and dry thoroughly.

TEA

Carpets

Sponge the area with cold water. Treat with the foam from a carpet shampoo or try 1001 carpet spray. Rinse and blot dry.

Fabrics

Rinse fresh stains in warm water and then wash as normal, using a biological detergent. Loosen dried stains with a pre-wash treatment before machine washing.

Upholstery

Rinse with cold water and then apply a biological detergent solution. Rinse thoroughly and blot dry. On stubborn stains try Carpet Devils No 4, but do not leave on for too long or it could affect the dye.

TYPING CORRECTION FLUID

For example, Tipp-Ex fluid, Liquid Paper.

Carpets and upholstery

Allow to dry and pick off as much of the deposit as possible, taking care not to snag the fabric. Treating with turpentine will fade but not remove the mark. The remainder can only be cleared by professional treatment.

Fabrics

Try acetone or turpentine followed by repeated washing. However, professional treatment is recommended.

URINE

Carpets

Flush the area with cold water and blot until nearly dry. Sponge with carpet shampoo solution such as 1001 Trouble Shooter Stain Remover with deodoriser or Carpet Devils No 3. Rinse well with cold water to which a few drops of disinfectant have been added. Blot to dry. If any odour persists try a deodorising product such as Neutrodol Carpet Deodorizer (see Useful Addresses).

Mattresses

Hold the mattress on its side while the treatment is being carried out. Sponge with a cold solution of washing-up liquid or upholstery shampoo. Wipe with cold water to rinse to which a few drops of disinfectant, such as Milton, has been added. Alternatively, try an upholstery spotting kit.

Non-washable fabrics

Fresh stains can be removed with a vinegar solution (1tbsp/15ml vinegar to 1 pint/500 ml warm water). Dried stains should be professionally treated.

Washable fabrics

Rinse and then soak in a biological detergent solution overnight. Then machine wash, as normal.

VOMIT

Carpet

Scoop up as much of the deposit as possible and flush through with a bicarbonate of soda solution. Blot well. Rub in the foam from a carpet shampoo solution such as 1001 Trouble Shooter Stain Remover containing deodoriser. Repeat until the stain has cleared. Rinse with warm water to which a few drops of antiseptic has been added. Blot well.

If any odour persists try a deodorising product such as Neutrodol Carpet Deodorizer (see Useful Addresses).

Fabrics

Remove any deposit and rinse well with cold water. Machine wash using a biological detergent if possible. Dry clean expensive or non-washable fabrics.

If any odour persists, try XO (see Useful Addresses).

Upholstery

Scoop up the surface deposit and sponge the area with warm water. Blot dry. Try an upholstery cleaner or foam from a carpet shampoo. If any odour persists try XO (see Useful Addresses).

WINE

Carpets

Sponge with sparkling water and blot to dry. Treat with a carpet shampoo and rinse well. If stains persist try a carpet spotting kit or Carpet Devils No 3 followed by shampooing.

Fabrics

Sponge fresh stains with white wine or sparkling water. Then follow with normal laundering.

Treat dried stains with Stain Devils Fruit and Wine Stain Remover or a hydrogen peroxide solution (one part 20-vol peroxide to six parts cold water). Follow by washing as normal.

Upholstery

Sponge the area with warm water and blot well. Treat with an upholstery shampoo or The Stain Slayer.

CREATIVE DIY

PAINTING AND DECORATING

It's never been easier or more fun to do your own decorating. All you need is a little imagination and some basic know-how to transform your home, help protect it – and save money too.

WHICH PAINT?

Every year sees the introduction of new, sophisticated paint finishes, such as solid emulsion, one-step gloss, environmentally-friendly 'green' paints, and tough sheens for kitchens and bathrooms.

With all these different and confusing products on the market, it may be a relief to know that there are only two main types of house paint: water-based; and solvent-based,\ which is traditionally, if not always accurately, called oil-based paint.

Water-based paints include emulsion, quick-drying eggshell and water-based gloss, while solvent-based paints range from traditional eggshell and gloss to durable sheen finishes and specialist lacquers or paints for metal. Some paints may have added ingredients such as vinyl, acrylic or polyurethane – to make them more durable or to increase coverage – but that doesn't alter their basic composition.

Water-based paints are ideal for walls and water-based eggshell or gloss can be used for most interior woodwork, while solvent-based paints are perfect for areas of hard wear: exterior as well as interior wood, and metal.

TIP Find out if a paint is water-based or solvent-based by reading the instructions given for thinning. If water is recommended, the paint will be water-based; if white spirit is advised, it's solvent-based.

PREPARATORY COATS

PRIMER

Primer seals absorbent surfaces and provides a key for the subsequent coats. Use it before painting bare timber, and when using gloss on bare metal. (Check the instructions to see if a special metal primer is required.) It's also possible to buy universal primer, for treating wood, plaster or metal.

Primer, undercoat and liquid gloss form the traditional three steps for painting wood but they are not always necessary today because you can buy combined primer/undercoat, which reduces the steps to two. Water-based primer (quick-drying primer or primer/ undercoat) dries in around two hours. It's ideal for use indoors.

Plaster primer (primer/sealer) and stabilising solutions are used for walls that are porous or liable to flake.

Solvent-based primer can be used outside. In white or the traditional pink, it needs 12 hours to dry before you can apply undercoat.

Aluminium primer is ideal for resinous woods. For added protection, apply two coats, thinning the first with 10 per cent white spirit.

UNDERCOAT

Undercoat provides a smooth, solid-coloured base for liquid gloss. It's a solvent-based paint that looks attractive in its own right, though the range of colours is limited. It tends to chip, so if using it without the top coat of gloss protect it with clear varnish.

TIP For the best effect, buy the same brand of primer, undercoat and gloss. They're designed to be used together.

EMULSION PAINT

Emulsion is the first choice for walls. It's a water-based paint, and normally contains vinyl, which makes it durable and easy to clean. It can be used on most sound, already painted surfaces.

If the area to be painted was previously covered with a different kind of paint, it may need some preparation. Sand gloss or eggshell surfaces lightly to provide a 'key' for the new coat. Varnish must be stripped completely.

Old-fashioned treatments like distemper and whitewash must be washed off before you can start. You're unlikely to encounter these today but you'll know if you do because new paint won't adhere to them.

Emulsion paint can be applied directly to new plaster or plasterboard, but it's best to first apply a 'mist' coat diluted with water to improve coverage. Modern emulsion is quick-drying: allow two to four hours between coats.

DESIGN TIPS

'Warm' colours (red, yellow, orange) appear to bring surfaces closer. Use them for cool north- or east-facing rooms, high ceilings (especially effective if you continue the paint down to picture rail level), and the end wall in a long passage.
'Cool' colours (blue, green, lilac) make surfaces look further away. Use them in warm, south- and west-facing rooms and in small areas.
Depth of colour can be used to modify the effect of warm and cool tones. Dark shades, which absorb light, seem to advance, while pastels, which reflect it, appear to recede.
Lose unwanted features such as cupboards, radiators and pipes by painting them the same colour as the wall. If you want to highlight features, use a contrasting colour.

COLOUR AND LIGHT

Artificial light can alter the effect of the colours you choose, so it's worth looking at samples at night as well as in daylight.
Standard tungsten light bulbs emphasise red tones but reduce blue and green, making colours look yellower than by day.
Fluorescent light can bring out blues and reduce shadows. Look for 'warm' fluorescents, which are closer to natural light.
Halogen lamps have a bright white light and colours may look harsher.
Reflected light is softer. Try using uplighters or spotlights that bounce light off the ceiling or wall.

TYPES OF EMULSION

There is a range of different consistencies and finishes for a variety of purposes.

Consistencies

Roller or solid emulsion paint (rather a misnomer, because it's more like cream cheese) is sold in trays for use with a roller. As it's virtually spatter-free, it's perfect for ceilings and stair-wells but more expensive than buying paint in tins.
'One-coat' emulsions are opaque enough to cover in a single application.
Flexible emulsion is designed to cover hairline cracks.

Finishes

Matt finish gives a soft, velvety look, and is

ideal for concealing flaws in plaster or uneven walls. Like all vinyl emulsions, it will wipe clean, but take care, because if you rub too hard, it starts to shine.

Silk finish has a delicate sheen that can highlight patterns on textured wall coverings but may also emphasise flaws.

Soft sheen is easier to clean than matt but is less shiny than silk finish.

Textured emulsion gives a random rippled effect. Like flexible emulsion, it will conceal flawed plaster, though it won't cover wide cracks, and it can be difficult to remove.

TIP Use emulsion paint rather than solvent-based paint or wallpaper on new plaster. Emulsion allows water to pass through as the plaster dries out.

PAINTS FOR WOODWORK

GLOSS PAINTS

Gloss paint is the traditional choice for wood and metalwork.

All solvent-based gloss has a high shine but for a truly mirror-like finish, it's best to opt for the liquid paint used over undercoat, a system favoured by professional decorators, especially for outside use. The one-coat non-drip formula designed for DIY use is much easier to apply, but sometimes brush marks are difficult to avoid. Self-undercoating gloss has added colour, and can be used directly over primer or existing paint.

Water-based acrylic gloss has more of a sheen than a shine. It's often recommended for use in children's rooms, because it's not toxic – completely lead and solvent free. Some acrylic gloss can be used outside, but check the tin before using it.

EGGSHELL PAINTS

Eggshell is a versatile sheen finish usually sold for indoor woodwork, though it can also be used on walls for a uniform look.

Solvent based

Traditional eggshell is solvent based but because it can be difficult to apply, it's sometimes re-formulated for domestic use and sold under another name: 'Satinwood' is one common example.

It has a rich sheen but is less shiny than gloss paint. It's ideal for metal, interior woodwork and walls in areas of hard wear or condensation, because it can virtually be scrubbed clean and seals the wall from damp. (Before painting bare plaster, apply a plaster primer.)

There are drawbacks, however, because it's expensive over a large area and the sheen will emphasise every possible irregularity in the wall. Traditional solvent-based eggshell can also produce troublesome fumes, but this is less of a problem now than it used to be with new, low-odour varieties.

PAINT SAFETY

- Solvent-based paint is flammable, so store it outside the house, but protected from frost and damp.
- Fumes from solvent-based gloss and eggshell are unpleasant so make sure the room is cool and well ventilated before you start painting.
- Lead is no longer added to paint, although a tiny amount exists naturally in gloss, solvent-based primer and undercoat. If you want to avoid it entirely, use water-based paints.

Water based

Newer 'quick-drying', 'green' or 'kitchen and bathroom' eggshell paints are water-based and are effectively emulsions.

It may be best to use water-based eggshell on walls, as it has less shine and doesn't give off fumes like solvent-based paints.

Water-based eggshell is ideal for most purposes indoors, but shouldn't be used on wood outdoors.

WOOD STAIN AND VARNISH

WOOD STAINS

Wood stains designed for use indoors are more decorative than protective, so cover them with two or more coats of clear varnish. Some products offer a degree of protection, but will still need varnishing in areas of heavy wear, such as skirtings, chairs or table tops.

Wood stains are designed to penetrate the wood and can only be removed with bleaching and sanding, so test the colour on an offcut or in an inconspicuous place before you start.

Stains for exterior use often contain a preservative to protect the timber and may not need varnishing. They include alternatives to creosote for use on rough-sawn wood such as fences and sheds, and mid-sheen finishes for planed wood on doors and window frames.

VARNISH

Varnish provides a clear, protective coating for paints and stains. It's available in matt, satin (mid-sheen) or high gloss finishes and in liquid or non-drip consistency. (Liquid varnish is difficult to apply so non-drip is much better for beginners.) A solvent-based product, it may have acrylic or polyurethane substances added for extra durability.

Yacht varnish is one of the most weather-resistant, but not all varnishes are suitable for use outside, or on floors, so check the label carefully before you buy.

Coloured varnish is available, usually in timber shades or occasionally in translucent tints, but when the top coat is chipped, the colour is removed too.

TIP Add a trace of white gloss paint to clear varnish, to stop it yellowing.

PAINTS FOR SPECIAL PURPOSES

Anti-condensation paint is an emulsion which insulates the wall, reducing the contrast in temperature that can cause condensation. It may contain glass particles and usually has a fungicide to prevent mould.

Anti-damp and anti-stain paints do not cure damp, but create a thick synthetic barrier that prevents damp marks and stain marks (from felt-tip pens, for example) from bleeding through to the surface. These paints are usually solvent-based.

Bituminous paint is tar-based. It will waterproof concrete and metal gutters but should not be covered by any other paint.

Enamel is a durable gloss available in smooth or hammered finishes and may contain metal particles. It is corrosion resistant and can be used on bare metal, though you may need to use a metal primer before applying it over existing paint.

It is ideal for household appliances, painting over tiles, or on china and glass, but you will need heat-resistant enamel for cookers and fireplaces and a special enamel for baths.

Enamel is expensive, which limits its use to small areas. Colours (such as hobby tins) are often bright, though the heat-resistant enamel sold for radiators is usually white or magnolia.

Flat oil paint, available from decorating specialists, is designed for use on walls, but because it is solvent-based, should be used over undercoat. It has a matt, velvety effect but marks easily and is difficult to clean.

Floor paint is usually solvent-based, though some designed for indoor use may be emulsions. These are relatively non-slip and resist abrasion.

Lacquer is a hard, gloss paint with a mirror-like shine. It's ideal for giving a colourful finish to doors, railings or furniture.

Microporous paints and stains are for outside use. They're designed to flex with the timber, keeping damp out but allowing the wood to 'breathe', but they won't work as well on previously painted surfaces. No primer or undercoat is needed, but preservative is required on bare wood.

Masonry paint is a tough emulsion for outside walls, usually strengthened with nylon, chips of silica or sand, giving a textured effect.

Matt black paint is used for beams and blackboards. It's a solvent-based paint with minimal shine.

Stove black is a heat-resistant paint that will withstand temperatures of up to 390°F/200°C. Use it for grates and fire backs.

PREPARATION FOR PAINTING

Preparation is essential, because paint and paper won't adhere to flaking surfaces and can magnify, rather than disguise, any flaws beneath. As a rule of thumb, allow two-thirds of your time for preparation and one-third for decoration. Clear the room as much as possible, removing light fittings and carpets if you can, and cover what's left with dust-sheets.

PAINT COVERAGE AND DRYING TIMES*

Type of paint	Area covered per litre	Touch dry	Re-coatable
Matt vinyl emulsion	12–14 sq m	2 hrs	4 hrs
Silk vinyl emulsion	12–14sq m	2 hrs	4 hrs
Soft sheen emulsion	13–15 sq m	2 hrs	4 hrs
Solid emulsion	11–13 sq	2 hrs	4 hrs
One-coat emulsion	10 sq m	2 hrs	4 hrs
Flexible emulsion	7–9 sq m	2 hrs	4 hrs
Textured emulsion	5–7 sq m	2 hrs	4 hrs
Water-based satin	14–16 sq m	2 hrs	4 hrs
Eggshell **	15–17 sq m	12 hrs	16 hrs
Liquid gloss	16–17 sq m	12 hrs	16 hrs
Non-drip gloss	10–12 sq m	1-3 hrs	5–6 hrs***
Water-based gloss	14–16 sq m	2 hrs	4 hrs
Self-undercoat gloss	10–12 sq m	2 hrs	4 hrs
Undercoat	15–17 sq m	8 hrs	12 hrs
Masonry paint	6–10 sq m	1 hr	4 hrs

* Coverage varies with the brand and absorbency of the surface. Times depend on moderate, dry conditions
** Solvent-based
*** Normally only one coat required

HOW TO FILL CRACKS

1 Open up small cracks with a putty knife or the end of a screwdriver to make them easier to fill.
2 Dampen with a small paintbrush dipped in water to clean out the crack and remove the dust.
3 Apply filler (available ready-mixed or in powder form) with a narrow-bladed filling knife, pushing it deeply into the crack so it fills it completely and leaving it raised above the level of the wall. (Deep cracks must be filled in layers, leaving each to dry before you add the next.)
4 When dry, sand the area down until it's flush with the wall and wipe clean.

Choose a flexible sealant for cracks between walls and window or door frames, which may expand or contract. If you use ordinary filler, the crack may open again.

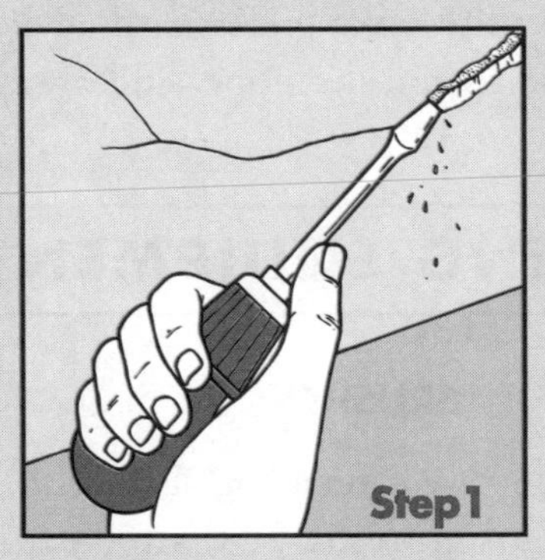

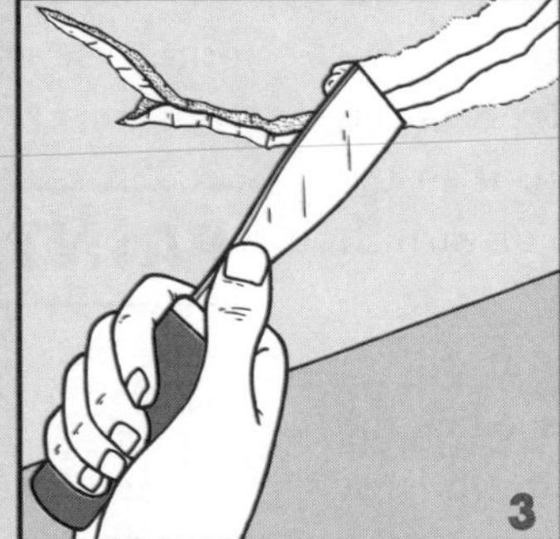

Keep a pair of old shoes for the job, and leave them by the door of the room being painted when you finish. This will help prevent treading paint and dust through the house when you leave the room.

Walls

If the walls are in good condition, simply wash them with a detergent solution, rinse and allow to dry.

If the walls are damp, you'll need to find the cause and tackle it before you decorate. Then wash any mould away with a solution of one part bleach to four parts water, leave for two days, and rinse.

TIP Wash walls from the bottom up, to prevent dirty streaks running down and making the task more difficult.

TIP To find the cause of damp, tape a piece of aluminium foil over the patch and leave for a week. After this period, if the outer surface of the foil is wet, the cause is probably condensation. If the foil is moist on the underside, the cause might be rising damp (from a faulty damp proof course) or penetrating damp, from walls that need re-pointing on the outside.

Lift off any patches of flaking plaster, fill dents and cracks, and sand until the repairs are level with the rest of the wall. Don't forget to sand any runs in old paintwork and lightly sand all over walls covered with eggshell or solvent-based paint to provide a key for the next coat. Apply a stabilising solution to powdery plaster, plaster primer to new plaster if necessary, and allow to dry.

WOODWORK

Remove all the door furniture (handles, finger plates and so on) and scrape old putty back from the window frames before you start.

If the paintwork is sound, simply sand the surface slightly to provide a key for the new coat, then clean with white spirit. Any blistered or flaking paint should be scraped back and sanded level with the surround.

New wood and bare patches must be primed before painting to seal the surface. This includes the bottom edge of new doors and any deep cracks.

Cracks should be stopped with flexible filler, but choose a wood filler and stain it to the shade you require if you intend to varnish natural wood.

Treat knots with knotting solution, to prevent resin seeping through and spoiling the new paint. If a knot does bleed through later, sand down to the bare wood, treat with the solution, and then prime before repainting.

TIP Silicon carbide sanding paper can be used dry, or wet, to keep down dust. Wrap it round a sanding block – an offcut of wood will do – for ease of use.

Stripping wood

There are several ways of stripping old paint or varnish from wooden surfaces:

Chemical wood stripper comes in liquid form; or as a paste or gel, which are ideal for ornate or vertical surfaces such as chair legs or banisters. The process takes time (from 15 minutes to 8 hours) and may need repeating.

Hot-air guns soften paint, making it easier to remove. Work from the bottom up to make the most of rising heat, and wear gloves to protect your hands.

Sanding can be done by hand, or with an electric orbital or belt sander. Drills may have disc sander attachments, which are suitable for rough work but won't give a fine finish.

Dry stripping is done with a shavehook (a small triangular, or combined straight and curved-edge scraper). You will also need a wide-bladed stripping knife to remove flaking paint. These tools are also useful to shift paint loosened by chemical or heat stripping.

Take care when stripping old paintwork. It may contain lead, which should not be released into the atmosphere. If the paint is very old and thick, take professional advice; otherwise use chemical stripper and always wear a mask.

PAINTING EQUIPMENT

BRUSHES

Brushes should have natural hog's-hair bristles, which pick up more paint than cheaper materials. Look for bristles that don't moult (run them through your hands a few times) and are tapered at the ends for a smooth finish – especially important when painting with eggshell and gloss.

Buy a range of widths (1, 2 and 3in/25, 50 and 75mm) for wood and metalwork, plus a ¾in/19mm angled cutting-in brush for painting the edge of the wall and a ½in/12 mm brush for the glazing bars on windows. If you want to paint the walls with a brush, choose a 4in/100mm wall brush, but make sure it's not too tiring to use.

ROLLERS

Rollers vary in width from 7–12in/ 175–300mm and come with a single frame (one end attached to the handle) or double (attached at both sides). A single-frame roller is easier to manipulate, especially in corners, but a double-frame roller helps you to exert even pressure – useful when painting ceilings or using an extension handle.

Roller sleeves made from lamb's wool (real or synthetic) are good for use with most paints, especially matt emulsion. Use on rough or textured surfaces. Mohair sleeves, which have a fine pile, are ideal for smooth surfaces with eggshell, silk emulsion and solid emulsion paint. Foam rollers are available, sometimes textured to create special effects. Although they are cheap, they tend to spatter. You'll also find small rollers especially designed for painting behind radiators.

PAINT PADS

Paint pads are easy to use but a fine finish can be difficult to achieve. They're available in sizes from an extra-wide 8in/200mm to a narrow 1in/25mm sash pad for windows. Like rollers, they're best for use on walls.

PAINT RECEPTACLES

Paint trays are sold with both rollers and paint pads. Most have ribs for removing excess paint.

A paint kettle is ideal for decanting liquid paint. Line it with foil to keep it clean and buy an old-fashioned S hook to hang it up by.

TIP Strain lumpy liquid paint through a stocking, or tie one loosely over the top of the tin to act as a filter when you dip in the brush.

TIP Jam the paint-tin lid on hard when you've finished painting and store the tin upside down, to prevent a skin forming.

WAYS WITH BRUSHES

- Hold a wide brush by the stock – the part that joins the bristles to the handle; hold a narrow one like a pencil.
- When dipping the brush into the paint, only cover half of the bristle area with emulsion, one-third with gloss. Remove the surplus by pressing the bristles against the side of the tin, not the rim, where paint may dry and lumps may fall into the tin, causing problems in the paint later.
- Tie a length of string tautly across the opening of a paint kettle or paint tin, so you can wipe excess paint off the brush as you lift it out of the paint.

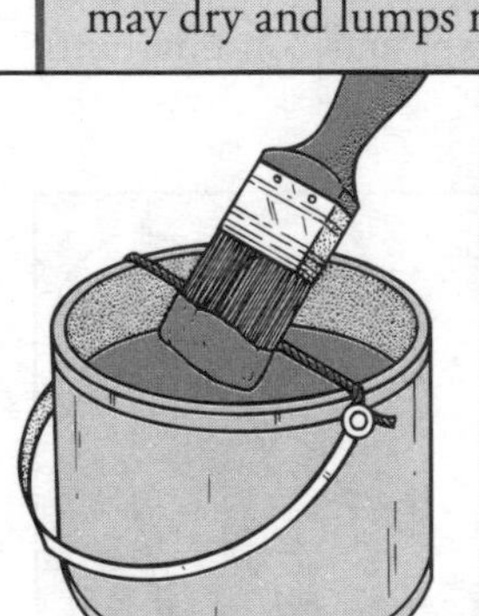

- For easy cleaning of a brush used with solvent-based paints, drill a hole through the handle of the brush and push a long nail through. Suspend it in a jar of white spirit.

- When you take a break from painting, wrap brushes in clingfilm so they don't dry out.
- As soon as you stop for the day, clean brushes in detergent for water-based paints, or white spirit for solvent-based. (Check the manufacturer's instructions.) Pat dry with kitchen paper.
- Store flat, or hang from a hole in the handle. Use a rubber band to keep all the bristles together neatly.

PAINTING A ROOM

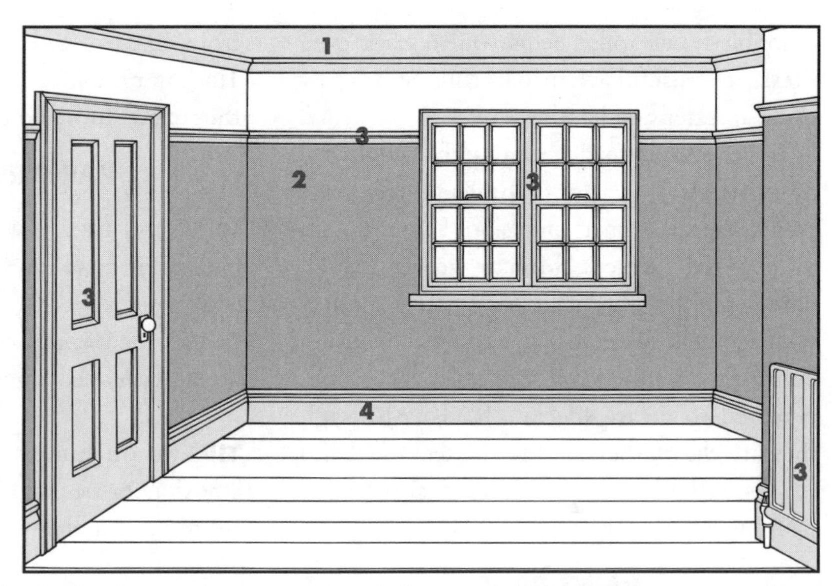

ORDER OF PAINTING

The following steps are the most orderly way to paint a room, and will avoid any drips or spills of one colour or type of paint on another.

1 Paint the ceiling. If there is a ceiling rose or other mouldings, give them an initial coat of paint and complete after finishing the ceiling.

2 Paint the walls, working away from the light source.

3 Paint window frames, picture rail (if any), radiators and doors.

4 Paint the skirting.

PAINTING A CEILING

Working with your arms above your head can be tiring, so choose a roller or paint pad for fast coverage and, if you can find the colour you want, use solid emulsion (roller paint), which makes less mess. Using extension handles makes access easier but can also affect the way you control the roller. It may be better to work from a plank between two sets of step ladders, but make sure they are stable.

ORDER OF PAINTING

1 Paint a narrow strip around the perimeter of the ceiling where the roller won't reach, using a narrow 'cutting in' brush.

2 Paint a wider strip parallel to one edge with a wide brush, paint pad or roller, leaving a small gap.

3 When you come to the end of the run, reverse the direction and use the brush, pad or roller to fill in the gap. Go over it again lightly to blend in the paint if necessary.

4 Recharge with paint and start a new line, again leaving a small gap, and continue until the ceiling is complete.

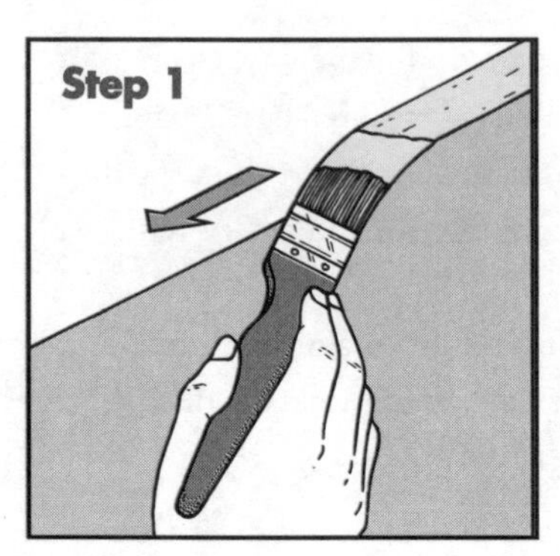

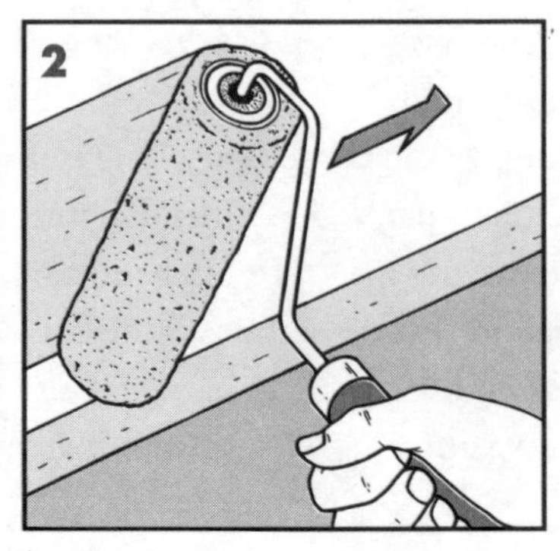

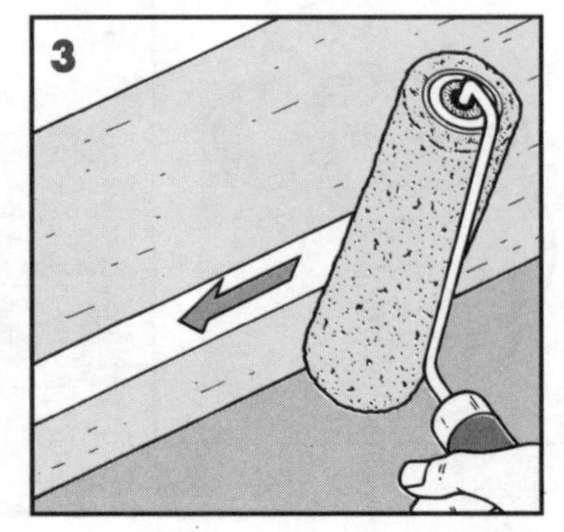

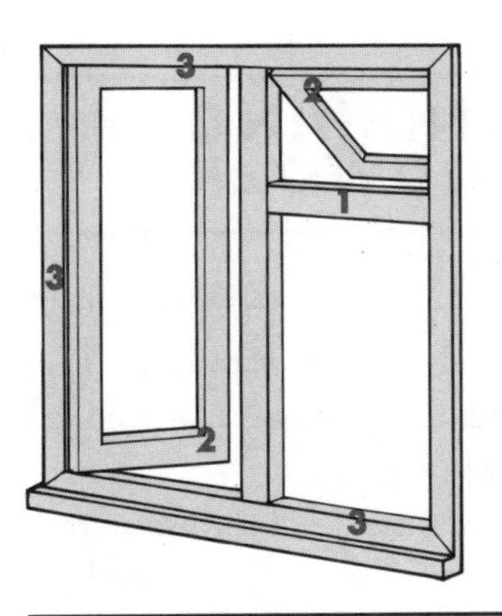

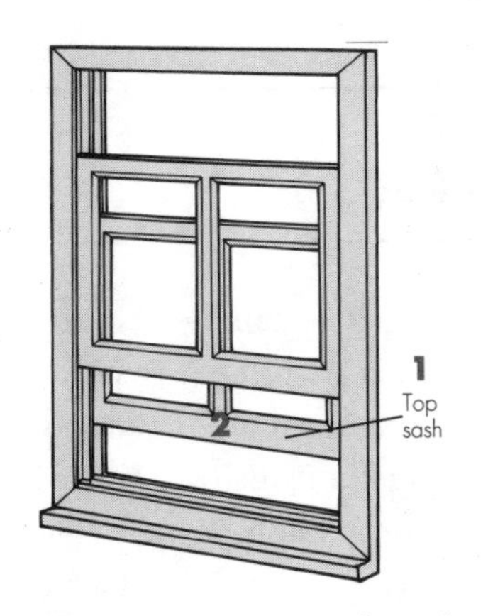

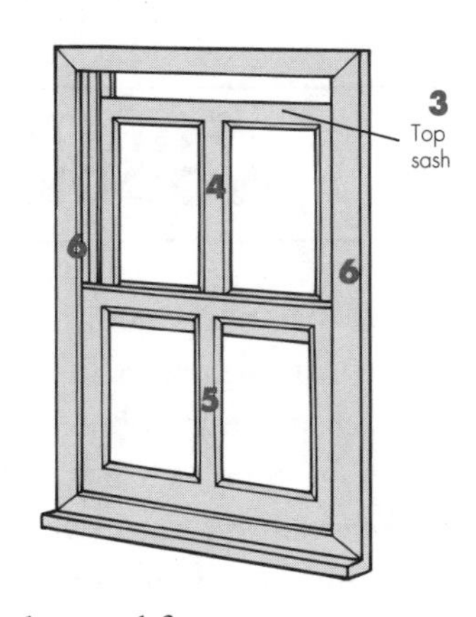

PAINTING WINDOWS

When protecting the glass with masking tape, let the paint overlap on to the glass by a millimetre to form a protective seal.

Casement (side opening) windows

1 Paint any glazing bars on the fixed window.
2 Paint the opening window, except for the outside edge which should match the exterior.
3 Paint the window frame and sill.

Sash windows

1 Open the window until the bottom sash and top sash overlap by about 8in/20cm.
2 Paint the bottom of the top sash.
3 Close the bottom sash and pull up the top sash so it's almost closed.
4 Paint the rest of the top sash.
5 Paint the bottom sash.
6 Paint the frame, avoiding the sash cords.

PAINTING PANELLED DOORS

1 Remove door 'furniture' (eg, handles, knobs and key plates, etc).
2 Paint the mouldings, if any.
3 Paint the panels.
4 Paint the vertical strips in the centre.
5 Paint the horizontals.
6 Paint the sides, edges and frame.

For the best effect, the outside edge of the door should match the paintwork of the room it opens into.

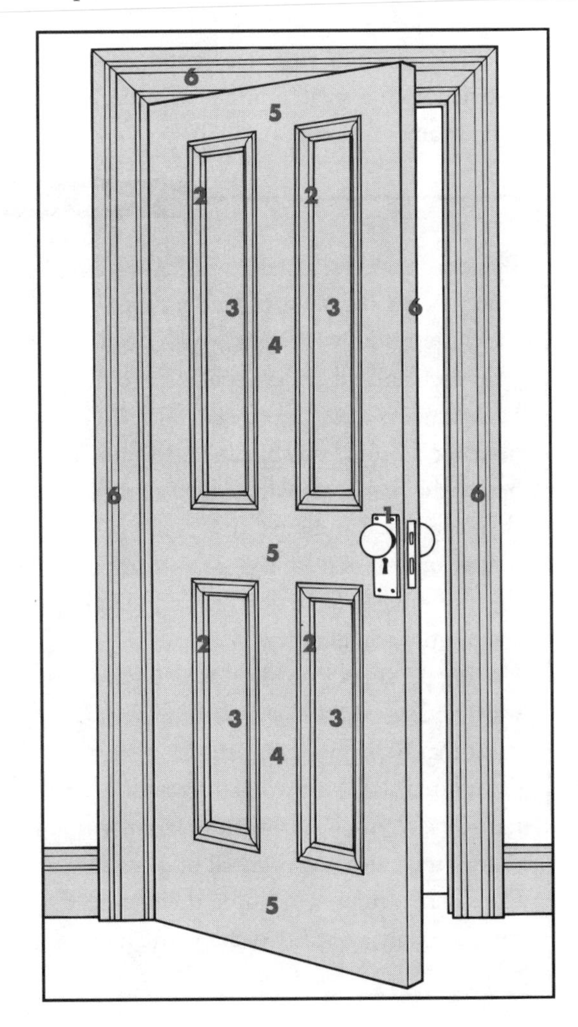

PAINTING WOODWORK

When painting wood, brush along the grain. On a narrow area, a single movement will be enough to cover it, but with wide areas, apply paint in parallel bands, reloading the brush before painting each strip. Aim for a smooth flowing movement for even coverage. After painting the second band, paint across the grain to join the two strips. 'Lay off' with light strokes along the grain for a smooth finish. Use two coats of undercoat when covering a dark base – cheaper than an extra coat of gloss.

TIP Make a 'tack rag' – a lint-free cloth moistened with a small amount of white spirit – to erase any mistakes.

VARNISHING WOODWORK

If covering a previously varnished or stained surface, sand and clean it. If varnishing bare wood or bare cork, apply a base coat thinned with 10 per cent white spirit.

Dip the brush into the tin of varnish so that half the bristle area is covered, and apply it along the grain, brushing out across the grain from the wet edge for even coverage. There's no pigment in varnish to disguise mistakes so take care to brush out overlaps and brush marks. Finish by brushing along the grain again with a single smooth stroke.

If more than one coat is needed, lightly sandith very fine abrasive paper when dry and clean with white spirit between each coat.

WHAT WENT WRONG?

Blisters are often caused by painting damp wood. Allow the paint to harden, then prick the blister. If it's wet inside, you'll need to strip back and fill the grain before repainting.
Crazing is caused by applying a second coat before the first coat is dry. Allow to dry, then rub down and repaint.
Cratering comes from too much damp in the atmosphere. Sand and repaint, keeping the room warm and dry.
Flaking paint is caused by powdery or dirty walls underneath the new coat, or gloss paint that hasn't been sanded. Emulsion paint often flakes off woodwork and radiators, so rub it down and repaint with a coat of solvent-based eggshell or gloss.
Runs come from overloading the brush. If there are only one or two, allow the paint to dry completely and then prick, rub down and touch in with a small paintbrush. Otherwise sand and start again.
Show through of what was originally underneath needs an additional top coat (emulsion) or an undercoat plus a new top coat (gloss).
Specks and stray bristles can be avoided if both wall and paint are clean and you use quality brushes. Either sand down and start again or, in a small area, sand or pick out the pieces, rub with wet abrasive paper and touch in. This also works for insects that have been trapped in wet paint.
Uneven coverage may occur if you try to spread paint too thinly or fail to prime large patches of filler or bare plaster. These are more absorbent than the rest of the wall and so take in more paint than primed areas.

SPECIAL PAINT EFFECTS

Fashions in decorating are always changing. Plain walls will be popular one year, patterns the next. At present, the trend is towards plains, but decorative paint finishes have the advantage of camouflaging defects and adding interest without defined pattern. You can buy special textured rollers that add a design for you, but it's often just as easy to use traditional materials. Here's what to do.

WALLS

Colour washing

This treatment gives a translucent finish.
Paint the wall with solvent-based eggshell (white will give a delicate effect) and leave to dry. For the top coat, mix 30 per cent transparent oil glaze with 50 per cent solvent-based eggshell and 20 per cent white spirit. If you want solid cover and a formal effect, use it straight; for a more casual, random effect, apply with a wall brush, moving it in all directions and leaving some areas uncovered to vary the depth of colour. Repeat when dry, covering the entire wall, still using criss-cross brush strokes.

You can protect the finish with a coat of polyurethane varnish in areas of hard wear but this will need to be removed when repainting.

TIP A similar effect can be achieved with emulsion paint. Paint the wall and leave to dry, then apply two coats of emulsion thinned with water, following the instructions on the tin. Use a wall brush, not a roller, and apply the paint with a random movement.

Best for cottagey living rooms, dining rooms and bedrooms.

Dragging

This needs solvent-based eggshell for the base coat and a top coat made up of 70 per cent transparent oil glaze, 20 per cent eggshell and 10 per cent white spirit, which is applied in bands about an arm's length wide. After painting each band, a dragging brush is pulled through the paint from the top of the wall down, which creates the characteristic effect.
Best for formal living rooms, studies, halls and bedrooms.

Sponging

An easy technique with emulsion paint, although solvent-based eggshell, which takes longer to dry, gives more time to create an effect. For the best results, use related colours, sponging the deeper colour over the paler one or vice versa. (Use three colours if you want a more elaborate effect.)

Pour a little paint into a saucer and apply with a natural sea sponge in a random direction, turning the sponge from time to time, until the wall is covered. You can use rags instead of a sponge if you prefer, choosing a textured cloth like stockinette or cheesecloth for greater definition.

TRANSPARENT OIL GLAZE

Also called scumble glaze, transparent oil glaze is essential for many paint treatments, especially those that take time to create, because it slows drying. It's available from specialist decorators (see Useful Addresses) and is often combined with solvent-based eggshell paint and white spirit as a top coat. A standard mix would be 70 per cent transparent oil glaze, 20 per cent eggshell and 10 per cent white spirit.

TIP Use solvent-based eggshell or acrylic emulsion paint in bathrooms for harder wear.

Best for bedrooms and bathrooms.

Rag rolling

This needs a base coat of solvent-based eggshell and a top coat made from 70 per cent transparent oil glaze, 20 per cent eggshell and 10 per cent white spirit. This is brushed on in vertical bands and rolled off with rags twisted into a sausage-shape, working from the top of the wall down.
Best for dining rooms and bedrooms.

Stippling

The subtlest way of producing broken colour. Paint the wall with solvent-based eggshell and, when dry, apply with a special stippling brush a top coat made from 70 per cent transparent oil glaze, 20 per cent eggshell, and 10 per cent white spirit. Keep the bristles at right angles to the wall, and wipe them from time to time so they don't become clogged.

You can also stipple walls by painting narrow (20in/50cm) strips of the top coat from top to bottom and then removing colour by using a clean, dry stippling brush.

TIP For speed, pour the top coat into a roller tray and apply with a stiff brush.

Best for all around the house.

Stencilling

Stencilling can create attractive borders and decorative motifs. Cutting your own stencils takes practice, so it's easiest to use ready-made stencils, available from most DIY superstores and decorating shops (such as Laura Ashley) as well as specialist suppliers such as The Stencil Store (see Useful Addresses). Whatever you choose, start with relatively simple designs, especially if you're stencilling a border, which can be time-consuming. Add variety by reversing the stencil from time to time, but to avoid smudges, remember to wipe it clean before you turn it over.

Use a stubby stencil brush and dab colour into the stencil until the design is filled in. You can use a variety of paints, from standard emulsion or eggshell (use solvent-based on woodwork) to acrylic or spray paint; special crayons are also available.

TIP Fix the stencil in place with masking tape or spray photo-mount, not Blu-Tak, which leaves a gap between the stencil and the wall and may lead to runs.

Best for borders, ceiling decorations, and motifs on furniture.

Murals

Murals can be painted in sections using simple picture-book designs.

Draw a grid over the original picture and number the squares, then draw a similar grid, the size of the finished mural, on the wall. Copy the outline of the design into each square, using chalk or soft pencil, then fill in, using one colour at a time and working from the top down. Rub off the grid marks when the mural is dry.
Best for passages and children's bedrooms.

WOODWORK

Bambooing

This decorative effect looks wonderful on turned wood as well as on bamboo furniture that has seen better days.

Paint with three coats of yellow-brown solvent-based eggshell and mottle the top coat with a rag while the paint is still damp. When

dry, draw circles of brown paint at intervals with a narrow brush. Paint a second, narrower and darker brown circle inside the first, followed by a final dark brown ring in the centre. You can also add the tiny spots and the V-shaped tail typical of natural bamboo.
Best for decorative pieces made from bamboo, cane or turned wood.

Colour rubbing

This gives a faded, weathered look. It involves brushing a milky glaze or a thin wash of water-based paint over the surface and then removing the excess before it dries, to highlight mouldings or emphasise the grain.

Alternatively, apply a base coat of solvent-based eggshell or wipe the bare wood with white spirit, and make a glaze from 75 per cent transparent oil glaze, 20 per cent solvent-based eggshell and 5 per cent white spirit. Brush this into the surface so that all the crevices are filled, and when it becomes tacky, rub along the grain with a soft cloth.
Best for doors, decorative fireplaces and floors (but not floors subject to hard wear).

Liming

Liming turns wood an attractive silvery grey and has been an especially popular finish for cupboard doors. Professionals use specialist products such as white shellac and liming wax, but you can achieve a similar look the following way.

Paint a base with white eggshell and allow to dry. Mix together 70 per cent transparent oil glaze, 20 per cent putty-coloured eggshell and 10 per cent white spirit. Brush this over the base coat, then tie a rag over a steel comb and drag over it from top to bottom. Finish by combing without a rag, using medium and fine combs. When dry, protect the finish with varnish, if needed.

TIP To vary the look, comb the sides only and leave a darker panel in the centre, rippled with a rag to look like real wood.

TIP For a verdigris look, paint a coat of turquoise eggshell over grey and drag the surface while still wet. Or, for a characteristic limed finish, try colour rubbing along the grain with grey-white paint.

Best for floors, doors.

Marbling

Paint with off-white solvent-based eggshell and, when dry, add a top coat made from 30 per cent transparent oil glaze, 50 per cent bone colour eggshell and 20 per cent white spirit. Dab with a rag to soften the effect and, while still wet, trace in the marble 'veins' in dark grey, using an artist's paint brush. Blur the lines with a special softening brush (or improvise with a rag) for a natural effect.
Best for table tops and floors.

Woodgraining

A way to make chipboard and pine look like oak or mahogany.

Give softwood and fibreboard a coat of wood filler thinned to the consistency of single cream, and sand when dry. Repeat this step, then paint with primer, undercoat and red-brown eggshell. (Make sure it's solvent-based.)

Mix several small batches of 60 per cent transparent oil glaze, 20 per cent eggshell and 20 per cent white spirit in progressively deeper shades of brown. Apply along the grain, starting with the lightest colour, using a comb or a special graining brush, and blur for a natural effect with a cloth or softening brush. Finish with button polish or polyurethane.
Best for small pieces of furniture, hand rails and panelling.

EXTERIOR PAINTING

Paint helps protect your home from wind, rain and sun. That is why the outside needs redecorating about every four years, or more often if you live near the sea or in an industrial area. It's best to paint at the end of the summer, when wood has had a long period in which to dry out.

Choose bright, still days if you can, following the sun on the house so that the paint is dried, but avoid painting in full sunlight or when it's windy. It's dangerous to use a ladder in high winds, and paint splashes on walls, caused by wind, can be very difficult to remove.

PREPARATION FOR PAINTING

- Tie back climbing plants.
- Check the state of roof and guttering and repair any leaks.
- Check for rot on fascias and barge-boards beneath the eaves, windows, doors (especially the base) and decorative wood. Replace where necessary, or repair by scraping back to sound wood, removing flaking paint and filling any cracks with exterior stopper.
- If rendering is falling apart, cut it back until you reach the part that is sound, then clean it and patch with mortar. Large areas will need professional attention.
- Clean out defective pointing and fill large cracks with ready-mixed mortar, small ones with exterior filler.
- To remove dirt on painted walls, brush with a stiff brush from the top down. Treat mould with one part bleach to four of water. Leave for two days and then brush the mould away with a stiff brush. Apply stabilising solution to flaky patches.
- Replace any cracked window panes and leave for two weeks before painting the frame, because the putty needs time to harden. Fill gaps between the wall and window frame with flexible exterior filler.
- Scrape metal downpipes and gutters and clean with a wire brush to remove flaking paint. Apply anti-rust primer to any rusty patches that remain. Sand sound paintwork lightly to provide a key.
- Remove peeling paint from window frames and fill and prime where necessary.
- Strip peeling varnish to the bare wood, sand, and apply a sealer coat of varnish thinned with white spirit.
- Clean, sand and dust off sound paintwork.

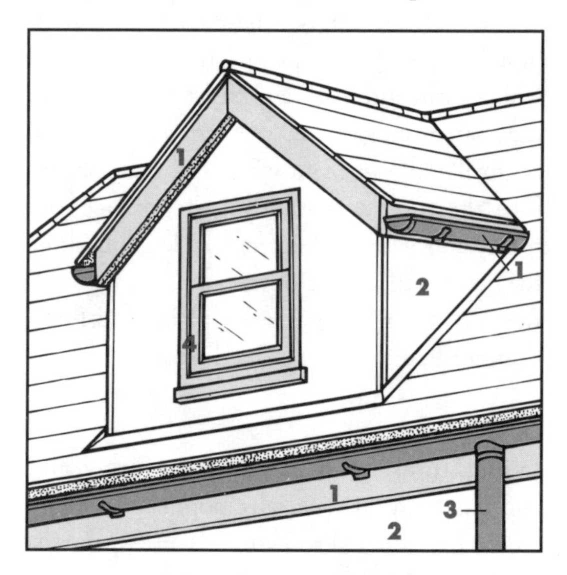

ORDER OF PAINTING

1 Paint fascias, barge-boards and gutters.
2 Paint walls in sections, starting in a corner and working from top to bottom.
3 Paint downpipes.
4 Paint windows and doors.

PAINTING WOOD AND METALWORK

Use gloss paint or stains on wood and gloss on metal. It's important to make sure they are suitable for outdoor use. In most cases, this

LADDER SAFETY

Ladders should be placed at ground level 3ft/1m away from the wall for every 4yds/4m of height. The top of the ladder should overlap the highest point and should be tied in place if possible. Secure at the base with a sandbag, or tie it to wooden pegs knocked into the ground. If the ground is soggy, place the ladder on a board to make sure it's secure.

A tower platform, available from hire shops, makes exterior decorating easier if your house is large, but never climb down the side, which will unbalance it. Special designs are available for chalet bungalows, wide bay windows or houses that have roofs on several levels.

means using a solvent-based paint, which is more weather resistant. But although paint systems especially designed for exterior use may specify two coats of undercoat plus one of liquid gloss for maximum durability, it's often possible to use non-drip one-coat products too – check the recommendations on the tin. Start from the top and work down, placing a piece of board behind downpipes to protect the wall from the paint.

PAINTING WALLS

Before you start, wrap downpipes in polythene or newspaper to protect them from paint splatters and cover plants and paths with plastic sheeting. Start by 'cutting in' – painting a narrow strip – next to barge-boards, doors and windows. Change to a wide wall brush for small areas, a long-pile roller for large ones, and apply the masonry paint with a criss-cross movement. Work from the top down in bands about an arm's length in width, and overlap each strip when you move on, for even coverage. Make sure you don't lean out too far when working at height.

WALLPAPER

Wallpaper is the fastest way to add texture or a floor-to-ceiling pattern to a room. In addition to traditional wallpaper, you'll find paper-backed vinyl, relief papers designed as a base for paint, and a range of textiles from silk to grasscloth. Some are much easier to hang than others, so if you're a novice at wallpaper hanging, look for a medium-weight traditional

DESIGN TIPS

- Large patterns seem to reduce space, while small patterns on a light ground, which give a sense of 'looking through' the design, appear to increase it.
- Stripes look best on even walls and walls where a picture rail or cornice provides a break between wall and ceiling.
- Small random patterns and textured designs may help disguise poor plaster.

wallpaper with a random design, which is unlikely to tear and won't need pattern matching. To avoid getting paint marks or splatters on the papered wall, make sure all the painting is completed before you paper.

TIP Coat plaster walls with 'size' made from wallpaper paste (you'll find instructions on the packet) to make it easier to guide the wallpaper into place.

WHICH WALLPAPER?

Lining paper provides a smooth base for wallpaper or paint. It's available in several weights: light (for covering with paint), medium (suitable for most wallpaper) and heavy (for use beneath relief wall coverings). Ideally it should be hung horizontally, so the joints don't coincide with those of the wallpaper on top.

Textured wallpapers can act as a base for paint. They include embossed designs, such as Anaglypta; high relief wall coverings, which have a more pronounced design and are made from paper plus cotton or clay, or vinyl; and woodchip, used for disguising uneven plaster, made from sawdust and woodchips bonded on to paper.

Printed wall coverings range from expensive,

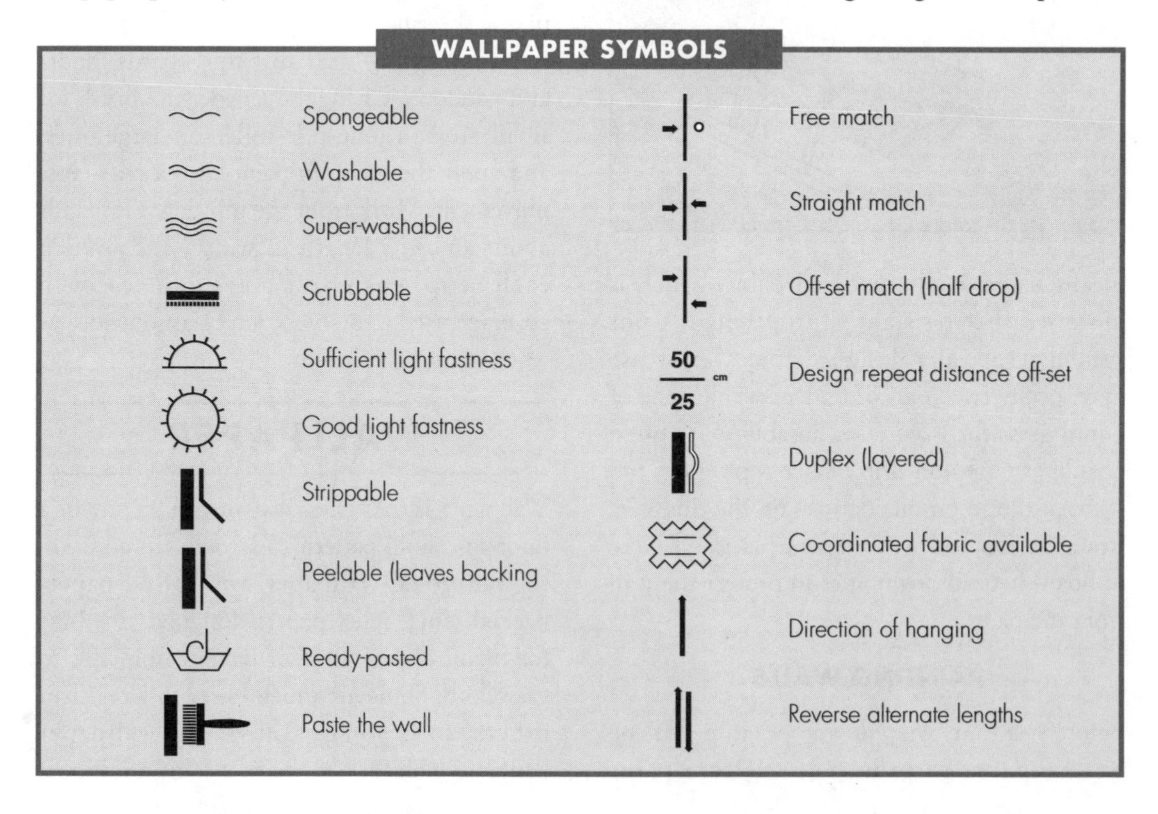

untrimmed, hand-printed designs, to cheap wall coverings when the pattern is printed direct on to paper. In between come papers with a coloured ground, and vinyl wall coverings with a paper backing, which is left behind when the surface is stripped. Because the pattern is printed directly on to the vinyl layer, they're usually more water resistant than washable wallpapers, which have a clear coating.

Textile wall coverings include paper-backed cork, hessian, grasscloth and silk, and flocked wallpapers, which are made from paper plus silk, cotton or wool, or vinyl and nylon. Because they're expensive, difficult to manipulate and liable to stain if adhesive comes into contact with the surface, all but the cheapest hessians and vinyl flocks should be professionally hung.

TIP Make sure all the rolls of wallpaper have the same batch number, because colours may vary between printings.

TIP Buy an extra roll of wallpaper and keep it for future repairs.

PREPARATION FOR WALLPAPERING

Any lumps and bumps on the walls are likely to show through wallpaper just as they do through paint, so walls should be filled and sanded smooth. Old wallpaper should be stripped away because it's rarely a satisfactory surface for the new layer. Wrinkles will be repeated, colour may bleed through, and the weight of the new paper may pull it all away from the wall.

Stripping wallpaper

1 Vinyls and paper-backed wallpapers are often designed for dry stripping, which means they can be peeled away from the backing. Try lifting a corner and pulling upwards and outwards. The backing can be used as lining paper if it's in good condition, especially if you intend to paint over the top or want to cover it with heavy wallpaper.

2 To remove standard wallpaper, first turn off the electricity at the mains. Then wet the wallpaper with detergent solution, working from the top of the wall down so the water runs over the wallpaper, giving it a chance to penetrate. (Be careful not to over-wet if you're working on plasterboard.)

3 If the wallpaper is coated or overpainted, you'll probably need to scrape the surface with a wire brush before wetting it to improve absorbency. Leave it to soak before you try to remove the wallpaper.

4 It's often worth hiring or buying a steam wallpaper stripper, which can speed things up if there are several layers of paper to remove.

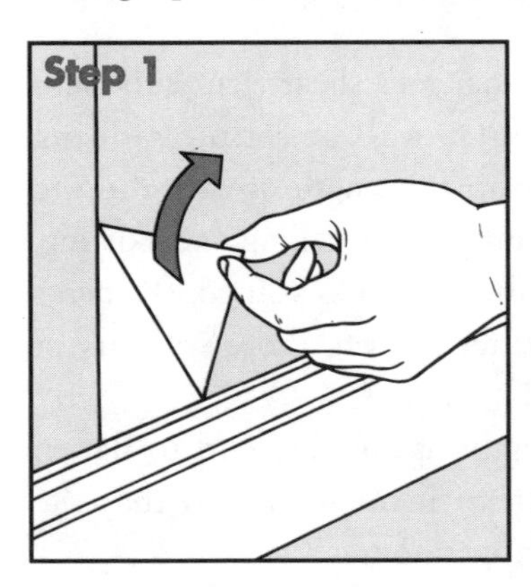

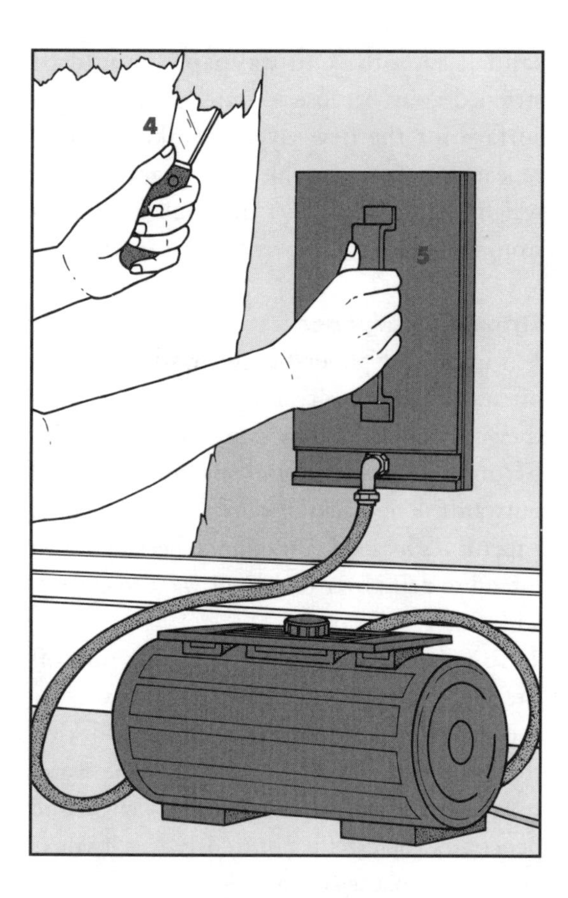

5 Using a scraper with a wide blade, start at the seams and base. With luck, you'll be able to remove a sizeable strip of wallpaper, but try not to damage the wall beneath, as any chips will need to be filled.

When all the paper has been removed, finish by sanding lightly to remove any small pieces of paper still stuck to the walls.

PLANNING PAPERING

Ideally you should start in a corner and work away from the light so that the joins between lengths are less noticeable. Before you start, it's worth marking where the joins will fall and adjusting your starting point if lengths meet in a prominent place. As a rule, where there are no special features, and unless you are left-handed, start at the wall to the right of the main window and work round the room.

ADHESIVES

- Standard wallpaper paste (available as powder or ready-mixed) is suitable for light and medium-weight wallpapers but heavy wallpaper needs a heavy-duty paste.
- Vinyls and plastic-coated wallpapers need a fungicidal adhesive to prevent mould.

However, if there is a chimney breast, paste the first length in the middle of it. Treat each half of the room separately, working towards the door and starting at the chimney breast again to paper the other side. This way, awkward joins can be minimised.

HOW TO HANG WALLPAPER

You will need

- Copydex or similar adhesive (for repairs)
- Paper-hanger's brush
- Paper-hanger's shears
- Paste brush
- Pasting table
- Pencil
- Plumb bob and line
- Ruler or tape measure
- Seam roller (to press down wallpaper edges)
- Wallpaper paste and bucket

1 Using paper-hanger's shears, cut sufficient drops for about a wall at a time, adding 2–3in/5–7.5cm to the length of each drop to allow for trimming at the ceiling and skirting, and matching the pattern as you go. (If there's a substantial pattern repeat, drops will vary in length.)
2 Roll the lengths against the curl to flatten them and then turn them over so that the pasting side is uppermost.

HOW MUCH WALLPAPER DO YOU NEED?

Standard rolls of wallpaper measure about 11yd/10.05m long by 21in/530mm wide, but American and continental sizes may differ. The following chart is based on standard wallpaper. Use it to work out the number of rolls you need.

Wall height from skirting	**Distance round the room (inc doors and windows)**																	
	30	34	38	42	46	50	54	58	62	66	70	74	78	82	86	90	94	98 **feet**
	9	10	12	13	14	15	16	17	18	19	21	22	23	24	26	27	28	30 **metres**
7–7 ½ft/ 2.15–2.30m	4	5	5	6	6	7	7	8	8	9	9	10	10	11	12	12	13	13
7 ½–8ft/ 2.30–2.45m	5	5	6	6	7	7	8	8	9	9	10	10	11	11	12	13	13	14
8–8 ½ft/ 2.45–2.60m	5	5	6	7	7	8	9	9	10	10	11	12	12	13	14	14	15	15
8 ½–9ft/ 2.60–2.75m	5	5	6	7	7	8	9	9	10	10	11	12	12	13	14	14	15	15
9–9 ½ft/ 2.75–2.90m	6	6	7	7	8	9	9	10	10	11	12	12	13	14	14	15	15	16
9 ½–10ft/ 2.90–3.05m	6	6	7	8	8	9	10	10	11	12	12	13	14	14	15	16	16	17
10–10 ½ft/ 3.05–3.20m	6	7	8	8	9	10	10	11	12	13	13	14	15	16	16	17	18	19

Ceilings:
To calculate the number of rolls required, work out the area in square metres and divide by five.

3 Mix the paste as instructed and brush it down the centre of the wallpaper with a pasting brush. (Tie a taut string across the bucket to remove excess paste from the brush.) Brush the paste out from the centre, first away from you and then towards you, so that the edges are covered.

Ready-pasted wall covering simply needs

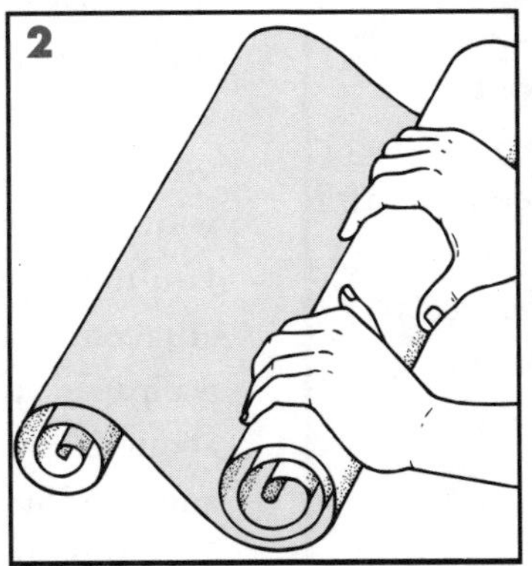

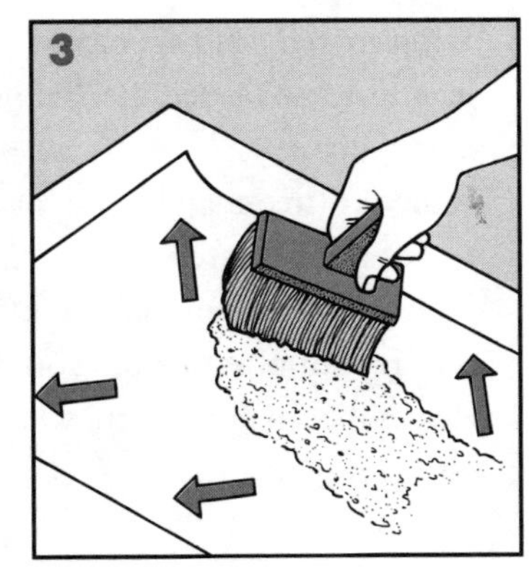

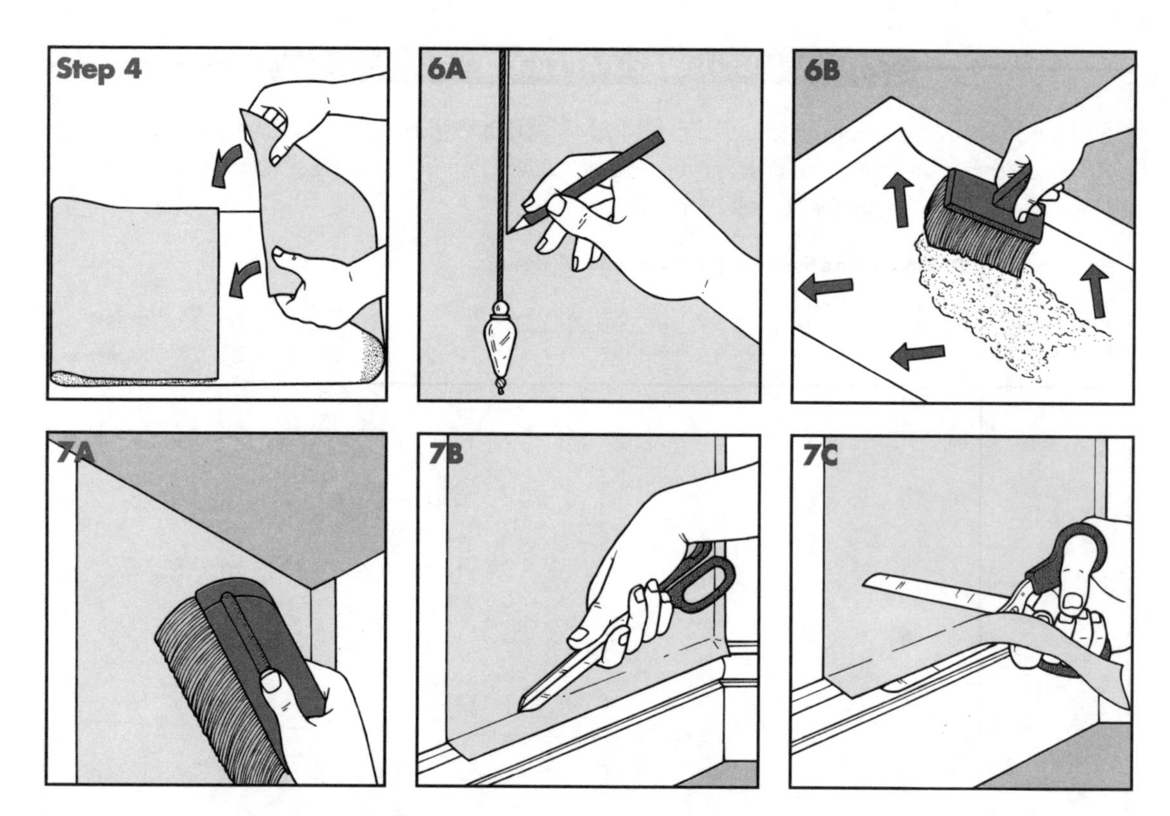

soaking in water in the trough provided and can be smoothed into place with a sponge. Apply Copydex to seams and edges if they have a tendency to lift.

4 Move the paper up and gently fold the paper over so the pasted surfaces meet. When you have pasted the whole drop, fold the other side so that the top and bottom meet in the centre. (When papering stairways and ceilings, you may have to concertina the paper to paste the longest lengths.)

5 Vinyls can be put up straight away but you should leave standard wallpaper to soak for five minutes and heavier relief designs for ten, so that the paper stretches and bubbles won't occur.

6 To make sure you hang the paper straight, find the vertical, using a plumb bob and line (a small weight on a string) as a guide (A). Mark a line 1in/25mm less than the wallpaper's width if you're starting at a corner (because you'll be turning this amount on to the adjacent wall) and hang the first piece of wallpaper, using this line as a guide, allowing about 2¾in/70mm to overlap on the ceiling. and 1in/25mm to turn round the corner (B).

7 Manoeuvre the top half into place and

PATTERN MATCHING

Straight-match wallpapers line up horizontally.

Drop-match wallpapers require adjoining lengths to be moved up or down to match up.

Random (free-match) designs don't need to be pattern matched.

Pattern repeats can make a difference to the amount of wallpaper you need. Remember to allow extra when estimating quantity.

HANGING LINING PAPER

Hang lining paper horizontally, working from the top downwards and joining lengths edge to edge (butt-joining). Overlap by about ⅝–1in/15–25mm at the corners for a neat, strong finish and to take in any irregularities in the wall. Walls are rarely straight. You must do this or the paper may peel back from the wall where the edges meet.

smooth down with a paper-hanger's brush, pushing it well into the corner (A). Release the bottom half, lower gently (it may stretch if dropped) and smooth into place. Mark a fold at skirting and ceiling level with the shears and trim to fit.

8 Hang the next length so it butts tightly up to the first, because the paper will shrink as it dries. Leave for five minutes and then press into place with a seam roller.

TIP Use a seam roller with care on relief wallpaper as it may crush the design.

WHAT WENT WRONG?

Bubbles form if the wallpaper isn't pasted thoroughly or isn't given time to soak. They can also occur if the length isn't smoothed out properly. It's sometimes possible to slit air bubbles with a razor blade and paste the edges into place.

Dirty marks can usually be removed with a white eraser (use with care) or a piece of stale white bread.

Gaps can appear if lengths are not pushed together or if the paper has been stretched too much when smoothed out and has shrunk back when dry.

Peeling is often caused by damp. If it's not substantial, trying lifting and re-pasting the edges with wallpaper paste or Copydex.

Tears may not be noticeable if they're stuck down carefully.

AWKWARD AREAS

Ceilings Paste the paper and fold into a concertina, then unfold as you press into place. Smooth down with a broom; this is best done by a partner walking behind you.

Corners (above) Unless the gap between the

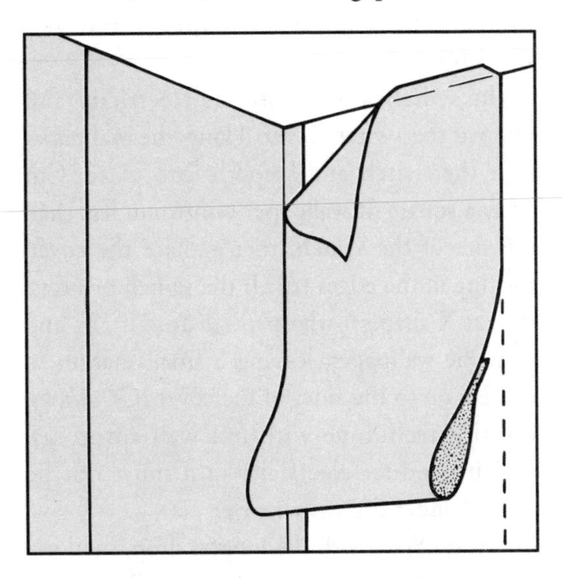

previous length of paper and the corner of the room is very narrow, cut the last length on the wall so that it turns the corner by about 1in/25mm. Find the vertical on the new wall and hang the first length on that wall so that it covers the overlaps. External (convex) corners (on alcoves and chimney breasts for example) may need a larger overlap to make sure seams don't coincide with the exposed corners, where they will undoubtedly tear.

TIP 'Feather' relief papers to make the edge thinner by tearing the edge and press down with a seam roller to minimise bulk when overlapping a corner.

Fixings Insert matches to mark the site of screws or picture hangers and allow them to

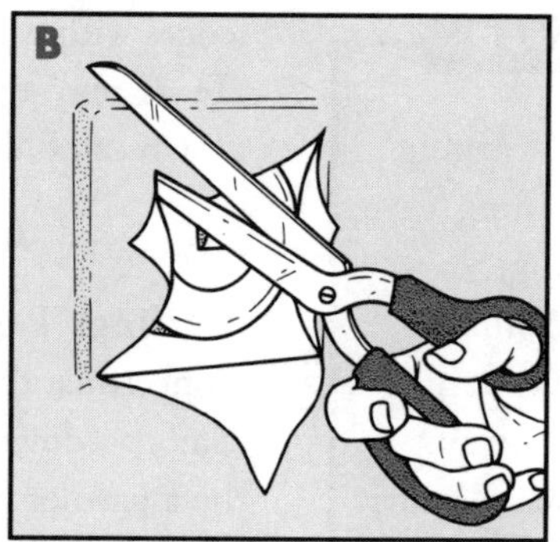

pierce through the wallpaper when you smooth it into place.

Light switches Turn off the electricity and remove the switch cover. Hang the wallpaper over the switch and smooth into place. Cut away a square of wallpaper ¼in/6mm less than the size of the switch, then replace the cover, tucking in the edges (A). If the switch projects, cut an X shape in the paper across it (B) and trim the wallpaper, leaving a small margin to overlap on to the sides of the cover (C). *Always* use this technique with foil wall coverings, which conduct electricity and must not be tucked under the switch cover.

Stairways Start with the longest drop, marking the vertical by fixing a piece of chalked string from top to bottom of the stair well, and snapping it against the wall. Cut each length separately, matching the pattern and making sure that the length is sufficient to take in the angled skirting.

Window sills Pull the paper over the corner of the sill and slit it before smoothing the paper into place.

BORDERS

Borders are available in wallpaper or ready-pasted vinyl, but though pasting techniques may differ, they are cut and fixed in more or less the same way.

You will need

Same equipment as for hanging wallpaper (page 384) plus

- Spirit-level

1 Mark the position of the border lightly in pencil, using a spirit level to find the horizontal. Then step back and see how it looks to the eye. It's sometimes better to have a border that follows the walls or ceiling than one that emphasises irregularities.

2 Cut the border, and paste or soak it.

3 Concertina the folds, matching pasted edge to pasted edge, and unwind carefully, smoothing into place as you go.

4 Butt join ends, making sure the pattern matches, and press the margins down firmly.

HOW TO MITRE A BORDER

If you want to create a panelled look with wallpaper borders, you'll need to mitre the corners for a perfect right angle.
1 Find the right-hand vertical with a plumb bob and line and mark with a pencil, then paste a strip of border into place, allowing 1in/25mm more than the finished size.
2 Check the horizontal with a spirit level and smooth the border across the top of the panel into place, allowing another 1in/25mm overlap on the right-hand side.
3 Mitre the corner by placing a ruler across the diagonal from the outer to the inner edge and cut along this line with a trimming knife. Take off the surplus triangle on top, then peel back the horizontal border and remove the excess from beneath. Smooth the edges into place.

OPENING UP A FIREPLACE

There are very few rooms that don't look better when a previously filled chimney breast is opened and the fireplace restored. The fireplace is the natural focal point of the room and the decorative impact it makes is well worth the sacrifice of wall space, even in quite small rooms.

Before you begin, look around for fireplaces that suit the style of your house. If you want an unusual design or one in a very small size, you may do best to look for authentic period pieces from specialists or architectural salvage firms. Alternatively, as grates and mantelpieces in good condition and a reasonable price can be difficult to find, you may find it easier to settle for a reproduction.

STEP-BY-STEP OPENING A FLUE

You will need

- Candle
- Hammer
- Bolster, or pointing chisel

1 Locate the chimney breast, which usually projects into the room but sometimes juts outside it. It may be covered by hardboard or plasterboard which are simple to remove, or it may be bricked in.
2 If the fireplace has been closed properly, you'll find an airbrick set into the wall to prevent damp. Insert the large chisel into the mortar surrounding it, and tap it with a hammer. Remove the airbrick carefully. If the fireplace has been filled with bricks and there is no airbrick, take out a few bricks about 12in/30cm from the floor.
3 Light a candle and place it the fireplace. If the flame is drawn upwards, the chimney is clear. If it goes out, ask a builder for advice.
4 If the chimney is clear, unblock the opening, taking care not to damage the lintel across the top of the fireplace.
5 Clean out the original fireplace and check that the fireback (which protects the wall from heat) is usable and not cracked, replacing it if necessary before you fit the new fireplace.

TIP For safety, have the chimney swept before you light the fire.

WALL TILES

Tiles are waterproof, last for years and need little more care than a swift wipe over with detergent. They're ideal for walls that are likely to get wet or need protection from steam or grease, but because they last so long, it's worth while choosing colours and designs that won't date and will look good with a variety of colour schemes.

Most wall tiles are ceramic, though glass mirror tiles are available too. The most popular size is 6in/152mm square, though 4in/100mm square tiles and rectangular tiles (usually 8 x 4in/200 x 100mm, or 8 x 6in/ 200 x 152mm) hexagonal and Provençal shapes are also available.

Craftsman-made and continental tiles are often smaller and chunkier; that goes for borders and dados too and, as a result, it can be difficult to mix and match unless you're certain of the depth of the tiles you want to use. If you can't compare samples directly, it may be safer to choose all your tiles from the same range.

TYPES OF TILE

'Universal' tiles have at least two glazed edges so you can use them anywhere, turning the glazed edges to the outside when you reach the end of a run. Bevelled-edge universal tiles butt together leaving a space for the grout so you won't need to use spacers.

Field tiles have unglazed edges for use in the centre of a panel. They may be self-spacing, with lugs on each side.

Border or edge tiles have one or two rounded edges, to finish the outside of a panel.

Quadrant tiles are narrow rounded strips, used to top standard tiles.

TILING STEP BY STEP

You will need

- Grout
- Hammer
- Metal rule
- Nails or tacks
- Notched tile-adhesive spreader (often supplied with the tile adhesive)
- Pincers for cutting random shapes (if necessary)
- Plastic tile spacers or matchsticks (if necessary)
- Sand paper (for stripping)
- Spirit-level
- Sponge
- Tile adhesive
- Tile file
- Tungsten carbide tile cutter
- Wooden battens

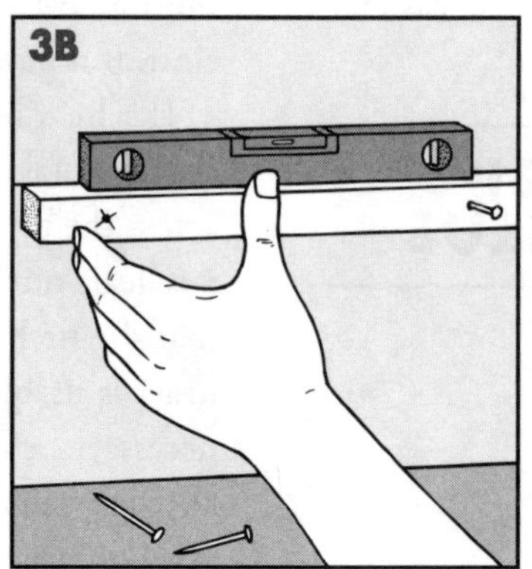

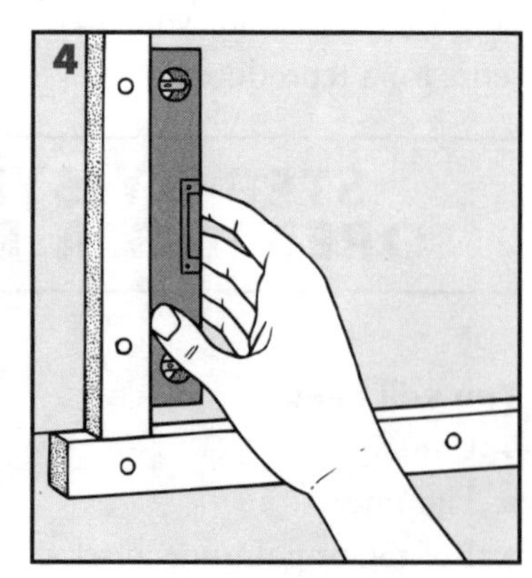

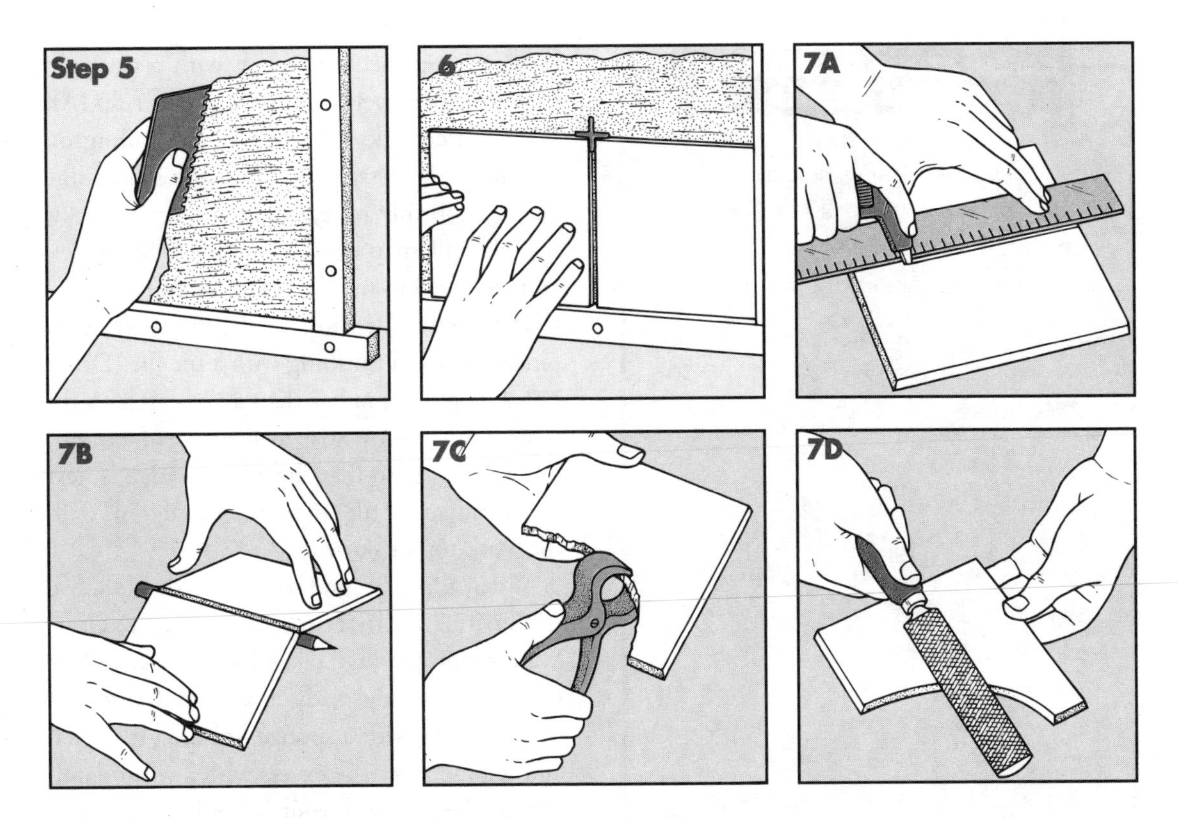

1 Wash down emulsion paint and sand solvent-painted surfaces to provide a key. Strip off all wallpaper before tiling.

TIP You can tile over old tiles if you rub down and seal with plaster primer to provide a key. You'll need a wooden strip or pieces of tile to conceal the double thickness at the top.

2 Work out where the cut tiles will fall. Have a 'dry run' and readjust if there are any very narrow pieces to cut at the end of a run. It's better to have two evenly cut tiles at each end.

3 Measure the distance of one tile up from the skirting or work-top (A) and find the true horizontal with a spirit-level (B). Mark with a pencil and nail or tack a slim wooden batten to the wall along this line.

4 Check the vertical with a spirit-level and fix a batten at the end of the last full row of tiles, to keep the tiles in line.

5 Starting in the corner where the battens meet, spread tile adhesive on to a square metre of wall, combing it with a notched spreader until it is even.

6 Press the tiles firmly into place without sliding them, inserting plastic spacers (to leave space for the grout) if necessary. Wipe off any adhesive on the surface of the tiles with a damp sponge as you go. Continue until all whole tiles have been fixed, checking the levels

DESIGN TIPS

- Use a row of border tiles to create a frieze on a wall of plain tiles.
- Panels of patterned tiles can make long, high walls seem shorter.
- To show off the design on odd or antique tiles, set them into a window ledge.
- Tile well-used coffee tables for a water and heat-resistant finish.

CALCULATING THE NUMBER OF TILES NEEDED

Measure the area you want to tile and divide by the size of the tiles or use this ready reckoner if you are using standard sizes. Add 10 per cent for breakages.

Area in:	4x4	6x6	4x8	12x12
cm:	10x10	15x15	10x20	30x30
sq yd/ sq m	**No tiles**			
1.1/1	100	44	50	12
2.2/2	200	87	100	23
3.3/3	300	130	150	34
4.4/4	400	174	200	45
5.5/5	500	217	250	56
6.6/6	600	260	300	67
7.7/7	700	303	350	78
8.8/8	800	347	400	89
9.9/9	900	390	450	100
11/10	1000	433	500	111

Per 1.1sq yd/1sq m:

Adhesive: 3⅓lb/1.5kg/1 litre

Grout: 6oz/150g

from time to time. Remove the battens when the adhesive is dry.

7 Now fix the cut tiles. Mark the cutting line on the tile and place it on a cutting board, right side up. Score through with a tungsten carbide cutter held against a metal rule (A). Place matchsticks or a pencil, depending on the tile's thickness, underneath the scored line and press firmly on each side. If you're lucky, the tile will snap evenly (B). For odd shapes, you will need to make a template and copy the shape on to the tile, nibbling away with pincers (C) and finishing with a tile file (D).

TIP Use pincers rather than a tile cutter to cut away a very narrow strip at the edge of a tile.

8 Fix cut tiles so that the smooth edge is next to the adjacent tile and the cut edge next to the work-top or skirting.

9 When tiling is complete, leave the adhesive to harden as instructed on the packet. Waterproof adhesive takes longer to dry. Mix the grout (or buy ready-mixed) and spread it over the gaps with a sponge, pushing it in well and wiping away the excess with a clean damp sponge. Neaten with your finger or a lolly stick just before the grout sets.

TIP Use flexible sealant between the tiles and bath or basin after you grout.

10 When dry, wipe with a damp sponge to remove the last traces of grout, and polish the tiles with a soft cloth.

TIP Don't rinse the sponges and cloths used for grouting under the tap. The grout residues may block the drain.

ALL ABOUT SHELVES

Shelves are the most flexible form of storage. Once you can put up a shelf, you'll have mastered the basic techniques needed for hanging everything from paintings and mirrors to wall cupboards. It's easy when you know how, as long as you make sure the shelf is absolutely level and choose suitable wall fixings so the brackets are secure.

It's wise to start by hanging a single decorative shelf rather than a floor to ceiling fitment, and if you've never used a drill before, to practise on different surfaces first, such as brick and wood.

WHICH SHELF?

Chipboard shelves can be finished with a layer of plastic laminate, like that used for kitchen cupboards, or melamine, a spray coating available in wood effect or plain colours. Plastic laminate shrugs off water and stains but melamine is less durable. It protects against damp but is easily marked.

Glass shelves must be plate glass and should have ground edges for safety.

Timber shelves range from unfinished pine, which you can paint, stain, varnish or polish, to expensive hardwoods. Most shelving for home use is made from softwoods, ready-cut or in lengths you can cut to size and then finish as you wish.

Supports can be made from pieces of wood fixed each side of a narrow alcove, individual brackets, or slotted uprights, which allow you to vary the height of the shelves. You can also buy horizontal metal supports designed to support the shelf along its entire length, which are more discreet than brackets or uprights.

SPACE SAVERS

Shelves provide an easy answer to a host of storage problems. Here are a few ideas.

- Put a shelf at the bottom of a wardrobe and store shoes underneath.
- Fit shelves in a tall cupboard and use for storing toys and games.
- A wide shelf with strong brackets can serve as a desk in a study or bedroom. Top with some bookshelves.
- Fix shallow shelves to the inside of kitchen cupboard doors or at the back of the larder or broom cupboard for extra storage.
- Line an under-stairs cupboard with shelves to keep light bulbs, plugs, small items and tools handy.
- Hang narrow decorative shelves beneath kitchen wall cupboards, for mugs or spices.
- Fit broad, widely-spaced shelves in children's rooms and use them to store toys in large plastic crates. (Make sure they're too high to be climbed or sat on.)
- Fit shelves in the garage and garden shed to hold tools and DIY equipment.
- Organise shelves in the bathroom or cloakroom: narrow glass ones for toiletries, wide wood or melamine for extra supplies and clean towels.
- Make an old-fashioned plate shelf with a slot to keep plates upright. Fix it round the room at picture rail level, to show off old china.
- Fix glass shelves across a dull window and cover with sun-loving plants; they'll thrive in the light.

WALLS AND FIXINGS

TYPE OF WALL

It's important to work out what the wall is made from, because that decides the type of fixing you use and the stability of the shelves.

TIP The dust from drilling is a guide to wall construction. Red dust indicates brick, which can take straightforward wall plugs. Grey powder is probably building blocks, which can also support conventional screw fixings. Black dust may mean breeze blocks, which need anchor fixings.

Solid walls are made from brick or building blocks. Most houses built before the First World War have solid exterior walls.
Cavity walls are made from two layers of brick or building blocks with a gap between for insulation. Houses built after the Second World War have exterior cavity walls.
Breeze blocks were sometimes used for interior walls in houses built between the 1930s and 60s. Although solid, breeze blocks do crumble easily and need reinforcement to support heavy loads.
Plasterboard is used to line walls and for stud walls, made from plasterboard on a timber frame. (Stud walls are sometimes used as interior walls in recently converted flats, or where doors have been filled in, or in small added extensions.) You can tell if a wall is made from plasterboard because it sounds hollow when knocked. Unless the load is very light, you'll need to locate the timber supports underneath the plasterboard on stud walls, or provide timber reinforcement on the wall behind for strength.
Lath and plaster walls consist of plaster supported by a web of timber slats, and are found in period homes. You can usually detect this type of construction because most of these wall are very irregular.
TIP Use a cable detector to locate the uprights in lath and plaster walls: it will light up when passed over the nails used to fix the laths.

WHICH FIXING?

If you're working on a solid wall, you can use standard wall plugs. Shelves fixed to timber uprights need strong screws which are screwed straight into the wood. If you want to fix shelving to breeze block or hollow plasterboard walls, you'll also need cavity fixings (which open out when screwed in to provide support behind the wall) or stronger toggle bolts.

PUTTING UP A SHELF STEP BY STEP

You will need
- Bradawl
- Pencil
- Power drill
- Screwdriver
- Shelves, brackets and fixings (including wall plugs if necessary)
- Spirit-level

1 Plan the distance between the shelves. Make sure they're broad enough and far apart enough for your needs.
TIP The heavier the load, the more supports you will need. Make sure brackets are a minimum of 16in/400mm apart for bookshelves or when fitting glass shelves.
2 Check that the screws are the right size for the brackets and that the wall plugs and drill bit size are compatible.
TIP 'Universal' wall plugs cover a range of common screw sizes.

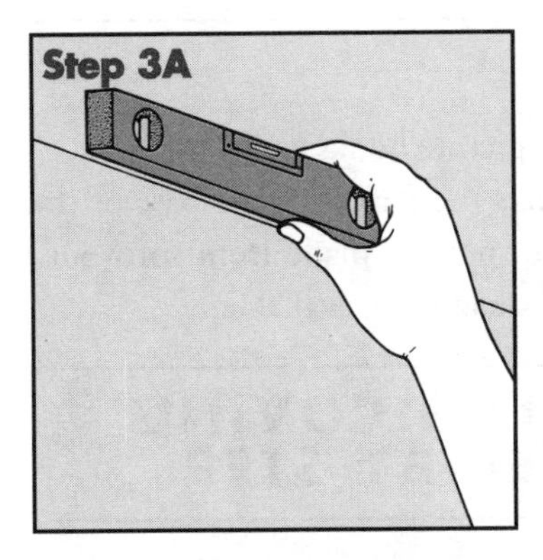

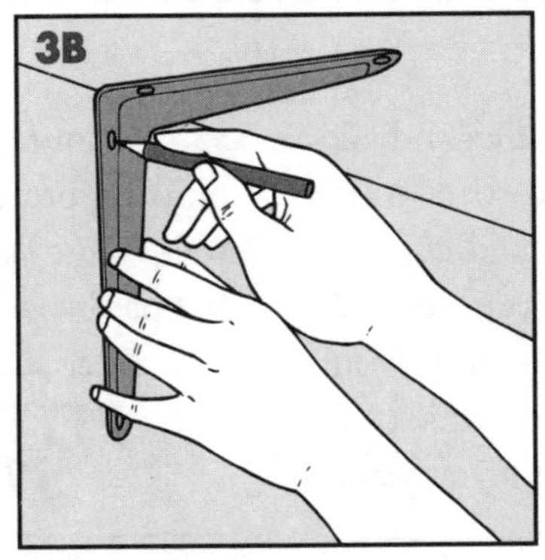

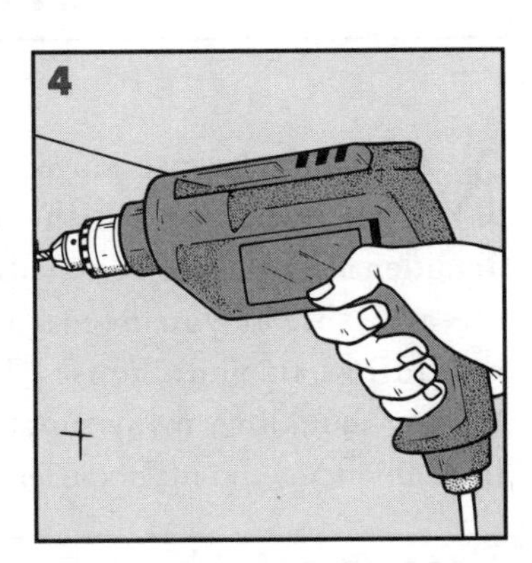

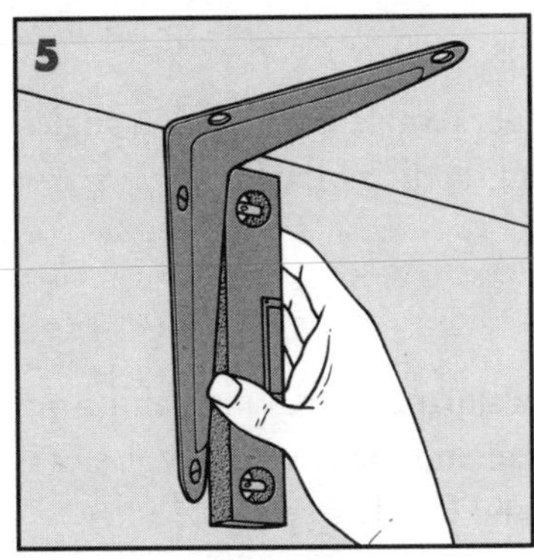

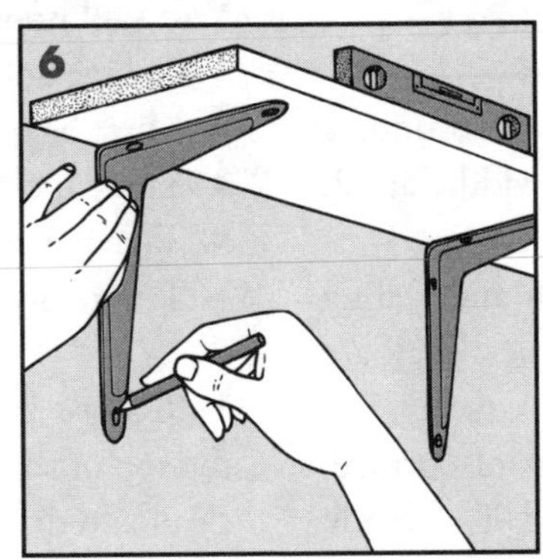

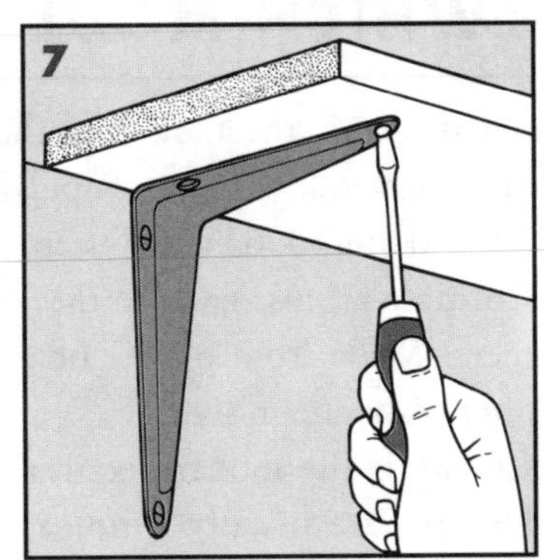

3 Mark a line along the wall where the shelf will be, using a spirit-level to check that it's straight (A). Hold the brackets in place and mark the screw holes (B), before checking the horizontal with a spirit-level once more.

4 With a solid wall, use a masonry drill bit to make holes for the first bracket, about 1½in/4cm deep where marked. (Work slowly to make sure the drill doesn't overheat.)

TIP To mark the drilling depth, twist a piece of Sellotape round the drill bit marking off the first 4cm.

For breeze block or hollow plasterboard walls, use an ordinary drill bit the correct size for the fixing. When working on wood, use a bradawl to start the screw holes as that will stop the timber splitting.

5 Push in the wall plugs until they are flush with the surface, and loosely screw the bracket into place, keeping a check that it is vertical with a spirit-level.

6 Repeat with the furthest bracket, and check both vertical and horizontal levels. Repeat until all the brackets are in place, carefully checking the levels each time, and making any adjustments necessary.

TIP Drill and screw just one hole for each bracket, marking the others in pencil until you are sure the shelf will be level, to avoid making unnecessary holes in the wall.

7 Screw the brackets firmly in place on the wall and put up the shelf. Mark the position of the small retaining screws that secure the shelf to the bracket. Remove the shelf and make small 'pilot' holes in it with a bradawl before replacing the shelf on the brackets and screwing into place manually.

TIP Make sure the screw is at least ¼in/6mm shorter than the depth of the shelf, so it won't pierce the surface.

TIP Rubbing screws with petroleum jelly makes them easier to remove later.

MOULDINGS

Mouldings balance a high ceiling and add a decorative finish to the wall. Traditional skirtings, picture rails and cornices are available if you need to replace the mouldings in your house. To match an existing moulding, many suppliers will copy from an offcut, and make the length you want.

WHICH MOULDING?

Architrave is the moulding that surrounds a door or window frame. Popular widths are 2, 2½ and 3in/50, 63 and 75mm.

Cornices are used where the wall and ceiling meet. Made from plaster or timber, they are often elaborate in style.

Coving is the modern equivalent of cornice. Designs are usually simple, and it is made from easy-to-handle plaster or polystyrene.

Dado rails are timber mouldings fixed about a metre from the ground. Originally called chair rails, they were once designed to protect the wall from knocks by furniture but are now often used to separate decorations, such as wallpaper above and paint below.

Frieze describes the area between the picture rail (see below) and cornice.

Picture rail is the timber moulding that runs round a wall above head height and has a special slot for picture hooks.

Skirting protects the plaster at the base of the wall. Most skirtings are made from softwood, but hardwood designs are available.

FITTING COVING STEP BY STEP

You will need

- Coving adhesive
- Mitre box/paper template for cutting angles
- Sandpaper and sanding block
- Tape measure
- Tenon saw

1 Remove any wallpaper or flaking paint from the top of the wall and make sure the plaster is clean and dry. Sand lightly to provide a key.

2 Measure the room, counting the corners, so you know how many angles you need to cut – both internal, such as in a recess, and external, where a chimney breast projects outwards.

3 Cut the lengths to the correct angle using a tenon saw and either a mitre box or a paper template. Smooth the edges by sanding lightly.

4 Apply adhesive generously to the reverse side and edges of the coving (A), and press into place (B). Use a clean cloth to wipe away any excess adhesive before it sets.

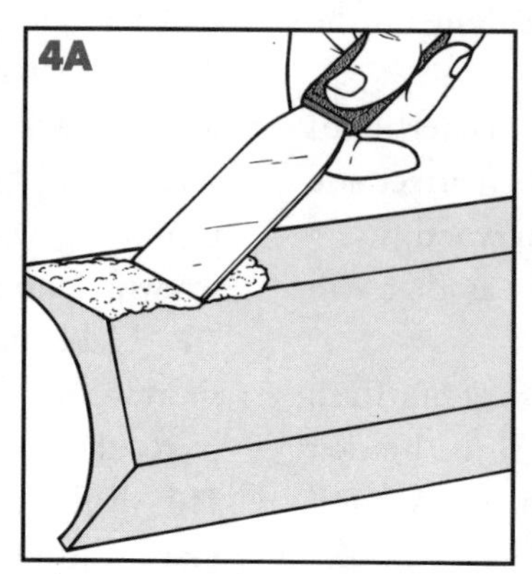

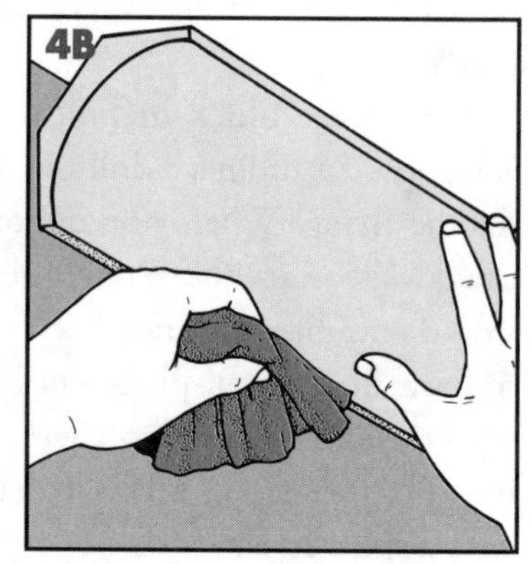

BASIC PICTURE FRAMING

There's no need to restrict the number of pictures you hang or let pictures and photos gather dust until you can afford professional framing. With a few simple tools and materials and basic DIY skills, you can produce excellent frames for minimum outlay. Use the following techniques for prints and inexpensive original paintings.

Anything that is particularly precious or antique should, however, be taken to a professional framer.

WHICH FRAME?

Wooden mouldings suit most pictures. They vary from ornate gilded designs for oil paintings, to waxed, limed or stained frames for water colours, and narrow, plain mouldings for prints. For your first attempt at framing, choose a basic moulding with a rebate (recess), to keep the picture and mount firmly in place.

Aluminium mouldings must be cut with a hacksaw, which can't be used with a mitre box. If you want aluminium frames, it may be better to buy a ready-cut kit.

Clip or 'no-frame' frames sandwich the picture between a hardboard backing and glass front, keeping it in place with clips. This is an economical way of hanging posters and children's paintings but won't protect pictures from dust or damp.

Box or shadow frames are like miniature glass-fronted cupboards. They're ideal for collections and collages that won't lie flat.

TIP To make sure the frame is strong enough to support the picture, the width of the moulding should measure at least 1/20th of the picture's longest side.

MAKING A FRAME AND MOUNT

You will need

Tools

- Bevelled mount cutter or sharp craft knife (if using a mount)
- Compasses (if cutting a circular mount)
- Fine-toothed tenon saw
- Corner or frame clamps
- Mitre box, to cut perfect corners. Fix it to a work bench or screw it to a block of wood and then clamp it to a table. (Cover the table with a piece of board to protect it.)
- Metal rule
- Nail punch
- Pin hammer
- Set square
- Small hand drill with very fine drill bit made from a cut-off veneer pin
- Woodwork vice – may be needed to hold wood for sawing

Materials

- Cord or picture wire for hanging
- Fine abrasive paper
- Glass: use non-reflective if light is a problem. Order glass cut to size (take the finished frame to the glazier). Glass is not necessary for oil paintings or prints that are block mounted.
- Hardboard for backing: 1/8in/3mm thick
- Masking tape
- Mounting card
- Veneer pins
- Screw eyes or D clips
- Turnclips
- Varnish, stain or paint
- PVA Wood glue

- Wood filler
- Wooden moulding with a rebate (recessed edge). (To find out how much you need, double the length and width of the picture, plus mount if any. Now add eight times the width of the moulding to allow for mitring the corners, plus 8in/20cm cutting allowance. The moulding can be cut in half for transport if necessary, because that will always allow enough for the longest edge.)

WHEN TO USE A MOUNT

Mounts are traditionally used with watercolours, prints and drawings to protect them and display the delicate colours to their best advantage. Techniques include sticking the picture on top of the mount most easily done using spray photo-mount on the back of the pictures, and (dry mounting) 'window' mounting, where the picture is seen through a hole cut in the mount, recommended for drawings and watercolours, that could be damaged if they came into contact with the glass.

Mount card is available from art shops in thicknesses graded from 1 to 12. Size 6 is a good general-purpose card. Choose a colour that enhances the painting to be framed, not one that competes with it, and look at the depth of colour too. A dark picture on a light mount generally appears smaller than a light picture on a dark mount. Dark mounts should be used with care, because they can detract from the impact of the picture.

TIP Combine two window mounts in different colours, one with a slightly smaller window under the other, to give an impression of depth.

A wide mount defines the picture and separates it from a busy background – worth bearing in mind if the walls are patterned. Very wide mounts are often used to emphasise miniatures though a narrower mount usually makes a picture appear larger.

Professional framers use a special formula when cutting mounts, which gives more depth at the base and makes the picture look central when displayed on the wall. The ratio is complicated, but cutting the mount allowing 10 to 20 per cent extra at the base gives similar results. For most purposes, a border of 2in/5cm at the top and sides and 2¼in/5.5cm beneath looks effective.

If the picture is wrinkled, dampen the back carefully with moist cotton wool before mounting. Leave for about ten minutes, then fix gummed paper to the top of the picture and lay the window mount over the front. Secure the other three sides with tape on the reverse and leave to dry. All but the deepest wrinkles should disappear as the paper contracts when it dries.

MAKING A MOUNT STEP BY STEP

1 Cut the mount board roughly to size using a straight metal rule, and a bevelled mount cutter or a sharp craft knife (A, right).

Cut the outer corners into perfect right angles, using a set square as a guide (B, right).

2 Cut backing the same size as the mount from thin card.

3 Using a set square, mark the window in the mount lightly in pencil. Use a bevelled mount cutter, or score along this line with a craft knife held against a metal ruler, keeping the blade at about 60° (to create a bevelled edge, which gives an illusion of depth) and pulling it towards you. Repeat until cut through.

4 Lift out the window, pressing with the craft knife to release the corners, and rubbing the sides gently with fine abrasive paper if necessary for a clean edge.

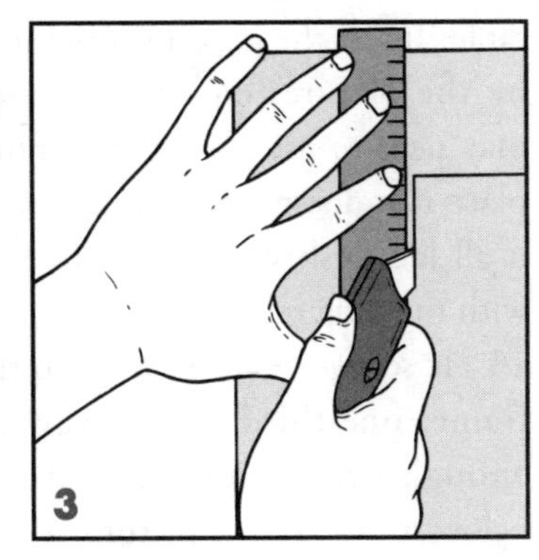

5 Stick the back and front of the mount together along the top edge, using double-sided sticky tape.

PICTURE FRAMING STEP BY STEP

1 Trim the picture if necessary to remove any rough edges and pin holes.

2 Work out the external measurements of the frame by using the following formula. Measure the width of the moulding, deducting the width of the rebate (recess). (See diagramme page 400.) Double this and add to the length and width measurements of the picture, adding an extra ⅛in/3mm to the length and width to allow for clearance.

3 Make sure the mitre box is firmly fixed and clamp the moulding into place, protecting it from denting with pieces of card. It should lie flat in the mitre box, with the rebate edge underneath and facing away from you.

TIP Practise mitring offcuts of wood until you're certain of cutting a clean edge and making sure the mitres go the right way.

4 Put the saw in the slot in the mitre box, and cut the first mitre at the end of one of the lengths of moulding.

5 Mark in pencil the external length of the longest side (as calculated in step 2) so you know where to cut. Cut the second mitre, angled in the opposite direction.

6 Using this length as a guide, measure and mitre the other long side.

7 Cut and mitre two pieces of moulding for the width.

8 Return the pieces of moulding to the mitre box and clamp into place to make sure they form a perfect right-angled corner.

9 Place a length of moulding in the vice with the longer outer edge uppermost and drill a tiny hole (two in a wide moulding) near the end of the moulding but not too close to the edges or the wood will split. (Experiment with wood offcuts.) Drill the hole at one end only. Repeat at one end of the other three mouldings.

10 Taking a long piece of moulding, put it in the vice and brush the cut edge of the undrilled end with glue (A, page 400). Place the pin-hole end of the shorter side on it to form two sides of the frame. Hammer in the pins, punch in and wipe away any glue that's squeezed out (B, page 400).

11 Remove the two pieces carefully and lay flat to dry. Repeat with the other side and then assemble the frame.

12 When dry, rub down with fine glass paper and stain or varnish the frame if required.

13 Cut the backing from hardboard with a hand saw, marking out the cutting lines with a pencil and set square.

14 Check that the glass (if used) and mount are clean and lay the frame face down on the

table. Insert the glass into the rebate, followed by the picture, mount and hardboard. You may need to use glazing sprigs to keep it all in place if it doesn't fill the rebate, or turnclips if it all lies flush with the surface. Seal the back with masking tape.

15 Fix screw eyes or D rings to the back of the frame, one-third of the way down. Attach enough cord or picture wire to come just below the top of the picture. Measure from the frame to the top of the picture wire or cord when fully stretched and mark the same point on the wall. Fix a picture hook to this point and hang the picture.

REPAIRING PICTURE FRAMES

Old picture frames can be more decorative than those available today and are often picked up at relatively little cost. Metal plates, from DIY and art shops, can be used for repairs and

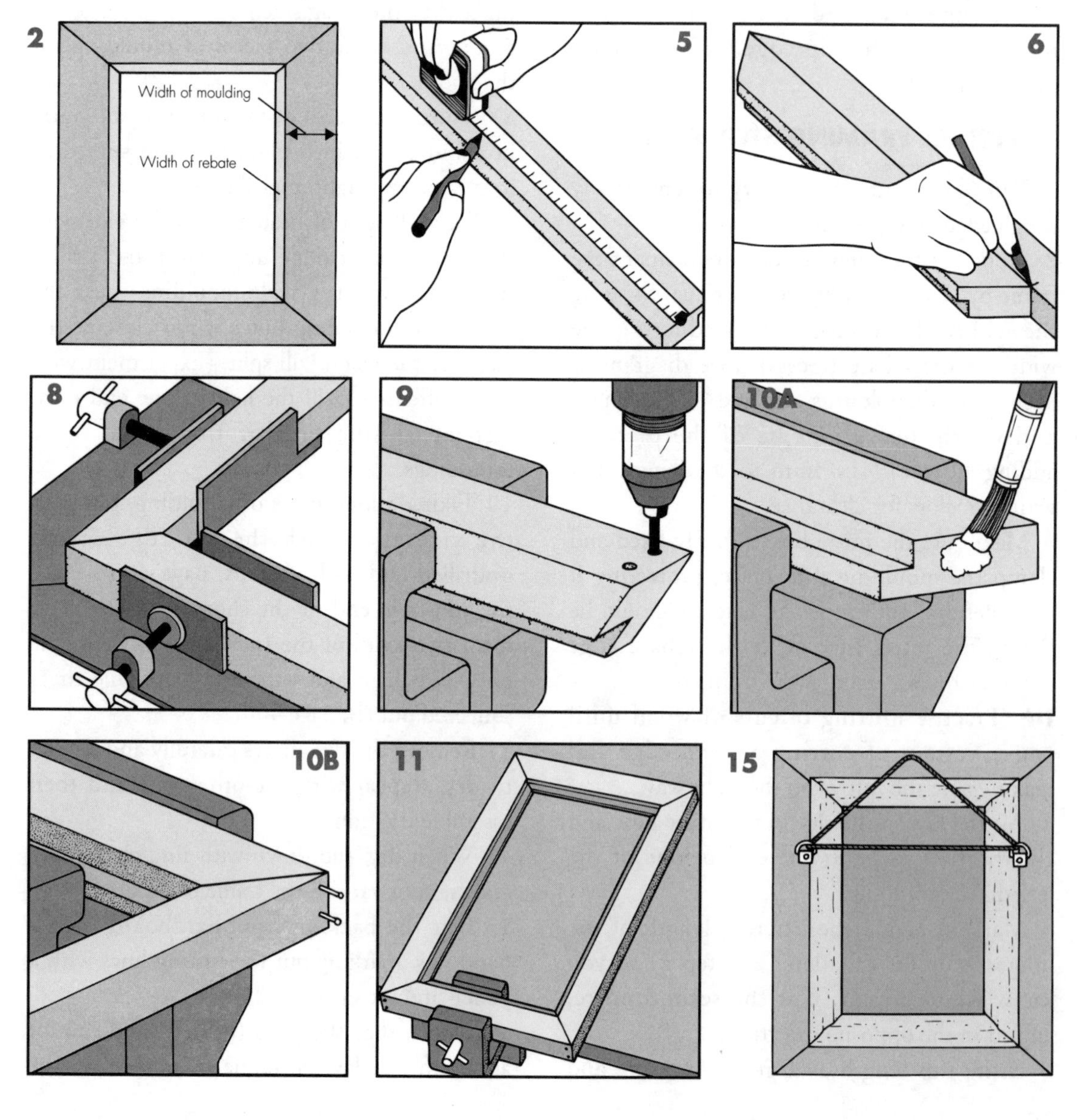

broken glass can be replaced by a glazier, who will cut a new piece to size. Secure your picture with a piece of thin hardboard fixed to the frame with panel pins or tape.

If the mitres are wobbly, remove the pins with pliers, fill the holes and re-fix. If the joints are damaged, it may be easier to cut the lengths and re-mitre them to make a smaller, sounder frame.

Check that the screw eyes and cords are in good condition, particularly if repairs make the frame heavier than before. You may need to substitute strong D rings for existing hangings and replace cord with picture wire.

RENEWING FRAME SURFACES

- Painted frames can be cleaned with white spirit, sanded and repainted with solvent-based undercoat and paint.
- Polished frames can be revived with methylated spirits that is rubbed in with fine wire wool.
- Gilded frames can be cleaned with methylated spirits, and sealed with lacquer.

DESIGN TIPS

- For a lacquered look on a smooth frame, repair chips with multi-purpose filler, and sand lightly when dry. Then apply two coats of enamel paint.
- Mock tortoiseshell has a deep, rich effect. Use artists' water-based acrylic paints that dry quickly and leave a slight sheen. On a smooth, clean base, apply one coat of orange acrylic paint. Allow to dry, sand lightly and wipe clean. Dab brown acrylic paint on top with a cosmetic sponge, allowing some of the first colour to show through. Finish by painting feathery streaks in black with an artist's paintbrush. Sand lightly when dry and protect with varnish.
- Lace relief work can disguise chips and cracks. Cover the frame with a ⅛in/3mm layer of ready-mixed filler and press a length of crisp lace into the surface. Pull the lace away carefully when the filler has dried and paint the surface as required.
- Sea-shells make an attractive surround on old mirror frames. Protect the mirror glass with paper and then cover the frame with a ¼in/6mm layer of ceramic tile cement. Press in a variety of shells and leave them for 24 hours or so, until completely dry. Finish with a layer of polyurethane varnish.
- Fabric can rescue damaged frames. Use strips of light cotton or silk, stiffened on the back with a stiff wallpaper paste. Remember to mitre the corners for a professional effect.

TIPS FOR HANGING PICTURES

Only large, imposing pictures look effective when hung alone in the centre of the wall. They should be positioned at eye level so they can be fully appreciated.

Other pictures are best hung in groups, 'anchored' to furniture or architectural details that provide a reference point. You can use all different shapes and sizes to add variety to the group, but as a rule, the largest should not be bigger than about one-third the size of the total, and the paintings should line up either at the top or the bottom. This arrangement works very well over tables, chests or sofas. You can also line them up along the right- or left-hand side as well as the top or bottom, which gives you room to extend the group.

An alternative is constant spacing, where all the paintings are hung the same distance apart: about 4in/10cm often works well. If you start with a central cluster of pictures, you can work upwards and outwards as your picture collection grows.

WINDOW TREATMENTS

Choosing curtains and blinds is one of the most creative aspects of home decorating. There's such a variety of fabrics, headings, tracks and poles to choose from that you're sure to find a style to suit your taste and your room. In fact, if there is a problem, it's that there's such a bewildering choice. Before you start shopping for material, jot down the effect you'd like to achieve and any considerations you should take into account. Ask yourself:

- Are there any practical features that will influence the style that you choose? For example, is there a radiator or window seat beneath the window? Does the window pivot? Is it a dormer, or French doors?
- What shape is the window, and do you want to alter it? A pelmet can help reduce the height of tall windows; long curtains can give importance to a small one. A square bay can be treated in several ways: as a single unit or with separate blinds or curtains.
- How many windows are there in the room? Identical windows can be given the same treatment, while windows that are very different in size and shape can be treated individually. If they're slightly different, or oddly proportioned, it's often best to copy the treatment chosen for the largest window, or to curtain the entire wall, if the windows are next to each other.
- How much clearance is there between the top of the window and the ceiling? This will affect the type of track and heading. Curtain poles need space above and below to look effective. If space is very limited, you may need a ceiling-hung track.
- Is privacy important? If the room is overlooked, you may need to screen the window with sheers or blinds during the day, as well as having curtains that close at night.
- Do you need extra insulation? Full-length lined and interlined curtains, when closed, can help keep precious heat inside the room.
- Will you need to wash the curtains or blinds? Lined curtains should be dry-cleaned even if both inner and outer fabric are made from cotton, because if washed they're liable to shrink at different rates and the seams will pucker. If you want curtains for a kitchen, bathroom or family room, it may be best to choose detachable linings or unlined sheers. Fabric blinds are usually not washed, but roller blinds can often be wiped with a damp cloth.
- Would you prefer an architectural solution? Window coverings don't need to be fabric. Other coverings include shutters, wood-slat blinds and shelves.
- Does the window really need covering? Oriel, round, and stained-glass windows are often best left to speak for themselves. Skylights and high, narrow windows rarely need covering for privacy though you may want to screen out the light. Their proportions may need minimising rather than emphasising so if you want to cover them, it may be best to choose a simple treatment in a colour that blends with the walls.
- Is security important? It's worth fitting simple locks to every window, but you may want to consider special blinds, security grilles or shutters for ground floor or basement windows, or if you live in a high risk area.

WHICH WINDOW?

The way a window opens can affect the window covering you choose, especially if it projects inwards rather than outwards and needs blinds or curtains that pull clear of the pane. Here are the main types to consider.

WINDOW FRAMES

Aluminium is popular for replacement windows, patio doors and double-glazed units. It can be coated as well as plain and is wiped clean easily but the cold metal may increase condensation. To prevent this, a plastic 'thermal break' is often provided in double-glazed windows, to improve insulation.
Plastic window frames are made from unplasticised polyvinyl chloride (uPVC) and reinforced with metal. They provide good insulation but should not be painted.
Galvanised metal windows may be found in some older houses, but are rarely used today because their poor insulation can cause condensation and rot. They need careful maintenance to prevent them from rusting.
Timber provides good insulation, minimising condensation round the frame, but needs to be painted or stained regularly to prevent rot. Timber frames should be treated with preservative, and softwood should be thoroughly seasoned before building, to prevent warping later.

Casement windows are side-opening. They usually have one fixed pane and one or two opening lights.
Sash or double-hung windows are made in two parts that can be raised and lowered independently, worked by sash cords or a metal spiral balance.
Tilting windows include pivoting designs, which turn through almost 180 degrees; projecting windows, which push forward on metal struts; tilting designs which can be tipped ajar for ventilation and pull inwards or pivot to open fully; and louvre (jalousie) windows, made from horizontal glass slats.
Sliding windows are usually patio doors, but small sliding windows are sometimes found in houses near the sea, where they're designed to resist buffeting by the wind.

COMPLEX WINDOW SHAPES

Bay windows extend the floor area of the room, letting in light on three sides. They can be square or angled, made from three separate windows, or a curved unit. You can cover a square bay with four curtains (two in the centre and one at each side); with three separate blinds; with a blind at the centre and show curtains on each side; or a single pair of curtains, provided you use track or poles that bend. You can also 'cut off' the bay by screening it with a pair of full-length curtains.

TIP Before you buy a curtain track, check the tightest angle recommended by the manufacturer for bending it. Some tracks for DIY use won't bend enough to fit a square bay.

Bow windows are curved windows set in a straight wall, and don't extend the room in the same way as a bay. You can fit curtains or blinds to cut off the bow, or hang them from curved track to emphasise the window's shape.
Dormer windows project from the roof. There's usually only one window (though some dormers have windows in the side like a miniature bay), plus a broad shelf underneath. Though charming to look at, dormers may not let much light in, so shutters, simple blinds, or narrow curtains that pull right back from the pane are often a good choice.

French windows and garden doors need curtains that pull clear on either side so that the doors can open easily. Tie-backs or hold-backs that secure the curtains when the doors are open help keep soiling to a minimum.
Picture windows and patio doors may take over most of the wall. In this case, it may be worth covering the entire wall, rather than the window alone, for the best effect.

CURTAIN TRACKS AND POLES

Curtain poles are designed for show; curtain track is often best hidden by a heading or pelmet. But just to confuse matters, there are now a number of curtain tracks that are attractive in their own right and can even be mistaken for poles. Here's a basic guide.

CURTAIN POLES

Poles are usually best for relatively short, straight runs, though it's possible to buy poles that bend to follow a bay. They are sold complete with fittings such as rings from which to hang the curtains, although it's usually possible to buy extra rings separately.

Poles are usually made from wood – either stained or sprayed or left natural before painting – or have a metal finish.

Most are fixed to the wall, though ceiling fixing is sometimes possible.

CURTAIN POLE DIAMETERS

Heavyweight
1⅛–1½in/28–38mm

Medium weight
1–1⅛in/22–25mm

Lightweight:
½–¾in/12–20mm

TIP If space is limited, look for 'short reach' brackets, which fix the pole close to the wall.

At the end of the pole is a finial (end piece), which keeps the last curtain ring in place. This can be removed if the pole is a very tight fit because the window is close to a corner.

The diameter of the pole is important. Long, lined curtains need substantial poles to bear the weight. Slim poles (under 1in/25mm thick) are best kept for short or sheer curtains. Long poles (over 8ft/2.4m) need a central support to prevent them sagging, and this can sometimes be used to join two lengths together. Larger poles may come ready corded, so the curtains don't need to be pulled by hand. It's possible to buy a draw rod, attached to the leading ring and concealed by the folds in the fabric, to pull uncorded curtains.

TIP Polish curtain poles from time to time with silicone polish so that the rings run up and down smoothly.

In addition to conventional poles, there are also sprung rods that will fit inside a window recess. These incude café rods for café curtains, and lightweight tension rods for lace curtains.

CURTAIN TRACKS

Curtain track can be fixed to walls or ceilings. The track is made from plastic, aluminium or steel and can be used with accessories such as cording sets (to open and close the curtains without handling them), a valance rail for fabric pelmets, or a net curtain track.

It's important to buy track that's strong enough for the curtains, as long, lined curtains and fabrics like velvet need double the support required by light cotton curtains. Many brands of track are suitable for DIY use but the heavier metal curtain tracks may need to be installed by a professional, especially if the window is a difficult shape.

You may need special type of track to fit a square bay window or to sweep each side of a bow window. Some types used by professional fitters will bend around 90 degrees.

TIP If you like the look of curtain poles but need the flexibility of track, consider a track that combines the features of both.

TIP To prevent the gliders sticking, spray curtain track with silicone-based polish or a lubricant such as WD-40.

FITTING CURTAIN TRACK

Make sure the track is the right length before you start. Curtain track is either cut or telescoped to fit; poles are cut to size.

Wall fixing

There's usually a concrete lintel above a window, so you will need to use a hammer drill and a masonry drill bit. (While it is possible to drill into a steel lintel, it is easier to hang curtains from the ceiling in this case.) Measure at least 2in/5cm above the window before you start to drill, and make sure the holes are at least 1½in/38mm deep so that you penetrate the wall beneath the plaster.

CURTAIN TRACK LOADS

	Maximum load/ length of track
Heavyweight	6½lb per ft/1kg per 10cm
Heavy/ mediumweight	2½lb per ft/375g per 10cm
Mediumweight	1½lb per ft/225g per 10 cm
Lightweight	1¼lb per ft/175g per 10cm

TIP If the plaster crumbles, try fixing a wooden batten to the lintel and screw the track to that. This will also cut down the number of holes drilled into the wall itself.

Ceiling fixing

It is very important to make sure the track is securely fixed into the timber joists above the ceiling plaster.

You can locate them by tapping the ceiling: Hollow areas will sound hollow and joists will sound duller. Then test with a bradawl, pushing through the plaster to find the wooden joists above. Alternatively, use a battery-operated joint and stud detector (see Putting up a shelf, page 394).

If the joists run parallel to the curtain track, you will need to take up the floorboards in the room above and fit strips of wood between the joists. It may be easier to fit track on the wall close to the ceiling.

MAKING A PELMET BOARD

This can be made from a standard 4in/10cm shelf or, for full-length curtains, as shelf 6in/15cm deep. Pelmet boards should be cut 2in/5cm wider each side than the curtain track, and fixed to the wall above the track with strong brackets.

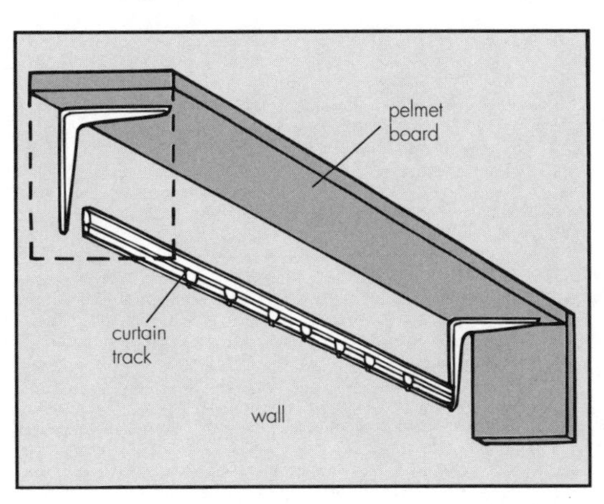

SAFETY AND SECURITY

HOME SAFETY

Accidents in the home are responsible for about 5,000 deaths a year, and at least three million people need medical attention for injuries sustained at home. Yet many of these injuries could easily be avoided with some common sense, safety measures and greater awareness of potential problems.

Every household is different, so take a good look at your home, room by room, and carry out a safety audit to see where the possible hazards lie.

KITCHEN

NEW

If you are planning a new kitchen, it's easy to get caught up with the overall look and the smart new appliances you would like to include, but don't forget to consider how practical and safe it will be. You'll need to consider the layout, design and positioning of appliances carefully (see Kitchen Planning, page 46).

INHERITING A KITCHEN

If, on the other hand, you have inherited a kitchen, you may also be taking in potential problem areas, and it is important to be aware of badly planned or problematic fitted kitchens, particularly if you have small children.

Ask yourself:

- Is the lighting adequate over the work surfaces?
- Are the plug sockets well positioned or will flexes trail near the sink or cooker?
- Are the edges of work tops or corners of tables sharp? Should you consider using covers for the tables?
- Is the kitchen ventilated adequately? Proper ventilation is vital, especially if you have gas appliances in the kitchen, and to provide a clean, airy environment.
- Are there unhygienic gaps in tiles on work surfaces? Seal with waterproof sealant. Germs can be harboured in crevices.
- Is there safe storage for hazardous cleaning chemicals or medicines?
- Are there glass fronted doors that would be safer with laminated glass?
- How even and ruck free is the flooring?
- Have you inherited electrical appliances with unknown histories? Get them serviced.
- Did the previous owners install the kitchen units themselves? Check how secure they are, especially wall units.
- How strong is the shelving? Don't overload shelves, and put heavy and fragile items in a low but secure position. Make sure the shelves have shelf retainers to prevent them tipping forward if a heavy weight is placed at the front.

KITCHEN HAZARDS

These are used every day and we often neglect to treat them with the respect they deserve.

COOKER

- Don't leave saucepans unattended.
- Try to get into the habit of using the pan that best fits the size of hob ring available. If possible, use the rings at the back of the hob and remember to turn saucepan handles inward (so that they don't hang over the edge of the cooker or get dangerously hot over another hob ring).
- Never fill the pan more than one-third full with oil, or two-thirds full when the food has been added.

- When cleaning, switch the cooker off at the wall panel.
- Don't be tempted to line any part of the cooker with kitchen foil to keep it clean – fat from foods may catch fire.

KETTLE

- If you have a corded kettle, buy a curly cord or check to see if you can wind the flex underneath so that the kettle cannot be sited too near the front of the work surface.
- Switch off and unplug at the wall socket before you fill or pour it. Fill with enough water to cover the element completely.
- If buying new, opt for a cordless kettle and site the power base near the back of the work surface.

KITCHEN KNIVES

- Don't keep sharp knives lose in the utensil drawer. Ideally, use a knife block at the back of the work surface, or a wall rack (but don't overload it).
- Knives should also be washed up separately from the rest of the cutlery to avoid bad cuts from hidden knives in soapy water.

TOASTER

- It's tempting to use a knife to loosen bread caught inside the toaster, but *never* do this without switching off and unplugging first, otherwise you may get an electric shock. Allow the toaster to cool, and only then remove the bread with a wooden spatula. (If buying a new toaster, look for one with an extra lift facility for easier access).
- Do not disturb the heat elements. Never poke about with a fork or similar metal object as you are likely to break them.
- Follow the maker's instructions for removing loose breadcrumbs. Many models now have removable crumb trays.

IRON

- Fill a steam iron before you plug it in. Make sure the iron base is dry before using it.
- Fit a flex holder to the ironing board. Do not wrap the flex around a hot iron, and never leave an iron face down.
- If you are worried about leaving the iron on after use, buy a model that automatically switches off if left in the ironing position after a few seconds.

MEDICINES

Always lock all medicines and chemicals away in a high cupboard, preferably in the kitchen where there are always more adults around than in a bathroom.

- Try to buy cleaning products and medicines in child-resistant containers.
- Never transfer gardening or cleaning liquids to squash bottles, in case children mistakenly think they are drinks.
- Don't take labels off anything: it may be potentially dangerous.
- If you have medicine left over, don't keep it or throw it in the dustbin. Take it back to a pharmacist so it can be destroyed.

HOUSEHOLD CLEANING AGENTS

This book is full of useful hints on how to cut cleaning costs by using cheap household chemicals but it is important to remember that some of them are potentially dangerous substances that should be treated with respect.

Caustic soda (Sodium hydroxide)

This is a very strong alkali. If using caustic-soda crystals remember they are corrosive and can burn the skin, so follow all the safety instructions on the can to the letter. Wear rubber gloves and avoid inhaling fumes. Always use in a well-ventilated room and if overcome by fumes, get to an open window as quickly as possible.

For accidental splashes on the skin, rinse the affected area well under running cold water.

Chlorine bleach (Sodium hypochlorite)

Always store bleach in a safe place. Don't be tempted to add it to any other household chemicals or proprietary cleaners to speed things up, as it may then give off toxic gases which can be extremely dangerous.

If you spill any on your skin, wash the affected area immediately with plenty of cold water. If any is accidentally swallowed, drink plenty of water followed by plenty of milk, then contact your doctor immediately.

Solvents

Include acetone and turpentine.

Keep all grease solvents well away from flames and sparks. Avoid inhaling fumes and vapours, and always work in a well-ventilated room. Avoid prolonged contact with the skin as it may make it feel dry. Keep well out of reach of children.

TIP If you are worried about children and solvent abuse contact the charity Re-Solv for advice (see Useful Addresses).

Ammonia

This is a poison. Don't allow it to be taken internally, and never open the bottle caps to smell the contents: the result can be most unpleasant. Avoid contact with the eyes, skin and clothing. Wear rubber gloves, always work in a well-ventilated room and store the bottle in a cool, dark place.

If spilt on the skin, flush liberally with cold water. If ammonia is swallowed, make the person drink plenty of cold water, then contact your doctor immediately.

BATHROOM

Many accidents take place in the bathroom. Inevitably, in an area where you are dealing with water and slippery surfaces there are a number of possible dangers.

- Baths should be filled with cold water first, then hot.
- Always use non-slip floor mats and non-slip bath mats. (For awkward shapes, try Slipsafe spray inside baths or shower trays, which bonds to most surfaces, see Useful Addresses).
- Make sure the areas around your bath and sink are properly sealed with bath sealant. This can be a breeding ground for germs in a hot, wet environment, and the sealant will prevent damage to the room below and also prevent wet rot.
- Consider fitting an extra bath grip for elderly members of the family to assist them in getting in or out of the bath.
- There should be no electrical plugs in the bathroom but if you live in an old house which has not been re-wired, watch for this and get in an electrician to advise you. All lights should be on pull cords, not switches.
- Make sure the shaver socket is situated well out of reach of children.
- Radiant heaters, towel rails and mirror lights must be fixed firmly to the wall. They should have permanent wiring (which means sockets) and pull-cord switches. Don't fix them above the bath or near a shower. Heaters must be out of reach of people using the bath and heaters with metal frames must be securely earthed and bonded to other metalwork in the bathroom. Have all work carried out by a qualified electrician.
- All shower heaters should have anti-scald thermal cut-outs. (If buying new, opt for thermostatic models that are designed to

stabilise any temperature changes while you're under the shower. Mechanical mixer showers are less expensive but do not offer the same degree of temperature control and safety.)

- If you have a gas water-heater in the bathroom, there should be adequate ventilation at all times.
- Hot-water thermostats should be set at 130°F/54°C.
- Always ensure that the radiators and towel rails are kept at a safe temperature.
- Install bath shower screens or curtains to reduce water escaping from the bath on to the bathroom floor.
- Take care not to leave medicines, cosmetics, household cleaners, razors and razor blades within reach of children.
- Never use loose rugs in bathrooms. All rugs should have safety grips
- Never use a portable electric fire, hairdryer, or other electrical equipment in the bathroom.

LIVING ROOM, STAIRS AND HALLWAY

HEATING

- Never hang things over a convector or storage heater.
- Don't place mirrors over fireplaces: it encourages people to stand too close to them.
- Portable heaters can start a fire if misused. When using, make sure the heater has a permanent safety guard, is used in a well-ventilated area and is clean and well maintained. Always turn them off before going to bed. Electric heaters should carry the British Electrotechnical Approvals Board (BEAB) approval mark. Portable gas heaters should carry the British Standard Kitemark (see page 54).

BEAB Approved

> **TIME SWITCHES**
>
> If you have any heaters on time switches, keep them well clear of curtains and furnishings. Never fit time-switched or delay controls to an electric fire.

- Open fires cause 1,400 house fires each year. Use a spark guard over the fire when you are not there to keep an eye on it. Don't forget to have the chimney swept each year.

TV AND STEREO

- Switch off when you are not using them and take the mains plug out of the supply socket.
- Never try to repair them yourself: call in a specialist.

LIGHTING

- Switch off light fittings before removing bulbs.
- To avoid causing a fire, do not use higher wattage bulbs than the makers recommend on shades and fittings.

FLOORING AND STEPS

- Don't polish floors under loose rugs or carpets, or place them at the base of stairs.
- Ensure stair rods are securely fixed and the stair carpet is not loose.
- Check that banisters and railings are firm.
- Stick down loose tiles and sheet vinyl. Neaten off frayed carpet edges.
- Make sure the lighting is adequate over the stairs.

WINDOWS

Each year, about 27,000 people in Britain are injured by glass in their homes. If you have

WHICH SAFETY GLASS?

There are various types, so for guidance, go to an expert: a member of the Glass and Glazing Federation. Use and look for glazing materials that meet BS 6206.

As a general guideline:

- Toughened glass is up to five times stronger than ordinary glass so is difficult to break. When it does, it shatters into thousands of pieces, rather like a car windscreen.
- Plastic safety film can be stuck on to one side of ordinary glass to hold the pieces together if the glass breaks.
- Laminated glass crazes but the pieces are held together by a strong, transparent interlayer, so minimising any injuries.

young children it may be worth considering safety glazing in fully glazed doors; door side panels, wet areas (eg shower screens), low level glazing and glass in furniture.

Glass in any window, whether it is double glazed or not, can be difficult to break. It is important to have at least one window wide enough to be used as an emergency exit in every room. With double glazing always make sure the key to the window is at hand (put it on a hook on the wall beside the window, out of reach of children).

BEDROOMS

ELECTRIC BLANKETS

Each year British fire brigades are called to some 1,500 fires caused by electric blankets. More than 20 people are killed and 250 injured in these fires. Only use electric blankets which conform to the BEAB approval mark (see page 411); BS 3999, Part 6, or BS EN 60967.

- Not all electric blankets can be left on all night: check the instructions.
- Over-blankets are designed to be tucked in at the sides and bottom of the bed, without

FIRE SAFETY AND FABRICS

If your upholstered furniture and bedding was made before the new fire safety regulations that came into effect in 1988, consider improving their resistance to fire.

If making loose covers for a sofa or armchair, look for match-resistant fabric (ask the advice of your fabric supplier).

Flame retardant sprays can be applied to fabrics, carpets and upholstery (see Useful Addresses). They may not always be as effective as fire resistance treatments that are applied by factory process. Check that the spray is suitable for the fabric on your furniture and follow the manufacturer's instructions carefully. Be warned: spray treatments that are not water resistant will simply wash out if liquids, eg tea, are spilled on the treated fabric.

If having your furniture re-upholstered, replacement covers and any material supplied in the course of a re-upholstering service must now meet the fire-resistance requirements. But you could also have the filling replaced with a fire resistant one or, at least, use a fire resistant interliner fitted between the new cover and the existing filling material to help protect the old fillings in the event of a fire.

any of the heated area being folded under.
- Follow the manufacturer's instructions, check blanket regularly for wear, and have it serviced every two to three years.

HAIRDRYERS

- Do not wrap the flex around the handle when you have finished with it.
- Disconnect when not in use.

SMOKING

- Never smoke in bed due to risk of fire.

CHILDREN

What may seem like a perfectly safe home can suddenly become an assault course of potential hazards once there is a child in the house. If you have young children then you've probably spotted most of the danger zones already, but there may be some which still lurk undetected. Pinpointing the hazards is more difficult when your home is only occasionally invaded by small children.

In the last two decades, accidents have emerged as the major health problem for children after the age of one. Home accidents are the biggest cause of death in under fours.

Babies

Babies less than nine months old have limited mobility, and accidents frequently result from the perilous positions they are put in by others. Over half the accidents in this age group are from falls such as rolling off furniture, or out of cots.

Toddlers

Toddlers (nine months to four years) often fall off and collide with furniture. They are also learning to climb stairs and are more likely to set off unaided. The increasingly mobile, active child can come into contact with medicines and household chemicals, small or hot objects, glass doors and other household hazards. A higher proportion of burning, poisoning and foreign body-type accidents occur to this age group.

CHILD-PROOFING YOUR HOME

Realistically, no home can be totally child-proof but here are some of the ways you can make a child's environment a little safer. Don't worry if you are not able to implement all the measures outlined below, but concentrate on those that are most applicable to your children depending on their age and inclinations.

STAIRS

- Fit stair gates: there's little to beat the challenge of climbing the stairs. Barriers or gates (from about £12) should be fitted at both the top and bottom of the staircase. Look for one that conforms to British Standard 4125 as this ensures that the spacing between the bars and the gap between the lower edge and the floor is much too small for a youngster to wriggle his/her head through.

TIP Buy a gate that can be opened easily with one hand.

- Install two-way light switches at the top and bottom of the stairway so you can light your way from either direction.
- Board up horizontal balcony rails so they cannot be used as a ladder.
- Never allow a child to play on or near stairs.
- Fix loose carpets and check that the carpet tacks are not poking up through worn patches.
- Keep halls well lit and fit a dimmer switch on the landing light, to keep the light on low through the night in case children want to go to the toilet.

WINDOWS

Small children love climbing up to peer out of windows but once up there it is all too easy for them to topple out.

- Vertical window bars may save a toddler's life but do make sure they can be removed quickly in the event of a fire. Less conspicuous are window limiters which only allow the window to be opened a little way – enough to allow fresh air in but not sufficient for a toddler to get out.
- Keep sash windows locked at the bottom.
- Don't put anything that a child can climb on to near a window.
- Check that patio doors, shower screens, glass tables and a conservatory are all made from safety glass. If they are they will be marked with the BS 6206 or Kitemark. If not, replace them with laminated or toughened glass, or at least cover them with safety film conforming to BS 6206.

IN THE KITCHEN

Young children are at risk of serious injury from hot liquids and cooking fat. Every year around 30,000 children go to hospital with scalds.

FIRST-AID TIP If a child is scalded, run cold water over the scald right away. Don't stop to remove clothing. Then get medical help for anything but the smallest accident.

- Always keep hot drinks well out of children's reach. Don't hold a baby when you are drinking. If you're passing a hot drink to someone else, make sure a child isn't underneath.
- Keep the kettle at the back of the work surface out of the reach of toddlers, and keep the lead as short as practical. Alternatively, buy a coiled flex for your kettle, keep it at the back of the work surface or use a kettle guard (which screws to the wall at the back of the work surface, cost about £5).
- Knives and utensils must always be locked away or stored well out of reach.
- Simple child-proof locks should be fitted to kitchen cupboards and medicine cabinets.
- Try to cook on the back rings of the hob, and always remember to point saucepan handles inwards or towards the rear. Use a cooker guard (£12 to £15) to prevent toddlers pulling pans off the hob.
- An oven built in above floor level ensures that at least one hot area is out of reach of children. If not, buy, an oven door guard which will at least diffuse some of the heat.
- Doors on washing machines, dishwashers and tumble driers should be kept closed always. Don't forget that the doors can get very hot during use (if they are not double insulated).

TIP To prevent children fiddling with the controls on a washing machine or tumble drier get a control visor to cover them.

- Never store soft drinks and alcohol in the same, low-level cupboard.
- Choose bottles with child-resistant lids where possible.
- Keep aerosol cans well out of reach.
- Make sure bookcases and wall units are well-secured and cannot be pulled over or used as climbing frames.

IN THE LIVING ROOM

- Guards should be fitted to all fires and radiators: BS 6539 on guards for open fires; BS1945 on guards for electric, gas and paraffin heaters. Check that there's at least 8in/20cm between the heat and the guard, otherwise the latter will become dangerously hot.
- Always extinguish cigarettes properly and

empty ashtrays. Always keep cigarettes, lighters and matches out of reach.

- Consider fitting door slam protectors to stop little fingers being crushed.
- Rugs can be fitted with adhesive underlay. (From specialist carpet retailers or contact The British Carpet Manufacturers' Association for stockists – see Useful Addresses.)
- House-plants should always be checked for poison and possible allergic reactions.
- Consider fixing ornaments and movable objects in position with sticky pads or other fixings.
- Play pens are advisable for toddlers on those occasions when you simply can't be in two places at once. Buy one made to BS 4863.
- Store any alcohol out of reach.

IN THE BATHROOM

- Try to ensure that the floor covering is water resistant without being slippery, and that any rugs have a non-slip backing. In the bath itself, a non-slip rubber bath mat will help prevent the child sliding under the water. Children can drown in only a few inches of water so never leave them alone in the bath – even for one moment.
- Ensure that children cannot reach the lock on the bathroom or toilet door, in case they lock themselves in. Move locks if necessary.
- Baths should always be filled with cold water before hot. Mix the water well and test the temperature with your elbow before you put a baby in.
- If bathing a baby in a baby bath, check that the stand for the bath is solid and fits the bath well. If the bath is part of a changing unit, make sure that the mat or cover lifts off or slides away completely, and cannot drop down on to the baby while in the bath. Once a child can stand unaided, stop using the baby bath on a stand. Either use an adult bath or put the baby bath inside the adult bath.
- For toddlers who delight in flushing toys, shoes, etc, down the toilet, buy a lid lock.

IN THE BEDROOM

- If the child has just graduated to his/her first grown-up bed, consider using a bed guard to stop them falling out. (This is a tubular frame with a soft, mesh infill. It is held in place with swivel arms which slide beneath the mattress and attach to the opposite side of the bed.)
- Non-toxic nursery paint should be used for children's rooms and furniture. Check that it conforms to BS 5665. (Available from specialist paint and hardware stores.)
- Encourage children to be tidy and put toys away after use, to avoid tripping and falling over objects on the floor.
- Check that the wardrobe doors can be opened from the inside in case your child gets stuck.
- Don't leave medicines (including the contraceptive pill), cosmetics, nail scissors, etc within a small child's reach.
- Don't put under-fives in the top deck of a bunk bed.
- Changing units: make sure the unit is stable when the drawers and cupboard are both open and closed. Make sure you can reach everything you need without leaving your baby alone on the unit.
- Nappy buckets: keep nappy sanitising powder out of reach. Your baby could swallow it and burn his/her mouth and throat. Keep nappy buckets out of the way of the baby. A child could drown in a full bucket or he/she could use the bucket as a step for climbing and reaching hazards like kettles.
- Cribs: make sure the stand for the crib is firm and that swinging cribs can be locked into a resting position.

- Moses baskets: make sure the fabric lining is stitched firmly into place and that there are no loose folds which could smother a baby.
- Cots and cot beds: always put the side up when the baby is in the cot. Drop the mattress base to the lowest position as soon as your baby can sit up. Don't put the cot near curtains or anything that might help the baby climb out.
- As soon as the baby starts trying to climb out of the cot, either switch to a bed or leave the drop side down. Keep the bedroom door closed or put a gate across it so that he/she cannot get out of the room at night.

TIP Move beds and other furniture away from windows to stop children climbing on them and falling out.

ELECTRICAL APPLIANCES

- Use covers on unused electrical sockets. Put furniture in front of electric sockets.
- Use a residual current device for areas in which your children live and play. It will automatically cut off the power in a fraction of a second, before your child receives a serious shock. It plugs into the socket, and you then plug the appliance into it.
- Make the TV and stereo strictly out of bounds. You can buy self-adhesive video shields to stop little fingers altering the programming.
- Look out for trailing flexes and clip them out of harm's way.
- Never leave a lamp without a bulb.

HELP WITH SAFETY EQUIPMENT

If you can't afford to buy items such as stair gate, car seats or fire guards, speak to your health visitor, GP or the Social Services about loan schemes in your area.

CHILDREN'S PLAY EQUIPMENT

- Check that outdoor play equipment is sturdy and well maintained.
- Paddling pools must always be emptied and ponds always covered when children are around. If you have a garden pond fence it or better still, drain it.
- Climbing frames or swings should be placed on a grassy surface or ground covered with bark chippings.
- Sand pits should always be covered when not in use to stop dogs or cats fouling them.

WATER, FIRE, GAS AND ELECTRICS

Most of us worry, at one time or another, whether we've unplugged the iron or switched off the gas cooker when we go out. But few people are aware of the full potential for accidents caused by the domestic services that we take so much for granted. Explosions caused by gas leaks don't just happen from leaving the cooker on accidentally: they are far more likely to be caused by appliances and central-heating systems that don't get regular servicing. Of course, the biggest fear is fire, but most people die without ever seeing any flames as they are overcome by smoke or toxic fumes first.

Make sure that all the family know the location of stoptaps, fuse-boxes, mains power switch, gas mains and what possible exit routes to use in case of fire.

GAS

- Have all gas appliances professionally installed and serviced regularly. Make sure there is adequate ventilation at all times.
- Switch off instant gas water-heaters before getting into the bath.

- Don't look for a gas leak with a naked flame and don't smoke near one. Open windows and phone the emergency gas service. (Look under Gas in the phone book, or better still, keep a list of emergency numbers handy (see Preparing for Emergencies, page 463).
- Always fill a paraffin heater outdoors, and never while it's still burning.
- Gas installers who are registered by CORGI (Council for Registered Gas Installers) must always be used for jobs involving gas appliances, by law.
- For further advice on gas safety and carbon monoxide poisoning, see Gas and Electricity, page 470.

ELECTRICITY

House wiring

Faults in wiring cause 2,200 fires and about ten deaths per year in Britain. You should have your household wiring checked every five years. This may sound excessive, but the cost is a small price to pay for electrical safety.

If your wiring circuits are more than 25 years old, or if your sockets are of the round, two-pin type you almost certainly need to renew them. Before checking or repairing wiring sockets or switches, turn off the power at the mains switch.

Get expert help for all repairs and wiring. If you think there may be a fault, immediately contact a contractor who is approved by the National Inspection Council for Electrical Installation Contracting (see Useful Addresses). There is a list of approved contractors at all Electricity Board showrooms. Always keep a torch handy in case it is needed during a power cut.

Plugs and flexes

Faulty flexes cause 1,000 fires and several deaths per year.

RESIDUAL CURRENT DEVICES

Residual current devices can be fitted by a professional at the mains supply where they offer protection throughout the home, or in a plug or socket suitable for portable equipment such as a lawn-mower, drill, or appliances which need an extension lead.

The RCD can detect damage to the cable and other faults through change in the current flow. It automatically disconnects the power, reducing the risk of an accident and warning you that there is a fault.

RCDs must be fitted to any electrical supply expected to serve appliances outdoors.

- Always buy shatter-proof plugs that meet BS 1363 or BS 1363/A, which are stronger than most. Make sure the clamp in the plug properly grips the outer plastic cover of the flex and not just the leads.
- Wire colour codes:
  Live = Brown
  Neutral = Blue
  Earth = Yellow/Green.
- Don't overload plug sockets. Use adaptors as little as possible. Ideally, you should use a separate socket for every appliance, but this is not always possible. If you regularly use two appliances from one point, fit a double socket.
- Make sure you are using the correct fuse for the appliance.

FIRE

No one should underrate the danger of fire. In this country every year there are about 50,000 accidental fires in the home which kill about 800 people and injure over 14,000 others.

Smoke alarms

Over 60 per cent of households now have a smoke alarm. Your chances of surviving a fire are two to three times greater if you have one fitted. Battery-operated models cost from as little as £4. You can also buy mains-powered alarms if you have a large house and need several alarms.You should preferably have one on each floor of the house.

Smoke alarm maintenance

Once you have fitted a smoke alarm, it is easy to forget about it. But it is important to maintain it properly: it could save your life.

- Make a note in your diary to replace the battery at least once a year.
- Test the battery once a week.

SMOKE ALARM CRITERIA

Smoke alarms should;

- Comply with BS 5446 and preferably carry the British Standard Kitemark.
- Be placed within 8yd/7m of rooms where fires are likely to start and within 3yd/3m of bedroom doors.
- Be placed at least 12in/30cm from any wall, or from a ceiling light fitting.
- If wall mounted, be between 6in–12in/15–30cm below the ceiling.
- Be fixed in positions that allow maintenance, testing and cleaning.
- Be sited well away from areas where steam, condensation or fumes could give false alarms.
- Be away from areas that get very hot or cold.

If installing mains-operated smoke alarms then they must comply with current IEE wiring regulations. Always use a qualified electrician for installation.

SMOKE ALARMS FOR THE HARD OF HEARING

Smoke alarms are available for those with hearing impairment. For details contact The Royal National Institute for the Deaf, see Useful Addresses.

- Vacuum dust from inside the alarm.
- Test sensor annually by waving a smoking candle under it.

Fire-fighting equipment

For most homes, a fire blanket in the kitchen (to BS 6575) and a multi-purpose dry powder, foam or water-type extinguisher in the hall (conforming to BS5423 or 6165 and the British Standard Kitemark) would be adequate. But it depends on the fire risks in your home and what you can afford. A multi-purpose dry powder or foam extinguisher in the garage, shed or car would complete the package.

If in doubt about which type to have, contact your local fire brigade for advice or contact The Fire Protection Association for useful leaflets (see Useful Addresses).

DIY SAFETY

One of the biggest causes of home accidents is the enthusiastic DIYer who overlooks the essential precautions when using power tools, hazardous chemicals or even climbing a ladder.

- Never cut corners, always use the right tool for the job and keep tools in good working order.
- When drilling walls, avoid areas adjacent to power sockets and the area at right angles and vertically above them. Power cables are usually routed in these locations.
- Always take care of hands when working,

and wear gloves whenever possible

- Always wear protective clothing – face masks, safety goggles, ear defenders or knee pads – when undertaking jobs which may be dangerous or harmful.
- Prepare yourself and your working area properly before you begin.
- Fuels, glue, cleaners, paints and lubricants all contain chemicals that can be harmful. Always follow the makers' safety guidelines. Ensure that you have adequate ventilation.
- Use residual circuit devices when operating power tools.
- Put blade covers on knives and chisels when not using them.
- Keep children away from all DIY work.

LADDER SAFETY

Falling off ladders and chairs is one of the most frequent DIY accidents.

- Always check ladders are suitable for the job.
- Use a special ladder tray that fits on to the ladder instead of carrying paint or tools.
- Never over-extend an extension ladder or exceed the recommended angle of a ladder.
- Use stabilising legs when using a ladder extension.
- Always wear a tool belt (to carry a number of tools) rather than carrying a handful.

THE GARDEN

The most obvious danger is the use of electrical equipment, such as mowers and hedge trimmers, but what about the hazards of barbecues and of course, plants themselves?

- Never use any electrical appliances outside when it's raining.
- When using mains-powered electrical appliances outside the home, wear rubber-soled shoes. Never mow the lawn or trim a hedge barefoot.
- Keep an electrical cable behind you, and continually check that it is still behind you.
- All electrical equipment should be unplugged during cleaning or adjustment and should be put away after use.

OUTDOOR WIRING

- Use a single flex without joins and never work with wet or worn flex.
- Do not run power tools from a lamp socket. Have a proper earthed socket fitted by a qualified electrician.
- If you use a socket to supply electricity to equipment outdoors, such as lawn-mowers or hedge-cutters, protect it with a residual current circuit breaker.
- Sockets installed outdoors must also be under cover, unless special weatherproof units in a waterproof box are used.

PLANTS

- Think carefully before siting hazardous plants where they will be accessible and attractive to children or animals. If in doubt about certain plants, take a clipping along to your local garden centre. (Be sure to wear protective gloves.)
- Rose bushes (and any other plants with thorns) should be well pruned.
- Dispose of broken or cracked plant pots.
- Always put away garden chemicals, ie. fertilisers, weed killers and insecticides.
- Be extremely careful of poisonous plants. The best-known are laburnum seeds, yew berries and foxgloves, but there are a number of other common plants with dangerous seeds or berries such as privet, laurel, rhododendron and hydrangea. Teach your child never to eat seeds or berries from the garden.
- If your child has eaten parts of, or been poisoned by, an unknown plant, seek medical

advice immediately. Don't make the affected person sick, and take a sample of the plant with you.

OUTDOOR GLAZING

Consider installing safety glazing (toughened glass, laminated glass or plastic sheet glazing) in the conservatory, patio doors, at low levels, and in any balustrades.

Contact the Glass and Glazing Federation for further advice and local member stockists; see Useful Addresses.

BARBECUES

- Site in a clear location away from fire hazards and children.
- Never sprinkle barbecue coals with flammable fluids. Read the instructions and follow the procedure for how to start or re-light a barbecue safely. The quality of charcoal varies from brand to brand. The better the quality the easier the barbecue will be to light and stay lit. (The British standard for barbecues is BS 5258.)

Barbecue problems

If your barbecue won't light, or the fire is flagging:

- Never use petrol, paraffin, methylated spirit or other flammable fuel to light or revive it.
- Do use special lighting fluid, pastes and fire lighters. Be sure they have totally burned away before you start cooking or they may taint the food with an unpleasant flavour.
- Add more charcoal, not fluid, to sides of barbecue.
- Try a different brand of charcoal.
- Try 'light the bag' instant-burn charcoal. (Place the whole bag in the barbecue bowl and light it.)
- Buy a grill starter (a mini chimney that uses burning newspaper and the pull of air up the chimney to light the coals. Then pour the hot coals into the barbecue bowl.)
- If the fire goes out, use tongs to place the coals in a steel bucket. Then start again with fresh charcoal.

FIRST AID

Many minor accidents can be effectively treated at home. Anyone can learn the basics of first aid and invest in a practical kit to cater for minor injuries, such as:

- sterile dressings of different sizes
- triangular and crepe bandages
- cotton wool
- individually wrapped assorted plasters
- sterile gauze pads
- safety pins
- thermometer
- mild painkillers
- protective gloves.

St John Ambulance and the British Red Cross both offer first-aid courses. They also have a variety of leaflets on safety and first aid. For details look in the telephone directory for your county headquarters, or see Useful Addresses.

TETANUS

Tetanus is extremely common in gardens, so ensure that all the family have had tetanus inoculations in case any garden accident should occur.

FURTHER SAFETY INFORMATION

For further information on safety in the home in general, contact The Royal Society for the Prevention of Accidents: see Useful Addresses.

HOME SECURITY

Every year, thousands of people suffer a burglary or break-in. The thought of a thief breaking into your home, picking through your personal belongings, and making off with the most valuable and resalable items is both unnerving and frightening. Yet, without turning your home into a fortress, you can employ a few simple precautions to make it less attractive – both to opportunists and to professional thieves.

Your greatest weapon against a burglar is time. The more barriers you place in front of him (such as fences, locked doors and windows) the less attractive your home will be. The chances are he'll give up and move on to the next house.

The area in which you live

Burglary isn't restricted to poor urban areas, although the chances of being burgled are greater in some areas of the country than others. There are, of course, centres of high risk but burglary is a national problem. According to Home Office statistics, you are least likely to be burgled in Dyfed and Powys in Wales, and most likely in the metropolitan area of London.

Be prepared for house contents insurance to be affected by the level of crime in your area. You may not know whether you live in a high-risk area but your insurers certainly will! Before buying expensive locks, etc, check with your insurer to see if he has any particular recommendations.

Planning home security

When considering home security measures, consider your lifestyle, what restrictions you are willing to impose on yourself and the practical aspects of any security devices.

CRIME FACTS

- The average burglary takes place in daylight.
- On average, each of us will be burgled twice in our time as home owners.
- Once burgled, you may have a repeat visit a few weeks later when the thief has calculated that you have received an insurance payment and have replaced your TV and video, etc.
- 80 per cent of thefts are opportunist.
- Most burglaries take place between 2pm and 4pm on a weekday afternoon.
- Thieves are usually aged between 15 and 18 and live locally.
- On average, it takes two minutes for a burglar to go through your home.

BASIC SECURITY PRECAUTIONS

Often people could do more to protect their homes and possessions but are put off by the cost. But many homes lack even basic security precautions that cost little or nothing at all. Here are some initial steps:

- Don't leave doors and windows open.
- Use the locks already installed.
- Don't make it easy for the burglar: lock up tools and ladders.
- Don't 'advertise' the valuables you have.
- Don't advertise your absence.
- Ask neighbours to be vigilant (and do the same for their property in return).
- Ask your local crime-prevention officer to visit your home and recommend ways to improve household security.

ENCOURAGING BURGLARS

Take a good look at your house from the outside, and consider whether any of these questions apply:

- Do you live in a quiet area?
- Is the house secluded or hidden from the road?
- Do you live in a poorly lit and neglected area?
- Could a burglar work unseen behind high walls and fences?
- Is there easy access to the rear, eg a footpath or a canal towpath?
- Do you have an open porch where a thief could hide?
- Does the house have side access which would allow a burglar to work unnoticed? Has the side passage been left unlocked?
- Are the locks on your external doors adequate?
- Is there a way through the garage to the house?
- Do you have valuables on display?
- Do you have a shed or garage containing tools, ladders, ropes, etc, that the thief could use to break in?
- If you have a garage (or coal bunker) with access to your house, are the locks adequate?

All these features could encourage a burglar to target your home, and remedying them will make your house less vulnerable to theft.

HOW BURGLARS BREAK IN

Front door	25%
Rear/side door	23%
Rear/side window	43%
Front window	3%
Upper window	3%

THE LIVED-IN LOOK

It is easy for a thief to tell who's in and who isn't. The house may be in darkness, post left in the letter box or milk bottles left out on the doorstep. Over 80 per cent of burglaries occur when a house is empty, so try to keep your house looking occupied when you are out, and even when you're away on holiday.

- If going away, don't leave your car full of luggage overnight. Load it just before you leave. Lock everything in the boot or under the cover of the hatchback if you're trying to save time in the morning.
- Cancel the milk and papers.

TIP Ring your local Royal Mail Customer Care Unit to find out if the Keepsafe scheme operates in your area. Under the scheme the Royal Mail will hold all your mail until you return home. (About £5 for two weeks, £7.50 for three and £10 for a month.)

- Curtains closed during the day make it look as if no one is home. It is better to leave them open and get security lighting (see below). If you have a large number of valuables, it may be worth considering an electric curtain-track system. You can programme it to open and close your curtains at pre-set times.
- Tell the local police station you'll be away.
- Mow the lawn before you go away.
- Buy a couple of automatic time switches for inside lights (from about £20). These can be used to turn on a light, TV or radio and help give the impression that you are in. They work at pre-set or random times.
- Don't announce that you're going away to a shop full of people. Only tell people who need to know.
- Don't leave valuable items like TVs, videos or stereos visible through windows.
- Don't have your home address showing on

your luggage for the outward journey. Put this only on the inside of your cases.

- If going out for an evening, leave a light on in a room, not the hall (many people leave the hall light on when they are out); and perhaps leave a radio playing.
- Ask a neighbour to keep an eye on the house, collect post and free newspapers left in the letter box, sweep up leaves, and even mow the lawn if you're going to be away longer than a fortnight. If they have two cars, perhaps one could be parked in your driveway. You can repay the favour by doing the same for them when they go away. Warn the key-holding neighbour not to put your surname, address or even house number on your keys in case they fall into the wrong hands.
- A message recorded by a strange voice on your answerphone announcing that a guest is staying in the house while you are away will fool everyone except close friends. Never leave a message saying you have gone away.
- Just before setting off on holiday, it's worth spending a quiet couple of minutes on the doorstep to check you've done everything, and have taken all you need with you.

HOME SITTERS

Leaving home for the pleasures of a holiday is often marred by the worry of burglary. Although you may be able to enlist neighbours to a degree, if you have pets or a conservatory full of precious plants, it may be worth considering a professional home sitter. Obviously you don't want just anyone living in your home, so be sure to choose a professional company that:

- Has been in business a reasonable length of time.
- Is registered and licensed by the Department of Employment.
- Vets its home sitters/caretakers carefully and takes references.
- Is insured against any problems that might occur such as the home sitter having an accident, simply not being up to the task, or damage to the home.
- Provides full back-up for the home sitter so that if he/she falls ill, or has to leave the assignment, the company is still bound to honour the contract.

The larger companies include Homesitters which employs all its people (charges include all PAYE and National Insurance contributions); Universal Aunts and Animal Aunts which are agencies which link self-employed sitters to homeowners. A sitter for two weeks will cost around £300 depending on your requirements (excluding travelling expenses and food).

TIP For peace of mind and to ensure everything runs smoothly, meet the prospective home sitter/caretaker before the day you hand over the keys.

DOOR SECURITY

Doors are the obvious point of entry for a thief. In 30 per cent of burglaries, life is made even easier by the owner leaving a door or window open.

DOOR LOCKS

Look on the front face of the lock for a BS Kitemark, which ensures that the lock is of a reasonable quality.

If in doubt about the suitability of your existing locks, check with your local crime prevention officer or a locksmith who is a member of the Master Locksmiths Association (see Useful Addresses). Also find out from your insurance company whether the locks are adequate to meet their requirements.

KEY TIPS

- Never leave a spare key in a convenient hiding place. Burglars instinctively know where to look.
- Change locks when you move into a new house, as you don't know how many sets of keys may be around.

When it comes to locks, most of us don't know our twin cylinders from our automatic deadlocks. Luckily, most lock manufacturers now put helpful advice on the packaging of their products to indicate which door it would be suitable for (front/back, internal/external).

TIP New guidelines from the Association of British Insurers recommend which locks householders need to fit to secure their homes adequately.

There are basically two kinds of door locks:

Mortice locks (usually seen on back doors) are sunk into the door so are more difficult to force out.

Cylinder rim locks (usually used on front doors) are screwed to the surface which makes them easier to fit.

When you are buying a lock for an entry/exit door, look for a deadlock, which means the bolts locks into the extended position and can be opened only with a key. This means a thief can't smash a nearby panel, reach round and open the door from the inside, nor can he enter by a window and then leave by that door.

FRONT DOOR

- The front door should be a minimum of 1¾in/44mm thick. Check this, especially if you live in a flat with a communal main door.
- It needs a high-security automatic deadlocking night latch with lockable internal knob or handle (to prevent entry by breaking glass and releasing the latch) and a five or seven-lever mortice deadlock (to BS 3621). These cost about £60. (A two-lever mortice lock isn't strong enough and should be used only on inside doors.)
- Fit a spyhole and a door chain (about £6 each).
- The letter box should be at least 15in/40cm away from the locks.
- Fit hinge bolts to reinforce the hinge side of the door (£4–£8 each).
- Check that the door frame is fixed firmly to the brickwork and is strong enough to hold the lock in place.

BACK DOOR

Over 60 per cent of burglaries occur through the back door so it needs particular attention.

- Fit a high-security two-bolt mortice lock, or ideally a five or seven lever-lock (to BS 3621).
- Fit mortice bolts top and bottom.

TIP Don't forget that it's no use having a £50 lock if the door itself is of poor quality and can easily be forced. You can strengthen a door by using a door-reinforcement kit which includes

IDENTIFYING MORTICE LOCKS

To find out if you only have a two-lever lock (which is really too lightweight for the back door and only suitable for internal doors) look at the face plate in the edge of the door. This may be marked with the number of levers.

If not, look at the key. If it looks cheap or has very few notches in the bit of the key then it's probably only a two or three-lever lock.

two solid plates which bolt on to each side of the door round the lock area (about £18 from ironmongers and locksmiths).

PATIO DOORS

Don't rely solely on factory-fitted locks for patio doors.

These should be fitted with multi-point locks (£14) and an anti-lift device (£6) to stop a thief from lifting the door off. If the hinges are visible from the outside, the doors should have hinge bolts as well.

GLASS-PANELLED DOORS

These should be fitted with laminated glass, which looks like ordinary glass, but is very hard to break. It may cost more than double the price of ordinary glass, but you should only have to put it in once.

Laminated glass is made of two or more layers of ordinary glass, bonded together with a strong, clear plastic interlayer. When attacked, the glass itself may break but the broken pieces will adhere to the interlayer and remain as a barrier. It's a good idea if there are many youngsters or vandals in the area, and it won't cause serious injury if you fall against it.

Laminated glass is available from members of the Glass and Glazing Federation. For further details contact the Laminated Glass Information Centre: see Useful Addresses.

Also fit a cylinder rim lock with a lockable inside handle. If a thief breaks the glass to reach in, the door cannot be opened.

WHO'S AT THE DOOR?

Most callers are genuine, but we've all heard tales of burglars getting into people's homes by pretending to be the gas man or from the council. So it's sensible to be cautious. If you live alone, be especially careful to check the identity of unknown callers.

- Ask to see the identity card of meter readers or service men.
- For blind or partially sighted people, electricity, gas and water services can arrange for their staff to use an identifying code word.
- If callers claim to be from local services, ask them to wait, shut the door and ring the office to check who they are.
- Call a neighbour or ask the visitor to come back when someone else is in.
- Don't keep a door chain on all the time. only put it on when someone calls, otherwise it may be difficult for others to get in in an emergency.
- Don't leave your handbag or wallet unattended in any room where a caller may need to enter. Stay with the caller and keep all other doors closed.

WINDOW SECURITY

The most common way for a burglar to break into your home is through a back window.

If you're not sure about whether a window is large enough for a thief to climb through, the rough rule is if you can get your head through an opening, he can squeeze inside.

TIP Do make sure there are no ladders left lying around and shut all windows – even small cloakroom ones – when you go out.

SECURITY TIPS

- Fit window locks. Over 60 per cent of homes still do not have window locks. You can buy them for casement, skylight or sash types (£3–£15). Pay particular attention to ground-floor windows and those above flat roofs, near drainpipes or fire escapes.
- Glue the slats of louvre windows in place with epoxy resin, or fit them with special

louvre locks.

- Consider replacing vulnerable downstairs windows with laminated glass.
- Install security grills on vulnerable windows, especially at the rear of the house. Many DIY stores and ironmongers sell decorative grills that can be attached to the wall quite easily with security screws.
- Shutters can be attached to the exterior wall, although they can be fitted on the interior if you do not want to change the appearance of your property. Both types are operated from the inside. They are usually aluminium or foam-filled aluminium which also provides insulation. Contact the British Blind and Shutter Association for a list of local suppliers: see Useful Addresses.
- Even small windows, like casement windows, skylights or bathroom fanlights might need locks.
- Check the window frames are in good repair. There's no point having a good lock if the burglar can simply push in a rotten frame.
- Always have internal beading on double glazing: otherwise thieves can simply slit around the rubber seal and remove the whole window with a suction pad.
- If you live in a bungalow, for secure ventilation use window limiters/child safety locks. These limit the window opening to no more than 15 degrees.

NEIGHBOURHOOD WATCH

Setting up a Neighbourhood/Home/Community or Tower Watch group can help reduce the level of crime and the fear of crime in a neighbourhood. They are not intended to encourage people to set up as a vigilante group, but just to be on the lookout for suspicious behaviour and to enhance the security of the members' own properties.

If you are interested in setting up a scheme in your area, find out first whether others share your enthusiasm before approaching the police.

SECURITY FOR FLATS

- As the front door of an individual flat is often not as strong as the main, outside door, it's worth upgrading a thin door with a more solid one. And it needs as many locks and bolts as the main communal door.
- If a fire escape runs up the side or back of the flats, make sure nearby doors and windows are secure.
- Talk to other residents, or the landlord, about installing a door telephone entry system. Bear in mind, however, these aren't foolproof and you must use them sensibly. Don't let anyone in for another flat or hold open the door for a stranger whose arrival coincides with yours.

SECURITY LIGHTING

The more visible the burglar is when he is trying to break into your house, the less he will like it. It will also make him less sure about whether the house is occupied if you have security lighting coming on and off while the house is actually empty.

PLUG-IN TIMER CONTROLLERS

These switch lights, radio, TV, etc, on and off while you are away so that the house appears to be occupied. They are simple to install, not difficult to set and several of them can be used around the home and moved around wherever you need them. They cost about £20. The most basic time switches simply plug into a socket outlet (like an adaptor) and then whatever you want the time switch to bring on – such as a lamp or TV – is plugged into it, to give the impression that you are home.

Electromechanical time switches are set by moving little markers or tappets around a dial. They operate, usually to the nearest 15 minutes, at the same time every day (or every week, with a seven-day timer) unless you move the tappets. Some switches will turn on at random within specified active periods. Electronic, programmable time switches can be set more accurately to the nearest minute. There may also be an option for setting different times each day.

SECURITY WALL SWITCHES

You can fit a security light switch (about £20) in place of a normal light switch to control a central room light, wall lights or an exterior porch light. It will normally be set so that it only brings on the light when it gets dark, but methods vary. There is a wide range of levels of sophistication.

- Simple photocells which turn lights on at dusk and off again at dawn.
- Switches that allow setting of the exact times at which lights will switch on and off.
- Switches that come on randomly.
- Switches that re-create the householder's own habits over a 24-hour period.

TIP You can't use time switches with fluorescent lights, but an adaptor is available for around £5.

OUTDOOR SECURITY LIGHTS

If you live in a large property, it may be worth considering illuminating large areas such as a drive or lawn with mains-wired floodlighting. This will spread an even, practical light, ideal both for deterring burglars from shady corners, and for alfresco entertaining in the summer.

Alternatively, spotlighting may be more effective. Key areas to spotlight are over the front door, garage, shed, passages and any other obvious entry points.

Rather than having lights that stay on all night and require you to turn them on and off, consider installing passive infra-red lighting. This only works when someone approaches: a passive infra-red detector senses body heat and automatically operates a light (turning it off again after a few minutes). You can buy both integral lights, or separate lights and passive infra-red sensors.

SAFETY WARNING

Unless you are competent at DIY, mains lighting should always be installed by a qualified electrician. There are strict safety standards for electrical installation to mains supply and you need a separate garden circuit with waterproof external plug sockets.

For a list of electricians in your area ring the National Inspection Council for Electrical Installation Contracting, or the Electrical Contractors' Association – see Useful Addresses.

TIPS FOR LIGHTING

- Don't forget that outdoor lighting should have separate wiring from your household system with external plug sockets, and should incorporate a Residual Current Device (RCD) and fuse. For installation, always use a qualified electrician.
- Mount light fittings high so no one can tamper with them and adjust the beam slightly off ground if you have cats or dogs, so they can't activate them accidentally.

• When positioning floodlighting or security lighting bear in mind that your neighbours may not want the night sky illuminated into the small hours. Be considerate.

SAFES

If you live in an area where burglary is common, a safe may be useful for small valuables and cash. Look for one that conforms to BS 7558. It's also worth checking with your insurer whether this will reduce your premium, and how much cover they will give for items in a safe.

Think carefully before buying secondhand (unless you are confident that the safe has been reconditioned to BS 7582). If you move into a house with an old safe, do not use it. Old safes may look quite secure, but the technology used will almost certainly be outdated, making them easy to break into.

The most common types of safe used in the home are wall safes (about £50) which can be set in brickwork or fixed to the wall, and floor safes (around £65) which are sited under the floorboards. You can buy small, free-standing safes (from around £120) but a thief may think you have something worth taking and decide to remove the whole safe.

It is important to ensure the safe is securely bolted to the floor or wall, and in a position where a thief would have difficulty prising it out. Have the safe professionally installed for maximum security. For a reputable company it's best to contact the Master Locksmith's Association (see Useful Addresses).

TIP To store cash, use a small portable unit, such as Safe-Can, which looks like an ordinary tin of food (about £5), or Safe Plug, a false double electrical wall socket. Both are available from DIY stores.

BURGLAR ALARMS

If after you've taken as many practical, physical and common-sense measures as you can you still feel insecure, then it may be worth considering fitting a burglar alarm. This isn't a substitute for having good locks, but may be worth it if you live in an inner city or a secluded spot and have a lot of valuables. You will have to use it conscientiously, even if out for only a few minutes – the major danger time for burglaries.

Don't be rushed into a decision by the offer of a discount, or frightening stories of crime levels. You will need to discuss your security risks with a local crime-prevention office. Do not deal with doorstep salesmen of burglar alarms. You'll also need to think about who you would appoint as your key holders for occasions when you are away. You will have to give them – and your family – full instructions on using the system.

If installing a burglar alarm you should always inform the police and environmental health department.

Some insurance companies offer discounted premiums if you have an 'approved' burglar-alarm system. But think carefully before trying to get a reduction on this basis as it often involves you in regular maintenance checks by an approved company and, in the event of a burglary, if the alarm wasn't on you may have difficulty claiming.

An 'approved' installer usually means one registered with the British Security Industry Association (the trade association) or the National Approval Council for Security Systems (NACOSS, the industry inspectorate) – see Useful Addresses.

Don't expect any insurance discounts for DIY-installed alarms.

COST

The cost of a professionally installed burglar alarm system will vary according to its level of sophistication. Installation charges, too, will reflect the type of house, its size, the number of entry points, etc. Expect to pay, on average, £400 to £700 for the installation and £35 upwards per year for the maintenance.

A DIY-installed system from your local DIY or hardware store will cost from £100, again depending on the complexity of the system. (See DIY Burglar Alarms on page 431 for further details).

To ensure you are charged the right price for the job, it is essential to obtain a minimum of three quotes from reputable installers before making your choice. Quotations are usually free and don't place you under any obligation. Remember, the cheapest installation is not necessarily the best option.

PROFESSIONAL ALARMS

- Check that the system meets BS 4737.
- Be suspicious of firms that offer you a ready-made package. For a burglar alarm to be really effective it needs to be tailored to your home and your particular needs. A professional installer should send someone to look at your home to determine what kind of lifestyle you lead so he can draw up the most appropriate form of protection before quoting. For instance, pets may cause a problem if allowed to run free in the area of movement detectors; or if you are elderly you may have visits from grandchildren who are attracted to personal-attack buttons placed at low level.
- Don't forget to ask how much servicing and maintenance will cost and who pays if the system breaks down, or there is a false alarm.
- You should also check that all equipment has a 12-month guarantee.
- Establish which part of the system you own. Signalling devices are invariably rented from the company. If the control equipment is rented you will lose this if you change alarm companies.

WHAT SYSTEM?

A burglar alarm consists of three main parts:

1 The detection device.

2 The control equipment. You should be able to set just part of the system, such as door, window and living-room detectors at night when you are asleep.

3 The signalling device/s.

Think of an alarm system as a stand-in for you: the detection devices are your eyes and ears, the control unit is your brain and the signalling device is your voice.

1 DETECTION DEVICES

These fall into two categories: fixed-point detectors and movement detectors.

Fixed point detectors

Normally fitted to doors and windows and can be:

- Switches that operate when a door or window is opened.
- Vibration sensors, which can be fitted on walls, windows or doors to detect physical vibration.
- Pressure sensors: hidden pressure pads that trigger the alarm when stepped on.

Movement detectors

Normally fixed to the corner of a wall near the ceiling and can be:

- Acoustic, to sense airborne vibrations such as the sound of breaking glass.
- Passive infra-red, which react to a change in temperature as an intruder moves within a

defined area.

- Air-activated, which sense changes in air pressure caused when doors or windows are opened or broken.

2 THE CONTROL PANEL

This is the nerve centre of the alarm system and is usually situated in a cupboard or under the stairs. Once activated by any of the detection devices it sets off the bell/siren, or the central monitoring station.

3 SIGNALLING DEVICES

Bell only

This sort of system makes a noise when set off. These are designed to draw immediate attention to the break-in but rely on neighbours or passers by to alert the police.

Bell-only systems are sometimes fitted with flashing lights fitted on the underside of the bell box. This gives a visual warning that the alarm has activated, which is useful for identification within a row of alarmed houses. The light will continue to flash even after the bell/sounder has cut out.

TIP It's worth having a bell that sounds inside the house as well as out. This is important as you may not be able to hear the outside bell: if you are in bed asleep, for example. It also stops a burglar from hearing what is going on outside, making him more vulnerable.

TIP Remember that a highly visible alarm-bell box will provide a deterrent, and if your house is vulnerable to attack from the rear, it may be worth fitting a dummy bell box at the back. Buy spares at DIY stores.

Monitored system

When a monitored alarm is set off, it sends a coded message down the phone to a central monitoring station, which in turn calls the police or a nominated relative or friend. This system comprises a bell-only system with the addition of a digital communicator to link the alarm to the monitoring station. All the major alarm companies run their own continuously manned monitoring stations.

The police will accept calls signalled over the phone line from these types of system, provided the alarm company is approved (usually if it is a member of NACOSS). A list is available from crime-prevention officers.

Personal-attack button

You press a personal-attack button (usually situated by the bed with a second one by the front door) if you sense an intruder. These are deliberately operated by a push button and reset via a key. This device is used to activate the alarm at any time, whether the control unit is switched on or off.

FALSE ALARMS

False alarms make up over 96 per cent of all alarm calls responded to by the police in England and Wales, wasting millions of pounds in lost police hours per year. If police are called out to false alarms at your property four times in a twelve-month period, you may receive a warning letter from the local police. If the false calls reach seven in a year, the police may stop responding completely.

It's not just the police who are inconvenienced by false alarms: it could cost you, the householder, dearly too. If your system has been installed by an approved engineer, the British Standard requires him to reset the system once it has been set off, accidentally or not, to prevent burglars cancelling the alarm. Your insurance cover and premium may also be affected if police cover is withdrawn. Find out what caused the false alarms and put it right. There's nothing guaranteed to annoy the neighbours more than an alarm bell continuously and needlessly going off.

DIY BURGLAR ALARMS

If you are a competent DIYer with experience in electrics, you will be able to fit your own system. Wire-free systems are the easiest to fit and should only take three or four hours, but you can also get DIY-wired alarms which are cheaper, but can take a day's work to install.

In a wire-free system there are no wires between the detection devices and the control panel. Each device contains a small transmitting device which signals to a receiver in the control unit. Apart from simplicity of installation, the advantages of having a wire-free system are that you can also use the system to protect garages and a garden shed, and take it with you if you move house.

Their main disadvantage is that the police won't accept calls signals from them. Therefore they are restricted to local, audible signalling or signals to nearby friends or neighbours.

POINTS TO REMEMBER

- Interfering signals from local police and taxis, etc, can prevent radio systems working properly, and some systems don't show this is happening.
- Effective range of radio systems can be dramatically reduced by internal walls and floors, especially if reinforced with steel.
- DTI approval: it is illegal to sell or advertise non-approved products. Certain radio frequencies have been allocated to these systems so that they don't interfere with the police, emergency services or cordless phones, etc. Talk to other alarm users and a couple of installers about the possibility of radio frequency interference if you happen to live near public services.
- Look for BS 6707 on Intruder Alarm Systems for Consumer Installation.
- Ensure that the control unit is accessible, but out of reach of young children and pets.
- Make sure you can close windows and doors so they don't rattle or vibrate when there is heavy traffic or wind. Physical vibration may set off the burglar alarm.
- If your system has an alarm clearly audible outside your home you should notify the local police station that you've installed an alarm within 48 hours of installation, and give them the names and addresses of at least two key holders. Show the key holders how to operate and silence the alarm. The bell or siren should be set to cut out after 20 minutes.
- Be warned: control panels and bell/siren boxes contain rechargeable batteries to keep the alarm working in the event of a power cut. These must be serviced regularly.

Local authorities' environmental health officers have power to switch off alarms causing a noise nuisance. You may also be liable to a fine if you do not notify the police or keyholders.

Rather than annoy your neighbours through noise, co-operate in looking after each others' property and taking notice if the alarm sounds, or suspicious activity takes place.

NEW HOUSES

If you're buying a brand-new house, look for the builder's Secured by Design symbol. This is awarded to flats and houses that meet police standards for home security, which include substantial door locks, secure boundaries and limited access to the rear.

Secured by Design is a police initiative involving builders and architects to improve home security. It has the support of the Association of British Insurers, the Home Office and the Department of Environment.

HOT PROPERTY

The most attractive items for burglars to steal are portable, high-value goods that can't be identified easily. If you mark your valuables, it will be harder for them to be sold and easier for the police to return them, if they're found.

- For absorbent surfaces, such as documents or fabrics, use a non-absorbent ultraviolet pen, which costs about £1.50 at a stationer.
- For hard surfaces, such as plastic or metal, use a hard-surface ultraviolet marker. Write in an inconspicuous place, as it's visible and can discolour some finishes.
- Etch your postcode, followed by the house number or the first two letters of the house name on to cameras and stereo equipment. Also make a record of serial numbers. Then if they are stolen and later found, the police can identify them and return them to you.
- Ask your local crime-prevention officer for postcoded property warning stickers to display in the front and back windows of your house.
- Keep a list of valuable items with the make, model number and serial number.
- Hide holdalls and suitcases, as thieves find them handy for taking valuables away.
- Keep a note of your credit cards, cashpoint card, pension/allowance book, bank and building society account numbers and the companies' emergency telephone numbers so you can advise them of the loss immediately.
- It's a good idea to have colour photographs taken of jewellery, antiques, silver, etc that can't be properly marked. Without an accurate description of stolen items there is little hope of them being recovered (see Recovering Stolen Goods, page 434).
- Valuables should be stored in the bank when you go on holiday, and items of lesser value hidden away.

BURGLARS' TOP TEN MOST VALUED ITEMS

Don't assume you have nothing worth stealing. This is what thieves like most:

1. Video recorders
2. Home computers
3. Cash
4. Stereo equipment
5. Chequebook, credit cards and documents (such as passports)
6. TVs
7. Jewellery
8. Gold and silver ware
9. Cameras
10. Antiques

TIP Antiques can be registered with The Art and Antiques Recording Service (see Useful Addresses). Photographic and written details of your valuables are stored on a database. If they are stolen, the details are then circulated to the appropriate authorities. It costs £150 to record ten items, or the same price for 25 items if you supply your own good-quality photographs.

HOUSE CONTENTS INSURANCE

There are over 100 insurers offering household insurance. All cover theft or attempted theft. Decide whether you want indemnity or new for old cover.

Indemnity reduces the amount paid out, to allow for wear and tear, and depreciation.

New for old cover pays out the cost of replacing an old item with a new one, so is more expensive.

Contact at least one independent intermediary to find a variety of quotes.

When you take out cover you will need to estimate the total, new replacement value of all your belongings (with the exception of linen and clothing. Nearly all policies make a deduction for wear and tear on these.)

Most insurers will now insist on you having certain minimum levels of security before they will give you cover. If you improve the security of your home above their minimum requirements, some insurers will give you a discount off your contents policy. For example, if you:

- belong to a Neighbourhood Watch Scheme;
- have locks approved to BS 3621 fitted to all front and back doors;
- have an alarm system fitted and serviced by a member of the National Approval Council for Security Systems (NACOSS).

Insurance tips

- Think carefully before installing an alarm. If you don't have it regularly serviced by a NACOSS-approved company and it wasn't switched on at the time of the burglary, you may invalidate your policy and be unable to make a claim.
- Fitting your own DIY kit alarm won't reduce an insurance premium.
- Check your policy for exclusion clauses. If you fit devices but don't use them, it may affect your cover.
- It's wise to check your policy for holiday cover. Leaving the house empty for over 30 days may restrict it.
- Policies often ask you to specify valuable items worth over £500.
- Check the policy covers garden items.

The Association of British Insurers issues a free leaflet, *Beat The Burglar*. For a copy, send a SAE – see Useful Addresses.

STRANGERS IN THE NIGHT

If you wake in the night and hear intruders, don't rush downstairs and confront them. Dial 999 immediately, if you can. Even if you can't give details, the police will respond. If you can't get to a phone, stay put until the thief has left and it's safe to move.

For the elderly or disabled who may not be able to reach a telephone during a break-in, a community alarm can be fitted. The alarms work as a normal telephone with the additional feature that they can automatically dial a control centre (run by local housing authorities, social services departments or commercial monitoring companies). It is triggered by pressing a button on the telephone or on a pendant around the neck. Prices for this service vary from nothing to over £4 a week. Contact your local housing authority, social services or Help the Aged.

TIP Help the Aged also produce an advice leaflet *Security In Your Home* (see Useful Addresses).

STOPPING GARDEN THIEVES

Did you know that there is a one in twenty chance that something will be stolen from your garden in the next two years, whether it is powered tools, plants or ornaments? Garden tools are often used to assist the burglar breaking into the house, with ladders and garden spades and forks particularly helpful to your unwanted visitor.

GARDEN SECURITY TIPS

- Put away all tools and equipment and ensure that all outside sheds and store cupboards are securely locked when not in use.
- Bring the tools inside if you do not have a garden shed or outbuilding.
- Install automatic security lighting outdoors (see Security Lighting, page 426).
- Use good-quality locks to secure your gates.
- If you have a burglar alarm, why not extend it to cover outbuildings and sheds?
- Photograph valuable garden plants or ornaments for identification if stolen.
- Postcode garden tools and equipment.
- Check that your household insurance policy covers theft from the garden and outbuildings.
- Use prickly plants to provide extra natural protection around your property. Suitable thorny defenders include Blue Spruce (dense blue, spiky needles), Creeping Juniper (thorny stem and foliage), Holly, Chinese Jujube (very spiny, pendulous branches), Firethorn (thorny stem), Juniper (prickly foliage), Blue Pine (spiky, needled stem).

RECOVERING STOLEN GOODS

If your home has been burgled, the chances of ever seeing your most valuable belongings again are, realistically, rare. If items are security marked the chances increase considerably, and if you have photographs and detailed descriptions of precious items, even better.

If the items are antiques, try contacting:

- The *Antiques Trade Gazette*, a weekly newspaper with a section on stolen goods, circulated to the antiques trade internationally. See Useful Addresses.
- *Trace* magazine publishes details of stolen works of art and antiques. Around 60 per cent of its advertisements are placed by private individuals. See Useful Addresses.
- The *Art Loss Register*: Any item worth over £500 in value can be registered for £20. The information is kept on a permanent database of stolen art and antiques and checked against auction catalogues. See Useful Addresses.

MALICIOUS PHONE CALLS AND HARASSMENT

A harassing or malicious phone caller can make you feel unpleasantly vulnerable in your own home. To combat such calls, both British Telecom and Mercury users should follow the procedure below.

- Call free on 0800 66 6700 for recorded advice on what to do if you get one of these calls. Such advice includes, for example: don't give your name or phone number, say nothing, walk away from the phone and gently hang up without saying anything after ten minutes. For personal advice, ring BT's Malicious Calls Bureau free on 0800 66 1441.
- The operator can intercept all your calls (usually for about two weeks) at no charge.
- Your telephone number can be changed.
- BT can organise Malicious Call Identification free of charge but only as part of a police investigation.

FURTHER INFORMATION

Further Information on crime prevention is provided in the 40-page handbook, *Practical Ways to Crack Crime.* For a free copy, contact The Home Office (see Useful Addresses).

And finally . . . Whatever security devices you fit, ensure they are simple enough for all the family to use *every day.*

LEGAL MATTERS

INTRODUCTION

The purpose of this section is to give you a guide to the law and explain your rights as they affect your acquisition of your home and your enjoyment of it. It is not intended as a substitute for taking legal advice, if you have a serious legal problem, or if you are about to enter into some important legal transaction. This is how the law affects you, and is aimed at encouraging you to be more confident in consulting a professional expert if it becomes necessary. It may also help you to understand the advice you are given.

Every attempt is made to give you an accurate outline of the law (as it stands on the 31st March 1994). But the law on many subjects is complex, and many detailed provisions and exceptions apply to particular situations. Furthermore, the law is subject to constant changes as a result of Acts of Parliament and decided cases, and the law in Scotland and Northern Ireland often differs from that in force in England and Wales.

You should not, therefore, use this outline of the law as if it is tailor-made to deal with your own particular case, and no liability can attach to the author or publisher of this work if you do.

If you are in doubt about whether or not to enter into a transaction, or whether or not to bring or defend a case against another party, you are strongly advised to seek professional legal help.

BUYING A HOUSE OR FLAT

EMPLOYING A SOLICITOR

Once you have chosen the home of your dreams and your offer has been accepted, you must decide who should be responsible for carrying out the legal side of the transaction.

It is perfectly possible to engage in do-it-yourself conveyancing. But if you want to undertake it, you will have to do a great deal of homework. If you get it right it will save you the cost of employing someone – about several hundred pounds or even a four figure sum. If some complication arises, or you get it wrong, it could cost you a great deal more.

The information set out in this book is not intended to be a guide to do-it-yourself conveyancing. It may, however, help you when dealing with a professional to have some idea what is being discussed and what is involved.

It has also to be said that solicitors prefer to deal with other solicitors, and although they will, of course, co-operate with a person conducting his or her own affairs, the whole operation runs more smoothly between professionals. Since buying a home is probably the biggest transaction you will ever make, you will probably not wish to add to your headaches by doing your own conveyancing.

Most people, therefore, employ a solicitor or sometimes a licensed conveyancer. If you do not already have a solicitor, try and get a friend to recommend one locally. Otherwise, do not hesitate to walk off the street into a solicitor's office and enquire about conveyancing.

ADVANTAGES OF EMPLOYING A SOLICITOR

One advantage is that he or she may be accepted by the building society or bank to deal on their behalf with the mortgage. Quite apart from his knowledge and experience of the procedure, items such as the transfer of funds can be dealt with more easily by him.

LICENSED CONVEYANCERS

In recent years, solicitors have faced competition from licensed conveyancers. They too are trained to take care of the legal aspects of buying and selling property. The purpose of licensing such people, who do not need to be trained in other aspects of the law, was to provide a cheaper alternative service. The effect has been to encourage solicitors to reduce their prices.

CAN I AFFORD A SOLICITOR?

Before you employ either a solicitor or a licensed conveyancer to undertake the legal work for you, make sure you ask for an estimate of the cost involved. The amount charged by different people varies considerably, and unless you happen to know a solicitor well, it is worth getting two or three quotations.

FINDING A SOLICITOR OR CONVEYANCER

The Law Society has a complete list of solicitors for any given area (see Useful Addresses). Your library should also have a directory of local solicitors, showing which ones do conveyancing.

The Council for Licensed Conveyancers (see Useful Addresses) also keeps a list of licensed conveyancers.

TIP There is no such thing as legal aid for conveyancing – you have to pay the costs yourself.

WHAT WILL THE SOLICITOR DO?

The solicitor's first job is to ensure that the property belongs to the seller: that is, that it is really his or hers to sell. It is vital to make sure that it is not subject to rights owned by others. For example, there could be tenants who have the right to stay in the property. Or a property apparently owned by a man could be subject to the rights of an estranged wife. It could even be subject to a mortgage which cannot be paid off, or there may be some other charge upon the property.

In addition, the solicitor will have to check to see what rights anybody else has in relation to the property, and what local plans there are which might affect it. He also has to make enquiries about the property from the sellers, and ascertain what is included in the sale. Most of this will usually be done before you enter into a binding contract.

HOW CAN I BE SURE THE PROPERTY WILL BE MINE?

The most fundamental task is to establish title to the property.

Nowadays, most properties are registered with the name of the owner at the Land Registry (see Useful Addresses). This means that there is a State guarantee that the person whose name is registered there is the owner of the property. When you complete the purchase, your own name will be recorded at the Land Registry as owner.

TIP The Land Registry keeps a record which includes a description and plan of the property, the name and address of the owner, and details of any mortgage outstanding on it.

Despite the scheme for compulsory registration of any conveyance, some properties which have been in the same ownership for a considerable time are still unregistered. Where this occurs, title has to be proved by establishing an unbroken chain of ownership for at least 15 years by having the deeds by which the property was conveyed each time. The idea is that each previous purchaser prior to that will have investigated the title for himself. You have to go back to the last sale before 15 years ago. Since the property may have been in the same hands for many years, the last sale which occurred more than 15 years ago may have been a very long time ago. Thus, some of the deeds produced may be quite old.

WHAT ARE 'SEARCHES'?

If the property is registered, before completion of the purchase a search is made by sending a form to the Land Registry. This is to ensure that no adverse interest has been established, such as a subsequent mortgage taken out by the vendor. Where the property is unregistered, a search has to be made by sending a form to the Land Charges Registry (which is a different body to the Land Registry, see Useful Addresses) to see if there are any charges upon the property.

TIP A record is kept at the Land Charges Registry of any charge against unregistered property, such as security for a loan, or an interest of a wife in the matrimonial home, where she is not actually a part owner.

Local searches are carried out by sending forms to the appropriate local council. The answers to these will show if any planning permission has been granted in relation to the property, and if any orders have been made which have an effect on the property.

The local council keeps a record of any planning permission granted for a change of use, building an extension, or any order affecting the property such as a tree-preservation order or smoke control order, and whether the local authority has any plans to widen the road into the front garden.

WHAT IS MEANT BY 'ENQUIRIES'?

Pre-contract enquiries are sent by your solicitor to the solicitor for the vendor. These enquiries are often in the form of a standard, printed form with some additions relevant to the particular property. They require the vendor to give answers, insofar as they are within his knowledge, about the condition of the property, any guarantees which there may be with it, any rights which neighbours may have, or any problems which have arisen with these rights.

The answers to these enquiries often do not take the matter much further forward. They tend to be of the nature 'not so far as is known to the vendor' or 'ask your surveyor' or 'ask the local authority'. They will also be designed to clarify what is included in the sale price, such as carpets, curtains, blinds and light fittings.

TIP If there is anything you are unsure about, for example, whether there is a gas supply, or if you suspect the next door neighbour may have a right to use the drive, ask your solicitor to include this query in the enquiries.

FREEHOLD OR LEASEHOLD: THE DIFFERENCE

Freehold

The property will belong to you and your heirs absolutely for all time, or until it is sold. No one else can claim rights of ownership over it. You own both the land and the building.

Leasehold

You may have bought the building (or part of it, as with a flat) but the freeholder still owns the land on which it stands. You will therefore have to pay ground rent upon it. The interest you have in the land is for a fixed term only.

Until fairly recently, this meant that after the lease had expired, the land, and with it anything built upon it, reverted to the owner of the freehold, and you were left with nothing. In the case of a long lease, this may be a long time in the future. Many leases were granted for 99 years or longer. But it meant that it was an asset with a diminishing value as the lease drew to an end. For that reason, building societies were reluctant to lend on leasehold property unless the lease still had a very long time to run: perhaps 25 years or more after the end of the mortgage period, which could mean a total of 50 years or more.

Recent legislation, however, has provided a remedy for this situation by creating a right to buy the freehold or extend the lease. Even if you do neither of these, the tenancy no longer automatically comes to an end. It will continue on a periodic basis until the freeholder takes action to bring it to an end.

TIP It is usually in your interest to buy the freehold or extend the lease, if you can.

If the property is a flat, it is almost certainly leasehold. When a developer builds a block of flats, he will grant a lease for each of the individual flats. These may be bought and sold many times, but the freehold remains vested in the developer or is sold to an individual or company as an investment. That person or company is then entitled to collect the rents and is responsible for keeping the whole block in a good state of repair and decoration. This is a service for which they will make a charge.

HOW CAN I BUY THE FREEHOLD?

Houses

If your home is a leasehold house, you can pay to extend the lease, or buy the freehold with the agreement of the freeholder. If you and your home fulfil certain qualifications, you can insist on buying the freehold, even if the owner of it does not agree.

This applies if you have a long lease and have lived in your house for three years or more. Even then it only applies to leases lasting longer than 21 years, and only if the rent is no more than two thirds of the rateable value and has been so at all times during the three years.

There is also a limitation based on the rateable value of the property. However this was raised by the Leasehold Reform Act 1993 to include higher value properties.

Flats

The 1993 Act has also extended the right to buy the freehold to qualifying tenants of flats, who have occupied them for 12 months or more. Such leaseholders now have a collective right to acquire the freehold of the building, subject to certain exceptions.

Those people who live in a block of flats sometimes club together to buy the freehold. This is normally done by forming a limited company in which the owners of each of the flats have a share. The company then owns the freehold, and the flat-owners have more control over their own affairs. In addition there is no one to make a profit from their ground rent and by charging commission on maintenance. Where a large enough number of the tenants qualify and at least two thirds of the tenants agree, they have the legal right to buy the freehold, even if the freeholder does not want to sell it.

Buying the freehold

In order to set the process in motion, you must serve notice on the landlord. You will have to pay a deposit, since you are liable for the landlord's costs of valuation, and legal fees. When you learn the cost of enfranchisement, (the cost of purchasing the freehold) you may withdraw, but may not serve notice again for another five years.

The method of calculating the value of the freehold is complicated and depends upon the rateable value of the property. The value is based on the market rate for the freehold bearing in mind that there is a tenant living in the house.

Further information can be obtained from a booklet entitled *Leasehold Flats: Your Right to Buy the Freehold of your Building or Renew your Lease*, published by the Department of the Environment and the Welsh Office; and *Buying your Freehold or Extending your Lease*, published by Leasehold Enfranchisement Ltd; see Useful Addresses.

Owning the freehold

Buying the freehold means you now own the property outright, as if you had bought it as a freehold property. It follows that you have no ground rent to pay, and that the lease will not run out at the end of a fixed period. You will also have a positive advantage in that the price you have to pay for the freehold will have been less than it is actually worth.

Extending the lease

You may prefer instead simply to extend the lease. First, you would need to qualify in the same way as for purchasing the freehold. You can extend the lease of a house for 50 years from the time when it would have ended. This takes effect as a new lease. Thus, if the old lease had 20 years to run, you would now acquire a lease for 70 years. The rent would be a ground rent for the site at current rates.

Under the 1993 Act, qualifying tenants of flats may acquire a new lease for 90 years at a peppercorn rent, on payment of a premium.

RENTING A HOME

Perhaps you have decided to rent a home rather than buying one at this stage. While some people do so on a permanent basis, others prefer renting for a temporary period.

The document which sets out the basis of the relationship between landlord and tenant is the lease. It is important to read this carefully before entering into an agreement to rent property, as this contains the express terms of the tenancy. But the law relating to landlord and tenant is complicated, and in addition to the terms set out in the lease there may be others implied by law.

TIP Read the lease with care before signing it; it may contain obligations which you do not wish to undertake.

WHAT IS A TENANCY?

A tenancy arises when one person grants to another an exclusive interest in a property less than that which he himself owns, and does so on a contractual basis. Thus, if a person who owns the freehold in a house lets it to another for three years, a tenancy is created. If a person who has a three year lease, lets the property to another on a weekly basis, that too creates a tenancy.

The nature of a tenancy is the exclusive right to occupation. Thus, if you are the tenant of a house or even part of a house, subject to special circumstances which are described later, you can keep the landlord out. In fact, he is a trespasser if he enters without your consent. If the agreement between the parties confers this exclusive right, it is one of tenancy no matter what word is used to describe it in the agreement. Suppose you have entered into an agreement which says you have a licence to occupy. If it is clear that the landlord may only enter under special conditions specified in the agreement, you probably have a tenancy, and all the rights given in law to a tenant.

Perhaps, on the other hand, the agreement merely gives you the right to occupy a room, but the landlord or others may come and go as they please. In this case the right you have acquired is a personal right to do something, rather than a right over the property. All you have is a licence to occupy, even if you pay regularly for it. Equally, if you are a lodger in a house where the owner provides bed linen and is responsible for cleaning, you do not become a tenant. Neither a licensee nor a lodger have the rights accorded by law to a tenant.

HOW DO I KNOW THE TERMS OF THE TENANCY?

If there is a formal agreement, the lease contains all the express terms of the tenancy. In particular, this includes details of the property, the length of the period for which the lease will last and the amount of rent payable, and when and how it should be paid. It also sets out the rights and duties of the landlord and the tenant with regard to the property, and who is responsible for carrying out repairs to different parts of the property. It will show what remedies there are and how they can be achieved in the event of a breach of the lease by either party.

In addition to the terms expressly set out in the lease, there are other terms which are implied by law, which are presumed to apply unless the lease says otherwise, or sometimes despite what is said in the lease. These additional terms are implied to clarify or amplify the express terms. The implied terms have developed as a result of various Acts of Parliament and decided legal cases. Furthermore, the parties do not have complete freedom to make any binding contract they like. For the law lays down certain requirements which must be met, irrespective of the agreement of the parties. And there are some legal terms which the parties cannot exclude by putting them in the lease.

The primary obligation of the landlord, whether expressly in the lease or not, is to afford to the tenant peaceful enjoyment of the property. This means that he must himself own rights to the property sufficient to put the tenant into lawful possession of it. He must allow the tenant to remain in peaceful occupation, undisturbed by any entry, eviction or other interruption by him or others acting on his behalf.

The tenant's principle obligation, on the other hand, is to pay the rent.

THE RENT

To start with, the amount of rent payable is a figure agreed between the parties. If there is a formal lease this is set out in that document. In certain cases, however, the law intervenes to overrule what the parties have agreed.

A number of Acts of Parliament have been enacted over the years, mostly for the protection of tenants. In circumstances specified by these either the landlord or the tenant can apply to the Rent Officer to register the rent. Most tenancies granted or agreed before the 15th January 1989 are called 'protected tenancies'. In the case of these, the Rent Officer will assess a 'fair rent' by reference to the market value, but not taking into account the scarcity element (ie the amount of housing available). Thus the fair rent could be substantially less than the amount of rent that could be obtained in a free market.

Most tenancies created after that date are called 'assured tenancies'. The premises must be let as a separate dwelling, and must be the tenant's only or principal home. There is no limit on the rent a landlord may charge, but a tenant may refer the rent to the Rent Assessment Committee in two instances. One is in the case of a periodic tenancy, (for example, from week to week or month to month) where the landlord proposes a rent increase. The other is where the landlord grants an assured shorthold tenancy for a fixed term, and the rent is too high (that is, significantly higher than that for comparable properties). In these cases the Rent Assessment Committee may determine the rent.

In some cases, where the landlord is resident in a separate part of a building (so long as it was not purpose built), or he provides food or other services, the tenancy agreement is called a 'restricted contract'. In these cases, either the landlord or tenant may apply to the Rent Tribunal to register a 'reasonable rent', an amount which takes into account all the different circumstances.

WHAT HAPPENS IF I CANNOT PAY THE RENT?

If you are in arrears the usual course taken by a landlord is to bring an action in the county court for payment of the arrears of rent. He does this simply by issuing a summons in the local county court and serving it on you. The hearing is not less than seven days later, and you have an opportunity to appear or otherwise pay admitted arrears to the court.

If the lease reserves a right of re-entry for breach of covenant to pay rent, the landlord may elect to forfeit the lease. The right of re-entry does not mean, however, that he can simply walk in and take over. It means that he may apply to the county court for an order that he should recover possession of the property, in which event your rights will come to an end. However, you can avoid this so long as you pay the money to the court at least five days before the hearing. Even if the court orders possession, it will not take effect for at least four weeks, and again you can obtain 'relief' from the forfeiture if you pay the money owing to the court. The court can extend this period in an appropriate case, and is likely to do so if you are making a realistic attempt to pay off the arrears.

TIP If you are unable to pay your rent because of lack of income, for example because you have lost your job, you should contact the local benefit office, with a view to applying for Income Support, and Housing Benefit from the local authority. Do not, in the meantime, simply allow the arrears of rent to accumulate, since this will only add to your problems.

OTHER PARTS OF THE LEASE

The lease will also show what restrictions are placed on the use of the property. For example, can it be used for business purposes as well as for a dwelling? Without an express restriction on use, the tenant may use the property for any lawful purpose subject to the requirements of planning permission.

The lease will also specify whether the property may be sub-let in whole or in part. For example, if you have a five-year lease, but are posted abroad for a year, could you let the property while you are away? Even if the lease prohibits it, would you be able to do so with the landlord's consent in writing? If the lease says you can do it with his consent, that consent may not be unreasonably withheld. Otherwise you may wish to rent out a room in order to help to pay the rent. You should check to see if the lease prohibits this altogether, or only prohibits it without the landlord's consent.

TIP If you wish to do something forbidden by the lease, ask the landlord's permission; if your request is reasonable it will probably be granted. If the lease requires consent it may have to be granted. You must ask first, though, because otherwise, you may find yourself forfeiting the lease.

RESPONSIBILITIES

The lease also sets out the responsibilities of the landlord and the tenant. It shows who is responsible for carrying out internal or external repairs or decoration. Once again, the law imposes obligations of its own.

Under the Housing Act, 1985, the landlord has repairing obligations where the lease is for a term of less than seven years. He must keep in proper repair the structure and exterior of the building. This includes the drains, gutters and external pipes as well as walls, chimneys and roof.

Where the lease is for a flat, contained in only part of the building, and the landlord maintains control of the common parts, he is obliged not only to maintain those parts but also any installation which is placed there, for example a boiler, which is in the part of the building controlled by him.

TIP If you want the landlord to carry out the repairs for which he is responsible, you must inform him by letter that the repair is needed; he is under no obligation to carry out repairs he did not know had become necessary.

On the long lease of a house it is normal for the tenant expressly to undertake the obligation to keep the property in proper repair. Where the property consists of a flat in a block, the usual course is for the landlord to undertake the structural and external repairs and charge each tenant for doing so, usually with a fee or commission for his own services in making the necessary arrangements.

DOES THE LANDLORD HAVE THE RIGHT TO VISIT MY HOME?

As we have already seen, when you rent a property you pay for the exclusive right to occupy it. But the landlord will probably have reserved certain specific rights to himself.

The rights of the landlord should be set out in the lease. This usually provides for entry by the landlord for the purpose of carrying out his duties to keep the property in good repair. Even if not specifically reserved, he has the implied right to enter for the limited purpose of carrying out work which he has an obligation to do. Normally, he will also reserve the right to enter to inspect the property to make sure you have also fulfilled any duties you may have, but can only do so at reasonable times and on giving reasonable notice.

If you refuse to let him in, he may obtain a court order. You would also be in breach of the terms of the lease, and this may result in him obtaining possession of the property.

CAN THE LANDLORD MAKE MY LIFE DIFFICULT?

It is a criminal offence if a landlord, or anyone acting on his behalf, acts in a way that is likely to interfere with the peace or comfort of the residential occupier or members of his household. It is also an offence if he persistently withdraws or withholds services. So, if your landlord cuts off your electricity, and leaves you without light and heat, he is committing a criminal offence for which he can be taken to court and fined, or in a bad case, even sent to prison.

Since he is not entitled to force you out, you can sue him if he tries. You can sue him for breach of his obligation to allow you enjoyment of the property, or for creating a nuisance, or for trespass to the property itself. You can also ask for a court order, called an injunction, to stop him harassing you.

If he succeeds in forcing you out of your home, the damages may be substantial. You may have to pay more to find accommodation elsewhere, particularly if the amount of your rent was limited to a registered figure. The landlord, meanwhile, will have made a substantial gain by having vacant possession of his property.

To offset this, you can claim his profit. This is the increase in the value of his interest in the property by virtue of acquiring vacant possession.

CAN HE BREAK IN?

The landlord is *not* entitled to break in, and is committing a crime if he does. It is a criminal offence for a landlord to use or threaten violence for the purposes of securing entry into any premises, providing that to his knowledge a person opposed to his entry is on the premises.

IS MY RIGHT TO STAY PROTECTED BY LAW?

As we have seen, many kinds of tenancy are subject to Acts of Parliament. When the lease expires, or when the notice to quit expires, you still have the right to remain there. If the landlord wishes you to leave he must serve on you a notice to quit. This gives you a specified time in which to leave, but is only valid if this is at least four weeks.

A notice to quit, however, does not entitle the landlord physically to eject you. In order to do that he must first obtain a court order. This allows you a right to attend the hearing and put your own case forward. It is not enough, however, simply to say he has no grounds to eject you. Unless you are protected by the Rent Acts he can serve notice at will.

WHEN IS A TENANCY PROTECTED?

For a tenant to be protected from eviction, certain conditions must apply. First, the property must be within the financial limits. Only very expensive properties are outside them.

Second, the landlord must be a private individual or company, not the local council, or the Crown, or in some cases housing associations, or colleges.

Third, the protection does not apply to furnished property. In order to be furnished the furniture must be substantial, not just a nominal couple of chairs.

Nor is protection offered in the case of a holiday let, or a let where the provision of services, such as meals, are an important part of what is being paid for.

In past years, because of the protection accorded to tenants, many people became reluctant to let out property and the stock, particularly of unfurnished homes, to rent on the market was diminished. This in turn led to high rents being charged. As a result 'shorthold tenancies' were created. A property let for two years or less is not subject to the Rent Acts. If the lease is extended or repeated, the Acts then start to apply.

Even when a property is protected, the landlord can regain possession in certain circumstances. For example, he can do so if you default in paying the rent, unless at a court hearing you persuade the court that you will pay within a specified time. The same applies if you are in breach of one of the other conditions of the lease.

Supposing a tenant is damaging the property, or removing items which form a part of it, or causing a nuisance to neighbours. This would entitle the landlord to have him evicted. He can also do so if he can offer the tenant suitable accommodation elsewhere, or in certain circumstances, if he wants the property back in order to make a home for himself, or for a relative.

If you are an owner-occupier who has been posted abroad for a spell, or who has to give up your home for a temporary period for some other reason, and this is made known to the tenant, you can recover the property on your return. Thus renting out your home may be a useful source of income in the meantime, and even enable you to pay the rent on your own temporary accommodation; and you can be sure of getting your home back on your return.

COUNCIL TENANTS

SECURITY

What right do I have to stay in my house or flat?

Tenants of a dwelling house have a secure tenancy where the landlord is a local authority or other public body, and certain conditions apply. The house must be let as a separate dwelling and must be the tenant's only or principal home. Long tenancies, that is those for over 21 years, do not qualify as secure tenancies, nor do lettings to students.

A secure tenancy means that when the term of the tenancy runs out, a periodic tenancy takes its place: that is, a tenancy from week to week or month to month, on more or less the same terms as before.

A secure tenancy lasts for life, unless determined (ie, brought to an end) by an order of the court. Such an order will only be made in limited circumstances. Examples are as a result of a breach of the terms under which the tenancy is held, such as non-payment of rent, or some bad behaviour on the part of the tenant. The tenancy can also be determined (see above) where the accommodation is inappropriate, that is, overcrowded or larger than is necessary, and alternative accommodation will be available for the tenant elsewhere.

So unless the council is offering you alternative accommodation for some good reason, you may stay in your council home so long as you have kept up payment of the rent, and have not behaved in some outrageous way, annoying the neighbours.

Supposing I die, would my grown up son be able to take over the tenancy?

Even after the death of the tenant, the tenancy may be passed on to the tenant's husband or wife, or another member of the family occupying the house as his only or principal home. He will then have the benefit of the secure tenancy. So long as your son actually lives there, and needs the property for his own accommodation and perhaps that of his family, he acquires the same rights as you had.

RIGHT TO BUY

Can I buy the council house I have lived in for the last 10 years?
Where there is a secure tenancy, the Housing Act of 1985 gave the tenant the right to buy the property from the council. This right applies where the tenant has occupied the dwelling for at least two years. If the property is a house, he may usually acquire the freehold (see Freehold or Leasehold, page 438). Where it is a flat, the tenant may acquire a long lease, for up to 125 years.

How much will it cost?
Where a council tenant exercises the right to buy the home in which he lives, the price is determined by the district valuer. He works out a figure based on the market value, assuming the house is sold with vacant possession, that is, without a sitting tenant. But the tenant does not pay the full market price. He gets a discount of between 32 per cent and 60 per cent of the market value depending on the length of time that he has been a secure tenant. So the price you pay will be less than the real value and will depend on how long you have lived there.

How will I pay for it?
On buying the property, the tenant is also entitled to borrow money to pay for it by creating a mortgage on the property. (See Getting a Mortgage, pages 18–25.)

As the property is worth substantially more than the purchase price, you may be able to buy it without having to produce any large lump sum. You will simply be making repayments on the mortgage loan instead of paying rent.

RESPONSIBILITY TO VISITORS

INJURIES

AM I RESPONSIBLE IF A VISITOR IS INJURED?

Every occupier of property, whether as an owner or tenant, has a duty of care towards those who visit. The duty is to take reasonable steps to ensure visitors' safety. If you fail in this duty you may find yourself liable to pay compensation if someone is injured.

Thus if your visitor breaks his leg due to a loose floorboard on the landing, or a loose tile falls and hits her on the head, you may find yourself liable to pay for the damage resulting from the injury, including pain, suffering and loss of earnings.

HOW WOULD I PAY FOR INJURIES?

Because damages for injuries can be very substantial, they are covered by standard insurance policies. Although there is no legal liability to have this cover it is obviously wise to do so.

The duty to take out such insurance lies with the occupier rather than the owner of property. This means that even if you are only renting the property you still owe a duty of care to your visitors and can be sued if you do not fulfil it. For this reason, the liability of an occupier of property is usually covered by household contents insurance, which you would be sensible to have, whether you are a tenant or owner-occupier.

TIP A person who fixes or places a flower pot, box or other heavy article in any upper window without sufficiently guarding it from being blown down can be fined under an Act of Parliament passed nearly 150 years ago.

The owner, on the other hand, is liable to compensate a person who is injured as a result of a failure on his part to do the repairs for which he is responsible under the lease. So he who is bound to ensure that the drains and gutters are in good repair will be liable if a piece of guttering detaches itself and hits the milkman on the head. For this reason, buildings insurance, normally taken out by the owner, should cover the liability of the owner of the property to others. Again it is not compulsory to have buildings insurance, but if you are borrowing money on a mortgage, the lenders will insist on your having cover.

TIP If you are the owner of a building, whether you live in it or not, make sure you have buildings insurance cover: if you are the occupier of a building, whether you own it or not, make sure you have contents insurance; make sure in both cases that they cover you for liability to third parties.

TO WHOM DOES MY RESPONSIBILITY EXTEND?

The responsibility for your visitors applies whether they are guests who are staying in the spare bedroom for the week or have just dropped in for a cup of tea. It applies equally to anyone who is lawfully on the premises, such as those who come there to work, like plumbers or electricians, and those who come to read the meters. Even those who get no further than the front garden are included, such as postmen and milkmen. It also extends to those who have an implied right to be there such as salesmen and people collecting for charity. You can forbid such people to enter by putting a notice on the gate, and they then become trespassers if they proceed.

It may go against the grain, but you even have a duty of care towards trespassers, so long as you can foresee that they are likely to be present. This would apply equally to someone walking across your garden, or to a group of squatters who have occupied your house. You are only under a duty to avoid taking positive steps to harm them. You do not have to protect them against existing features of your property which may happen to pose a potential hazard. So you are not liable to pay compensation for injury to a hiker who, much to your surprise, decides to take a shortcut across your land and falls into a ditch. But you are liable to a burglar for whom you set a hidden trap. You have foreseen that he is likely to be injured.

There is a special duty towards children whom you know are likely to be affected by danger. Whereas you might discharge your duty towards adults by putting up a notice saying 'danger, deep water', children cannot be expected to read or to have a high degree of common sense. So you may find yourself liable if a child falls in your pond, if you know that children are accustomed to play in your garden, even if they are trespassers there. You can fulfil your duty if you take reasonable steps either to safeguard them, or alternatively to keep them out.

Your liability to compensate your visitors extends to their property as well as to their persons. For example, if your guest's clothes are ruined in a flood resulting from your faulty plumbing, he will be able to claim against you. Again, damage to your visitor's possessions should be covered by your insurance.

WHAT HAPPENS IF MY DOG BITES THE POSTMAN?

If the injury had been caused by your pet tiger, you would be liable for it as the keeper, as your pet would belong to a dangerous species. In the case of a dog, the species as a whole is not dangerous; you are only liable if the injury caused by the dog was likely as a result of some unusual characteristics of which you were aware. Thus, if you knew perfectly well that the dog was liable to bite a stranger walking up the path, and allowed it out nevertheless, you would have to pay compensation.

TIP It is an offence under a 19th-century Act to keep at large an unmuzzled, ferocious dog.

TRESPASSERS

MAY I KILL A BURGLAR?

No, except under special circumstances. The normal rules of self-defence apply. This means that a person is entitled to use reasonable force to defend himself if he is either attacked or put in fear of an immediate attack. Of course, what is reasonable has to be seen in the context of what is happening. A person may easily be put in fear of attack by the discovery in the middle of the night of an intruder who did not in fact intend to harm him. Unless you are an expert in unarmed combat, however, it would be better to avoid violence and if possible make a telephone call to the police.

'TRESPASSERS WILL BE PROSECUTED'

No they won't, at least not at the moment. Although this is a sign commonly erected on land, it is not a *criminal* offence to trespass on someone else's property. Consequently trespassers cannot be prosecuted, at any rate not for trespassing. Of course if they steal your possessions while they are there, or commit criminal damage to the windows or front door in order to gain access, they could be prosecuted for that. Changes in the law of trespass have, however, been proposed, and may be made soon.

In civil law you can sue a trespasser, but you will only be able to claim anything more than nominal damages by way of compensation if he has damaged your property. If you are annoyed by someone regularly trespassing on your property, you might be able to get an injunction to stop him or her from entering.

HOW CAN I GET RID OF SQUATTERS?

Imagine returning from holiday to find that squatters have taken over your home. Perhaps they have established themselves and are living there as if it is their own home. You are permitted to use reasonable force to protect your property and to eject a trespasser. But as force is best avoided, how can the law help? Again, if they have damaged your property in order to gain entry, or even, for example, by drawing on the walls, they have committed a criminal offence, and you could ask the police to arrest them. Likewise if they have stolen your food from the freezer.

But there are special criminal offences associated with trespassing. It is an arrestable offence to remain on property when asked to leave by the owner. So if you ask them to go, giving them a reasonable time to gather their things together, and they refuse, you can get the police to arrest them. The police, on the other hand, would be reluctant to be involved in a civil dispute. In other words, if the squatters claim to be there as of right as tenants or licensees, you may have to go to the civil court in order to obtain an order for possession of the property.

Going to court

In order to obtain such an order you must go to the county court and issue what is called an 'originating application'. If you do not have a solicitor, the court staff will help as to what you need. You also have to swear an affidavit, a sworn statement stating your interest in the property. This could be as owner, or tenant; the important point is that you are entitled to immediate possession. You also have to say how it came about that the land was occupied without either your permission or consent.

Assuming that you do not know the names of the illegal occupiers, you should also say this. If you do know any of their names they must be named in the action. A copy of the application, specifying the date for hearing the case, must be delivered to the squatters personally. Alternatively, if their names are not known, the documents can be served by attaching them to the front door, and by putting them through the letter box in a sealed transparent envelope addressed to 'the occupiers'. Another method is to attach such envelopes to stakes placed in the ground at conspicuous parts of the occupied property.

The date fixed for the hearing must be at least five days after the day of service, including weekends. In cases of urgency, with the leave of the court, the date may be earlier. Anyone in occupation of the property who wishes to be heard may apply to become a party to the proceedings.

At the hearing, once your case has been proved by the affidavit, the court will make an order that you shall recover possession. Because the initial entry on to your property was illegal, the order is to take effect immediately. The bailiff will go to the property and evict anyone he finds there, whether parties to the proceedings or not, and hand possession of the premises to you.

If the squatters changed the locks, can I still get back in?

As a displaced residential person, you are free to break into your own home or one you rent, so long as you do so peacefully, that is, not as part of a violent act against the squatters. So you can go in to see to your own affairs, and rescue your belongings, or even to resume occupation.

DIFFICULT NEIGHBOURS

Disputes between neighbours are particularly likely to cause frustration and strife. Once a problem has arisen, it is impossible to walk away from it, and complaining about it often seems to aggravate the matter.

NOISE

Different ways of life often result in noise being made at inconvenient times. People have different ideas about what constitutes a reasonable level of music. Where people live in close proximity, in terraced houses or flats, thin walls mean that the problem can be especially acute.

Although the courts can sometimes find a remedy for the particular problem, there can never be a remedy for the ill-feeling which can arise, and which is likely to be exacerbated by going to court. If, therefore, the matter can be settled amicably it is far better than invoking the law. Your neighbour may not have realised how the powerful bass of his stereo carries into the flat upstairs, or that his late night do-it-yourself activities coincide with your bedtime.

CAN I STOP MY NEIGHBOUR PLAYING MUSIC IN THE EARLY HOURS?

If speaking to your neighbour about this problem does not produce results, the next step is to keep a proper record of what took place. This can take the form of a diary, but it should set out the nature of the nuisance and record the times and dates when it occurred.

It may be that if you show this to the neighbour it will dawn on him that his activities really are disturbing you, and take steps to curb them of his own accord. If not, it will provide valuable material from which you will be able to give evidence in support of your complaint.

It would also be helpful if you could get somebody else to be present on occasions when the noise is noticeable, since noise levels are difficult to establish without a scientific instrument, and may seem louder to some than to others.

Once you have your evidence, you can take your neighbour to court by issuing a summons in your local county court, asking for compensation in the form of damages, and seeking an injunction, ordering him to stop the noise. Be warned, however, that the process may be lengthy, and any compensation is likely to be small.

Instead of suing your neighbour in the county court, where the case is tried by a judge, you could take him or her instead to the local Magistrates' court. Here the case will probably be tried by the local magistrates. Although you will not get compensation, they can issue an order to stop the noise or restrict it to certain times. The procedure here is likely to be quicker and also cheaper, especially if you lose the case.

It is sometimes more effective, if you have a genuine grievance, to bring in the local authority. You can report the matter to the environmental health officer. He may monitor the noise, which will make the evidence much more effective. If he takes the view that there is a statutory nuisance, he will serve an abatement order, to prohibit or restrict the noise. If this is disobeyed, your neighbour could be fined up to £5,000, and £500 a day if the nuisance continues.

TIP Every person who beats or shakes any carpet, rug or mat in the street (except doormats, before 8 am) can be sent to prison for fourteen days under the Town Police Clauses Act 1847!

WHAT OTHER SORT OF NOISE IS CONSIDERED A NUISANCE?

Any type of noise is capable of constituting a nuisance. So a dog persistently barking, an alarm that seems to be always ringing and continual hammering are all examples of a nuisance which could result in a court case. It is all a question of what is reasonable in the circumstances. This depends not only on the level of the sound and the time of day, but also the area. What may be considered a nuisance in a quiet residential area is not necessarily so in a noisy industrial estate where there happen to be a few houses.

CAN I INSIST ON PEACE DURING MY AFTERNOON NAP?

You cannot expect the neighbours to cope with your unusual habits. Thus, if you sleep in the afternoon either because you need the extra sleep or because you work at nights, you will have no complaint in law unless the noise is sufficient to disturb people who are awake during normal hours.

WHAT ABOUT BUILDING WORK?

The same applies; it is all a question of what is reasonable. If repairs or alterations are being carried out on a nearby property, it is bound to create some disturbance. But you may have a case if it goes on late into the night or continues on Sunday.

OTHER NUISANCES

It is not only noise which can constitute a nuisance. Smells, smoke and vibration could also amount to a nuisance. The smoke from an occasional bonfire is not likely to be regarded as such however. Noisy children generally do not qualify, although you may think they are a sometimes a nuisance in non-legal terms.

SUPPOSING A NEIGHBOUR'S WATER FLOODS MY HOUSE?

If anything is permitted to escape from your neighbour's house which is likely to cause damage, you can claim compensation from him or her for the damage caused. Thus if his pipe bursts or bath overflows, and water penetrates your home causing damage to the carpets and decorations, you can make him pay for it.

CAN I MAKE MY NEIGHBOUR TIDY UP HIS GARDEN?

If you take the trouble to keep a tidy garden it is annoying to have an eyesore next door. There is no law against untidiness, however. Unless he is disobeying mutual covenants as to the state of the properties it is unlikely that you have a remedy, except in an extreme case. You could report the matter to the local council. If there is a pile of rubbish in the garden which is attracting mice and rats, the environmental health officer may insist on its removal. Or the council may take steps under its powers to preserve the amenity of the area.

CAN I PRUNE AN OVER-HANGING TREE?

Your neighbour has no right to encroach upon your territory with his trees, so you are entitled to chop off any branches which overhang your own garden or any roots which project into it from under the fence. If you do, however, he is entitled to whatever you have cut off, since even though it was growing on your side, it is still owned by him.

For example, you may not pick your

TYPES OF COURT

The differences between the various courts is not particularly clear cut, but here is a very brief guide to how the court system works.

Type of court	Type of dispute	Legal Representation Needed
Arbitration [1] (A lawyer or other expert in the field)	Any claim, but by agreement only	DIY, but solicitor or barrister recommended for big claims
Magistrates' court [2] (Usually lay magistrates)	Certain complaints, resulting in, for example, an order to stop noise	DIY or solicitor or barrister
Small claims arbitration (District judge or deputy)	Claims up to £1,000	DIY (no lawyer's costs allowed)
County court (County court judge or recorder)	Depending on the type of case, claims up to £50,000 (more by agreement)	Solicitor or barrister recommended
High Court (High Court judge)	Claims over £25,000; especially if over £50,000	Solicitor or barrister recommended

Note 1: Arbitration by an arbitrator is not to be confused with small claims arbitration. The latter takes place automatically when a small claim, begun in the the county court, is to be contested. Arbitration by an arbitrator takes place outside the court itself. The jurisdiction is unlimited but there must be agreement to submit to an award by the arbitrator. This can be a general agreement that any disputes arising from a contract will be decided by arbitration, or it can be an agreement to refer a dispute which has already arisen to arbitration instead of to the court. It is often quicker and less costly to have disputes decided in this way.

Note 2: A magistrates' court normally deals with criminal cases, resulting if proved in a fine, imprisonment or a community penalty. It also has other functions including hearing certain types of complaint, particularly where a local authority is involved. It has specific powers to stop or regulate certain types of act. The other courts are civil courts which decide disputes between two parties, usually resulting in an award of damages, ie financial compensation for breach of contract, or a civil wrong, resulting in personal injury, damage to property or other loss.

neighbour's apples and keep them, or even shake the branch causing them to fall, although you make keep those which fall naturally to the ground.

If your neighbour's tree is causing serious problems, say because the roots are affecting your foundations or penetrating your drains, he or she is responsible for the damage. You would therefore be entitled to claim compensation. As your buildings insurance policy should cover this sort of damage it is easier to claim under this and let the insurance company make the appropriate claim. It is likely that he/she too is insured to cover this sort of damage.

A tree subject to a preservation order may not be lopped without permission from the local authority, whether it is yours or your neighbour's. You could be subject to a fine if you do interfere with it. Likewise if you live in a conservation area.

CAN I STOP TREES OR FENCES FROM BLOCKING THE SUN?

There is no general right to light, and in particular no right to have the sun on your garden. So whether it is blocked by a tree growing ever taller and more bushy, or by a fence or wall that has just been erected, you cannot complain. There may be express covenants which have to obeyed by the owners of all the properties on a particular estate, restricting the height of fences. They are also the subject of the planning laws (see Alterations and Extensions, page 454). This does not apply to trees.

You can acquire the right to light to a particular window or for example to a greenhouse by having enjoyed it continuously for 20 years or more. This is a right to have a reasonable amount of light, not necessarily direct sunlight, and anyway you cannot complain if it is blocked by a tree or bush.

WHO IS RESPONSIBLE FOR THE FENCE?

Often, the answer to this is clear from the deeds of a house, or the lease in the case of a leasehold property.

Generally, you are responsible for any fences wholly on your own property. Sometimes there are party walls and fences. Then both sides are responsible. If the fence marks the boundary, there is a presumption that the party responsible is the one on whose side the fence posts are. This is rather anomalous as it probably means you have to go next door in order to repair it.

HOW DO I STOP PEOPLE NEXT DOOR TAKING SOME OF MY LAND?

Boundary disputes are frequently a source of trouble between neighbours. Although you might expect the Land Registry entry, or the deeds of a property to show exactly where the boundaries are, they are often not sufficiently detailed to do so. Furthermore, existing fencing is not always a reliable guide. It may have been put where someone once thought the boundary lay. Or it may have been built on the owner's land. Or it may even have been built on someone else's land in order to annex some of that property. If you treat land as your own for over 12 years (ten in Scotland) for example, by occupying it, or enclosing it with a fence, and the owner has not claimed it back, the land becomes yours.

If you do have a dispute which cannot be resolved in any other way you can bring an action in your local county court, but this can be complicated, lengthy and expensive.

CAN I STOP A NEIGHBOUR PARKING IN FRONT OF MY HOUSE?

You have no rights to the road outside your house. Even if you have parked there for years, you cannot stop your new neighbour from parking his car there. However, he may not park in such a way as to block the entrance to your drive or garage. Call the police or contact the local council if this happens regularly.

Another common problem occurs when neighbours opposite park outside their own house in such a position as to make it awkward to manoeuvre your own car into your driveway. However, unless they are actually obstructing your entrance you would have no ground to complain.

ALTERATIONS AND EXTENSIONS

Normally, you have to apply for planning permission from the local planning authority to erect or enlarge a building. In many cases, the enlargement, improvement or other alteration of a dwelling house is what is called 'permitted development'. This means that you can go ahead without obtaining planning permission. This does not necessarily apply to certain areas, including those designated as conservation areas, or areas of outstanding natural beauty. These are specially protected.

INTERNAL ALTERATIONS

In general, any maintenance, improvement or alterations, which affect only the interior of a building and which do not affect the outside appearance, are not regarded as a 'development' at all, and therefore planning permission is not required.

If the alteration is structural, you will still require building consent, but this is simply to make sure that the alteration is properly carried out.

If the alteration is to a kitchen or bathroom it may affect drainage or sewerage. Then the local authority should be consulted.

CAN I KNOCK DOWN A WALL BETWEEN TWO ROOMS?

As there is nothing to stop you making internal alterations which do not affect the outside appearance of the house, you may join two rooms into one by knocking down the dividing wall. Before embarking on a structural alteration, however, notice should be given to the building inspector at the local authority. This should be given by the builder, or by you if you are doing the job yourself or are employing direct labour.

The building inspector will visit the site and make whatever requirements he thinks fit to ensure compliance with the Building Regulations and good building practice. If you are knocking down a wall this may involve the need to use an RSJ (or steel beam) of a particular size to support the floor above. If you are building a wall it may involve providing foundations of a certain depth. If you are installing a new boiler, the building regulations may involve lining a chimney.

DO I NEED PLANNING PERMISSION FOR A LOFT CONVERSION?

In general, you do not need planning permission in order to convert your loft into living space, even if you have to alter the roof, for instance by putting in dormer windows, in order to do so.

This type of conversion will add to the amount of living space afforded by the house. The amount by which you can increase the cubic capacity is limited, just as it is with any other extension, but slightly more stringent limitations on the increase in size apply. Again, you must not raise the roof level above its original height. Although you may put in dormer windows in the back or side of the roof, you may not do anything which projects beyond the slope of the roof on the side facing the road. You would only be able to put in a skylight there. You must not alter the roof to such an extent that it results in a material alteration to the shape of the house.

EXTERNAL ALTERATIONS

CAN I BUILD AN EXTENSION TO MY HOUSE?

If the outside appearance is affected the alteration constitutes a 'development', but may be a 'permitted development', in which case again planning permission is not required. Painting the exterior of a house, so long as you are not painting up advertisements, not surprisingly comes under this category.

You can, however, do far more than this. You are also entitled to extend your property – within strict limits – without first obtaining planning permission. You may add up to 10 per cent or 65½cu yd/50cu m, whichever is the greater, to the original dwelling house if it is a terraced house; or 91½cu yd/70 cu m or 15 per cent if it is not terraced. The original dwelling house is the house as it was on the 1st July 1948 if it was built by then, or its original size if built since.

In no case may the addition:

- Exceed 150cu yd/115 cu m.
- Exceed the height of the original building.
- Be nearer to the road than the existing building, unless it is still 22yd/20m away.
- Be more than 4½yd/4m high, if it is within 2yd/2m of the boundary of the house or garden.
- Occupy more than half the garden.
- If it is built near the front of the house, extend beyond the house's nearest point to the road, and may not be nearer to the road than 2yd/2m.

CAN I BUILD A PORCH?

You are allowed to build a porch without planning permission, but again there are limitations. It must not occupy more than 3½sq yd/3sq m of ground space, or be more than 9ft 10in/3m high. It must not be within 6ft 6in/2m of the boundary of the garden.

CAN I ERECT A GARAGE?

You can build outbuildings such as a garage, or car port, or construct a swimming pool, without obtaining special permission, but only within certain limitations:

- It must not be for living purposes, and must be incidental to the enjoyment of the existing home. This includes providing a kennel for the dog, or a home for other domestic pets.
- It must not be nearer to the road than the house, or must be at least 22yd/20m away. If it is bigger than 13cu yd/10cu m, it must not be within 5m of the house.
- The height may not exceed 9ft 10in/3m (or 13ft 1in/4m if the roof is ridged).
- The total area covered by outhouses may not be more than half the garden. You can also make a hard surface, for example to provide hard standing for a car.

CAN I PUT UP A SATELLITE DISH?

You may have one satellite dish installed, so long as it obeys certain requirements:

- If it is attached to a chimney, it must not exceed 18in/45cm in any direction including mountings.
- If it is attached anywhere else it must not exceed 27½in/70cm or 36in/90cm, depending on the county in which you live.
- It must not exceed the height of any chimney or roof to which it is attached.

IS THERE ANY LIMIT ON THE HEIGHT OF FENCES?

Any fences, gates or walls must not exceed 6ft 6in/2m in height. If the wall or fence is adjacent to a road used by vehicles, it must not exceed 3ft 3in/1m.

OBTAINING PLANNING PERMISSION

If your property is a listed building or is in a conservation area, you cannot assume that your ideas will constitute 'permitted development'. Special provisions apply, and any alterations may be very restricted.

HOW DO I APPLY FOR PLANNING PERMISSION?

You must apply to the planning department of your local authority. Your application will set out details of your proposals and should include, as far as possible, drawings and specifications. These may be compiled by you, or by an architect employed by you. Outline drawings are sufficient, and the authority will tell you if further details are required.

Interested parties are given an opportunity to object to what you have in mind. If, for example, you have proposed an extension which affects your neighbour, you may have to amend your original proposal before you are given permission. Permission may be conditional on carrying out particular work.

If you have omitted to apply for planning permission when you should have done so, you may do so in retrospect, and if granted it will have the same effect as if granted in advance. It is risky to adopt this course deliberately, however, as the local authority has the power to order you to stop. If you fail to comply, you can be fined. Furthermore, the local authority can order you to pull down any construction which is contravention of the planning laws. So you could be liable for a great deal of expense without any result.

CHANGE OF USE

You also require planning permission for any change of use of a property. You may not, therefore, without permission use a dwelling house for another purpose, such as a fish-canning factory or a hairdressing shop. You may have a room which you use as a personal office or study within it, however. A dwelling house is one used as a sole or main residence by a single person or family, or by not more than six residents who are not part of a family but are living together as a single household.

It is, in particular, a change of use to convert a single dwelling house into two or more separate houses or flats.

PARTY WALLS

If your extension affects your neighbour's property directly, special considerations apply. For example, your loft conversion may involve an RSJ going into a wall that divides your neighbour's house from your own. If this is so, you should obtain his or her consent before the work begins. You may obtain a 'party wall award' which means that a surveyor will inspect the other property before and after the work to ensure that no damage has been caused by it, for which you would be liable. This procedure protects you as well as your neighbour, since if defects already exist, they could not then be attributable to the construction of your extension.

PLANNING PERMISSION, OR NOT?

If you are not sure whether planning permission is required, for any job, apply to the local council for a certificate that planning permission is not required; you are then safe from the suggestion that you acted without it, and cannot be required to remove the structure.

BUILDING WORK

There is no way of being sure that the work you have done in your home is of high quality, but at least you can minimise the risks involved.

HOW TO GET A GOOD JOB

First, you should get more than one quotation for the cost of the work. Once you have obtained, say, three quotations, you can choose the contractor, not necessarily selecting the cheapest, but also taking into account his approach to the work to be done, and any recommendation you have had from others. A good builder will be happy to show you work he has recently completed locally.

Once you have chosen your builder, make sure that he is covered by insurance. Then, if the house collapses because he provided insufficient support while pulling down a wall, you will have some comeback even if the builder goes bankrupt.

He may also belong to one of the recognised trade associations, or to the Building Guarantee Scheme, which offers a guarantee to cover the quality of his work.

Then tie up the legal side. Before the work starts it is important to have the main terms of your agreement with the builder clear. Reputable builders often have their own standard terms. If so, make sure you read them carefully before agreeing to anything. Otherwise you could use a standard form of contract such as the RIBA contract for small building works. With any standard form, you will have to fill in the details applicable to your own particular project.

Whether you use a standard form contract or not, it is best to have something in writing. The principal terms of the agreement should be set out. You should have a written agreement setting out the work to be done and the price to be charged. The work required should be set out in a schedule. The term concerning the price should also specify how it is to be paid. It should say whether any money is required in advance and whether payment is to be in stages during the work. If so, it should say who is responsible for deciding the value of work completed at any stage. If an architect is involved, for example, he should decide on the value of the work completed.

Sometimes it is difficult to quote accurately as it is not apparent until work begins exactly what is required. For example, if you are having work done on the roof it may not be clear until the tiles and lead are removed that some of the timbers need replacing. If a price is not quoted in advance for any work, you are liable to pay a reasonable amount for the work actually carried out with your agreement. Ideally, however, extra work should be specified, priced and agreed in writing before it is done.

The agreement should also contain details of when the work should start and finish, what standard of work is required, and on what basis either party can terminate the contract. If the time of finishing the work is important you should specify that 'time is of the essence'. Otherwise you will have no right to sue if work is not begun or ended on time. If time is important you may also specify what damages are payable on the failure of the builder to complete the work in time. If the sum shown is not related to an estimate of the actual cost to you, but is simply intended as a penalty, the clause will not be valid. It will only take effect if it is a genuine attempt to assess the costs likely to be suffered by you.

If the contract is silent on that point, there is an implied term in the agreement that the job will be carried out with reasonable skill and care, and that the builder will use suitable materials of merchantable quality. If he fails to fulfil either of these stipulations you can sue him for damages to compensate you for the cost of putting the work right. If the defect is fundamental, it would entitle you to set the agreement aside and employ someone else to re-do the work.

PROBLEMS WITH BUILDING WORK

MY NEW KITCHEN IS DEFECTIVE; WHAT CAN I DO?

Under the Supply of Goods and Services Act 1982, the contractor owes you a duty. He is failing in this duty if he has not acted with reasonable skill and care.

He also fails in his duty if he does not use materials of merchantable quality. This means you could take him to court to claim the cost of finishing the work properly. If the materials used are totally unsuitable, and the job as a whole is unfit for the purpose for which it was required, it is open to you to terminate the agreement, and have the whole kitchen replaced.

TIP Check units and materials before installation.

TIP You must make sure you see a fitted kitchen before it is installed. Showrooms are there so that you can feel the quality, try the drawers, give it a thump to see how substantial it is. At the least, ask for names and addresses of recent customers.

CAN I MAKE THE PLUMBER PAY FOR THE RUINED CARPET?

If a plumber has not only mended the pipe badly, but an ensuing flood has caused damage to the carpet in the room below, the plumber has been negligent, and has not complied with his agreement to carry out his work with reasonable skill and care. You can therefore bring an action against him for all foreseeable damage directly flowing from what he did. Damage to the carpet is clearly a foreseeable result of permitting the tap to leak badly, causing flooding.

THE ELECTRICIAN HAS OVERCHARGED; WILL I HAVE TO PAY?

If you have agreed the price with him in advance, you will have to pay the agreed price, even though the job only took a fraction of the time you thought it might take when you agreed. If there was no express agreement as to the price the electrician is entitled to charge you a reasonable price, by reference to what other skilled tradesmen charge.

If you have an emergency, be sure to enquire first whether there is a call-out charge.

DOUBLE GLAZING: CAN I GET MY MONEY BACK?

If the double glazing installed for you fails to work effectively then the same rules apply. The contractor has failed in his duties under the law, and if the failure is fundamental, as a last resort it would be possible to repudiate the contract and insist on the removal of the installation, as well as to claim damages for the inconvenience caused.

WHAT IF THERE WAS A GUARANTEE?

Much specialist work is the subject matter of guarantees. It includes wood preservation treatment, damp-course and roofing work. The guarantees are sometimes for as long as 30 years. If there is a repeat of the infestation during the period the company will return and treat the property again. Since a guarantee is part of what was supplied under the contract, you can sue under the guarantee. The guarantee is a valuable asset when it comes to selling the house, since it may be passed on to the purchaser.

Although a guarantee may say that it guarantees that there will be no recurrence of the infestation, it may not be a promise to pay for any damage caused to your house if there is. So although the company will come and re-treat the timbers if there is a recurrence, for example, of dry rot, the guarantee does not cover the cost of a wall falling down due to a rotten timber. You would have to sue the company on the contract in the normal way and prove that the workmanship was not up to standard.

Furthermore, the guarantee is only as good as the company giving it. The company may have gone into liquidation long before the 30 years are up, leaving any guarantee worthless.

TIP Try and choose a company whose guarantee is backed by another substantial firm, such as the manufacturer of the product used for treatment, or even better, an insurance company.

GUARANTEES AND WARANTIES

What is the difference between a guarantee and a warranty?

Although the different words have specific legal meanings, in the context in which they are used here, and in which they are used by companies selling goods, they are indistinguishable. They are simply the terms of the contract, setting out the circumstances in which the seller or manufacturer will repair or replace the goods or refund the money. The legal effect of them depends entirely on the words used.

The only point to note is that they will not usually prevent the buyer from exercising his or her statutory or common law rights, if these happen to be more extensive than those offered under the warranty or guarantee.

GOODS AND SERVICES

Both goods and services are governed by rules to protect consumer rights. Bear this informaton in mind when next buying an item or arranging for a service in your home.

SERVICES

Special rules concern the provision of services to your home. These include electricity, water, gas, telephone and even television. It is perhaps because, before privatisation, most of these services were public utilities. There is provision for entry by representatives of the bodies providing electricity, gas and water to enter your property for the purpose of reading meters, or in an appropriate case, cutting off your supply.

Criminal offences have also been provided by Parliament in connection with certain services. If you bypass the electric meter, for example, you can be accused of abstracting electricity. If you use a television in your home without a valid licence being in force, you can be fined. Again, there is special provision enabling entry for the purpose of enforcing this law.

JUNK MAIL AND UNWANTED GOODS

Everyone is bombarded nowadays with literature advertising all sorts of goods and services. Even if you have completed every available form endeavouring not to be on mailing lists, it is impossible to be completely immune to them. What often worries people, however, is being sent goods on approval or to try out, without ever having asked for them. They are sometimes accompanied by literature saying that if you do not send them back within a certain time you are assumed to have accepted them and will have to pay. This is sometimes called 'inertia selling'.

The rule is that no-one can impose an obligation on you to do something without your consent. It follows that if you do nothing, you cannot be deemed to have accepted the articles in question. You are under no obligation to return them. If you choose to use them, however, you may be deemed to have accepted them. Furthermore, if you place them outside so that they may be damaged by the rain, it may be regarded as causing damage wilfully or recklessly.

How then can you get rid of them? The law says that if the sender has not collected the goods within six months, you can treat them as a gift. That means you can either use them or throw them away as you choose. If you do not wish to wait this long, you should write to whoever sent them saying that the goods were unsolicited and stating a place where they may be collected. If they are not collected within 30 days, again you may treat them as a gift.

Meanwhile, it is a criminal offence for anyone to demand payment for goods, having supplied them in such circumstances.

Do be careful, though, that you have not signed some document asking for them to be sent on approval, without having read the small print.

If you don't wish to receive any more unrequested mail, write to the Mailing Preference Service (see Useful Addresses). This organisation will send you a form to fill in which will also help stop mail being sent to any member of your household with the same surname. This will not affect any company from which you currently order goods. This service is free of charge.

EMERGENCIES

PREPARING FOR EMERGENCIES

Knowing how to act in a household emergency is as much about understanding how your house works as staying cool in a crisis.

In an emergency you probably won't have time to read the advice in this chapter, so read it *now* and try to memorise the main points. Emergencies can happen at any time to anyone, so as well as learning what to do yourself, teach your older children.

ESSENTIAL PHONE NUMBERS

First, it's a good idea to keep a list of essential numbers by the phone. Ideally, these should include:

- Family doctor
- Nearest hospital with an accident and emergency unit
- Plumber
- Locksmith
- Glazier
- Electrician
- Electricity company's emergency number
- Local gas emergency number
- Local builder
- Local police station
- Vet (if applicable)
- Your and your partner's work numbers
- School and college numbers
- Relatives or friends that the children can ring in an emergency

TIP If choosing a tradesman for the first time, try to follow a personal recommendation from a neighbour, or at least choose a firm that is a member of a trade association that insists its members follow a code of practice, and that has a grievance procedure for customers to use should you need to complain, such as:

- Federation of Master Builders
- Institute of Plumbing
- National Association of Plumbing, Heating and Mechanical Services Contractors
- Electrical Contractors' Association
- National Inspection Council for Electrical Installation Contracting
- Council for Registered Gas Installers
- Glass and Glazing Federation

(See Useful Addresses.)

While making a list of emergency numbers, group other family details together that might come in handy, such as blood groups, medical card numbers, national insurance numbers and insurance policy numbers. Also list bank, building society and credit card numbers – and where to ring if they are lost or stolen.

FIRE

Take some time now to think carefully about how you and your family would escape from your house in a fire.

- Is there an alternative route down, as well as the stairs, in case they are blocked by fire?
- Is there a window in every room that could be used to climb out of?
- If you have double glazing, is the key kept by the window for easy unlocking?
- If you have secondary glazing, is there at least one window in each room that doesn't have it, that you could use to escape?

Finally, hold regular, family fire practice and make sure the whole family knows what to do if there really is a fire.

FIVE-POINT FIRE DRILL

1 Get everyone out.
2 Call the Fire Brigade by dialling 999.
3 Only attempt to tackle a fire in its earliest stages. Remember that fire extinguishers are only for 'first aid' fire fighting.
4 Wait for the Fire Brigade.
5 Don't go back to the house, until the fire officer tells you it's safe to do so

FIRE AT NIGHT

If you were to wake up at night and notice the smell of smoke, here's what to do:
1 Wake everyone up (calmly, without causing panic).
TIP Fit a smoke alarm (to BS 5446) on every floor of the house. It can increase your chances of tgetting out in a fire by two or three times, giving you precious extra minutes. (See Smoke Alarms, page 418.)
2 Try to establish where the heart of the fire is and close the door to that room if you can. Don't open any door that feels warm to the touch. (Use the back of your hand to touch it).
3 Use the stairs, if safe to do so, and get everyone out of the house. Call the Fire Brigade from a phone box or neighbour's house. Clearly state the address of the fire.
TIP Never store combustible materials, such as paint cans or solvents, under the stairs. They could give fuel to a fire and block your escape route.
4 If the stairs are blocked, use an upstairs window as an escape route – if you can do so safely. Otherwise go to a front bedroom, close the door, block any openings such as vents or skylights, and seal up the gap along the bottom of the door with rolled up clothes or bedding.
5 Go to the window and try to attract the attention of someone outside. Shout and wave something brightly coloured (or pale, that will be seen in the dark).
6 Don't try to get out unless you are forced to. If the room starts to fill with smoke, try not to become panicked. Tie a handkerchief or scarf around your mouth and lean out of the window to breathe. If this isn't possible, crouch down near the floor (the heat and smoke will be less there).
7 Only as a last resort, jump. Drop bedding or cushions to the ground to break your fall, and lower yourself feet first from the window sill to reduce the drop.

FIRE-FIGHTING EQUIPMENT

Kitchen: Fire blanket. Make sure it conforms to BS 6575 and is at least 3 x 3ft/90 x 90 cm in size.
Hall: Multi-purpose dry powder, foam or water type extinguisher (conforming to BS 5423 or 6165 and the British Standard Kitemark).

These would be adequate for most homes, but it depends on the fire risks in your home and what you can afford. A multi-purpose dry powder or foam extinguisher in the garage, shed or car would also be a good idea.

WHAT KIND OF FIRE?

Different kinds of fires require different measures: that is, extinguisher, water, etc.

CHIP PAN/FRYING PAN FIRE

1 Leave the pan where it is.
2 Turn off the heat if it is safe to do so.
3 Protecting your hands, place a damp cloth, a close fitting lid or a fire blanket over the pan

to smother the flames.

4 Leave the pan to cool for at least 30 minutes. (The fire can start again if the cover is removed too soon).

Ideally, use a thermostatically-controlled deep-fat fryer rather than an ordinary hob-top chip pan.

TIP Never use water or any type of extinguisher to fight an oil fire.

FURNITURE FIRES

Use a multi-purpose foam or a water fire extinguisher.

Fires in upholstered furniture can spread very quickly and produce poisonous fumes. Do not tackle the fire if it is burning fiercely or if there is already thick smoke. Get out immediately, shut the door properly, and call the fire brigade.

ELECTRICAL FITTING AND APPLIANCE FIRES

1 If possible, turn off the power. (Pull out the plug or switch off the appliance at the mains.)

2 Use a dry powder, carbon dioxide or halon extinguisher

Don't use a water-based extinguisher unless the appliance is disconnected from the mains – but never use one on TV sets, even when they are unplugged.

TIP Unplug TVs and computers and cover them with a damp blanket or a fire blanket to smother the fire. Don't use water.

FIRE PREVENTION

For further advice on fire protection in the home and how to choose and use a fire extinguisher contact your local fire safety officer. Alternatively, for general advice contact the Fire Protection Association. See Useful Addresses.

MAINS GAS APPLIANCES FIRES

1 Turn off the gas supply and wait until the gas flow stops.

2 Call the fire brigade immediately and tell them that mains gas is involved.

3 If the gas supply cannot be turned off, *do not* attempt to extinguish the burning gas jet, as this allows gas to escape and accumulate to explosive levels.

Tackling a gas leak

See Gas Leaks page 470.

CLOTHES ON FIRE

1 Lay the victim down so the flames cannot reach the face.

2 Douse the flames with water or any non-flammable liquid such as milk. Or smother the flames with a blanket or rug.

3 If water isn't readily available, wrap the victim in a fire blanket or rug.

4 Once the flames are out, check that there is no smouldering material.

5 Get medical help immediately.

SEVERE WEATHER

Excessive water or wind, or both at once, can cause major headaches for the householder.

FLOODING

After fire, a flood is the most destructive element that can hit your home. If you live near a river, reservoir, the sea or a water main, get in touch with your local authority who will advise you on the kind of flood precautions you should take.

READY SUPPLIES

It may be worthwhile having a supply of tinned and dried food and bottled water in case you are cut off for any length of time. It may also be useful to buy a camping light, camping cooker and candles, as the first thing you'll have to do in a flood is turn off the mains electricity.

If you have room in a garage or shed, keep a stock of plastic bags filled with sand or soil to block off outside doors and airbricks.

BE PREPARED

Even if a downpour looks as though it is going to turn into a flood, you should have a reasonable amount of time to prepare the house and your family.

- Block off outside doors and airbricks to try to keep water out of the house; place plastic carrier bags filled with soil against the outside faces of doors and airbricks.
- Turn off mains electricity, gas and water.
- Move your family, pets and what possessions you can (furniture, rugs, etc) to upper floors, or move out if in a bungalow.
- Take off downstairs internal doors, if possible. Severe flooding may damage them.

FLOOD SURVIVAL TIPS

- Get everyone to wrap up well, as the house may be cold, with no heating.
- Take an emergency supplies box with candles, a camping stove if you have one, tinned food and bottled water, etc.
- Flood water is almost certainly contaminated so don't use it for anything. Any cooking utensils which have been in the flood should be disinfected. Don't drink tap water until you hear from the local authority that it's all right to do so.

- Wait upstairs for the relief services to tell you what to do next.

CLEANING UP AFTER A FLOOD

Let the emergency services pump as much water out of the house as possible before trying to return. Once back inside, check the damage very carefully.

- If water has got into the electrics, it could be dangerous and you should get the local electricity company to test it as soon as possible. All appliances should also be examined and tested at the same time.
- Call in the local gas suppliers to check the system and any appliances.
- Check with the water company on the state of the water supplies.
- You should be able to hire a pump to clear any remaining water from cellars, and then use a three in one vacuum cleaner to remove any final pools of water.
- Check the loft for any damage. It may need temporary repairs to stop the roof letting in even more water. An uncovered water cistern in the loft may be contaminated and so you'll

need to drain it and clean it out. Throw out soaked loft insulation material.

- Remove furniture and lift floor coverings so you can hose walls and floors down. Scrub all affected surfaces thoroughly with strong disinfectant, as the flood water may have been contaminated with sewage.
- If you didn't get a chance to do this before the flood, take doors off their hinges and stack them flat so they can dry out without warping.
- Lift some floorboards so the underfloor area can dry out or be pumped out if necessary.
- Check that there is no water trapped underneath ground floors, in cellars or cavity walls. If water has got inside them, holes may have to be drilled from the outside to allow it to escape. Also check for trapped mud.
- Outside, make sure airbricks are free of debris. Unblock drains, clean out gully gratings and rod the drains to clear them.
- Keep windows and doors open as often as possible (security permitting) to give good ventilation, even when the heating is on. Good ventilation is crucial. Your greatest enemy is rotting timber.
- At night, you could use a dehumidifier (which removes moisture from the air and collects it in a container which you then empty). When you think the structural and joinery timbers are dry, call in a surveyor to check the moisture content.
- If the wallpaper is ruined, strip it off to help speed up drying out. Leave cupboard doors open and keep furniture away from walls.
- If walls are very damp, it may be necessary to have some of the inside plaster removed to aid drying out.

It can take weeks for the walls and floors, etc, of a house to dry out. A qualified surveyor will be able to tell you when the walls and structural timbers are dry and whether there has been any physical damage caused. It's a good idea to get the underfloor timbers inspected after about six months and again in a year's time, to check for rot.

Once the cleaning and drying is completed, get a qualified electrician to test the electrics for earth continuity and insulation resistance. Then ask him for an inspection certificate. Be on the lookout for any signs of trouble in the electrics such as sizzling, cracking or buzzing. If either occur turn off the supply immediately. Have your electrics inspected every month for the first six after the initial test and at least twice again in the following six months.

FLOOD INFORMATION

For further help, *How to Avoid Damage and Injuries during Wind Storms* and *Dealing with Flood Damage* are both available for £2 each from the Building Research Establishment. See Useful Addresses.

MINOR FLOODS

If you suddenly find your home flooding with water:

1 Turn off the electricity at the mains.

2 Find out what is causing the flood (such as an overflowing bath, a leaking washing machine) and if possible, turn it off.

3 If this doesn't stop the flow of water, turn off the water at the mains (see Cold Water Supply, page 218).

TIP To turn a mains water stoptap off, turn it clockwise as far as it will go, like a tap. Check where your stoptap is *now*. It is probably under the kitchen sink. In older houses, it could be in the cellar, or possibly outside the house under a small metal flap. Twice a year, check the stoptap hasn't seized up and that you can

turn it easily. If it is jammed, don't force it – turn off the one outside. If you don't know where that is ask your local water supplier.
4 Turn off the boiler, immersion heater, washing machine or anything that heats water.
5 If the flood is still in full flow, if possible, turn off the stoptap on the supply pipe from your cold-water cistern. If you cannot reach this easily, open cold taps and flush cisterns to empty the tank as quickly as possible. If water is coming from the hot-water system, turn off the stoptap adjacent to the hot-water cylinder (on its supply pipe).

DRYING OUT

- Once you have stopped the flood, assess the damage.
- If the ceiling plaster seems to be bulging downwards, under the weight of water from above, make a small hole with a skewer, screwdriver or knitting needle in the centre of the bulge, and put a bucket underneath to catch the water. This is important, otherwise the weight of water may bring the entire ceiling down.
- Wait to turn the power back on until any area with electrics in it has completely dried out. Check with a qualified electrician. You may be able to isolate the power and lighting circuits concerned by switching them off at your consumer unit (fuse box), so you have power to the rest of the house.
- Stand mattresses and foam cushions on their edge as seepage is slower on a vertical surface. Take up wet carpeting and loose-laid flooring. Carpets should be professionally cleaned. Don't replace furniture and heavy appliances until the floor has dried out completely, which may take several weeks. (See Flooding, page 465, for further advice.)
- Contact your insurance company (see Home Insurance, page 476).

STORMS

In an average year in Britain, the wind damages over 250,000 buildings.

You can find out about any approaching strong winds or storms through the Meteorological Office, which operates a severe-weather warning service.

GENERAL PRECAUTIONS

Keep your property in good repair and pay particular attention to the state of:
- Roofs (particularly ridges, eaves, etc)
- Chimney stacks
- Masonry boundary walls
- Aerials and satellite dishes
- Trees (particularly those close to buildings and taller than the building)

IF SEVERE WEATHER IS WARNED

1 Move under cover anything that might blow about, getting damaged or causing damage, such as garden furniture, dustbins, bikes, children's toys. Take pets indoors.
2 Close and fasten doors and windows. (Don't forget the greenhouse, shed or garage.)
3 Park vehicles in a garage, if possible. If not, move your car away from the house, where it might be hit by falling debris.
4 Close and secure trap doors with bolts.
5 Stay indoors as much as possible. (Don't go out to repair damage while the storm is in progress.)
6 Open internal doors only as needed and close them behind you.
7 Move away from windows. Sleep downstairs if you have any large trees sited near the house. (It will also be less noisy and safer if you are not directly beneath the roof).

TIP Keep buckets handy to deal with any leaks in the roof and, possibly, heavy-duty polythene sheeting, tacks and a hammer to cover broken windows. Check also that you have candles, matches and a torch to hand, in case of a power cut.

The aftermath

After the storm, check the chimney stack and roof slopes as the wind may have lifted flashings, dislodged tiles and ripped down your roof-top aerial. If you have a flat roof, check it for torn felt. Check for unstable trees, walls and fences.

Notify your insurance company of any damage for which you might want to claim.

PIPES AND DRAINS

FROZEN AND BURST PIPES

Freezing in winter and corrosion in the heating system often cause burst or frozen pipes. Don't panic. Disreputable plumbers thrive on this sort of problem but a burst pipe need not be a major disaster if you know how and where to turn off the water.

TIP Check your stoptap regularly by turning it off. This will help to stop it from scaling up.

BURST PIPES

1 Turn off the water to the affected pipe quickly. For a burst on the mains-pressure pipes (such as in the kitchen, or an outside tap), turn off at the rising main (see Cold Water Supply, page 218). For bursts on low-pressure pipes fed from the tank in the loft (such as taps in a bathroom or guest room), turn off gate valves if they are fitted or turn off the rising main stop-tap. Then open the hot and cold taps to empty all water from the affected pipes.

If the burst is on the heating pipework, switch off the boiler and turn off the stop-tap on the supply to the feed and expansion tank (if there is one) to stop it refilling. Then attach a length of hose to the lowest draincock on the system (such as from the washing machine) and take the other end to a drain outside (see Drainage Systems, page 221). A draincock is fitted to parts of your plumbing system which cannot be drained via a tap, for example, the boiler. Open the draincock valve to empty the system.

TIP Make sure you know where all the control valves and drain cocks are in your plumbing.

2 Now you have stemmed the flow of water, call in the plumber.

THINK AHEAD!

The most useful thing you can do to prevent internal flooding is to make sure that the cold-water pipes in your loft (and the top and side of the cold-water tank) are well insulated to prevent them freezing in winter. If you go away for a few days, leave the heating on low and prop the loft hatch open. If going for a longer period, drain down the plumbing system. This doesn't take long and may save a great deal of aggravation on your return!

WATER AND ELECTRICITY

The greatest danger from a burst pipe is to the electrical system. If water gets into power and lighting circuits it can make the whole plumbing system live. If in any doubt at all about dampness, switch off the electricity and work by torchlight. Then call in a qualified electrician to test the system.

FROZEN PIPES

1 Turn off your water at the mains, as above.

2 If the freeze is on a heating pipe, turn off the boiler as above.

3 Inspect the frozen pipes and try to find out whether they have burst. (You may see ice glistening in the pipe, or feel a split.) If it doesn't seem to have burst, very gently try to thaw it. Working back from the frozen tap, unwind any lagging and use a hairdryer, a warm air gun, a hot-water bottle or even hot cloths to thaw it.

TIP Never use a naked flame. Too much direct heat may cause the water in that section to boil and steam. Be patient.

5 If the pipe has split, bind rags tightly around the leak, or plug it with something, and place a bucket underneath to catch the water as the pipe thaws.

6 Call a qualified plumber.

TIP If replacing a pipe, flexible plastic pipes will allow a certain amount of expansion and although the water will still freeze it won't necessarily burst the pipe.

7 If possible, turn off the stoptap on the outlet to the cold water tank. If it is a hot-water tap that has burst, turn off the stoptap controlling the supply of water to the hot-water cistern.

TIP If escaping water cannot be controlled switch off the electrics at the mains, open all the cold taps and flush the cisterns in order to drain the system quickly. (Save some in the bath, jugs and bowls to use until the plumber comes). Then wait until the area has dried out completely before switching the electricity back on. If you can, isolate that circuit and switch on the power to the rest of the house.

BLOCKED TOILET

Most households have toilets with a wash-down pan: when flushed, two streams of water come from each side of the rim. The water should leave the pan smoothly, not eddying like a whirlpool.

- If the cistern is working properly but the bowl fails to clear, something is obstructing either the flush inlet or the toilet-pan outlet.
- If the flush water rises almost to the pan rim then ebbs away very slowly, there is most likely a blockage in the pan outlet, or possibly in the drain it discharges into.

UNBLOCKING A TOILET

You will need

- Plunger with long handle. (You may be able to use a mop or broom tied round with rags. Alternatively, stand on a stool and tip in a bucket of water in one go.)
- Flexible drain auger (plumber's snake)
- Bucket
- Rubber gloves
- Mirror

1 Remove all visible waste. You may be able to clear it with a bent wire pushed round the bend. Wait until the water level has dropped

and flush the toilet from a height with a bucket of water.
2 If this doesn't work take the plunger and push it sharply on to the bottom of the pan to cover the outlet. Then pump the handle up and down two or three times.
3 If this doesn't clear the pan, use a flexible drain auger (a plumber's snake) to probe the outlet and trap. If that doesn't work, you may need to call in a plumber or drain specialist to clear the underground drain. (See also Clearing a Blocked Drain, page 268.)
4 If when you flush the cistern, water is entering the pan poorly or unevenly, use a mirror to check the flushing rim. Probe the rim with your fingers for flakes of rust or debris from the cistern that may be obstructing the flush water.

BLOCKED WASTE PIPE

See Coping with Blockages, page 248.

GAS AND ELECTRICITY

GAS

Never carry out any DIY repairs to gas pipes, fittings or appliances. Gas installation and repair should only be carried out by a CORGI-registered gas installer (Council for Registered Gas Installers).

Make sure everyone in the family knows how to turn off the gas supply at the mains. If you don't know where your gas tap is, ask your meter reader next time he calls. (It is usually a small lever on the gas pipe near your meter).

THE GAS MAINS

OFF: Turn the lever until the notched line on the spindle points across the pipe. If your tap seems stiff, don't attempt to loosen it yourself: call your local gas service centre who will come and loosen it for you safely, free of charge.

ON: Before turning the gas on again, make sure that all appliances and pilot lights are turned off. The gas tap is on when the notched line on the spindle points along the pipe. After turning the supply on, re-light all pilot lights.

GAS LEAKS

If you smell gas:

- Turn off the mains gas tap (next to the gas meter).
- Put out all naked lights, don't smoke and don't operate any electrical equipment (including light switches and doorbells).
- Open doors and windows to increase ventilation and get rid of the gas.
- Ring the local gas board's 24-hour, 365-day-a-year emergency service: it's still all right to use the phone. Look under Gas in the phone book.

After the gas leak has been dealt with and the gas supply is back on, don't forget to re-light the pilot light.

CARBON MONOXIDE POISONING

If any of your fuel-burning appliances (including gas central-heating boilers, water-heaters, open fires and wood-burning stoves) use a flue, they must be kept clear. If the chimney or flue does get blocked, the waste gases could spill into the room, polluting the

DOMESTIC GAS AND CARBON MONOXIDE DETECTORS

Gas

Your sense of smell should tell you if there is a gas leak (which could lead to an explosion). But if you are worried about gas or have poor olfactory senses, consider having a gas detector installed (professionally, by wiring it directly to the mains).

There are different types for natural and bottled gas, and each must be installed correctly: high on a wall to detect the lighter-than-air methane in natural gas, and low down for the heavier-than-air propane and butane in bottled gas.

Carbon Monoxide

A carbon-monoxide detector will tell you if you have a leaky flue (which could lead to you getting poisoned).

You shouldn't rely on a gas or carbon monoxide detector to tell you if there is a leak. Carbon monoxide does not have a smell, so you will not be able to detect it unaided.

Follow the advice above if you are at all concerned about leaks. There is no substitute for making sure that all your gas appliances are properly maintained and serviced regularly.

If you are thinking about buying a gas or carbon-monoxide detector, ring the Gas Consumers Council for advice (see Useful Addresses) or ask at your local gas showroom.

air you breath with carbon monoxide. This could be fatal. Always ensure there is plenty of ventilation.

If you notice any of the following signs on your gas appliances, stop using the appliance and contact your local gas office immediately.

- Is the outer case discoloured?
- Is the decoration around the appliance stained or discoloured?
- Does the appliance burn with a yellow or orange flame?
- Is there a strange smell when the appliance is on?
- Is the flue damaged or broken?

ELECTRICITY

Unless you are highly competent at DIY, never tinker with electrical wiring or carry out repairs, except for very minor matters such as mending fuses and fitting plugs.

GET TO KNOW YOUR CONSUMER UNIT

This is the heart of your electrical installation, and every circuit in the house must pass through it. Go and take a look at it now, as these guidelines will then be easier to follow

- Every unit has a large, main switch that can turn off all the power to your house. These switches are called RCCBs (residual current circuit breakers).

TIP On some units, the main switch will trip automatically if a serious fault occurs, as well as being operable manually.

- With some consumer units you can't remove the outer cover without first turning off the main switch. If yours is not like this, stick a label on the cover to remind you to switch off before exposing any of the elements inside the unit.
- With the main switch off and the cover

removed, you can see how the unit is arranged.
TIP The cover must be replaced before the unit is switched on again – and remember that even when the unit is switched off, the cable connecting the meter to the main switch is still live, so take care.

- Look at the cables that feed the various circuits in the house (ideally they should all enter the consumer unit from the same direction) and should be labelled to tell you which area of electrics they cover.
- Each fuse covers a particular wiring circuit in the house. Check which has failed (lights, socket outlets, etc). If a faulty lamp or appliance is responsible, switch off the mains before replacing the fuse or closing a circuit breaker.

REPLACING A FUSE WIRE

To replace the fuse or fuse wire, first switch off the main switch on the consumer unit (or it may be on a separate switch box nearby).

Re-wirable fuses

1 On a blown re-wirable fuse you should be able to see the broken wire and scorch marks on the fuse carrier. If the fuse is one on which you cannot see the whole length of the fuse wire, pull gently on each end of the wire with the tip of a screwdriver to see if it is intact.
2 Loosen the two terminals holding the fuse and extract the broken pieces.
3 Wrap one end of a new length of wire (of the correct rating) clockwise round the terminal and tighten the screw on it.Then run the wire through the fuse carrier across to the other terminal, leaving it slightly slack, and attach it in the same way and cut off any surplus.
4 Replace the fuse carrier.
5 Refit the fuse-box cover and switch on the mains.

Cartridge fuses

1 Unscrew the fuse carrier.
2 Fit a new fuse of the correct rating.
3 Put together the carrier and screw tight.
4 Replace the fuse carrier and put back the fuse box cover.
5 Switch on the main switch.

MINIATURE CIRCUIT BREAKERS

Instead of the usual fuse holders, you may have MCBs. These are amp-rated, like fuses, but instead of removing an MCB to isolate the circuit you merely operate a switch or button to switch it to off. When a fault occurs the circuit breaker switches to the off position automatically, so the faulty circuit is obvious.
1 Turn the main switch off.
2 Correct the cause of the fault.
3 Close the switch on the MCB to reset it. (There is no fuse to replace.)
4 Switch on the mains.

RESIDUAL CURRENT DEVICES

If all the power to your house has gone off, it may be the residual current device (RCD) that has tripped. The RCD will operate quickly if there is an earth fault.
1 Correct the fault: unplug the faulty appliance or replace the light bulb.
2 Try to close the RCD.
3 If it opens again, switch off the mains,

WHICH FUSE TO FIT?

Always fit a fuse of the correct rating for the job.
5 amp: Lighting circuits
15 amp or 20 amp: Immersion heater
30 amp: Socket outlets and average sized cooker
45 amp: Large cooker

SAFETY AND FUSES

- If a fuse continues to blow or the breaker keeps opening, don't fit a larger fuse. If in doubt, consult a competent electrician.
- If the RCD re-opens, ring an electrician or your local electricity company. Don't try to repair the problem yourself.

For further advice on electricity in the home, visit your local electricity showroom for a range of practical leaflets.

remove all the circuit fuses or breakers and replace or reset them one at a time until you find the faulty circuit.

4 Leave the faulty fuse or breaker out and ring an electrician, or ask your local electricity company for help.

TIP Put a note on the consumer unit saying what you've done so that nobody else will try to replace that fuse.

5 Replace the cover before switching the electricity on again.

WHEN WILL A FUSE BLOW?

- When too many appliances are operated on a circuit the excessive demand for current will blow the fuse in that circuit.
- When current re-routes to earth because of a faulty appliance, the flow of current increases the circuit and blows the fuse. This is called short circuiting. You will have to deal with the original fault before replacing the fuse.

MAINS POWER CUT

1 Organise light: make sure that you know where to find torches or candles and matches.

2 Ring your local electricity company to report the problem and find out when you can expect a return of power.

3 Take care if using candles, putting them well out of reach of children. When the power comes back on again, make sure all candles are put out and that any appliances that you turned on before the power cut are not left on, such as a cooker, an iron or an electric blanket.

TIP Leave the fridge and freezer switched on. Check that the fridge drip tray is in position and keep the fridge door closed. Don't open your freezer; its contents will remain frozen for about eight hours. The more food inside, the longer the contents will keep without thawing. Food that has started to thaw shouldn't be re-frozen. To save uncooked but thawed meats and vegetables, make them into pies or casseroles, etc, and then re-freeze them.

4 When the power comes back on reset electric clocks, for example, on central heating, cooker and video.

BURGLARS AND INTRUDERS

BURGLARY

If you find you have been burgled, call the police immediately.

While waiting for them to arrive, don't move or touch anything except to minimise any damage. Check whether valuables have been stolen so you can give their details to the police when they arrive.

If you arrive home and think a burglar is still inside your house (due to an open door or window) don't go inside. Go to a neighbour's house or phone box and ring the police, then keep a discreet watch so you can give the police a description of anyone leaving.

Coming home to a burglar

If you arrive home to find an intruder in the house with you:

- Ask calmly what he wants.
- Don't get angry or attempt to prevent him from leaving: he may get violent.
- Try to remember what he looks like in as much detail as possible.
- Call the police as soon as he has gone.

If you suspect a prowler

If you hear a noise as though someone is in the house, or someone is trying to break in:

- Switch the lights on and make plenty of noise. Most burglars will flee immediately.
- Stay upstairs or out of the way, call the police if you have a bedroom/extension phone, and find something you can use as a weapon to defend yourself if you are attacked – but don't go in search of him.
- As soon as you hear the intruder leave, try to see what he looks like and what he is wearing, which way he goes and whether he has a car or van. Then ring the police.

TIP If you get a good look at an intruder, try to memorise details to help the police: age, sex, height, build, skin colour, hairstyle and colour, facial characteristics, clothing. For vehicles, note the type, model, colour and registration number.

IMPROVING HOME SECURITY

For comprehensive advice on how to keep burglars out of your home with sensible security measures, see Home Security, page 421.

MENDING A BROKEN WINDOW

A broken window is both a safety and a security risk and should be dealt with as soon as possible. It's not a difficult job to tackle yourself as long as you have or can borrow the right tools.

If the window is hard to reach, it's safer to remove the frame and work on it at ground level. Make sure you protect your hands with strong gloves and wear safety goggles.

There are two methods for fixing glass into a wood frame. With wood beading, you simply lever off the beading, replace the glass in mastic (sealant) and re-fix the beading. The method using putty is explained below, and applies equally to wooden and metal-framed windows.

You will need

Materials

- Glazing nails, ⅝in/15mm long, or glazing clips

- Glass: ask your glass merchant to advise you on the correct glass for your purpose as this will depend on the type and size of the frame and whether it is in a vulnerable position or area of high risk.
- Primer
- Putty

Tools

- Chisel
- Pincers
- Protective gloves
- Putty knife
- Safety spectacles
- Small hammer
- Steel measuring tape

1 Carefully remove all the loose glass and dispose of it safely (wrapped in newspaper).

TIP If the window is only cracked, stick tape over it in a criss-cross pattern to contain fragments and then tap out the pieces from the outside with a hammer.

2 Hack out the old putty and any remaining bits of glass from the rebate (the groove where the glass sits) with a chisel.

TIP With metal frames, the glass will have been held in by small clips. Take these out carefully with pincers as you uncover them, mark the hole positions on the frame and save them for later.

3 Brush out dust and loose bits of putty from the rebate and apply a coat of wood or metal primer to the rebate.

4 Measure up for the new glass. Check that the rebate is square by measuring all four sides, and use the smaller measurement in each case. Subtract $\frac{1}{8}$in/3mm from each measurement to allow for clearance. Then order the pane and appropriate putty from your glass merchant. If in doubt, cut a paper pattern and take this to your glass merchant.

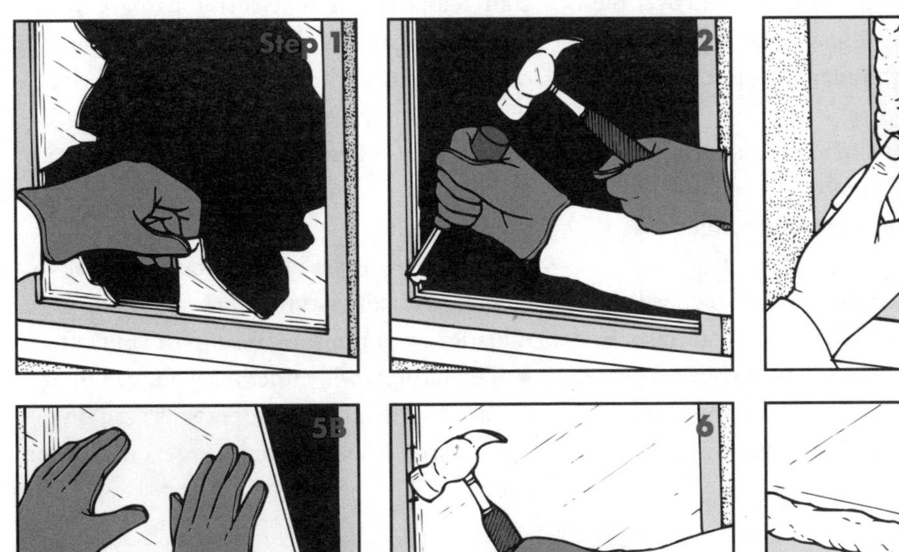

5 Put a layer of putty in a thinnish bead all around the rebate (A), rest the bottom edge of the pane in the rebate and push it gently and firmly into place, pressing round the edge rather than in the centre of the pane to compress the putty evenly (B).
6 To hold the glass in, tap glazing nails in the rebate, at about ½–⅝in/12–15cm intervals in a wooden frame, or use glazing clips in a metal one. Trim away excess putty from the inside of the frame with the putty knife.
7 Finish off with a layer of putty around the outside of the frame. Wet the blade of the putty knife to prevent it from sticking, and shape off at an angle. Finish off by trimming away the bedding putty where necessary and cleaning off the putty marks with methylated spirits.
8 Allow the putty to dry for two weeks before painting.

HOME INSURANCE

MAKING A CLAIM

If, unfortunately, you have to make a claim on your home insurance, here is how to make the process as smooth and fast as possible.

- Read your policy carefully. Does it cover the cause of the damage or loss? Should you claim under 'buildings' or 'contents'? Some policies cover both.
- Ring your insurer and ask for a claim form, quoting your policy number. Don't forget to quote the number on any correspondence as well, and keep copies.
- If temporary emergency repairs are needed, arrange these immediately and let your insurer know. The cost may form part of your overall claim, so keep all the bills and any damaged items as the insurers will probably want to see them. Take photos if necessary.
- Some insurers offer a 24-hour emergency help line which can give details of local tradespeople.
- While waiting to receive a claim form, get repair estimates from at least two specialist contractors, list all items lost or damaged, and find the original receipts if you can. If you can't, estimate their current value and check the price of replacements. Remember that some policies offer replacement as if the items had been new, while others take wear and tear into account.
- Complete the claim form and return it quickly, with any estimates, receipts and valuations you can find to support your case.
- The insurers will either pay your claim, or arrange for their claims inspector to call on you, or send a loss adjuster to assess the loss or damage.

CONVERSION TABLES & USEFUL ADDRESSES

CONVERSION FORMULAE

Imperial to Metric
Metric to Imperial

TO CONVERT	MULTIPLY BY
LENGTH	
Inches to centimetres	2.540
Centimetres to inches	0.3937
Feet to metres	0.3048
Metres to feet	3.281
Yards to metres	0.9144
Metres to yards	1.094
Miles to kilometres	1.609
Kilometres to miles	0.6214
AREA	
Sq inches to sq centimetres	6.452
Sq centimetres to sq inches	0.1550
Sq feet to sq metres	0.0929
Sq metres to sq feet	10.764
Sq yards to sq metres	0.8361
Sq metres to sq yards	1.196
Sq miles to sq kilometres	2.590
Sq kilometres to sq miles	0.3861
VOLUME	
Cu inches to cu centimetres	16.39
Cu centimetre to cu inches	0.06102
Cu feet to cu metres	0.02832
Cu metres to cu feet	35.315
Cu yards to cu metres	0.7645
Cu metres to cu yards	1.308
Cu inches to litres	0.01639
Litres to cu inches	61.024
Gallons to litres	4.546
Litres to gallons	0.219
WEIGHT	
Ounces to grams	28.35
Grams to ounces	0.03527
Pounds to kilograms	0.4536
Kilograms to pounds	2.205
Tons to kilograms	1016.05
Kilograms to tons	0.000984

TEMPERATURES

To convert °F to °C: (°F−32) x 5/9 = °C
To convert °C to °F: (°C x 9/5) + 32 = °F

LENGTH

Centimetres	Cm or Inches	Inches
2.54	1	0.39
5.08	2	0.79
7.62	3	1.18
10.16	4	1.58
12.70	5	1.97
15.24	6	2.36
17.78	7	2.76
20.32	8	3.15
22.86	9	3.54
25.40	10	3.94

WEIGHT

Kilograms	Kg or Pounds	Pounds
0.45	1	2.21
0.91	2	4.41
1.36	3	6.61
1.81	4	8.82
2.27	5	11.02
2.72	6	13.23
3.18	7	15.43
3.63	8	17.64
4.08	9	19.84
4.54	10	22.05

DISTANCE

Kilometres	Km or Miles	Miles
1.61	1	0.62
3.22	2	1.24
4.83	3	1.86
6.44	4	2.49
8.05	5	3.11
9.66	6	3.73
11.27	7	4.35
12.88	8	4.97
14.48	9	5.59
16.09	10	6.21

AREA

Hectares	Hectares or Acres	Acres
0.41	1	2.47
0.81	2	4.94
1.21	3	7.41
1.62	4	9.88
2.02	5	12.36
2.43	6	14.83
2.83	7	17.30
3.24	8	19.77
3.64	9	22.24
4.05	10	24.71

CAPACITY

Litres	Litres or Gallons	Gallons
4.55	1	0.22
9.09	2	0.44
13.64	3	0.66
18.18	4	0.88
22.73	5	1.10
27.28	6	1.32
31.82	7	1.54
36.37	8	1.76
40.91	9	1.98
45.46	10	2.20

TEMPERATURE

Celsius	°C or °F	Fahrenheit
-23	-10	14
-18	0	32
-12	10	50
-7	20	68
-1	30	86
4	40	104
10	50	122
16	60	140
21	70	158
27	80	176

WATER HARDNESS

Contact the local water company for a hardness reading.
It will be measured in mg/litre or ppm (parts per million).

1mg/l = 1 ppm

Naturally Soft Water: 50mg/l
Borderline between soft and hard: 100mg/l
Hard Water: 200mg/l and above

When using a dishwasher check the manufacturer's instructions for setting the water hardness regulator which controls the use of salt and rinse aid.

ENERGY UNITS AND RUNNING COSTS

GAS THERMS

To compare gas consumption with electricity quoted in Kwh (1 unit of electricity = 1 Kwh):

1 Multiply reading (cu ft) by 2.83, which equal the same reading in m^3.
2 Then multiply m^3 by the calorific value (quoted on gas bill, eg, 38.3MJ/m^3).
3 Divide by 3.6 = Kwh
4 If price is quoted as Kwh, multiply by pence per Kwh to give cost of gas

Summary: Reading x 2.83 x calorific value (38.3) x 3.6 = Kwh

LIGHT-BULB RATINGS

Conventional tungsten bulbs:	40w	60w	75w	100w
equivalent to				
Compact fluorescent bulb	9w	11w	15w	20w

CLOTHES SIZES

COLLARS

In	14½	15	15½	16	16½	17	17½
Cm	37	38	39–40	41	42	43	44

MEASUREMENTS

In	29	30	31	32	33	34	36	38	40	42	44	46
Cm	74	76	79	81	84	86	91	97	102	107	112	117

British Size	8	10	12	14	16	18
Continental	38	40	42	44	46	48
American	6	8	10	12	14	16

SHOE SIZES

Women

British	3½	4	4½	5	5½	6	6½	7	8	9
Continental	36	37	37½	38	39	39½	40	41	42	43
American	5	5½	6	6½	7	7½	8	8½	9½	10½

Men

British	6½	7	7½	8	8½	9	9½	10	10½	11	11½	12
Continental	40	41	41½	42	42½	43	44	44½	45	46	46½	47
American	7	7½	8	8½	9	9½	10	11	11½	12	12½	13

COOKING MEASUREMENTS

AMERICAN CUP MEASURES

One American cup measure equals

Butter	225g	8oz
Cheese		
- chedder (coarsely grated)	100g	4oz
- cottage	225g	8oz
Cocoa Powder	100g	4 oz
Cornflour	140g	4½oz
Cream	225ml	8 fl oz
Currants	150g	5oz
Flour		
- plain	150g	5oz
- wholemeal	165g	5½oz
Lard/Dripping	225g	8oz
Macaroni, uncooked	100g	4oz
Milk (fresh)	225ml	8 fl oz
Oats	75g	3 oz
Oils	225g	8 oz
Onions, chopped	150g	5 oz
Rice		
- long grain, uncooked	200g	7oz
- short grain, uncooked	215g	7½oz
Semolina	190g	6½oz
Suet, shredded	100g	4 oz
Sugar		
- granulated/caster	200g	7oz
- icing	100g	4oz
- moist brown (well packed)	200g	7oz
- demerara	200g	7oz
Syrup/treacle	350g	12oz

Liquid

4 tbsp = ¼ cup = 2 fl oz

16 tbsp = 1 cup = 8 fl oz

2 cups = 1 American pint= 16 fl oz

Eggs

1 cup = 4–6 whole eggs

1 cup = 8–10 egg whites

1 cup = 12–14 egg yolks

1 egg white = 1½ tbsp

1 egg yolk = 1 tbsp

COOKING TEMPERATURES

Gas Mark	¼	1	2	3	4	5	6	7	8	9
°F	250	275	300	325	350	375	400	425	450	475
°C	120	140	150	160	180	190	200	220	230	240

INGREDIENT MEASUREMENTS

1 teaspoon (tsp) = 5ml

1 tablespoon (tbsp) = 15ml

USEFUL ADDRESSES

BUYING A HOME

MOVING HOUSE

Department of the Environment
PO Box 151
London E15 2HF
Fax: 081 533 7700

Individual House Builders Association
107 Lancaster Gate
London W2 3WQ
Tel: 071 262 2218

National House-Building Council
Buildmark House
Chiltern Avenue
Amersham
Bucks HP6 5AP
Tel: 0494 43 4477

Zurich Insurance
Stanhope Road
Portsmouth
Hampshire PO1 1DU
Tel: 0705 82 2200

THE COST OF MOVING HOUSE

Council for Licenced Conveyancers
16 Glebe Road
Chelmsford
Essex CM1 1QG
Tel: 0245 349599

The Law Society
113 Chancery Lane
London WC2A 1PL
Tel: 071 242 1222

The Law Society of Scotland
26 Drumsheugh Gardens
Edinburgh EH3 7YR
Tel: 031 226 7411

GETTING A MORTGAGE

Age Concern England
Astral House
1268 London Road
London SW16 4ER
Tel: 081 679 8000

Age Concern Scotland
54A Fountainbridge
Edinburgh EH3 9PT
Tel: 031 228 5656

Office of Fair Trading
Field House
15–25 Bream's Building
London EC4A 1PR
Tel: 071 242 2858

Securities and Investments Board (SIB)
2–14 Bunhill Row
London EC1Y 8RA
Tel: 071 638 1240

HOUSE-HUNTING

Association of Relocation Agents
PO Box 108
Edinburgh EH7 5JQ
Tel: 031 558 3060

Incorporated Society of Valuers and Auctioneers
3 Cadogan Gate
London SW1X OAS
Tel: 071 235 2282

The Law Society
See The Cost of Moving House, page 482

National Association of Estate Agents
(National Homelink Service)
21 Jury Street
Coventry
Warwickshire CV34 4EH
Tel: 0926 496800
Homelink Hotline: 0926 410785

Royal Institution of Chartered Surveyors
12 Great George Street
Parliament Square
London SW1 3AD
Tel: 071 222 7000

THE MECHANICS OF BUYING

Architects and Surveyors Institute
15 St Mary's Street
Chippenham
Wiltshire SN15 3JN
Tel: 0249 444505

Council for Licensed Conveyancers
See The Cost of Moving House, page 482

The Law Society of Scotland
See The Cost of Moving House, page 482

Royal Institution of Chartered Surveyors
See House-Hunting, page 482

SELLING YOUR HOME

Incorporated Society of Valuers and Auctioneers
See House-Hunting, page 482

The Law Society of Scotland
See The Cost of Moving House, page 482

National Association of Estate Agents
See House-Hunting, left

Royal Institution of Chartered Surveyors
See House-Hunting, left

REMOVALS

British Association of Removers
3 Churchill Court
58 Station Road
North Harrow
Middlesex HA2 7SA
Tel: 081 861 3331

British Vehicle Rental and Leasing Association
13 St John's Street
Chichester
West Sussex PO19 1UU
Tel: 0243 786782

EQUIPPING YOUR HOME

EQUIPPING A KITCHEN

Alno (UK) Ltd
Unit 10
Hampton Farm Industrial Estate
Hampton Road West
Hanworth
Middlesex TW13 6DB
Tel: 081 898 4781

Blanco
Oxgate Lane
London NW2 7JN
Tel: 081 450 9100

The Building Bookshop
The Building Centre
26 Store Street
London WC1E 7BT
Tel: 071 637 3151

Council for Registered Gas Installers (CORGI)
4 Elmwood, Chinehan Business Park
Crockford Lane
Basingstoke
Hants RG24 8WG
Tel: 0256 707060

Department of the Environment
See Moving House, page 482

Federation of Master Builders
14–15 Great James Street
London WC1N 3DP
Tel: 071 242 7583

Institute of Plumbing
64 Station Lane
Hornchurch
Essex RM12 6NB
Tel: 0708 472791

Kitchen Specialists Association
PO Box 311
Worcester WR1 1DN
Tel: 0905 726066

Royal Institution of Chartered Surveyors
See House-Hunting, page 483

KITCHEN ESSENTIALS AND TABLEWARE

British Water
1 Queen Anne's Gate
London SW1H 9BT
(Enclose an A5 SAE)
Tel: 071 957 4554

Vacuvin
Vacu Products Ltd
130 New Street
Andover
Hants SP10 1DR
Tel: 0264 332821

WASTE DISPOSAL

Blanco
See Equipping a Kitchen, page 483

Waste Watch
Hobart House
Grosvenor Place
London SW1X 7AE.
Tel: 071 245 9718
(Enclose an A4 SAE)

HOUSEHOLD CLEANING APPLIANCES

Beam Built-in Vacuums Ltd
St Martins Gate
Worcester WR1 2DU
Tel: 0905 611041

BVC
Harbour Road
Gosport
Hants PO12 1BG
Tel: 0705 584281

FRZ
Austin White Ltd
38–44 Artizan Road
Northampton
Northamptonshire NN1 4HU
Tel: 0604 36335

Gemini Ironing System
Numatic International Ltd
Tapstone Road
Chard
Somerset TA20 2LW
Tel: 0460 68600

Miele
Fairacres
Marcham Road
Abingdon
Oxon OX14 1TW
Tel: 0235 554455

Nilfisk
Newmarket Road
Bury St Edmunds
Suffolk IP33 3SR
Tel: 0284 76 3163

Shirtmaster
BDP
Old Boundary House
London Road
Sunningdale SL5 0DW
Tel: 0344 87 3343

Univac Built-in Vacuum System Ltd
Unisafe House
Michigan Park
Michigan Avenue
Salford Quays
Manchester M5 2GY
Tel: 061 848 9900

LARGE KITCHEN APPLIANCES

Food Safety Advisory Centre
Tel: Freephone 0800 282 407

4 Hob
Homecare Products
Broomhill Road
London SW18 4JQ
Tel: 081 871 5027

Council for Registered Gas Installers (CORGI)
See Equipping a Kitchen, page 484

BATHROOM FIXTURES AND FITTINGS

Institute of Plumbing
See Equipping a Kitchen, page 484

National Inspection Council for Electrical Installation Contracting
Vintage House
37 Albert Embankment
London SE1 7UJ
Tel: 071 582 7746

BUYING A BED

British Waterbed Company
228 Withycombe Village Road
Exmouth
Devon EX8 3BD
Tel: 0395 27 0066

National Bed Federation
251 Brompton Road
London SW3 2EZ
Tel: 071 589 4888

CHOOSING BEDDING

Acton & Acton
Heybrook Mill
Hamer Lane
Rochdale
Lancs OL16 2UL
Tel: 0706 42361

Allerayde
Queens Head Court
42 Kirk Gate
Newark
Notts NG24 1AB
Tel: 0636 613444

Alprotec
Advanced Allergy Technologies
Royd House
224 Hale Road
Altringham WA15 8EB
Tel: 061 903 9293

Banamite Anti-Allergy Bedding
Medivac
Bollin House
Riverside Works
Manchester Road
Wilmslow SK9 1BJ
Tel: 0625 539401

Brinkhaus
Unit A
Bowers Hill
Branch Road
Barkisland
Halifax
West Yorks HX4 OAD
Tel: 0422 310206

Givans Irish Linen Store
207 Kings Road
London SW3 5ED
Tel: 071 352 6352

Holden Medical Ltd
Moss Rose Mill
Springfield Road
Kearsley
Bolton BL4 8JW
Tel: 0204 71686

Janet Turner Fine Linens
Axholme
1 Overcote Lane
Needingworth
Huntingdon
Cambs PE17 3TU
Tel: 0480 301773

Keys Of Clacton
132 Old Rd
Clacton
Essex CO15 3AJ
Tel: 0255 432518

Limericks Linens
Guildford House
Paycocke Rd
Basildon
Essex SS14 3DR
Tel: 0268 284405

Medibed Ltd
Burnley Wood Mill
Parliament Street
Burnley BB11 3JT
Tel: 0282 839700

SOFT FURNISHINGS

Crowson Fabrics
Crowson House
Bellbrook Park
Uckfield
East Sussex TN22 1QZ
Tel: 0825 761044

Ciba (Du Pont)
Hulley Road
Macclesfield
Cheshire SK10 2NX
Tel: 0625 618585

Dry Cleaning Information Bureau
7 Churchill Court
58 Station Road
North Harrow HA2 7SA
Tel: 081 863 8658

Rufflette
Sharston Road
Wythenshawe
Manchester M22 4TH
Tel: 061 998 1811

Safeclean
Helpline Tel: 0800 585693

Scotchguard Protector
3M United Kingdom plc
3M House
PO Box 1
Market Place
Bracknell RG12 1JU
Helpline Tel: 0800 581546

ServiceMaster Ltd
308 Melton Road
Leicester LE4 7SL
Tel: 0533 610761

Sewing Machine Trade Association Ltd
(SMTA)
24 Fairlawn Grove
Chiswick
London W4 5EH
Tel: 081 995 0411

LIGHTING

Daylight Studios
223A Portobello Road
London W11 1LU
Tel: 071 229 7812

Green Light
Jonathon Badger
11B High Street
Shepton Mallet
Somerset BA4 5AA
Tel: 0749 346135
For advice on energy-saving lighting.
Send a stamp for a catalogue.

HSS
Tel: 0800 282828

The National Inspection Council for Electrical
Installation Contracting
See Bathroom Fixtures and Fittings, page 485

Electrical Contractors' Association
ESCA House
34 Palace Court
London W2 4HY
Tel: 071 229 1266

STORAGE

Aero
96 Westbourne Grove
London W2 5RT
Tel: 071 221 1950

Betterware UK Ltd
Stanley House
Park Lane
Castle Vale
Birmingham B35 6LJ
Tel: 021 693 1111

Britannia Shelving Ltd
Unit 21
Haddenham Industrial Estate
Haddenham
Bucks HP17 8LJ
Tel: 0844 292856

Conservation Resources UK Ltd
Units 1, 2 and 4
Pony Road
Horspath Industrial Estate
Cowley
Oxford OX4 2RD
Tel: 0865 747755

The Conservation Unit of the Museums &
Galleries Commission
16 Queen Anne's Gate
London SW1H 9AA
Tel: 071 233 3683

Documentary Photography Archive
Cavendish Building
Cavendish Street
Manchester MI5 6 BG

The Domestic Paraphernalia Co
Unit 15
Marine Business Centre
Dock Road
Lytham
Lancs FY8 5AJ
Tel: 0253 736334

Institute of Paper Conservation
Leigh Lodge
Leigh
Worcester WR6 5LB
Tel: 0886 832323

Kleeneze Homecare Ltd
Martins Road
Hanham
Bristol BS15 3DY
Tel: 0272 670861

The London Wall Bed Company
263 The Vale
Acton
London W3 7QA
Tel: 081 743 1174

Lakeland Plastics Ltd
Alexandra Buildings
Windermere
Cumbria LA23 1BQ
Tel: 0539 488100

Momart plc
199–205 Richmond Road
London E8 3NJ
Tel: 081 986 3624

Muji
26 Great Marlborough Street
London WIV 1HL
Tel: 071 494 1197

National Carpet Cleaners Association Ltd
126 New Walk
De Montfort Street
Leicester LE1 7JA
Tel: 0533 554352

Paula Rosa Kitchens
Water Lane Trading Estate
Storrington
West Sussex RH20 3DS
Tel: 0903 743322

Royal Photographic Society
The Octagon
Milsom Street
Bath
Avon BA1 1DN
Tel: 0225 462841

Scotts of Stow
The Square
Stow on the Wold
Gloucestershire GL54 1AF
Tel: 0249 449111

Secol Ltd
Howlett Way
Thetford
Norfolk IP24 1HZ
Tel: 0842 752341

The Society of Bookbinders
Lower Hammonds Farm
Ripley Lane
West Horsley KT24 6JP
Tel: 0483 283175

Convert-a-Room
Strachan
3A Woodside Trading Estate
Low Lane
Horsforth
Leeds LS18 5PD
Tel: 0532 390777

United Kingdom Institute for Conservation of Historic and Artistic Works
6 Whitehorse Mews
Westminster Bridge Road
London SE1 7QD
Tel: 071 620 3371
Send SAE.

Woodfit Ltd
Kem Mill
Whittle-le-Woods
Chorley
Lancashire PR6 7EA
Tel: 0257 266421

FLOORING

Amtico Ltd
17 St George Street
London W1R 9DE
Tel: 071 629 6258

British Carpet Manufacturers' Association Ltd
72 Dean Street
London W1V 5HB
Tel: 071 734 9853

British Carpet Technical Centre
Wira House
West Park Ring Road
Leeds LS16 6QL
Tel: 0532 591999

Crucial Trading
PO Box 689
Craven Arms
Shropshire SY7 8ZZ
Tel: 0588 673666

Junckers Ltd
Wheaton Road
Witham
Essex CM8 3UJ
Tel: 0376 517512

Kahrs (UK) Ltd
Timberlaine Estate
Quarry Lane
Chichester
West Sussex PO19 2FJ
Tel: 0243 778747

National Carpet Cleaners' Association
See Storage, page 488

National Institute of Carpet Fitters
4D St Marys Place
Velace Market
Notts NG1 1PH
Tel: 0602 583077

National Master Tile Fixers Association
39 Upper Elmers End Road
Beckenham
Kent BR3 3QY
Tel: 081 663 0946

Qualitas Furnishing Standards Council
30 Harcourt Street
London W1H 2AA
Tel: 071 723 0297

Tarkett Ltd
Polye House
Blackthorne Road
Colnbrook
Slough
Berkshire
Tel: 0753 684533

Vigers Hardwood Flooring Systems
Beechfield Walk
Sewardstone Road
Waltham Abbey
Essex EN9 1AG
Tel: 0992 711133

Wicanders Ltd
Star Road
Partridge Green
Horsham
West Sussex RH13 8RA
Tel: 0403 710001

York Handmade Brick Company
Forest Lane
Alne
North Yorkshire YO6 2LU
Tel: 0347 838881

GARDEN EQUIPMENT

Henry Doubleday Research Association
Ryton Organic Gardens
Coventry CV8 3LG
Tel: 0203 303517

CARE & MAINTENANCE

HOW THE HOUSE WORKS

Electrical Contractors' Association
34 Palace Court
London W2 4HY
Tel: 071 229 1266

Electrical Contractors' Association of Scotland
Bush House
Bush Estate
Mid Lothian EM26 0SB
Tel: 031 445 5577

Institute of Plumbing
See Equipping a Kitchen, page 484

National Association of Plumbing, Heating and Mechanical Services Contractors
Ensign House
Ensign Business Centre
Westwood Way
Coventry CV4 8JA
Tel: 0203 470626

National Inspection Council for Electrical Installation Contracting
See Bathroom Fixtures and Fittings, page 485

Scottish and Northern Ireland Plumbing Employers' Federation
2 Walker Street
Edinburgh EH3 7LB
Tel: 031 225 2255

GIVE YOUR HOUSE A CHECK-UP

British Wood Preserving and Dampproofing Association
The Office Village
4 Romford Road
London E15 4EA
Tel: 081 519 2588

Building Conservation Directory
66 Strathleven Road
London SW2 5LB
Tel: 071 738 6462

Building Employers' Confederation
82 New Cavendish Street
London W1M 8AD
Tel: 071 580 5588

The Conservation Unit of the Museums & Galleries Commision
See Storage, page 487

English Heritage
23 Savile Row
London W1X 1AB
Tel: 071 973 3000

Georgian Group
37 Spital Square
London E1 6DY
Tel: 071 377 1722

Historic Scotland
20 Brandon Street
Edinburgh EH3 5RA
Tel: 031 244 2946

National House-Building Council
See Moving House, page 482

Salvo Directory
PO Box 1295
Bath
Avon BA1 3TJ
Tel: 0225 445387

Scottish Building Employers' Federation
13 Woodside Crescent
Glasgow G3 7UP
Tel: 041 332 7144

The Society for the Protection of Ancient Buildings
37 Spital Square
London E1 6DY
Tel: 071 377 1644

Twentieth Century Society
70 Cowcross Street
London EC1M 6BP
Tel: 071 250 3857

The Victorian Society
1 Priory Gardens, London W4 1TT
Tel: 081 994 1019

COPING WITH PROBLEMS

British Allergy Foundation
St Bartholomew's Hospital
West Smithfield
London EC1A 7BE
Send a large SAE.

British Pest Control Association
3 St James' Court
Friar Gate
Derby DE1 1ZU
Tel: 0332 294 288

British Wood Preserving and Dampproofing Association
See Give Your House a Check-up, page 490

Good Housekeeping
National Magazine House
72 Broadwick Street
London W1V 2BP
Tel: 0839 141414
Costs 49p/minute; open 9.30–5

Liquid Nitrogen Treatments

Cadogan Medical
95 Scrubs Lane
London NW10 6QU
Tel: 081 960 8020

Lycam
Bieldside
Balmullo
St Andrews KY16 OAY
Tel: 0334 870253

National Asthma Campaign
Providence House, Providence Place
London N1 ONT
Tel: 0345 010203

ServiceMaster
See Soft Furnishings, page 487

Solid Fuel Association
17 Wadham Road
Woodthorpe
Nottingham NG5 4JB
Tel: 0623 550411

WAYS TO KEEP WARM

British Plastic Windows Group
British Plastics Federation
6 Bath Place
Rivington Street
London E2A 3JE
Tel: 071 457 5000

British Standards Institution
389 Chiswick High Road
London W4 4AL
Tel: Not yet available

Council for Registered Gas Installers (CORGI)
See Equipping a Kitchen, page 484

Draught-proofing Advisory Association
PO Box 12
Haslemere
Surrey GU27 3AH
Tel: 0428 654011

Energy Efficiency Office
Department of the Environment
2 Marsham Street
London SW1P E3B
Tel: 071 276 0900

External Wall Insulation Association
See Draught-proofing Advisory Association, above

Glass and Glazing Federation
44–48 Borough High Street
London SE1 1XB
Tel: 071 403 7177

Heating and Ventilating Contractors' Association
34 Palace Court
London W2 4JG
Tel: 071 229 2488

MVM Starpoint Ltd
16 Park Place
Clifton
Bristol BS8 1JP
Tel: 0272 253769

National Association of Loft Insulation Contractors
See Draught-proofing Advisory Association, left

National Cavity Insulation Association
See Draught-proofing Advisory Association, left

The National Energy Foundation
Rockingham Drive
Linford Wood
Milton Keynes MK14 6EG
Tel: 0908 672787

A–Z OF HOUSEHOLD REPAIRS

BBC Engineering Information Department
Broadcasting House
London W1A 1AA
Tel: 081 576 7989

British Flat Roofing Council
38 Bridlesmith Gate
Nottingham NG1 2GQ
Tel: 0602 507733
Free guide.
Technical enquiry line: 0891 516876

Building Guarantee Scheme UK
143 Malone Road
Belfast BT9 6SU
Tel: 0232 661717

DMT Crystal Saver
Starkie and Starkie
118 South Knighton Road
Leicester LE2 3LQ
Tel: 0533 703212

Federation of Master Builders
See Equipping a Kitchen, page 484

National Federation of Roofing Contractors
24 Weymouth Street
London W1N 3FA
Tel: 071 436 0387

National Register of Warranted Builders
See Federation of Master Builders, above.

CLEANING IN THE HOME

HOW TO CLEAN SURFACES A–Z

Antiquax
James Briggs
Salmon Fields
Royton
Oldham
Lancs OL2 6HZ
Tel: 061 627 0983

Artisan Brighton Regency Leathers
4, The Parade
Valley Drive,
Brighton
East Sussex BN1 5FQ
Tel: 0273 557418
Suppliers of replacement leather tops.

Association of British Pewter Craftsmen
136 Hagley Road
Edgbaston,
Birmingham B16 9PN
Tel: 021 454 4141
Details of professionals who will remove tarnish from pewter.

Association of Master Upholsterers
Francis Vaughan House
102 Commercial Street
Newport
Gwent NP9 1LU
Tel: 0633 215454
Details of furniture restorers.

Autoglym
Works Road
Letchworth
Herts SG6 1LU
Tel: 0462 677766

Avonite
Sylmar Technology Ltd
Jenna House
Jenna Way
Newport Pagnell
Bucks MK16 9QA
Tel: 0908 210505

Bar Keepers Friend
See 4 Hob, Large Kitchen Appliances, page 485

British Antique Furniture Restorers Association
6 Whitehorse Mews
Westminster Bridge Road
London SE1 7QD
Tel: 071 620 3761
Details of furniture restorers.

British Bathroom Council
Federation House
Stoke-on-Trent
ST4 2RT
Tel: 0782 747074
Advice on choosing and using a bathroom. Provides a list of recommended cleaning products.

British Cutlery and Silverware Association
Light Trades House
3 Melbourne Avenue
Sheffield S10 2QJ
Tel: 0742 663084
For general advice on cutlery and silverware and details of members who carry out a re-plating service.

Cardinal Red Tile Polish
Reckitt & Colman
Dansom Lane
Hull HU8 7DS
Tel: 0482 26151

ColorFill
Unika
Unit 37B
North Tyne Industrial Estate
Longbenton
Newcastle upon Tyne NE12 9SZ
Tel: 091 270 0033

Corian Distributors CD (UK) Ltd
Unit 8
Centre 27
Bankwood Way
Birstall
West Yorkshire WF17 9TB
Tel: 0800 242525

Decosol Ltd
Decosol House
Shelf
Halifax
West Yorkshire HX3 7JT
Tel: 0422 205111

Descalite Chemical Supply Co
Unit 2
Maritime Close
Medway City Estate
Rochester
Kent ME2 4DJ
Tel: 0634 294455

4 Hob
See Large Kitchen Appliances, page 485

HG Marble Polish
HG Cleaners
Worldpoint Ltd
Unit 8
Grange Way Business Park
Whitehall Road Industrial Estate
Colchester
Essex CO2 8HF
Tel: 0206 795200

Institute of Paper Conservation
Leigh Lodge,
Leigh
Worcester WR6 5LB
Tel: 0886 832323
Advice on the repair and restoration of paintings, pictures and books.

Just Desks
20 Church Street
London NW8 8EP
Tel: 071 723 7976
Supplier of replacement leather tops.

Liberon Waxes
Mountfield Industrial Estate
Learoyd Road
New Romney
Kent TN28 8XU
Tel: 0679 67555

Lift Off scale remover
See Descalite, page 494

Lloyd Look Furniture
Kellet Gate
Low Fulney
Spalding
Lincolnshire PE12 6EH
Tel: 0775 712111
Supplier of a repair kit for Lloyd Loom furniture.

Mancha, Graham
Weston Turnville
Buckinghamshire HP22 5TG
Tel: 0296 615121
Specialist restorer of Lloyd-Loom furniture.

Manger's Stainex
Kalon Specialist Products
Wide Lane
Morley
Leeds
West Yorkshire LS27 9BL
Tel: 0532 381555

Manor House Decanter Drier
Hurley Style Ltd
The Manor House
Hurley
Berkshire SL6 5NB
Tel: 0628 824303

Marble
A Bell & Company
Kingsthorpe Road
Kingsthorpe
Northampton NN2 6LT
Tel: 0604 712505

Metal Finishing Association
10 Vyse Street
Birmingham B18 6LT
Tel: 021 236 2657
Details of professional lacquerers of metal items.

National Association of Goldsmiths
78a Luke Street
London EC2A 4PY
Tel: 071 613 4445
Details of jewellers who will carry out repairs.

Petal Fresh
Shootlands Farm
Abinger Common
Dorking
Surrey RH5 6JX
Tel: 0306 731413

Plasti-Kote Ltd
London Road Industrial Estate
Sawston
Cambridge CB2 4TR
Tel: 0223 836400

Quickshine Descaler Bag
QSP Ltd
Unit 7
The Empire Centre
Imperial Way
Watford WD2 4YY
Tel: 0923 246276

Rustins
Waterloo Road
Cricklewood
London NW2 7TX
Tel: 081 450 4666

Scoopy
Lakeland Plastics Ltd
Alexandra Buildings
Windermere
Cumbria LA23 1BQ
Tel: 0539 488100

Screenclens and Foamclene
Automation Facilities
Westworth House
Blakes Road
Wargrave
Berkshire RG10 8AW
Tel: 0734 403012

Silkstone
Astracast plc
PO Box 20
Oakwell Way
Birstall
West Yorkshire WF7 9XD
Tel: 0924 477466

Stone Federation
82 New Cavendish Street
London W1M 8AD
Tel: 071 580 5404
Supply and fix stone, including granite and marble.

Thermos Ltd
Ongar Road
Brentwood
Essex CM15 9AY
Tel: 0277 213404

Tile Guard
Cannie Products Ltd
Unit A, Horton Trading Estate
Stanwell Road
Horton
Slough
Berkshire SL3 9PF
Tel: 0753 686767

Vitreous Enamel Development Council Ltd
Charnwood
Frenze Road
Diss
Norfolk IP22 3PB
Tel: 0379 650340
Advice on the care and use of enamel surfaces. Provides a list of recommended cleaners and a list of professional restorers who will re-enamel baths etc.

Worshipful Company of Goldsmiths
Goldsmiths Hall
Foster Lane
London EC2V 6BN
Tel: 071 606 7010
Professional advice on specialist silverware and jewellery repair.

Zebo
Reckitt & Colman
Dansom Lane
Hull HU8 7DS
Tel: 0482 26151

WASH-DAY WISDOM

Independent test houses for fabric analysis

British Leather Confederation
Kings Park Road
Moulton Park
Northampton NN3 1ED
Tel: 0604 49 4131

British Textile Technology Group
See British Carpet Technical Centre, Flooring, page 489

Drycleaning Technology Centre
8 Wells Promenade
Ilkley
West Yorkshire LS29 9LF
Tel: 0943 81 6545

Fabric Care Research Association
Forest House Laboratories
Knaresborough Road
Harrogate
North Yorkshire HG2 7LZ
Tel: 0423 88 5977

Scot Innovation and Development Ltd
Netherdale
Galashields
Selkirkshire TD1 3EY
Tel: 0896 2196

National Association of Launderette Industries
79 Glen Eyre Road
Southampton
SO2 3NN
Tel: 0703 766328

Textile Services Association
7 Churchill Court
58 Station Road
North Harrow
Middlesex HA2 7SA
Tel: 081 863 7755

A–Z FABRIC CARE

Barbour, J
Simonside
South Shields
Tyne and Wear NE34 9PD
Tel: 091 455 4444

Dreamland Appliances Ltd
Vine Mill
Middleton Road
Royton
Lancashire OL2 5LN
Tel: 061 628 8018

Dry Cleaning Information Bureau
7 Churchill Court
58 Station Road
North Harrow
Middlesex HA2 7SA
Tel: 081 863 8658

Berger, Harry
25 Station Road
Cheadle Hulme
Cheshire SK8 5AF
Tel: 061 485 3421

Jeeves of Belgravia
30–48 Lawrence Road
Tottenham
London N15 4EX
Tel: 081 809 3232

Johnson and Calverley
George Street
Ellend
West Yorkshire HX5 ONE
Tel: 0422 376320

Mars Oil Co
Withycombe Farmhouse
Drayton
Banbury
Oxfordshire OX15 6EE
Tel: 0295 262844

Meltonian Grease and Tar Remover
Sara Lee Household and Personal Care
225 Bath Road
Slough SL1 4AU
Tel: 0753 52 3971

National Carpet Cleaners' Association
See Storage, page 488

Nikwax
Durgates Industrial Estate
Wadhurst
East Sussex TN5 6DF
Tel: 0892 783855

Royal School of Needlework
Appartment 12A
Hampton Court Palace
East Molesey
Surrey KT8 9AU
Tel: 081 943 1432

Textile Services Association
See Wash-day Wisdom, page 497

Warmabed Ltd
Hollingworth Lane
Knottingley
West Yorkshire WF11 9DF
Tel: 0977 67 2051

Warmalux
Springwood Mills
Holywell Green
Halifax HX4 9BH
Tel: 0422 37 4801

A–Z OF STAIN REMOVAL

Beckmann and Stain Devils
DDD Group
94 Rickmansworth Road
Watford
Hertfordshire WD1 7JJ
Tel: 0923 229251

Bissell
Jubilee Avenue
Larkshall Road
Highams Park
London E4 9HN
Tel: 081 503 3233

British Carpet Manufacturers' Association
See Flooring, page 489

Cuprinol
Adderwell
Frome
Somerset BA11 1NL
Tel: 0373 465151

Dabitoff
See Meltonian Grease and Tar Remover, Sara Lee, above left

Dip
See Meltonian Grease and Tar Remover, Sara Lee, above left

Dylon
Worsley Bridge Road
Sydenham
London SE26 5HD
Tel: 081 650 4801

Meltonian
See A–Z Fabric Care, above left

Mykal
Unit 5
Morris Close
Park Farm
Wellingborough NN8 6XF
Tel: 0933 402822

National Carpet Cleaners Association
See Storage, page 488

Neutradol
Quadrant House
The Quadrant
Richmond
Surrey
TW9 1DG
Tel: 081 332 2333

1001 Products
Cussons UK Ltd
Kersal Vale
Manchester M7 3GL
Tel: 061 792 6111

Rentokil Group PLC
Felcourt
East Grinstead
West Sussex OH19 2JY
Tel: 0342 833022

Secto
Carlinghurst Road
Blackburn BB2 1PW
Tel: 0254 261632

Shaws Pet Products Ltd
50 Weston Road
Ashton Clinton
Aylesbury
Bucks HP22 5EH
Tel: 0296 630121

Stain Devils
See Beckmann and Stain Devils A–Z Stain Removal, page 498

The Stain Slayer
JCB Developments
17 City Business Centre
Basin Road
Chichester
West Sussex PO19 1LH
Tel: 0243 531319

Victoria and Albert Museum
Cromwell Road
London SW7
Tel: 071 938 8500

White Wizard
American Marketing Systems
13b Palmer Avenue
Blackpool FY1 5JP
Tel: 0253 401872

XO
157 Redland Road
Bristol
BS6 6YE
Tel: 0272 683898.

CREATIVE DIY

PAINTING AND DECORATING

J W Bollom and Co
15 Theobald's Road
London WC1X 8SN
Tel: 071 242 0313
Stocks a wide range of paints, varnishes and brushes.

Henry Gates & Son
70 Alderman's Hill
London N13 4BP
Tel: 081 882 3237
Stocks a wide range of paints, including transparent oil glaze and metal leaf.

Craig and Rose plc
172 Leith Walk
Edinburgh EH6 5EB
Tel: 031 554 1131
Sells paints, varnishes, stains and glazes.

Green and Stone
259 Kings Road
London SW3 5EL
Tel: 071 352 0837
Stocks a range of paints, glazes and brushes.

J H Ratcliffe and Paints Co Ltd
135A Linaker Street
Southport PR8 5DF
Tel: 0704 537999
Manufactures paint and glazes. Also sells specialist tools and brushes.

The Stencil Store
91 Lower Sloane Street
London SW1W 8DA
Tel: 071 730 0728
Mail Order:
PO Box 30
Rickmansworth
Herts WD3 5LG
Send £2 check made out to Elrose Products.

WINDOW TREATMENTS

Cope and Timmins Ltd
Angel Road Works
Angel Road
London N18 3AY
Tel: 081 803 6481
Specialist in curtain tracks.

SAFETY AND SECURITY

SAFETY

British Carpet Manufacturers' Association
See Flooring, page 489

British Red Cross
9 Grosvenor Crescent
London SW1X 7EJ
Tel: 071 235 5454

Fire Protection Association
140 Aldersgate Street
London EC1A 4HX
Tel: 071 606 3757

Flame-retardant sprays
Cope and Timmins Ltd
See Window Treatments, left

Glass and Glazing Federation
See Ways to Keep Warm, page 492

National Inspection Council for Electrical Installation Contracting
See Bathroom Fixtures and Fittings, page 485

Re-Solv
30A High Street
Stone
Staffordshire ST15 8AW
Tel: 0785 817885

Royal National Institute for Deaf People
105 Gower Street
London WC1E 6AH
Tel: 071 387 8033

The Royal Society for the Prevention of Accidents
Cannon House
The Priory
Queensway
Birmingham B4 6BS
Tel: 021 200 2461

St Johns Ambulance
1 Grosvenor Crescent
London SW1 X 7EF
Tel: 071 235 5231

Slipsafe
BTC
409 Victory Business Centre
Somers Road North
Portsmouth PO1 1PJ
Tel: 0705 861622

SECURITY

Antiques Trade Gazette
17 Whitcomb Street
London WC2H 7PL
Tel: 071 930 7195

The Art and Antiques Recording Service
Control Risks Group
83 Victoria Street
London SW1H OHW
Tel: 071 222 1552

Art Loss Register
13 Grosvenor Place
London SW1X 7HH
Tel: 071 235 3393

Association of British Insurers
51 Gresham Street
London EC2V 7HQ
Tel: 071 600 3333

British Blind and Shutter Association
Heath Street
Tamworth
Staffordshire B79 7JH
Tel: 0827 52337

British Security Industry Association
Security House
Barbourne Road
Worcester WR1 1RS
Tel: 0905 21464

Electrical Contractors' Association
See How the House Works, page 490

Help the Aged
St James's Walk
London EC1R OBE
Tel: 071 253 0253

Home Office
PO Box 999
Sudbury
Suffolk CO10 6FS

Laminated Glass Information Centre
299 Oxford Street
London W1R 1LA
Tel: 071 499 1720.

Master Locksmiths Association
Units 4/5
The Business Park
Woodford Halse
Daventry
Northants NN11 6PZ
Tel: 0327 62255

National Approval Council for Security Systems (NACOSS)
Queensgate House
14 Cookham Road
Maidenhead
Berkshire SL6 8AJ
Tel: 0628 37512

National Inspection Council for Electrical Installation Contracting
See Bathroom Fixtures and Fittings, page 485

Trace Magazine
38 New Street
The Barbican
Plymouth
Devon PL1 2NA
Tel: 0752 228727

LEGAL MATTERS

Council for Licensed Conveyancers
See The Cost of Moving House, page 482

Department of the Environment
See Moving House, page 482

Land Charges Registry
Drake's Hill Court
Burrington Way
Plymouth PL5 3LP
Tel: 0752 779831

The Law Society
See The Cost of Moving House, page 482

The Law Society of Scotland
See The Cost of Moving House, page 482

Leasehold Enfranchisement Limited
Chartered Surveyors
The Swan Centre
Fishers Lane
Chiswick
London W4 1RX
Tel: 081 742 8829

Mail Preference Service
Freepost 22
London W1E 7EZ

EMERGENCIES

Building Research Establishment
Garston
Watford WD2 7JR
Tel: 0923 664444

Council for Registered Gas Installers
(CORGI)
See Equipping a Kitchen, page 484

Electrical Contractors' Association
See How the House Works, page 490

Federation of Master Builders
Gordon Fisher House
14–15 Great James Street
London WC1N 3D
Tel: 071 242 7583

Fire Protection Association
See Safety, page 500

Gas Consumers Council
6th Floor
Abford House
15 Wilton Road
London SW1V 1LT
Tel: 071 931 0977

Glass and Glazing Federation
See Ways to Keep Warm, page 492

Institute of Plumbing
See Equipping a Kitchen, page 484

National Association of Plumbing, Heating
and Mechanical Services Contractors
See How the House Works, page 490

National Inspection Council for Electrical
Installation Contracting
See Bathroom Fixtures and Fittings, page 485

INDEX